Study Guide to Accompany
Modern Anatomy & Physiology

Prepared and Edited by Abour H. Cherif
Reviewed by Dianne M. Jedlicka, Ateegh Al-Arabi, Bob Aron, and Linda Michel

Taken from:

Study Guide: Anatomy & Physiology, Second Edition
by Elaine N. Marieb

Study Guide: Fundamentals of Anatomy & Physiology, Seventh Edition, by Frederic H. Martini
by Charles M. Seiger

PEARSON
Custom
Publishing

PEARSON
Benjamin
Cummings

Cover photograph by Paul Gilham, courtesy of Getty Images.

Taken from:

Study Guide: Anatomy & Physiology, Second Edition
by Elaine N. Marieb
Copyright © 2005 by Pearson Education, Inc.
Published by Benjamin Cummings
San Fransicso, California 94111

Study Guide: Fundamentals of Anatomy and Physiology, Seventh Edition, by Frederic H. Martini
by Charles M. Seiger
Copyright © 2006 by Pearson Education, Inc.
Published by Benjamin Cummings

This special edition published in cooperation with Pearson Custom Publishing.

Printed in the United States of America

8 9 10 V0CR 14 13 12

ISBN 0-536-53201-X

2008460026

RG/RH

Please visit our web site at *www.pearsoncustom.com*

PEARSON CUSTOM PUBLISHING
501 Boylston Street, Suite 900, Boston, MA 02116
A Pearson Education Company

Contents

Chapters 1–2, 7–8, 10, 12, 18, 20, 24–27 taken from *Study Guide: Fundamentals of Anatomy and Physiology*, Seventh Edition, by Frederic H. Martini, by Charles M. Seiger.

Chapters 3–6, 9, 11, 13–16, 17, 19, 21–23 taken from *Study Guide: Anatomy & Physiology*, Second Edition, by Elaine N. Marieb.

Preface*

This study guide is intended to accompany *Modern Anatomy & Physiology*, a custom textbook based on two well known titles authored by Frederic Martini and Elaine Marieb. It uses Bloom's Taxonomy to provide a logical framework for the progressive development of skills as students advance through material of increasing levels of complexity. It is intended to help health professional and life science students master the basic concepts of human anatomy and physiology through aggressive review and reinforcement exercises. The topic order of the study guide reflects the organization of the parent text, *Modern Anatomy & Physiology*, customized and edited by Al-Arabi, Cherif, Jedlicka, and Aron.

The graduates of health science programs, for whom this course is developed, are valued for what they can do and how they can apply concepts. To help students achieve this goal, each study guide chapter begins with a listing of Student Objectives, and selected chapters include a short overview. In addition, we have used various types of exercises to maximize student understanding of the subject matter. Throughout, we have emphasized terminal course objectives designed for allied health programs.

Scope of Educational Exercises and Activities

The exercises in the Study Guide review human anatomy using a systems approach while consistently focusing on knowledge of the human body and its application to the real world. Collectively, the exercises will help students to achieve a better understanding of each of the separate chapters as well as providing an integrated approach to understanding how the human body as a whole functions. Where relevant, Pathophysiology and clinical aspects of study are covered with each system so that students can apply their learning.

Every chapter contains a variety of exercises, including some or all of the following: Coloring exercises, selecting from key choices, multiple choice, matching terms with appropriate descriptions, defining important terms, diagram labeling, concept mapping, elimination questions, correcting true/false questions, completion, essay, constructing graphs and completing tables, visualization exercises, challenge questions, closer connections, and covering all your bases. The authors used Bloom's Taxonomy to design and select questions for each type of educational exercise and activity.

The use of coloring exercises helps promote visualization of key structures and processes. Coloring exercises have proven to be a unique motivating approach for learning and reinforcement. Each illustration has been carefully prepared to show sufficient detail for learning key concepts without overwhelming the student with complexity or tedious repetition of coloring. There are many coloring exercises in this Study Guide. When completed, the colored diagrams provide an ideal reference and review tool.

Other question formats in this section include selecting from key choices, matching terms with appropriate descriptions, defining important terms, and labeling diagrams. Elimination questions require the student to discover similarities and dissimilarities among a number of structures or processes. Correcting true/false questions adds a new dimension to this traditional exercise format. In addition, students are asked to construct graphs and complete tables, exercises that not only reinforce learning but also provide a handy study aid. When applicable, a given chapter also contains a visualization exercise, another unique feature of this Study Guide. These *Incredible Journey* exercises ask students to imagine themselves in miniature traveling through various organs and systems within the body.

Challenging Yourself: These exercises, typically consist of two groups of questions—questions in "At the Clinic" focus on applying knowledge to clinical situations, whereas those in "Stop and Think" stress comprehension of principles pertaining to non-clinical situations. For the most part, the clinical questions are written to approximate real situations and require short answers. The "Stop and Think" questions require critical thinking. They cross the lines between topics and prod the student to put two and two together, to synthesize old and new information, and to think logically.

Closer Connections: Checking the Systems, these questions encourage the student to see the connections between body systems, to describe the interrelationships considered in previous chapters, and to recognize the application of this understanding for professional practice.

Covering All Your Bases: This section reintroduces concepts already covered but tests them via different formats. It includes multiple-choice questions and a section called "Word Dissection" that asks the student to define word roots encountered in the chapter and to come up with an example.

As Elaine Marieb wrote, the study of human anatomy and physiology has its own special terminology. It requires that students become familiar with the basic concepts of chemistry to understand physiology. It is our hope that this Study Guide will help simplify the task and maximize the learning and understanding of the intended learning objectives. We sincerely hope that when it is used in conjunction with its customized parent, *Modern Anatomy & Physiology* (edited by Al-Arabi, Cherif, Jedlicka, and Aron), it will not only excite students about this course but also provide valuable reinforcement of difficult concepts by challenging students to increase their knowledge, comprehension, retention, and appreciation of the structure and function of the human body.

Answers for all of the educational exercises and activities are provided at the end of this study guide in the Appendices.

Abour Cherif, Ph.D. & Bob Aron, Ph.D.

April 2008

*This preface and study guide were adapted with modification from the prefaces and study guides that accompany Anatomy & Physiology, Second Edition, *by Elaine N. Marieb, and* Foundations of Anatomy and Physiology, *by Frederic Martini.*

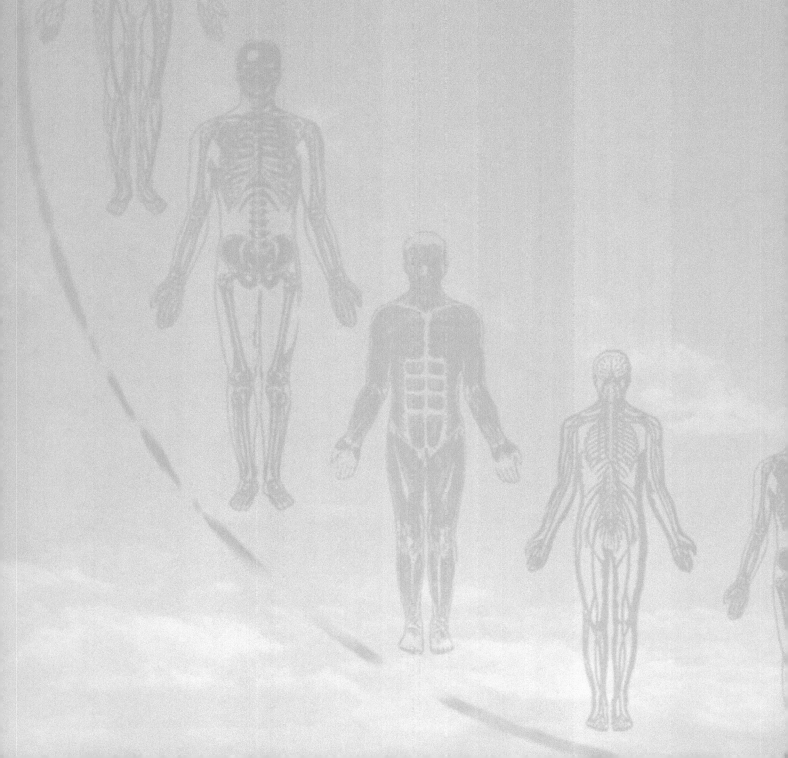

PART 1

BIOS 250

1

AN INTRODUCTION
TO ANATOMY AND PHYSIOLOGY

Overview

Are you interested in knowing something about your body? Have you ever wondered what makes your heart beat or why and how muscles contract to produce movement? If you are curious to understand the what, why, and how of the human body, then the study of anatomy and physiology is essential for you. The term *anatomy* is derived from a Greek word that means to cut up or anatomize (dissect) representative animals or human cadavers, which serve as the basis for understanding the structure of the human body. *Physiology* is the science that attempts to explain the physical and chemical processes occurring in the body. Anatomy and physiology provide the foundation for personal health and clinical applications.

Chapter 1 is an introduction to anatomy and physiology *citing* some of the basic functions of living organisms, *defining* various specialties of anatomy and physiology, *identifying* levels of organization in living things, *explaining* homeostasis and regulation, and *introducing* some basic anatomical terminology. The information in this chapter will provide the framework for a better understanding of anatomy and physiology, and includes basic concepts and principles necessary to get you started on a successful and worthwhile trek through the human body.

LEVEL 1   Review of Chapter Objectives

1. Define anatomy and physiology and describe the various specialties of each discipline.

2. Identify the major levels of organization in organisms from the simplest to the most complex.

3. Identify the organ systems of the human body and the major components of each system.

4. Explain the concept of homeostasis and its significance for organisms.

5. Describe how positive and negative feedback are involved in homeostatic regulation.

6. Use anatomical terms to describe body sections, body regions, and relative positions.

7. Identify the major body cavities and their subdivisions.

[L1] Multiple Choice

Place the letter corresponding to the correct answer in the space provided.

OBJ. 1 _____ 1. Anatomy is the study of _____ and physiology is the study of _____.
   a. function; structure
   b. animals; plants
   c. cells; microorganisms
   d. structure; function

OBJ. 1 _____ 2. The study of general form and superficial anatomical markings is called:
   a. developmental anatomy
   b. surface anatomy
   c. comparative anatomy
   d. systemic anatomy

OBJ. 1 _____ 3. The anatomical specialty that provides a bridge between the realms of macroscopic anatomy and microscopic anatomy is:
   a. gross anatomy
   b. regional anatomy
   c. developmental anatomy
   d. surgical anatomy

OBJ. 1 _____ 4. The specialized study that analyzes the structure of individual cells is:
   a. histology
   b. microbiology
   c. cytology
   d. pathology

OBJ. 1 _____ 5. The scientist who studies the effects of *diseases* on organ or system functions would be classified as a:
   a. histophysiologist
   b. cell physiologist
   c. system physiologist
   d. pathological physiologist

OBJ. 2 _____ 6. The smallest *living* units in the body are:
   a. elements
   b. subatomic particles
   c. cells
   d. molecules

OBJ. 2 _____ 7. The level of organization that reflects the interactions between organ systems is the:
   a. cellular level
   b. tissue level
   c. molecular level
   d. organism

OBJ. 3 _____ 8. The two regulatory systems in the human body include the:
   a. nervous and endocrine
   b. digestive and reproductive
   c. muscular and skeletal
   d. cardiovascular and lymphatic

OBJ. 4 _____ 9. *Homeostasis* refers to:
   a. the chemical operations under way in the body
   b. individual cells becoming specialized to perform particular functions
   c. changes in an organism's immediate environment
   d. the existence of a stable internal environment

OBJ. 5 _____ 10. When a variation outside of normal limits triggers an automatic response that corrects the situation, the mechanism is called:
   a. positive feedback
   b. crisis management
   c. negative feedback
   d. homeostasis

OBJ. 5 _____ 11. When the initial stimulus produces a response that exaggerates the stimulus, the mechanism is called:
   a. autoregulation
   b. negative feedback
   c. extrinsic regulation
   d. positive feedback

OBJ. 6 _____ 12. An erect body, with the feet together, eyes directed forward, and the arms at the side of the body with the palms of the hands turned forward, represents the:
   a. supine position
   b. prone position
   c. anatomical position
   d. proximal position

OBJ. 6 _____ 13. Moving from the wrist toward the elbow is an example of moving in a _____ direction.
   a. proximal
   b. distal
   c. medial
   d. lateral

OBJ. 6 _____ 14. RLQ is an abbreviation used as a reference to designate a specific:
   a. section of the vertebral column
   b. area of the cranial vault
   c. region of the pelvic girdle
   d. abdominopelvic quadrant

OBJ. 6 _____ 15. Making a sagittal section results in the separation of:
   a. anterior and posterior portions of the body
   b. superior and inferior portions of the body
   c. dorsal and ventral portions of the body
   d. right and left portions of the body

OBJ. 6 _____ 16. The process of choosing one sectional plane and making a series of sections at small intervals is called:
   a. parasagittal sectioning
   b. resonance imaging
   c. serial reconstruction
   d. sectional planing

OBJ. 7 _____ 17. The subdivisions of the dorsal body cavity include the:
   a. thoracic and abdominal cavity
   b. abdominal and pelvic cavity
   c. pericardial and pleural cavity
   d. cranial and spinal cavity

OBJ. 7 _____ 18. The subdivisions of the ventral body cavity include the:
   a. pleural and pericardial cavity
   b. thoracic and abdominopelvic cavity
   c. pelvic and abdominal cavity
   d. cranial and spinal cavity

OBJ. 7 _____ 19. The heart and the lungs are located in the _____ cavity.
   a. pericardial
   b. thoracic
   c. pleural
   d. abdominal

OBJ. 7 _____ 20. The ventral body cavity is divided by a flat muscular sheet called the:
   a. mediastinum
   b. pericardium
   c. diaphragm
   d. peritoneum

OBJ. 7 _____ 21. The procedure used to monitor circulatory pathways using radiodense dyes produces an x-ray image known as:
   a. an MRI
   b. a CT scan
   c. an echogram
   d. an angiogram

OBJ. 7 _____ 22. Checking for tumors or other tissue abnormalities is best accomplished by the use of:
   a. computerized tomography
   b. X-ray
   c. ultrasound
   d. magnetic resonance imaging

[L1] Completion

Using the terms below, complete the following statements.

autoregulation	endocrine	pericardial	positive feedback
organs	histologist	physiology	medial
regulation	mediastinum	distal	peritoneal
tissues	digestive	equilibrium	molecules
integumentary	liver	embryology	urinary
transverse			

OBJ. 1   1. A person who specializes in the study of tissue is called a _____.

OBJ. 1   2. The study of early developmental processes is called _____.

OBJ. 1   3. The study of the *functions* of the living cell is called cell _____.

OBJ. 2   4. In complex organisms such as the human being, cells unite to form _____.

OBJ. 2   5. At the chemical level of organization, chemicals interact to form complex _____.

OBJ. 2   6. The cardiovascular system is made up of structural units called _____.

OBJ. 3   7. The kidneys, bladder, and ureters are organs that belong to the _____ system.

OBJ. 3   8. The esophagus, large intestine, and stomach are organs that belong to the _____ system.

OBJ. 3   9. The organ system to which the skin belongs is the _____ system.

OBJ. 4   10. The term that refers to the adjustments in physiological systems is _____.

OBJ. 4   11. When opposing processes or forces are in balance, it can be said that they have reached a state of _____.

OBJ. 5   12. When the activities of a cell, tissue, organ, or system change automatically due to environmental variation, the homeostatic mechanism that operates is called _____.

OBJ. 5   13. A response that is important in accelerating processes that must proceed to completion rapidly is called _____.

OBJ. 5   14. The two systems often controlled by negative feedback mechanisms are the nervous and _____ system.

OBJ. 6   15. Tenderness in the right upper quadrant (RUQ) might indicate problems with the _____.

OBJ. 6   16. A term that means "close to the long axis of the body" is _____.

OBJ. 6   17. A term that means "away from an attached base" is _____.

OBJ. 6   18. A horizontal or cross-section view of the human body at a right angle to the long axis of the body is a _____ view.

OBJ. 7   19. The subdivision of the thoracic cavity that houses the heart is the _____ cavity.

OBJ. 7   20. The large central mass of connective tissue that surrounds the pericardial cavity
              and separates the two pleural cavities is the _____.

OBJ. 7   21. The abdominopelvic cavity is also known as the _____ cavity.

[L1] Matching

Match the terms in column B with the terms in column A. Use letters for answers
in the spaces provided.

Part I	Column A	Column B
OBJ. 1 _____	1. cytology	A. disease
OBJ. 1 _____	2. histology	B. organelles
OBJ. 1 _____	3. gross anatomy	C. endocrine
OBJ. 1 _____	4. pathology	D. study of tissues
OBJ. 2 _____	5. internal cell structures	E. cardiovascular
OBJ. 3 _____	6. heart	F. study of cells
OBJ. 3 _____	7. pituitary	G. macroscopic

Part II	Column A	Column B
OBJ. 4 _____	8. homeostasis	H. skull
OBJ. 4 _____	9. automatic system change	I. control
OBJ. 5 _____	10. receptor	J. steady state
OBJ. 5 _____	11. nervous system	K. ventral body cavity
OBJ. 6 _____	12. cranial	L. stimulus
OBJ. 6 _____	13. prone	M. abdominopelvic
OBJ. 7 _____	14. peritoneal	N. autoregulation
OBJ. 7 _____	15. coelom	O. face down

[L1] Drawing/Illustration Labeling

Identify each numbered structure by labeling the following figures:

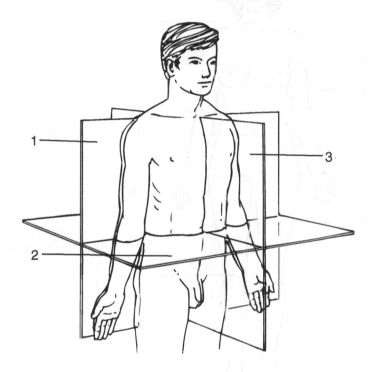
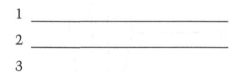

1 _____

2 _____

3 _____

OBJ. 6   **Figure 1.1 Planes of the Body**

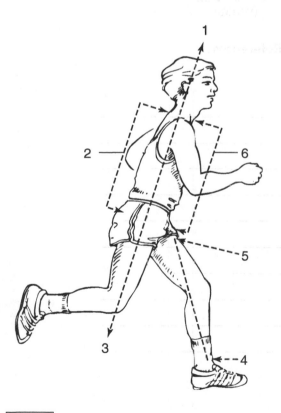

1 _____

2 _____

3 _____

4 _____

5 _____

6 _____

OBJ. 6   **Figure 1.2 Human Body Orientation and Direction**

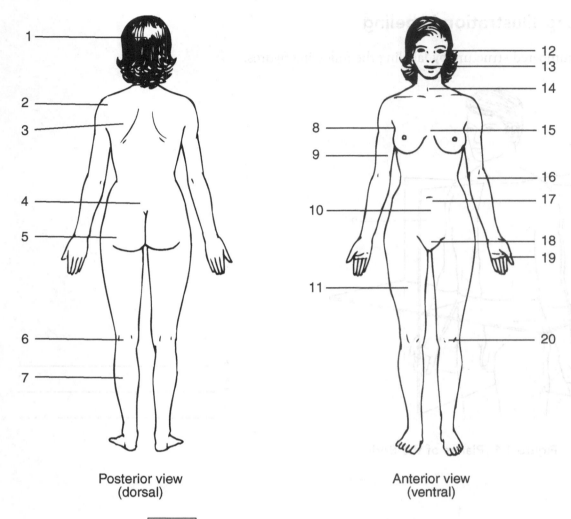

Posterior view
(dorsal)

Anterior view
(ventral)

OBJ. 6   **Figure 1.3 Regional Body References**

1 _____   11 _____

2 _____   12 _____

3 _____   13 _____

4 _____   14 _____

5 _____   15 _____

6 _____   16 _____

7 _____   17 _____

8 _____   18 _____

9 _____   19 _____

10 _____   20 _____

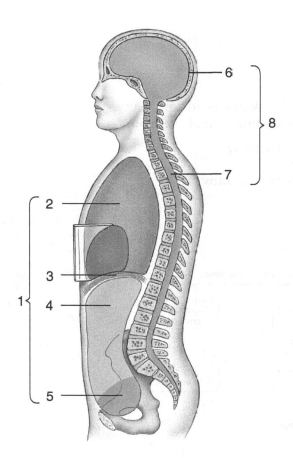

1	_____
2	_____
3	_____
4	_____
5	_____
6	_____
7	_____
8	_____

OBJ. 6   **Figure 1.4 Body Cavities—Sagittal View**

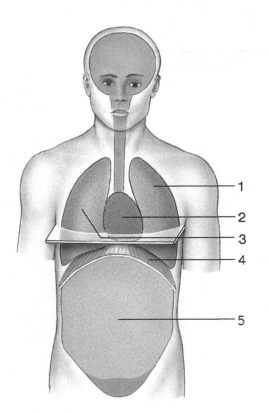

1	_____
2	_____
3	_____
4	_____
5	_____

OBJ. 6   **Figure 1.5 Body Cavities—Anterior View**

LEVEL 2 Concept Synthesis

Concept Map I

Using the following terms, fill in the circled, numbered, blank spaces to complete the concept map. Follow the numbers to comply with the organization of the map.

Surgical Anatomy   Regional Anatomy
Embryology   Cytology
Tissues   Macroscopic Anatomy
Structure of Organ Systems

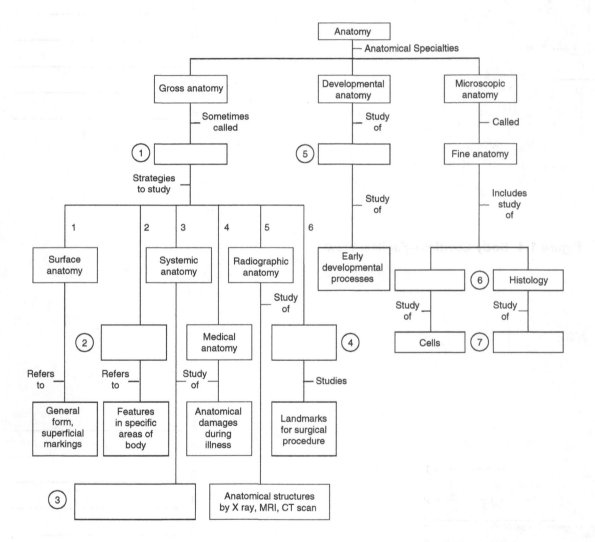

Concept Map II

Using the following terms, fill in the circled, numbered, blank spaces to complete the concept map. Follow the numbers to comply with the organization of the map.

Pathological Physiology
Functions of Living Cells
Exercise Physiology
Functions of Anatomical
    Structures

Histophysiology
Specific Organ Systems
Body Function Response to Athletics
Body Function Response to Changes
    in Atmospheric Pressure

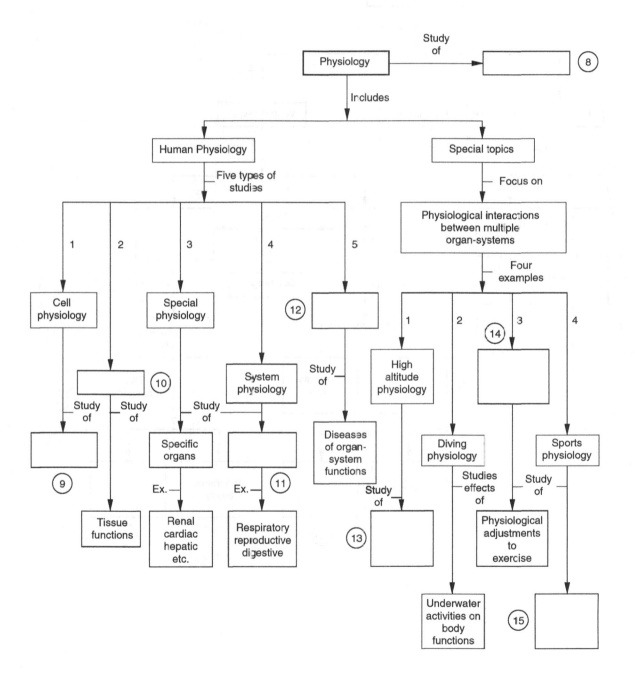

Concept Map III

Using the following terms, fill in the circled, numbered, blank spaces to complete the concept map. Follow the numbers to comply with the organization of the concept map.

Pelvic Cavity   Spinal Cord   Cranial Cavity
Heart   Abdominopelvic Cavity   Two Pleural Cavities

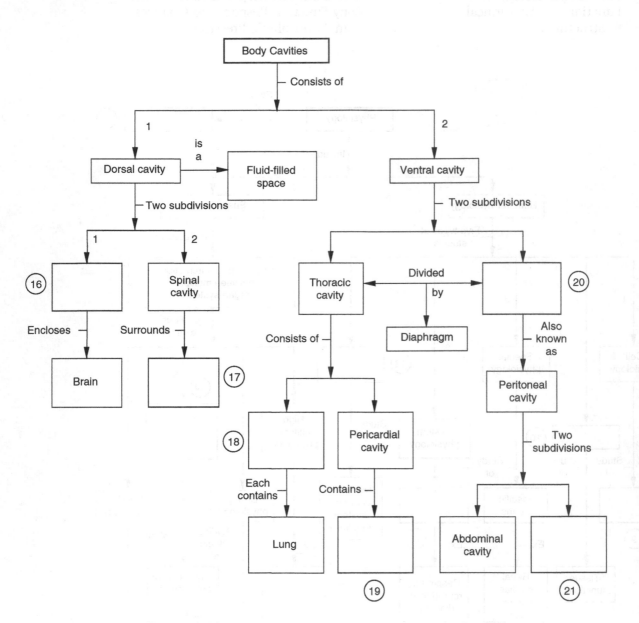

Concept Map IV

Using the following terms, fill in the circled, numbered, blank spaces to complete the concept map. Follow the numbers to comply with the organization of the concept map.

Angiogram   High-energy radiation   CT Scans
Echogram   Radio Waves   Radiologist

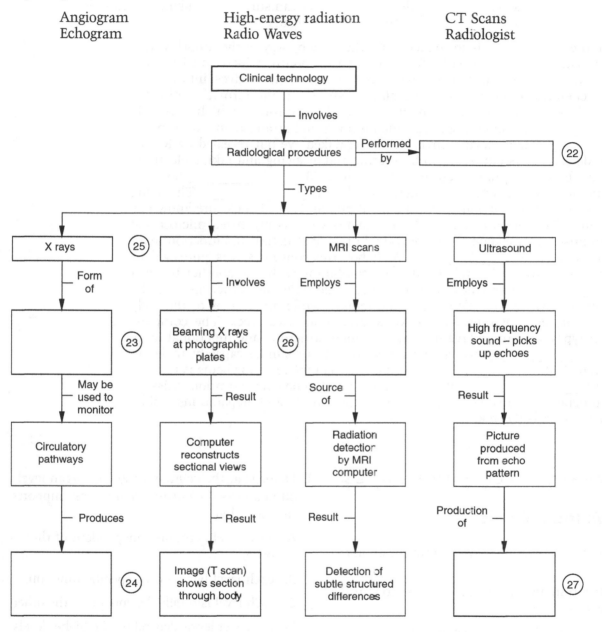

Body Trek

Using the terms below, fill in the blanks to complete the trek through the *levels of organization* in the human body.

Tissues   Organelles   Cells   Organism   Subatomic particles
Atoms   Systems   Molecules   Organs

Robo, the micro-robot, is introduced into the body by way of the mouth where immediate contact is made with the lining of the mouth, which consists of a mucous epithelium. Immediate feedback to Mission Control gives information about the chemical interactions taking place, resulting in the formation of cells. Robo discloses that protons, neutrons, and electrons, which are (1) _____, are combining in specific numbers and arrangements to form (2) _____. There, forms, invisible to the naked eye but revealed by Robo's advanced detection system, seem to be sharing and/or giving and taking electrons and forming bonds that hold them together to make (3) _____. Some of these structures are organized into structures called (4) _____. The living matter is surrounded by a double phospholipid-protein layered enclosure known as a membrane. The enclosed living substance along with its organized microscopic forms comprises the makeup of the individual units of structure and function in all living things called (5)_____. As Robo's trek continues, it is quite evident that there are many of the individual units combining with one another to form (6)_____. Four kinds are detected as Robo treks into other areas of the body. Epithelial was rather plentiful in the mouth, while other areas of the body include the presence of muscular, nervous, and connective types. The complex, multi-unit types form more organized and complex structural and functional units called (7) _____, which, when performing in a similar capacity, make up the eleven body (8)_____. The complex, complete, living being is referred to as an (9)_____. With the completion of Robo's investigation, Mission Control programs a convenient exit by way of the mouth, and preparations will be made for the next body trek.

COVERING ALL YOUR BASES

[L2] Multiple Choice

Select the best answer or answers from the choices given.

1. Variation in an organism's response to stimuli over time is:

   A. differentiation   C. positive feedback
   B. homeostasis   D. adaptability

2. Beginning with cells and proceeding through increasing levels of complexity, the correct sequence is:

   A. cells, tissues, organs, system
   B. cells, organs, tissues, system
   C. cells, system, tissues, organs
   D. system, organs, tissues, cells

3. Damage at the cellular, tissue, or organ level often affects the entire system. This supports the view that:

   A. each level is totally independent of the others
   B. each level has its own specific function
   C. each level is totally dependent on the other
   D. the lower levels depend on the higher levels

4. Anatomical position refers to a person standing erect, feet facing forward and:

   A. arms hanging to sides and palms of hands facing anteriorly and the thumbs located medially
   B. arms in a raised position and palms of hands facing forward with the thumbs located laterally

C. arms hanging to sides and palms of hands facing forward with the thumbs located laterally

D. arms in a raised position and palms of hands facing dorsally with the thumbs located medially

5. From the following selections, identify the directional terms in *correct sequence* that apply to the areas of the human body. (ventral, posterior, superior, inferior)

A. anterior, dorsal, cephalic, caudal

B. dorsal, anterior, caudal, cephalic

C. caudal, cephalic, anterior, posterior

D. cephalic, caudal, posterior, anterior

6. Which of the following pairs of anatomical terms are correctly associated with their opposites?

A. distal, coronal

B. cranial, caudal

C. proximal, lateral

D. cephalic, posterior

7. Resistance to x-ray penetration is called radiodensity. From the following selections, choose the one that correctly shows the order of *increasing* radiodensity of materials in the human body.

A. air, liver, fat, blood, bone, muscle

B. air, fat, liver, blood, muscle, bone

C. air, fat, blood, liver, muscle, bone

D. air, liver, blood, fat, muscle, bone

8. From the organ systems listed below, select the organs in correct sequence that are found in each of the systems. (cardiovascular, digestive, endocrine, urinary, integumentary)

A. blood vessels, pancreas, kidneys, lungs, nails

B. heart, stomach, lungs, kidneys, hair

C. heart, liver, pituitary gland, kidneys, skin

D. lungs, gall bladder, ovaries, bladder, sebaceous glands

9. In a negative feedback system, the mechanism that triggers an automatic response that corrects the situation is:

A. the presence of a receptor area and an effector area

B. an exaggeration of the stimulus

C. temporary repair to the damaged area

D. a variation outside of normal limits

10. Suppose an individual's body temperature is 37.3° C, which is outside the "normal" range. This variation from the "normal" range may represent:

A. an illness that has not been identified

B. individual variation rather than a homeostatic malfunction

C. the need to see a physician immediately

D. a variability that is abnormal

11. If the temperature of the body climbs above 99° F, negative feedback is triggered by:

A. increased heat conservation by restricted blood flow to the skin

B. the individual experiences shivering

C. activation of the positive feedback mechanism

D. an increased heat loss through enhanced blood flow to the skin and sweating

12. The term *medial surface* refers to the area:

A. close to the long axis of the body

B. away from the long axis of the body

C. toward an attached base

D. away from an attached base

13. Diagnostic procedures have not changed significantly in a thousand years. The four basic components used by physicians when conducting a physical examination are:

A. X-ray, CT scans, MRI scans, ultrasound

B. inspection, palpation, percussion, auscultation

C. blood pressure, urinalysis, x-ray, check reflexes

D. use of otoscope, ophthalmoscope, blood pressure, urinalysis

14. In order for a hypothesis to be valid, the three necessary characteristics are that it will be:

    A. intuitive, theoretical, and conclusive

    B. modifiable, reliable, scientific

    C. testable, unbiased, and repeatable

    D. A, B, and C are correct

15. Using the scientific method to investigate a problem begins by:

    A. designing an experiment to conduct the investigation

    B. collecting and analyzing data

    C. evaluating data to determine its relevance and validity

    D. proposing a hypothesis

[L2] Completion

Using the terms below, complete the following statements.

appendicitis	adaptability	stethoscope
sternum	knee	elbow
nervous	lymphatic	extrinsic regulation
cardiovascular		

1. As a result of exposure to increased sunlight, the skin produces pigments that absorb damaging solar radiation and provide a measure of protection. This process is called _____.

2. The system responsible for internal transport of cells and dissolved materials, including nutrients, wastes, and gases, is the _____ system.

3. The system responsible for defense against infection and disease is the _____.

4. Activities of the nervous and endocrine systems to control or adjust the activities of many different systems simultaneously are _____.

5. The system that performs crisis management by directing rapid, short-term, and very specific responses is the _____ system.

6. The popliteal artery can be found near the _____.

7. Tenderness in the right lower quadrant of the abdomen may indicate _____.

8. Moving proximally from the wrist brings you to the _____.

9. Auscultation is a technique that employs the use of a _____.

10. If a surgeon makes a midsagittal incision in the inferior region of the thorax, the incision would be made through the _____.

[L2] Short Essay

Briefly answer the following questions in the spaces provided below.

1. Despite obvious differences, all living things perform the same basic functions. List at least six (6) functions that are active processes in living organisms.

2. Show your understanding of the *levels of organization* in a complex living thing by using arrows and listing in correct sequence from the simplest level to the most complex level.

3. What is homeostatic regulation and how is it physiologically important?

4. What is the major difference between negative feedback and positive feedback?

5. References are made by the anatomist to the *front, back, head,* and *tail* of the human body. What directional reference terms are used to describe each one of these directions? Your answer should be in the order listed above.

6. What is the difference between a *sagittal* section and a *transverse* section?

7. Identify the body cavity in which each of the following organs or organ systems are found:

   a. brain, spinal cord

   b. cardiovascular, digestive, and urinary system

   c. heart, lungs

   d. stomach, intestines

8. List the basic sequence of the steps involved in the development of a scientific theory. (Use arrows to show stepwise sequence.)

LEVEL 3 Critical Thinking/Application

Using principles and concepts learned in *Introduction to Anatomy and Physiology*, answer the following questions. Write your answers on a separate sheet of paper.

1. Unlike the abdominal viscera, the thoracic viscera is separated into two compartments by an area called the mediastinum. What is the clinical importance of this compartmental arrangement?

2. The events of childbirth are associated with the process of positive feedback. Describe the events that confirm this statement.

3. A radioactive tracer is induced into the heart to trace the possibility of a blockage in or around the uterus. Give the sequence of *body cavities* that would be included as the tracer travels in the blood from the heart through the aorta and the uterine artery.

4. Suppose autoregulation fails to maintain homeostasis in the body. What is the process called that takes over by initiating activity of both the nervous and endocrine systems? What are the results of this comparable homeostatic mechanism?

5. Monitoring fetal development may be dangerous for the fetus if improper diagnostic techniques are used. Why is ultrasound an effective means of monitoring fetal development?

6. Gastroenterologists use x-rays to check for ulcers or other stomach and upper digestive tract disorders. Before the x-rays are taken, why is it necessary for the patient to drink large quantities of a solution that contains barium ions?

7. Body temperature is regulated by a control center in the brain that functions like a thermostat. Assuming a normal range of 98°–99° F, identify from the graph below what would happen if there was an increase or decrease in body temperature beyond the normal limits. Use the following selections to explain what would happen at no. 1 and no. 2 on the graph.

- body cools
- shivering
- increased sweating
- temperature declines

- body heat is conserved
- ↑ blood flow to skin
- ↓ blood flow to skin
- temperature rises

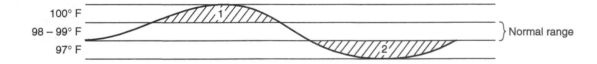

2

THE CHEMICAL LEVEL
OF ORGANIZATION

Overview

Technology within the last 40 to 50 years has allowed humans to "see and understand" the unseen within the human body. Today, instead of an "organ system view" of the body, we are able to look through the eyes of scientists using sophisticated technological tools and see the "ultra-micro world" within us. Our technology has permitted us to progress from the "macro-view" to the "micro-view" and to understand that the human body is made up of atoms, and that the interactions of these atoms control the physiological processes within the body.

The study of anatomy and physiology begins at the most fundamental level of organization, namely, individual atoms and molecules. The concepts in Chapter 2 provide a framework for understanding how simple components combine to make up the more complex forms that comprise the human body. Information is provided that shows how the chemical processes need to continue throughout life in an orderly and timely sequence if homeostasis is to be maintained.

The student activities in this chapter stress many of the important principles that make up the science of chemistry, both inorganic and organic. The tests are set up to measure your knowledge of chemical principles and to evaluate your ability to apply these principles to the structure and functions of organ systems within the human body.

LEVEL 1 Review of Chapter Objectives

1. Describe an atom and how atomic structure affects interactions between atoms.
2. Compare the ways in which atoms combine to form molecules and compounds.
3. Use chemical notation to symbolize chemical reactions.
4. Distinguish among the major types of chemical reactions that are important for studying physiology.
5. Describe the crucial role of enzymes in metabolism.
6. Distinguish between organic and inorganic compounds.
7. Explain how the chemical properties of water make life possible.
8. Discuss the importance of pH and the role of buffers in body fluids.
9. Describe the physiological roles of inorganic compounds.
10. Discuss the structure and function of carbohydrates, lipids, proteins, nucleic acids, and high-energy compounds.

[L1]   Multiple Choice

Place the letter corresponding to the correct answer in the space provided.

OBJ. 1   ____   1. The smallest chemical units of matter of which no chemical change can alter their identity are:

    a. electrons

    b. mesons

    c. protons

    d. atoms

OBJ. 1   ____   2. The three subatomic particles that are stable constituents of atomic structure are:

    a. carbon, hydrogen, oxygen

    b. protons, neutrons, electrons

    c. atoms, molecules, compounds

    d. cells, tissues, organs

OBJ. 1   ____   3. The protons in an atom are found only:

    a. outside the nucleus

    b. in the nucleus or outside the nucleus

    c. in the nucleus

    d. in orbitals

OBJ. 2   ____   4. The unequal sharing of electrons in a molecule of water is an example of:

    a. an ionic bond

    b. a polar covalent bond

    c. a double covalent bond

    d. a strong covalent bond

OBJ. 2   ____   5. The formation of cations and anions illustrates the attraction between:

    a. ionic bonds

    b. polar covalent bonds

    c. nonpolar covalent bonds

    d. double covalent bonds

OBJ. 3   ____   6. The symbol 2H means:

    a. one molecule of hydrogen

    b. two molecules of hydrogen

    c. two atoms of hydrogen

    d. a, b, and c are correct

OBJ. 4   ____   7. From the following choices, select the one that diagrams a typical *decomposition* reaction:

    a. $A + B \rightleftarrows AB$

    b. $AB + CD \rightarrow AD + CB$

    c. $AB \rightarrow A + B$

    d. $C + D \rightarrow CD$

OBJ. 4 ____ 8. A + B ⇄ AB is an example of a(n) _____ reaction.
   a. reversible
   b. synthesis
   c. decomposition
   d. a, b, and c are correct

OBJ. 4 ____ 9. AB + CD ⇄ AD + CB is an example of a(n) _____ reaction.
   a. reversible
   b. synthesis
   c. exchange
   d. a, b, and c are correct

OBJ. 5 ____ 10. The presence of an appropriate enzyme affects only the:
   a. rate of a reaction
   b. direction of the reaction
   c. products that will be formed from the reaction
   d. a, b, and c are correct

OBJ. 5 ____ 11. Organic catalysts made by a living cell to promote a specific reaction are called:
   a. nucleic acids
   b. buffers
   c. enzymes
   d. metabolites

OBJ. 6 ____ 12. The major difference between inorganic and organic compounds is that *inorganic* compounds are usually:
   a. small molecules held together partially or completely by ionic bonds
   b. made up of carbon, hydrogen, and oxygen
   c. large molecules that are soluble in water
   d. easily destroyed by heat

OBJ. 6 ____ 13. The four major classes of organic compounds are:
   a. water, acids, bases, and salts
   b. carbohydrates, fats, proteins, and water
   c. nucleic acids, salts, bases, and water
   d. carbohydrates, lipids, proteins, and nucleic acids

OBJ. 7 ____ 14. The ability of water to maintain a relatively constant temperature and then prevent rapid changes in body temperature is due to its:
   a. solvent capacities
   b. molecular structure
   c. boiling and freezing points
   d. capacity to absorb and distribute heat

OBJ. 8 ____ 15. To maintain homeostasis in the human body, the normal pH range of the blood must remain at:
   a. 6.80 to 7.20
   b. 7.35 to 7.45
   c. 7.0
   d. 6.80 to 7.80

OBJ. 8 _____ 16. The human body generates significant quantities of acids that may promote a disruptive:
   a. increase in pH
   b. pH of about 7.40
   c. decrease in pH
   d. sustained muscular contraction

OBJ. 9 _____ 17. The ideal medium for the absorption and/or transport of inorganic or organic compounds is:
   a. oil
   b. water
   c. blood
   d. lymph fluid

OBJ. 9 _____ 18. A solute that dissociates to release hydrogen ions and causes a decrease in pH is:
   a. a base
   b. a salt
   c. an acid
   d. water

OBJ. 9 _____ 19. Of the following ionic compounds, the one that is *least* likely to affect the concentrations of H^+ and OH^- ions is:
   a. a base
   b. a salt
   c. an acid
   d. a colloid

OBJ. 10 _____ 20. A carbohydrate molecule is made up of:
   a. carbon, hydrogen, oxygen
   b. monosaccharides, disaccharides, polysaccharides
   c. glucose, fructose, galactose
   d. carbon, hydrogen, nitrogen

OBJ. 10 _____ 21. Carbohydrates, lipids, and proteins are classified as:
   a. eicosanoids
   b. inorganic compounds
   c. organic compounds
   d. noncaloric compounds

OBJ. 10 _____ 22. The building blocks of proteins consist of chains of small molecules called:
   a. peptide bonds
   b. amino acids
   c. R groups
   d. amino groups

OBJ. 10 _____ 23. Special proteins that are involved in metabolic regulation are called:
   a. transport proteins
   b. contractile proteins
   c. structural proteins
   d. enzymes

OBJ. 10   _____ 24. The three basic components of a *single nucleotide* of a nucleic acid are:

      a. purines, pyrimidines, sugar

      b. sugar, phosphate group, nitrogen base

      c. guanine, cytosine, thymine

      d. pentose, ribose, deoxyribose

OBJ. 10   _____ 25. The most important high-energy compound found in the human body is:

      a. DNA

      b. UTP

      c. ATP

      d. GTP

[L1] Completion

Using the terms below, complete the following statements.

glucose	protons	mass number	buffers
H_2	acidic	carbonic acid	solvent
decomposition	ionic bond	organic	exergonic
salt	covalent bonds	cation	dehydration synthesis
catalysts	solute	water	prostaglandins
inorganic	endergonic		

OBJ. 1   1. The atomic number of an atom is determined by the number of _____.

OBJ. 1   2. The total number of protons and neutrons in the nucleus is the _____.

OBJ. 2   3. Atoms that complete their outer electron shells by sharing electrons with other atoms result in molecules held together by _____.

OBJ. 2   4. When one atom loses an electron and another accepts that electron, the result is the formation of a(n) _____.

OBJ. 3   5. The chemical notation that would indicate "one molecule of hydrogen composed of two hydrogen atoms" would be _____.

OBJ. 3   6. A chemical with a charge of +1 due to the loss of one electron refers to a _____.

OBJ. 4   7. A reaction that breaks a molecule into smaller fragments is called _____.

OBJ. 4   8. Reactions that release energy are said to be_____, and reactions that absorb heat are called _____ reactions.

OBJ. 5   9. Compounds that accelerate chemical reactions without themselves being permanently changed are called _____.

OBJ. 6   10. Compounds that contain the elements carbon and hydrogen, and usually oxygen, are _____ compounds.

OBJ. 6   11. Acid, bases, and salts are examples of _____ compounds.

OBJ. 7   12. The fluid medium of a solution is called the _____, and the dissolved substance is called the _____.

OBJ. 7   13. The most important constituent of the body, accounting for up to two-thirds of the total body weight, is _____.

OBJ. 8   14. A solution with a pH of 6.0 is _____.

OBJ. 8   15. Compounds in body fluids that maintain pH within normal limits are _____.

OBJ. 9   16. The interaction of an acid and a base in which the hydrogen ions of the acid are replaced by the positive ions of the base results in the formation of a(n) _____.

OBJ. 9   17. An example of a weak acid that serves as an effective buffer in the human body is _____.

OBJ. 10   18. The most important metabolic "fuel" in the body is _____.

OBJ. 10   19. The linking together of chemical units by the removal of water to create a more complex molecule is called _____.

OBJ. 10   20. The eicosanoids derived from arachidonic acid, which may produce the sensation of pain, are the _____.

[L1] Matching

Match the terms in column B with those in column A. Use letters for answers in the spaces provided.

Part I   **Column A**   **Column B**

OBJ. 1   _____   1. electron   A. two products; two reactants

OBJ. 2   _____   2. N_2 B. sodium chloride

OBJ. 2   _____   3. polar covalent bond   C. negative electric charge

OBJ. 3   _____   4. NaCl   D. inorganic base

OBJ. 4   _____   5. exchange reaction   E. triple covalent bond

OBJ. 5   _____   6. enzyme   F. unequal sharing of electrons

OBJ. 6   _____   7. HCl   G. catalyst

OBJ. 6   _____   8. NaOH   H. inorganic acid

Part II   **Column A**   **Column B**

OBJ. 7   _____   9. ionization   I. hydroxyl group

OBJ. 7   _____   10. hydrolysis   J. uracil

OBJ. 8   _____   11. OH^- K. thymine

OBJ. 8   _____   12. H^+ L. bicarbonate ion

OBJ. 9   _____   13. HCO_3^- M. hydrogen ion

OBJ. 10   _____   14. DNA-N base   N. dissociation

OBJ. 10   _____   15. RNA-N base   O. reactivity

[L1]   Drawing/Illustration Labeling

Identify each numbered structure by labeling the following figures:

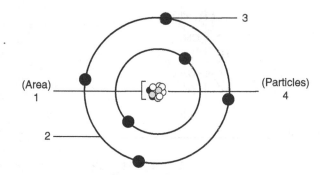

1 _____

2 _____

3 _____

4 _____

OBJ. 1   **Figure 2.1   Diagram of an Atom**

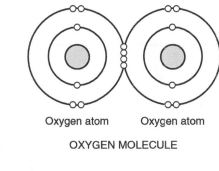

1 _____

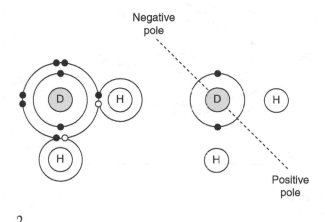

2 _____

OBJ. 2   **Figure 2.2   Identification of Types of Bonds**

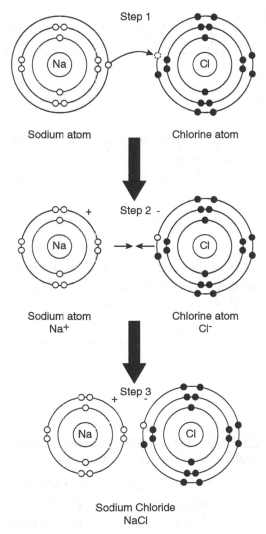

3 _____

1 _____

2 _____

3 _____

4 _____

5 _____

6 _____

7 _____

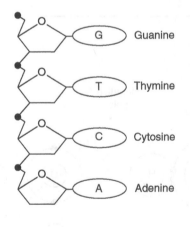

8 _____

OBJ. 10   **Figure 2.3   Identification of Organic Molecules**
(Select from the following terms to identify each molecule.)

polysaccharide	cholesterol	monosaccharide
amino acid	DNA	saturated fatty acid
disaccharide	polyunsaturated fatty acid	

LEVEL 2 Concept Synthesis

Concept Map I

Using the following terms, fill in the circled, numbered, blank spaces to complete
the concept map. Follow the numbers to comply with the organization of the map.

Monosaccharides   Sucrose   Complex carbohydrates
Glucose   Glycogen   Bulk, fiber
Disaccharides

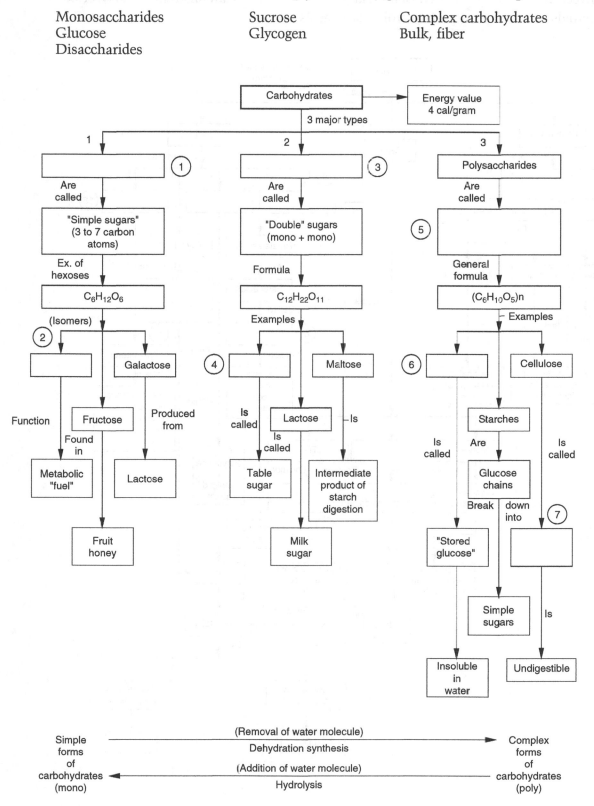

Concept Map II

Using the following terms, fill in the circled, numbered, blank spaces to complete
the concept map. Follow the numbers to comply with the organization of the map.

Local hormones   Di-   Saturated
Glyceride   Phospholipid   Carbohydrate + diglyceride
Steroids   Glycerol + fatty acids

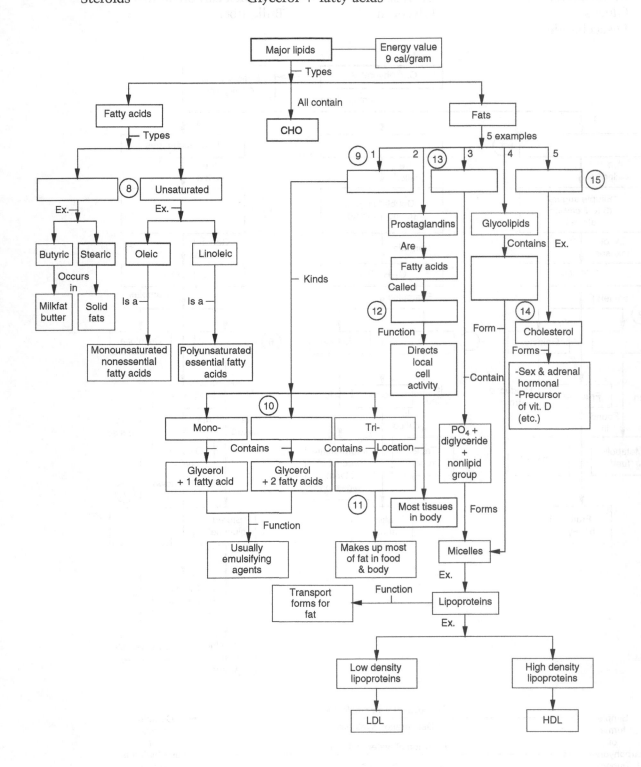

Concept Map III

Using the following terms, fill in the circled, numbered, blank spaces to complete the concept map. Follow the numbers to comply with the organization of the concept map.

Variable group   –COOH   Globular proteins
Enzymes   Elastin   Quaternary
Structural proteins   Amino acids   Alpha helix
Amino group   Primary

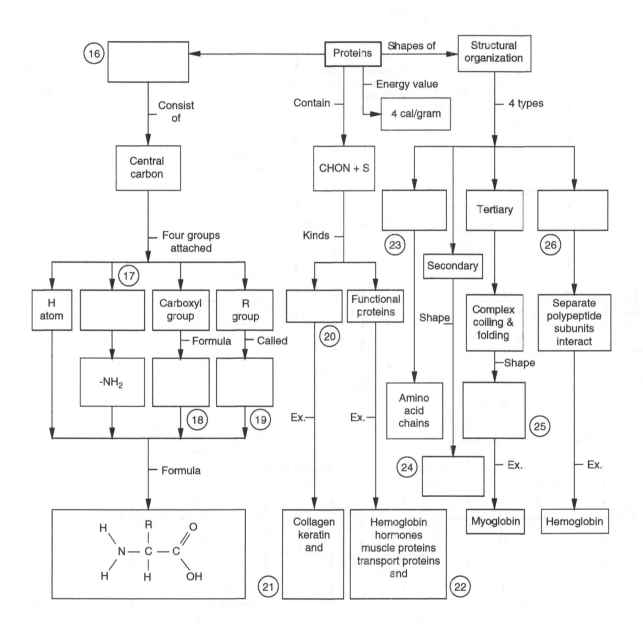

Concept Map IV

Using the following terms, fill in the circled, numbered, blank spaces to complete the concept map. Follow the numbers to comply with the organization of the concept map.

Ribonucleic acid   Deoxyribose nucleic acid   N bases
Pyrimidines   Adenine   Thymine
Deoxyribose   Purines   Ribose

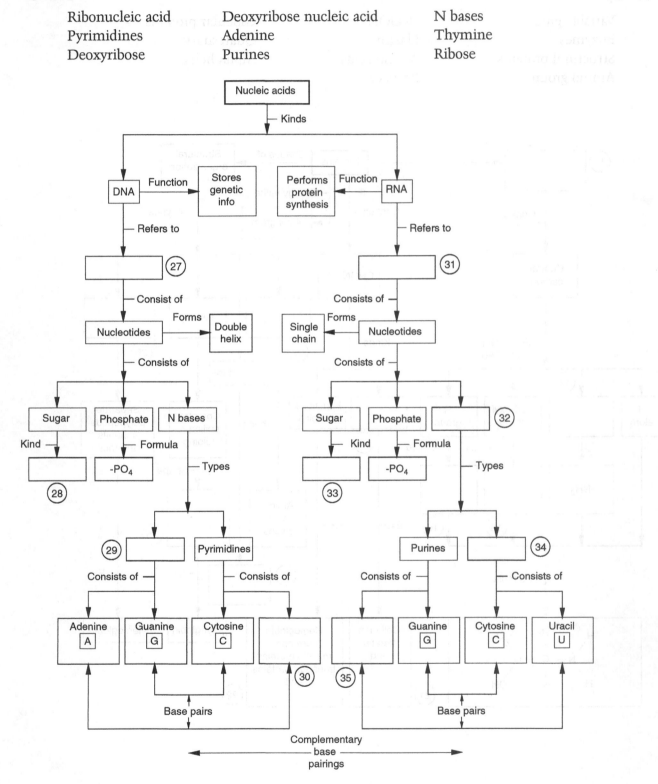

Body Trek

Using the terms below, fill in the blanks to complete the trek through the chemical organization in the human body.

Heat capacity	Neutrons	Six	Polar covalent
Glycogen	Protein	Zero	Solvent
Polypeptide	Isotope	66	Water
Phosphorylation	Oxygen	ATP	Negatively
DNA	Deuterium	Eight	Electrons
Protons	Lowering	100	Glucose
Molecule	Hydrophobic	RNA	Monosaccharide
Hydrophilic	Oxygen gas	Orbitals	Hydrolysis
Nucleus	Dehydration synthesis	Double covalent bond	

Robo's task to monitor chemical activity begins with a trek outside the body. The robotic "engineers" have decided to place Robo in a cyclotron, an apparatus used in atomic research. The robotic sensors immediately detect an environment that has negative particles called (1) _____, which are whirling around in cloudlike formations called (2) _____. The particles are travelling at a high rate of speed and appear to be circling stationary particles in a central region called the (3) _____. The central region contains positive charges called (4) _____ and, with the exception of hydrogen in its natural state, all the areas "observed" contain particles that are neutral called (5) _____. Robo's electronic systems appear to be overloaded and there is difficulty monitoring all the activity in the surrounding environment. Feedback to Mission Control reads, "Oops! There goes one that looks exactly like hydrogen, but it has two neutrons looking like a heavier hydrogen called (6) _____, which is chemically identified as a(n) (7) _____ commonly used as a radioactive tracer in research laboratories." Robo signals the presence of an "area" that contains eight positive charges, eight neutral particles, and eight negative charges, which is identified as a(n) (8) _____ atom. Atoms of this kind appear to be chemically active because the outermost cloud only has (9) _____ negative particles and a full complement of (10) _____ is necessary if the atom is to maintain chemical stability. In the atmosphere these "active atoms" are constantly in "search" of atoms of their own kind. When two of these atoms contact one another there is a chemical interaction evidenced by each one sharing two electrons and forming a(n) (11) _____, resulting in one (12) _____ of (13) _____. When a single oxygen atom comes into contact with two hydrogen atoms, a(n) (14) _____ bond is formed due to an unequal sharing of electrons. The result is a region around the oxygen atom that is (15) _____ charged and the region around the hydrogen atoms is positively charged.

After removal of the micro-robot from the cyclotron, preparation is made for Robo to be catheterized through the heart to begin the body trek. The robot is immediately swept from the heart into the large aorta where it is transported in a "sea" of liquid with suspended solid particles. As it treks along, it is obvious that the liquid portion of the surrounding solution is (16) _____, which comprises about (17) _____ percent of the total body weight. Mission Control requests more information about this liquid medium. An immediate response confirms that the medium can withstand extremes of cold temperatures reaching a freezing point of (18) _____ °C and a boiling point of (19) _____ °C. The molecules of this medium have a high (20) _____, which prevents rapid changes in body temperature, and the heat absorbed during evaporation makes perspiration an effective means of losing heat and (21) _____ body temperature. The robot senses the dissolving of numerous organic and inorganic compounds establishing the (22) _____ property of the aqueous medium. The readily dissolved molecules are said to be (23) _____, and some of the body's fat deposits, which are insoluble, are said to be (24) _____. Robo's adventure through the bloodstream is briefly interrupted by a trek through the liver. The robot's sensors are fully activated to cope with all the information available in the liver. Robo is surrounded by a sweet substance, (25) _____ , a (26) _____ , which is the body's most important metabolic fuel. The molecules of this sweet stuff are "sticking" together because water is "leaking out" and molecules of (27) _____ are forming due to the process of (28) _____. What a chemical show! Robo detects a signal that indicates additional sugar is needed for energy in other parts of the body and the molecules formed by the "sticking" together of the sugar molecules need to be separated so other cells can use this fuel for energy. The liver responds by engaging in the process of (29) _____ and sending the "ready fuel" by way of the bloodstream to where it is needed. Other cells are involved in protein synthesis. As the (30) _____ in the nucleus transcribes onto (31) _____, a message will translate into the production of (32) _____ chains resulting in the formation of large (33) _____ molecules that have both structural and functional roles in the body. The process of (34) _____ in the mitochondria of the liver cells is producing a high-energy compound called (35) _____. The end of Robo's trek is imminent and an exit route is facilitated via the hepatic vein with eventual arrival in the brachial vein where the process of bloodletting will release the robot. What a trek!

COVERING ALL YOUR BASES

[L2] Multiple Choice

Select the best answer or answers from the choices given.

1. The chemical properties of every element are determined by:

   A. the number and arrangement of electrons in the outer energy level

   B. the number of protons in the nucleus

   C. the number of protons and neutrons in the nucleus

   D. the atomic weight of the atom

2. Whether an atom will react with another atom will be determined primarily by:

   A. the number of protons present in the atom

   B. the number of electrons in the outermost energy level

   C. the atomic weight of the atom

   D. the number of subatomic particles present in the atom

3. In the formation of *nonpolar* covalent bonds there is:

   A. equal sharing of protons and electrons

   B. donation of electrons

   C. unequal sharing of electrons

   D. equal sharing of electrons

4. The symbol $2H_2O$ means that two identical molecules of water are each composed of:

   A. 4 hydrogen atoms and 2 oxygen atoms

   B. 2 hydrogen atoms and 2 oxygen atoms

   C. 4 hydrogen atoms and 1 oxygen atom

   D. 2 hydrogen atoms and 1 oxygen atom

5. The reason water is particularly effective as a solvent is:

   A. polar molecules are formed due to the closeness of hydrogen atoms

   B. cations and anions are produced by hydration

   C. hydrophobic molecules have many polar covalent bonds

   D. it has a high heat capacity, which dissolves molecules

6. The formation of a complex molecule by the removal of water is called:

   A. dehydration synthesis

   B. hydrolysis

   C. activation energy

   D. reversible reaction

7. A *salt* may best be described as:

   A. an organic molecule created by chemically altering an acid or base

   B. an inorganic molecule that buffers solutions

   C. an inorganic molecule created by the reaction of an acid and a base

   D. an organic molecule used to flavor food

8. The chemical makeup of a lipid molecule is different from a carbohydrate in that the lipid molecule:

   A. contains much less oxygen than a carbohydrate having the same number of carbon atoms

   B. contains twice as much oxygen as the carbohydrate

   C. contains equal amounts of carbon and oxygen in its molecular structure

   D. the chemical makeup is the same

9. Lipid deposits are important as *energy reserves* because:

   A. they appear as fat deposits on the body

   B. they are readily broken down to release energy

   C. the energy released from lipids is metabolized quickly

   d. lipids provide twice as much energy as carbohydrates

10. Proteins differ from carbohydrates in that they:

    A. are not energy nutrients

    B. do not contain carbon, hydrogen, and oxygen

    C. always contain nitrogen

    D. are inorganic compounds

11. Compared to the other major organic compounds, nucleic acids are unique in that they:

    A. contain nitrogen

    B. store and process information at the molecular level

    C. are found only in the nuclei of cells

    D. control the metabolic activities of the cell

12. In the human body, compounds that stabilize the pH of a solution by removing or replacing hydrogen ions are called:

    A. suspensions

    B. colloids

    C. hydrophilic

    D. buffers

13. From the selections that follow, choose the one that represents the symbols for each of the following elements in the correct order. (carbon, sodium, phosphorus, iron, oxygen, nitrogen, sulfur)

    A. C, So, Ph, I, O, Ni, S

    B. C, Na, P, I, O, N, S

    C. C, Na, P, Fe, O, N, S

    D. C, Na, P, Fe, O_2, N_2, S

14. If an atom has an atomic number of 92 and its atomic weight is 238, how many protons does the atom have?

    A. 238

    B. 92

    C. 146

    D. 54

15. If the second energy level of an atom has one electron, how many more does it need to fill it to its maximum capacity?

    A. 1

    B. 2

    C. 5

    D. 7

16. The atomic structure of hydrogen looks like which one of the following?

A.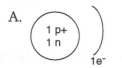

C.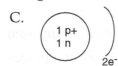

B.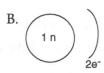

d.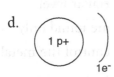

17. The number of neutrons in $_8O^{17}$ is:

    A. 8

    B. 9

    C. 7

    D. 17

18. Which one of the following selections represents the pH of the *weakest* acid?

    A. 7.0

    B. 1.3

    C. 3.2

    D. 6.7

19. The type of bond that has the most important effects on the properties of water and the shapes of complex molecules is the:

    A. hydrogen bond

    B. ionic bond

    C. covalent bond

    D. polar covalent bond

20. If oxygen has an atomic weight of 16, what is the molecular weight of an oxygen molecule?

    A. 16

    B. 8

    C. 32

    D. 2

21. If the concentration of hydrogen ions is (0.000001) what is the pH?

    A. 1

    B. 5

    C. 6

    D. 7

22. Two simple sugars joined together form a disaccharide. The reaction involved for this to occur necessitates:

    A. the removal of water to create a more complex molecule

    B. the addition of water to create a more complex molecule

    C. the presence of cations and anions to initiate electrical attraction

    D. the disassembling of molecules through hydrolysis

23. The presence of a *carboxylic acid group* at the end of a carbon chain demonstrates a characteristic common to all:

    A. amino acids

    B. inorganic acids

    C. nucleic acids

    D. organic acids

24. The three important functions of triglycerides or neutral fats are:

    A. solubility, reactivity, and lubrication

    B. energy, insulation, and protection

    C. support, movement, and transport

    D. buffering, metabolic regulation, and defense

[L2]   Completion

Using the terms below, complete the following statements.

nucleic acids	isomers	molecular weight
peptide bond	ions	hydrolysis
ionic bonds	hydrophobic	inorganic compounds
mole	saturated	dehydration synthesis
molecule	alkaline	alpha particles

1. The helium nucleus, consisting of two protons and two neutrons, describes the characteristics of _____.

2. For every element, a quantity that has a mass in grams equal to the atomic weight will contain the same number of atoms. The name given to this quantity is a(n) _____.

3. A chemical structure containing more than one atom is a(n) _____.

4. Atoms or molecules that have positive or negative charges are called _____.

5. Electrical attraction between opposite charges produces a weak _____.

6. The sum of the atomic weight of the components in a compound is the _____.

7. Small molecules held together partially or completely by ionic bonds are _____.

8. Molecules that have few if any polar covalent bonds and do not dissolve in water are _____.

9. If the pH is above 7 with hydroxyl ions in the majority, the solution is _____.

10. Of the four major classes of organic compounds, the one responsible for storing genetic information is the _____.

11. Molecules that have the same molecular formula but different structural formulas are _____.

12. The process that breaks a complex molecule into smaller fragments by the addition of a water molecule is _____.

13. Glycogen, a branched polysaccharide composed of interconnected glucose molecules, is formed by the process of _____.

14. Butter, fatty meat, and ice cream are examples of sources of fatty acids that are said to be _____.

15. The attachment of a carboxylic acid group of one amino acid to the amino group of another forms a connection called a(n) _____.

[L2]   Short Essay

Briefly answer the following questions in the spaces provided below.

1. Suppose an atom has eight protons, eight neutrons, and eight electrons. Construct a diagram of the atom and identify the subatomic particles by placing them in their proper locations.

2. From the following simulated reaction, identify the *decomposition* reaction (a) and the synthesis reaction (b).

   a. $A-B-C-D-E + H_2O \rightarrow A-B-C-H + HO-D-E$

   b. $A-B-C-H + HO-D-E \rightarrow A-B-C-D-E + H_2O$

3. Why are the elements helium, argon, and neon called *inert gases*?

4. In a water (H_2O) molecule the unequal sharing of electrons creates a *polar covalent bond*. Why?

5. Compute the molecular weight (MW) of one molecule of glucose ($C_6H_{12}O_6$). [Note: atomic weights C = 12; H = 1; O = 16]

6. List six important characteristics of water that make life possible.

7. List the four major classes of organic compounds found in the human body and give an example for each one.

8. Differentiate between a saturated and an unsaturated fatty acid.

9. Using the four kinds of nucleotides that make up a DNA molecule, construct a model that will show the correct arrangement of the components that make up each nucleotide. *Name each nucleotide*.

10. What are the three components that make up one nucleotide of ATP?

LEVEL 3 Critical Thinking/Application

Using principles and concepts learned in Chapter 2, answer the following questions. Write your answers on the answer sheet provided.

1. Using the letters AB and CD, show how each would react in an exchange reaction.

2. Why might "baking soda" be used to relieve excessive stomach acid?

3. Using the glucose molecule ($C_6H_{12}O_6$), demonstrate your understanding of dehydration synthesis by writing an equation to show the formation of a molecule of sucrose ($C_{12}H_{22}O_{11}$). [Make sure the equation is balanced.]

4. Even though the recommended dietary intake for carbohydrates is 55 to 60 percent of the daily caloric intake, why do the carbohydrates account for less than 3 percent of our total body weight?

5. Why can a drug test detect the use of marijuana for days after the drug has been used?

6. Why is it potentially dangerous to take excessive amounts of vitamins A, D, E, and K?

7. You are interested in losing weight so you decide to eliminate your intake of fats completely. You opt for a fat substitute such as *Olestra*, which contains compounds that cannot be used by the body. Why might this decision be detrimental to you?

8. A friend of yours is a bodybuilder who takes protein supplements with the idea that this will increase the body's muscle mass. What explanation might you give your friend to convince him/her that the purchase of protein supplements is a waste of money?

3

CELLS:
THE LIVING UNITS

Student Objectives

When you have completed the exercises in this chapter, you will have accomplished the following objectives:

Overview of the Cellular Basis of Life

1. Define *cell*.
2. List the three major regions of a generalized cell and indicate the function of each.

The Plasma Membrane: Structure and Functions

3. Describe the chemical composition of the plasma membrane and relate it to membrane functions.
4. Compare the structure and function of tight junctions, desmosomes, and gap junctions.
5. Relate plasma membrane structure to active and passive transport mechanisms. Differentiate between these transport processes relative to energy source, substances transported, direction, and mechanism.
6. Define *membrane potential* and explain how the resting membrane potential is maintained.
7. Describe the role of the plasma membrane when cells interact with their environment.
8. List several roles of membrane receptors.

The Cytoplasm

9. Describe the composition of the cytosol; define *inclusions* and list several types.
10. Discuss the structure and function of mitochondria.
11. Discuss the structure and function of ribosomes, the endoplasmic reticulum, and the Golgi apparatus including functional interrelationships among these organelles.

12. Compare the functions of lysosomes and peroxisomes.
13. Name and describe the structure and function of cytoskeletal elements.
14. Describe the roles of centrioles in mitosis and in the formation of cilia and flagella.

The Nucleus

15. Describe the chemical composition, structure, and function of the nuclear membrane, nucleolus, and chromatin.

Cell Growth and Reproduction

16. List the phases of the cell life cycle and describe the events of each phase.
17. Describe the process of DNA replication.
18. Define *gene* and *genetic code* and explain the function of genes.
19. Name the two phases of protein synthesis and describe the roles of DNA, mRNA, tRNA, and rRNA in each phase. Contrast triplets, codons, and anticodons.
20. Describe the function of ubiquitin in degradation of soluble protein.

Extracellular Materials

21. Name and describe the composition of extracellular materials.

The basic unit of structure and function in the human body is the cell. Each of a cell's parts, or organelles, as well as the entire cell, is organized to perform a specific function. Cells have the ability to metabolize, grow, reproduce, move, and respond to stimuli. The cells of the body differ in shape, size, and specific roles in the body. Cells that are similar in structure and function form tissues, which, in turn, form the various body organs.

Student activities in this chapter include questions relating to the structure and functional abilities of the generalized animal cell.

BUILDING THE FRAMEWORK

Overview of the Cellular Basis of Life

1. Answer the following questions by inserting your responses in the answer blanks.

    1. List the four concepts of the cell theory. _____

    _____

    _____

    _____

    2. List three different cell shapes. _____

    _____

    3. Name the three major parts of any cell. _____

    _____

    4. Define *generalized* or *composite cell*. _____

    _____

    _____

    _____

The Plasma Membrane: Structure and Functions

1. Figure 3.1 is a diagram of a portion of a plasma membrane. Select four different colors and color the coding circles and the corresponding structures in the diagram. Then respond to the questions that follow, referring to Figure 3.1 and inserting your answers in the answer blanks.

   ◯ Phospholipid molecules   ◯ Carbohydrate molecules

   ◯ Protein molecules   ◯ Cholesterol molecules

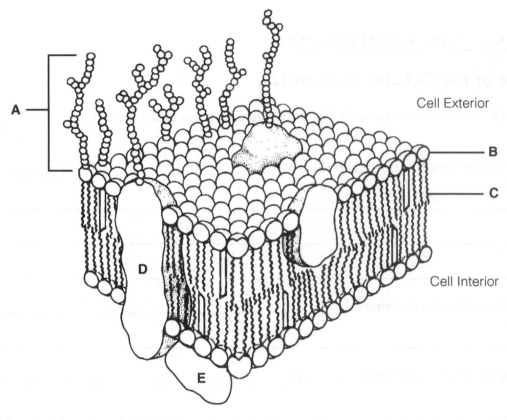

Figure 3.1

1. What name is given to this model of membrane structure? _____

2. What is the function of cholesterol molecules in the plasma membrane? _____

   _____

3. Name the carbohydrate-rich area at the cell surface (indicated by bracket A). _____

4. Which label, B or C, indicates the nonpolar region of a phospholipid molecule? _____

5. Does nonpolar mean hydrophobic or hydrophilic? _____

6. Which label, D or E, indicates an integral protein and which a peripheral protein? _____

   _____

2. Label the specializations of the plasma membrane, shown in Figure 3.2, and color the diagram as you wish. Then, answer the questions provided that refer to this figure.

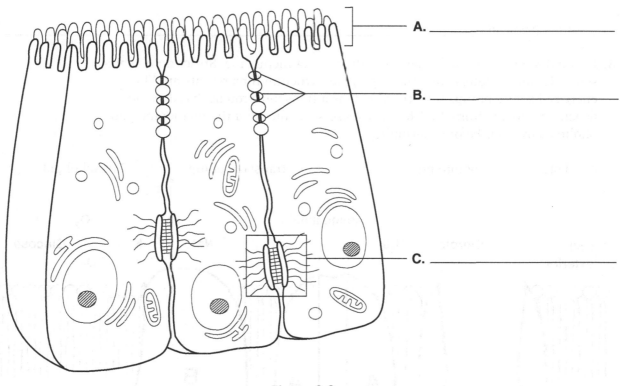

A. _____

B. _____

C. _____

Figure 3.2

1. What is the structural significance of microvilli? _____

   _____

2. What type of cell function(s) does the presence of microvilli typically

   indicate? _____

3. What protein acts as a microvilli "stiffener"? _____

4. Name two factors in addition to special membrane junctions that help

   hold cells together. _____

5. Which cell junction forms an impermeable barrier? _____

6. Which cell junction is a buttonlike adhesion? _____

7. Which junction has linker proteins spanning the intercellular space? _____

8. Which cell junction (not shown) allows direct passage from one cell's

   cytoplasm to the next? _____

9. What name is given to the transmembrane proteins that allow this

   direct passage? _____

3. Figure 3.3 is a simplified diagram of the plasma membrane. Structure A represents channel proteins constructing a pore, structure B represents an ATP-energized solute pump, and structure C is a transport protein that does not depend on energy from ATP. Identify these structures and the membrane phospholipids by color before continuing.

   ◯ Pore   ◯ Solute pump   ◯ Passive transport pump   ◯ Phospholipids

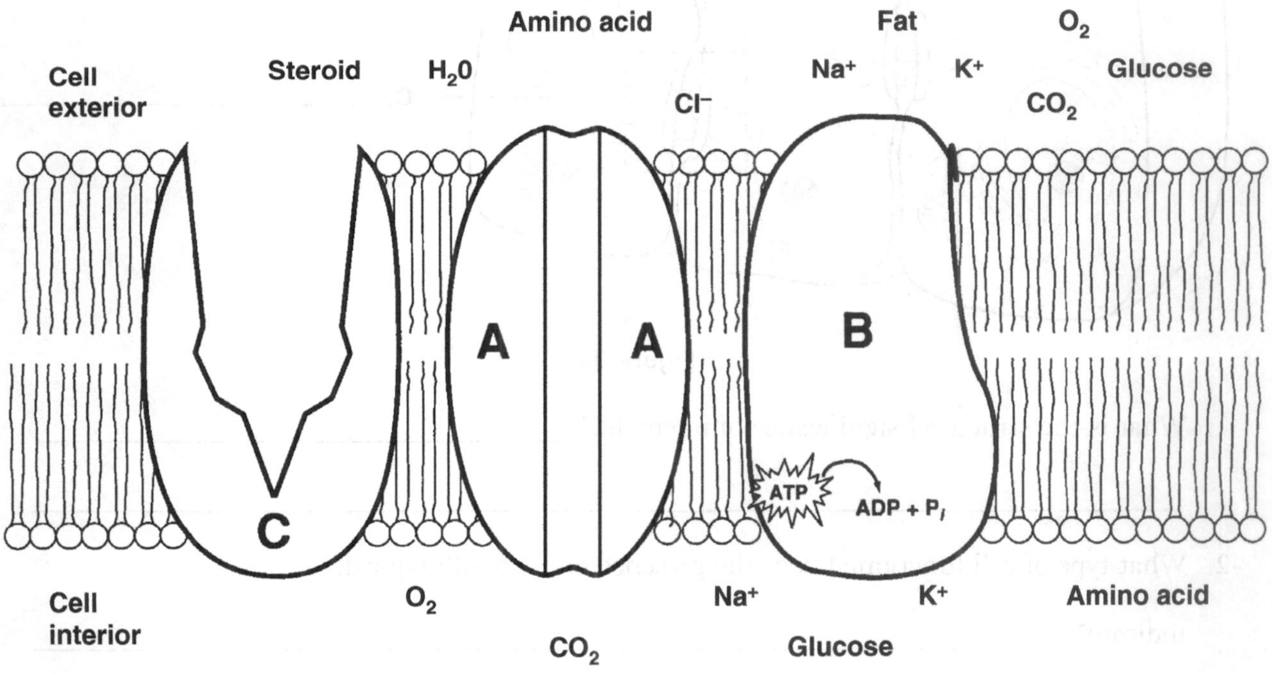

Figure 3.3

Now add arrows to Figure 3.3 as instructed next: For each substance that moves through the plasma membrane, draw an arrow indicating its (most likely) direction of movement (into or out of the cell). If it is moved actively, use a red arrow; if it is moved passively, use a blue arrow.

Finally, answer the following questions referring to Figure 3.3:

1. Which of the substances shown move passively *through the lipid* part

   of the membrane? _____

2. Which of the substances shown enter the cell by attachment to a passive-

   transport protein carrier? _____

3. Which of the substances shown moves passively through the membrane

   by moving through its pores? _____

4. Which of the substances shown would have to use a solute pump to be

   transported through the membrane? _____

4. Select the key choices that characterize each of the following statements. Insert
   the appropriate answers in the answer blanks.

Key Choices

A. Caveolin-coated pit   D. Exocytosis   G. Pinocytosis

B. Diffusion, simple   E. Filtration   H. Receptor-mediated endocytosis

C. Diffusion, osmosis   F. Phagocytosis   I. Solute pumping

_____   1. Engulfment processes that require ATP

_____   2. Driven by molecular energy

_____   3. Driven by hydrostatic (fluid) pressure (typically blood pressure
                               in the body)

_____   4. Moves down (with) a concentration gradient

_____   5. Moves up (against) a concentration gradient; requires a carrier

_____   6. Uses a clathrin-coated vesicle ("pit")

_____   7. Typically involves *coupled systems*; that is, symports or antiports

_____   8. Examples of vesicular transport

_____   9. A means of bringing fairly large particles into the cell

_____   10. Used to eject wastes and to secrete cell products

_____   11. May provide signaling platforms

5. Figure 3.4 shows three microscope fields containing red blood cells. Arrows indicate the direction of net osmosis. Select three different colors and use them to color the coding circles and the corresponding cells in the diagrams. Then, respond to the questions below, referring to Figure 3.4 and inserting your answers in the spaces provided.

◯ Water moves into the cells   ◯ Water enters and exits the cells at the same rate

◯ Water moves out of the cells

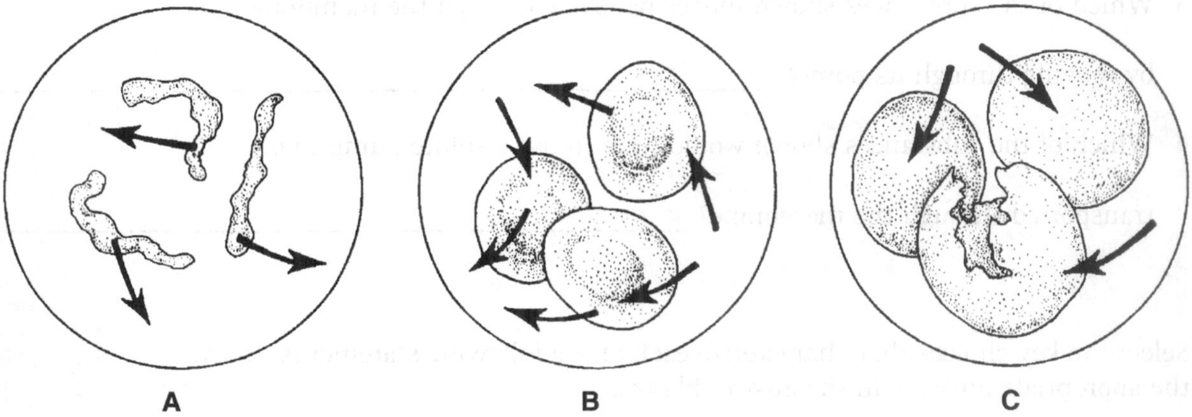

A   B   C

Figure 3.4

1. Name the type of tonicity illustrated in diagrams A, B, and C.

   A. _____   B. _____   C. _____

2. Name the terms that describe the cellular shapes in diagrams A, B, and C.

   A. _____   B. _____   C. _____

3. What does *isotonic* mean? _____

4. Why are the cells in diagram C bursting? _____

   _____

5. What is the difference between tonicity and osmolarity? _____

   _____

6. The differential permeability of the plasma membrane to sodium (Na^+) and potassium (K^+) ions results in the development of a voltage (resting membrane potential) of about –70 mV across the membrane as indicated in the simple diagram in Figure 3.5.

First, draw in some Na^+ and K^+ ions in the cytoplasm and extracellular fluid, taking care to indicate their *relative* abundance in the two sites.

Second, add positive and negative signs to the inner and outer surfaces of the "see-through" cell's plasma membrane to indicate its electrical polarity.

Third, draw in arrows and color them to match each of the coding circles associated with the conditions noted just below.

○ Potassium electrical gradient   ○ Sodium electrical gradient

○ Potassium concentration gradient   ○ Sodium concentration gradient

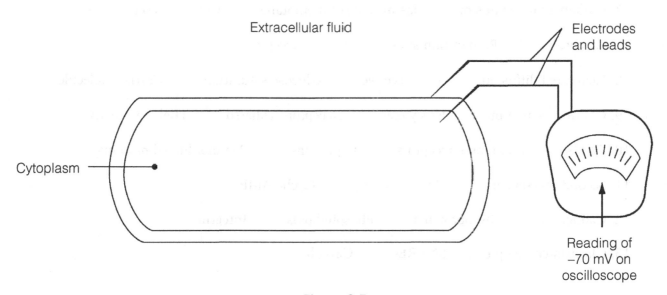

Figure 3.5

7. Referring to plasma membranes, circle the term or phrase that does not belong in each of the following groupings.

1. Fused protein molecules of adjacent cells   Tight junction   Lining of digestive tract

   Communication between adjacent cells   No intercellular space

2. Lipoprotein filaments   Binding of tissue layers   Heart muscle

   Impermeable junction   Desmosomes

3. Impermeable intercellular space   Molecular communication   Embryonic cells

   Gap junction   Protein channel

4. Resting membrane potential   High extracellular potassium ion (K⁺) concentration

   High extracellular sodium ion (Na⁺) concentration   Nondiffusible protein anions

   Separation of cations from anions

5. –50 to –100 millivolts   Electrochemical gradient   Inside membrane negatively charged

   K⁺ diffuses across membrane more rapidly than Na⁺   Protein anions move out of cell

6. Active transport   Sodium-potassium pump   Polarized membrane

   More K⁺ pumped out than Na⁺ carried in   ATP required

7. Carbohydrate chains on cytoplasmic side of membrane   Cell adhesion

   Glycocalyx   Recognition sites   Antigen receptors

8. Facilitated diffusion   Nonselective   Glucose saturation   Carrier molecule

9. Clathrin-coated pit   Exocytosis   Receptor-mediated   High specificity

10. CAMs   Membrane receptors   G proteins   Channel-linked proteins

11. Second messenger   NO Ca^{2+} Cyclic AMP

12. Cadherins   Glycoproteins   Phospholipids   Integrins

13. Clathrin-coated pit   SNAREs   Caveolin

The Cytoplasm

1. Define *cytosol*. _____

_____

2. Differentiate clearly between *organelles* and *inclusions*. _____

_____

_____

_____

3. Using the following terms, correctly label all cell parts indicated by leader lines in Figure 3.6. Then select different colors for each structure and use them to color the coding circles and the corresponding structures in the illustration.

◯ Plasma membrane   ◯ Mitochondrion   ◯ Nuclear membrane   ◯ Centrioles

◯ Chromatin threads   ◯ Nucleolus   ◯ Golgi apparatus   ◯ Microvilli

◯ Rough endoplasmic reticulum (rough ER)   ◯ Smooth endoplasmic reticulum (smooth ER)

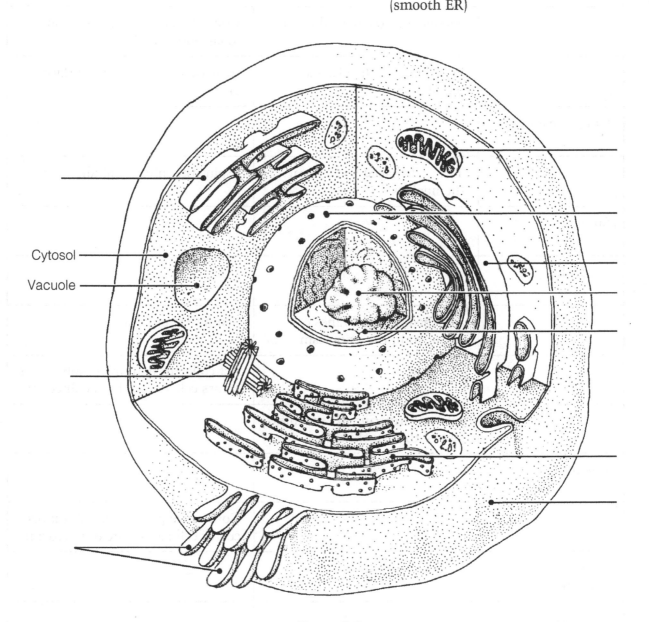

Cytosol

Vacuole

Figure 3.6

4. Complete the following table to fully describe the various cell parts. Insert your responses in the spaces provided under each heading.

Cell structure	Location	Function
	External boundary of the cell	Confines cell contents; regulates entry and exit of materials
Lysosome		
	Scattered throughout the cell	Controls release of energy from foods; forms ATP
	Projections of the plasma membrane	Increase the membrane surface area
Golgi apparatus		
	Two rod-shaped bodies near the nucleus	"Spin" the mitotic spindle
Smooth ER		
Rough ER		
	Attached to membranes or scattered in the cytoplasm	Synthesize proteins
		Act collectively to move substances across cell surface in one direction
	Internal structure of centrioles; part of the cytoskeleton	
Peroxisomes		
		Contractile protein (actin); moves cell or cell parts; core of microvilli
Intermediate filaments	Part of cytoskeleton	
Inclusions		

5. Relative to cellular organelles, circle the term or phrase that does not belong in each of the following groupings.

1. Peroxisomes   Enzymatic breakdown   Centrioles   Lysosomes

2. Microtubules   Intermediate filaments   Cytoskeleton   Cilia

3. Ribosomes   Smooth ER   Rough ER   Protein synthesis

4. Mitochondrion   Cristae   Self-replicating   Vitamin A storage

5. Centrioles   Basal bodies   Mitochondria   Cilia   Flagella

6. ER   Endomembrane system   Ribosomes   Secretory vesicles

7. Nucleus   DNA   Lysosomes   Mitochondria

6. Name the cytoskeletal element (microtubules, microfilaments, or intermediate filaments) described by each of the following phrases.

_____ 1. give the cell its shape

_____ 2. resist tension placed on a cell

_____ 3. radiate from the cell center

_____ 4. interact with myosin to produce contractile force

_____ 5. are the most stable

_____ 6. have the thickest diameter

7. Different organelles are abundant in different cell types. Match the cell types with their abundant organelles by selecting a letter from the key choices.

Key Choices

A. mitochondria   C. rough ER   E. microfilaments   G. intermediate filaments

B. smooth ER   D. peroxisomes   F. lysosomes   H. Golgi apparatus

_____ 1. cell lining the small intestine (assembles fats)

_____ 2. white blood cell; a phagocyte

_____ 3. liver cell that detoxifies carcinogens

_____ 4. muscle cell (contractile cell)

_____ 5. mucus–secreting cell (secretes a protein product)

_____ 6. cell at external skin surface (withstands friction and tension)

_____ 7. kidney tubule cells (makes and uses large amounts of ATP)

8. Describe the components and importance of the endomembrane system.

_____

_____

_____

_____

_____

The Nucleus

1. Complete the following brief table to describe the nucleus and its parts. Insert your responses in the spaces provided.

Nuclear structure	General location/appearance	Function
Nucleus		
Nucleolus		
Chromatin		
Nuclear membrane		

2. Figure 3.7 shows a portion of the proposed model of a chromatin fiber. Select two different colors for the coding circles and the corresponding structures on the figure. Then respond to the two questions that follow.

◯ DNA helix   ◯ Nucleosome

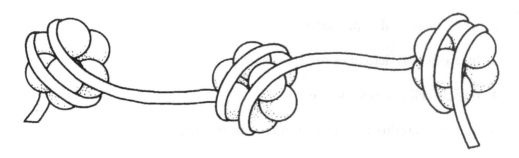

Figure 3.7

1. What is the chemical composition of a nucleosome? (Be specific.) _____

2. What is the function of the nucleosome components named above? _____

_____

Cell Growth and Reproduction

1. The cell life cycle consists of interphase and _____, during

which the cell _____. Name the three phases of interphase in
order, and indicate the important events of each phase.

Phase of interphase	Important events

2. Diagram (by making a pie-shaped graph) the relative lengths of time of the G_1,
S, G_2, and M phases for the cell types listed:

A. Rapidly dividing cell type   **B.** Slowly dividing cell type

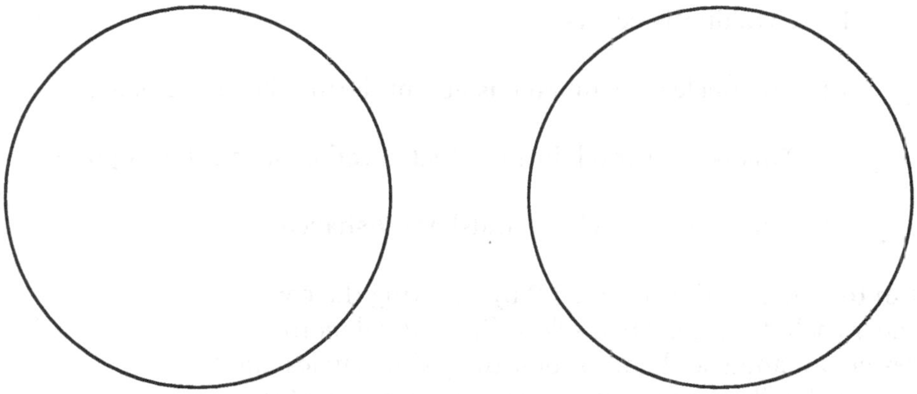

Figure 3.8

3. Complete the following statements concerning control of cell division.

_____   1.   A complex of two proteins called __(1)__ gives the "OK" signal
for a cell to begin mitosis. One of these proteins, called __(2)__,
_____   2.   is always present. The other, a regulatory protein called __(3)__,
is regenerated anew with each cycle.

_____   3.

4. The following statements describe events that occur during the different phases of mitosis. Identify the phase by choosing the correct responses from the key choices and inserting the answers in the answer blanks.

Key Choices

A. Anaphase   B. Metaphase   C. Prophase   D. Telophase   E. None of these

_____ 1. Chromatin coils and condenses to form deeply staining bodies.

_____ 2. Centromeres break, and chromosomes begin migration toward opposite poles of the cell.

_____ 3. The nuclear membrane and nucleoli reappear.

_____ 4. Chromosomes cease their poleward movement.

_____ 5. Chromosomes align on the equator of the spindle.

_____ 6. The nucleoli and nuclear membrane disappear.

_____ 7. The spindle forms through the migration of the centrioles.

_____ 8. DNA replication occurs.

_____ 9. Chromosomes obviously are duplex structures.

_____ 10. Chromosomes attach to the spindle fibers.

_____ 11. Cytokinesis occurs.

_____ 12. The nuclear membrane is absent during the entire phase.

_____ 13. This is the period during which a cell is not in the M phase.

_____ 14. Chromosomes (chromatids) are V-shaped.

5. Identify the phases of mitosis depicted in Figure 3.9 by inserting the correct terms in the blanks under each diagram. Then select different colors to represent the structures below, and use them to color the coding circles and the corresponding structures in the illustration. When you have completed the work on Figure 3.9, identify all of the mitotic stages provided with leader lines in the photomicrograph of an onion root tip in Figure 3.10.

◯ Nuclear membranes, if present   ◯ Centrioles   ◯ Chromosomes

◯ Nucleoli, if present   ◯ Spindle fibers, if present

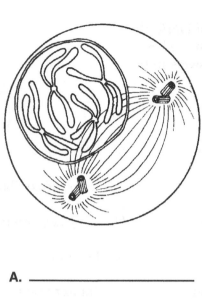

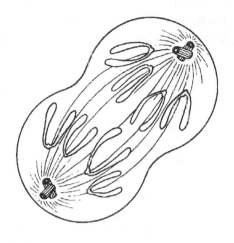

Figure 3.9

A. _____

B. _____

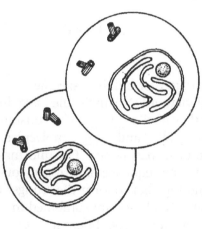

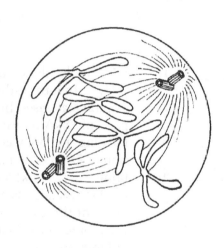

C. _____

D. _____

Figure 3.10

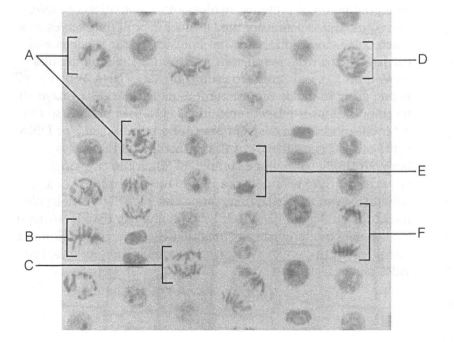

A. _____

B. _____

C. _____

D. _____

E. _____

F. _____

6. The following statements provide an overview of the structure of DNA (the genetic material) and its role in the body. Choose responses from the key choices that complete the statements. Insert the appropriate answers in the answer blanks.

Key Choices

A. Adenine

B. Amino acids

C. Bases

D. Codons

E. Complementary

F. Cytosine

G. Enzymes

H. Genes

I. Growth

J. Guanine

K. Helix

L. New

M. Nucleotides

N. Old

O. Phosphate

P. Proteins

Q. Replication

R. Repair

S. Ribosome

T. Sugar (deoxyribose)

U. Template, or model

V. Thymine

W. Transcription

X. Uracil

_____ 1.

_____ 2.

_____ 3.

_____ 4.

_____ 5.

_____ 6.

_____ 7.

_____ 8.

_____ 9.

_____ 10.

_____ 11.

_____ 12.

_____ 13.

_____ 14.

_____ 15.

_____ 16.

_____ 17.

_____ 18.

DNA molecules contain information for building specific __(1)__. In a three-dimensional view, a DNA molecule looks like a spiral staircase; this is correctly called a __(2)__. The constant parts of DNA molecules are the __(3)__ and __(4)__ molecules, forming the DNA-ladder uprights, or backbones. The information of DNA is actually coded in the sequence of nitrogen-containing __(5)__, which are bound together to form the "rungs" of the DNA ladder. When the four DNA bases are combined in different three-base sequences, called triplets, different __(6)__ of the protein are called for. It is said that the N-containing bases of DNA are __(7)__, which means that only certain bases can fit or interact together. Specifically this means that __(8)__ can bind with guanine, and adenine binds with __(9)__.

The production of proteins involves the cooperation of DNA and RNA. RNA is another type of nucleic acid that serves as a "molecular slave" to DNA. That is, it leaves the nucleus and carries out the instructions of the DNA for the building of a protein on a cytoplasmic structure called a __(10)__. When a cell is preparing to divide, in order for its daughter cells to have all its information, it must oversee the __(11)__ of its DNA so that a "double dose" of genes is present for a brief period. For DNA synthesis to occur, the DNA must uncoil, and the bonds between the N-bases must be broken. Then the two single strands of __(12)__ each act as a __(13)__ for the building of a whole DNA molecule. When completed, each DNA molecule formed is half __(14)__ and half __(15)__. The fact that DNA replicates before a cell divides ensures that each daughter cell has a complete set of __(16)__. Cell division, which then follows, provides new cells so that __(17)__ and __(18)__ can occur.

7. Figure 3.11 is a diagram illustrating protein synthesis.

First, select four different colors and use them to color the coding circles and the corresponding structures in the diagram.

Second, using the letters of the genetic code, label the nitrogen bases on the encoding strand (strand 2) of the DNA double helix, on the mRNA strands, and on the tRNA molecules.

Third, answer the questions that follow, referring to Figure 3.11 and inserting your answers in the answer blanks.

◯ Backbones of the DNA double helix   ◯ tRNA molecules

◯ Backbone of the mRNA strands   ◯ Amino acid molecules

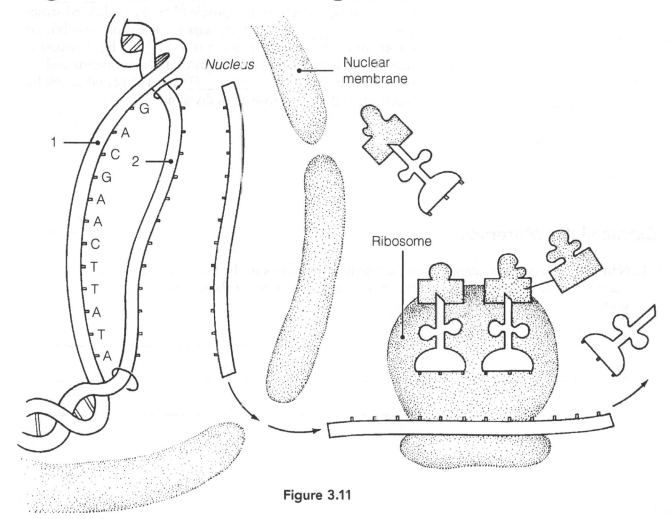

Figure 3.11

1. Transfer of the genetic message from DNA to mRNA is called _____.

2. Assembly of amino acids according to the genetic information carried by mRNA is called

_____.

3. All three types of RNA are made on the _____.

4. The set of three nitrogen bases on tRNA that is complementary to an mRNA codon is called a _____. The complementary three-base sequence on DNA is called a _____.

5. Define *gene*. _____

_____

8. Complete the following statements. Insert your answers in the answer blanks.

_____ 1.

_____ 2.

_____ 3.

_____ 4.

_____ 5.

_____ 6.

_____ 7.

Division of the __(1)__ is referred to as mitosis. Cytokinesis is division of the __(2)__. The major structural difference between chromatin and chromosomes is that the latter are __(3)__. Chromosomes attach to the spindle fibers by undivided structures called __(4)__. If a cell undergoes nuclear division but not cytoplasmic division, the product is a __(5)__. The structure that acts as a scaffolding for chromosomal attachment and movement is called the __(6)__. __(7)__ is the period of cell life when the cell is not involved in division.

Extracellular Materials

1. Name the three major categories of extracellular materials in the body, provide examples of each class, and cite some of the important roles of these substances.

1. _____

2. _____

3. _____

A Visualization Exercise for the Cell

A long, meandering membrane with dark globules clinging to its outer surface now comes into sight.

1. Complete the narrative by inserting the missing words in the answer blanks.

_____	1.	For this journey, you will be miniaturized to the size of a small protein molecule and will travel in a microsubmarine, specially
_____	2.	designed to enable you to pass easily through living membranes. You are injected into the intercellular space between
_____	3.	two epithelial cells, and you are instructed to observe one cell firsthand and to identify as many of its structures as possible.
_____	4.	You struggle briefly with the controls and then maneuver your microsub into one of these cells. Once inside the cell, you find
_____	5.	yourself in a kind of "sea." This salty fluid that surrounds you is the ___(1)___ of the cell.
_____	6.	
		Far below looms a large, dark oval structure, much larger than
_____	7.	anything else. You conclude that it is the ___(2)___. As you move downward, you pass a cigar-shaped structure with strange-
_____	8.	looking folds on its inner surface. Although you have a pretty good idea that it must be a ___(3)___, you decide to investigate
_____	9.	more thoroughly. After passing through the membrane of the structure, you are confronted with yet another membrane.
_____	10.	Once past this membrane, you are inside the strange-looking structure. You activate the analyzer switch in your microsub for a readout on which molecules are in your immediate vicinity.

As suspected, there is an abundance of energy-rich ___(4)___ molecules. Having satisfied your curiosity, you leave this structure to continue the investigation.

A long, meandering membrane with dark globules clinging to its outer surface now comes into sight. You maneuver closer and sit back to watch the activity. As you watch, amino acids are joined together and a long, threadlike protein molecule is built. The globules must be ___(5)___, and the membrane, therefore, is the ___(6)___. Once again you head toward the large dark structure seen and tentatively identified earlier. On approach, you observe that this huge structure has very large openings in its outer wall; these openings must be the ___(7)___. Passing through one of these openings, you discover that from the inside the color of this structure is a result of dark, coiled, intertwined masses of ___(8)___ which your analyzer confirms contain genetic materials, or ___(9)___ molecules. Making your way through this tangled mass, you pass two round, dense structures that appear to be full of the same type of globules you saw outside. These two round structures are ___(10)___. All this information confirms your earlier identification of this cellular structure, so now you move to its exterior to continue your observations.

_____ 11. Just ahead, you see what appears to be a mountain of flattened sacs with hundreds of small vesicles at its edges. The vesicles
_____ 12. appear to be migrating away from this area and heading toward the outer edges of the cell. The mountain of sacs must be the __(11)__ . Eventually you come upon a rather simple-looking membrane-bounded sac. Although it doesn't look too exciting and has few distinguishing marks, it does not resemble anything else you have seen so far. Deciding to obtain a chemical analysis before entering this sac, you activate the analyzer, and on the screen you see "Enzymes—Enzymes—Danger—Danger." There is little doubt that this apparently innocent structure is actually a __(12)__ .

Completing your journey, you count the number of organelles identified so far. Satisfied that you have observed most of them, you request retrieval from the intercellular space.

CHALLENGING YOURSELF

At the Clinic

1. An infant is brought in with chronic diarrhea, which her mother says occurs whenever the baby drinks milk. The doctor diagnoses lactose intolerance. She explains to the parents that their baby is unable to digest milk sugar and suggests adding lactase to the baby's milk. How would lactose intolerance lead to diarrhea? How does adding lactase prevent diarrhea?

2. Anaphylaxis is a systemic (bodywide) allergic reaction in which capillaries become excessively permeable. This results in increased filtration and fluid accumulation in the tissues, leading to edema. Why is this condition life-threatening even if no frank bleeding occurs?

3. Some people have too few receptors for the cholesterol-carrying low-density lipoprotein (LDL). As a result, cholesterol builds up in blood vessel walls, restricting blood flow and leading to high blood pressure. By what cellular transport process is cholesterol taken up from the blood in a person with normal numbers of LDL receptors?

4. Sugar (glucose) can appear in the urine in nondiabetics if sugar intake is exceptionally high (when you pig out on sweets!). What functional aspect of carrier-mediated transport does this phenomenon demonstrate?

5. Plasma proteins such as albumin have an osmotic effect. In normally circulating blood, the proteins cannot leave the bloodstream easily and, thus, tend to remain in the blood. But, if stasis (blood flow stoppage) occurs, the proteins will begin to leak out into the interstitial fluid (IF). Explain why this leads to edema.

6. Hydrocortisone is an anti-inflammatory drug that acts to stabilize lysosomal membranes. Explain how this effect reduces cell damage and inflammation. Why is this steroid hormone marketed in a cream (oil) base and used topically (applied to the skin)?

7. Streptomycin (an antibiotic) binds to the small ribosomal subunit of bacteria (but not to the ribosomes of the host cells infected by bacteria). The result is the misreading of bacterial mRNA and the breakup of polysomes. What process is being affected, and how does this kill the bacterial cells?

Stop and Think

1. Think *carefully* about the chemistry of the plasma membrane, then answer this question: Why is minor damage to the membrane usually not a problem?

2. Knowing that diffusion rate is inversely proportional to molecular weight, predict the results of the following experiment: Cotton balls are simultaneously inserted in opposite ends of a 1-meter-long glass tube. One cotton ball is saturated with ammonium hydroxide (NH_4OH), the other with sulfuric add (H_2SO_4). The two gases diffuse until they meet, at which point a white precipitate of ammonium chloride is formed. At what relative point along the tube does the precipitate form?

3. The upper layers of the skin constantly slough off. Predict the changes in the integrity of desmosomes as skin cells age (and move closer to the skin's surface).

4. Some cells produce lipid-soluble products. Can you deduce how such products are stored, that is, prevented from exiting the cell?

5. List three examples of folding of cellular membranes to increase membrane surface area.

6. Should the existence of mitochondrial ribosomes come as a complete surprise? Explain your response.

7. If a structure (such as the lens and cornea of the eye) contains no blood vessels (that is, is *avascular*), is it likely to be very thick? Why or why not?

8. Examine the organelles of the cells depicted in Figure 3.12 A and B. Predict the product of each cell and state your reasons.

Figure 3.12

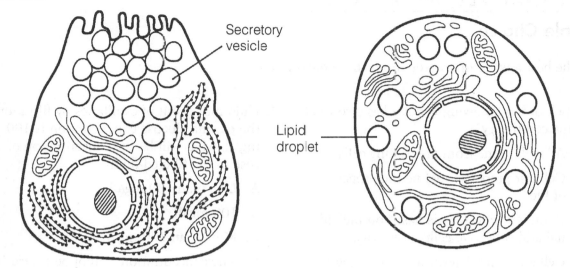

A. Acinar cell from pancreas   **B. Interstitial cell from testis**

9. In Figure 3.13, an artificial cell with an aqueous solution enclosed in a selectively permeable membrane has just been immersed in a beaker containing a different solution. The membrane is permeable to water and to the simple sugars glucose and fructose, but is completely impermeable to the disaccharide sucrose. Answer the following questions pertaining to this situation.

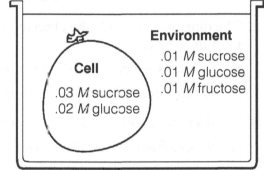

Figure 3.13

1. Which solute(s) will exhibit net diffusion into the cell?

2. Which solute(s) will exhibit net diffusion out of the cell?

3. In which direction will there be net osmotic movement of water?

4. Will the cell crenate or swell?

10. Using the information provided:

mRNA codon:	AUG	AAC	CGU	GAA	AGU	UAG
amino acid:	Met	Asn	Arg	Glu	Ser	Stop

and given the DNA sequence TAC G C A T C A C T T T T GATC:

1. What is the amino acid sequence encoded?

2. If the nucleotides that are underlined were deleted by mutation, what would the resulting amino acid sequence be?

Multiple Choice

Select the best answer or answers from the choices given.

1. Which of the following is not a basic concept of the cell theory?

   A. All cells come from preexisting cells.

   B. Cellular properties define the properties of life.

   C. Organismic activity is based on individual and collective cellular activity.

   D. Cell structure determines and is determined by biochemical function.

   E. Organisms can exhibit properties that cannot be explained at the cellular level.

2. The dimension outside the observed range for human cells is:

   A. 10 micrometers   C. 2 nanometers

   B. 30 centimeters long   D. 1 meter long

3. A cell's plasma membrane would not contain:

   A. phospholipid   D. cholesterol

   B. nucleic acid   E. glycolipid

   C. protein

4. Which of the following would you expect to find in or on cells whose main function is absorption?

   A. Microvilli   D. Gap junctions

   B. Cilia   E. Secretory vesicles

   C. Desmosomes

5. Adult cell types expected to have gap junctions include:

   A. skeletal muscle   C. heart muscle

   B. bone   D. smooth muscle

6. For diffusion to occur, there must be:

   A. a selectively permeable membrane

   B. equal amounts of solute

   C. a concentration difference

   D. some sort of carrier system

   E. all of these

7. Fluid moves out of capillaries by filtration. If the plasma glucose concentration is 100 mg/dl, what will be the concentration of glucose in the filtered fluid?

   A. Less than 100 mg/dl

   B. 100 mg/dl

   C. More than 100 mg/dl

   D. The concentration cannot be determined.

8. Lack of cholesterol in the plasma membrane would result in the membrane's:

   A. excessive fluidity

   B. instability

   C. increased protein content

   D. excessive fragility

   E. reduced protein content

9. Which of the following membrane components is involved in glucose transport?

   A. Phospholipid bilayer

   B. Transmembrane protein

   C. Cholesterol

   D. Peripheral protein

   E. Glycocalyx

10. If a 10% sucrose solution within a semipermeable sac causes the fluid volume in the sac to increase a given amount when the sac is immersed in water, what would be the effect of replacing the sac solution with a 20% sucrose solution?

    A. The sac would lose fluid.

    B. The sac would gain the same amount of fluid.

    C. The sac would gain more fluid.

    D. There would be no effect.

11. Intestinal cells absorb glucose, galactose, and fructose by carrier-mediated transport. Poisoning the cells' mitochondria inhibits the absorption of glucose and galactose but not that of fructose. By what processes are these sugars absorbed?

    A. All are absorbed by facilitated diffusion.

    B. All are absorbed by active transport.

    C. Glucose and galactose are actively transported, but fructose is moved by facilitated diffusion.

    D. Fructose is actively transported, but glucose and galactose are moved by facilitated diffusion.

12. In a polarized cell:

    A. sodium is being pumped out of the cell

    B. potassium is being pumped out of the cell

    C. sodium is being pumped into the cell

    D. potassium is being pumped into the cell

13. Which of the following are possible functions of the glycocalyx?

    A. Determination of blood groups

    B. Binding sites for toxins

    C. Aiding the binding of sperm to egg

    D. Guiding embryonic development

    E. Increasing the efficiency of absorption

14. A cell stimulated to increase steroid production will have abundant:

    A. ribosomes   D. Golgi apparatus

    B. rough ER   E. secretory vesicles

    C. smooth ER

15. A cell's ability to replenish its ATP stores has been diminished by a metabolic poison. What organelle is most likely to be affected?

    A. Nucleus

    B. Plasma membrane

    C. Centriole

    D. Microtubule

    E. Mitochondrion

16. Steroid hormones increase protein synthesis in their target cells. How would this stimulus be signified in a bone-forming cell, which secretes the protein collagen?

    A. Increase in heterochromatin

    B. Increase in endocytosis

    C. Increase in lysosome formation

    D. Increase in formation of secretory vesicles

    E. Increase in amount of rough ER

17. In certain nerve cells that sustain damage, the rough ER disbands and most ribosomes are free. What does this indicate?

    A. Decrease in protein synthesis

    B. Increase in protein synthesis

    C. Increase in synthesis of intracellular proteins

    D. Increase in synthesis of secreted proteins

18. What cellular inclusions increase in number in a light-skinned human after increased exposure to sunlight?

    A. Melanin granules

    B. Lipid droplets

    C. Glycogen granules

    D. Mucus

    E. Zymogen granules

19. A cell with abundant peroxisomes would most likely be involved in:

    A. secretion

    B. storage of glycogen

    C. ATP manufacture

    D. movement

    E. detoxification activities

20. Biochemical tests show a cell with replicated DNA, but incomplete synthesis of proteins needed for cell division. In what stage of the cell cycle is this cell most likely to be?

    A. M   C. S

    B. G_2 D. G_1

21.–23. Consider the following information for Questions 21–23:

A DNA segment has this nucleotide sequence:

A A G C T C T T A C G A A T A T T C

21. Which mRNA matches or is complementary?

A. A A G C T C T T A C G A A T A T T C

B. T T C G A G A A T G C T T A T A A G

C. A A G C U C U U A C G A A U A U U C

D. U U C G A G A A U G C U U A U A A G

22. How many amino acids are coded in this segment?

A. 18   C. 6

B. 9   D. 3

23. What is the tRNA anticodon sequence for the fourth codon from the left?

A. G   C. GCU

B. GC   D. CGA

24. The organelle that consists of a stack of 3–10 membranous discs associated with vesicles is:

A. Mitochondrion   C. Golgi apparatus

B. Smooth ER   D. Lysosome

25. Which statement concerning lysosomes is false?

A. They have the same structure and function as peroxisomes.

B. They form by budding off the Golgi apparatus.

C. They are abundant in phagocytes.

D. They contain their digestive enzymes to prevent general cytoplasmic damage.

26. The fundamental structure of the plasma membrane is determined almost exclusively by:

A. phospholipid molecules

B. peripheral proteins

C. cholesterol molecules

D. integral proteins

27. Centrioles:

A. start to duplicate in G_1

B. reside in the centrosome

C. are made of microtubules

D. lie parallel to each other

28. The *trans* face of the Golgi apparatus:

A. is where products are dispatched in vesicles

B. is its convex face

C. receives transport vesicles from the rough ER

D. is in the center of the Golgi stack

29. The protein that tags cytoplasmic proteins for destruction is:

A. Ubiquitin   C. Proteosome

B. Cyclin   D. Histone

Word Dissection

For each of the following word roots, fill in the literal meaning and give an example, using a word found in this chapter.

Word root	Translation	Example
1. chondri	_____	_____
2. chrom	_____	_____

Word root	Translation	Example
3. crist	_____	_____
4. cyto	_____	_____
5. desm	_____	_____
6. dia	_____	_____
7. dys	_____	_____
8. flagell	_____	_____
9. meta	_____	_____
10. mito	_____	_____
11. nucle	_____	_____
12. onco	_____	_____
13. osmo	_____	_____
14. permea	_____	_____
15. phag	_____	_____
16. philo	_____	_____
17. phobo	_____	_____
18. pin	_____	_____
19. plasm	_____	_____
20. telo	_____	_____
21. tono	_____	_____
22. troph	_____	_____
23. villus	_____	_____

4

TISSUES

Student Objectives

When you have completed the exercises in this chapter you will have accomplished the following objectives:

Epithelial Tissue

1. List several structural and functional characteristics of epithelial tissue.
2. Classify the epithelia.
3. Name and describe the various types of epithelia; also indicate their chief function(s) and location(s).
4. Define *gland*. Differentiate between exocrine and endocrine glands and unicellular and multicellular glands.
5. Describe how multicellular exocrine glands are classified structurally and functionally.

Connective Tissue

6. Describe common characteristics of connective tissue, and list and describe its structural elements.

7. Describe the types of connective tissue found in the body and indicate their characteristic functions.

Covering and Lining Membranes

8. Describe the structure and function of the three varieties of epithelial membranes.

Nervous Tissue

9. Indicate the general characteristics of nervous tissue.

Muscle Tissue

10. Compare and contrast the structures and body locations of the three types of muscle tissue.

Tissue Repair

11. Outline the process of tissue repair involved in the normal healing of a superficial wound.

In the human body, as in any multicellular body, every cell has the ability to perform all activities necessary to remain healthy and alive. In the multicellular body, however, the individual cells are no longer independent. Instead, they aggregate, forming cell communities made of cells similar to one another in form and function. Once specialized, each community is committed to performing a specific activity that helps to maintain homeostasis and serves the body as a whole.

Fully differentiated cell communities are called tissue (from *tissu*, meaning "woven"). Tissues, in turn, are organized into functional units called organs (such as the heart and brain). Because individual tissues are unique in cellular shape and structure, they are readily recognized and are often named for the organ of origin—for example, muscle tissue and nervous tissue.

Student activities in Chapter 4 include questions relating to the structure and function of tissues, membranes, glands and glandular tissue, tissue repair, and the developmental aspects of tissues.

BUILDING THE FRAMEWORK

Overview of Body Tissues

1. Circle the term that does not belong in each of the following groupings.

   1. Columnar   Areolar   Cuboidal   Squamous

   2. Collagen   Cell   Matrix   Cell product

   3. Cilia   Flagellum   Microvilli   Elastic fibers

   4. Glands   Bones   Epidermis   Mucosae

   5. Adipose   Hyaline   Osseous   Nervous

   6. Blood   Smooth   Cardiac   Skeletal

   7. Polarity   Cell-to-cell junctions   Regeneration possible   Vascular

   8. Matrix   Connective tissue   Collagen   Keratin

   9. Cartilage   GAGs   Vascular   Water retention

2. Twelve tissue types are diagrammed in Figure 4.1. Identify each tissue type by inserting the correct name in the blank below each diagram. Select different colors for the following structures and use them to color the coding circles and corresponding structures in the diagrams.

◯ Epithelial cells

◯ Nerve cells

◯ Muscle cells

◯ Matrix (Where found, matrix should be colored differently from the living cells of that tissue type. Be careful. This may not be as easy as it seems!)

A _____

B _____

C _____

D _____

E _____

F _____

Figure 4.1

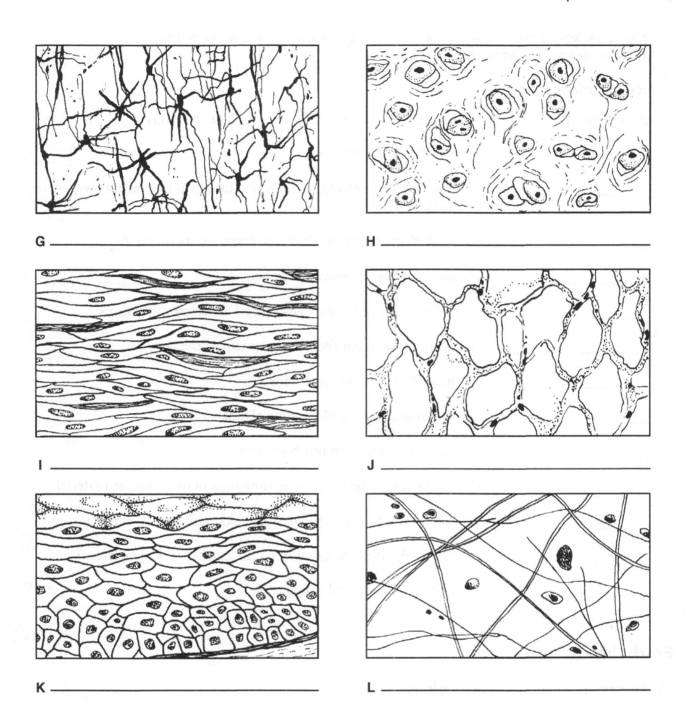

G _____   H _____

I _____   J _____

K _____   L _____

Figure 4.1 (continued)

3. Using the key choices, correctly identify the following *major* tissue types. Enter the appropriate answer in the answer blanks.

Key Choices

A. Connective   B. Epithelium   C. Muscle   D. Nervous

_____   1. Forms membranes

_____   2. Allows for movement of limbs and for organ movements within the body

_____   3. Uses electrochemical signals to carry out its functions

_____   4. Supports and reinforces body organs

_____   5. Cells of this tissue may absorb and/or secrete substances

_____   6. Basis of the major controlling system of the body

_____   7. Its cells shorten to exert force

_____   8. Forms endocrine and exocrine glands

_____   9. Surrounds and cushions body organs

_____   10. Characterized by having large amounts of extracellular material

_____   11. Allows you to smile, grasp, swim, ski, and throw a ball

_____   12. Widely distributed; found in bones, cartilages, and fat depots

_____   13. Forms the brain and spinal cord

Epithelial Tissue

1. List the six major functions of epithelium. _____

_____

2. List six special characteristics of epithelium. _____

_____

_____

_____

3. For 1–5, match the epithelial type named in Column B with the appropriate *location* in Column A.

Column A	Column B
_____ 1. Lines the stomach and most of the intestines	A. Pseudostratified ciliated columnar
_____ 2. Lines the inside of the mouth	B. Simple columnar
_____ 3. Lines much of the respiratory tract	C. Simple cuboidal
_____ 4. Endothelium and mesothelium	D. Simple squamous
_____ 5. Lines the inside of the urinary bladder	E. Stratified columnar
	F. Stratified squamous
	G. Transitional

For 6–10, match the epithelium named in Column B with the appropriate *function* in Column A.

Column A	Column B
_____ 6. Protection	H. Endothelium
_____ 7. Small molecules pass through rapidly	I. Simple columnar
_____ 8. Propel sheets of mucus	J. A ciliated epithelium
_____ 9. Absorption, secretion, or ion transport	K. Stratified squamous
_____ 10. Stretches	L. Transitional

4. Arrange the following types of epithelium from 1 to 5 in order of increasing *protectiveness*.

_____ A. Simple squamous _____ D. Pseudostratified

_____ B. Stratified squamous _____ E. Simple columnar

_____ C. Simple cuboidal

5. Arrange the following types of epithelium from 1 to 4 in order of increasing *absorptive* ability.

_____ A. Simple squamous _____ C. Simple cuboidal

_____ B. Stratified squamous _____ D. Simple columnar

6. Epithelium exhibits many of the plasma membrane modifications described in conjunction with our discussion of the composite cell in Chapter 3. Figure 4.2 depicts some of these modifications.

First: Choose a color for the coding circles and the corresponding structures in the figure.

◯ Epithelial cell cytoplasm   ◯ Connective tissue

◯ Epithelial cell nucleus   ◯ Blood vessel

◯ Nerve fibers

Second: Correctly identify the following structures or regions by labeling appropriate leader lines using terms from the list below:

A. Epithelium   E. Connective tissue   I. Cilia

B. Basal region   F. Basement membrane   J. Reticular lamina

C. Apical region   G. Basal lamina   K. Tight junctions

D. Capillary   H. Microvilli   L. Desmosome

Figure 4.2

7. Identify the structural class of each gland described here:

_____ 1. Flask-shaped gland, unbranched ducts

_____ 2. Slender, straight gland, unbranched ducts

_____ 3. Combination of gland shapes

_____ 4. Branched ducts

8. Write T in the answer blank if a statement is true. If a statement is false, correct the underlined word(s) by writing the correct word(s) in the answer blank.

_____ 1. Exocrine glands are classified <u>functionally</u> as merocrine, holocrine, or apocrine.

_____ 2. The above classification refers to the way <u>ducts branch</u>.

_____ 3. Most exocrine glands are <u>apocrine</u>.

_____ 4. In <u>apocrine</u> glands, secretions are produced and released immediately by exocytosis.

_____ 5. <u>Holocrine</u> glands store secretions until the cells rupture. Ruptured cells are replaced through mitosis.

_____ 6. In apocrine glands, the secretory cells <u>die</u> when they pinch off at the apex to release secretions.

_____ 7. A sweat gland is an example of a <u>holocrine</u> gland.

_____ 8. The mammary gland is the most likely example of an <u>apocrine</u> gland.

9. Using the key choices, correctly identify the types of glands described below. Enter the appropriate answers in the answer blanks.

Key Choices

A. Endocrine   B. Exocrine   C. Neither of these

_____ 1. Duct from this gland type carries secretions to target organ or location

_____ 2. Examples are the thyroid and adrenal glands

_____ 3. Glands secrete regulatory hormones directly into blood or lymph

_____ 4. The more numerous of the two types of glands

_____ 5. Duct from ovary that carries ovum (egg) to uterus

_____ 6. Examples are the liver, which produces bile, and the pancreas, which produces digestive enzymes

10. Complete the following statements by filling in the appropriate answers.

_____ 1. Endocrine and exocrine glands are formed from __(1)__ tissue.
Unicellular exocrine glands called __(2)__ are found in the

_____ 2. intestinal mucosae, where they secrete __(3)__, a lubricating,
water-soluble glycoprotein. Multicellular glands are composed

_____ 3. of three structures: __(4)__, __(5)__, and __(6)__. Exocrine
glands classified as compound tubular are glands with __(7)__

_____ 4. ducts and with secretory cells located in __(8)__ secretory units.

_____ 5.

_____ 6.

_____ 7.

_____ 8.

Connective Tissue

1. Using the key choices, identify the following connective tissue types. Insert the
appropriate answers in the answer blanks.

Key Choices

A. Adipose connective tissue   G. Fibrocartilage

B. Areolar connective tissue   H. Hyaline cartilage

C. Dense regular connective   I. Mucous connective

D. Dense irregular connective   J. Osseous tissue

E. Elastic cartilage   K. Reticular connective tissue

F. Elastic connective tissue   L. Vascular tissue

_____ 1. Parallel bundles of collagenic fibers provide strength; found
in tendons

_____ 2. Stores fat

_____ 3. The skin dermis

_____ 4. Hardest tissue of our "skull cap"

_____ 5. Composes the basement membrane; surrounds and cushions
blood vessels and nerves; its gel-like matrix contains all
categories of fibers and many cell types

_____ 6. Forms the embryonic skeleton; covers surfaces of bones at joints;
reinforces the trachea

_____ 7. Insulates the body

_____ 8. Firm, slightly "rubbery" matrix; milky white and "glassy" in appearance

_____ 9. Cells are arranged in concentric circles around a nutrient canal; matrix is hard due to calcium salts

_____ 10. Contains collagenous fibers; found in intervertebral discs

_____ 11. Makes supporting framework of lymphoid organs

_____ 12. Found in umbilical cord

_____ 13. Found in external ear and auditory tube

_____ 14. Provides the medium for nutrient transport throughout the body

_____ 15. Forms the "stretchy" ligaments of the vertebral column

2. Areolar connective tissue is often considered to be the prototype of connective tissue proper because of its variety of cell types and fibers. Figure 4.3 shows most of these elements. Identify all structures or cell types provided with leader lines. Color the diagram as your fancy strikes you.

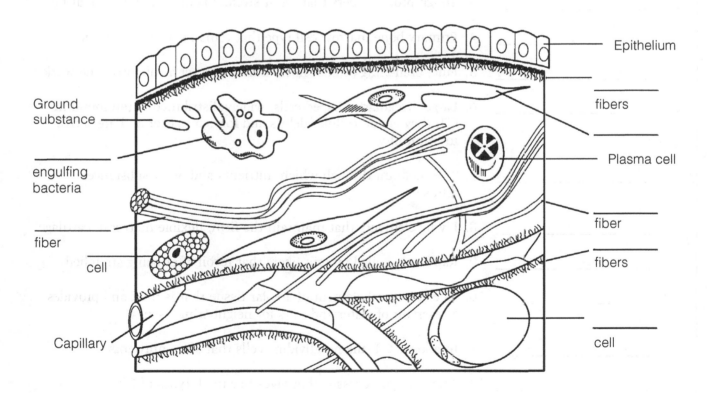

Figure 4.3

3. Arrange the following tissue types from 1 to 3 in order of *decreasing* vascularity.

_____ A. Cartilage

_____ B. Areolar connective

_____ C. Dense connective

4. Using the key choices, select the structural or related elements of connective tissue (CT) types that permit specialized functions. Insert the appropriate answers in the answer blanks.

Key Choices

A. Adipocytes   D. Elastic fibers   G. Macrophages   J. Osteocytes

B. Chondrocytes   E. Ground substance   H. Matrix   K. Osteoblasts

C. Collagen fibers   F. Hemocytoblast   I. Mesenchyme   L. Reticular fibers

_____ 1. Composed of ground substance and structural protein fibers

_____ 2. Composed of glycoproteins and water-binding glycosaminoglycans

_____ 3. Tough protein fibers that resist stretching or longitudinal tearing

_____ 4. Primary bone marrow cell type that remains actively mitotic

_____ 5. Fine, branching protein fibers that construct a supportive network

_____ 6. Large, irregularly shaped cells, widely distributed, often found in CT; they engulf cellular debris and foreign matter and are active in immunity

_____ 7. The medium through which nutrients and other substances diffuse

_____ 8. Living elements that maintain the firm, flexible matrix in cartilage

_____ 9. Randomly coiled protein fibers that recoil after being stretched

_____ 10. The structural element of areolar tissue that is fluid and provides a reservoir of water and salts for neighboring tissues

_____ 11. In a loose CT, the nondividing cells that store nutrients

_____ 12. The embryonic tissue that gives rise to all types of CT

_____ 13. Cellular elements that produce the collagen fibers of bone matrix

Covering and Lining Membranes

1. Five simplified diagrams are shown in Figure 4.4. Select different colors for the membranes listed below and use them to color the coding circles and the corresponding structures.

◯ Mucosae

◯ Visceral pleura (serosa)

◯ Parietal pleura (serosa)

◯ Visceral pericardium (serosa)

◯ Parietal peritoneum (serosa)

◯ Visceral peritoneum (serosa)

◯ Mesentery

◯ Endothelium

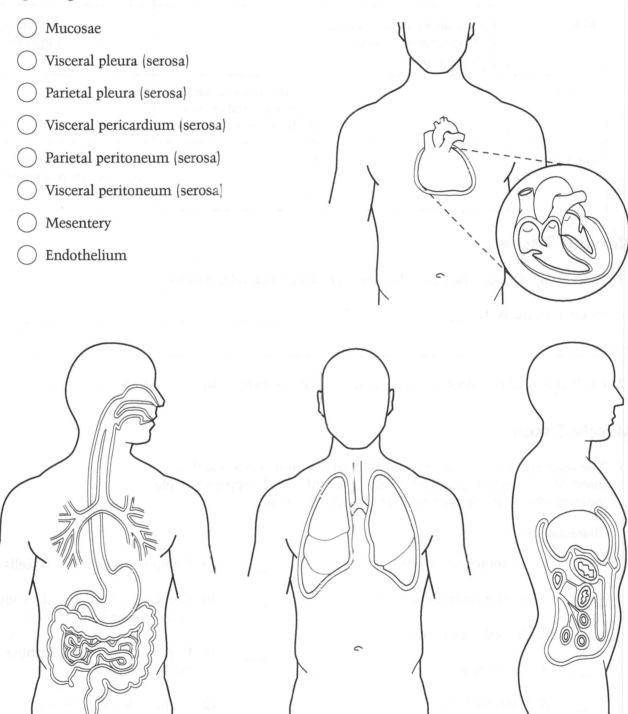

Figure 4.4

2. Complete the following table relating to epithelial membranes. Enter your responses in the areas left blank.

Membrane	Tissue type (epithelial/connective)	Common locations	Functions
Mucous	Epithelial sheet with underlying connective tissue (lamina propria)		Protection, lubrication, secretion, absorption
Serous		Lines internal ventral cavities and covers their organs	
Cutaneous			Protection from external insults; protection from water loss

Nervous Tissue

1. Describe briefly how the particular structure of a neuron relates to its

function in the body. _____

_____

2. Circle the word that does *not* apply to neuroglia: Support   Insulate   Conduct   Protect

Muscle Tissue

1. The three types of muscle tissue exhibit certain similarities and differences. Insert Sk (skeletal), C (cardiac), or Sm (smooth) into the appropriate blanks to indicate which muscle type exhibits each characteristic.

Characteristic

_____ 1. Voluntarily controlled

_____ 2. Involuntarily controlled

_____ 3. Banded appearance

_____ 4. Uninucleate

_____ 5. Multinucleate

_____ 6. Found attached to bones

_____ 7. Enables you to swallow

_____ 8. Found in the walls of the small intestine, uterus, bladder, and veins

_____ 9. Contains spindle-shaped cells

_____ 10. Contains cylindrical cells with branching ends

_____ 11. Contains long, nonbranching cylindrical cells

_____ 12. Displays intercalated disks

_____ 13. Concerned with locomotion of the body as a whole

_____ 14. Changes the internal volume of an organ as it contracts

_____ 15. Tissue of the circulatory pump

Tissue Repair

1. For each of the following statements about tissue repair that is true, enter T in the answer blank. For each false statement, correct the underlined word(s) by writing the correct word(s) in the answer blank.

_____ 1. The nonspecific response of the body to injury is called <u>regeneration</u>.

_____ 2. Intact capillaries near an injury dilate, leaking plasma, blood cells, and <u>antibodies</u>, which cause the blood to clot. The clot at the surface dries to form a scab.

_____ 3. During organization, the first phase of tissue repair, capillary buds invade the clot, forming a delicate pink tissue called <u>endodermal</u> tissue.

_____ 4. <u>Fibroblasts</u> synthesize fibers across the gap.

_____ 5. When damage is not too severe, the surface epithelium migrates beneath the dry scab and across the surface of the granulation tissue. This repair process is called <u>proliferation</u>.

_____ 6. If tissue damage is very severe, tissue repair is more likely to occur by <u>fibrosis</u>, or scarring.

_____ 7. During fibrosis, fibroblasts in the granulation tissue lay down <u>keratin</u> fibers, which form a strong, compact, but inflexible mass.

_____ 8. The repair of cardiac muscle and nervous tissue occurs only by <u>fibrosis</u>.

_____ 9. <u>Organization</u> is replacement of a blood clot by granulation tissue.

_____ 10. Granulation tissue resists infection by secreting <u>virus-inhibiting</u> substances.

_____ 11. Problems associated with <u>regeneration</u> include shrinking, loss of elasticity, and formation of adhesions.

CHALLENGING YOURSELF

At the Clinic

1. Since adipocytes are incapable of cell division, how is weight gain accomplished?

2. A histological examination of the brain during an autopsy reveals an extremely high number of microglial cells in an area that had suffered recent trauma. What do these cells signify?

3. Why do cartilage and tendons take so long to heal?

4. In mesothelial cancer of the pleura, serous fluid is hypersecreted. How does this contribute to respiratory problems?

5. In cases of ruptured appendix, what serous membrane is likely to become infected? Why can this be life-threatening?

Stop and Think

1. Try to come up with some *advantages* of the avascularity of epithelium and cartilage. Also, try to deduce why tendons are poorly vascularized.

2. Structurally speaking, why is simple columnar epithelium more resistant to being torn apart than simple squamous epithelium?

3. What types of tissue can have microvilli? Cilia?

4. Why do endocrine glands start out having ducts?

5. On his anatomy test, Bruno answered two questions incorrectly. He confused a basal lamina with a basement membrane, and a mucous membrane with a sheet of mucus. What are the differences between each of these sound-alike pairs of structures?

6. Time for an educated guess. Do you think the elastic connective tissue layer in the large arteries is regularly or irregularly arranged? Explain your reasoning.

7. What kind of tissue surrounds a bone shaft?

8. Why are skeletal muscle cells multinucleate?

COVERING ALL YOUR BASES

Multiple Choice

Select the best answer or answers from the choices given.

1. Scar tissue is a type of:
   A. epithelium   C. muscle
   B. connective tissue D. nervous tissue

2. Which of the following terms/phrases could *not* be applied to epithelium?
   A. Basement membrane D. Strong matrix
   B. Free surface   E. Ciliated
   C. Desmosomes present

3. Which is not a type of epithelium?
   A. Reticular
   B. Simple squamous
   C. Pseudostratified
   D. Transitional
   E. Stratified columnar

4. In which of the following tissue types might you expect to find goblet cells?
   A. Simple cuboidal
   B. Simple columnar
   C. Simple squamous
   D. Stratified squamous
   E. Transitional

5. Mesothelium is found in:
   A. kidney tubules
   B. mucous membranes
   C. serosae
   D. the liver
   E. the lining of cardiovascular system organs

6. An epithelium "built" to withstand friction is:
   A. simple squamous
   B. stratified squamous
   C. simple cuboidal
   D. simple columnar
   E. pseudostratified

7. Functions of keratin include:
   A. absorbing sunlight
   B. energy storage
   C. directing protein synthesis
   D. waterproofing
   E. providing toughness

8. What cellular specialization causes fluid to flow over the epithelial surface?
   A. Centrioles   D. Microvilli
   B. Flagella   E. Myofilaments
   C. Cilia

9. The gland type that secretes its product continuously, by exocytosis, into a duct is:
   A. merocrine   C. endocrine
   B. holocrine   D. apocrine

10. Which of the following is not a function of some kind of connective tissue?
    A. Binding   D. Sensation
    B. Support   E. Repair
    C. Protection

11. The original embryonic connective tissue is:
    A. mucous connective
    B. mesenchyme
    C. vascular
    D. areolar connective
    E. connective tissue proper

12. Components of connective tissue matrix include:
    A. hyaluronic acid   C. proteoglycans
    B. basal lamina   D. glycosaminoglycans

13. Which of the following fibrous elements gives a connective tissue high tensile strength?
    A. Reticular fibers   C. Collagen fibers
    B. Elastic fibers   D. Myofilaments

14. The cell that forms bone is the:
    A. fibroblast   D. osteoblast
    B. chondroblast   E. reticular cell
    C. hematopoietic stem cell

15. Which of the following cell types secretes histamine and perhaps heparin?
    A. Macrophage   D. Fibroblast
    B. Mast cell   E. Histiocyte
    C. Reticular cell

16. Resistance to stress applied in a longitudinal direction is provided best by:
    A. fibrocartilage
    B. elastic connective
    C. reticular connective
    D. dense regular connective
    E. areolar connective

17. What kind of connective tissue acts as a sponge, soaking up fluid when edema occurs?
    A. Areolar connective
    B. Adipose connective
    C. Dense irregular connective
    D. Reticular connective
    E. Vascular tissue

18. Viewed through the microscope, most cells in this type of tissue have only a rim of cytoplasm.
    A. Reticular connective
    B. Adipose connective
    C. Areolar connective
    D. Osseous tissue
    E. Hyaline cartilage

19. The major function of reticular tissue is:
    A. nourishment   D. protection
    B. insulation   E. movement
    C. stroma formation

20. What type of connective tissue prevents muscles from pulling away from bones during contraction?
    A. Dense irregular connective
    B. Dense regular connective
    C. Areolar
    D. Elastic connective
    E. Hyaline cartilage

21. The type of connective tissue that provides flexibility to the vertebral column is:
    A. dense irregular connective
    B. dense regular connective
    C. reticular connective
    D. areolar
    E. fibrocartilage

22. Phrases that describe cartilage include:
    A. highly vascularized
    B. holds large volumes of water
    C. has no nerve endings
    D. grows both appositionally and interstitially
    E. can get quite thick

23. Which type of cartilage is most abundant throughout life?
    A. Elastic cartilage
    B. Fibrocartilage
    C. Hyaline cartilage

24. Select the one false statement about mucous and serous membranes.
    A. The epithelial type is the same in all serous membranes, but there are different epithelial types in different mucous membranes.

    B. Serous membranes line closed body cavities, while mucous membranes line body cavities open to the outside.
    C. Serous membranes always produce serous fluid, and mucous membranes always secrete mucus.
    D. Both membranes contain an epithelium plus a layer of loose connective tissue.

25. Serous membranes:
    A. line the mouth
    B. have parietal and visceral layers
    C. consist of epidermis and dermis
    D. have a connective tissue layer called the lamina propria
    E. secrete a lubricating fluid

26. Which of the following terms describe cardiac muscle?
    A. Striated   D. Involuntary
    B. Intercalated discs E. Branching
    C. Multinucleated

27. Events of tissue repair include:
    A. regeneration   D. fibrosis
    B. organization   E. inflammation
    C. granulation

28. The prototype connective tissue is:
    A. areolar connective tissue
    B. mesenchyme
    C. dense fibrous
    D. reticular

29. Examples of GAGs include:
    A. chondroitin sulfate
    B. hyaluronic acid
    C. laminin
    D. histamine

Word Dissection

For each of the following word roots, fill in the literal meaning and give an example, using a word found in this chapter.

Word root	Translation	Example
1. ap	_____	_____
2. areola	_____	_____
3. basal	_____	_____
4. blast	_____	_____
5. chyme	_____	_____
6. crine	_____	_____
7. endo	_____	_____
8. epi	_____	_____
9. glia	_____	_____
10. holo	_____	_____
11. hormon	_____	_____
12. hyal	_____	_____
13. lamina	_____	_____
14. mero	_____	_____
15. meso	_____	_____
16. retic	_____	_____
17. sero	_____	_____
18. squam	_____	_____
19. strat	_____	_____

5

THE INTEGUMENTARY SYSTEM

Student Objectives

When you have completed the exercises in this chapter, you will have accomplished the following objectives:

The Skin

1. Name the specific tissue types composing the epidermis and dermis. List the major layers of each and describe the function of each layer.
2. Describe the factors that normally contribute to skin color. Briefly describe how changes in skin color may be used as clinical signs of certain disease states.

Appendages of the Skin

3. List the parts of a hair follicle and explain the function of each part. Describe the functional relationship of arrector pili muscles to the hair follicle.
4. Name the regions of a hair and explain the basis of hair color. Describe the distribution, growth, and replacement of hairs and the changing nature of hair during the life span.

5. Compare the structure and most common locations of sweat and oil glands. Also compare the composition and functions of their secretions.
6. Compare and contrast eccrine and apocrine glands.
7. Describe the structure of nails.

Functions of the Integumentary System

8. Describe how the skin accomplishes at least five different functions.

Homeostatic Imbalances of Skin

9. Explain why serious burns are life-threatening. Describe how to determine the extent of a burn and differentiate between first-, second-, and third-degree burns.
10. Name the three major types of skin cancers.

The integumentary system consists of the skin and its derivatives—glands, hairs, and nails. Although the skin is very thin, it provides a remarkably effective external shield that acts to protect our internal organs from what is outside the body.

This chapter reviews the anatomical characteristics of the skin (composed of the dermis and the epidermis) and its derivatives. It also reviews the manner in which the skin responds to both internal and external stimuli to protect the body.

BUILDING THE FRAMEWORK

The Skin

1. 1. Name the tissue type composing the epidermis.

    2. Name the tissue type composing the dermis.

2. The more superficial cells of the epidermis become less viable and ultimately die. What two factors account for this natural demise of the epidermal cells?

    1. _____

    2. _____

    _____

3. Several types of skin markings may reveal structural characteristics of the dermis. Complete the following statements by inserting your responses in the answer blanks.

    _____   1. Skin cuts that run parallel to __(1)__ gape less than cuts running across these skin markings.

    _____   2. A more scientific term for "stretch marks" is __(2)__.

    _____   3. Skin markings that occur where the dermis is secured to deeper structures are called __(3)__.

    _____   4. __(4)__ appear when dermis elasticity declines from age or excessive sun exposure.

4. Figure 5.1 depicts a longitudinal section of the skin. Label the skin structures
   and areas indicated by leader lines and brackets on the figure. Select different
   colors for the structures below and color the coding circles and the corresponding structures on the figure.

   ◯ Arrector pili muscle   ◯ Nerve fibers

   ◯ Adipose tissue   ◯ Sweat (sudoriferous) gland

   ◯ Hair follicle   ◯ Sebaceous gland

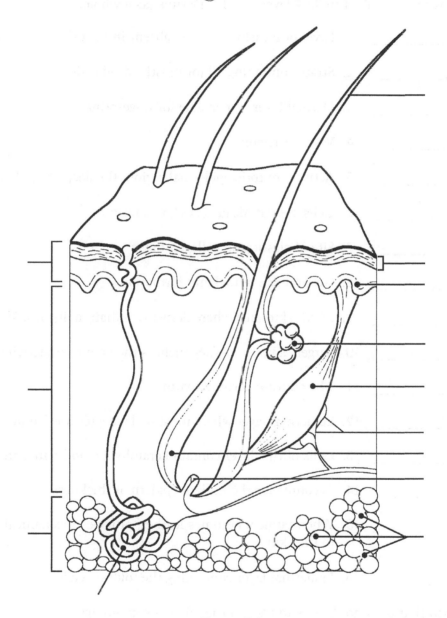

Figure 5.1

5. Using the key choices, choose all responses that apply to the following descriptions. Enter the appropriate letters and/or terms in the answer blanks. (Note: S. = stratum)

Key Choices

A. S. basale	D. S. lucidum	G. Reticular layer	J. Hypodermis
B. S. corneum	E. S. spinosum	H. Epidermis (as a whole)	
C. S. granulosum	F. Papillary layer	I. Dermis (as a whole)	

_____ 1. Layer of translucent cells, absent in thin skin

_____ 2. Strata containing all (or mostly) dead cells

_____ 3. Dermal layer responsible for fingerprints

_____ 4. Vascular region

_____ 5. Actively mitotic epidermal region, the deepest epidermal layer

_____ 6. Cells are flat, dead "bags" of keratin

_____ 7. Site of elastic and collagen fibers

_____ 8. General site of melanin formation

_____ 9. Major skin area where derivatives (hair, nails) *reside*

_____ 10. Largely adipose tissue; anchors the skin to underlying tissues

_____ 11. The stratum germinativum

_____ 12. Epidermal layer where most melanocytes are found

_____ 13. Cells of this layer contain keratohyalin and lamellated granules

_____ 14. Accounts for the hulk of epidermal thickness

_____ 15. When tanned, becomes leather; provides mechanical strength to the skin

_____ 16. Epidermal layer containing the "oldest" cells

6. Circle the term that does not belong in each of the following groupings.

1. Reticular layer   Keratin   Dermal papillae   Meissner's corpuscles

2. Melanin   Freckle   Wart   Malignant melanoma

3. Prickle cells   Stratum basale   Stratum spinosum   Cell shrinkage

4. Langerhans' cells   Epidermal dendritic cells   Keratinocytes   Macrophages

5. Meissner's corpuscles   Pacinian corpuscles   Merkel cells   Arrector pili

6. Waterproof substance   Elastin   Lamellated granules   Produced by keratinocytes

7. Mast cells   Macrophages   Fibroblasts   Melanocytes

8. Intermediate filaments   Keratin fibrils   Keratohyaline   Lamellated granules

9. Keratinocyte   Fibroblast   Merkel cell   Langerhans' cell

7. This exercise examines the relative importance of three pigments in determining skin color. Indicate which pigment is identified by the following descriptions by inserting the appropriate answer from the key choices in the answer blanks.

Key Choices

A. Carotene   B. Hemoglobin   C. Melanin

_____ 1. Most responsible for the skin color of dark-skinned people

_____ 2. Provides an orange cast to the skin

_____ 3. Provides a natural sunscreen

_____ 4. Most responsible for the skin color of Caucasians

_____ 5. Phagocytized by keratinocytes

_____ 6. Found predominantly in the stratum corneum

_____ 7. Found within red blood cells in the blood vessels

8. Abnormalities of skin color can be helpful in alerting a physician to certain pathologies. Match the clinical terms in Column B with the possible-cause descriptions in Column A. Place the correct letter in each answer blank.

Column A

_____ 1. A bluish cast of the skin resulting from inadequate oxygenation of the blood

_____ 2. Observation of this condition might lead to tests for anemia or low blood pressure

_____ 3. Accumulation of bile pigments in the blood; may indicate liver disease

_____ 4. Clotted mass of blood that may signify bleeder's disease

_____ 5. A common result of inflammation, allergy, and fever

Column B

A. Cyanosis

B. Erythema

C. Hematoma

D. Jaundice

E. Pallor

Appendages of the Skin

1. Figure 5.2 shows longitudinal and cross-sectional views of a hair follicle.

Part A

1. Identify and label all structures provided with leader lines.

2. Select different colors to identify the structures described below and color both the coding circles and the corresponding structures on the diagram.

   ◯ Contains blood vessels that nourish the growth zone of the hair

   ◯ Secretes sebum into the hair follicle

   ◯ Pulls the hair follicle into an upright position during fright or exposure to cold

   ◯ The follicle sheath that consists of dermal tissue

   ◯ The follicle sheath that consists of epidermal tissue

   ◯ The actively growing region of the hair

3. Draw in the nerve fibers and blood vessels hat supply the follicle, the hair, the hair root, and the arrector pili.

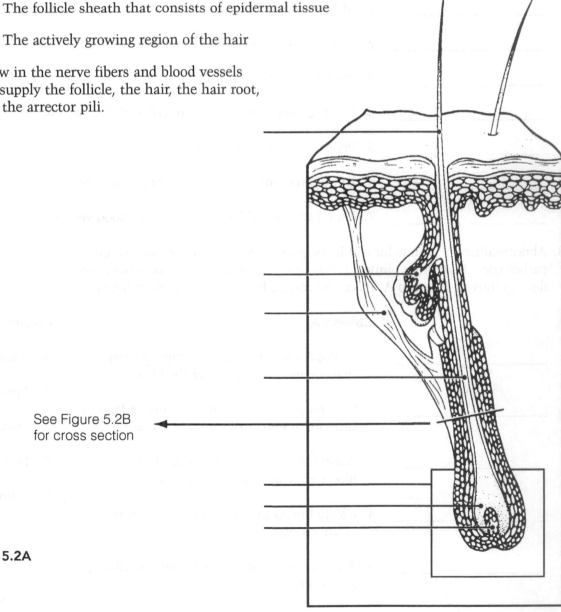

See Figure 5.2B
for cross section

Figure 5.2A

Part B

4. Identify the two portions of the follicle wall by placing the correct name of the sheath at the end of the appropriate leader line.

5. Color these regions using the same colors used for the identical structures in Part A.

6. Label, color code, and color these three regions of the hair:

   ◯ Cortex   ◯ Cuticle   ◯ Medulla

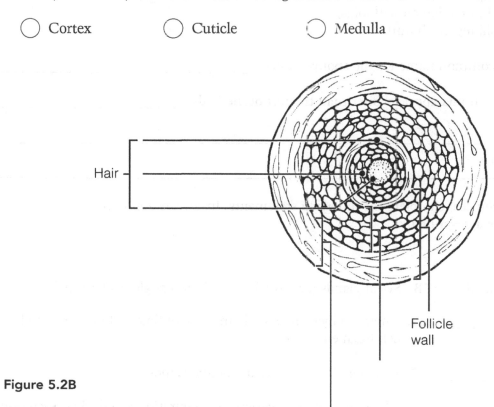

Hair

Follicle
wall

Figure 5.2B

2. Circle the term that does not belong in each of the following groupings.

   1. Luxuriant hair growth   Testosterone   Poor nutrition   Good blood supply

   2. Vitamin D   Cholesterol   UV radiation   Keratin

   3. Stratum corneum   Nail matrix   Hair bulb   Stratum basale

   4. Scent glands   Eccrine glands   Apocrine glands   Axilla

   5. Terminal hair   Vellus hair   Dark, coarse hair   Eyebrow hair

   6. Hard keratin   Hair shaft   Desquamation   Durable

   7. Growth phase   Resting phase   Atrophy   Inactive

3. What is the scientific term for baldness? _____

4. Name four factors that can cause hair loss and hair thinning *other than*

nutritional or circulatory factors. _____

_____

5. Draw a simple diagram of a fingertip *bearing a fingernail* in the space at the right. Identify and label the following nail regions on your sketch: free edge, body, lunula, lateral nail folds, proximal nail fold (eponychium).

1. What is the common name for the eponychium? _____

2. Why does the lunula appear whiter than the rest of the nail? _____

_____

_____

6. Using the key choices, complete the following statements. Insert the appropriate letters in the answer blanks.

Key Choices

A. Sebaceous glands   B. Sweat glands (apocrine)   C. Sweat glands (eccrine)

_____ 1. Their products are an oily mixture of lipids, cholesterol, and cell fragments.

_____ 2. Functionally, these are merocrine glands.

_____ 3. The less numerous variety of perspiration gland, their secretion (often milky in appearance) contains proteins and other substances that favor bacterial growth.

_____ 4. Their ducts open to the external environment via a pore.

_____ 5. These glands are found everywhere on the body except the palms of the hands and soles of the feet.

_____ 6. Their secretions contain bactericidal substances.

_____ 7. They become more active at puberty under the influence of androgens.

_____ 8. Their secretions, when oxidized, are seen on the skin surface as a blackhead.

_____ 9. The ceruminous glands that produce ear wax are a modification of this gland variety.

_____ 10. These glands are involved in thermoregulation.

Functions of the Integumentary System

1. The skin protects the body by providing three types of barriers. Classify each of the protective factors listed below as an example of a chemical barrier (C), a biological barrier (B), or a mechanical (physical) barrier (M).

    _____ 1. Langerhans' cells and macrophages   _____ 4. Keratin

    _____ 2. Intact epidermis   _____ 5. Melanin

    _____ 3. Bactericidal secretions   _____ 6. Acid mantle

2. Substances that can penetrate the skin in limited amounts include (circle all that apply):

    Fat-soluble vitamins   Steroid hormones   Water-soluble substances

    Organic solvents   Oxygen   Mercury, lead, and nickel

3. In what way does a sunburn impair the body's ability to defend itself?

    (Assume the sunburn is mild.) _____

    _____

4. Explain the role of sweat glands in maintaining body temperature homeostasis.

    In your explanation, indicate how their activity is regulated. _____

    _____

    _____

    _____

5. Complete the following statements. Insert your responses in the answer blanks.

    _____ 1.

    _____ 2.

    _____ 3.

    _____ 4.

    _____ 5.

    _____ 6.

    _____ 7.

    The cutaneous sensory receptors that reside in the skin are actually part of the __(1)__ system. Four types of stimuli that can be detected by certain of the cutaneous receptors are __(2)__ , __(3)__ , __(4)__ , and __(5)__ .

    Vitamin D is synthesized when modified __(6)__ molecules in the __(7)__ of the skin are irradiated by __(8)__ light. Vitamin D is important in the absorption and metabolism of __(9)__ ions.

    _____ 8.

    _____ 9.

Homeostatic Imbalances of Skin

1. Overwhelming infection is one of the most important causes of death in burn patients. What is the other major problem they face, and what are its possible consequences?

   _____

   _____

2. This section reviews the severity of burns. Using the key choices, select the correct burn type for each of the following descriptions. Enter the correct answers in the answer blanks.

   Key Choices

   A. First-degree burn   B. Second-degree burn   C. Third-degree burn

   _____   1. Full-thickness burn; epidermal and dermal layers destroyed; skin is blanched

   _____   2. Blisters form

   _____   3. Epidermal damage, redness, and some pain (usually brief)

   _____   4. Epidermal and some dermal damage; pain; regeneration is possible

   _____   5. Regeneration impossible; requires grafting

   _____   6. Pain is absent because nerve endings in the area are destroyed

3. What is the importance of the "rule of nines" in the treatment of burn patients?

   _____

4. Fill in the type of skin cancer that matches each of the following descriptions:

   _____   1. Cells of the stratum spinosum develop lesions; metastasizes to lymph nodes.

   _____   2. Cells of the lowest level of the epidermis invade the dermis and hypodermis; exposed areas develop ulcer; slow to metastasize.

   _____   3. Rare but deadly cancer of pigment-producing cells.

5. What does ABCD mean in reference to examination of pigmented areas? _____

   _____

   _____

THE INCREDIBLE JOURNEY

A Visualization Exercise for the Skin

Your immediate surroundings resemble huge, grotesquely twisted vines . . . you begin to climb upward.

1. Complete the narrative by inserting the missing words in the answer blanks.

_____ 1.

_____ 2.

_____ 3.

_____ 4.

_____ 5.

_____ 6.

_____ 7.

_____ 8.

For this trip, you are miniaturized for injection into your host's skin. Your journey begins when you are injected into a soft gel-like substance. Your immediate surroundings resemble huge, grotesquely twisted vines. But when you peer carefully at the closest "vine," you realize you are actually seeing connective tissue fibers. Most of the fibers are fairly straight, although tangled together, and look like strong cables. You identify these as the __(1)__ fibers. Here and there are fibers that resemble coiled springs. These must be the __(2)__ fibers that help give skin its springiness. At this point, there is little question that you are in the __(3)__ region of the skin particularly since you can also see blood vessels and nerve fibers around you.

Carefully, using the fibers as steps, you begin to climb upward. After climbing for some time and finding that you still haven't reached the upper regions of the skin, you stop for a rest. As you sit, a strange-looking cell approaches, moving slowly with parts alternately flowing forward and then receding. Suddenly you realize that this must be a __(4)__ that is about to dispose of an intruder (you) unless you move in a hurry! You scramble to your feet and resume your upward climb. On your right is a large fibrous structure that looks like a tree trunk anchored in place by muscle fibers. By scurrying up this __(5)__ sheath, you are able to escape from the cell and again scan your surroundings. Directly overhead are tall cubelike cells, forming a continuous sheetlike membrane. In your rush to escape you reached the __(6)__ region of the skin. As you watch the activity of the cells in this layer, you notice that many of the cells are pinching in two and that the daughter cells are being forced upward. Obviously, this is the specific layer that continually replaces cells that rub off the skin surface, and these cells are the __(7)__ cells.

Looking through the transparent cell membrane of one of the basal cells, you see a dark mass hanging over the nucleus. You wonder if this cell could have a tumor; but then, looking through the membranes of the neighboring cells, you find that they also have dark umbrella-like masses hanging over their nuclei. As you consider this matter, a black cell with long tentacles begins to pick its way carefully between the other cells. As you watch, one of the transparent cells engulfs the end of a tentacle of the black cell, and within seconds contains some of its black substance. Suddenly, you remember that one of the skin's protective functions is to protect the deeper layers from sun damage; the black substance must be the protective pigment __(8)__ .

_____ 9. Once again you begin your upward climb and notice that the cells are becoming shorter and harder and are full of a tough,

_____ 10. waxy substance. This substance has to be __(9)__, which would account for the increasing hardness of the cells. Climbing still higher, the cells become flattened like huge shingles. The only material apparent in the cells is the waxy substance; there is no nucleus, and there appears to be no activity in these cells. Considering the clues—shinglelike cells, no nuclei, full of the waxy substance, no activity—these cells are obviously __(10)__ and therefore are very close to the skin surface.

Suddenly, you feel a strong agitation in your immediate area. The pressure is tremendous. Looking upward through the transparent cell layers, you see your host's fingertips vigorously scratching the area directly overhead. You wonder if you are causing his skin to sting or tickle. Then, within seconds, the cells around you begin to separate and fall apart, and you are catapulted out into the sunlight. Since the scratching fingers might descend once again, you quickly advise your host of your whereabouts.

CHALLENGING YOURSELF

At the Clinic

1. Xeroderma pigmentosum is a severe, genetically linked skin cancer in which DNA repair mechanisms are impaired. Why would sufferers of this condition need to stay out of the sun?

2. A new mother brings her infant to the clinic, worried about a yellowish, scummy deposit that has built up on the baby's scalp. What is this condition called, and is it serious?

3. Hives are welts, or reddened "bumps," that indicate sites of local inflammation. They are often a sign of an allergic reaction. Recall from Chapter 3 the role of capillary permeability and plasma loss in causing edema. Would systemic hives be cause for worry?

4. A worker in a furniture refinishing establishment fell into a vat of paint stripper, but quickly removed his clothes and rinsed off in the safety shower. Were his safety measures adequate? What vital organs might suffer early damage from poisoning through skin by organic solvents?

5. What two factors in the treatment of critical third-degree burn patients are absolutely essential?

6. Mr. Bellazono, a fisherman in his late 60s, comes to the clinic to complain of small ulcers on both forearms as well as on his face and ears. Although he has had them for several years, he has not had any other problems. What is the likely diagnosis, and what is the likely cause?

7. The hypodermis of the face is quite loose and has few connections to the deep fascia of the muscles. Explain how this relates to the greater need to suture cuts on the face compared to other body regions.

8. Martha, the mother of a 13-month-old infant, brings her child to the clinic because his skin has turned orange. Why does the pediatrician inquire about the child's diet?

9. Mrs. Ibañez volunteered to help at a hospital for children with cancer. When she first entered the cancer ward, she was upset by the fact that most of the children had no hair. What is the explanation for their baldness?

10. Carmen slipped on some ice and split open the skin of her chin on the sidewalk. As the physician in the emergency room was giving her six stitches, he remarked that the split was straight along a cleavage line. How cleanly is her wound going to heal, and is major scarring likely to occur?

Stop and Think

1. How can the skin be both a membrane and an organ?

2. Why does the border between the epidermis and the dermis undulate?

3. The skin covering your shins is *not* freely movable. Palpate (feel) your shins and compare that region to the other regions of the body. Then try to deduce why there is little free movement of the skin of the shins.

4. In terms of both function and benefit, why are surface keratinocytes dead?

5. What nerve endings in the skin respond to the lightest touch?

6. Why does sunburned skin peel in sheets?

7. Would increasing protein intake (such as by taking gelatin supplements) increase hair and nail strength in an otherwise healthy individual?

8. Studies have shown that women who live or work together tend to develop synchronized monthly cycles. What aspect of the integumentary system might explain this sexual signaling?

9. If our cells and body fluids are hyperosmotic to the water of a swimming pool (and they *are*), then why do we not swell and pop when we go for a swim?

COVERING ALL YOUR BASES

Multiple Choice

Select the best answer or answers from the choices given.

1. Which is *not* part of the skin?

   A. Epidermis   C. Dermis

   B. Hypodermis   D. Superficial fascia

2. Which of the following is *not* a tissue type found in the skin?

   A. Stratified squamous epithelium

   B. Loose connective tissue

   C. Dense irregular connective tissue

   D. Ciliated columnar epithelium

   E. Vascular tissue

3. Epidermal cells that aid in the immune response include:

   A. Merkel cells   C. melanocytes

   B. Langerhans' cells   D. spinosum cells

4. Which organelle is most prominent in cells manufacturing the protein keratin?

   A. Ribosomes

   B. Golgi apparatus

   C. Smooth endoplasmic reticulum

   D. Lysosomes

5. Which epidermal layer has the highest concentration of Langerhans' cells, and has numerous desmosomes and thick bundles of keratin filaments?

   A. Stratum corneum

   B. Stratum lucidum

   C. Stratum granulosum

   D. Stratum spinosum

6. Fingerprints are caused by:

   A. the genetically determined arrangement of dermal papillae

   B. the conspicuous epidermal ridges

   C. the sweat pores

   D. all of these

7. Find the *false* statement concerning vitamin D.

   A. Dark-skinned people make no vitamin D.

   B. If vitamin D production is inadequate, one may develop weak bones.

   C. If the skin is not exposed to sunlight, one may develop weak bones.

   D. Vitamin D is needed for the uptake of calcium from food in the intestine.

8. Use logic to deduce the answer to this question. Given what you now know about skin color and skin cancer, which of the following groups would have the highest rate of skin cancer?

   A. Blacks in tropical Africa

   B. Scientists in research stations in Antarctica

   C. Whites in northern Australia

   D. Norwegians in the southern part of the U.S.

   E. Blacks in the U.S.

9. Which structure is not associated with a hair?

   A. Shaft

   B. Cortex

   C. Eponychium

   D. Matrix

   E. Cuticle

10. Which of the following hair colors is not produced by melanin?

    A. Blonde

    B. Brown

    C. Black

    D. Gray

    E. White

11. Which is the origin site of cells that are directly responsible for growth of a hair?

    A. Hair bulb

    B. Hair follicle

    C. Papilla

    D. Hair bulge

    E. Matrix

12. Concerning movement of hairs:

    A. Movement is the function of the arrector pili.

    B. Movement is sensed by the root hair plexus.

    C. Muscle contraction flattens the hair against the skin.

    D. Muscle contraction is prompted by cold or fright.

13. A particular type of tumor of the adrenal gland causes excessive secretion of sex hormones. This condition expresses itself in females as:

    A. male pattern baldness

    B. hirsutism

    C. increase in growth of vellus hairs over the whole body

    D. increase in length of terminal hairs

14. At the end of a follicle's growth cycle:

    A. the follicle atrophies

    B. the hair falls out

    C. the hair elongates

    D. the hair turns white

15. What is the major factor accounting for the waterproof nature of the skin?

    A. Desmosomes in stratum corneum

    B. Glycolipid between stratum corneum cells

    C. The thick insulating fat of the hypodermis

    D. The leathery nature of the dermis

16. In investigating the cause of thinning hair, which of the following questions needs to be asked?

    A. Is the diet deficient in proteins?

    B. Is the person taking megadoses of vitamin C?

    C. Has the person been exposed to excessive radiation?

    D. Has the person recently suffered severe emotional trauma?

17. Which structures are not associated with a nail?

    A. Nail bed   C. Nail folds

    B. Lunula   D. Nail follicle

18. One of the following is not associated with production of perspiration. Which one?

    A. Sweat glands   D. Eccrine gland

    B. Sweat pores   E. Apocrine gland

    C. Holocrine gland

19. Components of sweat include:

    A. water   D. ammonia

    B. sodium chloride   E. vitamin D

    C. sebum

20. Which of the following is *true* concerning oil production in the skin?

    A. Oil is produced by sudoriferous glands.

    B. Secretion of oil is via the holocrine mode.

    C. The secretion is called sebum.

    D. Oil is usually secreted into hair follicles.

21. A disorder *not* associated with oil glands is:

    A. seborrhea   C. acne

    B. cystic fibrosis   D. whiteheads

22. Contributing to the chemical barrier of the skin is/are:

    A. perspiration

    B. stratified squamous epithelium

    C. Langerhans' cells

    D. sebum

    E. melanin

23. Which of the following provide evidence of the skin's role in temperature regulation?

    A. Shivering   D. Sensible perspiration

    B. Flushing   E. Acid mantle

    C. Blue fingernails

24. Contraction of the arrector pili would be "sensed" by:

    A. Merkel discs

    B. Meissner's corpuscles

    C. root hair plexuses

    D. Pacinian corpuscles

25. A dermatologist examines a patient with lesions on the face. Some of the lesions appear as a shiny, raised spot; others are ulcerated with a beaded edge. What is the diagnosis?

    A. Melanoma

    B. Squamous cell carcinoma

    C. Basal cell carcinoma

    D. Either squamous or basal cell carcinoma

26. A burn patient reports that the burns on her hands and face are not painful, but she has blisters on her neck and forearms and the skin on her arms is very red. This burn would be classified as:

    A. first-degree only

    B. second-degree only

    C. third-degree only

    D. critical

27. Which of the following is associated with vitamin synthesis in the body?

A. Cholesterol

B. Calcium metabolism

C. Carotene

D. Ultraviolet radiation

E. Melanin

28. A patient has a small (about 1 mm), regular, round, pale mole. Is this likely to be melanoma?

A. Yes

B. No, because it is small

C. No, because it is pale

D. No, because it is round

E. No, because it is regular

Word Dissection

For each of the following word roots, fill in the literal meaning and give an example, using a word found in this chapter.

Word root	Translation	Example
1. arrect		
2. carot		
3. case		
4. cere		
5. corn		
6. cort		
7. cutic		
8. cyan		
9. derm		
10. folli		
11. hemato		
12. hirsut		
13. jaune		
14. kera		
15. lanu		
16. lunul		
17. medull		

Word root	Translation	Example
18. melan	_____	_____
19. pall	_____	_____
20. papilla	_____	_____
21. pili	_____	_____
22. plex	_____	_____
23. rhea	_____	_____
24. seb	_____	_____
25. spin	_____	_____
26. sudor	_____	_____
27. tegm	_____	_____
28. vell	_____	_____

6

BONES AND SKELETAL TISSUES

Student Objectives

When you have completed the exercises in this chapter, you will have accomplished the following objectives:

Skeletal Cartilages

1. Explain the functional properties of the three types of cartilage tissue.

2. Locate the major cartilages of the adult skeleton.

3. Explain how cartilage grows.

Functions of the Bones

4. List and describe five important functions of bones.

Classification of Bones

5. Compare and contrast the structure of the four bone classes and provide examples of each class.

Bone Structure

6. Describe the gross anatomy of a typical long bone and flat bone. Indicate the locations and functions of red and yellow marrow, articular cartilage, periosteum, and endosteum.

7. Indicate the functional importance of bone markings.

8. Describe the histology of compact and spongy bone.

9. Discuss the chemical composition of bone and the relative advantages conferred by its organic and its inorganic components.

Bone Development

10. Compare and contrast intramembranous ossification and endochondral ossification.

11. Describe the process of long bone growth that occurs at the epiphyseal plates.

Bone Homeostasis: Remodeling and Repair

12. Compare the locations and remodeling functions of the osteoblasts, osteocytes, and osteoclasts.

13. Explain how hormones and physical stress regulate bone remodeling.

14. Describe the steps of fracture repair.

Homeostatic Imbalances of Bone

15. Contrast the disorders of bone remodeling seen in osteoporosis, osteomalacia, and Paget's disease.

Bone and cartilage are the principal tissues that provide support for the body; together they make up the skeletal system. The early skeleton is formed largely from cartilage. Later, the cartilage is replaced almost entirely by bone. Bones provide attachments for muscles and act as levers for the movements of body parts. Bones perform additional essential functions. They are the sites for blood cell formation and are storage depots for many substances, such as fat, calcium, and phosphorus.

Bone tissue has an intricate architecture that is both stable and dynamic. Although it has great strength and rigidity, bone tissue is able to change structurally in response to a variety of chemical and mechanical factors.

Chapter 6 topics for student review include an overview of skeletal cartilages, the structures of long and flat bones, the remodeling and repair of bone, and bone development and growth.

BUILDING THE FRAMEWORK

Skeletal Cartilages

1. Use the key choices to identify the type of cartilage tissue found in the following body locations:

Key Choices

A. Elastic cartilage   B. Fibrocartilage   C. Hyaline cartilage

_____   1. At the junction of a rib and the sternum

_____   2. The skeleton of the external ear

_____   3. Supporting the trachea walls

_____   4. Forming the intervertebral discs

_____   5. Forming the epiglottis

_____   6. At the ends of long bones

_____   7. Most of the fetal skeleton

_____   8. Knee menisci

2. In comparing bone and cartilage tissue, indicate whether each of the following statements is true (T) or false (F).

_____ 1. Cartilage is more resilient than bone.

_____ 2. Cartilage is especially strong in resisting shear (bending and twisting) forces.

_____ 3. Cartilage can grow faster than bone in the growing skeleton.

_____ 4. In the adult skeleton, cartilage regenerates faster than bone when damaged.

_____ 5. Neither bone nor cartilage contains capillaries.

_____ 6. Bone tissue contains relatively little water compared to cartilage tissue, which contains a large amount of water.

_____ 7. Nurtients diffuse quickly through cartilage matrix but very poorly through solid bone matrix.

3. What single structural characteristic accounts for the resilience of cartilage and its ability to grow rapidly in the developing skeleton?

_____

_____

Functions of the Bones

1. List and explain five important functions of bones. Write your answers in the answer blanks below.

1. _____

2. _____

3. _____

4. _____

5. _____

Classification of Bones

1. Identify each of the following bones as a member of one of the four major bone categories. Use L for long bone, S for short bone, F for flat bone, and I for irregular bone. Enter the appropriate letters in the answer blanks.

_____ 1. Calcaneus   _____ 4. Humerus   _____ 7. Radius

_____ 2. Frontal   _____ 5. Mandible   _____ 8. Sternum

_____ 3. Femur   _____ 6. Metacarpal   _____ 9. Vertebra

Bone Structure

1. Figure 6.1A is a drawing of a sagittal section of the femur. Do not color the articular cartilage. Leave it white. Select different colors for the bone regions listed at the coding circles below. Color the coding circles and the corresponding regions on the drawing. Complete Figure 6.1A by labeling compact bone and spongy bone.

   Figure 6.1B is a mid-level, cross-sectional view of the diaphysis of the femur. As in A, identify by color the area where yellow marrow is found. Label the membrane that lines the cavity and the membrane that covers the outside surface. Indicate by an asterisk (*) the membrane that contains both osteoblasts and osteoclasts.

   ○ Diaphysis   ○ Area where red marrow is found

   ○ Epiphyseal plate   ○ Area where yellow marrow is found

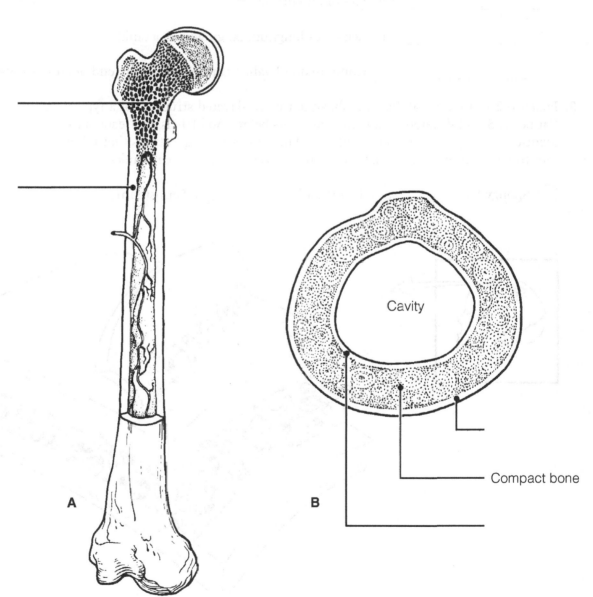

Figure 6.1

2. Using the key choices, characterize the following statements relating to the structure of a long bone. Enter the appropriate answers in the answer blanks.

Key Choices

A. Diaphysis   C. Epiphysis   E. Yellow marrow cavity

B. Epiphyseal plate   D. Red marrow

_____ 1. Location of spongy bone in an adult's bone

_____ 2. Location of compact bone in an adult's bone

_____ 3. Site of hematopoiesis in an adult's bone

_____ 4. Scientific name for bone shaft

_____ 5. Site of fat storage

_____ 6. Region of longitudinal growth in a child

_____ 7. Composed of hyaline cartilage until the end of adolescence

3. Figure 6.2 is a sectional diagram showing the five-layered structure of a typical flat bone. Select different colors for the layers below. Add labels and leaders to identify Sharpey's fibers and trabeculae. Then answer the questions that follow, referring to Figure 6.2 and inserting your answers in the answer blanks.

◯ Spongy bone   ◯ Compact bone   ◯ Periosteum

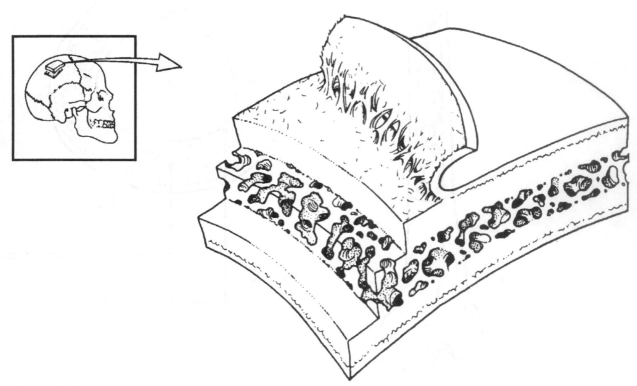

Figure 6.2

1. Which layer is called the diploë? _____

2. Name the membrane that lines internal bone cavities. _____

4. Five descriptions of bone structure are provided in Column A.

First, identify the structure by choosing the appropriate term from Column B and placing the corresponding answer in the answer blank.

Second, consider Figure 6.3A, a diagrammatic view of a cross section of bone, and Figure 6.3B, a higher-magnification view of compact bone tissue. Select different colors for the structures and bone areas in Column B and use them to color the coding circles and corresponding structures on the diagrams. Since concentric lamellae would be difficult to color without confusing other elements, identify one lamella by using a bracket and label.

Column A	Column B
_____ 1. Layers of calcified matrix	A. Central (Haversian) canal ◯
_____ 2. "Residences" of osteocytes	B. Concentric lamellae ◯
_____ 3. Longitudinal canal, carrying blood vessels and nerves	C. Lacunae ◯
	D. Canaliculi ◯
_____ 4. Nonliving, structural part of bone	E. Bone matrix ◯
_____ 5. Tiny canals connecting lacunae	F. Osteocyte ◯

A

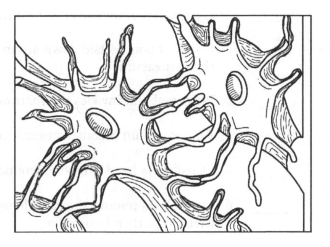

B

Figure 6.3

5. Classify each of the following terms as a projection (P), a depression (D), or an opening (O). Enter the appropriate letter in the answer blanks.

_____ 1. Condyle   _____ 4. Foramen   _____ 7. Ramus   _____ 10. Fossa

_____ 2. Crest   _____ 5. Head   _____ 8. Spine   _____ 11. Facet

_____ 3. Fissure   _____ 6. Meatus   _____ 9. Tuberosity   _____ 12. Sinus

6. Circle the term that does not belong in each of the following groupings.

1. Rigidity   Calcium salts   Hydroxyapatites   Collagen   Hardness

2. Hematopoiesis   Red marrow   Yellow marrow   Spongy bone   Diploë

3. Lamellae   Cellular extensions   Canaliculi   Circulation   Osteoclasts

4. Osteon   Marrow cavity   Volkmann's canals   Haversian canal   Canaliculi

5. Epiphysis   Articular cartilage   Periosteum   Hyaline cartilage

6. Perichondrium   Periosteum   Appositional growth   Osteoblasts

7. Spongy   Cancellous   Woven   Lamellar   Trabecular

Bone Development

1. The following events apply to the endochondral ossification process as it occurs in the primary ossification center. Put these events in their proper order by assigning each a number (1–6).

_____ 1. Cavity formation occurs within the hyaline cartilage.

_____ 2. Collar of bone is laid down around the hyaline cartilage model just beneath the periosteum.

_____ 3. Periosteal bud invades the marrow cavity.

_____ 4. Perichondrium becomes vascularized to a greater degree and becomes a periosteum.

_____ 5. Osteoblasts lay down bone around the cartilage spicules in the bone's interior.

_____ 6. Osteoclasts remove the cancellous bone from the shaft interior, leaving a marrow cavity that then houses fat.

2. For each statement that is true, insert T in the answer blank. For false statements, correct the underlined words by inserting the correct words in the answer blanks.

_____ 1. When a bone forms from a fibrous membrane, the process is called underline{endochondral} ossification.

_____ 2. <u>Membrane</u> bones develop from hyaline cartilage structures.

_____ 3. The organic bone matrix is called the <u>osteoid</u>.

_____ 4. The enzyme alkaline phosphatase encourages the deposit of <u>collagen fibers</u> within the matrix of developing bone.

_____ 5. When trapped in lacunae, osteoblasts change into <u>osteocytes</u>.

_____ 6. Large numbers of <u>osteocytes</u> are found in the inner periosteum layer.

_____ 7. During endochondral ossification, the <u>periosteal bud</u> invades the deteriorating hyaline cartilage shaft.

_____ 8. <u>Primary</u> ossification centers appear in the epiphyses.

_____ 9. Epiphyseal plates are made of <u>spongy bone</u>.

_____ 10. In appositional growth, bone reabsorption occurs on the <u>periosteal</u> surface.

_____ 11. "Maturation" of newly formed (noncalcified) bone matrix takes about <u>10 days</u>.

3. Follow the events of intramembranous ossification by writing the missing words in the answer blanks.

_____ 1. The initial supporting structure for this type of ossification is a fibrous membrane formed by __(1)__. The first recognizable

_____ 2. event is a clustering of the __(1)__ cells to form a(n) __(2)__ in the fibrous membrane. These cells then differentiate into

_____ 3. __(3)__ which begin secreting __(4)__ around the fibers of the membrane. Within a few days, calcium salt deposit or __(5)__

_____ 4. occurs, producing true __(6)__. The first network of trabeculae formed are arranged irregularly. This early membrane bone is

_____ 5. referred to as __(7)__ bone. As it forms, a layer of vascular __(8)__ condenses on the external face of the bone structure,

_____ 6. forming a __(9)__. Eventually lamellar bone replaces __(7)__, and the vascular tissue within the __(10)__ differentiates into red

_____ 7. marrow. The final result is a flat bone.

_____ 8.

_____ 9.

_____ 10.

4. Figure 6.4 is a diagram representing the histological changes in the epiphyseal plate of a growing long bone.

First, select different colors for the types of cells named below. Color the coding circles and the corresponding cells in the diagram.

◯ Region of ossification   ◯ Dividing cartilage cells

◯ Older, enlarging, vesiculating cells

Second, identify bracketed zones A–C on the diagram as: *growth*, *osteogenic*, or *transformation*.

Third, complete the statements, referring to Figure 6.4 and the labeled regions on the diagram. Insert the correct words in the spaces provided.

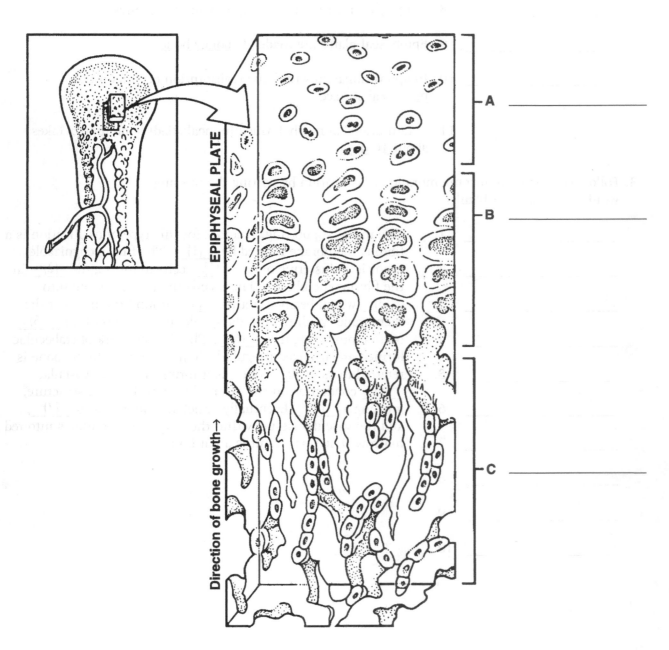

Figure 6.4

_____ 1. The cell type in region A is ___(1)___.

_____ 2. The type of cell in region B is ___(2)___.

_____ 3. Calcification of the cartilage matrix begins in region ___(3)___.

_____ 4. The cartilaginous matrix begins to deteriorate in region ___(4)___.

_____ 5. The type of cell found in region C is ___(5)___.

_____ 6. The matrix being deposited in region C is ___(6)___ matrix.

Bone Homeostasis: Remodeling and Repair

1. Using the key choices, insert the correct answers in the answer blanks below.

Key Choices

A. Atrophy   C. Gravity   E. Osteoclasts   G. Parathyroid hormone

B. Calcitonin   D. Osteoblasts   F. Osteocytes   H. Stress and/or tension

_____ 1. When blood calcium levels begin to drop below homeostatic levels, ___(1)___ is released, causing calcium to be released from bones.

_____ 2. Mature bone cells, called ___(2)___, maintain bone in a viable state.

_____ 3. Disuse such as that caused by paralysis or severe lack of exercise results in muscle and bone ___(3)___.

_____ 4. Large tubercles and/or increased deposit of bony matrix occur at sites of ___(4)___.

_____ 5. Immature, or matrix-depositing, bone cells are referred to as ___(5)___.

_____ 6. ___(6)___ causes blood calcium to be deposited in bones as calcium salts.

_____ 7. Bone cells that liquefy bone matrix and release calcium to the blood are called ___(7)___.

_____ 8. Astronauts must perform isometric exercises when in outer space because bones atrophy under conditions of weightlessness or lack of ___(8)___.

2. Circle the term that does not belong in each of the following groupings.

1. Bone deposit   Injury sites   Growth zones   Repair sites   Bone resorption

2. Osteoid   Organic matrix   Calcium salts   Osteoblasts $10\,\mu$ wide

3. Hypercalcemia   Hypocalcemia   Calcium   Salt deposit in soft tissue

   Ca^{2+} over 11 mg/100 ml blood

4. Mechanical forces   Gravity   Muscle pull   Blood calcium levels   Wolff's law

5. Growth in diameter   Growth in length   Appositional growth

   Increase in thickness

3. According to Wolff's law, bones form according to the stresses placed upon them. Figure 6.5 is a simple diagram of the proximal end of a femur (thighbone). There are two sets of double arrows and two single arrows. Your job is to decide which of the single or paired arrows represents each of the following conditions and indicate those conditions on the diagram. Color the arrows to agree with your coding circles.

◯ Site of maximal compression   ◯ Load (body weight) exertion site

◯ Site of maximal tension   ◯ Point of no stress

Explain why long bones can "hollow out" without jeopardy to their integrity (soundness of structure).

_____

_____

_____

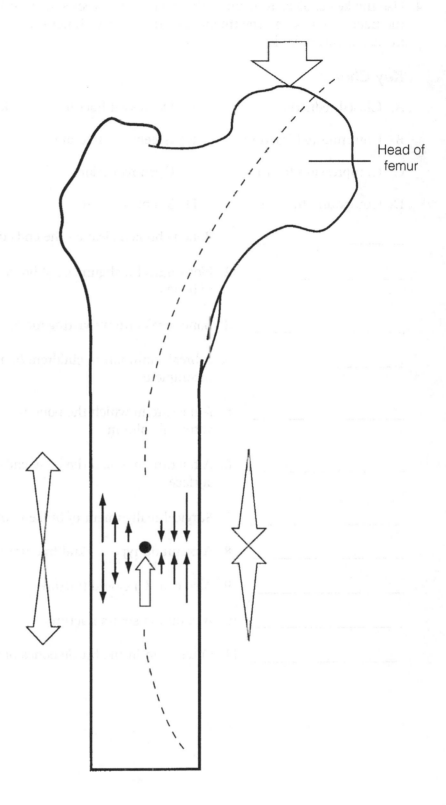

Head of
femur

Figure 6.5

4. Use the key choices to identify the fracture (fx) types shown in Figure 6.6 and the fracture types and treatments described below. Enter the appropriate answer in each answer blank.

Key Choices

A. Closed reduction   E. Depressed fracture   I. Spiral fracture

B. Comminuted fracture   F. Greenstick fracture

C. Compression fracture   G. Open reduction

D. Compound fracture   H. Simple fracture

_____ 1. Bone is broken cleanly; the ends do not penetrate the skin

_____ 2. Nonsurgical realignment of broken bone ends and splinting of bone

_____ 3. Bone breaks from twisting forces

_____ 4. A break common in children; bone splinters, but break is incomplete

_____ 5. A fracture in which the bone is crushed; common in the vertebral column

_____ 6. A fracture in which the bone ends penetrate through the skin surface

_____ 7. Surgical realignment of broken bone ends

_____ 8. A common type of skull fracture

_____ 9. Also called a closed fracture

_____ 10. A common sports fracture

_____ 11. Often seen in the brittle bones of the elderly

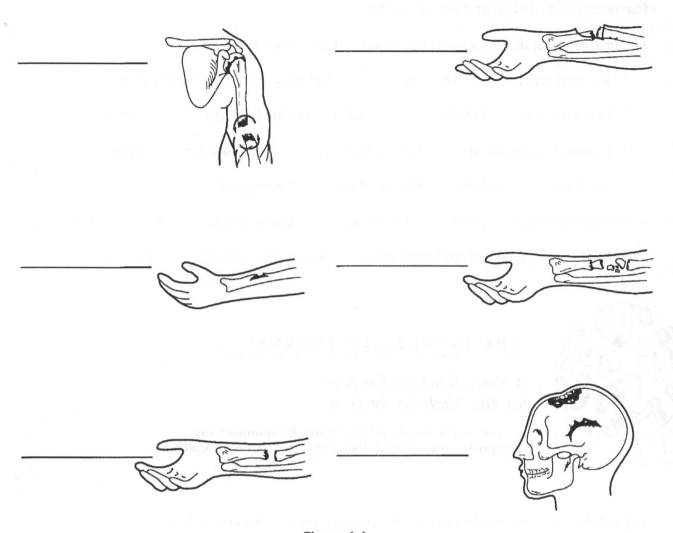

Figure 6.6

5. For each of the following statements about bone breakage and the repair
process that is true, insert T in the answer blank. For false statements, correct
the underlined words by inserting the correct words in the answer blanks.

_____ 1. A <u>hematoma</u> usually forms at a fracture site.

_____ 2. Deprived of nutrition, <u>osteocytes</u> at the fracture site die.

_____ 3. Nonbony debris at the fracture site is removed by <u>fibroblasts</u>.

_____ 4. <u>Osteocytes</u> produce collagen fibers that span the break.

_____ 5. Osteoblasts from the <u>medullary cavity</u> migrate to the fracture site.

_____ 6. The <u>fibrocartilaginous callus</u> is the first repair mass to splint the
broken bone.

_____ 7. The bony callus is composed of <u>compact</u> bone.

Homeostatic Imbalances of Bone

1. Circle the term that does not belong in each of the following groupings.

1. Bacterial infection   Osteoporosis   Inflammation   Osteomyelitis

2. Osteomalacia   Elderly   Vertebral compression fractures   Osteoporosis

3. Increased reabsorption   Decreased density   Paget's disease   Elderly

4. Soft bones   Rickets   Osteomalacia   Porous bones

5. Bone-filled marrow cavity   Pagetic bone   Osteomalacia   Bone thickenings

6. Rickets   Calcified epiphyseal discs   Vitamin D deficiency   Children

THE INCREDIBLE JOURNEY

A Visualization Exercise for the Skeletal System

. . . you look around and find yourself examining the stalagmite- and stalactitelike structures that surround you.

1. Complete the narrative by inserting the missing words in the answer blanks.

_____   1.   For this journey you are miniaturized and injected into the interior of the largest bone of your host's body, the __(1)__ . Once
_____   2.   inside this bone, you look around and find yourself examining the stalagmite- and stalactitelike structures that surround you.
_____   3.   Although you feel as if you are in an underground cavern, you know that it has to be bone. Since the texture is so full of holes,
_____   4.   it obviously is __(2)__ bone.

_____   5.   Although the arrangement of these bony spars seems to be haphazard, as if someone randomly had dropped straws, they are
_____   6.   precisely arranged to resist points of __(3)__ . All about you is frantic, hurried activity. Cells are dividing rapidly, nuclei are being ejected, and disclike cells are appearing. You decide that

these disclike cells are __(4)__ and that this is the __(5)__ cavity. As you explore further, strolling along the edge of the cavity, you spot many tunnels leading into the solid bony area on which you are walking. Walking into one of these drainpipe-like openings, you notice that it contains a glistening white rope-like structure, a __(6)__ , and blood vessels running the length of the tube. You eventually come to a point in the channel where the horizontal passageway joins with a vertical passage that runs with the

_____ 7.

_____ 8.

_____ 9.

_____ 10.

_____ 11.

_____ 12.

longitudinal axis of the bone. This is obviously a __(7)__ canal. Since you would like to see how nutrients are brought into __(8)__ bone, you decide to follow this channel. Reasoning that there is no way you can possibly scale the slick walls of the channel, you leap up and grab onto a white cord hanging down its length. Since it is easier to slide down than to try to climb up the cord, you begin to lower yourself, hand over hand. During your descent, you notice small openings in the wall, which are barely large enough for you to wriggle through. You conclude that these are the __(9)__ that connect all the __(10)__ to the nutrient supply in the central canal. You decide to investigate one of these tiny openings and begin to swing on your cord, trying to get a foothold on one of the openings. After managing to anchor your-self, and squeezing into an opening, you use a flashlight to illuminate the passageway in front of you. You are startled by a giant cell with many dark nuclei that appears to be plastered around the entire lumen directly ahead of you. As you watch this cell, the bony material beneath it, the __(11)__ , begins to liquefy. The cell apparently is a bone-digesting cell, or __(12)__ , and since you are unsure whether or not its enzymes can also liquefy you, you slither backward hurriedly and begin your trek back to your retrieval site.

CHALLENGING YOURSELF

At the Clinic

1. Mrs. Bruso, a woman in her 80s, stumbled slightly while walking and then felt a terrible pain in her hip. At the hospital, X rays reveal that her hip is broken and that she has compression fractures in her lower vertebral column and extremely low bone density in her vertebrae, hip bones, and femurs. What are the condition, cause, and treatment?

2. A child with a "red-hot" infected finger is brought into the clinic a week after the infection has set in. Why does the doctor order an X ray?

3. An X ray of the arm of an accident victim reveals a faint line curving around and down the shaft. What kind of fracture might this indicate?

4. A woman taking triple the recommended calcium supplement is suffering from lower back pains. X rays reveal that she has kidney stones. What is the name of the condition that causes this problem?

5. Larry, a 6-year-old boy, is already 5 feet tall. For what hormone will the pediatrician order a blood test?

6. Old Norse stories tell of a famous Viking named Egil who lived around 900 AD. His skull was greatly enlarged and misshapen, and the cranial bones were hardened and thickened (6 cm, or several inches, thick!). After he died, his skull was dug up and it withstood the blow of an ax without damage. In life, he had headaches from the pressure exerted by enlarged vertebrae on his spinal cord. What bone disorder did Egil probably have?

7. Ming posed the following question: "If the epiphyseal growth plates are growing so fast, why do they stay thin? Growing things are supposed to get larger or thicker, but these plates remain the same thickness." How would you answer her?

Stop and Think

1. Which appears first, the blood vessels within an osteon or the lamellae of bone matrix around the central canal?

2. Is there any form of interstitial growth in bone tissue? (Explain)

3. Contrast the arrangement and articulation of long bones and short bones.

4. Which type of cell, osteoclast or osteoblast, is more active in the medullary cavity of a growing long bone? On the internal surface of cranial bones?

5. Compare the vascularity of bone to that of the fibrous and cartilaginous tissues that precede it.

6. While walking home from a meeting of his adult singles support group, 52-year-old Ike broke a bone and damaged a knee cartilage in a fall. Assuming no special tissue grafts are made, which will probably heal faster, the bone or the cartilage? Why?

7. Eric, a radiologic tech student, was handed an X ray of the right femur of a 10-year-old boy. He noted that the area of the epiphyseal plate was beginning to show damage from osteomyelitis (the boy's diagnosis). Eric expressed his concern about the future growth of the boy's femur to the head radiologist. Need he have worried? Why or why not?

8. In several early cultures, bone deformation was a sign of social rank. For example, in the Mayan culture, head binding was done to give the skull a flattened forehead and a somewhat pointed top. Explain this in terms of Wolff's law.

9. Signs of successful (or at least nonfatal) brain surgery can be found on skulls many thousands of years old. How can an anthropologist tell that the patient didn't die from the surgery?

10. Explain (a) why cartilages are springy and (b) why cartilage can grow so quickly in the developing skeleton.

COVERING ALL YOUR BASES

Multiple Choice

Select the best answer or answers from the choices given.

1. Important bone functions include:

   A. support of the pelvic organs

   B. protection of the brain

   C. providing levers for movement of the limbs

   D. protection of the skin and limb musculature

   E. storage of water

2. Which of the following are correctly matched?

   A. Short bone—wrist

   B. Long bone—leg

   C. Irregular bone—sternum

   D. Flat bone—cranium

3. Terms that can be associated with any type of bone include:

   A. periosteum   D. cancellous bone

   B. diaphysis   E. medullary cavity

   C. diploë

4. Which would be common locations of osteoblasts?

   A. Osteogenic layer of periosteum

   B. Lining of red marrow spaces

   C. Covering articular cartilage

   D. Lining central canals

   E. Aligned with Sharpey's fibers

5. Which of the listed bone markings are sites of muscle or ligament attachment?

   A. Trochanter   D. Spine

   B. Meatus   E. Condyle

   C. Facet

6. Which of the following are openings or depressions?

   A. Fissure   D. Fossa

   B. Tuberosity   E. Tubercle

   C. Meatus

7. A passageway connecting neighboring osteocytes in an osteon is a:

   A. central canal   D. canaliculus

   B. lamella   E. perforating canal

   C. lacuna

8. Between complete osteons are remnants of older, remodeled osteons known as:

   A. circumferential lamellae

   B. concentric lamellae

   C. interstitial lamellae

   D. lamellar bone

   E. woven bone

9. Which of these could be found in cancellous bone?

   A. Osteoid   D. Central canals

   B. Trabeculae   E. Osteoclasts

   C. Canaliculi

10. Elements prominent in osteoblasts include:

    A. rough ER   D. smooth ER

    B. secretory vesicles   E. heterochromatin

    C. lysosomes

11. Which of the following are prominent in osteoclasts?

    A. Golgi apparatus   C. Microfilaments

    B. Lysosomes   D. Exocytosis

12. Endosteum is in all these places, except:

    A. around the exterior of the femur

    B. on the trabeculae of spongy bone

    C. lining the central canal of an osteon

    D. often directly touching bone marrow

13. Which precede(s) intramembranous ossification?

    A. Chondroblast activity

    B. Mesenchymal cells

    C. Woven bone

    D. Collagen formation

    E. Osteoid formation

14. Which of the following is (are) part of the process of endochondral ossification and growth?

    A. Vascularization of the fibrous membrane surrounding the cartilage template

    B. Formation of diploë

    C. Destruction of cartilage matrix

    D. Appositional growth

    E. Mitosis of chondroblasts

15. What is the earliest event (of those listed) in endochondral ossification?

    A. Ossification of proximal epiphysis

    B. Appearance of the epiphyseal plate

    C. Invasion of the shaft by the periosteal bud

    D. Cavitation of the cartilage shaft

    E. Formation of secondary ossification centers

16. Which zone of the epiphyseal plate is most influenced by sex hormones?

    A. Zone of resting cartilage

    B. Zone of hypertrophic cartilage

    C. Zone of proliferating cartilage

    D. Zone of calcification

17. The region active in appositional growth is:

    A. osteogenic layer of periosteum

    B. within central canals

    C. endosteum of red marrow spaces

    D. internal callus

    E. epiphyseal plate

18. Deficiency of which of the following hormones will cause dwarfism?

    A. Growth hormone

    B. Sex hormones

    C. Thyroid hormones

    D. Calcitonin

    E. Parathyroid hormone

19. A remodeling unit consists of:

    A. osteoblasts

    B. osteoid

    C. osteocytes

    D. osteoclasts

    E. chondroblasts

20. The calcification front marks the location of:

    A. newly formed osteoid

    B. newly deposited hydroxyapatite

    C. actively mitotic osteoblasts

    D. active osteoclasts

    E. the activity of alkaline phosphatase

21. A deficiency of calcium in the diet would lead to:

    A. an increase of parathyroid hormone in the blood

    B. an increase in calcitonin secretion

    C. an increase in somatomedin levels in the blood

    D. increased secretion of growth hormone

22. Ionic calcium plays a role in:

    A. the transmission of nerve impulses

    B. blood clotting

    C. muscle contraction

    D. cytokinesis

    E. the activity of sudoriferous glands

23. Which of the following is not associated with Wolff's law?

    A. Compression

    B. Gravity

    C. Growth hormone

    D. Orientation of trabeculae

    E. Bone atrophy following paralysis

24. The initial event following a bone fracture is:

    A. formation of granulation tissue

    B. ossification of internal callus

    C. hemorrhage and hematoma formation

    D. remodeling

    E. endochondral ossification

25. Women suffering from osteoporosis are frequent victims of _____ fractures of the vertebrae.

    A. compound   D. compression

    B. spiral   E. depression

    C. comminuted

26. Which of the listed bone disorders is (are) caused by hormonal imbalances?

    A. Osteomalacia   D. Achondroplasia

    B. Osteoporosis   E. Paget's disease

    C. Gigantism

27. At birth, ossification has progressed to the point where:

    A. only intramembranous ossification has begun

    B. endochondral ossification is complete

    C. some secondary ossification centers have appeared

    D. only major long bones have primary centers of ossification

    E. appositional growth has yet to begin

28. The growth spurt of puberty is triggered by:

    A. high levels of sex hormones

    B. the initial, low levels of sex hormones

    C. growth hormone

    D. parathyroid hormone

    E. calcitonin

Word Dissection

For each of the following word roots, fill in the literal meaning and give an example, using a word found in this chapter.

Word root	Translation	Example
1. call		
2. cancel		
3. clast		
4. fract		
5. lamell		
6. malac		
7. myel		
8. physis		
9. poie		
10. soma		
11. trab		

7

THE AXIAL SKELETON

Overview

The skeletal system in the human body is composed of 206 bones, 80 of which are found in the axial division, and 126 of which make up the appendicular division. Chapter 7 includes a study of the bones and associated parts of the axial skeleton, located along the body's longitudinal axis and center of gravity. They include 22 skull bones, 6 auditory ossicles, 1 hyoid bone, 26 vertebrae, 24 ribs, and 1 sternum. This bony framework protects and supports the vital organs in the dorsal and ventral body cavities. In addition, the bones serve as areas for muscle attachment, articulate at joints for stability and movement, assist in respiratory movements, and stabilize and position elements of the appendicular skeleton.

Your study and review for this chapter includes the identification and location of bones, the identification and location of bone markings, the functional anatomy of bones, and the articulations that comprise the axial skeleton.

LEVEL 1 Review of Chapter Objectives

1. Identify the bones of the axial skeleton and specify their functions.
2. Identify the bones of the cranium and face and explain the significance of the markings on the individual bones.
3. Describe the structure of the nasal complex and the functions of the individual bones.
4. Explain the function of the paranasal sinuses.
5. Describe key structural differences in the skulls of infants, children, and adults.
6. Identify and describe the curvatures of the spinal column and their functions.
7. Identify the vertebral regions and describe the distinctive structural and functional characteristics of each vertebral group.
8. Explain the significance of the articulations between the thoracic vertebrae and ribs, and between the ribs and sternum.

[L1]   Multiple Choice

Place the letter corresponding to the correct answer in the space provided.

OBJ. 1 _____ 1. The axial skeleton can be recognized because it:

     a. includes the bones of the arms and legs

     b. forms the longitudinal axis of the body

     c. includes the bones of the pectoral and pelvic girdles

     d. a, b, and c are correct

OBJ. 1 _____ 2. The axial skeleton provides an extensive surface area for the attachment of muscles that:

     a. adjust the positions of the head, the neck, and the trunk

     b. perform respiratory movements

     c. stabilize or position parts of the appendicular skeleton

     d. all of the above

OBJ. 1 _____ 3. Of the following selections, the one that includes bones found exclusively in the axial skeleton is:

     a. ear ossicles, scapula, clavicle, sternum, hyoid

     b. vertebrae, ischium, ilium, skull, ribs

     c. skull, vertebrae, ribs, sternum, hyoid

     d. sacrum, ear ossicles, skull, scapula, ilium

OBJ. 1 _____ 4. The axial skeleton creates a framework that supports and protects organ systems in:

     a. the dorsal and ventral body cavities

     b. the pleural cavity

     c. the abdominal cavity

     d. the pericardial cavity

OBJ. 2 _____ 5. The bones of the *cranium* that exclusively represent *single*, unpaired bones are:

     a. occipital, parietal, frontal, temporal

     b. occipital, frontal, sphenoid, ethmoid

     c. frontal, temporal, parietal, sphenoid

     d. ethmoid, frontal, parietal, temporal

OBJ. 2 _____ 6. The *paired* bones of the cranium are:

     a. ethmoid and sphenoid

     b. frontal and occipital

     c. occipital and parietal

     d. parietal and temporal

OBJ. 2 _____ 7. The *associated* bones of the skull include the:

     a. mandible and maxilla

     b. nasal and lacrimal

     c. hyoid and auditory ossicles

     d. vomer and palatine

OBJ. 2 _____ 8. The *single, unpaired* bones that make up the skeletal part of the face are the:
   a. mandible and vomer
   b. nasal and lacrimal
   c. mandible and maxilla
   d. nasal and palatine

OBJ. 2 _____ 9. The *sutures* that articulate the bones of the skull are:
   a. parietal, occipital, frontal, temporal
   b. calvaria, foramen, condyloid, lacerum
   c. posterior, anterior, lateral, dorsal
   d. lambdoidal, sagittal, coronal, squamosal

OBJ. 2 _____ 10. The bones that make up the *eye socket* or *orbit* include:
   a. lacrimal, zygomatic, maxilla
   b. ethmoid, temporal, zygomatic
   c. lacrimal, ethmoid, sphenoid
   d. temporal, frontal, sphenoid

OBJ. 2 _____ 11. *Foramina*, located on the bones of the skull, serve primarily as passageways for:
   a. airways and ducts for secretions
   b. sound and sight
   c. nerves and blood vessels
   d. muscle fibers and nerve tissue

OBJ. 2 _____ 12. The lines, tubercles, crests, ridges, and other processes on the bones represent areas that are used primarily for:
   a. attachment of muscles to bones
   b. attachment of bone to bone
   c. joint articulation
   d. increasing the surface area of the bone

OBJ. 2 _____ 13. Areas of the head that are involved in the formation of the skull are called:
   a. fontanels
   b. craniocephalic centers
   c. craniulums
   d. ossification centers

OBJ. 3 _____ 14. The *sinuses* or internal chambers in the skull are found in:
   a. sphenoid, ethmoid, vomer, lacrimal bones
   b. sphenoid, frontal, ethmoid, maxillary bones
   c. ethmoid, frontal, lacrimal, maxillary bones
   d. lacrimal, vomer, ethmoid, frontal bones

OBJ. 3 _____ 15. The nasal complex consists of the:
   a. frontal, sphenoid, and ethmoid bones
   b. maxilla, lacrimal and ethmoidal concha
   c. inferior concha
   d. a, b, and c are correct

`OBJ. 4` _____ 16. The air-filled chambers that communicate with the nasal cavities are the:
   a. condylar processes
   b. paranasal sinuses
   c. maxillary foramina
   d. mandibular foramina

`OBJ. 4` _____ 17. The primary function(s) of the paranasal sinus mucus epithelium is to:
   a. lighten the skull bones
   b. humidify and warm incoming air
   c. trap foreign articulate matter such as dust or microorganisms
   d. all of the above

`OBJ. 5` _____ 18. The reason the skull can be distorted without damage during birth is:
   a. fusion of the ossification centers is completed
   b. the brain is large enough to support the skull
   c. fibrous connective tissue connects the cranial bones
   d. shape and structure of the cranial elements are elastic

`OBJ. 5` _____ 19. At birth, the bones of the skull can be distorted without damage because of the:
   a. cranial foramina
   b. fontanels
   c. alveolar process
   d. cranial ligaments

`OBJ. 5` _____ 20. The most significant growth in the skull occurs before age five because:
   a. the brain stops growing and cranial sutures develop
   b. brain development is incomplete until maturity
   c. the cranium of a child is larger than that of an adult
   d. the ossification and articulation process is completed

`OBJ. 6` _____ 21. The primary spinal curves that appear late in fetal development:
   a. help shift the trunk weight over the legs
   b. accommodate the lumbar and cervical regions
   c. become accentuated as the toddler learns to walk
   d. accommodate the thoracic and abdominopelvic viscera

`OBJ. 6` _____ 22. An abnormal lateral curvature of the spine is called:
   a. kyphosis
   b. lordosis
   c. scoliosis
   d. amphiarthrosis

`OBJ. 6` _____ 23. The vertebrae that indirectly effect changes in the volume of the rib cage are the:
   a. cervical vertebrae
   b. thoracic vertebrae
   c. lumbar vertebrae
   d. sacral vertebrae

OBJ. 7 _____ 24. The most massive and least mobile of the vertebrae are the:

    a. thoracic

    b. cervical

    c. lumbar

    d. sacral

OBJ. 7 _____ 25. Of the following selections, the one that correctly identifies the sequence of the vertebra from superior to inferior is:

    a. thoracic, cervical, lumbar, coccyx, sacrum

    b. cervical, lumbar, thoracic, sacrum, coccyx

    c. cervical, thoracic, lumbar, sacrum, coccyx

    d. cervical, thoracic, sacrum, lumbar, coccyx

OBJ. 7 _____ 26. When identifying the vertebra, a numerical shorthand is used such as C_3. The C refers to:

    a. the region of the vertebrae

    b. the position of the vertebrae in a specific region

    c. the numerical order of the vertebrae

    d. the articulating surface of the vertebrae

OBJ. 7 _____ 27. C_1 and C_2 have specific names, which are the:

    a. sacrum and coccyx

    b. atlas and axis

    c. cervical and costal

    d. atlas and coccyx

OBJ. 7 _____ 28. The sacrum consists of five fused elements that afford protection for:

    a. reproductive, digestive, and excretory organs

    b. respiratory, reproductive, and endocrine organs

    c. urinary, respiratory, and digestive organs

    d. endocrine, respiratory, and urinary organs

OBJ. 7 _____ 29. The primary purpose of the coccyx is to provide:

    a. protection for the urinary organs

    b. protection for the anal opening

    c. an attachment site for leg muscles

    d. an attachment site for a muscle that closes the anal opening

OBJ. 8 _____ 30. The first seven pairs of ribs are called true ribs, while the lower five pairs are called *false* ribs because:

    a. the fused cartilages merge with the costal cartilage

    b. they do not attach directly to the sternum

    c. the last two pair have no connection with the sternum

    d. they differ in shape from the true ribs

OBJ. 8 _____ 31. The skeleton of the chest or thorax consists of:

    a. cervical vertebrae, ribs, and sternum

    b. cervical vertebrae, ribs, and thoracic vertebrae

    c. cervical vertebrae, ribs, and pectoral girdle

    d. thoracic vertebrae, ribs, and sternum

OBJ. 8 ___ 32. The three components of the adult sternum are the:
  a. pneumothorax, hemothorax, and tuberculum
  b. manubrium, body, and xiphoid process
  c. head, capitulum, and tuberculum
  d. angle, body, and shaft

[L1]   Completion

Using the terms below, complete the following statements.

centrum	costal	floating
axial	cranium	capitulum
fontanels	cervical	"soft spot"
mucus	paranasal	foramen magnum
compensation	xiphoid process	inferior concha
muscles		

OBJ. 1
1. The part of the skeletal system that forms the longitudinal axis of the body is the _____ division.

OBJ. 1
2. The bones of the skeleton provide an extensive surface area for the attachment of _____.

OBJ. 2
3. The part of the skull that provides protection for the brain is the _____.

OBJ. 2
4. The opening that connects the cranial cavity with the canal enclosed by the spinal column is the _____.

OBJ. 3
5. The paired scroll-like bones located on each side of the nasal septum are the _____.

OBJ. 3
6. The airspaces connected to the nasal cavities are the _____ sinuses.

OBJ. 4
7. Irritants are flushed off the walls of the nasal cavities because of the presence of _____.

OBJ. 5
8. At birth, the cranial bones are connected by areas of fibrous connective tissues called _____.

OBJ. 5
9. The anterior fontanel that is often easily seen by new parents is referred to as the _____.

OBJ. 6
10. The spinal curves that assist in allowing a child to walk and run are called _____ curves.

OBJ. 7
11. The medium, heart-shaped, flat face that serves as a facet for rib articulation on the *thoracic* vertebrae is called the _____.

OBJ. 7
12. The vertebrae that stabilize relative positions of the brain and spinal cord are the _____ vertebrae.

OBJ. 8
13. The cartilaginous extensions that connect the ribs to the sternum are the _____ cartilages.

OBJ. 8
14. A typical rib articulates with the vertebral column at the area of the rib called the _____.

OBJ. 8   15. The last two pairs of ribs that do not articulate with the sternum are called
_____ ribs.

OBJ. 8   16. The smallest part of the sternum that serves as an area of attachment for the muscular
diaphragm and rectus abdominis muscles in the _____.

[L1] Matching

Match the terms in column B with the terms in column A. Use letters for answers in the spaces
provided.

Part I		Column A	Column B
OBJ. 1	_____	1. hyoid bone	A. calvaria
OBJ. 1	_____	2. respiratory movement	B. premature closure of fontanel
OBJ. 2	_____	3. skullcap	C. infant skull
OBJ. 2	_____	4. sphenoid bone	D. vomer
OBJ. 3	_____	5. nasal septum	E. paranasal sinuses
OBJ. 4	_____	6. air-filled chambers	F. sella turcica
OBJ. 5	_____	7. fontanel	G. elevation of rib cage
OBJ. 5	_____	8. craniostenosis	H. stylohyoid ligaments

Part II		Column A	Column B
OBJ. 6	_____	9. primary curves	I. jugular notch
OBJ. 7	_____	10. cervical vertebrae	J. ribs 8–10
OBJ. 7	_____	11. lumbar vertebrae	K. C_1
OBJ. 7	_____	12. atlas	L. C_2
OBJ. 7	_____	13. axis	M. ribs 1–7
OBJ. 8	_____	14. vertebrosternal ribs	N. accommodation
OBJ. 8	_____	15. vertebrochondral ribs	O. neck
OBJ. 8	_____	16. manubrium	P. lower back

[L1]   Drawing/Illustration Labeling

Identify each numbered structure by labeling the following figures:

[OBJ. 1]   **Figure 7.1   Bones of the Axial Skeleton**

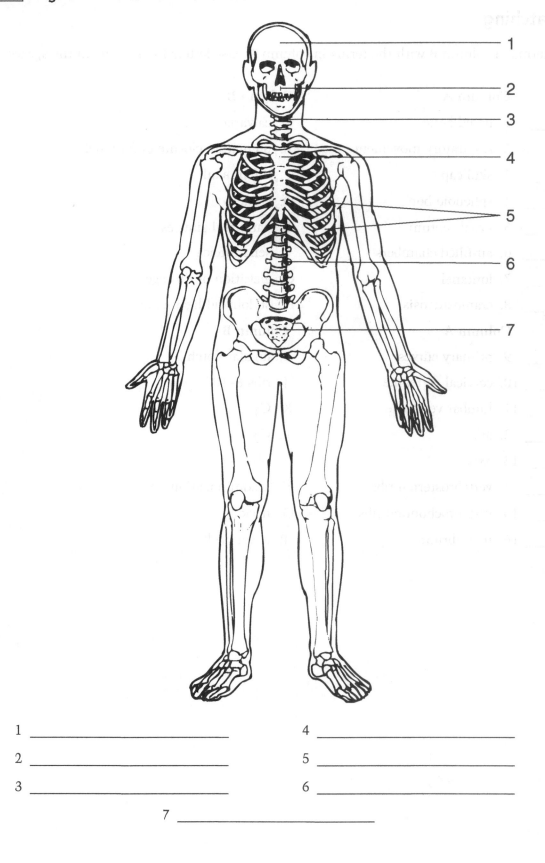

1 _____   4 _____

2 _____   5 _____

3 _____   6 _____

                      7 _____

OBJ. 2
OBJ. 3

Figure 7.2   Anterior View of the Skull

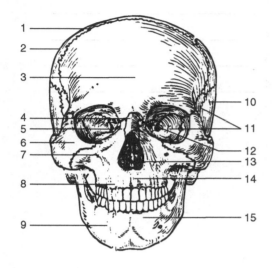

1 _____   8 _____
2 _____   9 _____
3 _____   10 _____
4 _____   11 _____
5 _____   12 _____
6 _____   13 _____
7 _____   14 _____
15 _____

OBJ. 2
OBJ. 3

Figure 7.3   Lateral View of the Skull

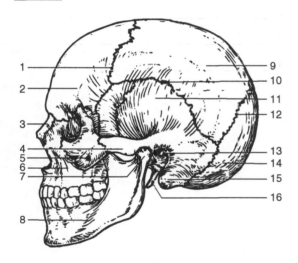

1 _____   9 _____
2 _____   10 _____
3 _____   11 _____
4 _____   12 _____
5 _____   13 _____
6 _____   14 _____
7 _____   15 _____
8 _____   16 _____

OBJ. 2
OBJ. 3

Figure 7.4   Inferior View of the Skull

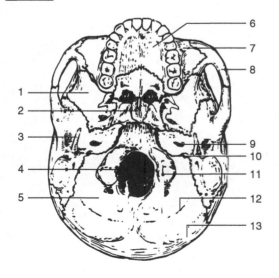

1 _____   7 _____
2 _____   8 _____
3 _____   9 _____
4 _____   10 _____
5 _____   11 _____
6 _____   12 _____
13 _____

Figure 7.5   Paranasal Sinuses

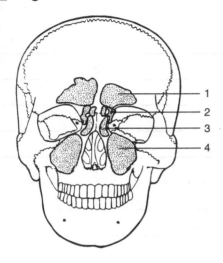

1 _____
2 _____
3 _____
4 _____

Figure 7.6   Fetal Skull—Lateral View

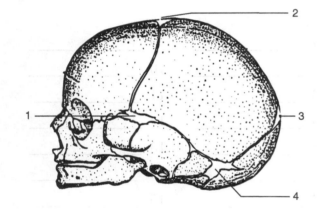

1 _____
2 _____
3 _____
4 _____

Figure 7.7   Fetal Skull—Superior View

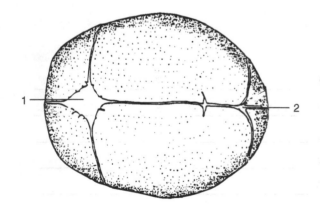

1 _____
2 _____

OBJ. 7 **Figure 7.8 The Vertebral Column**

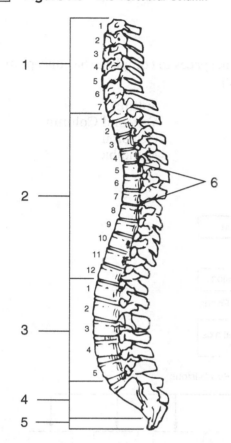

1 _____
2 _____
3 _____
4 _____
5 _____
6 _____

OBJ. 8 **Figure 7.9 The Ribs**

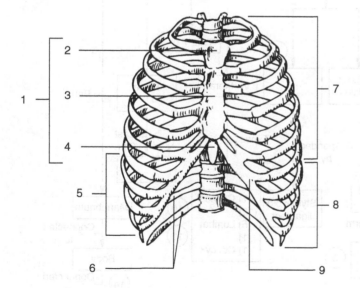

1 _____
2 _____
3 _____
4 _____
5 _____
6 _____
7 _____
8 _____
9 _____

LEVEL 2 Concept Synthesis

Concept Map I

Using the following terms, fill in the circled, numbered, blank spaces to complete the concept map. Follow the numbers to comply with the organization of the map.

Floating ribs, 2 pair	Temporal	Sutures
Hyoid	Sacral	Vertebral Column
Lacrimal	Xiphoid process	Occipital
Sternum	Skull	Mandible
Thoracic	Coronal	

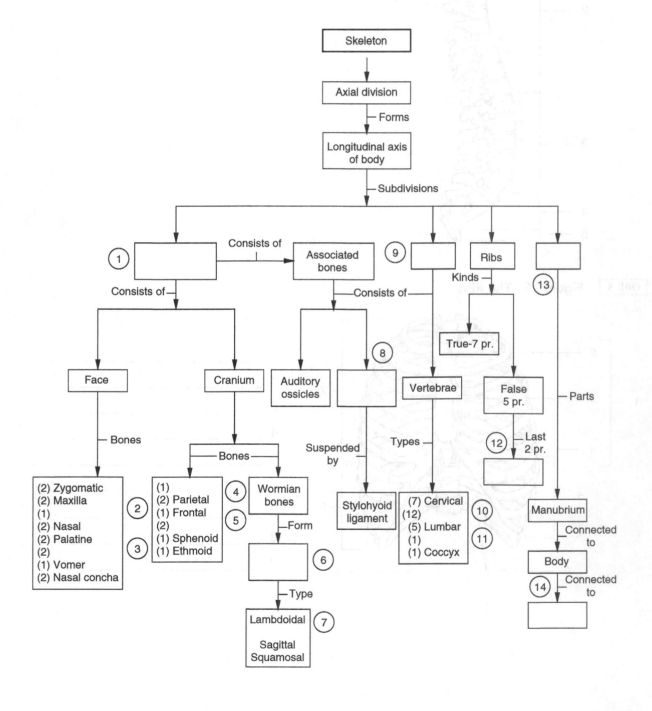

Body Trek

Using the terms below, fill in the blanks to complete the study of the axial skeleton.

Mandible	Thoracic	Sternum	Xiphoid process
Hyoid	Sacrum	Skull	Cranium
True	Occipital	Parietal	Zygomatic
Ribs	Vertebrae	Lumbar	Lacrimal
Axial	Sphenoid	False	Nasal
Sutures	Cervical	Manubrium	Sagittal
Floating			

Because of the difficulties involved with trekking from bone to bone inside the body, Robo is placed in an anatomy laboratory to monitor the activities of students who are using a skeleton to locate and name the bones of the axial skeleton. The students are initially unaware of the robot's presence. It is programmed to offer sounds of encouragement as the study proceeds.

The students are quick to recognize that the bones of the (1) _____ division of the skeleton form the longitudinal axis of the body. A suggestion is made to identify all the components of the division first and then study each part separately. [Robo: "Wow, what an idea!"] The most superior part, the (2) _____, consists of the (3) _____, the face, and associated bones. Just below the neck, and looking anteriorly at the skeleton, the students immediately identify the twelve pairs of (4) _____ and the (5) _____, a broad-surfaced bone with three individual articulated parts. Turning the skeleton around for a posterior view, the twenty-six artistically, articulated (6) _____ are exposed. After identifying the component parts, the class is divided into small groups to study each part. Members of each group share with the entire class what their study has revealed.

The first group has chosen the skull. Having identified the face as a part of the skull, group members notice the presence of six paired bones, which include the (7) _____, maxilla, (8) _____, palatine, (9) _____, and the nasal concha. The (10) _____ and the vomer bone comprise the single bones of the face. The cranial part of the skull includes four unpaired bones, the (11) _____, frontal, (12) _____, and the ethmoid. The paired bones of the cranium are the (13) _____ and the temporal. [Robo: "Good job!"] The students laugh and are curious to know who or what is making the muffled sounds. [Robo: "Continue."] The first group continues by locating the Wormian bones, which appear in (14) _____ of the skull. These immovable joints have names such as lambdoidal, coronal, squamosal, and (15) _____. The associated skull bones include the ear ossicles and the (16) _____, the only bone in the body not articulated with another bone. [Robo: "Excellent observation!"]

The students chuckle as the second group notices the uniqueness of the vertebral column. Twenty-six vertebrae are counted and categorized into regions according to their location. The first seven make up the (17) _____ area; the next twelve the (18) _____ region; the five that follow, the (19) _____; and the last two fused areas, the (20) _____ and the coccyx. [Robo: "Very interesting!"] The students ignore the comment.

The third group, which is studying the ribs, is debating which ones are the true ribs and which ones are the false ribs. [Robo: "Count them!"] Students look around, seem confused, but decide to count. They conclude that one through seven are the (21) _____ ribs, and eight through twelve are the (22) _____ ribs. [Robo: "Easy, wasn't it?"] Students laugh. Someone in the group notices that the last two pairs do not attach to the cartilage above. Another responds, "That is the reason they are called the (23) _____ ribs."

The fourth group appears intrigued with the structure of the sternum owing to its three-part articulated form, which includes the superiorly located (24) _____, the body, and the (25) _____ located at the inferior end. [Robo: "Easy job, but good work!"]

The lab instructor finally removes the mirco-robot from its location inside the skull of the skeleton and informs the students that Robo will return to the lab when they study the appendicular division of the skeleton.

COVERING ALL YOUR BASES

[L2]   Multiple Choice

Place the letter corresponding to the correct answer in the space provided.

1. Brain growth, skull growth, and completed cranial suture development occur:

   A. before birth

   B. right after birth

   C. before age 5

   D   between age 5 and 10

2. The area of the greatest degree of flexibility along the vertebral column is found from:

   A. C_3–C_7 C. T_7–T_{12}

   B. T_1–T_6 D L_1–L_5

3. After a hard fall, compression fractures or compression/dislocation fractures most often involve the:

   A. last thoracic and first two lumbar vertebrae

   B. first two cervical vertebrae

   C. sacrum and coccyx

   D   fifth lumbar and the sacrum

4. Intervertebral discs are found in between all the vertebrae except:

   A. between C_1 and T_1, and T_{12} and L_1; sacrum and coccyx

   B. the sacrum and the coccyx

   C. between L_5 and the sacrum

   D   between C_1 and C_2 and the sacrum and coccyx

5. Part of the loss in *height* that accompanies aging results from:

   A. degeneration of osseous tissue in the diaphysis of long bones

   B. degeneration of skeletal muscles attached to bones

   C. the decreasing size and resiliency of the intervertebral discs

   D   the reduction in the number of vertebrae due to aging

6. The skull articulates with the vertebral column at the:

   A. foramen magnum

   B. occipital condyles

   C. lambdoidal sutures

   D C_1 and C_2

7. The long framework of the sphenoid bone that houses the pituitary gland is the:

   A. crista galli

   B. styloid process

   C. sella turcica

   D   frontal squama

8. The growth of the cranium is usually associated with:

   A. the expansion of the brain

   B. the development of the fontanels

   C. the closure of the sutures

   D   the time of birth

9. Beginning at the superior end of the vertebral canal and proceeding inferiorally:

   A. the diameter of the cord and the size of the neural arch increase

   B. the diameter of the cord increases and the size of the neural arch decreases

   C. the diameter of the cord decreases and the size of the neural arch increases

   D   the diameter of the cord and the size of the neural arch decrease

10. The vertebrae that are directly articulated with the ribs are:

    A. cervical and thoracic

    B. thoracic only

    C. cervical only

    D   thoracic and lumbar

11. During CPR, proper positioning of the hands is important so that an excessive pressure will not break the:

A. manubrium

B. xiphoid process

C. body of the sternum

D costal cartilages

[L2] Completion

Using the terms below, complete the following statements.

kyphosis
auditory ossicles
metopic
compensation

mental foramina
lordosis
tears

pharyngotympanic
alveolar processes
scoliosis

1. The structure that ends inside the mass of the temporal bone, which connects the airspace of the middle ear with the pharynx, is the _____ tube.

2. At birth the two frontal bones that have not completely fused are connected at the _____ suture.

3. The lacrimal bones house the structures that are associated with the production and release of _____.

4. The associated skull bones of the middle ear that conduct sound vibrations from the tympanum to the inner ear are the _____.

5. The oral margins of the maxillae that provide the sockets for the teeth are the

_____.

6. Small openings that serve as nerve passageways on each side of the body of the mandible are the _____.

7. The lumbar and cervical curves that appear several months after birth and help to position the body weight over the legs are known as _____ curves.

8. A normal thoracic curvature that becomes exaggerated, producing a "roundback" appearance, is a _____.

9. An exaggerated lumbar curvature or "swayback" appearance is a _____.

10. An abnormal lateral curvature that usually appears in adolescence during periods of rapid growth is _____.

[L2] Short Essay

Briefly answer the following questions in the spaces provided below.

1. What are the four primary functions of the axial skeleton?

2. A. List the *paired bones* of the *cranium*.

   B. List the *unpaired* (single) bones of the *cranium*.

3. A. List the *paired* bones of the *face*.

   B. List the *unpaired* (single) bones of the *face*.

4. Why are the auditory ossicles and hyoid bone referred to as associated bones of the skull?

5. What is *craniostenosis* and what are the results of this condition?

6. What is the difference between a *primary curve* and a *secondary curve* of the spinal column?

7. Distinguish among the abnormal spinal curvature distortions of kyphosis, lordosis, and scoliosis.

8. What is the difference between the *true* ribs and the *false* ribs?

LEVEL 3 Critical Thinking/Application

Using principles and concepts learned about the axial skeleton, answer the following questions. Write your answers on a separate sheet of paper.

1. What senses are affected by the cranial and facial bones that protect and support the sense organs?

2. A friend of yours tells you that she has been diagnosed as having TMJ. What bones are involved with this condition, how are they articulated, and what symptoms are apparent?

3. Your nose has been crooked for years and you have had a severe sinus condition to accompany the disturbing appearance of the nose. You suspect there is a relationship between the crooked nose and the chronic sinus condition. How do you explain your suspicion?

4. During a car accident you become a victim of *whiplash*. You experience pains in the neck and across the upper part of the back. Why?

5. During a child's routine physical examination it is discovered that one leg is shorter than the other. Relative to the spinal column, what might be a plausible explanation for this condition?

6. A clinical diagnosis has been made that substantiates the presence of a herniated disc and a severe case of sciatica. What is the relationship between the two conditions?

8

THE APPENDICULAR SKELETON

Overview

How many things can you think of that require the use of your hands? Your arms? Your legs? Your feet? If you are an active person, the list would probably be endless. There are few daily activities, if any, that do not require the use of the arms and/or legs performing in a dynamic, coordinated way to allow you to be an active, mobile individual. This intricately articulated framework of 126 bones comprises the appendicular division of the skeleton. The bones consist of the pectoral girdle and the upper limbs, and the pelvic girdle and the lower limbs. The bones in this divi-

sion provide support, are important as sites for muscle attachment, articulate at joints, are involved with movement and mobility, and are utilized in numerous ways to control the environment that surrounds you every second of your life.

Your study and review for Chapter 8 includes the identification and location of bones and bone markings, and the functional anatomy of the bones and articulations that comprise the appendicular skeleton.

LEVEL 1 Review of Chapter Objectives

1. Identify the bones that form the pectoral girdle, their functions, and their superficial features.

2. Identify the bones of the upper limbs, their functions, and their superficial features.

3. Identify the bones that form the pelvic girdle, their functions, and their superficial features.

4. Identify the bones of the lower limbs, their functions, and their superficial features.

5. Discuss structural and functional differences between the pelvis of females and that of males.

6. Explain how study of the skeleton can reveal significant information about an individual.

7. Summarize the skeletal differences between males and females.

8. Describe briefly how the aging process affects the skeletal system.

[L1]   Multiple Choice

Place the letter corresponding to the correct answer in the space provided.

OBJ. 1   _____   1. The clavicles articulate with a bone of the sternum called the:
   a. xiphoid process
   b. scapula
   c. manubrium
   d. deltoideus

OBJ. 1   _____   2. The surfaces of the scapulae and clavicles are extremely important as sites for:
   a. muscle attachment
   b. positions of nerves and blood vessels
   c. nourishment of muscles and bones
   d. support and flexibility

OBJ. 1   _____   3. The conoid tubercle and costal tuberosity are processes located on the:
   a. scapulae
   b. clavicle
   c. sternum
   d. manubrium

OBJ. 1   _____   4. The bones of the *pectoral* girdle include:
   a. clavicle and scapula
   b. ilium and ischium
   c. humerus and femur
   d. ulna and radius

OBJ. 1   _____   5. The large posterior process on the scapula is the:
   a. coracoid process
   b. acromion process
   c. olecranon fossa
   d. styloid process

OBJ. 2   _____   6. The primary function of the *pectoral* girdle is to:
   a. protect the organs of the thorax
   b. provide areas for articulation with the vertebral column
   c. position the shoulder joint and provide a base for arm movement
   d. support and maintain the position of the skull

OBJ. 2   _____   7. The parallel bones that support the forearm are the:
   a. humerus and femur
   b. ulna and radius
   c. tibia and fibula
   d. scapula and clavicle

OBJ. 2   _____   8. The large rough elevation on the lateral surface of the shaft of the humerus is the:
   a. greater tubercle
   b. radial fossa
   c. deltoid tuberosity
   d. lesser tubercle

OBJ. 3 _____ 9. The bones of the *pelvic* girdle include:
   a. tibia and fibula
   b. ilium, pubis, and ischium
   c. ilium, ischium, and acetabulum
   d. coxa, patella, and acetabulum

OBJ. 3 _____ 10. The amphiarthrotic articulation, which limits movements between the two pubic bones, is the:
   a. pubic symphysis
   b. obturator foramen
   c. greater sciatic notch
   d. pubic tubercle

OBJ. 4 _____ 11. The large medial bone of the lower leg is the:
   a. femur
   b. fibula
   c. tibia
   d. humerus

OBJ. 4 _____ 12. A prominent deviation that runs along the center of the posterior surface of the femur, which serves as an attachment site for muscles that abduct the femur, is the:
   a. greater trochanter
   b. trochanteric crest
   c. trochanteric lines
   d. linea aspera

OBJ. 5 _____ 13. The general appearance of the pelvis of the female compared to the male is that the female pelvis is:
   a. heart-shaped
   b. robust, heavy, and rough
   c. relatively deep
   d. broad, light, and smooth

OBJ. 5 _____ 14. The shape of the pelvic inlet in the female is:
   a. heart-shaped
   b. triangular
   c. oval to round
   d. somewhat rectangular

OBJ. 6 _____ 15. Of the following selections, the one that would be used to estimate muscular development and body weight is:
   a. sex and age
   b. degenerative changes in the normal skeletal system
   c. normal timing of skeletal development
   d. development of various ridges and general bone mass

OBJ. 6 _____ 16. An indication of the individual's medical history may include the:
   a. sex and age of the person
   b. person's muscle mass and muscular development

c. condition of the teeth or the presence of healed fractures

d. appearance of ridges and general bone mass

OBJ. 7 _____ 17. The two specific *areas* of the skeleton that are generally used to identify significant differences between a male and female are:

a. arms and legs

b. ribs and vertebral column

c. skull and pelvis

d. a, b, and c are correct

OBJ. 7 _____ 18. The two important *skeletal elements* that are generally used to determine sex and age are:

a. teeth and healed fractures

b. presence of muscular and fatty tissue

c. condition of the teeth and muscular mass

d. bone weight and bone markings

OBJ. 8 _____ 19. In determining the age of a skeleton, which of the following selections would be used?

a. the presence/absence of epiphyseal plates

b. the size and roughness of bone markings

c. the mineral content of the bones

d. a, b, and c are correct

[L1] Completion

Using the terms below, complete the following statements.

knee	styloid	glenoid fossa	pelvis
pubic symphysis	clavicle	acetabulum	teeth
malleolus	age	childbearing	acromion
coxae	wrist	pectoral girdle	

OBJ. 1   1. The clavicle articulates with a process of the scapulae called the _____.

OBJ. 1   2. The only direct connection between the pectoral girdle and the axial skeleton is the _____.

OBJ. 1   3. The shoulder area and its component bones comprise a region referred to as the _____.

OBJ. 1   4. The scapula articulates with the proximal end of the humerus at the _____.

OBJ. 2   5. The ulna and the radius both have long shafts that contain like processes called _____ processes.

OBJ. 2   6. The radiocarpal articulations and the intercarpal articulations are responsible for the movements in the region of the _____.

OBJ. 3   7. The pelvic girdle consists of six bones collectively referred to as the _____.

OBJ. 3   8. Ventrally the coxae are connected by a pad of fibrocartilage at the _____ .

OBJ. 4   9. The process that the tibia and fibula have in common that acts as a shield for the ankle is the _____ .

OBJ. 4   10. At the hip joint to either side, the head of the femur articulates with the _____ .

OBJ. 4   11. The popliteal ligaments are responsible for reinforcing the back of the _____ .

OBJ. 5   12. An enlarged pelvic outlet in the female is an adaptation for _____ .

OBJ. 6   13. A major means of determining the medical history of a person is to examine the condition of the individual's _____ .

OBJ. 7   14. Skeletal differences between males and females are usually identified axially on the skull and/or the appendicular aspects of the _____ .

OBJ. 8   15. Reduction in mineral content of the bony matrix is an example of a skeletal change related to _____ .

[L1]   Matching

Match the terms in column B with the terms in column A. Use letters for answers in the spaces provided.

		Column A		Column B
OBJ. 1	_____	1. scapular process	A.	lower arm bones
OBJ. 1	_____	2. pectoral girdle	B.	involved with running
OBJ. 1	_____	3. clavicle	C.	hip bones
OBJ. 2	_____	4. radius, ulna	D.	lower leg bones
OBJ. 3	_____	5. pelvic girdle	E.	oval to round
OBJ. 4	_____	6. patella	F.	acromion process
OBJ. 4	_____	7. tibia, fibula	G.	sternal end
OBJ. 5	_____	8. female pelvic inlet	H.	heavier bone weight
OBJ. 5	_____	9. male pelvic inlet	I.	smooth bone markings
OBJ. 6	_____	10. talar arch	J.	shoulder girdle
OBJ. 7	_____	11. male characteristic	K.	heart-shaped
OBJ. 8	_____	12. process of aging	L.	kneecap

[L1]   Drawing/Illustration Labeling

Identify each numbered structure by labeling the following figures:

OBJ. 1, 2, 3, 4   **Figure 8.1   Appendicular Skeleton**

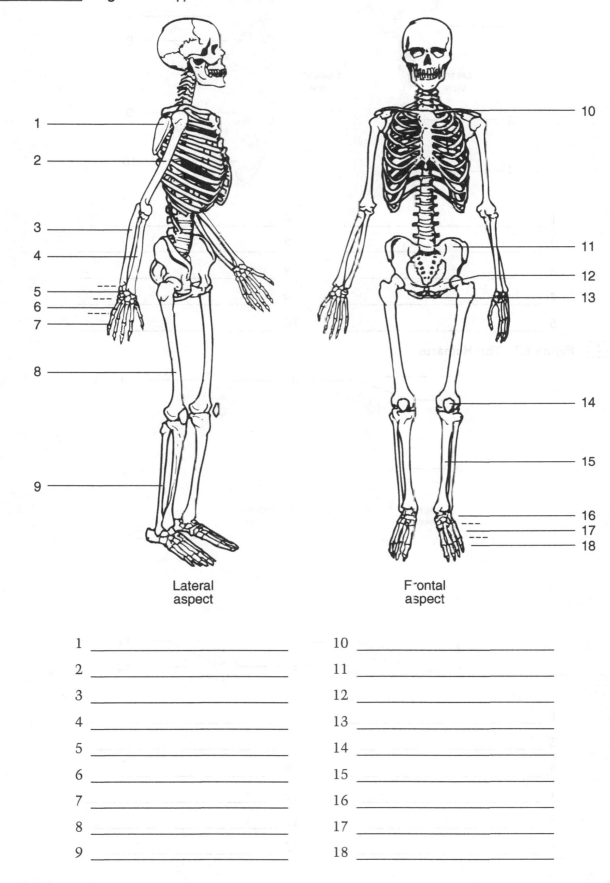

Lateral aspect   Frontal aspect

1	_____		10	_____
2	_____		11	_____
3	_____		12	_____
4	_____		13	_____
5	_____		14	_____
6	_____		15	_____
7	_____		16	_____
8	_____		17	_____
9	_____		18	_____

OBJ. 1 **Figure 8.2 The Scapula**

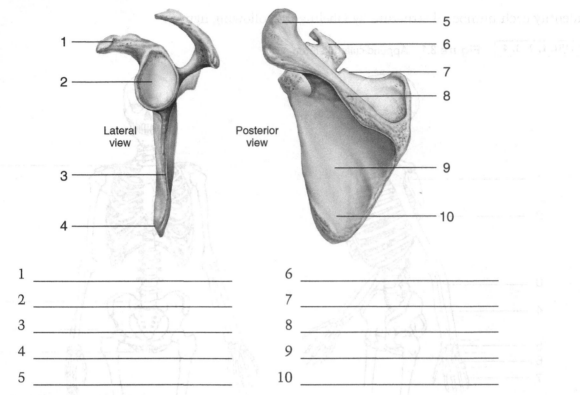

Lateral view

Posterior view

1	_____	6	_____
2	_____	7	_____
3	_____	8	_____
4	_____	9	_____
5	_____	10	_____

OBJ. 2 **Figure 8.3 The Humerus**

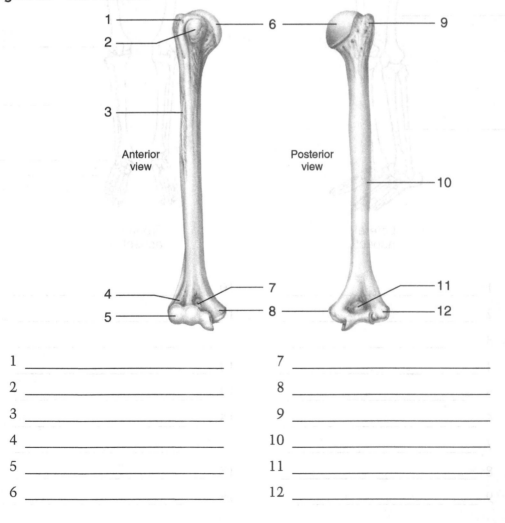

Anterior view

Posterior view

1	_____	7	_____
2	_____	8	_____
3	_____	9	_____
4	_____	10	_____
5	_____	11	_____
6	_____	12	_____

OBJ. 2   **Figure 8.4   The Radius and Ulna**

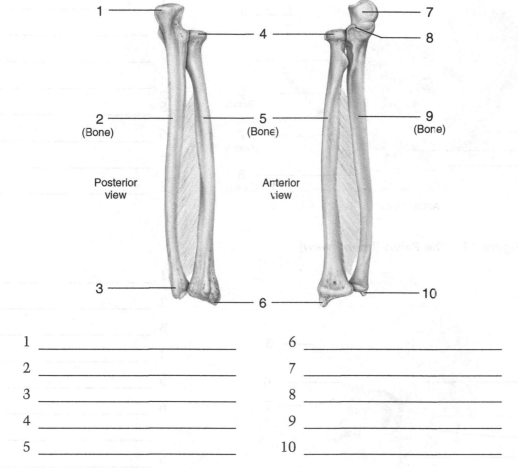

Posterior
view

Arterior
view

1 _____   6 _____

2 _____   7 _____

3 _____   8 _____

4 _____   9 _____

5 _____   10 _____

OBJ. 2   **Figure 8.5   Bones of the Wrist and Hand**

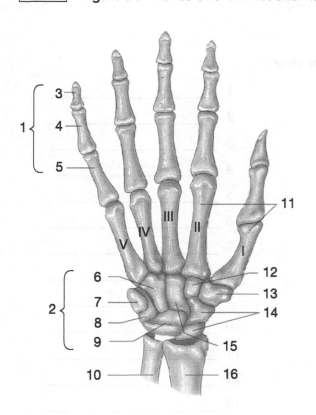

1 _____

2 _____

3 _____

4 _____

5 _____

6 _____

7 _____

8 _____

9 _____

10 _____

11 _____

12 _____

13 _____

14 _____

15 _____

16 _____

OBJ. 3   **Figure 8.6   The Pelvis (anterior view)**

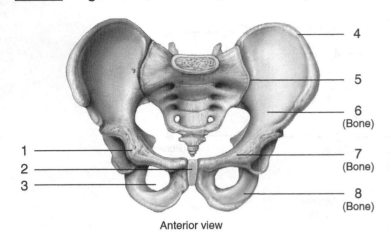

Anterior view

1 _____
2 _____
3 _____
4 _____
5 _____
6 _____
7 _____
8 _____

OBJ. 3   **Figure 8.7   The Pelvis (lateral view)**

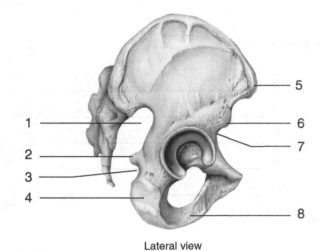

Lateral view

1 _____
2 _____
3 _____
4 _____
5 _____
6 _____
7 _____
8 _____

OBJ. 4   **Figure 8.8   The Femur (anterior and posterior views)**

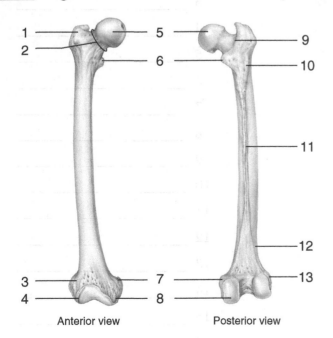

Anterior view   Posterior view

1 _____
2 _____
3 _____
4 _____
5 _____
6 _____
7 _____
8 _____
9 _____
10 _____
11 _____
12 _____
13 _____

OBJ. 4   **Figure 8.9   The Tibia and Fibula**

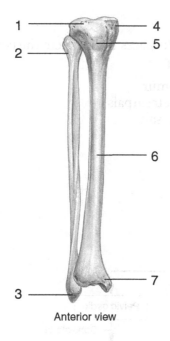

Anterior view

1 _____
2 _____
3 _____
4 _____
5 _____
6 _____
7 _____

OBJ. 4   **Figure 8.10   Bones of the Ankle and Foot**

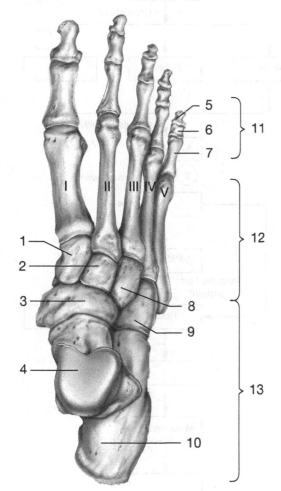

1 _____
2 _____
3 _____
4 _____
5 _____
6 _____
7 _____
8 _____
9 _____
10 _____
11 _____
12 _____
13 _____

LEVEL 2 Concept Synthesis

Concept Map I

Using the following terms, fill in the circled, numbered, blank spaces to complete the concept map. Follow the numbers to comply with the organization of the map.

Fibula   Ischium   Femur

Humerus   Pectoral girdle   Metacarpals

Phalanges   Radius   Tarsals

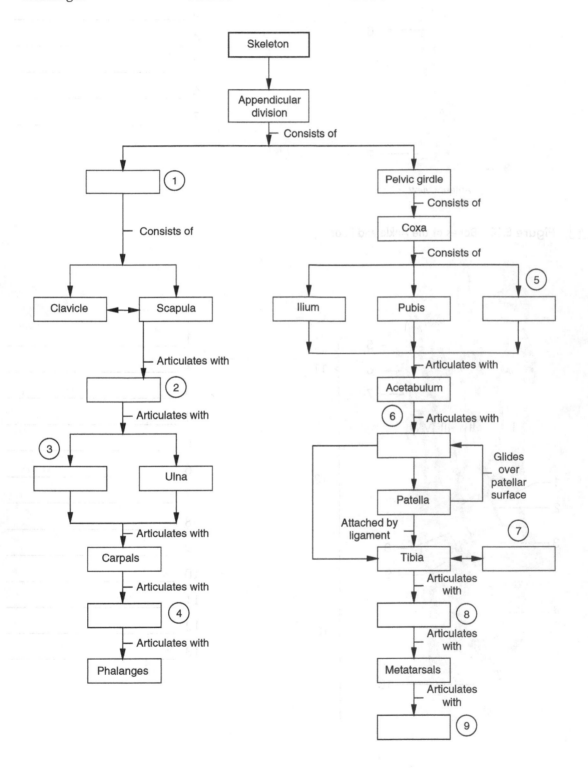

Body Trek

Using the terms below, fill in the blanks to complete the study of the appendicular skeleton.

Patella	Tibia	Metacarsals	Pubis
Metacarpals	Ilium	Ulna	Femur
Tarsals	Hinge	Fibula	Radius
Clavicle	Pectoral	Brachium	Scapula
Carpals	Pelvic	Ball and socket	Ischium
Phalanges	Humerus	Knee	Shoulder
Finger bones	Acetabulum	Elbow	

Robo is returned to the lab to monitor the activities of the students as they use a skeleton to locate and name the bones and joints of the appendicular skeleton. The students are aware of the robot's presence, but unsure of its location. They look forward to the "verbal" encouragement Robo offers. The four groups that studied the axial skeleton remain intact, and each group is assigned an area of the appendicular skeleton to identify and study. Group 1 is assigned the pectoral girdle and the shoulder joint; group 2 the bones of the upper and lower arm and the elbow joint; group 3 the pelvic girdle and hip joint; and group 4 the bones of the upper and lower leg and the knee joint.

Group 1 locates and identifies the scapula and the (1) _____, the bones that make up the (2) _____. Group members notice that the shoulder joint is shaped like a (3) _____ because the rounded convex surface of the upper arm bone fits into a cuplike socket of the (4) _____. [Robo: "Just like I would have done it!"] Students can't believe that a robot can talk.

Group 2 notices that there is only one long bone in the upper arm, the (5) _____, and two long bones in the lower arm, the (6) _____, which is always located on the thumb side, and the (7) _____. The long bone of the (8) _____, or upper arm, is joined with the two long bones of the lower arm by the elbow joint, which functions like a (9) _____. The distal ends of the lower arm bones are articulated with the wrist bones, the (10) _____, which join with the hand bones, the (11) _____, which are connected to the phalanges or (12) _____. [Robo: "Wish I had arms and hands!"] A student shouts, "As small as you are we wouldn't be able to see them." Others laugh.

Settling down, group 3 has difficulty differentiating among the largest bone of the pelvic girdle, the (13) _____, from the (14) _____ and the (15) _____, which forms a joint at the inferior part of the pelvis. Group members observe that the pelvic socket, the (16) _____, is comprised of all three bones of the (17) _____ girdle. [Robo: "What a job! Can't wait to hear the next group get 'it' all together."]

Group 4 responds enthusiastically to Robo's comment by locating the longest and heaviest bone in the body, in the upper leg, the (18) _____, which has a ball-like head that fits into the pelvic socket and forms a joint that functions like the (19) _____ joint. Students point out that the large bone articulates at the distal end with a long thin bone, the (20) _____, and the larger and thicker (21) _____, both of which make up the bones of the lower leg. The (22) _____, a bone that glides across the articular surface of the femur, is embedded within a tendon in the region of the (23) _____ joint, which functions like the (24) _____ joint. [Robo: "I'm impressed!"] Students laugh. Distally, the long bones of the lower leg articulate with the ankle bones called (25) _____, which join with the bones of the foot, the (26) _____, which are connected to the toe bones called (27) _____. [Robo: "Wish I had legs and feet so I could escape from this acetabulum."] Students are amused and raise questions about the technology involved in producing micro-robots and their potential uses for monitoring activity within the human body. Robo is removed from its location and returned to Mission Control to begin preparation for the next trek.

COVERING ALL YOUR BASES

[L2]   Multiple Choice

Select the best answer or answers from the choices given.

1. An example of sesamoid bones in the appendicular skeleton include the:

    a. lunate, scaphoid, and cuboid

    b. talus and calcaneus

    c. patella and pisiform

    d. radius, clavicle, and manubrium

2. The bone of the axial skeleton to which the pectoral girdle attaches is the:

    a. sternum   c. scapula

    b. clavicle   d. humerus

3. The bone of the axial skeleton to which the pectoral girdle attaches is the:

    a. sternum   c. scapula

    b. clavicle   d. humerus

4. The process on the humerus located near the head that establishes the contour of the shoulder is the:

    a. intertubercular groove

    b. deltoid tuberosity

    c. lateral epicondyle

    d. greater tubercle

5. The four *proximal* carpals are:

    a. trapezium, trapezoid, capitate, and hamate

    b. trapezium, triquetal, capitate, and lunate

    c. scaphoid, trapezium, lunate, and capitate

    d. scaphoid, lunate, triquetal, and pisiform

6. The *distal* carpals are:

    a. scaphoid, lunate, triquetal, and pisiform

    b. trapezium, trapezoid, capitate, and hamate

    c. trapezium, scaphoid, trapezoid, and lunate

    d. scaphoid, capitate, triquetal, and hamate

7. The bone that is sometimes referred to as the "sit down" bone is the:

    a. ischium   c. pubis

    b. illium   d. gluteus maximus

8. The only ankle bone that articulates with the tibia and the fibula is the:

    a. calcaneus   c. navicular

    b. talus   d. cuboid

9. Severe fractures of the femoral neck have the highest complication rate of any fracture because:

    a. primary limits are imposed by the surrounding muscles

    b. of the restrictions imposed by ligaments and capsular fibers

    c. of the thickness and length of the bone

    d. the blood supply to the region is relatively limited

10. From the following selections, which pair of terms is correctly associated?

    a. pubic symphysis; pectoral girdle

    b. patella; acetabulum

    c. radius; phalanges

    d. femur; linea aspera

11. The femur in older individuals, particularly small women, can be distinguished by:

    a. being stronger than other bones of the pelvis

    b. having a greater number of trabecular than those of younger individuals

    c. a greater tendency to bend with the stress of weight bearing

    d. being the most likely site of a breach when the person suffers a broken hip

12. Of the two bones of the forearm, the one which articulates with the carpal bones of the wrist is the:

    a. ulna   c. radius

    b. humerus   d. tibia

13. When a ligament is stretched to the point where some of the collagen fibers are torn, the injury is called a:

    a. dislocation   c. sprain

    b. strain   d. dancer's fracture

14. Abnormalities that affect the bones can have a direct effect on the muscles because:

    a. when a muscle gets larger, the bones become stronger

    b. most of the body's calcium is tied up in the skeleton

    c. when a bone gets more massive, the muscle enlarges proportionately

    d. a, b, and c are correct

[L2]   Completion

Using the terms below, complete the following statements.

calcaneus	hallux	bursitis	thumb
clavicle	fibula	ilium	metacarpals
femur	arthroscopy	pelvis	bursae
ulna	scapula	acetabulum	

1. The bone that cannot resist strong forces and provides the only fixed support for the pectoral girdle is the _____.

2. At its proximal end, the round head of the humerus articulates with the _____.

3. The bone that forms the medial support of the forearm is the _____.

4. The bones that form the palm of the hand are the _____.

5. Chambers lined by synovial membrane and filled with synovial fluid are the _____.

6. Propping your head above a desk while struggling through your A & P textbook may result in "student's elbow," which is a form of _____.

7. At the proximal end of the femur, the head articulates with the curved surface of the _____.

8. The largest coxal bone is the _____.

9. The coxae, the sacrum, and the coccyx form a composite structure called the _____.

10. The longest and heaviest bone in the body is the _____.

11. The bone in the lower leg that is completely excluded from the knee joint is the _____.

12. The large heel bone that receives weight transmitted to the ground by the inferior surface of the talus is the _____.

13. If a person has dislocated his pollex, he has injured his _____.

14. The first toe is anatomically referred to as the _____.

15. The technique that uses fiber optics to permit exploration of a joint without major surgery is _____.

[L2] Short Essay

Briefly answer the following questions in the spaces provided below.

1. What are the primary functions of the appendicular skeleton?

2. What are the basic components of the appendicular skeleton?

3. What bones comprise the pectoral girdle? The pelvic girdle?

4. What are the structural and functional similarities and differences between the ulna and the radius?

5. Functionally, what is the relationship between the elbow joint and the knee joint?

6. What are the structural and functional similarities and differences between the tibia and the fibula?

7. Functionally, what is the commonality between the shoulder joint and the hip joint?

8. How are the articulations of the carpals of the wrist comparable to those of the tarsals of the ankle?

9. How are muscles and bones physiologically linked?

LEVEL 3 Critical Thinking/Application

Using principles and concepts learned about the appendicular skeleton, answer the following questions. Write your answers on a separate sheet of paper.

1. The carpals are arranged in two rows of four each. In order for tendons, nerves, and blood vessels to pass into the hand from the wrist, a ligament stretches across the wrist, which forms a tunnel on the anterior surface of the wrist called the *carpal tunnel*. Tingling, burning, and numbness in the hand are symptoms that result from *carpal tunnel syndrome*. What causes these symptoms to occur?

2. A recent headline on the sports page of the newspaper read, "Football player dies awaiting leg surgery." The player was expected to be sidelined for a matter of weeks with a broken leg but died suddenly due to lung hemorrhaging and inability to oxygenate his blood. What is the relationship between a fractured leg and pulmonary hemorrhaging that caused the death of this young athlete?

3. What structural characteristics of the female pelvis, compared to those of the male, make it adaptable for delivery of the newborn?

4. What is the association between the metabolic disorder known as *gout*, which affects the joints, and damage to the kidney?

5. From time to time it is fashionable to wear pointed shoes. How might a decision to wear pointed shoes contribute to the formation of a bunion?

6. What is the commonality and what are the differences of "housemaid's knee," "weaver's bottom," and "student's elbow"?

9

JOINTS AND ARTICULATIONS

Student Objectives

When you have completed the exercises in this chapter, you will have accomplished the following objectives:

1. Define *joint* or *articulation*.

Classification of Joints
2. Classify joints structurally and functionally.

Fibrous Joints
3. Describe the general structure of fibrous joints. Name and give an example of each of the three common types of fibrous joints.

Cartilaginous Joints
4. Describe the general structure of cartilaginous joints. Name and give an example of each of the two common types of cartilaginous joints.

Synovial Joints
5. Describe the structural characteristics of synovial joints.

6. List three natural factors that stabilize synovial joints.
7. Compare the structures and functions of bursae and tendon sheaths.
8. Name and describe (or perform) the common types of body movements.
9. Name and provide examples of the six types of synovial joints based on the type of movement allowed.
10. Describe the elbow, knee, hip, and shoulder joints relative to articulating bones, anatomical characteristics of the joint, movement allowed, and joint stability.

Homeostatic Imbalances of Joints
11. Name the most common joint injuries and discuss the symptoms and problems associated with each.
12. Compare and contrast the common types of arthritis.

Joints are structures that connect adjoining bones. Except for the hyoid bone, and sesamoid bones like the patella, each bone contacts at least one other bone at a joint. A typical joint includes the adjacent surfaces of the bones and the fibrous tissue or ligaments that bind the bones together. In addition to binding the bones together, joints provide the skeleton with the flexibility to permit body movements.

Since joints vary in structure and range of motion, it is convenient to classify them on the basis of their structure (fibrous, cartilaginous, or synovial) and function (the degree of joint movement allowed).

Topics for review in Chapter 9 include the classification of joints, the structures of selected synovial joints, joint impairment, and changes in the joints throughout life.

BUILDING THE FRAMEWORK

Classification of Joints

1. Write your answers to the following questions in the answer blanks.

1. What are the two major functions of joints? _____

_____

2. List three criteria used to classify joints. _____

_____

_____

3. For each of the structural joint categories—fibrous, cartilaginous, and synovial—give the *most common* functional classification and describe the degree of movement.

_____

_____

_____

Fibrous, Cartilaginous, and Synovial Joints

1. For each joint described below, select an answer from Key A. Then, if the Key A selection is *other than C* (synovial joint), classify the joint further by making a choice from Key B.

Key A: A. Cartilaginous   **Key B:** 1. Gomphosis   4. Syndesmosis

B. Fibrous   2. Suture   5. Synchondrosis

C. Synovial   3. Symphysis   6. Synostosis

_____ 1. Characterized by hyaline cartilage connecting the bony portions

_____ 2. All have a fibrous capsule lined with a synovial membrane surrounding a joint cavity

_____ 3. Bone regions united by fibrous connective tissue

_____ 4. Joints between skull bones

_____ 5. Joint between atlas and axis

_____ 6. Hip, elbow, knee, and inter-carpal joints

_____ 7. Intervertebral joints (between vertebral bodies)

_____ 8. Pubic symphysis

_____ 9. All are reinforced by ligaments

_____ 10. Costosternal joints 2–7

_____ 11. Joint providing the most protection to underlying structures

_____ 12. Often contains a fluid-filled cushion

_____ 13. Child's epiphyseal plate made of hyaline cartilage

_____ 14. Most joints of the limbs

_____ 15. Teeth in body alveolar sockets

_____ 16. Joint between first rib and manubrium of sternum

_____ 17. Ossified sutures

_____ 18. Distal tibiofibular joint

2. Which structural joint type is *not* commonly found in the axial skeleton

and why not? _____

_____

_____

3. Figure 9.1 shows the structure of a typical synovial joint. Select different colors to identify and color the following areas. Then label the following: the more proximal epiphyseal line, the more distal epiphyseal line, spongy bone, periosteum.

◯ Articular cartilage of bone ends   ◯ Synovial membrane

◯ Fibrous capsule   ◯ Joint cavity

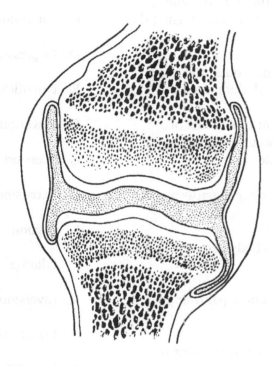

Figure 9.1

4. Match the key choices with the descriptive phrases below, to properly characterize selected aspects of synovial joints.

Key Choices

A. Articular cartilage   C. Ligaments and fibrous capsule

B. Synovial fluid   D. Muscle tendons

_____ 1. Keeps bone ends from crushing when compressed; resilient

_____ 2. Resists tension placed on joints

_____ 3. Lubricant that minimizes friction and abrasion of joint surfaces

_____ 4. Keeps joints from overheating

_____ 5. Helps prevent dislocation

5. Match the body movement terms in Column B with the appropriate description in Column A. (More than one choice may apply.)

Column A

Column B

_____ 1. Movement along the sagittal plane that decreases the angle between two bones

_____ 2. Movement along the frontal plane, away from the body midline; raising the arm laterally

_____ 3. Circular movement around the longitudinal bone axis; shaking the head "no"

_____ 4. Slight displacement or slipping of bones, as might occur between the carpals of the wrist

_____ 5. Describing a cone-shaped pathway with the arm

_____ 6. Lifting or raising a body part; shrugging the shoulders

_____ 7. Moving the hand into a palm-up (or forward) position

_____ 8. Movement of the superior aspect of the foot toward the leg; standing on the heels

_____ 9. Turning the sole of the foot medially

_____ 10. Movement of a body part anteriorly; jutting the lower jaw forward

_____ 11. Common angular movements

A. Abduction

B. Adduction

C. Circumduction

D. Depression

E. Dorsiflexion

F. Elevation

G. Eversion

H. Extension

I. Flexion

J. Gliding

K. Inversion

L. Plantar flexion

M. Pronation

N. Protraction

O. Retraction

P. Rotation

Q. Supination

6. Figure 9.2 illustrates types of movements allowed by synovial joints. Match the letters on the figure with the types of movements listed below. Insert your answers in the answer blanks. Then color the drawing to suit your fancy.

_____ 1. Flexion

_____ 2. Plantar flexion

_____ 3. Abduction

_____ 4. Rotation

_____ 5. Pronation

_____ 6. Protraction

_____ 7. Circumduction

_____ 8. Adduction

_____ 9. Extension

_____ 10. Dorsiflexion

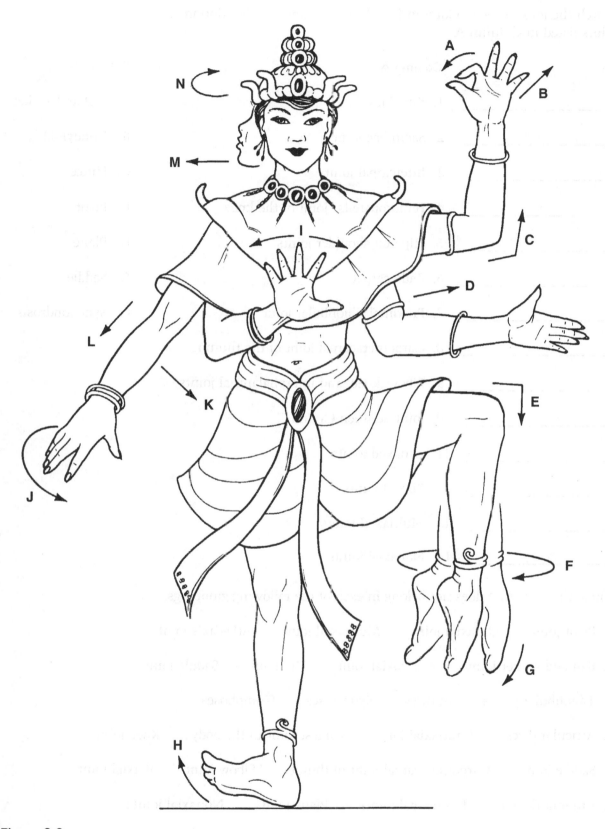

Figure 9.2

7. Match the joint types in Column B with the examples or descriptions of joints listed in Column A.

	Column A	Column B
_____	1. Knuckles	A. Ball and socket
_____	2. Sacroiliac joints	B. Condyloid
_____	3. Intercarpal joints	C. Hinge
_____	4. Femoropatellar joint of the knee	D. Pivot
_____	5. Hip and shoulder joints	E. Plane
_____	6. Radiocarpal	F. Saddle
_____	7. Proximal tibiofibular joint	G. Synchondrosis
_____	8. Carpometacarpal joint of the thumb	
_____	9. Elbow, knee, and interphalangeal joints	
_____	10. Joint between C_1 and C_2	
_____	11. Uniaxial joints	
_____	12. Biaxial joints	
_____	13. Multiaxial joints	
_____	14. Nonaxial joints	

8. Circle the term that does not belong in each of the following groupings.

1. Pivot joint   Uniaxial joint   Multiaxial joint   Atlas/axis joint

2. Ball and socket joint   Multiaxial joint   Hip joint   Saddle joint

3. Tibiofibular joints   Sutures   Synostoses   Gomphoses

4. Articular discs   Multiaxial joint   Largest joint in the body   Knee joint

5. Saddle joint   Carpometacarpal joint of thumb   Elbow joint   Biaxial joint

6. Amphiarthrotic   Intercarpal joints   Plane joints   Nonaxial joints

7. Intervertebral joints   Bursae   Cartilaginous joints   Symphyses

8. Hinge joint   Condyloid joint   Elbow joint   Uniaxial joint

9. Muscle tendon reinforcement   Shoulder joint   Biaxial joint

   Most freely moving joint in the body

9. Several characteristics of specific synovial joints are described below. Identify each of the joints described by choosing a response from the key choices.

Key Choices

A. Elbow   B. Hip   C. Knee   D. Shoulder

_____   1. Rotator cuff muscles are important in stabilizing this joint; capsule reinforced only anteriorly by ligaments; articular surfaces shallow.

_____   2. Three joints in one; capsule incomplete anteriorly; has menisci and intracapsular cruciate ligaments.

_____   3. Capsule is loose; reinforced by medial and lateral collateral ligaments; articular surfaces most important in ensuring joint stability.

_____   4. Articular surfaces deep and secure; capsule heavily reinforced by ligaments and muscle tendons; intracapsular ligamentum teres. Extremely stable joint.

10. Figure 9.3 shows diagrams of two synovial joints. Identify each joint by inserting the name of the joint in the blank below each diagram. Then select different colors and use them to color the coding circles and the structures in the diagrams. Finally, add labels and leader lines on the diagrams to identify the following structures: the ligamentum teres, the anterior cruciate ligament, the posterior cruciate ligament, the suprapatellar bursa, the subcutaneous prepatellar bursa, and the deep infrapatellar bursa.

◯ Fibrous capsule (lined with synovial membrane)   ◯ Joint cavity

◯ Articular cartilage of bone ends   ◯ Acetabular labrum

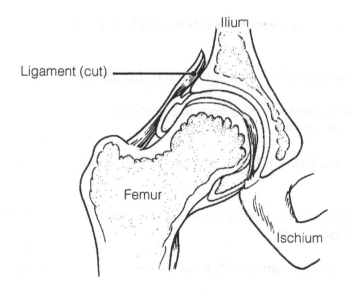

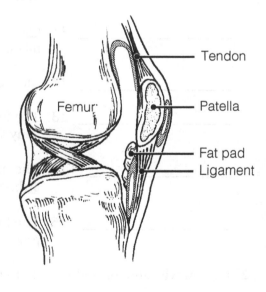

A. _____   B. _____

Figure 9.3

Homeostatic Imbalances of Joints

1. For the following statements that are true, insert T in the answer blanks. For false statements, correct the underlined words and insert your corrections in the answer blanks.

_____ 1. The term <u>arthritis</u> refers to bone ends that are forced out of their normal positions in a joint cavity.

_____ 2. In a <u>sprain</u>, the ligaments reinforcing a joint are excessively stretched or torn.

_____ 3. Erosion of articular cartilages and formation of painful bony spurs are characteristic of <u>gouty arthritis</u>.

_____ 4. "Housemaid's knee" is an example of inflammation of the <u>tendon sheaths</u>.

_____ 5. <u>Chronic</u> arthritis usually results from bacterial invasion.

_____ 6. Healing of a partially torn ligament is slow because its hundreds of fibrous strands are poorly <u>aligned</u>.

_____ 7. <u>Acute</u> arthritis is an autoimmune disease.

_____ 8. Hyperuricemia may lead to <u>rheumatoid</u> arthritis.

_____ 9. Torn menisci of the knee rarely heal because cartilage is <u>avascular</u>.

_____ 10. In rheumatoid arthritis, the initial pathology is inflammation of the <u>bursae</u>.

_____ 11. <u>Gouty</u> arthritis involves several joints that are affected in a bilateral manner.

_____ 12. Most cartilage injuries of the knee involve torn <u>ligaments</u>.

_____ 13. The function of the bursae is to <u>absorb the shock</u> between bony structures in a joint.

_____ 14. The most common form of chronic arthritis is <u>rheumatoid arthritis</u>.

_____ 15. The local swelling seen in bursitis is caused by excessive production of <u>plasma</u> fluid.

2. Explain why sprains and injuries to joint cartilages are particularly troublesome.

_____

_____

A Visualization Exercise for the Knee Joint

This place is like an underground cave, and you flip on your back to swim in the shallow pool.

1. Complete the narrative by inserting the missing words in the answer blanks.

_____ 1.

_____ 2.

_____ 3.

_____ 4.

_____ 5.

_____ 6.

_____ 7.

_____ 8.

_____ 9.

_____ 10.

_____ 11.

_____ 12.

_____ 13.

_____ 14.

_____ 15.

For this journey, you are miniaturized and injected into the knee joint of a football player who is resting before the game. You find yourself standing on a firm, white, flexible, C-shaped structure, a __(1)__ , which prevents side-to-side rocking of the __(2)__ on the __(3)__ . The space you are in, the __(4)__ , is filled with a clear, viscous liquid, the __(5)__ , which serves to __(6)__ the glassy-smooth articulating surfaces. You note that this place is like an underground cave, and you flip on your back to swim in the shallow pool. As you gaze upward, you see, almost touching your head, two enormous boulderlike structures. At first, you're afraid they might fall on you, but then, of course, you recognize them as the __(7)__ of the femur. After becoming accustomed to this environment, you begin to wonder what this football player is doing with his knee joint. Because you see that his __(8)__ ligament is taut, you surmise that his knee joint must be in extension.

Suddenly, the liquid around you becomes less viscous, and you are swept upward, past a rather small, flat, roundish bone, which you identify as the __(9)__ , into an enormous ocean of that same viscous liquid. You note that it is surrounded by a membrane. After some puzzlement, you realize that this must be the suprapatellar __(10)__ !

Knowing that your football player is no longer at rest, you swim, with great effort, back to the joint cavity to watch his knee joint in action. Within a moment, a hard, lateral blow to the knee sends him (and you) spinning. You examine his joint and note that the meniscus has been torn from its attachment at the __(11)__ margins of the __(12)__ and that the extracapsular lateral collateral __(13)__ has also suffered some damage. Since you know that cartilage rarely heals because it has no __(14)__ for nourishment, you predict that your football player will most likely undergo surgery for removal of his __(15)__ . Since you prefer not to wait until then to leave your host, you signal headquarters that you are ready to be picked up by the syringe.

CHALLENGING YOURSELF

At the Clinic

1. Jenny's father loved to hold his 4-year-old daughter by her hand and swing her around in great circles. One day, Jenny's glee was suddenly replaced by tears and she screamed that her left elbow hurt. When examined, the little girl was seen to hold her elbow semiflexed and her forearm pronated. What is your diagnosis?

2. A patient complains of pain starting in the jaw and radiating down the neck. Upon questioning, he states that when he is under stress he grinds his teeth. What joint is causing his pain?

3. In the condition *cleidocranial dysostosis*, ossification of the skull is delayed and clavicles may be completely absent. What effect would you predict that this condition has on the function and appearance of the shoulders?

4. Mrs. Carlisle, an elderly woman, suffered sharp pain in her shoulder while trying to raise a stuck window. Examination reveals degeneration and rupture of the rotator cuff. What is the function of the rotator cuff, and how does its rupture affect the function of the shoulder joint?

5. A complete fracture of the femoral neck will not result in death of the femoral head, unless the ligamentum teres is ruptured. What does this ligament contribute to maintain the integrity of the femoral head?

6. At work, a box fell from a shelf onto Bertha's acromial region. In the emergency room, the physician could feel that the head of her humerus had moved into the axilla. What had happened to Bertha?

7. What type of cartilage is damaged in a case of "torn cartilage"?

8. Marjorie, a middle-aged woman, comes to the clinic complaining of stiff, painful joints. A glance at her hands reveals knobby, deformed knuckles. What condition will be tested for?

Stop and Think

1. Name all the diarthrotic joints in the axial skeleton.

2. What joints are involved in pronation and supination? How are these joints classified?

3. Explain the significance of the interdigitating and interlocking surfaces of sutures.

4. What microscopic feature marks the end of the periosteum and the beginning of an intrinsic ligament?

5. Is the lining of a joint cavity an epithelial membrane? If so, what type? If not, what is it?

6. What is the role of menisci in the jaw and sternoclavicular joints?

7. What is the effect of years of poor posture on the posterior vertebral ligaments?

8. Only one joint flexes posteriorly. Which one?

9. Is the head capable of circumduction? Why or why not?

10. How does the knee joint differ from a typical hinge joint?

Multiple Choice

Select the best answer or answers from the choices given.

1. Which of the joints listed would be classified as synarthrotic?

   A. Vertebrocostal   D. Distal tibiofibular

   B. Sternocostal (most)   E. Epiphyseal plate

   C. Acromioclavicular

2. Cartilaginous joints include:

   A. syndesmoses   C. synostoses

   B. symphyses   D. synchondroses

3. Which of the following may be an amphiarthrotic fibrous joint?

   A. Syndesmosis   C. Sternocostal

   B. Suture   D. Intervertebral

4. Joints that eventually become synostoses include:

   A. fontanels

   B. first rib—sternum

   C. ilium-ischium-pubis

   D. epiphyseal plates

5. Which of the following joints have a joint cavity?

   A. Glenohumeral

   B. Acromioclavicular

   C. Intervertebral (at bodies)

   D. Intervertebral (at articular processes)

6. Joints that *contain* fibrocartilage include:

   A. symphysis pubis   C. acromioclavicular

   B. knee   D. atlanto-occipital

7. Considered to be part of a synovial joint are:

   A. bursae   C. tendon sheath

   B. articular cartilage   D. capsular ligaments

8. Synovial fluid:

   A. is indistinguishable from fluid in cartilage matrix

   B. is formed by synovial membrane

   C. thickens as it warms

   D. nourishes and lubricates

9. Which joint type would be best if the joint receives a moderate to heavy stress load and requires moderate flexibility in the sagittal plane?

   A. Gliding   C. Condyloid

   B. Saddle   D. Hinge

10. In comparing two joints of the same type, what characteristic(s) would you use to determine strength and flexibility?

    A. Depth of the depression of the concave bone of the joint

    B. Snugness of fit of the bones

    C. Size of bone projections for muscle attachments

    D. Presence of menisci

11. Which of the following is a multiaxial joint?

    A. Atlanto-occipital

    B. Atlantoaxial

    C. Glenohumeral

    D. Metacarpophalangeal

12. Plane joints allow:

    A. pronation   C. rotation

    B. flexion   D. gliding

13. The temporomandibular joint is capable of which movements?

    A. Elevation   C. Hyperextension

    B. Protraction   D. Inversion

14. Abduction is:

    A. moving the right arm out to the right

    B. spreading out the fingers

    C. wiggling the toes

    D. moving the sole of the foot laterally

15. Which of the joints listed is classified as a hinge joint functionally but is actually a condyloid joint structurally?

    A. Elbow

    B. Interphalangeal

    C. Knee

    D. Temporomandibular

16. Which of the following joints has the greatest freedom of movement?

    A. Interphalangeal

    B. Saddle joint of thumb

    C. Distal tibiofibular

    D. Coxal

17. In what condition would you suspect inflammation of the superficial olecranal bursa?

    A. Student's elbow

    B. Housemaid's knee

    C. Target shooter's trigger finger

    D. Teacher's shoulder

18. Contributing substantially to the stability of the hip joint is the:

    A. ligamentum teres

    B. acetabular labrum

    C. patellar ligament

    D. iliofemoral ligament

19. The ligament located on the posterior aspect of the knee joint is the:

    A. fibular collateral   C. oblique popliteal

    B. tibial collateral   D. posterior cruciate

20. Which of the following apply to a sprain?

    A. Dislocation

    B. Slow healing

    C. Surgery for ruptured ligaments

    D. Grafting

21. Examining a person's skeleton would enable one to learn about his or her:

    A. age   C. muscular strength

    B. gender   D. height

22. Erosion of articular cartilage and subsequent formation of bone spurs occur in:

    A. ankylosis   C. torn cartilage

    B. ankylosing spondylitis   D. osteoarthritis

23. An autoimmune disease resulting in inflammation and eventual fusion of diarthrotic joints is:

    A. gout   C. degenerative joint disease

    B. rheumatoid arthritis   D. pannus

24. Which of the following is correlated with gouty arthritis?

    A. High levels of antibodies

    B. Hyperuricemia

    C. Hypouricemia

    D. Hammertoe

25. Synovial joints are richly innervated by nerve fibers that:

    A. monitor how much the capsule is stretched

    B. supply articular cartilages

    C. cause the joint to move

    D. monitor pain if the capsule is injured

26. Which specific joint does the following description identify? "Articular surfaces are deep and secure, multiaxial; capsule heavily reinforced by ligaments; labrum helps prevent dislocation; the first joint to be built artificially; very stable."

    A. Elbow   C. Knee

    B. Hip   D. Shoulder

27. How does the femur move with respect to the tibia when the knee is locking during extension?

    A. Glides anteriorly   D. Rotates medially

    B. Flexes   E. Rotates laterally

    C. Glides posteriorly

Word Dissection

For each of the following word roots, fill in the literal meaning and give an example, using a word found in this chapter.

Word root	Translation	Example
1. ab	_____	_____
2. ad	_____	_____
3. amphi	_____	_____
4. ankyl	_____	_____
5. arthro	_____	_____
6. artic	_____	_____
7. burs	_____	_____
8. cruci	_____	_____
9. duct	_____	_____
10. gompho	_____	_____
11. labr	_____	_____
12. luxa	_____	_____
13. menisc	_____	_____
14. ovi	_____	_____
15. pron	_____	_____
16. rheum	_____	_____
17. spondyl	_____	_____
18. supine	_____	_____

10

MUSCLE TISSUE

Overview

It would be impossible for human life to exist without muscle tissue. This is because many functional processes and all our dynamic interactions internally and externally with our environment depend on movement. In the human body, muscle tissue is necessary for movement to take place. The body consists of various types of muscle tissue, including cardiac, which is found in the heart; smooth, which forms a substantial part of the walls of hollow organs; and skeletal, which is attached to the skeleton. Smooth and cardiac muscles are involuntary and are responsible for transport of materials within the body. Skele-

tal muscle is voluntary and allows us to maneuver and manipulate in the environment; it also supports soft tissues, guards entrances and exits, and serves to maintain body temperature.

The review exercises in this chapter present the basic structural and functional characteristics of skeletal muscle tissue. Emphasis is placed on muscle cell structure, muscle contraction and muscle mechanics, the energetics of muscle activity, muscle performance, and integration with other systems.

LEVEL 1 Review of Chapter Objectives

1. Specify the functions of skeletal muscle tissue.
2. Describe the organization of muscle at the tissue level.
3. Explain the unique characteristics of skeletal muscle fibers.
4. Identify the structural components of a sarcomere.
5. Identify the components of the neuromuscular junction and summarize the events involved in the neural control of skeletal muscles.
6. Explain the key steps involved in the contraction of a skeletal muscle fiber.
7. Describe the mechanism responsible for tension production in a muscle fiber, and discuss the factors that determine the peak tension developed during a contraction.
8. Discuss the factors that affect peak tension production during the contraction of an entire skeletal muscle, and explain the significance of the motor unit in the process.

9. Compare the different types of muscle contractions.
10. Describe the mechanisms by which muscle fibers obtain the energy to power contractions.
11. Discuss the factors that contribute to muscle fatigue, and discuss the stages and mechanisms involved in the muscle's subsequent recovery.
12. Relate the types of muscle fibers to muscle performance.
13. Distinguish between aerobic and anaerobic endurance, and explain their implications for muscular performance.
14. Identify the structural and functional differences between skeletal muscle fibers and cardiac muscle cells.
15. Identify the structural and functional differences between skeletal muscle fibers and smooth muscle cells.
16. Discuss the role that smooth muscle tissue plays in systems throughout the body.

[L1] Multiple Choice

Place the letter corresponding to the correct answer in the space provided.

OBJ. 1 _____ 1. Muscle tissue consists of cells that are highly specialized for the function of:
   a. excitability
   b. contraction
   c. extensibility
   d. a, b, and c are correct

OBJ. 1 _____ 2. The primary function(s) performed by skeletal muscles is (are):
   a. to produce skeletal movement
   b. to guard entrances and exits
   c. to maintain body temperature
   d. a, b, and c are correct

OBJ. 1 _____ 3. Skeletal muscles move the body by:
   a. using the energy of ATP to form ADP
   b. activation of the excitation-coupling reaction
   c. means of neural stimulation
   d. pulling on the bones of the skeleton

OBJ. 2 _____ 4. Skeletal muscles are often called voluntary muscles because:
   a. ATP activates skeletal muscles for contraction
   b. the skeletal muscles contain myoneural junctions
   c. they contract when stimulated by motor neurons of the central nervous system
   d. connective tissue harnesses generated forces voluntarily

OBJ. 2 _____ 5. The three layers of connective tissue compressing each muscle are the:
   a. skeletal, cardiac, and smooth
   b. epimysium, perimysium, and endomysium
   c. voluntary, involuntary, and resting
   d. satellite cells, tendons, and aponeurosis

OBJ. 3 _____ 6. The smallest functional unit of the muscle fiber is:
   a. thick filaments
   b. thin filaments
   c. Z line
   d. sarcomere

OBJ. 3 _____ 7. Nerves and blood vessels are contained within the connective tissues of the:
   a. epimysium and endomysium
   b. the endomysium only
   c. epimysium and perimysium
   d. the perimysium only

OBJ. 4 _____ 8. The *thin* filaments consist of:

   a. a pair of protein strands wound together to form chains of actin molecules
   b. a helical array of actin molecules
   c. a pair of protein strands wound together to form chains of myosin molecules
   d. a helical array of myosin molecules

OBJ. 4 _____ 9. The *thick* filaments consist of:

   a. a pair of protein strands wound together to form chains of myosin molecules
   b. a helical array of myosin molecules
   c. a pair of protein strands wound together to form chains of actin molecules
   d. a helical array of actin molecules

OBJ. 5 _____ 10. All of the muscle fibers controlled by a single motor neuron constitute a:

   a. motor unit
   b. sarcomere
   c. myoneural junction
   d. cross-bridge

OBJ. 5 _____ 11. The tension in a muscle fiber will vary depending on:

   a. the structure of individual sarcomeres
   b. the initial length of muscle fibers
   c. the number of cross-bridge interactions within a muscle fiber
   d. a, b, and c are correct

OBJ. 5 _____ 12. The reason there is *less* precise control over leg muscles compared to the muscles of the eye is:

   a. single muscle fibers are controlled by many motor neurons
   b. many muscle fibers are controlled by many motor neurons
   c. a single muscle fiber is controlled by a single motor neuron
   d. many muscle fibers are controlled by a single motor neuron

OBJ. 6 _____ 13. The *sliding filament theory* explains that the *physical* change that takes place during contraction is:

   a. the thick filaments are sliding toward the center of the sarcomere alongside the thin filaments
   b. the thick and thin filaments are sliding toward the center of the sarcomere together
   c. the Z lines are sliding toward the H zone
   d. the thin filaments are sliding toward the center of the sarcomere alongside the thick filaments

OBJ. 6 _____ 14. Troponin and tropomyosin are two proteins that can prevent the contractile process by:

   a. combining with calcium to prevent active site binding
   b. causing the release of calcium from the sacs of the sarcoplasmic reticulum
   c. covering the active site and blocking the actin–myosin interaction
   d. inactivating the myosin to prevent cross-bridging

OBJ. 6 _____ 15. The first step in excitation–contraction coupling is the:
- a. stimulation of the sarcolemma
- b. neuronal activation in the CNS
- c. release of calcium ions from the sarcoplasmic reticulum
- d. production of tension at the neuromuscular junction

OBJ. 7 _____ 16. The amount of tension produced by an individual muscle fiber ultimately depends on the:
- a. number of calcium ions released
- b. number of contracting sarcomeres
- c. number of pivoting cross-bridges
- d. all-or-none principle

OBJ. 7 _____ 17. Skeletal muscle fibers contract most forcefully when stimulated over a:
- a. narrow range of resting lengths
- b. wide range of resting lengths
- c. decrease in the resting sarcomere length
- d. resting sarcomere is as short as it can be

OBJ. 8 _____ 18. The amount of tension produced in the skeletal muscle as a whole is determined by the:
- a. internal tension produced by the stimulated muscle fibers
- b. external tension produced by the stimulated muscle fibers
- c. total number of muscle fibers stimulated
- d. a, b, and c are correct

OBJ. 8 _____ 19. Peak tension production occurs when all motor units in the muscle contract in a state of:
- a. treppe
- b. twitch
- c. wave summation
- d. complete tetanus

OBJ. 9 _____ 20. In an *isotonic* contraction:
- a. the tension in the muscle varies as it shortens
- b. the muscle length doesn't change due to the resistance
- c. the cross-bridges must produce enough tension to overcome the resistance
- d. tension in the muscle decreases as the resistance increases

OBJ. 9 _____ 21. In an *isometric* contraction:
- a. tension rises but the length of the muscle remains constant
- b. the tension rises and the muscle shortens
- c. the tension produced by the muscle is greater than the resistance
- d. the tension of the muscle increases as the resistance decreases

OBJ. 10 _____ 22. A high blood concentration of the enzyme creatine phosphokinase (CPK) usually indicates:

    a. the release of stored energy

    b. serious muscle damage

    c. an excess of energy is being produced

    d. the mitochondria are malfunctioning

OBJ. 10 _____ 23. Mitochondrial activities are relatively efficient, but their rate of ATP generation is limited by:

    a. the presence of enzymes

    b. the availability of carbon dioxide and water

    c. the energy demands of other organelles

    d. the availability of oxygen

OBJ. 11 _____ 24. Of the following selections, the one that has been correlated with muscle fatigue is:

    a. an increase in metabolic reserves within the muscle fibers

    b. a decline in pH within the muscle altering enzyme activities

    c. an increase in pH within the muscle fibers affecting storage of glycogen

    d. increased muscle performance due to an increased pain threshold

OBJ. 11 _____ 25. During the recovery period, the body's oxygen demand is:

    a. elevated above normal resting levels

    b. decreased below normal resting levels

    c. unchanged

    d. an irrelevant factor during recovery

OBJ. 12 _____ 26. The three major types of skeletal muscle fibers in the human body are:

    a. slow, fast resistant, and fast fatigue

    b. slow, intermediate, and fast

    c. SO, FR, and FF

    d. a, b, and c are correct

OBJ. 12 _____ 27. Extensive blood vessels, mitochondria, and myoglobin are found in the greatest concentration in:

    a. fast fibers

    b. slow fibers

    c. intermediate fibers

    d. Type II fibers

OBJ. 13 _____ 28. The length of time a muscle can continue to contract while supported by mitochondrial activities is referred to as:

    a. anaerobic endurance

    b. aerobic endurance

    c. hypertrophy

    d. recruitment

OBJ. 13 _____ 29. Altering the characteristics of muscle fibers and improving the performance of the cardiovascular system results in improving:

  a. thermoregulatory adjustment

  b. hypertrophy

  c. anaerobic endurance

  d. aerobic endurance

OBJ. 14 _____ 30. The property of cardiac muscle that allows it to contract without neural stimulation is:

  a. intercalation

  b. automaticity

  c. plasticity

  d. pacesetting

OBJ. 14 _____ 31. The type of muscle tissue that does not contain sarcomeres is:

  a. cardiac

  b. skeletal

  c. smooth

  d. a and c are correct

OBJ. 15 _____ 32. Structurally, smooth muscle cells differ from skeletal muscle cells because smooth muscle cells:

  a. contain many nuclei

  b. contain a network of T tubules

  c. lack myofibrils and sarcomeres

  d. possess striations

OBJ. 15 _____ 33. Smooth muscle tissue differs from other muscle tissue in that:

  a. calcium ions interact with calmodulin to trigger muscle contraction

  b. calcium ions combine with troponin to trigger muscle contraction

  c. smooth muscle doesn't require the release of calcium ions to trigger muscle contraction

  d. the myofibrils in smooth muscle release potassium ions to trigger muscle contractions

OBJ. 16 _____ 34. Smooth muscle contractions in the respiratory passageways would cause:

  a. increased resistance to air flow

  b. decreased resistance to air flow

  c. immediate death

  d. resistance to air flow will not be affected

OBJ. 16 _____ 35. Layers of smooth muscle in the reproductive tract of the female are important in:

  a. movement of ova

  b. movement of sperm if present

  c. expelling of the fetus at delivery

  d. a, b, and c are correct

[L1] Completion

Using the terms below, complete the following statements.

endurance	epimysium	skeletal muscle	lactic acid
twitch	white muscles	glycolysis	action potential
tendon	sarcomeres	ATP	sarcolemma
body movement	smooth muscle	fascicles	red muscles
sphincter	T tubules	treppe	recruitment
troponin	pacemaker	oxygen debt	cross-bridges
motor unit	incomplete tetanus	plasticity	complete tetanus
Z lines	tension		

OBJ. 1	1. Muscle tissues are highly specialized for producing _____.
OBJ. 2	2. The dense layer of collagen fibers surrounding a muscle is called the _____.
OBJ. 2	3. Bundles of muscle fibers are called _____.
OBJ. 2	4. The dense regular connective tissue that attaches skeletal muscle to bones is known as a _____.
OBJ. 3	5. The cell membrane that surrounds the cytoplasm of a muscle fiber is called the _____.
OBJ. 3	6. Structures that help distribute the command to contract throughout the muscle fiber are called _____.
OBJ. 3	7. Muscle cells contain contractible units called _____.
OBJ. 4	8. Because they connect thick and thin filaments, the myosin heads are also known as _____.
OBJ. 4	9. The boundary between adjacent sarcomeres is marked by the _____.
OBJ. 5	10. The conducted charge in the transmembrane potential is called a(n) _____.
OBJ. 5	11. The smooth but steady increase in muscular tension produced by increasing the number of active motor units is called _____.
OBJ. 6	12. Active site exposure during the contraction process occurs when calcium binds to _____.
OBJ. 6	13. The interactions between the thick and the thin filaments produce _____.
OBJ. 7	14. When the calcium ion concentration in the cytoplasm prolongs the contraction state, making it continuous, the contraction is called _____.
OBJ. 7	15. A muscle producing peak tension during rapid cycles of contraction and relaxation is said to be in _____.
OBJ. 8	16. An indication of how fine the control of movement can be is determined by the size of the _____.
OBJ. 8	17. By controlling the number of activated muscle fibers, you can control the amount of tension produced by the _____.
OBJ. 9	18. The "staircase" phenomenon during which the peak muscle tension rises in stages is called _____.

OBJ. 9   19. A single stimulus–contraction–relaxation sequence in a muscle fiber is a _____.

OBJ. 10   20. When muscles are actively contracting, the process requires large amounts of energy in the form of _____.

OBJ. 11   21. At peak activity levels, most of the ATP is provided by glycolysis, leading the to production of _____.

OBJ. 11   22. A skeletal muscle continues to contract even when mitochondrial activity is limited by the availability of oxygen due to the process of _____.

OBJ. 12   23. Muscles dominated by fast fibers are sometimes referred to as _____.

OBJ. 12   24. Muscles dominated by slow fibers are sometimes referred to as _____.

OBJ. 13   25. The amount of oxygen used in the recovery period to restore normal pre-exertion conditions is referred to as _____.

OBJ. 13   26. The amount of time for which the individual can perform a particular activity is referred to as _____.

OBJ. 14   27. The timing of contractions in cardiac muscle tissues is determined by specialized muscle fibers called _____ cells.

OBJ. 15   28. The ability of smooth muscle to function over a wide range of lengths is called _____.

OBJ. 15   29. Spindle-shaped cells with a single, centrally located nucleus are characteristic of _____.

OBJ. 16   30. In the digestive and urinary systems, the rings of smooth muscle that regulate the movement of materials along internal passageways are called _____.

[L1] Matching

Match the terms in column B with the terms in column A. Use letters for answers in the spaces provided.

	Column A	Column B
OBJ. 1	_____ 1. skeletal muscle	A. thick filaments
OBJ. 2	_____ 2. fascicles	B. resting tension
OBJ. 2	_____ 3. aponeurosis	C. synaptic cleft
OBJ. 2	_____ 4. tendons	D. cardiac muscle fibers
OBJ. 3	_____ 5. myoblasts	E. muscle bundles
OBJ. 4	_____ 6. myosin	F. lactic acid
OBJ. 5	_____ 7. neuromuscular junction	G. red muscles
		H. peak tension
OBJ. 6	_____ 8. cross-bridging	I. smooth muscle cell
OBJ. 7	_____ 9. contraction phase	J. produce body movements
OBJ. 8	_____ 10. myogram	K. actin–myosin interaction
OBJ. 9	_____ 11. muscle tone	L. embryonic cells
OBJ. 10	_____ 12. energy reserve	M. creatine phosphate

OBJ. 11	____ 13. lactic acid	N. measures external tension
OBJ. 12	____ 14. slow fibers	
OBJ. 13	____ 15. anaerobic glycolysis	O. lowers intracellular pH
OBJ. 14	____ 16. intercalated discs	P. rhythmic cycles
OBJ. 15	____ 17. no striations	Q. bundle of collagen fibers
OBJ. 16	____ 18. pacemaker cells	R. broad sheet

[L1]   Drawing/Illustration Labeling

Identify each numbered structure by labeling the following figures:

OBJ. 2   **Figure 10.1   Organization of Skeletal Muscles**

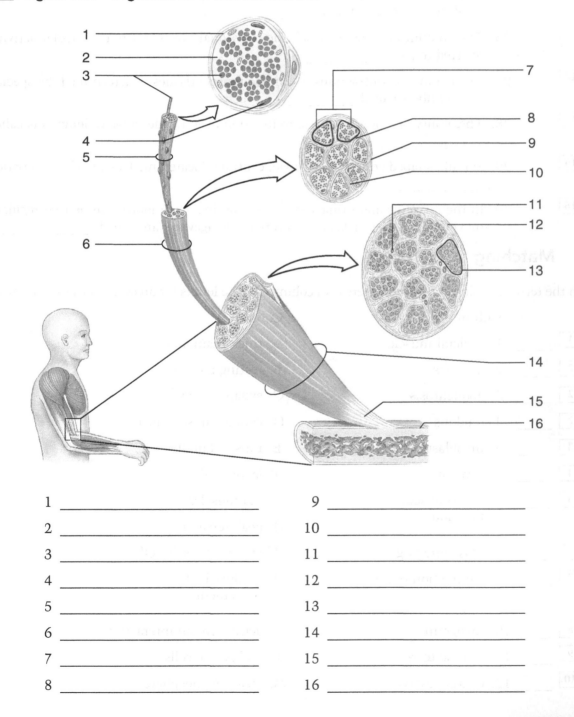

1 _____   9 _____

2 _____   10 _____

3 _____   11 _____

4 _____   12 _____

5 _____   13 _____

6 _____   14 _____

7 _____   15 _____

8 _____   16 _____

OBJ. 3   **Figure 10.2   The Histological Organization of Skeletal Muscles**

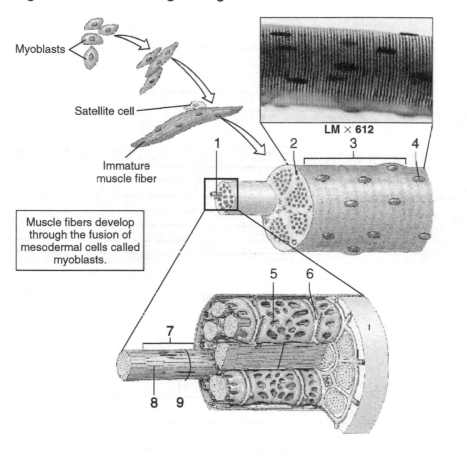

Myoblasts

Satellite cell

Immature
muscle fiber

Muscle fibers develop
through the fusion of
mesodermal cells called
myoblasts.

LM × 612

1 _____   6 _____

2 _____   7 _____

3 _____   8 _____

4 _____   9 _____

5 _____

OBJ. 3   **Figure 10.3   Types of Muscle Tissue**

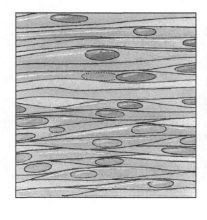
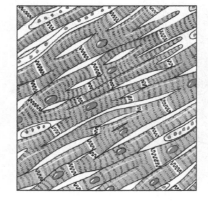
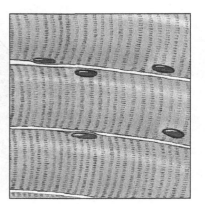

1 _____   2 _____   3 _____

OBJ. 4   **Figure 10.4   Structure of a Sarcomere**

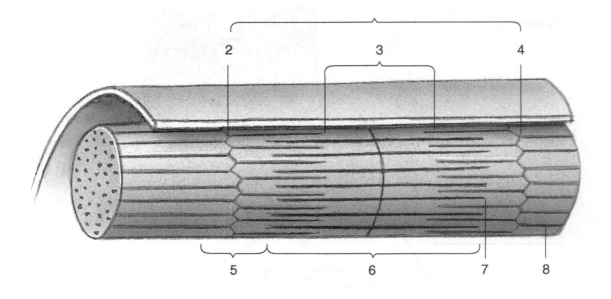

1 _____   5 _____

2 _____   6 _____

3 _____   7 _____

4 _____   8 _____

OBJ. 5   **Figure 10.5   Neuromuscular Junction**

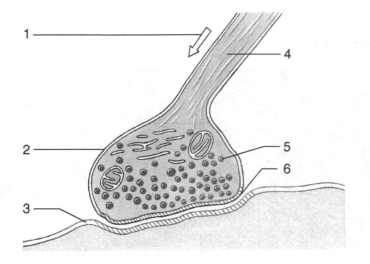

1 _____

2 _____

3 _____

4 _____

5 _____

6 _____

LEVEL 2 Concept Synthesis

Concept Map I

Using the following terms, fill in the circled, numbered, blank spaces to complete the concept map. Follow the numbers to comply with the organization of the map.

Smooth   Involuntary   Striated
Multinucleated   Bones   Non-striated
Heart

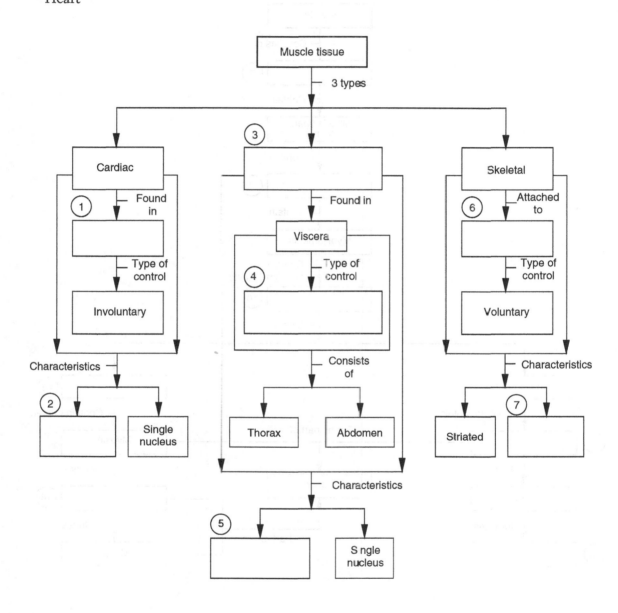

Concept Map II

Using the following terms, fill in the circled, numbered, blank spaces to complete the concept map. Follow the numbers to comply with the organization of the map.

Z lines   Muscle bundles (fascicles)   Myofibrils
Actin   Thick filaments   Sarcomeres
H zone

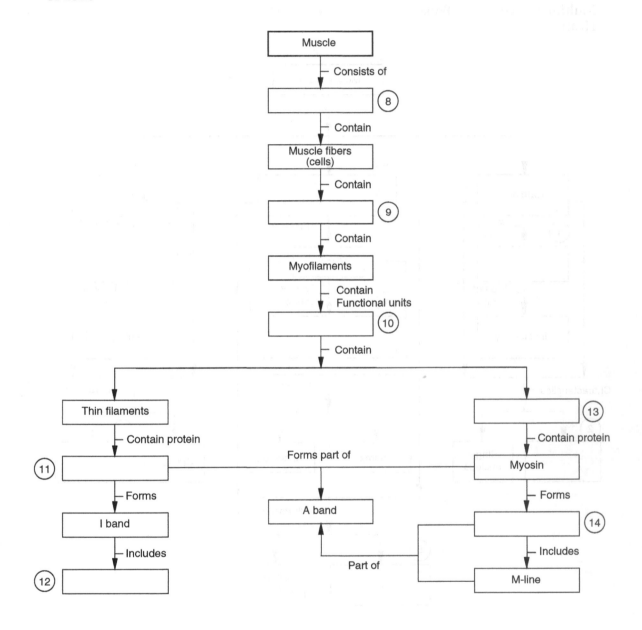

Concept Map III

Using the following terms and/or phrases, fill in the numbered, blank spaces to complete the concept map on muscle contraction. Follow the numbers to comply with the organization of the map.

        Cross-bridging (heads of myosin attach to turned-on thin filaments)

        Energy + ADP + phosphate

        Release of Ca++ from sacs of sarcoplasmic reticulum

        Shortening, i.e., contraction of myofibrils and muscle fibers they compose

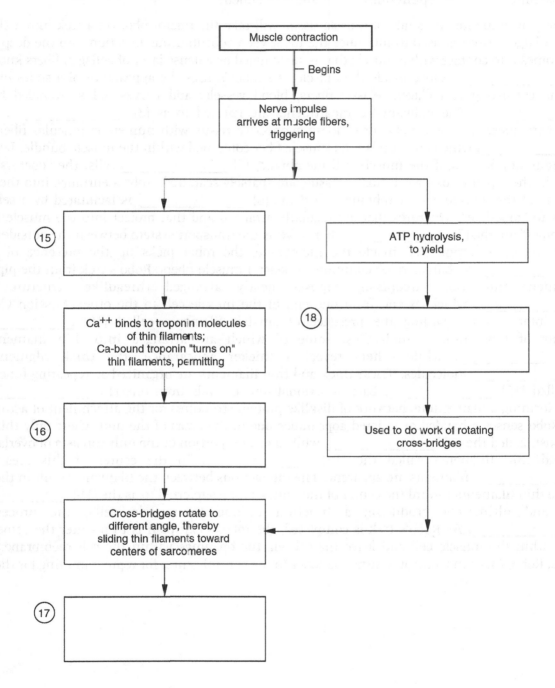

Body Trek

Using the terms below, fill in the blanks to complete the trek through the muscle tissue.

thick	nuclei	fascicles	actin
contraction	Z line	endomysium	A band
myosin	sarcomeres	sarcolemma	T tubules
myofibrils	I band	myofilaments	perimysium
satellite	epimysium	sliding filament	

Robo's programming for the study of muscle tissue will take the micro-robot on a trek into a skeletal muscle. A large syringe is used to introduce the robot via a subcutaneous injection into the deep fascia until it comes into contact with a muscle that is surrounded by a dense layer of collagen fibers known as the (1) _____. Once inside the muscle, the robot senses the appearance of a series of compartments consisting of collagen, elastic fibers, blood vessels, and nerves, all surrounded by the (2) _____. The individual compartments are referred to as (3) _____. Probing deeper, there appears to be a network of loose connective tissue with numerous reticular fibers, the (4) _____, which surrounds each muscle fiber contained within the muscle bundle. Between this surrounding layer and the muscle cell membrane, (5) _____ cells, the "doctors" that function in the repair of damaged muscle tissue, are sparsely scattered. Robo's entrance into the muscle by way of the muscle cell membrane, called the (6) _____, is facilitated by a series of openings to "pipe-like" structures that are regularly arranged and that project into the muscle fibers. These "pipes" are the (7) _____ that serve as the transport system between the outside of the cell and the cell interior. Just inside the membrane, the robot picks up the presence of many (8) _____, a characteristic common to skeletal muscle fibers. Robo's trek from the pipe-like environment into the sarcoplasm exposes neatly arranged threadlike structures, the (9) _____, which extend from one end of the muscle cell to the other. Mission Control receives information regarding the presence of smaller filaments called (10) _____, consisting of large protein molecules, some of which are arranged into thin filaments or (11) _____, while others reveal a thicker appearance, the thick filaments or (12) _____ molecules. These thick and thin filaments are organized as repeating functional units called (13) _____. Each functional unit extends from one (14) _____ to another, forming a filamentous network of disklike protein structures for the attachment of actin molecules. Robo senses a banded or striated appearance due to the areas of the unit where only thin filaments exist, called the (15) _____, while a greater portion of the unit consists of overlapping thick and thin filaments called the (16) _____. In the center of this area, only (17) _____ filaments are apparent. The interactions between the filaments result in the sliding of the thin filaments toward the center of the unit, a process referred to as the (18) _____ theory, and ultimately producing a function unique to muscle cells, the process of (19) _____. As Robo's trek is completed, the robot's exit plan is to re-enter the "pipe-like" system within the muscle cell and leave the cell via the openings within the cell membrane. After retrieving Robo, Mission Control returns the robot to the control center for reprogramming for the next task.

COVERING ALL YOUR BASES

[L2] Multiple Choice

Select the best answer or answers from the choices given.

1. Muscle contraction occurs as a result of:

    A. interactions between the thick and thin filaments of the sarcomere

    B. the interconnecting filaments that make up the Z lines

    C. shortening of the A band, which contains thick and thin filaments

    D. shortening of the I band, which contains thin filaments only

2. The area of the A band in the sarcomere consists of:

    A. Z line, H band, and M line

    B. M line, H band, and zone of overlap

    C. thin filaments only

    D. overlapping thick and thin filaments

3. The process of cross-bridging, which occurs at an active site, involves a series of sequential-cyclic reactions that include:

    A. attach, return, pivot, and detach

    B. attach, pivot, detach, and return

    C. attach, detach, pivot, and return

    D. attach, return, detach, and pivot

4. Excitation–contraction coupling forms the link between:

    A. the release of Ca^{++} to bind with the troponin molecule

    B. depolarization and repolarization

    C. electrical activity in the sarcolemma and the initiation of a contraction

    D. the neuromuscular junction and the sarcoplasmic reticulum

5. When Ca^{++} binds to troponin, it produces a change by:

    A. initiating activity at the neuromuscular junction

    B. causing the actin–myosin interaction to occur

    C. decreasing the calcium concentration at the sarcomere

    D. exposing the active site on the thin filaments

6. The phases of a single twitch in sequential order include:

    A. contraction phase, latent phase, relaxation phase

    B. latent period, relaxation phase, contraction phase

    C. latent period, contraction phase, relaxation phase

    D. relaxation phase, latent phase, contraction phase

7. After contraction, a muscle fiber returns to its original length through:

    A. the active mechanism for fiber elongation

    B. elastic forces and the movement of opposing muscles

    C. the tension produced by the initial length of the muscle fiber

    D. involvement of all the sarcomeres along the myofibrils

8. A muscle producing peak tension during rapid cycles of contraction and relaxation is said to be in:

    A. complete tetanus

    B. incomplete tetanus

    C. treppe

    D. recruitment

9. The process of reaching *complete tetanus* is obtained by:

    A. applying a second stimulus before the relaxation phase has ended

    B. decreasing the concentration of calcium ions in the cytoplasm

    C. activation of additional motor units

    D. increasing the rate of stimulation until the

relaxation phase is completely eliminated

10. The total force exerted by a muscle as a whole depends on:

    A. the rate of stimulation

    B. how many motor units are activated

    C. the number of calcium ions released

    D. a, b, and c are correct

11. The primary energy reserves found in skeletal muscle cells are:

    A. carbohydrates, fats, and proteins

    B. DNA, RNA, and ATP

    C. ATP, creatine phosphate, and glycogen

    D. ATP, ADP, and AMP

12. The two mechanisms used to generate ATP from glucose are:

    A. aerobic respiration and anaerobic glycolysis

    B. ADP and creatine phosphate

    C. cytoplasm and mitochondria

    D. a, b, and c are correct

13. In *anaerobic glycolysis*, glucose is broken down to pyruvic acid, which is converted to:

    A. glycogen

    B. lactic acid

    C. acetyl-CoA

    D. citric acid

14. The maintenance of normal body temperature is dependent upon:

    A. the temperature of the environment

    B. the pH of the blood

    C. the production of energy by muscles

    D. the amount of energy produced by anaerobic glycolysis

15. Growth hormone from the pituitary gland and the male sex hormone, testosterone, stimulate:

    A. the rate of energy consumption by resting and active skeletal muscles

    B. muscle metabolism and increased force of contraction

    C. synthesis of contractile proteins and the enlargement of skeletal muscles

    D. the amount of tension produced by a muscle group

16. The hormone responsible for stimulating muscle metabolism and increasing the force of contraction during a sudden crisis is:

    A. epinephrine

    B. thyroid hormone

    C. growth hormone

    D. testosterone

17. The type of skeletal muscle fibers that have low fatigue resistance are:

    A. fast fibers

    B. slow fibers

    C. intermediate fibers

    D. Type I fibers

18. An example of an activity that requires *anaerobic endurance* is:

    A. a 50-yard dash

    B. a 3-mile run

    C. a 10-mile bicycle ride

    D. running a marathon

19. Athletes training to develop anaerobic endurance perform:

    a. few, long, relaxing workouts

    b. a combination of weight training and marathon running

    C. frequent, brief, intensive workouts

    D. stretching, flexibility, and relaxation exercises

20. The major support that the muscular system gets from the cardiovascular system is:

    a. a direct response by controlling the heart rate and the respiratory rate

    b. constriction of blood vessels and decrease in heart rate for thermoregulatory control

    C. nutrient and oxygen delivery and carbon dioxide removal

    D. decreased volume of blood and rate of flow for maximal muscle contraction

[L2]   Completion

Using the terms below, complete the following statements.

satellite   myoblasts   fatigue
isotonic   tetanus   motor unit
rigor   muscle tone   absolute refractory periods
A bands

1. Specialized cells that function in the repair of damaged muscle tissue are called
_____ cells.

2. During development, groups of embryonic cells that fuse together to create individual muscle fibers are called _____.

3. Resting tension in a skeletal muscle is called _____.

4. A rise of a few degrees in temperature within a muscle may result in a severe
contraction called _____.

5. The time when a muscle cell cannot be stimulated because repolarization is occurring is the _____.

6. The condition that results when a muscle is stimulated but cannot respond is
referred to as _____.

7. In a sarcomere, the dark bands (anisotropic bands) are referred to as
_____.

8. A single cranial or spinal motor neuron and the muscle fibers it innervates
comprise a _____.

9. At sufficiently high electrical frequencies, the overlapping twitches result in one
strong, steady contraction referred to as _____.

10. When the muscle shortens but its tension remains the same, the contraction is
_____.

[L2]   Short Essay

Briefly answer the following questions in the spaces provided below.

1. What are the five functions performed by skeletal muscles?

2. What are the three layers of connective tissue that are part of each muscle?

3. Draw an illustration of a sarcomere and label the parts according to the unit
organization.

4. Cite the five interlocking steps involved in the contraction process.

5. Describe the major events that occur at the neuromuscular junction to initiate the contractive process.

6. Identify the types of muscle contractions illustrated at points A, B, and C on the diagram below.

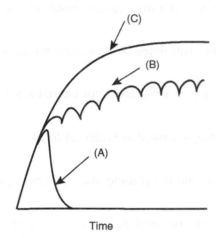

Time

7. What are the differences between an isometric and an isotonic contraction?

8. What is the relationship among fatigue, anaerobic glycolysis, and oxygen debt?

9. Why do fast fibers fatigue more rapidly than slow fibers?

LEVEL 3 Critical Thinking/Application

Using principles and concepts learned about skeletal muscle tissue, answer the following questions. Write your answers on a separate sheet of paper.

1. When a person drinks an excessive amount of alcohol, that individual becomes drunk or intoxicated, a condition resulting in a lack of muscular control and coordination. How does the alcohol cause this condition?

2. Suppose you are assigned the responsibility of developing training programs tailored to increase both aerobic and anaerobic endurance. What types of activities would be necessary to support these training programs?

3. During a lecture on death and dying, a student asks, "Is rigor mortis the same as physiological contracture?" How would you as the lecturer describe the similarities/differences between these two conditions?

4. An individual who has been on a diet that eliminates dairy products complains of muscular spasms and nervousness. Why might these symptoms result from such a diet?

5. What does the bacterium *Clostridium botulinum* and the *poliovirus* have in common that ultimately affects the condition of muscles in the human body?

11

THE MUSCULAR
SYSTEM

Student Objectives

When you have completed the exercises in this chapter, you will have accomplished the following objectives:

Muscle Mechanics: The Importance of Fascicle Arrangement and Leverage

1. Define *lever*, and explain how a lever operating at a mechanical advantage differs from a lever operating at a mechanical disadvantage.

2. Name the three types of lever systems and indicate the arrangement of effort, fulcrum, and load in each. Also note the advantages of each type of lever system.

3. Name the common patterns of muscle fascicle arrangement and relate these to power generation.

Interactions of Skeletal Muscles in the Body

4. Describe the function of prime movers, antagonists, synergists, and fixators.

Naming Skeletal Muscles

5. List the criteria used in naming muscles. Provide an example to illustrate the use of each criterion.

Major Skeletal Muscles of the Body

6. Name and identify the major muscles of the human body.

All contractile tissues—smooth, cardiac, and skeletal muscle—are muscles, but the muscular system is concerned only with skeletal muscles, the organs composed of skeletal muscle tissue, and connective tissue wrappings. The skeletal muscles clothe the bony skeleton and make up about 40% of body mass. Skeletal muscles, also called voluntary muscles, help shape the body and enable you to smile, run, shake hands, grasp things, and otherwise manipulate your environment.

The topics of Chapter 11 include principles of leverage, classification of muscles on the basis of their major function, identification of voluntary muscles, and a description of their important actions and interactions.

BUILDING THE FRAMEWORK

Muscle Mechanics: The Importance of Fascicle Arrangement and Leverage

1. Complete the following short paragraph, which considers the operation of lever systems in the body. Insert your responses in the answer blanks.

   _____   1.   In the body, lever systems involve the interaction of __(1)__ , which provide the force, and __(2)__ , which provide the lever

   _____   2.   arms. The force is exerted where __(3)__ . The site at which movement occurs in each case is the intervening __(4)__ , which

   _____   3.   acts as the fulcrum.

   _____   4.

2. Circle all of the elements that characterize a lever that operates at a mechanical disadvantage:

   Fast   Moves a large load over a small distance   Requires maximal shortening

   Slow   Moves a small load over a large distance   Requires minimal shortening

   Muscle force greater than the load   Muscle force less than load moved

3. Figure 11.1 illustrates the elements of three different lever systems on the left and provides examples of each lever system from the body on the right. Select different colors for the lever elements listed above the figure and use them to color the diagrams of each lever system. Complete this exercise by following the steps below for each muscle diagram.

1. Add a red arrow to indicate the point at which the effort is exerted.

2. Draw a circle enclosing the fulcrum.

3. Indicate whether the lever shown is operating at a mechanical advantage or disadvantage by filling in the line below the diagram.

4. Color the load yellow.

◯ Effort   ◯ Fulcrum   ◯ Load (resistance)

A. First-class lever

B. Second-class lever

C. Third-class lever

Figure 11.1

4. The brachialis is a short stout muscle inserting close to the fulcrum of the elbow joint; the brachioradialis is a slender muscle inserting distally, well away from the fulcrum of the elbow joint. Which muscle is associated with mechanical advantage and which with mechanical disadvantage?

5. Four fascicle arrangements are shown in Figure 11.2; these same arrangements are described below. First, correctly identify each fascicle arrangement by (1) writing the appropriate term in the answer blank and (2) writing the letter of the corresponding diagram in the answer blank. Second, on the remaining lines beside the diagrams, reidentify the fasicle arrangement and then name two muscles that have the fascicle arrangement shown.

_____ 1. Fascicles insert into a midline tendon from both sides.

_____ 2. Muscle fibers are arranged in concentric array around an opening.

_____ 3. Fascicles run with the long axis of the muscle.

_____ 4. Fascicles angle from a broad origin to a narrow insertion.

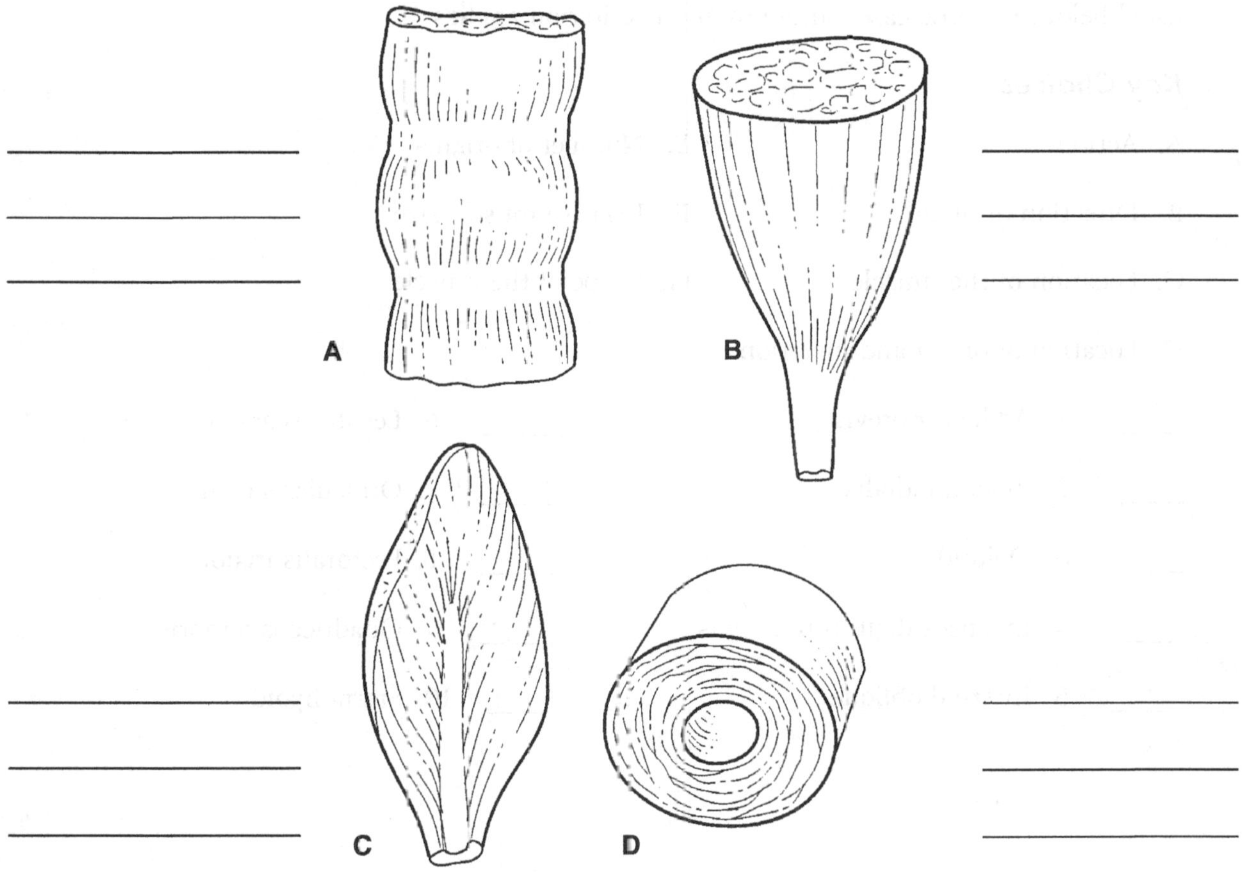

Figure 11.2

Interactions of Skeletal Muscles in the Body

1. The terms in the key choices are often applied to the manner in which muscles interact with other muscles. Select the terms that apply to the following definitions and insert the correct answers in the answer blanks.

Key Choices

A. Antagonist   B. Fixator   C. Prime mover   D. Synergist

_____ 1. Holds parts of the body in proper position for the action of other muscles, primarily postural muscles

_____ 2. Bears the major responsibility for producing a particular movement

_____ 3. Acts to reverse or act against the action of another muscle

_____ 4. Assists an agonist by a like contraction movement or by holding a joint over which an agonist acts immobile

Naming Skeletal Muscles

1. From the key choices, select the criteria that are used in naming the muscles listed below. In some cases, more than one criterion applies.

Key Choices

A. Action

B. Direction of fibers

C. Location of the muscle

D. Location of origin and insertion

E. Number of origins

F. Relative muscle size

G. Shape of the muscle

_____ 1. Adductor brevis

_____ 2. Brachioradialis

_____ 3. Deltoid

_____ 4. Extensor digitorum longus

_____ 5. Internal oblique

_____ 6. Levator scapulae

_____ 7. Orbicularis oculi

_____ 8. Pectoralis major

_____ 9. Quadriceps femoris

_____ 10. Sternohyoid

Major Skeletal Muscles of the Body

1. Match the names of the suprahyoid and infrahyoid muscles listed in Column B with their descriptions in Column A. (Note that not all muscles in Column B are described.) For each muscle that has a color-coding circle, color the coding circles and the corresponding muscles on Figure 11.3 as you like, but color the hyoid bone yellow and the thyroid cartilage blue.

Column A		Column B
◯ _____	1. Most medial muscle of the neck; thin; depresses larynx	A. Digastric
◯ _____	2. Slender muscle that parallels the posterior belly of the digastric muscle; elevates and retracts hyoid bone	B. Geniohyoid
		C. Mylohyoid
◯ _____	3. Consists of two bellies united by an intermediate tendon; prime mover to open the mouth; also depresses mandible	D. Omohyoid
		E. Sternohyoid
◯ _____	4. Lateral and deep to sternohyoid; pulls thyroid cartilage inferiorly	F. Sternothyroid
◯ _____	5. Flat triangular muscle deep to digastric; elevates hyoid, enabling tongue to force food bolus into the pharynx	G. Stylohyoid
		H. Thyrohyoid
◯ _____	6. Narrow muscle in the midline running from chin to hyoid; widens pharynx for receiving food as it elevates the hyoid bone	
◯ _____	7. Superior continuation of the sternothyroid	

Hyoid bone

Thyroid cartilage of the larynx

Sternocleidomastoid

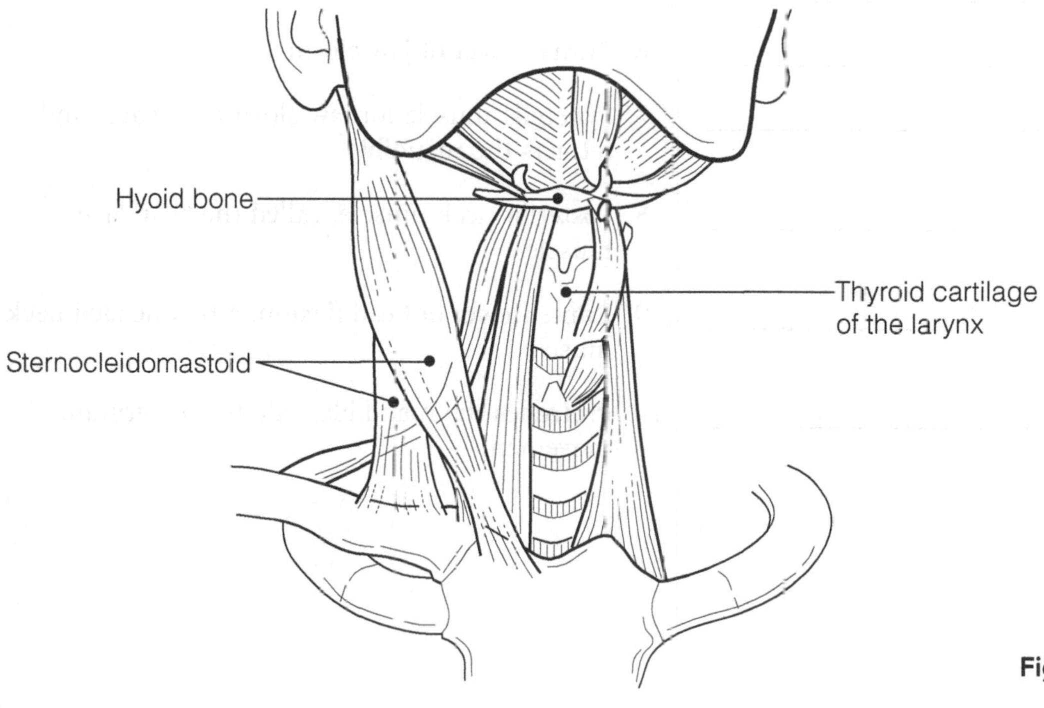

Figure 11.3

2. Match the muscle names in Column B to the facial muscles described in Column A.

<table>
<tr><td colspan="2">Column A</td><td>Column B</td></tr>
<tr><td>_____</td><td>1. Squints the eyes</td><td>A. Corrugator supercilii</td></tr>
<tr><td>_____</td><td>2. Furrows the forehead horizontally</td><td>B. Depressor anguli oris</td></tr>
<tr><td>_____</td><td>3. Smiling muscle</td><td>C. Frontalis</td></tr>
<tr><td>_____</td><td>4. Puckers the lips</td><td>D. Occipitalis</td></tr>
<tr><td>_____</td><td>5. Draws the corners of the lips laterally and downward</td><td>E. Orbicularis oculi</td></tr>
<tr><td></td><td></td><td>F. Orbicularis oris</td></tr>
<tr><td>_____</td><td>6. Pulls the scalp posteriorly</td><td></td></tr>
<tr><td></td><td></td><td>G. Platysma</td></tr>
<tr><td>_____</td><td>7. Tensed during shaving of the chin and neck</td><td>H. Zygomaticus</td></tr>
</table>

3. Relative to muscles of the head and neck, name the major muscles described here. Select a different color for each muscle and color the coding circles and corresponding muscles on Figure 11.4. Notice that the last muscle to be identified lacks a coding circle.

◯ _____ 1. Used to show you're happy

◯ _____ 2. Compresses the cheek; holds food between the teeth

◯ _____ 3. Used in winking

◯ _____ 4. Used to raise your eyebrows

◯ _____ 5. The "kissing" muscle

◯ _____ 6. Prime mover of jaw closure

◯ _____ 7. Synergist muscle for jaw closure; elevates and retracts the mandible

◯ _____ 8. Posterior neck muscle, called the "bandage" muscle

◯ _____ 9. Prime mover of head flexion, a two-headed neck muscle

_____ 10. Protrudes the mandible; side-to-side grinding movements

Zygomatic bone

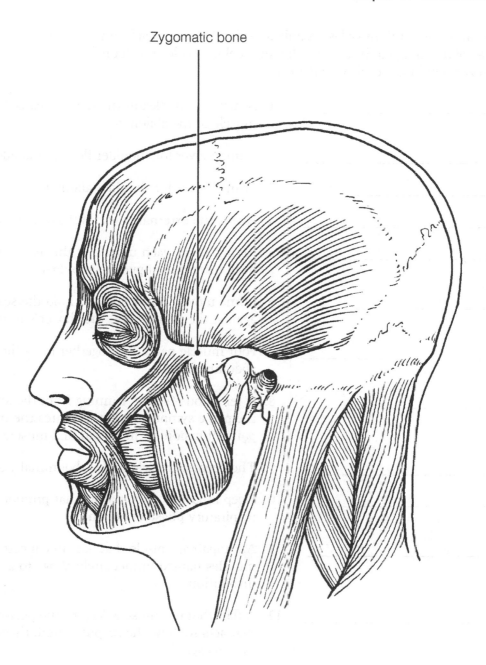

Figure 11.4

4. Describe briefly the function of the pharyngeal constrictor muscles.

_____

_____

5. Name the anterior trunk muscles described below. Then, for each muscle name
that has a color-coding circle, select a different color to color the coding circle
and the corresponding muscle on Figure 11.5.

○ _____   1. A major spine flexor; the name means "straight muscle of the abdomen"

○ _____   2. Prime mover for shoulder flexion and adduction

○ _____   3. Prime mover for shoulder abduction

○ _____   4. Forms the external lateral walls of the abdomen

○ _____   5. Acting alone, each muscle of this pair turns the head toward the opposite shoulder

○ _____   6. Prime mover to protract and hold the scapula against the thorax wall; the "boxer's muscle"

○ _____   7. Four muscle pairs that together form the so-called abdominal girdle

_____   8. A tendinous "seam" running from the sternum to the pubic symphysis that indicates the midline point of fusion of the abdominal muscle sheaths

○ _____   9. The deepest muscle of the abdominal wall

_____   10. Deep muscles of the thorax that promote the inspiratory phase of breathing

_____   11. An unpaired muscle that acts in concert with the muscles named immediately above to accomplish inspiration

_____   12. A flat, thoracic muscle deep to the pectoralis major that acts to draw the scapula inferiorly or to elevate the rib cage

6. What is the functional reason the muscle group on the dorsal leg (calf) is so
much larger than the muscle group in the ventral region of the leg?

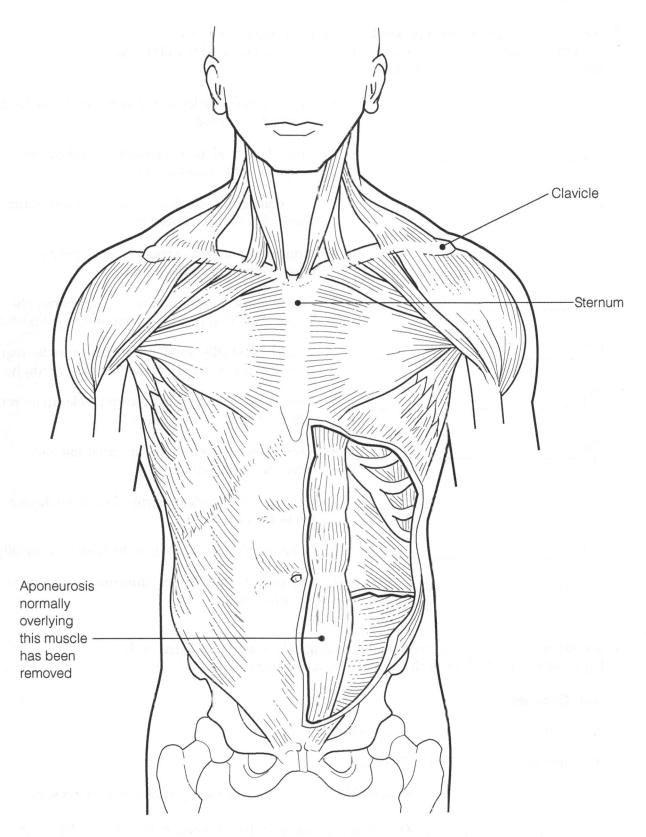

Clavicle

Sternum

Aponeurosis
normally
overlying
this muscle
has been
removed

Figure 11.5

7. Name the posterior trunk muscles described below. Select a different color for each muscle with a color-coding circle and color the coding circles and the corresponding muscles on Figure 11.6.

○ _____ 1. A muscle that enables you to shrug your shoulders or extend your head

○ _____ 2. A muscle that adducts the shoulder and causes extension of the shoulder joint

○ _____ 3. The shoulder muscle that is the antagonist of the muscle described in Question 2 above

_____ 4. Prime mover of back extension; a composite muscle consisting of three columns

_____ 5. A fleshy muscle forming part of the posterior abdominal wall that helps to maintain upright posture

○ _____ 6. Acting individually, small rectangular muscles that rotate the glenoid cavity of the scapulae inferiorly

○ _____ 7. Synergist of the trapezius in scapular elevation; act to flex the head to the same side

○ _____ 8. Synergist of latissimus dorsi in extension and adduction of the humerus

○ _____ 9. A rotator cuff muscle; prevents downward dislocation of the humerus

○ _____ 10. A rotator cuff muscle; rotates the humerus laterally

○ _____ 11. A rotator cuff muscle; lies immediately inferior to the infraspinatus

8. Several muscles that act to move and/or stabilize the scapula are listed in the key choices. Match them to the appropriate descriptions below.

Key Choices

A. Levator scapulae   C. Serratus anterior

B. Rhomboids   D. Trapezius

_____ 1. Muscle that holds the scapula tightly against the thorax wall

_____ 2. Kite-shaped muscle pair that elevates, stabilizes, and depresses the scapulae

_____ 3. Small rectangular muscles that square the shoulders as they act together to retract the scapula

_____ 4. Small muscle pair that elevates the scapulae

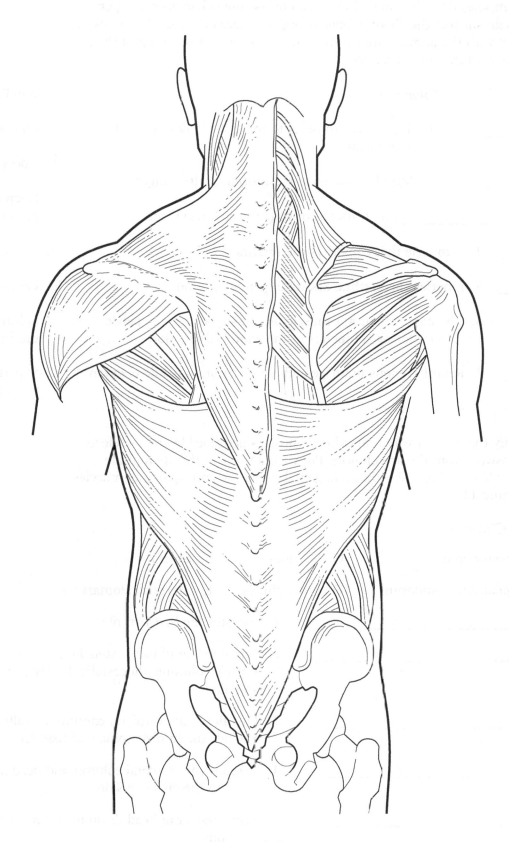

Figure 11.6

9. The muscles described in Column A comprise the pelvic floor and perineum and help support the abdominopelvic organs. Match the muscle names in Column B with the appropriate descriptions in Column A by filling in the answer blanks with the correct letters.

Column A	Column B
_____ _____ 1. Two paired muscles forming the bulk of the pelvic diaphragm	A. Bulbospongiosus
	B. Coccygeus
_____ _____ 2. Muscles that form the urogenital diaphragm	
	C. Deep transverse perineus
_____ _____ _____ 3. Muscles forming the superficial space	
_____ 4. A muscle that constricts the urethra	D. Ischiocavernosus
_____ 5. Empties the urethra; assists in penile erection	E. Levator ani
_____ 6. The most important muscle pair in supporting the pelvic viscera; forms sphincters at the anorectal junction	F. Sphincter urethrae
_____ 7. Retards venous drainage and helps maintain penile erection	G. Superficial transverse perineus

10. Identify the neck or vertebral column muscles described below by selecting answers from the key choices. Put each answer in the appropriate answer blank, then color the coding circles and the corresponding muscles on Figure 11.7.

Key Choices

A. Erector spinae   C. Scalenes   E. Splenius

B. Quadratus lumborum   D. Semispinalis   F. Sternocleidomastoid

_____ 1. Elevates the first two ribs

◯ _____ 2. Prime mover of back extension; consists of three muscle columns (iliocostalis, longissimus, and spinalis)

◯ _____ 3. One flexes the vertebral column laterally; the pair extends the lumbar spine and fixes the 12th rib

◯ _____ 4. Extends the vertebral column and head and rotates them to the opposite side

_____ 5. Prime mover of head flexion; spasms of one causes torticolis

_____ 6. Acting together, the pair extends the head; one rotates the head and bends it laterally

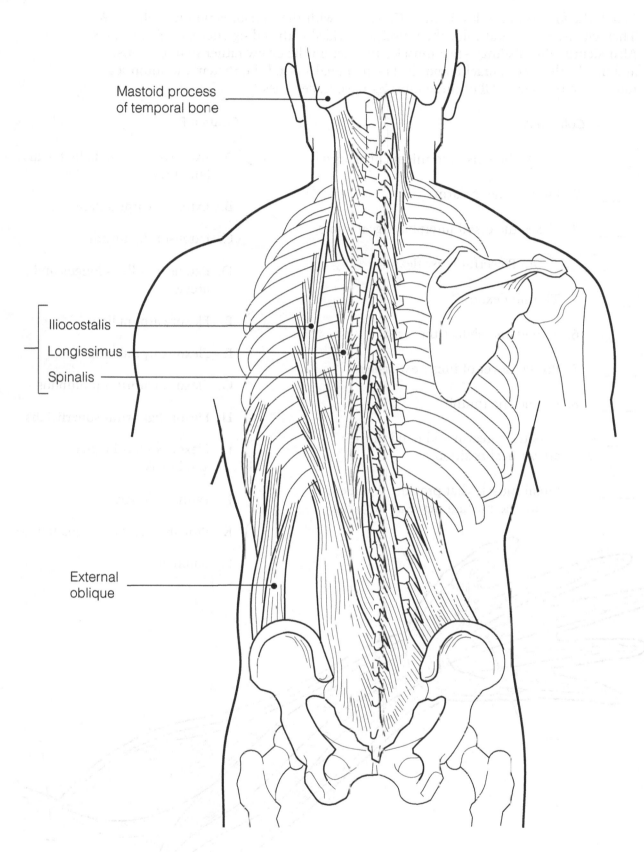

Mastoid process
of temporal bone

Iliocostalis

Longissimus

Spinalis

External
oblique

Figure 11.7

11. Match the forearm muscles listed in Column B with their major action in Column A. Then choose colors and color the muscles provided with coding circles on Figure 11.8. Also identify (by labeling)—two muscles that act on the elbow rather than the wrist and hand—the biceps brachii and the brachioradialis—and the thenar and lumbrical muscles of the hand. All of these muscles have leader lines.

Column A

_____ 1. Flexes the wrist and middle phalanges

_____ 2. Pronate the forearm

_____ 3. Flexes the distal interphalangeal joints

_____ _____ 4. Powerful wrist flexors

_____ 5. Thumb flexors

_____ 6. Extend and abduct the wrist

_____ 7. Prime mover of finger extension

_____ 8. Extend the thumb

_____ 9. Puts the forearm and hand in the anatomical position

_____ 10. Small muscle that provides a guide to locate the median nerve at the wrist

Column B

◯ A. Extensor carpi radialis longus (and brevis)

B. Extensor carpi ulnaris

C. Extensor digitorum

D. Extensor pollicis longus and brevis

◯ E. Flexor carpi radialis

◯ F. Flexor carpi ulnaris

G. Flexor digitorum profundus

◯ H. Flexor digitorum superficialis

◯ I. Flexor pollicis longus and brevis

◯ J. Palmaris longus

◯ K. Pronators teres and quadratus

L. Supinator

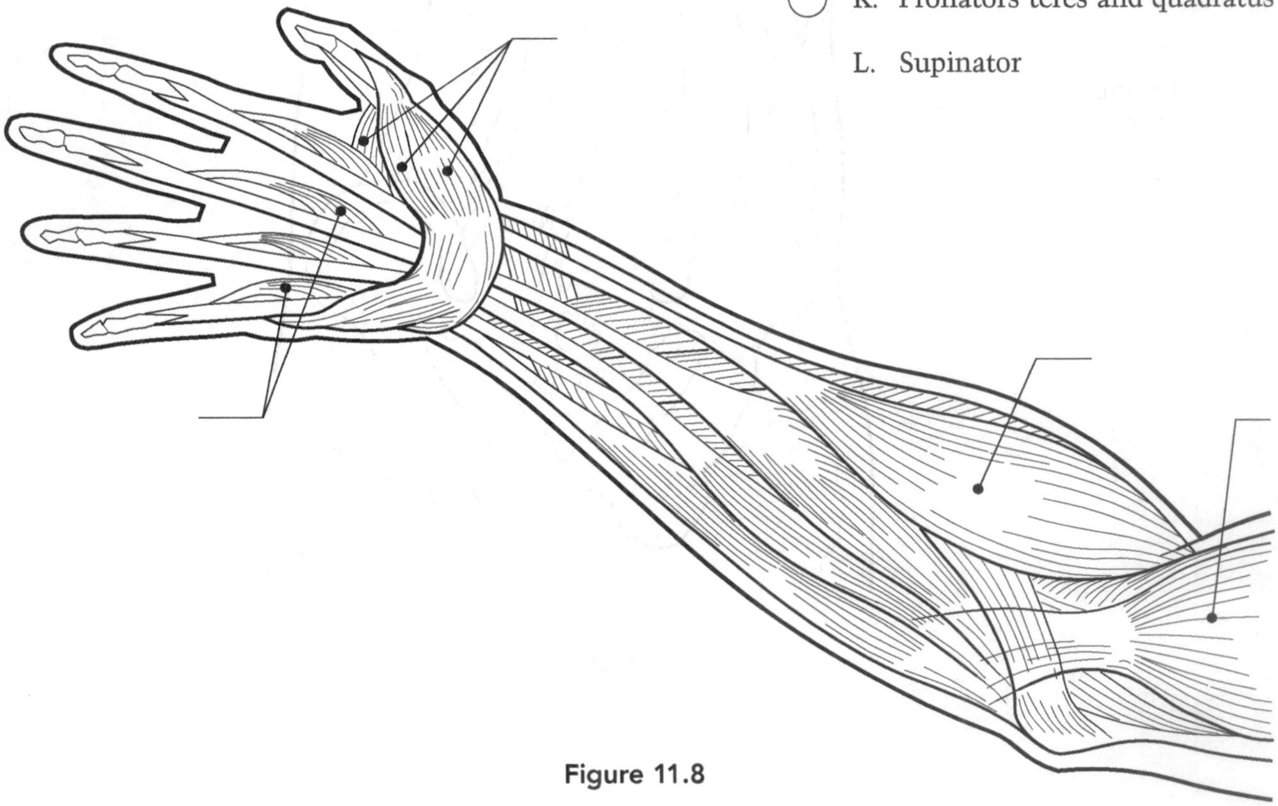

Figure 11.8

12. Name the upper limb muscles described below. Then select a different color for each muscle that has a color-coding circle and color the muscles on Figure 11.9.

1. Wrist flexor that follows the ulna

   ○ _____

2. The muscle that extends the fingers

   ○ _____

3. Two elbow flexor muscles: the first also supinates

   ○ _____

4. The second is a synergist at best

   ○ _____

5. The muscle that extends the elbow: prime mover

   ○ _____

6. A short muscle; synergist of triceps brachii

   ○ _____

7. A stocky muscle, deep to the biceps brachii; a prime mover of elbow flexion

   _____

8.–9. Two wrist extensors that follow the radius

   ○ _____

   ○ _____

10. The muscle that abducts the thumb

   ○ _____

11. The muscle that extends the thumb

   ○ _____

12. A powerful shoulder abductor; used to raise the arm overhead

   ○ _____

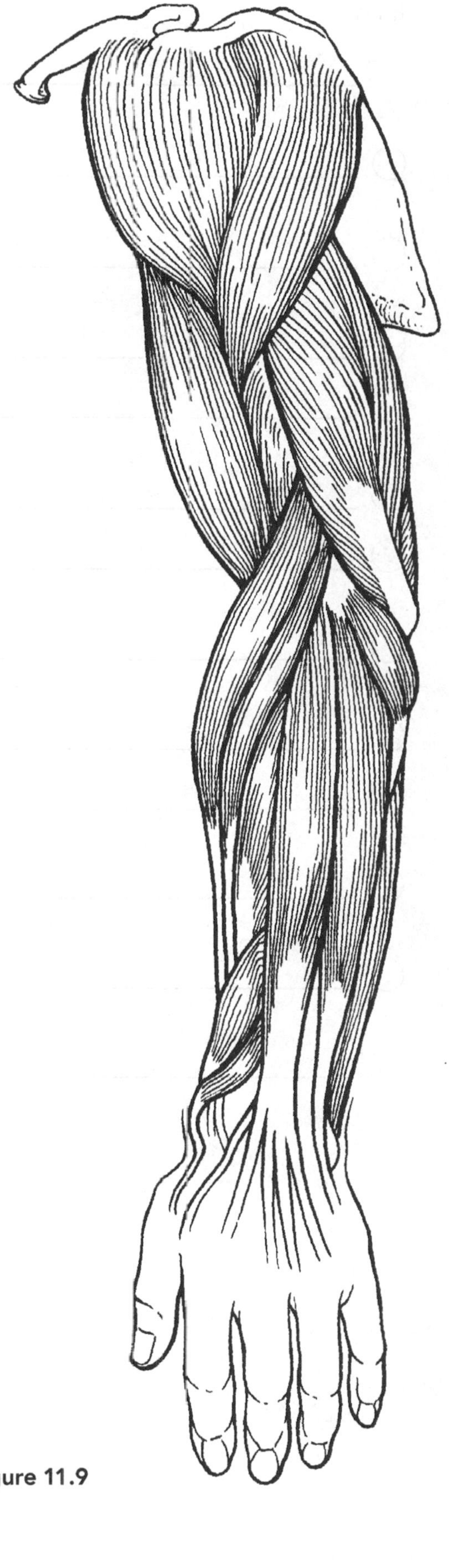

Figure 11.9

13. Name the muscles of the lower limb described below. Select a different color for each muscle that has a color-coding circle and color the circles and the muscles on Figure 11.10. Complete the illustration by labeling those muscles with leader lines.

_____ 1. Strong hip flexor, deep in pelvis; a composite of two muscles

○ _____ 2. Power extensor of the hip; forms most of buttock mass

○ _____ 3. Prime mover of plantar flexion; a composite of two muscles

○ _____ 4. Inverts and dorsiflexes the foot

○ _____ 5. The group that enables you to draw your legs to the midline of your body, as when standing at attention

○ _____ 6. The muscle group that extends the knee

○ _____ 7. The muscle group that extends the thigh and flexes the knee

○ _____ 8. The smaller hip muscle commonly used as an injection site

○ _____ 9. The thin superficial muscle of the medial thigh

○ _____ 10. A muscle enclosed within fascia that blends into the iliotibial tract; a synergist of the iliopsoas

○ _____ 11. Dorsiflexes and everts the foot; prime mover of toe extension

○ _____ 12. A superficial muscle of the lateral leg; plantar flexes and everts foot

_____ 13. A muscle deep to the soleus; prime mover of foot inversion; stabilizes the medial longitudinal arch of the foot and plantar flexes the ankle

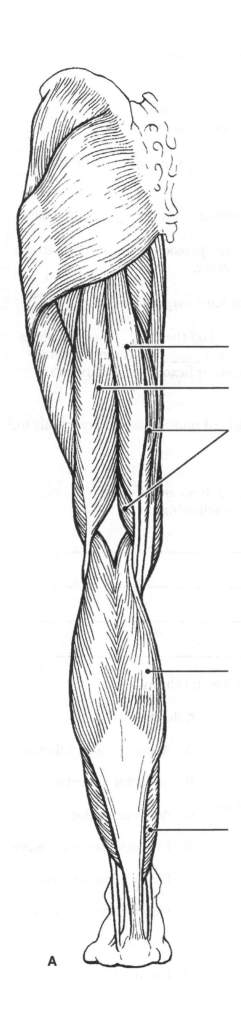

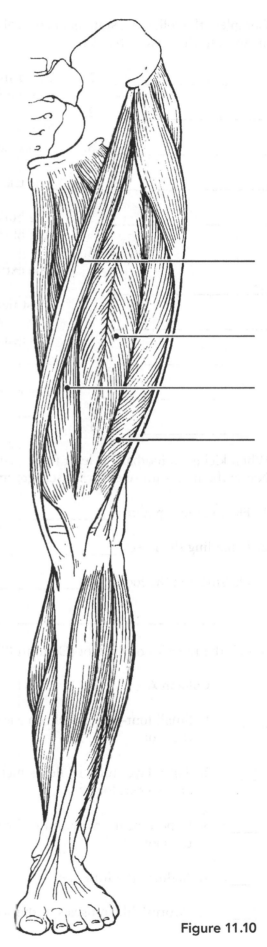

A

B

Figure 11.10

14. Complete the following statements describing muscles. Write the correct answers in the answer blanks.

_____ 1.   Three muscles, _____(1), _____(2), and _____(3), are commonly used for intramuscular injections.

_____ 2.

The insertion tendon of the _____(4) group contains a large

_____ 3.   sesamoid bone, the patella.

_____ 4.   The triceps surae insert in common into the _____(5) tendon.

_____ 5.   The bulk of the tissue of a muscle tends to lie _____(6) to the part of the body it causes to move.

_____ 6.

The extrinsic muscles of the hand originate on the _____(7).

_____ 7.

Most flexor muscles are located on the _____(8) aspect of the

_____ 8.   body; most extensors are located _____(9). An exception to this generalization is the extensor-flexor musculature of the

_____ 9.   _____(10).

_____ 10.   The pectoralis major and deltoid muscles act synergistically to _____(11) the arm.

_____ 11.

15. When kicking a football, at least three major actions of the lower limb are involved. Name the major muscles (or muscle groups) responsible for the following:

1. Flexing the hip joint: _____

2. Extending the knee: _____

3. Dorsiflexing the foot: _____

_____

16. Match the muscles of the foot (Column B) with their descriptions in column A.

Column A

_____ 1. Small four-part muscle on the dorsal aspect of the foot

_____ 2. Third layer muscle; flexes metatarsophalangeal joint of the great toe

_____ 3. Important in maintaining the transverse arch of the foot

_____ 4. Abducts the little toe

_____ 5. "Worm"-like muscles of the second muscle layer

Column B

A. Abductor digiti minimi

B. Abductor hallucis

C. Adductor hallucis

D. Extensor digitorum brevis

E. Flexor digitorum brevis

F. Flexor hallucus brevis

G. Interossei

H. Lumbricals

_____   6. Fourth layer muscles; abduct and adduct the toes

_____   7. Abducts the great toe

17. Now that you have begun your study of the skeletal muscles of the body, use what you have learned to match a specific muscle to its fascicle arrangement:

	Column A	Column B
_____	1. Deltoid	A. Convergent
_____	2. Rectus femoris	B. Fusiform
_____	3. Gracilis	C. Circular
_____	4. Gluteus maximus	D. Bipennate
_____	5. Vastus medialis	E. Multipennate
_____	6. Sphincter urethrae	F. Parallel
_____	7. Biceps brachii	G. Unipennate

18. Circle the term that does not belong in each of the following groupings.

1. Vastus lateralis   Vastus medialis   Knee extension   Biceps femoris

2. Latissimus dorsi   Pectoralis major   Synergists   Adduction of shoulder

   Antagonists

3. Gluteus minimus   Lateral rotation   Gluteus maximus   Piriformis

   Obturator externus

4. Adductor magnus   Vastus medialis   Rectus femoris   Origin on os coxa

   Iliacus

5. Lateral rotation   Teres minor   Supraspinatus   Infraspinatus

6. Tibialis posterior   Flexor digitorum longus   Fibularis longus   Foot inversion

7. Supraspinatus   Rotator cuff   Teres major   Teres minor   Subscapularis

19. Identify the numbered muscles in Figure 11.11. Match each number with one of the following muscle names. Then select a different color for each muscle that has a color-coding circle and color each muscle group on Figure 11.11.

○ _____   1. Orbicularis oris

○ _____   2. Pectoralis major

○ _____   3. External oblique

○ _____   4. Sternocleidomastoid

○ _____   5. Biceps brachii

○ _____   6. Deltoid

○ _____   7. Vastus lateralis

○ _____   8. Frontalis

○ _____   9. Rectus femoris

○ _____   10. Sartorius

○ _____   11. Gracilis

○ _____   12. Adductor group

○ _____   13. Fibularis longus

○ _____   14. Temporalis

○ _____   15. Orbicularis oculi

○ _____   16. Zygomaticus

○ _____   17. Masseter

○ _____   18. Vastus medialis

○ _____   19. Tibialis anterior

○ _____   20. Transversus abdominus

○ _____   21. Tensor fascia lata

○ _____   22. Rectus abdominis

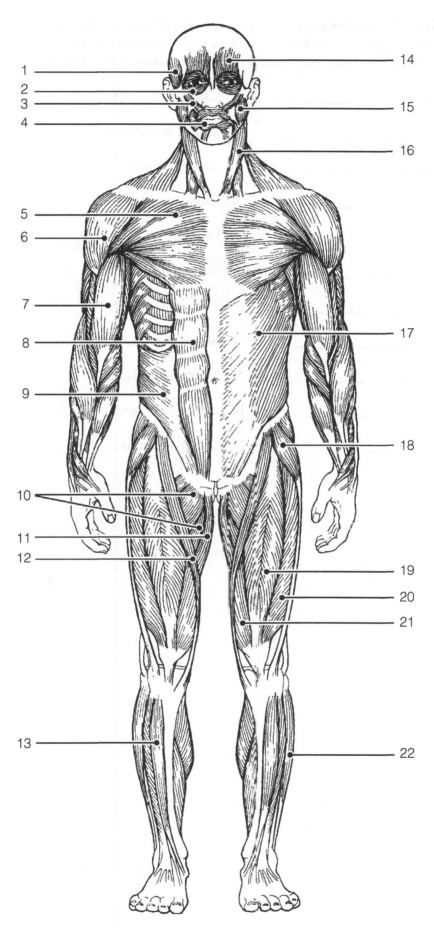

1
2
3
4
5
6
7
8
9
10
11
12
13

14
15
16
17
18
19
20
21
22

Figure 11.11

20. Identify each of the numbered muscles in Figure 11.12. Match each number with one of the following muscle names. Then select different colors for each muscle and color the coding circles and corresponding muscles on Figure 11.12.

◯ _____	1. Gluteus maximus
◯ _____	2. Adductor muscles
◯ _____	3. Gastrocnemius
◯ _____	4. Latissimus dorsi
◯ _____	5. Deltoid
◯ _____	6. Semitendinosus
◯ _____	7. Trapezius
◯ _____	8. Biceps femoris
◯ _____	9. Triceps brachii
◯ _____	10. External oblique
◯ _____	11. Gluteus medius

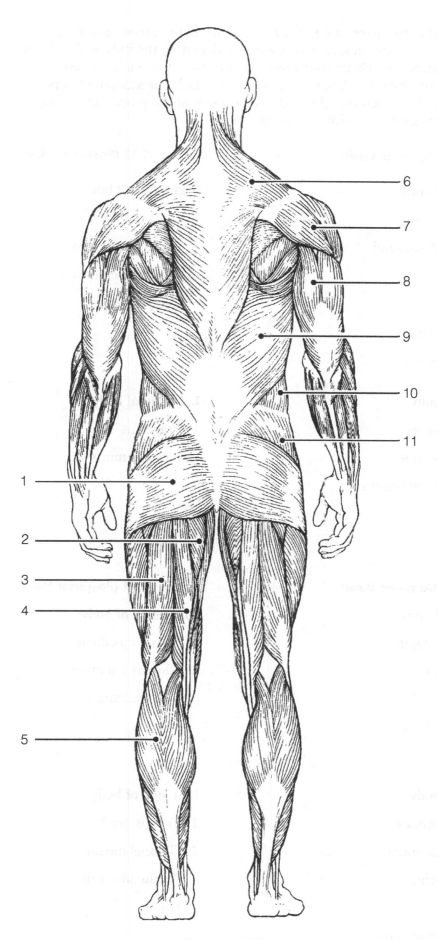

Figure 11.12

21. On the following two pages are skeleton diagrams, both anterior and posterior views. Listed below are muscles that should be drawn on the indicated sides of the skeleton diagrams. Using your muscle charts and, if necessary, referring back to bone landmarks in Chapter 7, draw the muscles as accurately as possible. Be sure to draw each muscle on the correct side of the proper figure; the muscles are grouped to minimize overlap.

Figure 11.13 (Anterior View)

Right side of body

1. Orbicularis oculi
2. Sternocleidomastoid
3. Deltoid
4. Brachialis
5. Vastus medialis
6. Vastus lateralis

Left side of body

1. Rectus femoris
2. Tibialis anterior
3. Quadratus lumborum
4. Frontalis
5. Platysma

Figure 11.13 (Posterior View)

Right side of body

1. Deltoid
2. Gluteus minimus
3. Semimembranosus
4. Occipitalis

Left side of body

1. Trapezius
2. Biceps femoris

Figure 11.14 (Anterior View)

Right side of body

1. Pectoralis major
2. Psoas major
3. Iliacus
4. Adductor magnus
5. Gracilis

Left side of body

1. Pectoralis minor
2. Rectus abdominis
3. Biceps brachii
4. Sartorius
5. Vastus intermedius

Figure 11.14 (Posterior View)

Right side of body

1. Latissimus dorsi
2. Gluteus maximus
3. Gastrocnemius

Left side of body

1. Triceps brachii
2. Gluteus medius
3. Semitendinosus
4. Soleus

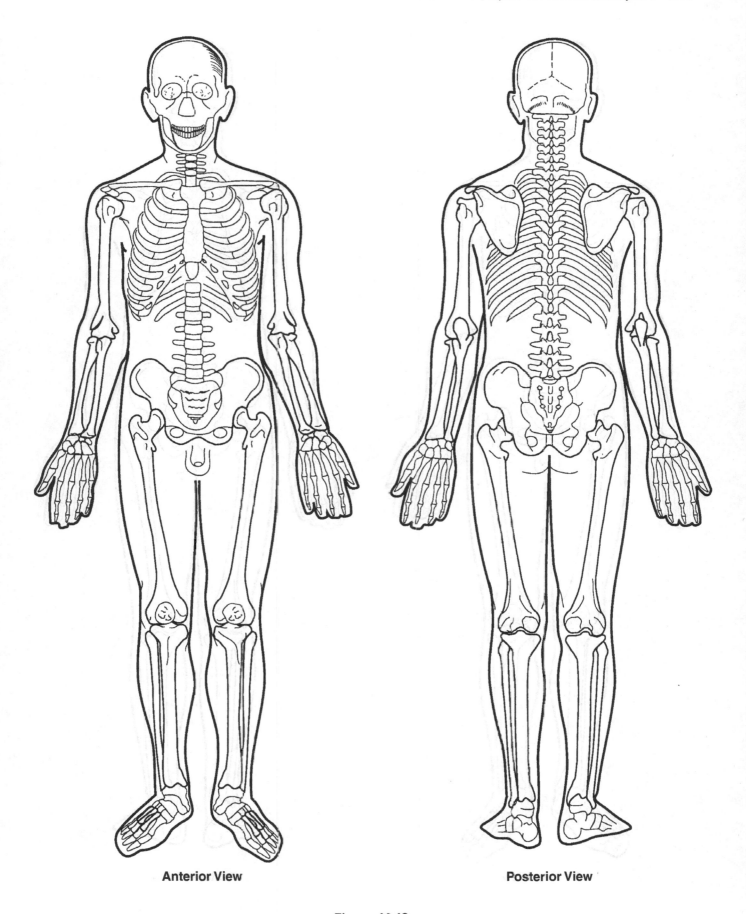

Anterior View   **Posterior View**

Figure 11.13

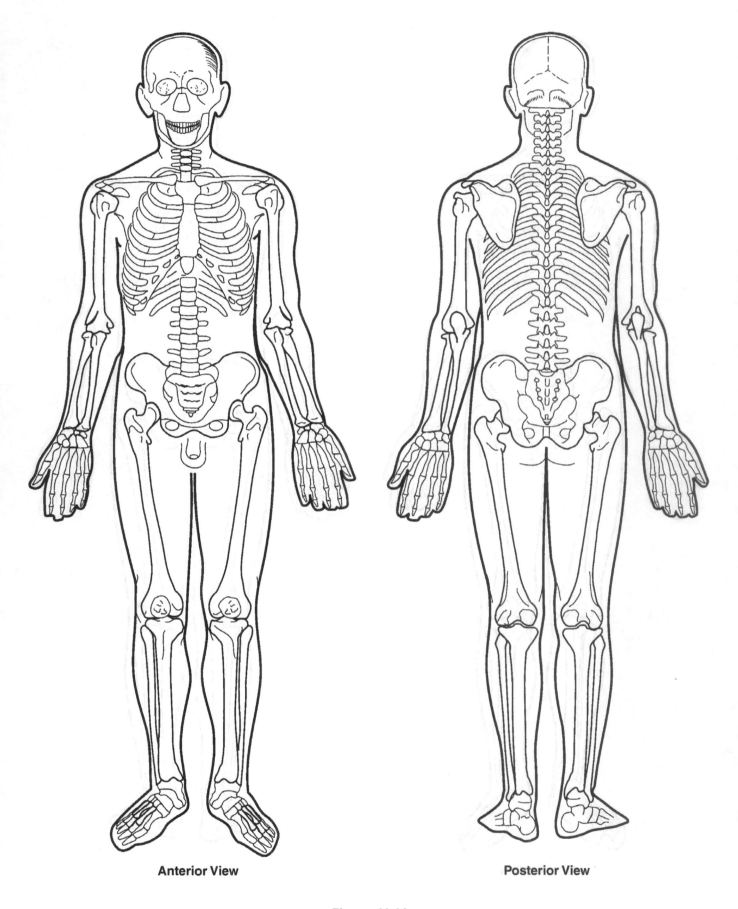

Anterior View   **Posterior View**

Figure 11.14

CHALLENGING YOURSELF

At the Clinic

1. An elderly man is brought to the clinic by his distraught wife. Among other signs, the nurse notices that the muscles on the right side of his face are slack. What nerve is not functioning properly?

2. Pete, who has been moving furniture all day, arrives at the clinic complaining of painful spasms in his back. He reports having picked up a heavy table by stooping over. What muscle group has Pete probably strained, and why are these muscles at risk when one lifts objects improperly?

3. An accident victim (who was not wearing a seat belt) was thrown from a vehicle and pronounced dead at the scene. The autopsy reveals the cause of death to be spinal cord injury resulting in paralysis of the phrenic and intercostal nerves. Why is this injury fatal?

4. Mr. Posibo has had gallbladder surgery. Now he is experiencing weakness of the muscles on his right side only, the side in which the incision was made through the abdominal musculature. Consequently, the abdominal muscles on his left side contract more strongly, throwing his torso into a lateral flexion. Mr. Posibo needs physical therapy. What abnormal spinal curvature will result if he doesn't get it and why?

5. An emergency appendectomy is performed with the incision made at the lateral edge of the right iliac abdominopelvic region. Was the rectus abdominis cut?

6. In some women who have borne several children, the uterus prolapses (everts through the weakened pelvic diaphragm). The weakening of what muscles allows this to happen?

7. What muscles must be immobilized to prevent movement of a broken clavicle?

8. Out of control during a temper tantrum, Malcolm smashed his fist through a glass door and severed several tendons at the anterior wrist. What movements are likely to be lost if tendon repair is not possible?

9. During an overambitious workout, a high school athlete pulls some muscles by forcing his knee into extension when his hip is already fully flexed. What muscles does he pull?

10. Susan, a massage therapist, was giving Mr. Graves a back rub. What two broad superficial muscles of the back were receiving the "bulk" of her attention?

11. An elderly woman with extensive osteoarthritis of her left hip joint entered the hospital to have total hip joint replacement (prosthesis implantation). After surgery, her left hip was maintained in adduction to prevent dislocation of the prosthesis while healing was occurring. Physical therapy was prescribed to prevent atrophy of the gluteal muscles during the interval of disuse. Name the gluteal muscles and describe which of their actions were being prevented while the hip was adducted.

Stop and Think

1. Do all skeletal muscles attach to a bone? If not, what else do they attach to, and how is the result different from muscle attachment to bone?

2. Are the *stated* origins and insertions always the *functional* origins and insertions? That is, is the stated origin always fixed, and does the stated insertion always move?

3. State, in general terms, how to tell by a muscle's *location* what its *action* will be.

4. How can the latissimus dorsi, which is on the back, aid in medial, instead of lateral, rotation of the humerus?

5. Where is the insertion of the tibialis anterior, which is able to invert the foot? Where is the insertion of the fibularis longus, a foot everter?

6. What is the functional reason why the muscle group on the dorsal leg (calf) is so much larger than the muscle group in the ventral region of the leg?

Closer Connections: Checking the Systems— Covering, Support, and Movement

1. People with chronic back pain occasionally get relief from a "tummy tuck." How does this help?

2. Which of the systems in this unit has the most crucial need for calcium? Why?

3. Where in each system's tissues would you find collagen fibers?

4. Which system in this unit has the most mitotically active cells? Which has the least active?

5. Which systems play a role in homeostasis of body temperature, and how do they do so?

6. Which systems have protection as a basic function? How is this function carried out?

COVERING ALL YOUR BASES

Multiple Choice

Select the best answer or answers from the choices given.

1. Which one of the following muscles has the most motor units relative to its size?

   A. Flexor pollicis longus

   B. Rectus femoris

   C. Soleus

   D. Latissimus dorsi

2. Which muscle has the largest motor units?

   A. Fibularis brevis   C. Frontalis

   B. Gluteus maximus   D. Platysma

3. Head muscles that insert on a bone include the:

   A. zygomaticus   C. buccinator

   B. masseter   D. temporalis

4. Which muscles change the position or shape of the lips?

   A. Zygomaticus   C. Platysma

   B. Orbicularis oris   D. Mentalis

5. Chewing muscles include the:

   A. buccinator   C. lateral pterygoid

   B. medial pterygoid   D. sternothyroid

6. Which of the following plays a role in swallowing?

   A. Lateral pterygoid   C. Digastric

   B. Styloglossus   D. Geniohyoid

7. The hyoid bone provides an insertion for the:

   A. digastric   C. sternothyroid

   B. pharyngeal constrictor muscles   D. thyrohyoid

8. Muscles that function in head rotation include:
   A. scalenes
   B. sternocleidomastoid
   C. splenius
   D. semispinalis capitis

9. Lateral flexion of the torso involves:
   A. erector spinae
   B. rectus abdominis
   C. quadratus lumborum
   D. external oblique

10. Muscles attached to the vertebral column include:
    A. quadratus lumborum
    B. external oblique
    C. diaphragm
    D. latissimus dorsi

11. Which of the following muscles attach to the hip bones?
    A. Transversus abdominis
    B. Rectus femoris
    C. Vastus medialis
    D. Longissimus group of erector spinae

12. Muscles that attach to the rib cage include:
    A. scalenes
    B. internal oblique
    C. trapezius
    D. psoas major

13. Which muscles are part of the pelvic diaphragm?
    A. Superficial transverse perineus
    B. Deep transverse perineus
    C. Levator ani
    D. Sphincter urethrae

14. Which of the following insert on the arm?
    A. Biceps brachii
    B. Triceps brachii
    C. Trapezius
    D. Coracobrachialis

15. Rotator cuff muscles include:
    A. supraspinatus
    B. infraspinatus
    C. teres minor
    D. teres major
    E. subscapularis

16. Muscles that help stabilize the scapula and shoulder joint include:
    A. triceps brachii
    B. biceps brachii
    C. trapezius
    D. rhomboids

17. Which muscles insert on the radius?
    A. Triceps brachii
    B. Biceps brachii
    C. Flexor carpi radialis
    D. Pronator teres

18. Which muscles insert on the femur?
    A. Quadratus lumborum
    B. Iliacus
    C. Gracilis
    D. Tensor fasciae latae

19. Which of these thigh muscles causes movement at the hip joint?
    A. Rectus femoris
    B. Biceps femoris
    C. Vastus lateralis
    D. Semitendinosus

20. Leg muscles that can cause movement at the knee joint include:
    A. tibialis anterior
    B. fibularis longus
    C. gastrocnemius
    D. soleus

21. Muscles that function in lateral hip rotation include:
    A. gluteus medius
    B. gluteus maximus
    C. obturator externus
    D. tensor fasciae latae

22. Hip adductors include:
    A. sartorius
    B. gracilis
    C. vastus medialis
    D. pectineus

23. Which muscles are in the posterior compartment of the leg?
    A. Flexor digitorum longus
    B. Flexor hallucis longus
    C. Extensor digitorum longus
    D. Fibularis tertius

24. Which of the following insert distal to the tarsus?
    A. Soleus
    B. Tibialis anterior
    C. Extensor hallucis longus
    D. Fibularis longus

25. Which muscles are contracted while standing at attention?
    A. Iliocostalis
    B. Rhomboids
    C. Tensor fascia latae
    D. Flexor digitorum longus

26. The main muscles used when doing chin-ups are:

    A. triceps brachii and pectoralis major

    B. infraspinatus and biceps brachii

    C. serratus anterior and external oblique

    D. latissimus dorsi and brachialis

27. In walking, which two lower limb muscles keep the forward-swinging foot from dragging on the ground?

    A. pronator teres and popliteus

    B. flexor digitorum longus and popliteus

    C. adductor longus and abductor digiti minimi in foot

    D. gluteus medius and tibialis anterior

28. The major muscles used in doing push-ups are:

    A. biceps brachii and brachialis

    B. supraspinatus and subscapularis

    C. coracobrachialis and latissimus dorsi

    D. triceps brachii and pectoralis major

29. Someone who sticks out a thumb to hitch a ride is _____ the thumb.

    A. extending   C. adducting

    B. abducting   D. opposing

30. Which are ways in which muscle names have been derived?

    A. Attachments   C. Function

    B. Size   D. Location

Word Dissection

For each of the following word roots, fill in the literal meaning and give an example, using a word found in this chapter.

Word root	Translation	Example
1. agon		
2. brevis		
3. ceps		
4. cleido		
5. gaster		
6. glossus		
7. pectus		
8. perone		
9. rectus		

12

NEURAL TISSUE

Overview

The nervous system is the control center and communication network of the body, and its overall function is the maintenance of homeostasis. The nervous system and the endocrine system acting in a complementary way regulate and coordinate the activities of the body's organ systems. The nervous system generally affects short-term control, whereas endocrine regulation is slower to develop and the general effect is long-term control.

In this chapter the introductory material begins with an overview of the nervous system and the cellular organization in neural tissue. The emphasis for the remainder of the chapter concerns the structure and function of neurons, information processing, and the functional patterns of neural organization.

The integration and interrelation of the nervous system with all the other body systems is an integral part of understanding many of the body's activities, which must be controlled and adjusted to meet changing internal and external environmental conditions.

LEVEL 1 Review of Chapter Objectives

1. Describe the anatomical and functional divisions of the nervous system.
2. Sketch and label the structure of a typical neuron and describe the functions of each component.
3. Classify neurons on the basis of their structure and function.
4. Describe the locations and functions of neuroglia.
5. Explain how the resting potential is created and maintained.
6. Describe the events involved in the generation and propagation of an action potential.
7. Discuss the factors that affect the speed with which action potentials are propagated.
8. Describe the general structure of synapses in the CNS and PNS.
9. Discuss the events that occur at a chemical synapse.
10. Describe the major types of neurotransmitters and neuromodulators, and discuss their effects on post-synaptic membranes.
11. Discuss the interactions that make possible the processing of information in neural tissue.

[L1]   Multiple Choice

Place the letter corresponding to the correct answer in the space provided.

OBJ. 1 _____ 1. The two major anatomical subdivisions of the nervous system are:
 a. central nervous system (CNS) and peripheral nervous system (PNS)
 b. somatic nervous system and autonomic nervous system
 c. neurons and neuroglia
 d. afferent division and efferent division

OBJ. 1 _____ 2. The central nervous system (CNS) consists of:
 a. afferent and efferent division
 b. somatic and visceral division
 c. brain and spinal cord
 d. autonomic and somatic division

OBJ. 1 _____ 3. The primary function(s) of the nervous system include:
 a. providing sensation of the internal and external environments
 b. integrating sensory information
 c. regulating and controlling peripheral structures and systems
 d. a, b, and c are correct

OBJ. 2 _____ 4. Neurons are responsible for:
 a. creating a three-dimensional framework for the CNS
 b. performing repairs in damaged neural tissue
 c. information transfer and processing in the nervous system
 d. controlling the interstitial environment

OBJ. 2 _____ 5. The region of a neuron with voltage-gated sodium channels is the:
 a. soma
 b. dendrite
 c. axon hillock
 d. perikaryon

OBJ. 3 _____ 6. Neurons are classified on the basis of their *structure* as:
 a. astrocytes, oligodendrocytes, microglia, ependymal
 b. efferent, afferent, association, interneurons
 c. motor, sensory, association, interneurons
 d. anaxonic, unipolar, bipolar, multipolar

OBJ. 3 _____ 7. Neurons are classified on the basis of their *function* as:
 a. unipolar, bipolar, multipolar
 b. motor, sensory, association
 c. somatic, visceral, autonomic
 d. central, peripheral, somatic

OBJ. 4 _____ 8. The two major cell populations of neural tissue are:
 a. astrocytes and oligodendrocytes
 b. microglia and ependymal cells
 c. satellite cells and Schwann cells
 d. neurons and neuroglia

OBJ. 4 _____ 9. The types of glial cells in the central nervous system are:

    a. astrocytes, oligodendrocytes, microglia, ependymal cells

    b. unipolar, bipolar, multipolar cells

    c. efferent, afferent, association cells

    d. motor, sensory, interneuron cells

OBJ. 4 _____ 10. The white matter of the CNS represents a region dominated by the presence of:

    a. astrocytes

    b. oligodendrocytes

    c. neuroglia

    d. unmyelinated axons

OBJ. 5 _____ 11. Depolarization of the membrane will shift the membrane potential toward:

    a. −90 mV

    b. −85 mV

    c. −70 mV

    d. 0 mV

OBJ. 5 _____ 12. The resting membrane potential (RMP) of a typical neuron is:

    a. −85 mV

    b. −60 mV

    c. −70 mV

    d. 0 mV

OBJ. 6 _____ 13. If resting membrane potential is −70 mV and the threshold is −60 mV, a membrane potential of −62 mV will:

    a. produce an action potential

    b. depolarize the membrane to 0 mV

    c. repolarize the membrane to −80 mV

    d. not produce an action potential

OBJ. 6 _____ 14. At the site of an action potential the membrane contains:

    a. an excess of negative ions inside and an excess of negative ions outside

    b. an excess of positive ions inside and an excess of negative ions outside

    c. an equal amount of positive and negative ions on either side of the membrane

    d. an equal amount of positive ions on either side of the membrane

OBJ. 6 _____ 15. If the resting membrane potential is −70 mV, a hyperpolarized membrane is:

    a. 0 mV

    b. +30 mV

    c. −80 mV

    d. −65 mV

OBJ. 7 _____ 16. A node along the axon represents an area where there is:

    a. a layer of fat

    b. interwoven layers of myelin and protein

    c. a gap in the cell membrane

    d. an absence of myelin

OBJ. 7 ____ 17. The larger the diameter of the axon:

    a. the slower an action potential is conducted

    b. the greater the number of action potentials

    c. the faster an action potential will be conducted

    d. the less effect it will have on action potential conduction

OBJ. 7 ____ 18. The two most important factors that determine the rate of action potential conduction are:

    a. the number of neurons and the length of their axons

    b. the strength of the stimulus and the rate at which the stimulus is applied

    c. the presence or absence of a myelin sheath and the diameter of the axon

    d. a, b, and c are correct

OBJ. 8 ____ 19. At an electrical synapse, the presynaptic and postsynaptic membranes are locked together at:

    a. gap junctions

    b. synaptic vesicles

    c. myelinated axons

    d. neuromuscular junctions

OBJ. 8 ____ 20. Chemical synapses differ from electric synapses, because chemical synapses:

    a. involve direct physical contact between cells

    b. involve a neurotransmitter

    c. contain integral proteins called connexons

    d. propagate action potentials quickly and efficiently

OBJ. 8 ____ 21. The effect of a neurotransmitter on the postsynaptic membrane depends on the:

    a. nature of the neurotransmitter

    b. properties of the receptor

    c. overall condition of the synapse

    d. all of the above

OBJ. 9 ____ 22. Exocytosis and the release of acetylcholine into the synaptic cleft is triggered by:

    a. calcium ions leaving the cytoplasm

    b. calcium ions flooding into the axoplasm

    c. reabsorption of calcium into the endoplasmic reticulum

    d. active transport of calcium into synaptic vesicles

OBJ. 9 ____ 23. The normal stimulus for neurotransmitter release is the depolarization of the synaptic knob by the:

    a. release of calcium ions

    b. binding of Ach receptor sites

    c. opening of voltage-regulated calcium channels

    d. arrival of an action potential

OBJ. 10 ____ 24. Inhibitory or hyperpolarizing CNS neurotransmitters include:

    a. acetylcholine and norepinephrine

    b. dopamine and serotonin

    c. glutamate and aspartate

    d. substance P and endorphins

OBJ. 10 _____ 25. An excitatory postsynaptic potential (EPSP) is:

a. an action potential complying with the all-or-none principle

b. a result of a stimulus strong enough to produce threshold

c. the same as a nerve impulse along an axon

d. a depolarization produced by the arrival of a neuro-transmitter

OBJ. 10 _____ 26. An inhibitory postsynaptic potential (IPSP) is a:

a. depolarization produced by the effect of a neurotransmitter

b. transient hyperpolarization of the postsynaptic membrane

c. repolarization produced by the addition of multiple stimuli

d. reflection of the activation of an opposing transmembrane potential

OBJ. 11 _____ 27. The most important determinants of neural activity are:

a. EPSP–IPSP interactions

b. the presence or absence of myelin on the axon of the neuron

c. the type and number of stimuli

d. the strength of the stimuli and the rate at which the stimuli are applied

OBJ. 11 _____ 28. The reason(s) that active neurons need ATP is to support:

a. the synthesis, release, and recycling of neurotransmitter molecules

b. the recovery from action potentials

c. the movement of materials to and from the soma via axoplasmic flow

d. a, b, and c are correct

OBJ. 11 _____ 29. Sensory neurons are responsible for carrying impulses:

a. to the CNS

b. away from the CNS

c. to the PNS

d. from the CNS to the PNS

OBJ. 11 _____ 30. Interneurons, or associated neurons, differ from sensory and motor neurons because of their:

a. structural characteristics

b. inability to generate action potentials

c. exclusive location in the brain and spinal cord

d. functional capabilities

OBJ. 11 _____ 31. Efferent pathways consist of axons that carry impulses:

a. toward the CNS

b. from the PNS to the CNS

c. away from the CNS

d. to the spinal cord and into the brain

OBJ. 11 _____ 32. Graded potentials that develop in the postsynaptic membrane in response to a neurotransmitter are:

a. presynaptic facilitators

b. presynaptic inhibitors

c. presynaptic potentials

d. postsynaptic potentials

OBJ. 11 _____ 33. The addition of stimuli occurring in rapid succession is:

    a. temporal summation

    b. spatial summation

    c. facilitation

    d. the absolute refractory period

[L1]   Completion

Using the terms below, complete the following statements.

cholinergic	temporal summation	saltatory
proprioceptors	autonomic nervous system	threshold
afferent	neuromodulators	adrenergic
collaterals	divergence	IPSP
electrochemical gradient	electrical	skeletal muscle fiber
spatial summation	microglia	

OBJ. 1   1. The visceral motor system that provides automatic, involuntary regulation of smooth and cardiac muscle and glandular secretions is the _____.

OBJ. 2   2. The "branches" that enable a single neuron to communicate with several other cells are called _____.

OBJ. 3   3. Sensory information is brought to the CNS by means of the _____ fibers.

OBJ. 4   4. In times of infection or injury the type of neuroglia that will increase in numbers is _____.

OBJ. 5   5. The sum of all the chemical and electrical forces active across the cell membrane is known as the _____.

OBJ. 6   6. An action potential occurs only if the membrane is lowered to the level known as _____.

OBJ. 7   7. The process that conducts impulses along an axon at a high rate of speed is called _____ conduction.

OBJ. 8   8. The type of synapse where direct physical contact between the cells occurs is a(an) _____.

OBJ. 8   9. The neuromuscular junction is a synapse where the postsynaptic cell is a(an) _____.

OBJ. 9   10. Chemical synapses that release the neurotransmitter acetylcholine are known as _____ synapses.

OBJ. 9   11. Chemical synapses that release the neurotransmitter norepinephrine are known as _____ synapses.

OBJ. 10   12. Compounds that influence the postsynaptic cells' response to a neurotransmitter are called _____.

OBJ. 11   13. Addition of stimuli occurring in rapid succession at a single synapse is called _____.

OBJ. 11   14. Addition of stimuli arriving at different locations of the nerve cell membrane is called _____.

OBJ. 11   15. Sensory neurons that monitor the position of skeletal muscles and joints are called _____.

OBJ. 11   16. The spread of nerve impulses from one neuron to several neurons is called
_____.

OBJ. 11   17. A graded hyperpolarization of the postsynaptic membrane is referred to
as a(n) _____.

[L1] Matching

Match the terms in column B with the terms in column A. Use letters for answers in the spaces provided.

Part I	Column A	Column B
OBJ. 1 _____	1. somatic nervous system	A astrocytes
OBJ. 1 _____	2. autonomic nervous system	B –70 mV
		C interoceptors
OBJ. 2 _____	3. axons	D transmit action potentials
OBJ. 3 _____	4. visceral sensory neurons	E +30 mV
OBJ. 3 _____	5. somatic sensory neurons	F involuntary control
OBJ. 4 _____	6. neuroglia	G supporting brain cells
OBJ. 4 _____	7. maintain blood–brain barriers	H voluntary control
		I exteroceptors
OBJ. 5 _____	8. sodium channel inactivation	
OBJ. 5 _____	9. resting membrane potential (neuron)	

Part II	Column A	Column B
OBJ. 6 _____	10. potassium ion movement	J gap synapsis
OBJ. 7 _____	11. unmyelinated axons	K cAMP
OBJ. 7 _____	12. nodes of Ranvier	L continuous conduction
OBJ. 8 _____	13. electrical synapses	M serotonin
OBJ. 9 _____	14. norepinephrine	N depolarization
OBJ. 9 _____	15. GABA	O saltatory conduction
OBJ. 10 _____	16. CNS neurotransmitter	P simultaneous multiple synapses
OBJ. 11 _____	17. second messenger	
OBJ. 11 _____	18. EPSP	Q repolarization
OBJ. 11 _____	19. spatial summation	R inhibitory effect
		S adrenergic synapse

[L1]   Drawing/Illustration Labeling

Identify each numbered structure by labeling the following figures:

OBJ. 3
OBJ. 4
Figure 12.1   **Structure and Classification of Neurons**

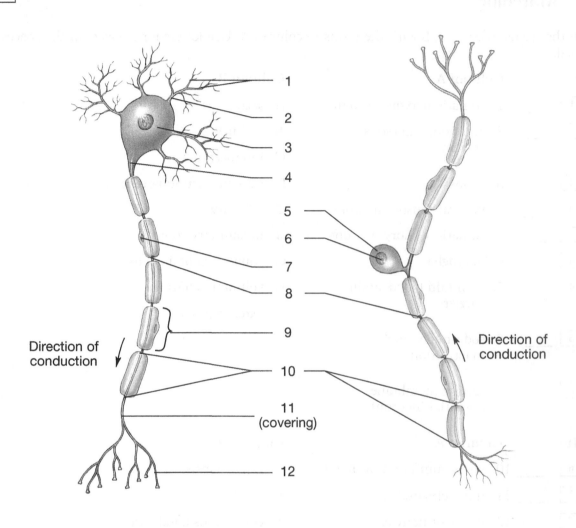

	← Based on function →	
(13)		(14)
(type of neuron)		(type of neuron)

1 _____	8 _____
2 _____	9 _____
3 _____	10 _____
4 _____	11 _____
5 _____	12 _____
6 _____	13 _____
7 _____	14 _____

OBJ. 3   **Figure 12.2   Neuron Classification (Based on Structure)**
(Identify the types of neurons)

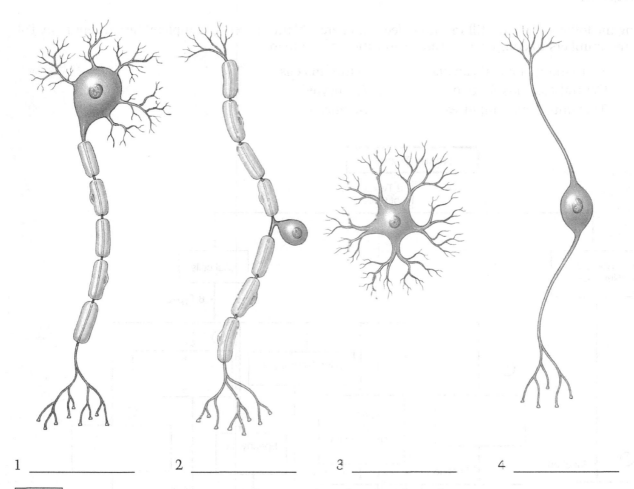

1 _____   2 _____   3 _____   4 _____

OBJ. 11   **Figure 12.3   Organization of Neuronal Pools (Identify each process)**

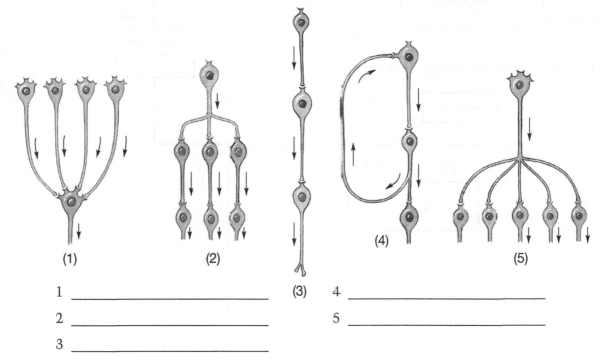

(1)   (2)   (3)   (4)   (5)

1 _____   (3)   4 _____

2 _____   5 _____

3 _____

LEVEL 2 Concept Synthesis

Concept Map I

Using the following terms, fill in the circled, numbered, blank spaces to complete the concept map. Follow the numbers to comply with the organization of the map.

Surround peripheral ganglia   Schwann cells
Central Nervous System   Astrocytes
Transmit Nerve Impulses   Microglia

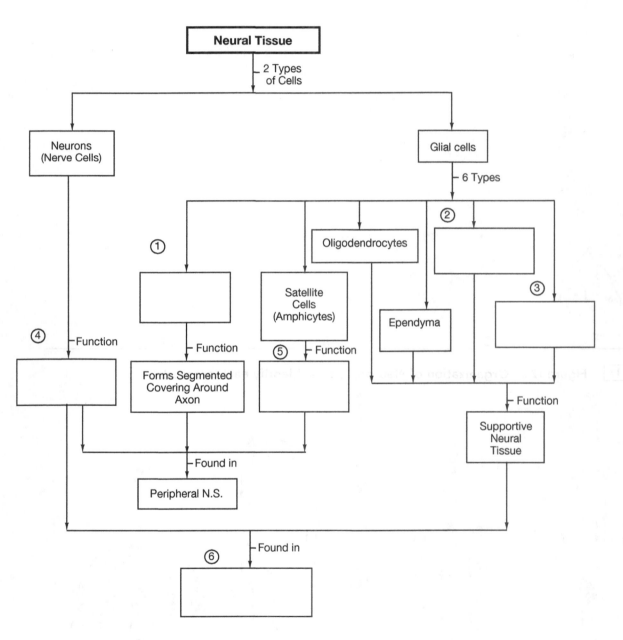

Concept Map II

Using the following terms, fill in the circled, numbered, blank spaces to complete the concept map. Follow the numbers to comply with the organization of the map.

Brain   Peripheral nervous system
Afferent division   Smooth muscle
Sympathetic N.S.   Somatic Nervous System
Motor System

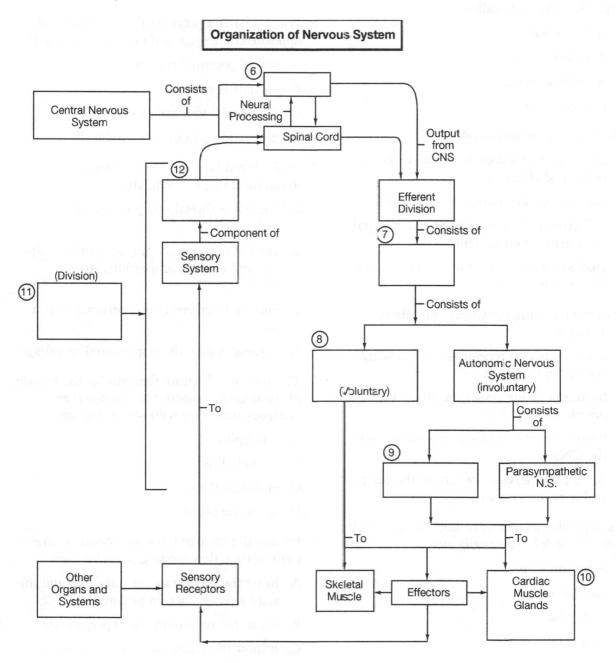

| COVERING ALL YOUR BASES |

[L2]   Multiple Choice

Select the best answer or answers from the choices given.

1. When sensory information is relayed from one processing center to another in the brain, the pattern is called:

   A. convergence

   B. divergence

   C. serial processing

   D. reverberation

2. Interneurons are responsible for:

   A. carrying instructions from the CNS to peripheral effectors

   B. delivery of information to the CNS

   C. collecting information from the external or internal environment

   D. analysis of sensory inputs and coordination of motor outputs

3. Sensory (ascending) pathways distribute information:

   A. from peripheral receptors to processing centers in the brain

   B. from processing centers in the brain to peripheral receptors

   C. from motor pathways to interneurons in the CNS

   D. the central nervous system to the peripheral nervous system

4. The type of cells that surround the nerve cell bodies in peripheral ganglia are:

   A. Schwann cells

   B. satellite cells

   C. microglia

   D. oligodendrocytes

5. Schwann cells are glial cells responsible for:

   A. producing a complete neurilemma around peripheral axons

   B. secretion of cerebrospinal fluid

   C. phagocytic activities in the neural tissue of the PNS

   D. surrounding nerve cell bodies in peripheral ganglia

6. When a barrier prevents the movement of opposite charges toward one another, a a(n):

   A. action potential occurs

   B. current is produced

   C. potential difference exists

   D. generation potential is produced

7. In the formula, Current = Voltage/Resistance, i.e., $I = V/R$, the

   A. current is directly proportional to resistance

   B. current is inversely proportional to voltage and directly proportional to resistance

   C. current is inversely proportional to voltage

   D. current is directly proportional to voltage

8. The neuromodulators that inhibit the release of the neurotransmitter *substance P* at synapses that relay pain sensations are:

   A. endorphins

   B. enkephalins

   C. endomorphins

   D. all of the above

9. During the relative refractory period a larger-than-normal depolarizing stimulus can:

   A. bring the membrane to threshold and initiate a second action potential

   B. cause the membrane to hyperpolarize

   C. inhibit the production of an action potential

   D. cause a membrane to reject a response to further stimulation

10. Saltatory conduction conducts impulses along an axon:

    A. two to three times more slowly than continuous conduction

    B. five to seven times faster than continuous conduction

    C. at a rate determined by the strength of the stimulus

    D. at a velocity determined by the rate at which the stimulus is applied

11. In type C fibers action potentials are conducted at speeds of approximately:

    A. 2 mph

    B. 40 mph

    C. 150 mph

    D. 500 mph

12. The larger the diameter of the axon, the:

    a. slower the rate of transmission

    B. greater the resistance

    C. faster the rate of transmission

    D. size of the axon doesn't affect rate of transmission or resistance

13. *Facilitation* in the neuron's transmembrane potential toward threshold refers to:

    a. any shift that makes the cell more sensitive to further stimulation

    B. repolarization produced by the addition of multiple stimuli

    C. transient hyperpolarization of a postsynaptic membrane

    D. a, b, and c are correct

14. Sensory neurons that provide information about the external environment through the sense of sight, smell, hearing, and touch are called:

    a. proprioceptors

    B. exteroceptors

    C. enviroceptors

    D. interoceptors

15. The main functional difference between the autonomic nervous system and the somatic nervous system is that the activities of the ANS are:

    a. primarily voluntary controlled

    B. primarily involuntary or under "automatic" control

    C. involved with affecting skeletal muscle activity

    D. involved with carrying impulses to the CNS

16. Motor (descending) pathways begin at CNS centers concerned with motor control and end at:

    a. the cerebral cortex in the brain

    B. the cerebrum for conscious control

    C. the skeletal muscles they control

    D. reflex arcs within the spinal cord

17. *Reverberation* in neural circuits refers to collateral axons that:

    a. involve several neuronal pools processing the same information at one time

    B. relay sensory information from one processing center to another in the brain

    C. synapse on the same postsynaptic neuron

    D. use positive feedback to stimulate presynaptic neurons

18. *Presynaptic facilitation* refers to the:

    a. calcium channels remaining open for a longer period, thus increasing the amount of neurotransmitter released

    B. reduction of the amount of neurotransmitter released due to the closing of calcium channels in the synaptic knob

    C. a larger than usual depolarizing stimulus necessary to bring the membrane potential to threshold

    D. shift in the transmembrane potential toward threshold, which makes the cell more sensitive to further stimulation

[L2]   Completion

Using the terms below, complete the following statements.

association	tracts	preganglionic fibers	current
gated	stroke	postganglionic fibers	convergence
perikaryon	voltage	hyperpolarization	nuclei
parallel	ganglia	nerve impulse	

1. The cytoplasm that surrounds a neuron's nucleus is referred to as the
   _____.

2. Nerve cell bodies in the PNS are clustered together in masses called
   _____.

3. Movement of charged objects, such as ions, is referred to as _____.

4. The potential difference that exists across a membrane or other barrier is expressed
   as a(n) _____.

5. Ion channels that open or close in response to specific stimuli are called
   _____ channels.

6. The loss of positive ions, which causes a shift in the resting potential to as much
   as –80 mV, is referred to as _____.

7. An action potential traveling along an axon is called a(n) _____.

8. Interruption of blood supply to the brain by a circulatory blockage or other vascular
   problem is called a(n) _____.

9. Axons extending from the CNS to a ganglion are called _____.

10. Axons connecting the ganglionic cells with peripheral effectors are known as
    _____.

11. Neurons that may be situated between sensory and motor neurons are called
    _____ neurons.

12. Several neurons synapsing on the same postsynaptic neuron are called
    _____.

13. Several neuronal pools processing the same information at one time are called
    _____ processing.

14. Collections of nerve cell bodies in the CNS are termed _____.

15. The axonal bundles that make up the white matter of the CNS are called
    _____.

[L2]   Short Essay

Briefly answer the following questions in the spaces provided below.

1. What are the four major functions of the nervous system?

2. What are the major components of the central nervous system and the peripheral nervous system?

3. What four types of glial cells are found in the central nervous system?

4. Functionally, what is the major difference between neurons and neuroglia?

5. Using a generalized model, list and describe the four steps that describe an action potential.

6. What role do the nodes of Ranvier play in the conduction of an action potential?

7. What functional mechanism distinguishes an adrenergic synapse from a cholinergic synapse?

8. What is the difference between an EPSP and an IPSP and how does each type affect the generation of an action potential?

9. How are neurons categorized functionally and how does each group function?

10. What is the difference between *divergence* and *convergence*?

LEVEL 3 Critical Thinking/Application

Using principles and concepts learned about the nervous system, answer the following questions. Write your answers on a separate sheet of paper.

1. How does starting each day with a few cups of coffee and a cigarette affect a person's behavior and why?

2. Guillain-Barré syndrome is a degeneration of the myelin sheath that ultimately may result in paralysis. What is the relationship between degeneration of the myelin sheath and muscular paralysis?

3. Even though microglia are found in the CNS, why might these specialized cells be considered a part of the body's immune system?

4. Substantiate the following statement concerning neurotransmitter function: "The effect on the postsynaptic membrane depends on the characteristics of the receptor, not on the nature of the neurotransmitter."

5. What physiological mechanisms operate to induce threshold when a single stimulus is not strong enough to initiate an action potential?

13

THE CENTRAL NERVOUS SYSTEM

Student Objectives

When you have completed the exercises in this chapter, you will have accomplished the following objectives:

The Brain

1. Describe the process of brain development.
2. Name the major regions of the adult brain.
3. Define the term *ventricle* and indicate the location of the ventricles of the brain.
4. Indicate the major lobes, fissures, and functional areas of the cerebral cortex.
5. Explain lateralization of hemisphere function.
6. Differentiate between commissures, association fibers, and projection fibers.
7. State the general function of the basal nuclei.
8. Describe the location of the diencephalon and name its subdivisions.
9. Identify the three major regions of the brain stem, and note the general function of each area.
10. Describe the structure and function of the cerebellum.
11. Localize the limbic system and the reticular formation and explain the role of each functional system.

Higher Mental Functions

12. Define *EEG* and distinguish between alpha, beta, theta, and delta waves.
13. Compare and contrast the events and importance of slow-wave and REM sleep, and indicate how their patterns change through life.
14. Describe consciousness in clinical terms.
15. Compare and contrast the stages and categories of memory.
16. Describe the relative roles of the major brain structures believed to be involved in fact and skill memories.

Protection of the Brain

17. Describe how meninges, cerebrospinal fluid, and the blood-brain barrier protect the CNS.
18. Describe the formation of cerebrospinal fluid, and follow its circulatory pathway.
19. Describe the cause (if known) and major signs and symptoms of cerebrovascular accidents, Alzheimer's disease, Huntington's disease, and Parkinson's disease.

The Spinal Cord

20. Describe the gross and microscopic structure of the spinal cord.
21. List the major spinal cord tracts and classify each as a motor or sensory tract.
22. Distinguish between flaccid and spastic paralysis and between paralysis and paresthesia.

Diagnostic Procedures for Assessing CNS Dysfunction

23. List and explain several techniques used to diagnose brain disorders.

The human brain is a marvelous biological computer. It can receive, store, retrieve, process, and dispense information with almost instantaneous speed. Together, the brain and spinal cord make up the central nervous system (CNS). By way of inputs from the peripheral nervous system, the CNS is advised of changes in both the external environment and internal body conditions. After perception, integration, and coordination of this knowledge, the CNS dispatches instructions to initiate appropriate responses.

Included in Chapter 13 are student exercises on the regions and associated functions of the brain and spinal cord. Traumatic and degenerative disorders of the central nervous system are also considered, as are topics such as EEGs, sleep, and selected higher mental functions.

BUILDING THE FRAMEWORK

The Brain

1. Figure 13.1 (which continues on the next page) shows diagrams of embryonic development. Arrange the diagrams in the correct order by numbering each one. Where possible, insert the time, in days or weeks, of each stage of development. Label all structures that have leader lines.

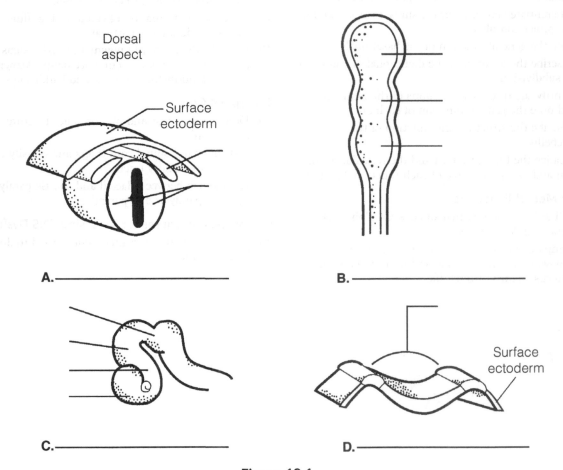

Figure 13.1

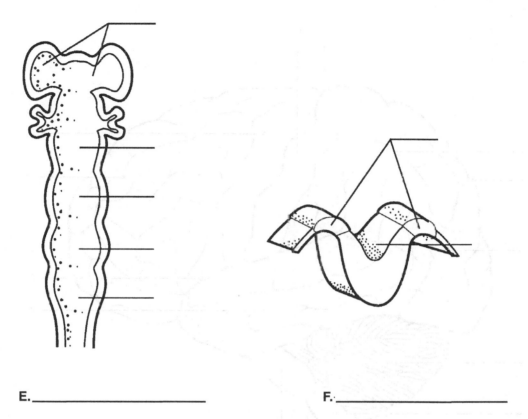

E._____   F._____

Figure 13.1

2. Figure 13.2 is a diagram of the right lateral view of the human brain. First, match the letters on the diagram with the following list of terms and insert the appropriate letters in the answer blanks. Then, select different colors for each of the areas of the brain with a color-coding circle and use them to color the diagram. If an identified area is part of a lobe, use the color you selected for the lobe but use stripes for that area.

○ ____ 1. Frontal lobe   ____ 7. Lateral fissure

○ ____ 2. Parietal lobe   ____ 8. Central sulcus

○ ____ 3. Temporal lobe   ○ ____ 9. Cerebellum

○ ____ 4. Precentral gyrus   ○ ____ 10. Medulla

____ 5. Parieto-occipital fissure   ○ ____ 11. Occipital lobe

○ ____ 6. Postcentral gyrus   ○ ____ 12. Pons

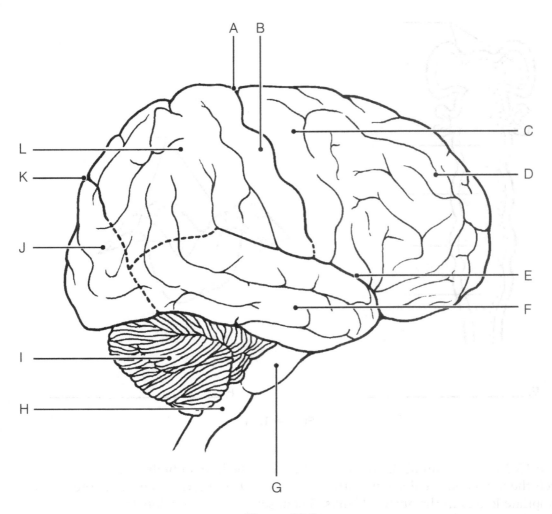

Figure 13.2

3. Fill in the table below by indicating the adult brain structures formed from each of the secondary brain vesicles and the adult neural canal regions. Some of that information has already been entered.

Secondary brain vesicle	Adult brain structures	Neural canal regions
Telencephalon		Lateral ventricles
Diencephalon	Diencephalon	
Mesencephalon		
Metencephalon	Brain stem: pons; cerebellum	
Myelencephalon		

4. Figure 13.3 illustrates a "see-through" brain showing the positioning of the ventricles and connecting canals or apertures. Correctly identify all structures having leader lines by using the key choices provided below. One of the lateral ventricles has already been identified. Color the spaces filled with cerebrospinal fluid blue.

Key Choices

A. Anterior horn   D. Fourth ventricle   G. Lateral aperture

B. Central canal   E. Inferior horn   H. Third ventricle

C. Cerebral aqueduct   F. Interventricular foramen

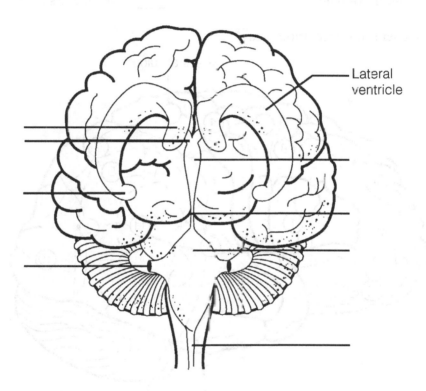

Lateral
ventricle

Figure 13.3

5. Figure 13.4 shows a left lateral view of the brain with some of its functional areas indicated by numbers. These areas are listed below. Identify each cortical area by its corresponding number on the diagram. Color the diagram as you wish.

_____	Primary motor cortex	_____	Primary somatosensory cortex
_____	Premotor cortex	_____	Somatosensory association area
_____	Visual cortex	_____	Auditory cortex
_____	Prefrontal cortex	_____	Broca's area
_____	Frontal eye field	_____	Wernicke's area
_____	General interpretation area		

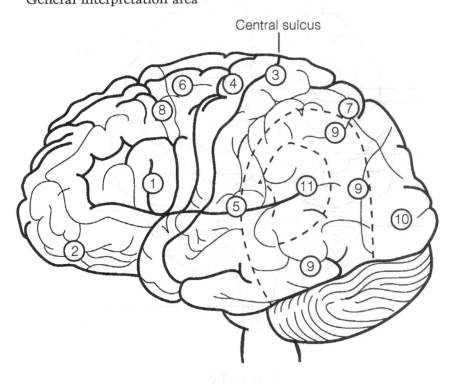

Figure 13.4

6. Some of the following brain structures consist of gray matter; others are white matter. Write G (for gray) or W (for white) as appropriate.

_____ 1. Cortex of cerebellum   _____ 5. Pyramids

_____ 2. Internal capsule   _____ 6. Olives

_____ 3. Anterior commisure   _____ 7. Thalamic nuclei

_____ 4. Medial lemniscus   _____ 8. Cerebellar peduncle

7. If a statement is true, write the letter T in the answer blank. If a statement is false, correct the underlined word(s) and write the correct word(s) in the answer blank.

_____ 1. The primary somatosensory area of the cerebral hemisphere(s) is found in the <u>precentral</u> gyrus.

_____ 2. Cortical areas involved in audition are found in the <u>occipital</u> lobe.

_____ 3. The primary motor area in the <u>temporal</u> lobe is involved in the initiation of voluntary movements.

_____ 4. The specialized motor speech area is located at the base of the precentral gyrus in an area called <u>Wernicke's</u> area.

_____ 5. The right cerebral hemisphere receives sensory input from the <u>right</u> side of the body.

_____ 6. The <u>pyramidal</u> tract is the major descending voluntary motor tract.

_____ 7. The primary motor cortex is located in the <u>postcentral</u> gyrus.

_____ 8. Centers for control of repetitious or stereotyped motor skills are found in the <u>primary motor</u> cortex.

_____ 9. The largest parts of the motor humunculus are the lips, tongue, and <u>toes</u>.

_____ 10. Sensations such as touch and pain are integrated in the <u>primary sensory cortex</u>.

_____ 11. The primary visual cortex is in the <u>frontal</u> lobe of each cerebral hemisphere.

_____ 12. In most humans, the area that controls the comprehension of language is located in the <u>left</u> cerebral hemisphere.

_____ 13. Elaboration of the <u>visual</u> cortex sets humans apart from other animals.

_____ 14. Complex sensory memory patterns are stored in an area called the <u>general interpretation</u> area.

_____ 15. Areas in the cerebral hemisphere opposite the ones containing Broca's and Wernicke's areas are centers for <u>cognitive</u> language.

_____ 16. Cerebral dominance designates the hemisphere that is dominant for <u>memory</u>.

_____ 17. The right cerebral hemisphere of <u>left</u>-handed humans is usually involved with intuition, poetry, and creativity.

8. Using the key choices, select the terms identified in the following descriptions by inserting the appropriate letters in the answer blanks.

Key Choices

A. Basal nuclei   D. Cerebral hemispheres   G. Septum pellucidum

B. Brain stem   E. Cortex   H. Ventricles

C. Cerebellum   F. Diencephalon   I. White matter

_____ 1. The four major subdivisions of the adult brain

_____ 2. Contain cerebrospinal fluid

_____ 3. Masses of gray matter embedded deep within the cerebral white matter

_____ 4. Myelinated fiber tracts

_____ 5. Consists of the midbrain, pons, and medulla

_____ 6. Separates the lateral ventricles

_____ 7. Thin layer of gray matter on outer surface of cerebral hemispheres and cerebellum

_____ 8. Account for more than 60% of the total brain weight

_____ 9. Consists of the hypothalamus, thalamus, and epithalamus

9. Figure 13.5 is a diagram of the sagittal view of the human brain. First, match the letters on the diagram with the following list of terms and insert the appropriate letters in the answer blanks. Then, color the brain stem areas blue and the areas where cerebrospinal fluid is found yellow.

_____ 1. Cerebellum

_____ 2. Cerebral aqueduct

_____ 3. Cerebral hemisphere

_____ 4. Cerebral peduncle

_____ 5. Choroid plexus

_____ 6. Corpora quadrigemina

_____ 7. Corpus callosum

_____ 8. Fornix

_____ 9. Fourth ventricle

_____ 10. Hypothalamus

_____ 11. Medulla oblongata

_____ 12. Optic chiasma

_____ 13. Pineal body

_____ 14. Pituitary gland

_____ 15. Pons

_____ 16. Thalamus (intermediate mass)

_____ 17. Third ventricle

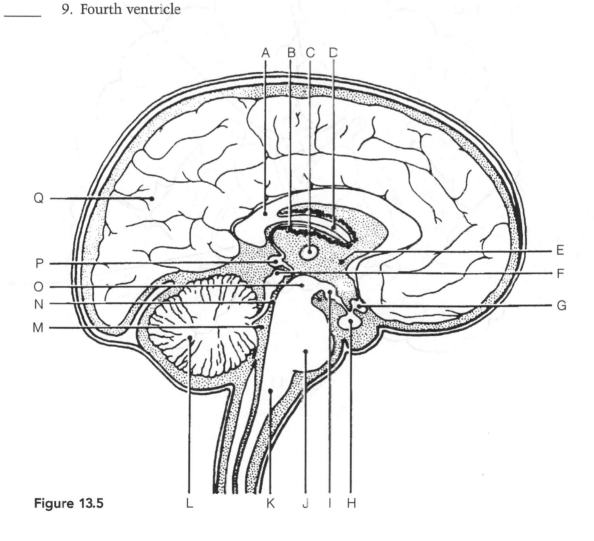

Figure 13.5

10. Figure 13.6 is a diagram of a frontal section through the brain, as indicated on the orientation diagram. Label the ventricles and the longitudinal fissure, both of which are indicated by leader lines. Color code and color the structures listed below.

◯ Cerebral cortex   ◯ Corpus callosum

◯ Basal nuclei   ◯ Internal capsule

◯ Thalamus   ◯ Hypothalamus

◯ Cerebral white matter ◯ Septum pellucidum

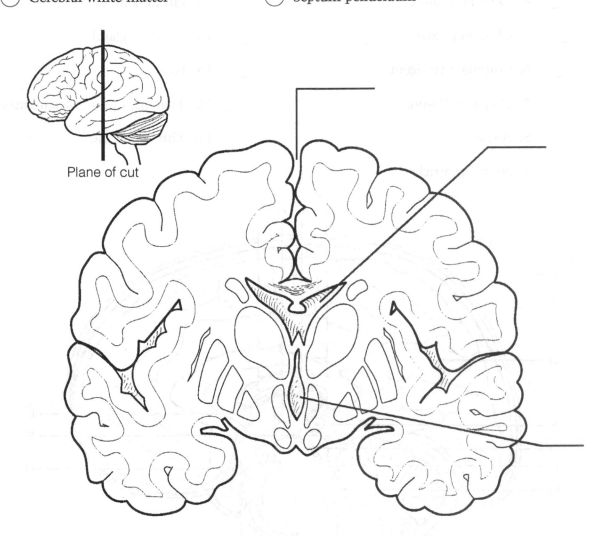

Plane of cut

Figure 13.6

11. Referring back as necessary to the brain areas listed in Exercise 9, match the appropriate brain structures with the following descriptions. Insert the terms selected in the answer blanks.

_____   1. Site of regulation of water balance, body temperature, rage, and pain centers; the main visceral (autonomic) center of brain

_____   2. Reflex centers involved in regulating respiratory rhythm in conjunction with lower brain stem centers

_____   3. Responsible for the regulation of posture and coordination of skeletal muscle movements

_____   4. Important relay station for afferent fibers, traveling to the sensory cortex for interpretation

_____   5. Contains autonomic centers that regulate blood pressure and respiratory rhythm, as well as coughing and sneezing centers

_____   6. Midbrain area consisting of large, descending motor tracts

_____   7. Influences body rhythms; interacts with the biological clock

_____   8. Location of middle cerebellar peduncles

_____   9. Locations of visual and auditory reflex centers

12. In the horizontal section shown in Figure 13.7 (see plane of cut in inset), identify by color coding and coloring, the structures listed below.

◯ Caudate nucleus   ◯ Choroid plexus   ◯ Putamen

◯ Claustrum   ◯ Pineal body   ◯ Thalamus

◯ Corpus callosum

Then, using the leader lines provided, correctly identify the fornix, inferior horn of the lateral ventricle, third ventricle, insula, internal capsule, and septum pellucidum.

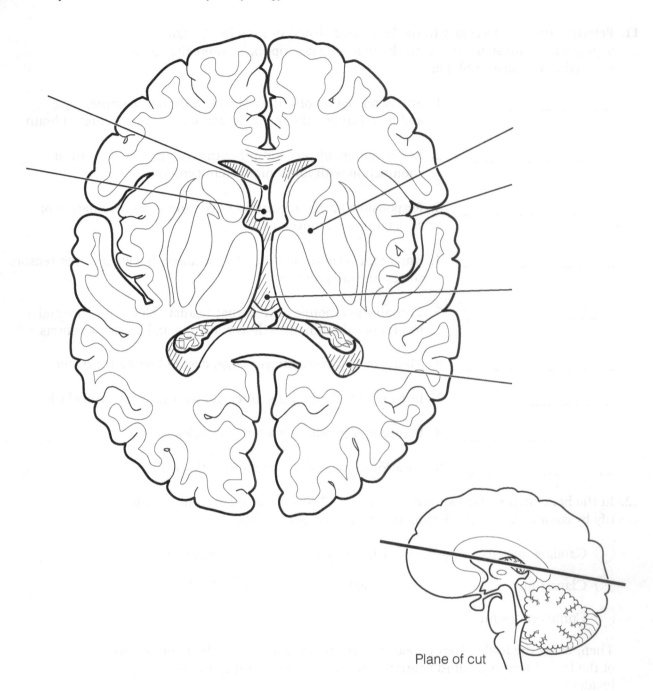

Figure 13.7

13. Figure 13.8 shows the brain stem and associated diencephalon. Using the key choices, label all structures provided with leader lines. Then, color code and color the following structures or groups of structures.

◯ All cranial nerves   ◯ Medulla oblongata   ◯ Midbrain

◯ Diencephalon   ◯ Pons   ◯ Infundibulum

Key Choices

A. Abducens nerve (VI)

B. Accessory nerve (XI)

C. Cerebral peduncle

D. Decussation of the pyramids

E. Facial nerve (VII)

F. Glossopharyngeal nerve (IX)

G. Hypoglossal nerve (XII)

H. Infundibulum

I. Lateral geniculate body

J. Mammillary body

K. Oculomotor nerve (III)

L. Optic chiasma

M. Optic nerve (II)

N. Optic tract

O. Pons

P. Spinal chord

Q. Thalamus

R. Trigeminal nerve (V)

S. Vagus nerve (X)

T. Vestibulocochlear nerve (VIII)

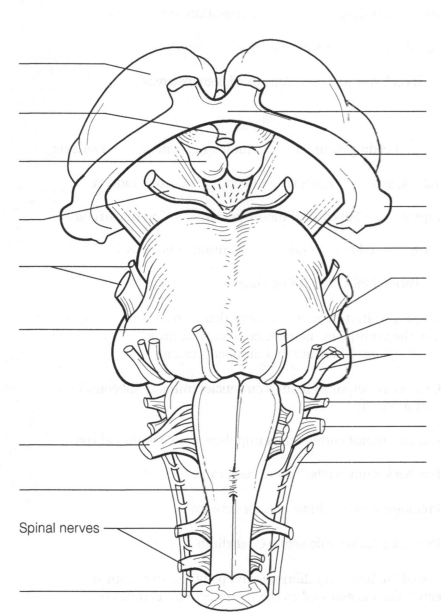

Spinal nerves

Figure 13.8

14. Circle the term that does not belong in each of the following groupings.

    1. Connects cerebral hemispheres   Corpus callosum   Cerebral peduncles

       Commissure

    2. Hypophysis cerebri   Pineal gland   Produces hormones   Pituitary gland

    3. Medulla oblongata   Pons   Cardiac center   Decussation of pyramids

    4. Prefrontal cortex   Distractability   Loss of initiative   Paralysis

    5. Nonverbal components   Speech disorder   Affective language areas

       Loss of vocal expression

    6. Lack of cerebral dominance   Reading disorder   Motor impairment   Dyslexia

    7. Projection fibers   Internal capsule   Association fibers   Corona radiata

    8. Basal nuclei   Internal capsule   Subcortical motor nuclei   Corpora striata

    9. Caudate nucleus   Putamen   Globus pallidus   Lentiform nucleus

    10. Cerebellum   Vermis   Parietal lobe   Arbor vitae

15. Below is a listing of events involved in voluntary motor activity that also considers the role of the cerebellum. Put the event(s) in their correct temporal (time) sequence by numbering them 1 to 5. (*Note:* There are *two* number 5 events.)

_____   1. Cerebellar output to brain stem nuclei initiates subconscious motor output.

_____   2. Primary motor cortex sends impulses along pyramidal tracts.

_____   3. Feedback from cerebellum to cerebrum.

_____   4. Premotor cortex initiates motor activity.

_____   5. Pyramidal collaterals signal cerebellum.

_____   6. Visual, auditory, equilibrium, and body sensory input to cerebellum is assessed as the motor activity is initiated.

16. Relative to the limbic and reticular systems, identify the correct system for each characteristic described below. Insert L for the limbic system or R for the reticular system in the answer blanks.

_____ 1. Maintains cortex in a conscious state

_____ 2. Includes the RAS

_____ 3. Originates in primitive rhinencephalon

_____ 4. Its hypothalamus is the gatekeeper for visceral responses

_____ 5. Site of rage and anger; moderated by cerebral cortex

_____ 6. Has far-flung axonal connections

_____ 7. Functioning may be associated with psychosomatic illness

_____ 8. Helps distinguish and filter out unimportant stimuli

_____ 9. Depressed by alcohol and some drugs; severe injury may cause coma

_____ 10. Severe injury may result in personality changes

_____ 11. Extends through the brain stem

_____ 12. Includes cingulate gyrus, hippocampus, and some thalamic nuclei

_____ 13. Contains raphe nuclei, large-celled and small-celled regions

_____ 14. Located in the medial aspect of both hemispheres

Higher Mental Functions

1. Using the key choices, identify the brain wave patterns described below. Write your answers in the answer blanks. (*Note:* Hz = hertz or cycles per second.)

Key Choices

A. Alpha   B. Beta   C. Delta   D. Theta

_____ 1. Slow, synchronous waves with an average frequency of 10 Hz

_____ 2. More irregular than beta waves; normal in children but abnormal in awake adults

_____ 3. Recorded when a person is awake and relaxed, with eyes closed

_____ 4. High-amplitude waves with a very low frequency (4 Hz or less)

_____ 5. Recorded during sleep or anesthesia

_____ 6. Recorded when a person is awake and fully alert

2. Complete the following statements by writing the missing terms in the answer blanks.

_____ 1.

_____ 2.

_____ 3.

_____ 4.

_____ 5.

_____ 6.

_____ 7.

_____ 8.

_____ 9.

1. A recording of the electrical activity of the brain is called an __(1)__ . Brain wave patterns are identified by their __(2)__ , which are measured in __(3)__ . When large numbers of neurons fire synchronously, the __(4)__ of the waves increases, a condition typical of the normal adult in a state of __(5)__ . Brain waves that are abnormally slow or fast are typical when __(6)__ is interfered with. Very fast brain waves with large spikes are common in a patient who suffers from uncontrollable seizures, a condition called __(7)__ . The most severe form of this disease is called __(8)__ , during which a sensory "aura" is followed by unconsciousness and intense convulsions. A record showing the complete absence of brain waves is clinical evidence of __(9)__ .

3. For any of the following statements about sleep that are true, write T in the answer blanks. For any false statements, correct the underlined word by writing the correct word in the answer blanks. (*Note:* EEG = electro-encephalogram; REM = rapid eye movements; RAS = reticular activating system; NREM = non-rapid eye movements.)

_____ 1. Circadian rhythms recur every <u>12</u> hours.

_____ 2. The unconscious state, when arousal is not possible, is called <u>sleep</u>.

_____ 3. During sleep, vital <u>cortical</u> activities continue.

_____ 4. The sleep-wake cycle is most likely timed by the <u>RAS</u>.

_____ 5. During deep sleep, vital signs decline, and EEG waves <u>decrease</u> in amplitude.

_____ 6. During REM sleep, vital signs increase, most muscle movement is inhibited, and the EEG shows <u>alpha</u> waves.

_____ 7. In normal adults, NREM and REM sleep periods alternate, with <u>REM</u> sleep accounting for the greatest proportion of sleeping time.

_____ 8. Most dreaming occurs during REM sleep, when certain brain neurons release more norepinephrine and <u>serotonin</u>.

_____ 9. Deprivation of <u>NREM</u> sleep may lead to emotional instability.

_____ 10. In the elderly, <u>slow wave (stage 4)</u> sleep declines and may disappear.

_____ 11. Two important sleep disorders are insomnia and <u>coma</u>.

4. State the definition of *consciousness* as proposed by cognitive scientists, and list the three underlying suppositions.

_____

_____

_____

_____

5. List the four clinical states of consciousness, starting with the highest state of cortical activity.

_____ , _____ , _____ , _____

6. Categorize the following descriptions as characteristic of either long-term memory (L) or short-term memory (S). Insert your answers in the answer blanks.

_____ 1. Very brief   _____ 4. May last a lifetime

_____ 2. Lasts from seconds to hours   _____ 5. Limited capacity

_____ 3. Enormous capacity   _____ 6. Association process required

7. List four factors that promote memory consolidation (the transfer of information from short-term to long-term memory).

1. _____

2. _____

3. _____

4. _____

8. Distinguish between fact memory and skill memory by defining each term and by comparing how each type of memory is best remembered.

1. Fact memory _____

_____

_____

2. Skill memory _____

_____

_____

9. Several proposed pathways and regions, including the amygdala, hippocampus, thalamus, hypothalamus, prefrontal cortex, and basal forebrain, may be involved in the consolidation of fact memory. In terms of these pathways, respond to the questions that follow by writing your answers in the answer blanks.

_____ 1. According to present assumptions, are the initial connections between old memories and the new perceptions made in the cortex or in the subcortical structures?

_____ 2. The feedback pathway makes connections between which structure and the cerebral sensory cortex?

_____ 3. This feedback pathway seems to transform the initial perception into what?

_____ 4. Which structure appears to associate memories formed through different senses?

_____ 5. What is the result if both the amygdala and the hippocampus are destroyed?

_____ 6. Can a person with amnesia still learn skills?

_____ 7. Does widespread cortical damage appear to impair memory?

_____ 8. Human memory is characterized by great redundancy. If you had to find memory traces or "engrams," where would you look?

_____ 9. As opposed to fact memory, skill memory is believed to be processed/mediated by which brain regions?

Protection of the Brain

1. Figure 13.9 shows a frontal view of the meninges of the brain at the level of the superior sagittal (dural) sinus. First, label arachnoid villi and falx cerebri on the figure. Then, select different colors for each of the following structures and use them to color the diagram.

   ○ Dura mater   ○ Pia mater

   ○ Arachnoid   ○ Subarachnoid space

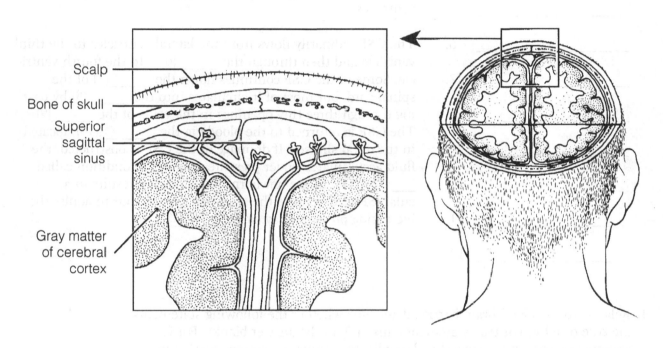

Scalp

Bone of skull

Superior sagittal sinus

Gray matter of cerebral cortex

Figure 13.9

2. Referring again to the structures in Figure 13.9, identify the meningeal (or associated) structures described here. Write the correct terms in the answer blanks.

   _____ 1. Innermost covering of the brain; delicate and vascular

   _____ 2. Structures that return cerebrospinal fluid to the venous blood in the dural sinuses

   _____ 3. Its outer layer forms the periosteum of the skull

   _____ 4. Contains cerebrospinal fluid

   _____ 5. Location of major arteries and veins

   _____ 6. Contains venous blood

   _____ 7. Attaches to crista galli of the ethmoid bone

3. Complete the following statements by inserting the missing terms in the answer blanks.

_____ 1.

_____ 2.

_____ 3.

_____ 4.

_____ 5.

_____ 6.

_____ 7.

_____ 8.

_____ 9.

_____ 10.

_____ 11.

_____ 12.

1. The composition of the cerebrospinal fluid (CSF) is similar to
   _____(1), from which it arises. The concentration of _____(2)
2. in the CSF is important in the control of cerebral blood flow
   and breathing.
3.
   The CSF is formed by capillary knots called _____(3), which
4. hang from the roof of each _____(4). Circulation of the CSF is
   aided by the beating cilia of the _____(5) cells lining the
5. ventricles.

6. The CSF ordinarily flows from the lateral ventricles to the third
   ventricle and then through the _____(6) to the fourth ventri-
7. cle. Some of the CSF continues down the _____(7) of the
   spinal cord, but most of it circulates into the _____(8) by pass-
8. ing through three tiny openings in the walls of the _____(9).
   The CSF is returned to the blood via the _____(10), located
9. in the dural sinuses. If drainage of the CSF is obstructed, the
   fluid accumulates under pressure, causing a condition called
10. _____(11). In the newborn, the condition results in an
    enlarged head because the skull can expand, but in adults the
11. increasing pressure may cause _____(12).

4. Relative to the blood-brain barrier, determine whether the following statements
are true or false. For true statements, insert T in the answer blanks. For false
statements, correct the underlined word(s) by writing the correct word(s) in the
answer blanks.

_____ 1. Desmosomes are the epithelial structures that make brain capillaries relatively impermeable.

_____ 2. Water, glucose, and metabolic wastes pass freely from the blood
   into the brain, but proteins and most drugs are normally
   prevented from entering the brain.

_____ 3. Calcium ions, in particular, are actively pumped from the brain
   because they modify neural thresholds.

_____ 4. The blood-brain barrier is absent in the cerebrum.

_____ 5. Alcohol and other water-soluble molecules easily cross the blood-
   brain barrier.

_____ 6. The blood-brain barrier is incompletely developed in newborns.

5. Match the brain disorders listed in Column B with the conditions described in Column A. Place the correct answers in the answer blanks.

Column A	Column B
_____ 1. Slight and transient brain injury	A. Alzheimer's disease
_____ 2. Traumatic injury that destroys brain tissue	B. Cerebral edema
_____ 3. Total nonresponsiveness to stimulation	C. Cerebrovascular accident (CVA)
_____ 4. May cause medulla oblongata to be wedged into foramen magnum by pressure of blood	D. Coma
_____ 5. After head injury, retention of water by brain	E. Concussion
_____ 6. Results when a brain region is deprived of blood or exposed to prolonged ischemia; probably reflects excessive NO release	F. Contusion
_____ 7. Reversible CVA	G. Intracranial hemorrhage
_____ 8. Progressive degeneration of the brain with abnormal protein deposits	H. Multiple sclerosis
_____ 9. Autoimmune disorder with extensive demyelination	I. Transient ischemic attack (TIA)

The Spinal Cord

1. Using the key choices, select the correct terms as defined by the following descriptions. Write the correct letters in the answer blanks.

Key Choices

A. Decussation	C. Gray matter	E. Sensory
B. Funiculus	D. Motor	F. Somatotopy

_____ 1. Its central location separates white matter into columns

_____ 2. Crossing of fibers from one side to the other side of the cord

_____ 3. Precise spatial relationship of most spinal cord pathways to an orderly mapping of the body

_____ 4. Pathways from the brain to the spinal cord

_____ 5. Ascending spinal cord pathways

_____ 6. A white column of the cord containing several tracts

2. Figure 13.10 is a cross-sectional view of the spinal cord. First identify the areas listed in the key choices by inserting the correct letters next to the appropriate leader lines on parts A and B of the figure. Then, color the bones of the vertebral column in part B gold.

Key Choices

A. Central canal

B. Columns of white matter

C. Conus medullaris

D. Dorsal (posterior) horn

E. Dorsal root

F. Dorsal root ganglion

G. Filum terminale

H. Spinal nerve

I. Ventral (anterior) horn

J. Ventral root

On part A, color the butterfly-shaped gray matter gray, and color the spinal nerves and roots yellow. Finally, select different colors to identify the following structures and use them to color the figure.

◯ Pia mater   ◯ Dura mater   ◯ Arachnoid

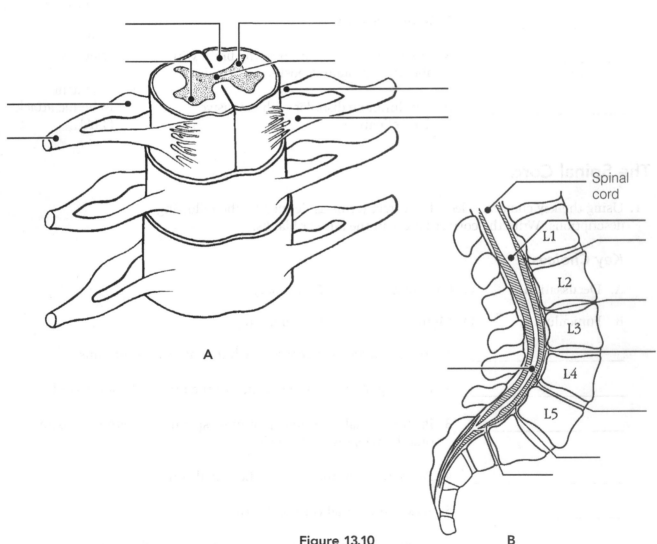

A

Spinal cord

L1

L2

L3

L4

L5

Figure 13.10   B

3. Complete the following statements by writing the missing terms in the answer blanks.

_____ 1.

_____ 2.

_____ 3.

_____ 4.

_____ 5.

_____ 6.

_____ 7.

_____ 8.

_____ 9.

The spinal cord extends from the _____(1) of the skull to the _____(2) region of the vertebral column. The meninges, which cover the spinal cord, extend more inferiorly to form a sac, from which cerebrospinal fluid can be withdrawn without damage to the spinal cord. This procedure is called a _____(3). _____(4) pairs of spinal nerves arise from the cord. Of these, _____(5) pairs are cervical nerves, _____(6) pairs are thoracic nerves, _____(7) pairs are lumbar nerves, and _____(8) pairs are sacral nerves. The tail-like collection of spinal nerves at the inferior end of the spinal cord is called the _____(9).

4. Classify the following inputs and outputs as somatic sensory (SS), visceral sensory (VS), somatic motor (SM), or visceral motor (VM) relative to regions of the spinal cord involved in transmission.

_____ 1. Pain from skin

_____ 2. Proprioception

_____ 3. Efferent innervation of a gland

_____ 4. Efferent innervation of your gluteus maximus

_____ 5. A stomachache

_____ 6. A sound you hear

_____ 7. Efferent innervation of the muscle of the urinary bladder wall

5. First, examine the pathway in Figure 13.11 to determine whether this ascending pathway (spinal cord tract) is a *specific* or *nonspecific* pathway. Label accordingly on the left line beneath the pathway. Next, identify the pathway more precisely by selecting one of the choices below, and insert your response on the right line beneath the figure.

Spinocerebellar   Fasciculus cuneatus   Fasciculus gracilis   Spinothalamic

Then, color code the following structures and identify them by coloring them on the diagram.

○ First-order neuron   ○ Sensory receptor   ○ Thalamus

○ Second-order neuron   ○ Sensory homunculus   ○ Postcentral gyrus

○ Third-order neuron   ○ Spinal cord

Finally, circle all sites of synapse, and indicate your reasons for identifying

this pathway as you did. _____

_____

_____

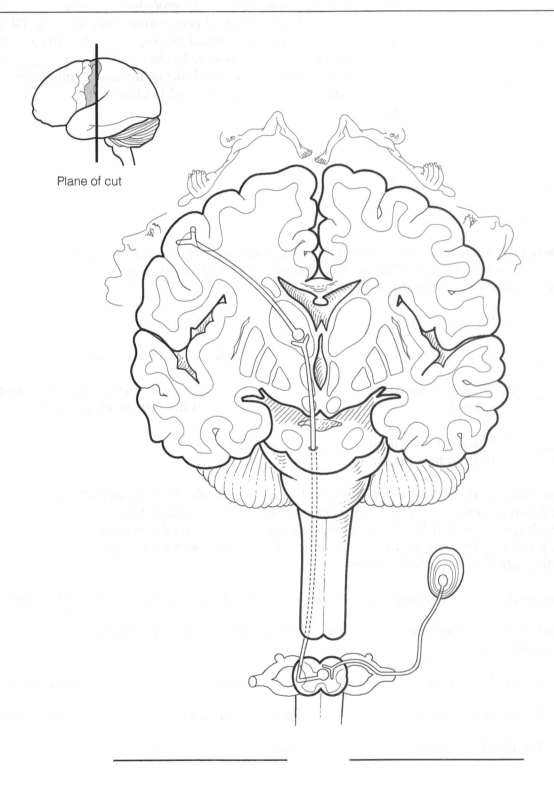

Plane of cut

Figure 13.11

6. Complete the following statements by writing the missing terms in the answer blanks.

_____ 1.

_____ 2.

_____ 3.

_____ 4.

_____ 5.

_____ 6.

_____ 7.

_____ 8.

_____ 9.

_____ 10.

The spinal cord sheath is composed of the single __(1)__ layer of the dura mater. Soft, protective padding around the spinal cord fills the __(2)__ space. The space between the arachnoid and pia mater meninges is filled with __(3)__. The anterior groove extending the length of the cord is called the __(4)__. The interior central gray matter mass is surrounded by __(5)__ matter. The two sides of the central gray mass are connected by the __(6)__. Neurons in the __(7)__ horn are somatic motor neurons that serve the skeletal muscles, whereas neurons in parts of the __(3)__ horn are autonomic motor neurons serving the visceral organs. If the dorsal root of a spinal nerve is severed, loss of __(9)__ function follows. If the ventral root is damaged, loss of __(10)__ function occurs.

7. First, examine the diagram in Figure 13.12 to determine whether it is an example of a *direct* or *indirect* motor pathway. Write your response on the line below the figure. Next, determine what specific tracts are depicted by carefully examining the two locations where the fiber tract has been "lassoed" by a leader line, and label the pathways appropriately on the diagram. Then, color code the structures provided with coloring circles and identify them by coloring them on the diagram.

◯ Basal nuclei   ◯ Brain stem motor nuclei   ◯ Cerebellum

◯ Alpha motor neuron   ◯ Primary motor cortex   ◯ Effector

◯ Motor homunculus   ◯ Medullary pyramid   ◯ Internal capsule

◯ Thalamus

Finally, indicate on the diagram which of these structures is the point of decussation.

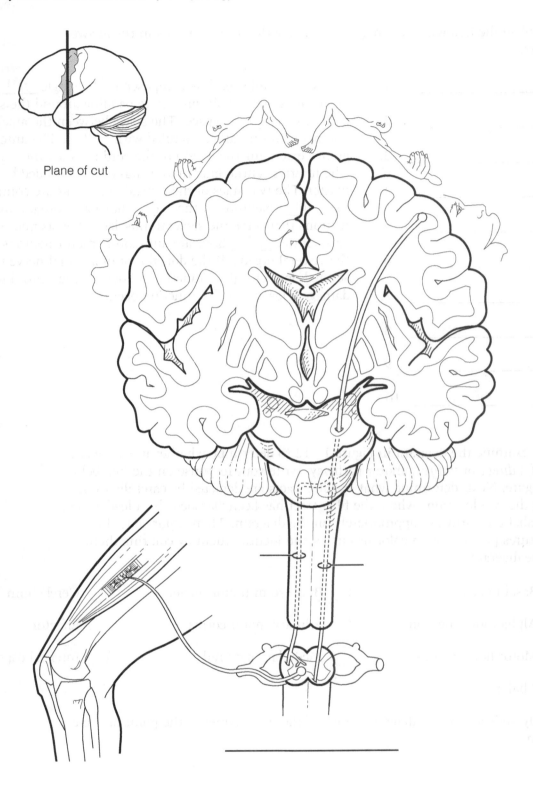

Plane of cut

Figure 13.12

8. Match the terms listed in Column B with the injuries described in Column A.

	Column A		Column B
_____	1. Loss of sensation		A. Flaccid paralysis
_____	2. Paralysis without atrophy		B. Hemiplegia
_____	3. Loss of motor function		C. Paralysis
_____	4. Traumatic flexion and/or extension of the neck		D. Paraplegia
_____	5. Result of transection of the cord between T_{11} and L_1		E. Paresthesia
_____	6. Transient period of functional loss induced by trauma to the cord		F. Quadriplegia
_____	7. Result of permanent injury to the cervical region of the cord		G. Spastic paralysis
_____	8. Paralysis of one side of the body that usually reflects brain injury rather than injury to the spinal cord		H. Spinal shock
			I. Whiplash

Diagnostic Procedures for Assessing CNS Dysfunction

1. If a statement is true, write the letter T in the answer blank. If a statement is false, change the underlined word(s) and write the correct word(s) in the answer blank.

_____ 1. An X ray of gas-filled ventricles is called <u>electroencephalogram</u>.

_____ 2. A flat electroencephalogram is clinical evidence of brain <u>death</u>.

_____ 3. Damage to the cerebral arteries of TIA victims is usually assessed by a <u>PET scan</u>.

_____ 4. The biochemical activity of the brain may be monitored by <u>MRI</u>.

_____ 5. A lumbar puncture is done below L_1 because the spinal cord ends <u>below</u> that level.

THE INCREDIBLE JOURNEY

A Visualization Exercise
for the Nervous System

You climb on the first cranial nerve you see . . .

1. Complete the following narrative by inserting the missing words in the answer blanks.

_____ 1.

_____ 2.

_____ 3.

_____ 4.

_____ 5.

_____ 6.

Nervous tissue is quite densely packed, and it is difficult to envision strolling through its various regions. Imagine instead that each of the various functional regions of the brain has a computerized room in which you might observe what occurs in that particular area. Your assignment is to determine where you are at any given time during your journey through the nervous system.

You begin your journey after being injected into the warm pool of cerebrospinal fluid in your host's fourth ventricle. As you begin your stroll through the nervous tissue, you notice a huge area of branching white matter overhead. As you enter the first computer room, you hear an announcement through the loudspeaker: "The pelvis is tipping too far posteriorly—please correct—we are beginning to fall backward and will soon lose our balance." The computer responds immediately, decreasing impulses to the posterior hip muscles and increasing impulses to the anterior thigh muscles. "How is that, proprioceptor 1?" From this information, you determine that your first stop is the _____(1).

At the next stop, you hear "Blood pressure to head is falling; increase sympathetic nervous system stimulation of the blood vessels." Then, as it becomes apparent that your host has not only stood up but is going to run, you hear "Increase rate of impulses to the heart and respiratory muscles—we are going to need more oxygen and a faster blood flow to the skeletal muscles of the legs." You recognize that this second stop must be the _____(2).

Computer room 3 presents a problem. There is no loudspeaker here; instead, incoming messages keep flashing across the wall, giving only bits and pieces of information. "Four hours since last meal—stimulate appetite center. Slight decrease in body temperature—initiate skin vasoconstriction. Mouth dry—stimulate thirst center. Um, a stroke on the arm—stimulate pleasure center." Looking at what has been recorded here—appetite, temperature, thirst, and pleasure—you conclude that this has to be the _____(3).

Continuing your journey upward toward the higher brain centers, finally you are certain you have reached the cerebral cortex. The first center you visit is quiet, like a library with millions of encyclopedias of facts and recordings of past input. You conclude that this must be the area where _____(4) are stored and that you are probably in the _____(5) lobe. The next stop is close by. As you enter the computer center, you once again hear a loudspeaker: "Let's have the motor instructions to say tintinnabulation—we don't want them to think we're tongue-tied." This area is obviously _____(6). Your final stop in the cerebral cortex is a very hectic center. Electrical impulses are traveling back and forth between giant neurons, sometimes in different directions and sometimes back and forth between a small number of neurons. Watching intently, you try to make some sense out of these

_____ 7.

_____ 8.

_____ 9.

_____ 10.

_____ 11.

_____ 12.

interactions, and you suddenly realize that this *is* what is happening here. The neurons are trying to make some sense out of something, which helps you decide that this must be the brain area where _____(7) occurs in the _____(8) lobe.

You hurry out of this center and retrace your steps back to the cerebrospinal fluid, deciding en route to observe a cranial nerve. You decide to pick one randomly and follow it to the organ it serves. You climb onto the first cranial nerve you see and slide down past the throat. Picking up speed, you quickly pass the heart and lungs and see the stomach and small intestine coming up fast. A moment later you land on the stomach, and now you know that this wandering nerve has to be the _____(9). As you look upward, you see that the nerve is traveling almost straight up and decide you'll have to find an alternative route back to the cerebrospinal fluid. You begin to walk posteriorly until you find a spinal nerve, which you follow until you reach the vertebral column. You squeeze between two adjacent vertebrae to follow the nerve to the spinal cord. With your pocket knife, you cut away the tough connective tissue covering the cord. Thinking that the _____(10) covering deserves its name, you finally manage to cut an opening large enough to get through, and you return to the warm bath of cerebrospinal fluid that these membranes enclose. At this point you are in the _____(11), and from here you swim upward until you get to the lower brain stem. Once there, it should be an easy task to find the holes leading into the _____(12) ventricle, where your journey began.

CHALLENGING YOURSELF

At the Clinic

1. Following a train accident, Sharon Money, a woman with an obvious head injury, is observed stumbling about the scene. An inability to walk properly and loss of balance are quite obvious. What brain region was injured?

2. A child is brought to the clinic with a high temperature. The doctor states that the child's meninges are inflamed. What name is given to this condition and how is it diagnosed?

3. Jemal, an elderly man with a history of TIAs, complained to his daughter that he had a severe headache. Shortly thereafter, he lapsed into a coma. At the hospital, he was diagnosed as having a brain hemorrhage. Which part of the brain was damaged by the hemorrhage?

4. A young man has just received serious burns resulting from standing with his back too close to a bonfire. He is muttering that he never felt the pain; otherwise, he would have smothered the flames by rolling on the ground. What part of his CNS might be malfunctioning?

5. Elderly Mrs. Barker has just suffered a stroke. She is able to understand verbal and written language, but when she tries to respond, her words are garbled. What cortical region has been damaged by the stroke?

6. An elderly man is brought to the clinic by his wife, who noticed that his speech is slurred, the right side of his face is slack, and he has difficulty swallowing. In which area of the brain would a stroke be suspected?

7. Sufferers of Tourette's syndrome have an excess of dopamine in the basal nuclei. They tend to exhibit explosive, uncontrollable verbal episodes of motor activity. The drug haloperidol reduces dopamine levels and returns voluntary control to the patient. What condition would an overdose of haloperidol mimic?

8. Huntington's disease results from a genetic defect that causes degeneration of the basal nuclei and, eventually, the cerebral cortex. Its initial symptoms involve involuntary motor activity, such as arm flapping. Would it be treated with a drug that increases or decreases dopamine levels?

9. Cindy's parents report that she has "spells," lasting 15 to 20 minutes, during which the 4-year-old is unresponsive although apparently awake. What is Cindy's probable diagnosis? Is improvement likely?

10. A young woman comes to the clinic complaining that she is plagued with spells during which she goes on emotional rampages, and after which she is extremely disoriented for a while. From what type of epilepsy is she suffering?

11. Mrs. Tonegawa is brought to the hospital in a semiconscious state after falling from a roof. She did not lose consciousness immediately, and she was initially lucid. After a while, though, she became confused and then unresponsive. What is a likely explanation of her condition?

12. Beth is brought to the clinic by her frantic husband. He explains that she has gradually lost control of her right hand. No atrophy of the muscles is apparent. Should upper *or* lower motor neuron damage be investigated?

13. A woman brings her elderly father to the clinic. He has been having more and more difficulty caring for himself and now even dressing and eating are a problem. The nurse notes the man's lack of change of facial expression; slow, shuffling gait; and tremor in the arms. What are the likely diagnosis and treatment?

14. Mary, an elderly woman, complains that she cannot sleep at night. She says she sleeps no more than four hours a night, and she demands sleeping medication. Is Mary's sleep pattern normal? Will a sleeping aid help her?

15. An alcoholic in his 60s is brought to the clinic in a stupor. When he has regained consciousness, a PET scan is ordered. The PET scan shows no activity in parts of the limbic system. The man has no memory of what befell him; in fact, he has no memory of the last 20 years! What type of amnesia does he have? Will it affect his ability to learn new skills?

Stop and Think

1. Why do you think so much of the cerebral cortex is devoted to sensory and motor connections to the eyes?

2. Electroconvulsive therapy (ECT) can be used to treat severe clinical depression. After ECT, patients exhibit some memory loss. The electrical current apparently wipes out reverberating circuits, resulting in lifting of the depression as it causes loss of information. Is ECT more likely to affect STM or LTM?

3. Do all tracts from the cerebrum to the spinal cord go through the entire brain stem?

4. Contrast damage to the primary visual cortex with damage to the visual association cortex.

5. Any CSF accumulation will cause hydrocephalus, which in a fetus will lead to expansion of the skull. In a fetus, would blockage of CSF circulation in the cerebral aqueduct have a different effect than blockage of the arachnoid villi?

6. What does mannitol's ability to make capillary cells shrivel tell you about the cells' permeability to mannitol?

7. A victim of a motorcycle accident fractured vertebra T_{12}, and there was concern that the spinal cord was crushed at the level of this vertebra. At what spinal cord segment was the damage expected? Choose and explain: (a) between C_4 and C_8, and the ability to move the arms was tested, (b) at C_1, and the respiratory movements of the diaphragm were tested, (c) spinal-cord level L_3, (d) there could be no deficits because the cord always ends above T_{12}.

8. Why is hemiplegia more likely to be a result of brain injury than of spinal cord injury?

9. Which would more likely result from injury exclusively to the posterior side of the spinal cord—paresthesia or paralysis? Explain your answer.

10. Ralph had brain surgery to remove a small intracranial hematoma (blood mass). He was allergic to general anesthesia, so the operation was done under local anesthesia. Ralph remained conscious while the surgeon removed a small part of the skull. The operation went well, and Ralph asked the surgeon to mildly stimulate his (unharmed) postcentral gyrus with an electrode. The surgeon did so. What happened? Choose and explain: (a) Ralph was seized with uncontrollable rage; (b) he saw things that were not there; (c) he asked to see what was touching his hand, but nothing was; (d) he started to kick; (e) he heard his mother's voice from 30 years ago.

COVERING ALL YOUR BASES

Multiple Choice

Select the best answer or answers from the choices given.

1. The secondary brain vesicle that is least developed in the adult brain is the:

   A. telencephalon C. metencephalon

   B. mesencephalon D. rhombencephalon

2. Which is an incorrect association of brain region and ventricle?

   A. Mesencephalon—third ventricle

   B. Cerebral hemispheres—lateral ventricles

   C. Pons—fourth ventricle

   D. Medulla—fourth ventricle

3. Which of the following is not part of the brain stem?

A. Medulla   C. Pons

B. Cerebellum   D. Midbrain

4. Connecting a ventricle to the subarachnoid space is the function of the:

A. interventricular foramen

B. cerebral aqueduct

C. lateral aperture

D. median aperture

5. The discrete correlation of body regions to CNS structures is:

A. a homunculus   C. lateralization

B. somatotopy   D. cephalization

6. Which is not associated with the frontal lobe?

A. Olfaction

B. Motor control of the eyes

C. Prefrontal cortex

D. Skilled motor programs

7. Regions involved with language include:

A. auditory association area

B. prefrontal cortex

C. Wernicke's area

D. Broca's area

8. When neurons in Wernicke's area send impulses to neurons in Broca's area, the white matter tracts utilized are:

A. commissural fibers

B. projection fibers

C. association fibers

D. anterior funiculus

9. The basal nuclei include:

A. hippocampus

B. caudate nucleus

C. lentiform nucleus

D. mammillary bodies

10. Which of the brain areas listed are involved in normal voluntary muscle activity?

A. Amygdala   C. Medullary pyramids

B. Putamen   D. Precentral gyrus

11. If impulses to the cerebral cortex from the thalamus were blocked, which of the following sensory inputs would get through to the appropriate sensory cortex?

A. Visual impulses

B. Auditory impulses

C. Olfactory impulses

D. General sensory impulses

12. Functions controlled by the hypothalamus include:

A. crude interpretation of pain

B. regulation of many homeostatic mechanisms

C. setting of some biological rhythms

D. secretion of melatonin

13. The pineal gland is located in the:

A. hypophysis cerebri

B. mesencephalon

C. epithalamus

D. corpus callosum

14. Which of the following are part of the midbrain?

A. Corpora quadrigemina

B. Cerebellar peduncles

C. Substantia nigra

D. Nucleus of cranial nerve V

15. Cranial nerves with their nuclei in the pons include:

A. facial   C. trigeminal

B. vagus   D. trochlear

16. Functions that are at least partially overseen by the medulla are:

A. regulation of the heart

B. maintaining equilibrium

C. regulation of respiration

D. visceral motor function

17. Which of the following are important in cerebellar processing?

    A. Feedback to cerebral motor cortex

    B. Input from body parts

    C. Output for subconscious motor activity

    D. Direct impulses from motor cortex via a separate cerebellar pathway

18. Parts of the limbic system include:

    A. cingulate gyrus   C. fornix

    B. hippocampus   D. septal nuclei

19. Inability to prevent expressing one's emotions most likely indicates damage to the:

    A. affective brain

    B. cognitive brain

    C. affective brain's control of the cognitive brain

    D. cognitive brain's control of the affective brain

20. Which statements concerning the reticular activating system are true?

    A. It consists of neural columns extending through the brain stem.

    B. Its connections reach as far as the cerebral cortex.

    C. It is housed primarily in the thalamus.

    D. It filters sensory input to the cerebrum.

21. Relative to the cranial meninges:

    A. the arachnoid produces CSF

    B. the dura contains several blood sinuses

    C. the pia mater has two layers

    D. three dural folds help support brain tissue

22. Which structures are directly involved with formation, circulation, and drainage of CSF?

    A. Ependymal cilia

    B. Ventricular choroid plexuses

    C. Arachnoid villi

    D. Serous layers of the dura mater

23. Which of the following are associated with the conus medullaris?

    A. Filum terminale

    B. The end of the dural sheath

    C. Cauda equina

    D. Location of lumbar puncture

24. The spinal cord feature associated with the leash of nerves supplying the upper limbs is the:

    A. brachial plexus

    B. brachial enlargement

    C. cervical enlargement

    D. lateral gray horns

25. Features associated with the anterior surface of the spinal cord include the:

    A. ventral horns of gray matter

    B. median fissure

    C. median sulcus

    D. root ganglia

26. Poliomyelitis affects the:

    A. posterior white columns

    B. posterior gray horns

    C. anterior white columns

    D. anterior gray horns

27. Which spinal cord tracts carry impulses for conscious sensations?

    A. Fasciculus gracilis

    B. Lateral spinothalamic

    C. Anterior spinocerebellar

    D. Fasciculus cuneatus

28. Damage to which descending tract would be suspected if a person had unilateral poor muscle tone and posture?

    A. Reticulospinal   C. Tectospinal

    B. Rubrospinal   D. Vestibulospinal

29. Damage to the lower motor neurons may result in:
    A. paresthesia   C. spastic paralysis
    B. flaccid paralysis   D. paraplegia

30. Which neuron parts occupy the gray matter in the spinal cord?
    A. Tracts of long axons
    B. Motor neuron cell bodies
    C. Sensory neuron cell bodies
    D. Nerves

31. A professor unexpectedly blew a loud horn in his anatomy classroom, and all his students looked up, startled. These reflexive movements of their neck and eye muscles were mediated by:
    A. cerebral cortex   C. raphe nuclei
    B. inferior olives   D. inferior colliculus

32. Which of the following is (are) associated with the medial lemniscal pathways?
    A. Fasciculus gracilis
    B. Fasciculus cuneatus
    C. Ventral posterior thalamic nucleus
    D. Trigeminal nerves

33. Both specific and nonspecific pathways:
    A. transmit impulses to the thalamus
    B. initiate interpretation of emotional aspects of sensation
    C. stimulate the RAS
    D. cross over within the CNS

34. Relaxation of muscles prior to and during sleep is due to:
    A. increased inhibition at the projection level
    B. decreased stimulation by the vestibular nuclei
    C. increased activity of the RAS
    D. inhibition of the reticular nuclei

35. An adult male is having an EEG. The recording shows irregular waves with a frequency of 4–7 Hz. This is:
    A. normal
    B. normal in REM sleep
    C. normal in deep sleep
    D. abnormal in an awake adult

36. During REM sleep:
    A. alpha waves appear
    B. oxygen utilization of the brain increases
    C. rapid eye movement occurs
    D. dreaming occurs

37. Consciousness involves:
    A. discrete, localized stimulation of the cortex
    B. activity concurrent with localized activities
    C. simultaneous, interconnected activity
    D. stimulation of the RAS

38. States of unconsciousness include:
    A. sleep
    B. grand mal seizure
    C. syncope
    D. narcoleptic seizure

39. Fact memory involves:
    A. the hippocampi
    B. rehearsal
    C. language areas of the cortex
    D. consolidation

40. The sleep neurotransmitter is said to be:
    A. serotonin
    B. norepinephrine
    C. dopamine
    D. acetylcholine

Word Dissection

For each of the following word roots, fill in the literal meaning and give
an example, using a word found in this chapter.

Word root	Translation	Example
1. campo		
2. collicul		
3. commis		
4. cope		
5. enceph		
6. epilep		
7. falx		
8. forn		
9. gyro		
10. hippo		
11. infundib		
12. isch		
13. lemnisc		
14. nigr		
15. rhin		
16. rostr		
17. uncul		
18. uncus		

14

THE PERIPHERAL NERVOUS SYSTEM

Student Objectives

When you have completed the exercises in this chapter you will have accomplished the following objectives:

1. Define *peripheral nervous system* and list its components.

Sensory Receptors and Sensation

2. Classify the general sensory receptors by structure, stimulus detected, and body location.

3. Outline the events that lead to sensation and perception.

4. Describe receptor and generator potentials and sensory adaptation.

5. Describe the main aspects of sensory perception.

6. Describe the location, structure, and afferent pathways of taste and smell receptors, and explain how these receptors are activated.

7. Describe the structure and function of accessory eye structures, eye tunics, lens, and humors of the eye.

8. Trace the pathway of light through the eye to the retina and explain how light is focused for distant and close vision.

9. Describe the events involved in the stimulation of photoreceptors by light, and compare and contrast the roles of rods and cones in vision.

10. Note the cause and consequences of astigmatism, cataract, glaucoma, hyperopia, myopia, and color blindness.

11. Compare and contrast light and dark adaptation.

12. Trace the visual pathway to the optic cortex and briefly describe the process of visual processing.

13. Describe the structure and general function of the outer, middle, and inner ears.

14. Describe the sound conduction pathway to the fluids of the inner ear and follow the auditory pathway from the organ of Corti to the temporal cortex.

15. Explain how one is able to differentiate pitch and loudness and localize the source of sounds.

16. Explain how the balance organs of the semicircular canals and the vestibule help maintain dynamic and static equilibrium.

17. List possible causes and symptoms of otitis media, deafness, Ménière's syndrome, and motion sickness.

Transmission Lines:
Nerves and Their Structure and Repair

18. Define *ganglion* and indicate the general body location of ganglia.

19. Describe the general structure of a nerve, and follow the process of nerve regeneration.

20. Name the twelve pairs of cranial nerves and indicate the body region and structures innervated by each.

21. Describe the formation of a spinal nerve and describe the general distribution of its rami.

22. Define *plexus*. Name the major plexuses and describe the distribution and function of the peripheral nerves arising from each plexus.

Motor Endings and Motor Activity

23. Compare and contrast the motor endings of somatic and autonomic nerve fibers.

24. Outline the three levels of the motor hierarchy.

25. Compare the roles of the cerebellum and basal nuclei in controlling motor activity.

Reflex Activity

26. Name the components of a reflex and distinguish between autonomic and somatic reflexes.

27. Compare and contrast stretch, flexor, and crossed extensor reflexes.

The part of the nervous system that lies outside the brain and spinal cord is called the peripheral nervous system (PNS). The PNS consists of sensory receptors, all peripheral nerves (12 pairs of cranial nerves, 31 pairs of spinal nerves) and their associated ganglia, and the motor endings. The PNS serves as the two-way communication network between the environment (both inside and outside the body) and the central nervous system (CNS), where the sensory information generated by the PNS is received, interpreted, and used to maintain homeostasis.

The topics for study in Chapter 14 are the sensory receptors, the structure and function of the special sense organs, the structure and types of PNS nerves, their pathways, the body regions they serve, and motor endings and the basics of motor activity. Reflex activities are also studied in this chapter.

BUILDING THE FRAMEWORK

1. Complete the following statements by writing the missing terms in the answer blanks.

_____ 1.

_____ 2.

_____ 3.

_____ 4.

_____ 5.

_____ 6.

_____ 7.

_____ 8.

The two functional divisions of the PNS are the _____(1) division, in which the nerve fiber type called _____(2) carries impulses toward the CNS, and the _____(3) division, in which the nerve fiber type called _____(4) carries impulses away from the CNS. The motor division of the PNS includes two types of fibers, the _____(5) and _____(6) motor nerve fibers. Skeletal muscles are innervated by _____(7) fibers, whereas visceral organs are innervated by _____(8) fibers.

2. By assigning them numbers from 1 to 9, arrange the following elements in order of stimulation. (*Note:* two of the elements will be used twice.)

Spinal nerve   Ventral ramus of spinal nerve   Dorsal root of spinal nerve

Sensory nerve fiber   Motor nerve fiber   Receptor   Effector

Sensory Receptors and Sensation

1. Complete the following statements by writing the missing terms in the answer blanks.

_____ 1. _____(1) is the awareness of internal and external stimuli. The conscious interpretation of such stimuli is called _____(2).

_____ 2.

Sensory receptors transduce stimulus energy into _____(3). As

_____ 3. stimulus energy is absorbed by the receptor, the _____(4) of the receptor membrane changes. This allows ions to flow through

_____ 4. the membrane and results in a _____(5) potential called the receptor potential. If the receptor potential reaches _____(6) a

_____ 5. generator potential is produced and a(n) _____(7) potential is generated and transmitted.

_____ 6.

The nonspecific ascending pathways are also called the

_____ 7. _____(8) pathways, whereas the specific ascending pathways are also known as the _____(9) system. Of these, the

_____ 8. _____(10) are more concerned with the emotional aspects of perception. The brain region that acts as a relay station and

_____ 9. projects fibers to the sensory cortex is the _____(11).

_____ 10.

_____ 11.

2. If a statement about the three levels of sensory integration is true, write T in the answer blank. If a statement is false, change the underlined word(s) and write the correct word(s) in the answer blank.

_____ 1. Sensation occurs in the <u>sensory association cortex</u>.

_____ 2. The stronger the stimulus, the greater is the <u>velocity</u> of impulse transmission.

_____ 3. <u>Specific</u> ascending pathways are formed by the spinothalamic tracts.

_____ 4. <u>Nonspecific</u> ascending pathways transmit information about pain, touch, pressure, and temperature.

_____ 5. Second-order neurons of both specific and nonspecific ascending circuits terminate in the <u>medulla</u>.

_____ 6. The fasciculus cuneatus, fasciculus gracilis, and median lemniscal tracts form the <u>nonspecific</u> ascending pathways.

_____ 7. The cell bodies of <u>second-order</u> neurons are located in the dorsal root ganglia.

_____ 8. To accommodate precise, discriminatory information, impulses are carried by <u>specific</u> ascending pathways.

3. Classify the receptor types described below by *location* (make a choice from Key A) and then by *stimulus type detected* (make a choice from Key B).

Key A: A. Exteroceptor   **Key B:** 1. Chemoreceptor   4. Photoreceptor

        B. Interoceptor   2. Mechanoreceptor   5. Thermoreceptor

        C. Proprioceptor   3. Nociceptor

_____, _____ 1. In skeletal muscles; respond to muscle stretch

_____, _____ 2. In the walls of blood vessels; respond to oxygen content of surrounding interstitial fluid

_____, _____ 3. In the skin; respond to a hot surface

_____, _____ 4. In the eyes; respond to light

_____, _____ 5. In the inner ear; respond to sound

_____, _____ 6. In the skin; respond to acid splashing on the skin

_____, _____ 7. In the wall of blood vessels; respond to blood pressure

_____, _____ 8. In the stomach wall; respond to an over-full stomach

_____, _____ 9. In the nose; respond to a skunk's spray (Yuk!)

4. In relation to sensory receptors, circle the term that does not belong in each of the following groupings.

1. Cutaneous receptors   Free dendritic endings   Tendon stretch   Pain and touch

2. Meissner's corpuscle   Encapsulated dendritic endings   Dermal papillae

   Numerous in muscle

3. Largest of corpuscular receptors   Light touch   Pacinian corpuscle

   Multiple layers of supporting cells

4. Thermoreceptor   Hair movement   Light touch   Root hair plexus

5. Merkel discs   Meissner's corpuscle   Muscle spindle   Touch receptor

6. Proprioceptors   Nociceptors   Sensitive to tendon stretch   Muscle spindle

7. Merkel discs   Sensitive to joint orientation   Articular capsules

   Joint kinesthetic receptors

8. Mechanoreceptor Photoreceptor Interoceptor Chemoreceptor

9. Free dendritic endings Root hair plexuses Merkel discs

  Modified free dendritic endings

5. Identify the highly simplified cutaneous receptors shown in Figure 14.1 and color the figure as it strikes your fancy.

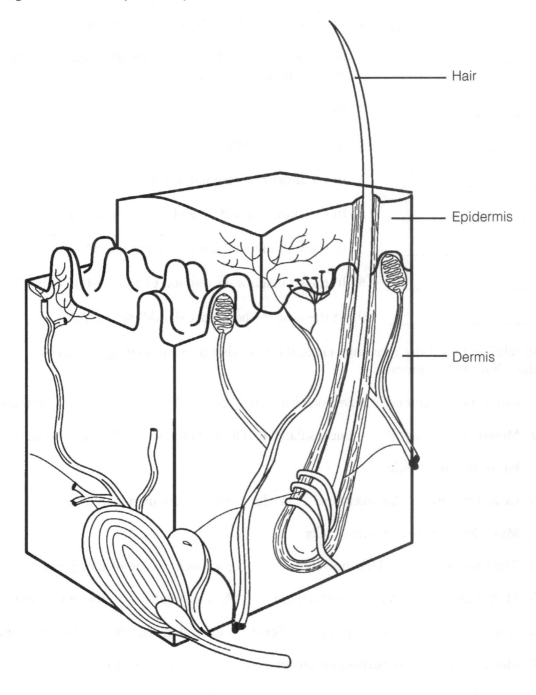

Figure 14.1

6. Certain activities and sensations are listed below. Using the key choices, select the specific receptor type that would be activated by the activity or sensation. Insert the correct letters in the answer blanks. Note that more than one receptor type may be activated in some cases.

Key Choices

A. Free dendritic endings (pain)

B. Golgi tendon organ

C. Meissner's corpuscle

D. Merkel discs

E. Muscle spindle

F. Pacinian corpuscle

G. Joint kinesthetic receptor

H. Root hair plexuses

I. Ruffini's corpuscle

_____ 1. Standing on hot pavement (identify two)

_____ 2. Feeling a pinch (identify two)

_____ 3. Leaning on a shovel (identify four)

_____ 4. Muscle sensations when rowing a boat (identify three)

_____ 5. Feeling a caress (identify three)

_____ 6. Feeling the coldness of an iced-tea glass

_____ 7. Reading braille

7. Complete the following statements by writing the missing terms in the answer blanks.

_____ 1.

_____ 2.

_____ 3.

_____ 4.

_____ 5.

_____ 6.

1. The gustatory and olfactory senses rely on _____(1), meaning that chemicals dissolved in fluid will stimulate these receptors.
2. The receptors for _____(2) taste, in the back of the tongue, are thought to be protective since many poisons stimulate these
3. receptors. The sensation we call taste is reduced when the nasal passages are swollen; this indicates that "taste" relies
4. heavily on the _____(3) sense. The loss of smell that accompanies a cold is the result of the less-than-optimal position of the
5. olfactory epithelium, on the _____(4) of the nasal cavity. The pathway for the sense of smell also runs to the _____(5)
6. system and thus has emotional ties. It is the only sensory input that does not pass through the _____(6) in the diencephalon to reach its destination in the cerebral cortex.

8. On Figure 14.2A, label the two types of tongue papillae containing taste buds. On Figure 14.2B, color the taste buds green. On Figure 14.2C, color the gustatory cells red, the supporting cells blue, the basal cells purple, and the sensory fibers yellow. Add appropriate labels at the leader lines to identify the *taste pore* and *microvilli* of the gustatory cells.

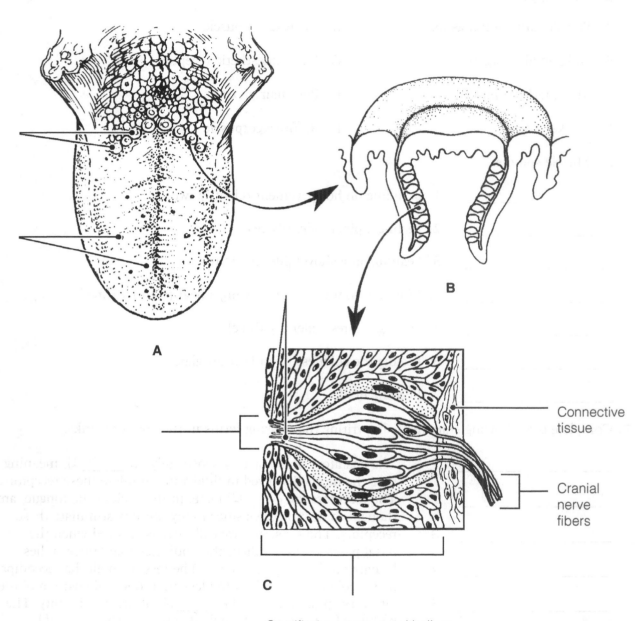

A

B

Connective tissue

Cranial nerve fibers

C

Stratified squamous epithelium

Figure 14.2

9. Figure 14.3 illustrates the site of the olfactory epithelium in the nasal cavity (part A is an enlarged view of the olfactory receptor area). Select different colors to identify the structures listed below and use them to color the illustration. Then add labels and leader lines to identify the filaments of the olfactory nerve, the fibers of the olfactory tract, the mitral cells, and the olfactory "hairs," and add arrows to indicate the direction of impulse transmission. Finally, respond to the questions following the diagrams.

○ Olfactory neurons (receptor cells)

○ Supporting cells

○ Glomeruli

○ Olfactory bulb

○ Cribriform plate of the ethmoid bone

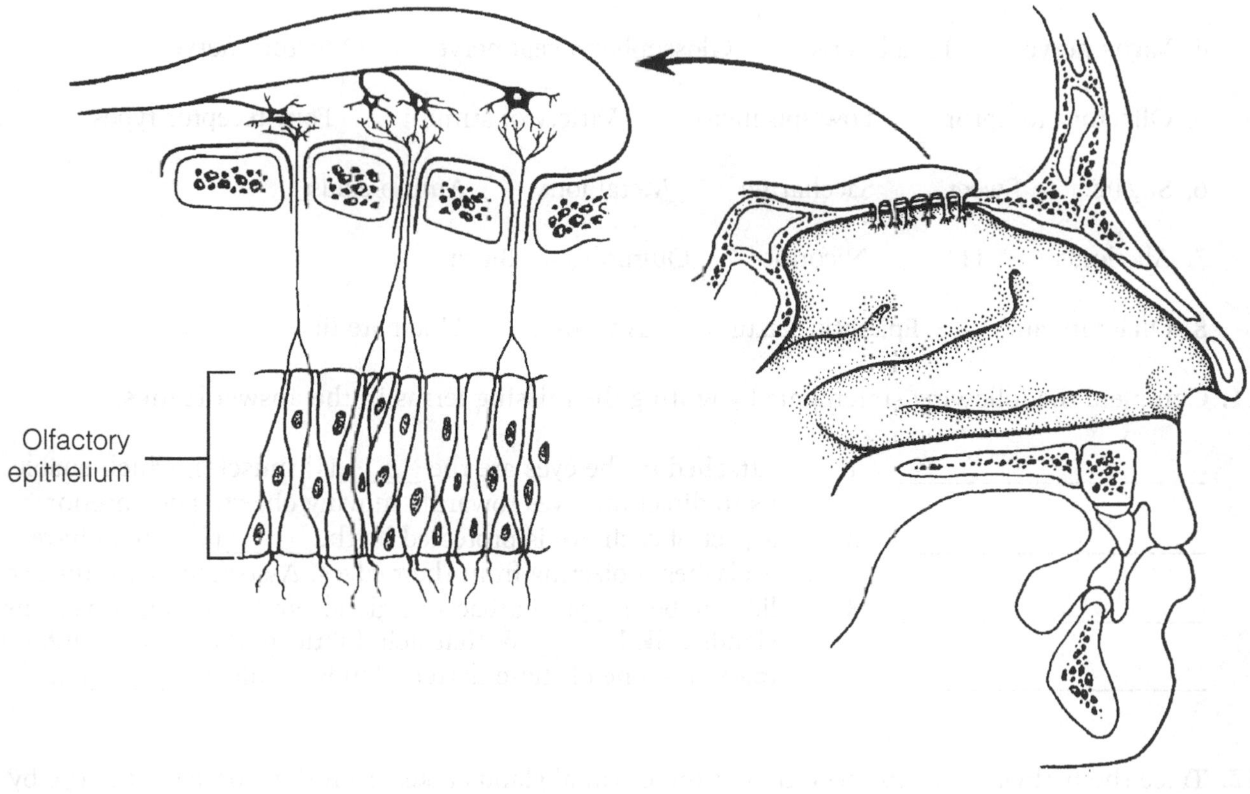

Figure 14.3 **A** **B**

Olfactory epithelium

1. Explain briefly the role of the mitral cells found in the glomeruli. _____

_____

2. What name is given to the complex spherical structures that house the mitral cells? _____

3. What cells also found in the olfactory bulbs can act to inhibit the mitral cells and what is

   the result when such inhibition occurs? _____

4. List two brain regions to which olfactory tract fibers project, other than the olfactory cortex in the temporal lobes. _____

_____

10. Circle the term that does not belong in each of the following groupings.

    1. Sweet   Musky   Sour   Bitter   Salty

    2. Bipolar neuron   Epithelial cell   Olfactory receptor   Ciliated

    3. Gustatory cell   Taste pore   Microvilli   Yellow-tinged epithelium

    4. Vagus nerve   Facial nerve   Glossopharyngeal nerve   Olfactory nerve

    5. Olfactory receptor   Low specificity   Variety of stimuli   Four receptor types

    6. Sugars   Sweet   Saccharine   Metal ions   Amino acids

    7. Alkaloids H^+ Nicotine   Quinine   Bitter

    8. Olfactory aura   Epileptic seizure   Anosmia   Uncinate fit

11. Complete the following statements by writing the missing terms in the answer blanks.

    _____   1.   Attached to the eyes are the _____(1) muscles, which enable us to direct our eyes toward a moving object. The anterior
    _____   2.   aspect of each eye is protected by the _____(2), which have eyelashes projecting from their edges. Associated with the eye-
    _____   3.   lids are both typical sebaceous glands and modified sebaceous glands called _____(3) that help lubricate the eyes. An inflam-
    _____   4.   mation of one of these (latter) glands is called a _____(4).

12. Trace the pathway that the secretion of the lacrimal glands takes from the surface of the eye by assigning a number to each structure.

    _____ 1. Lacrimal sac   _____ 3. Nasolacrimal duct

    _____ 2. Nasal cavity   _____ 4. Lacrimal canals

13. Identity each of the eye muscles indicated by leader lines in Figure 14.4. Color each muscle a different color. Then, in the blanks below, indicate the eye movement caused by each muscle.

1. Superior rectus _____   4. Lateral rectus _____

2. Inferior rectus _____   5. Medial rectus _____

3. Superior oblique _____   6. Inferior oblique _____

_____   _____

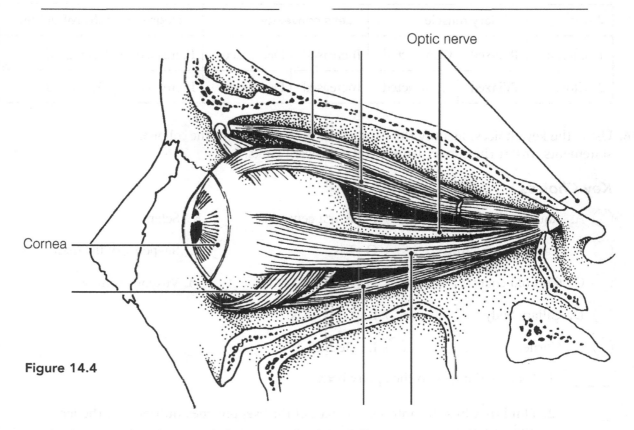

Figure 14.4

14. Circle the term that does not belong in each of the following groupings.

1. Choroid   Sclera   Vitreous humor   Retina

2. Inferior oblique   Iris   Superior rectus   Inferior rectus

3. Pupil constriction   Far vision   Accommodation   Bright light

4. Mechanoreceptors   Rods   Cones   Photoreceptors

5. Ciliary body   Iris   Suspensory ligaments   Lens

6. Uvea   Choroid   Ciliary body   Pigmented retina   Iris

7. Retina   Neural layer   Pigmented layer   Transparent   Contains photoreceptors

8. Optic disc   Blind spot   Lacks photoreceptors   Macula lutea

9. Cornea   Active sodium ion pump   Transparent   Richly vascular

   Many pain fibers

10. Inner segment   Outer segment   Photoreceptor pigments   Receptor region

11. Conjunctiva   Meibomian glands   Tarsal plate   Lacrimal gland

15. In the following table, circle each word that correctly describes events occurring within the eye during close and distant vision.

Vision	Ciliary muscle		Lens convexity		Degree of light refraction	
1. Distant	Relaxed	Contracted	Increased	Decreased	Increased	Decreased
2. Close	Relaxed	Contracted	Increased	Decreased	Increased	Decreased

16. Using the key choices, identify the parts of the eye described in the following statements. Insert the correct letters in the answer blanks.

Key Choices

◯ A. Aqueous humor   ◯ F. Fovea centralis   ◯ K. Sclera

◯ B. Canal of Schlemm   ◯ G. Iris   ◯ L. Suspensory ligaments

◯ C. Choroid coat   ◯ H. Lens   ◯ M. Vitreous humor

◯ D. Ciliary body   ◯ I. Optic disk

◯ E. Cornea   ◯ J. Retina

_____ 1. Secures the lens to the ciliary body

_____ 2. Fluid that fills the anterior segment of the eye; provides nutrients to the lens and cornea

_____ 3. Fibrous tunic, white and opaque

_____ 4. Area of retina that lacks photoreceptors

_____ 5. Muscular structure that manipulates the lens

_____ 6. Nutritive (vascular) tunic of the eye

_____ 7. Drains the aqueous humor of the eye

_____ 8. Tunic concerned with image formation

_____ 9. Gel-like substance, filling the posterior segment of the eyeball; helps reinforce the eyeball

_____ 10. Heavily pigmented tunic that prevents light scattering within the eye

_____ 11. _____ 12. Smooth muscle structures (sites of intrinsic eye muscles)

_____ 13. Area of acute or discriminatory vision

_____ 14. _____ 15. _____ 16. _____ 17. Refractory media of the eye

_____ 18. Anteriormost clear part of the fibrous tunic

_____ 19. Pigmented "diaphragm" of the eye

17. Using the key choices in Exercise 16, identify the structures indicated by leader lines on the diagram of the eye in Figure 14.5. Select different colors for all the structures with a color-coding circle in Exercise 16 and color the structures on the figure.

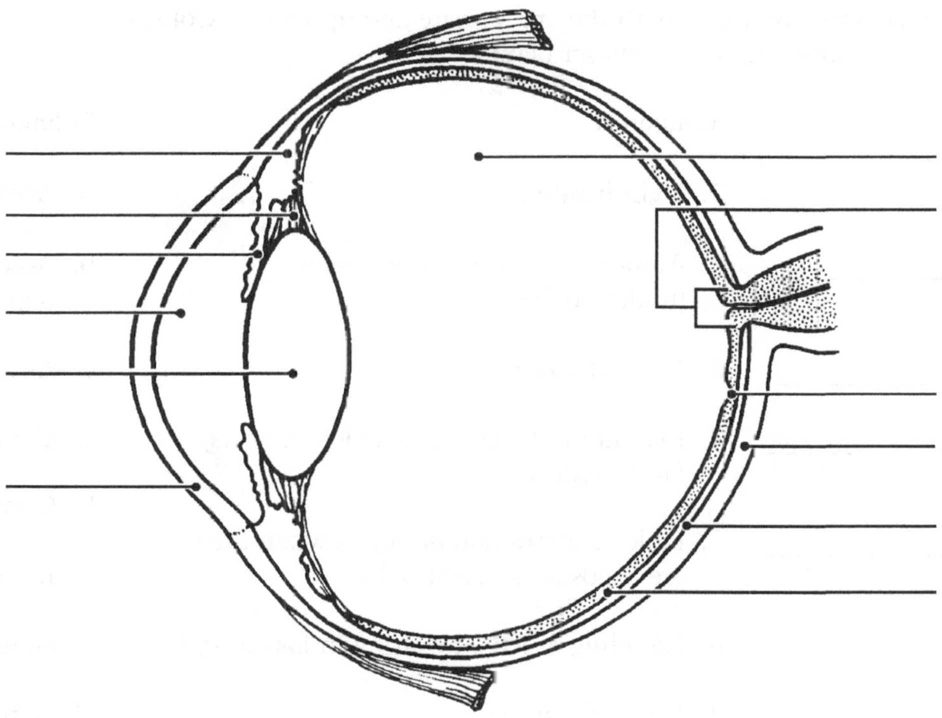

Figure 14.5

18. Explain why it helps to look up and gaze into space after reading for a prolonged period.

_____

_____

_____

19. Match the key choices with the following descriptions concerning optics.

Key Choices

A. Concave lens   C. Far point of vision   E. Near point of vision

B. Convex lens   D. Focal point   F. Visible light

_____ 1. The closest point at which clear focus is possible

_____ 2. The electromagnetic waves to which the photoreceptors of the eyes respond

_____ 3. The point at which light rays are converged by a convex lens

_____ 4. A lens that is thickest at the edges; diverges the light rays

_____ 5. The point beyond which accommodation is unnecessary

20. Match the terms in Column B with the appropriate descriptions in Column A. Insert the correct answers in the answer blanks.

	Column A	Column B
_____	1. Light bending	A. Accommodation
_____	2. Ability to focus for close vision (under 20 feet)	B. Accommodation pupillary reflex
_____	3. Normal vision	C. Astigmatism
_____	4. Inability to focus well on close objects; farsightedness	D. Cataract
_____	5. Reflex constriction of pupils when they are exposed to bright light	E. Convergence
_____	6. Clouding of lens, resulting in loss of sight	F. Emmetropia
_____	7. Nearsightedness	G. Glaucoma
_____	8. Blurred vision, resulting from unequal curvatures of the lens or cornea	H. Hyperopia
_____	9. Condition of increasing pressure inside the eye, resulting from blocked drainage of aqueous humor	I. Myopia
_____	10. Medial movement of the eyes during focusing on close objects	J. Night blindness
_____	11. Reflex constriction of the pupils when viewing close objects	K. Photopupillary reflex
_____	12. Inability to see well in the dark; often a result of vitamin A deficiency	L. Refraction

21. Complete the following statements by writing the missing terms in the answer blanks.

_____ 1.   There are _____(1) varieties of cones. One type responds most
vigorously to _____(2) light, another to _____(3) light, and

_____ 2.   still another to _____(4) light. The ability to see intermediate
colors such as purple results from the fact that more than one

_____ 3.   cone type is being stimulated _____(5). Lack of all color receptors results in _____(6). Because this condition is sex linked, it

_____ 4.   occurs most commonly in _____(7). Black and white or dim
light vision is a function of the _____(8). The density of cones

_____ 5.   is greatest in the _____(9) , whereas rods are densest in the
_____(10).

_____ 6.

_____ 7.

_____ 8.

                _____ 9.   _____ 10.

22. Answer the following questions concerning rod photopigment and physiology,
or complete the statements as indicated.

1. The bent 11-*cis* form of retinal is combined with a protein called _____

   to form the photoreceptor pigment called _____ .

2. The light-induced event during which the photoreceptor pigment breaks down to its two

   components and retinal assumes its straighter _____ shape is

   called _____ .

3. Retinal is produced from vitamin _____ , which is ordinarily

   stored in large amounts by the _____ .

4. What ionic and electrical events occur in the photoreceptors (rods) when it is dark?

   _____

   _____

5. How is this changed in the light? _____

   _____

   _____

23. Name in sequence the neural elements of the visual pathway, beginning
with the retina and ending with the optic cortex.

Retina ⟶ _____ ⟶ _____ ⟶ _____

synapse in thalamus ⟶ _____ ⟶ optic cortex

24. Check (✓) all of the following conditions that pertain to dark adaptation.

_____ 1. Retinal sensitivity increases   _____ 7. Retinal sensitivity decreases

_____ 2. Rhodopsin accumulates   _____ 8. Rhodopsin is broken down rapidly

_____ 3. The cones are inactive   _____ 9. The cones are active

_____ 4. Rods are activated   _____ 10. Rods are inactivated

_____ 5. Visual acuity increases   _____ 11. Visual acuity decreases

_____ 6. Pupils constrict   _____ 12. Pupils dilate

25. Using the key choices, select the terms that apply to the following descriptions.
Place the correct letters in the answer blanks.

Key Choices

A. Anvil (incus)   F. Hammer (malleus)   K. Semicircular canals

B. Auditory tube   G. Oval window   L. Stirrup (stapes)

C. Cochlea   H. Perilymph   M. Tympanic membrane

D. Endolymph   I. Pinna   N. Vestibule

E. External auditory canal   J. Round window

_____ 1. _____ 2. _____ 3. Structures composing the outer ear

_____ 4. _____ 5. _____ 6. Elements of the bony or osseous labyrinth

_____ 7. _____ 8. _____ 9. The ossicles

_____ 10. Ear structures not involved with hearing

_____ 11. Allows middle ear pressure to be equalized with atmospheric pressure

_____ 12. Transmits sound vibrations to the ossicles

_____ 13. Contains the organ of Corti

_____ 14. Passage from the nasopharynx to the middle ear; also called the
pharyngotympanic tube

_____ 15. _____ 16. House receptors for the sense of equilibrium

_____ 17. Transfers vibrations from the stirrup to the fluid in the inner ear

_____ 18. Fluid inside the membranous labyrinth

_____ 19. Fluid within the osseous labyrinth, and surrounding the membranous
labyrinth

_____ 20. Fits into the oval window

26. Figure 14.6 is a diagram of the ear. Use anatomical terms (as needed) from the key choices in Exercise 1 to correctly identify all structures in the figure with leader lines. Color all external ear structures yellow, color the ossicles red, color the equilibrium areas of the inner ear green, and color the inner ear structures involved with hearing blue.

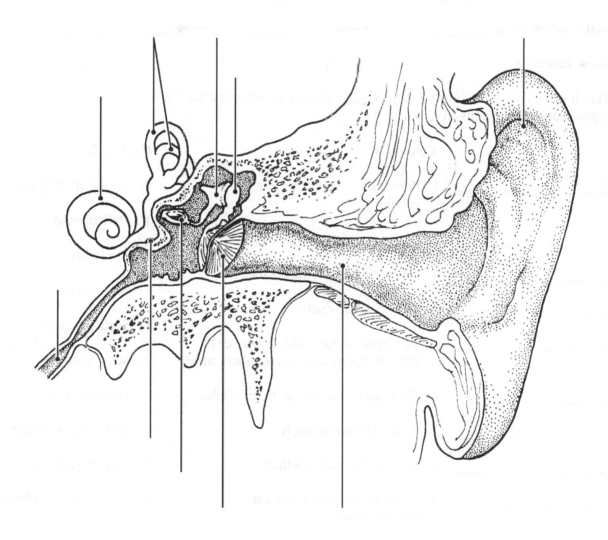

Figure 14.6

27. Sound waves hitting the eardrum set it into vibration. Trace the pathway through which vibrations and fluid currents travel to finally stimulate the hair cells in the organ of Corti. Name the appropriate ear structures in their correct sequence.

Eardrum ⟶ _____ ⟶ _____ ⟶ _____ ⟶

oval window ⟶ _____ ⟶ _____ ⟶ _____

⟶ hair cells.

28. Match the terms in Column B concerning cochlear structures with the appropriate descriptions in Column A.

Column A	Column B
_____ 1. Bony pillar supporting the coiled cochlea	A. Basilar membrane
	B. Helicotrema
_____ 2. Superior cavity of the cochlea	
_____ 3. Inferior cavity of the cochlea	C. Modiolus
	D. Scala media
_____ 4. The cochlear duct	
_____ 5. The apex of the cochlea; where the perilymph-containing chambers meet	E. Scala tympani
	F. Scala vestibuli
_____ 6. Shelflike extension of the modiolus	G. Spiral lamina
_____ 7. Forms the endolymph	H. Spiral organ of Corti
_____ 8. Roof of the cochlear duct	I. Stria vascularis
_____ 9. Supports the organ of Corti; membranous	J. Vestibular membrane

29. Figure 14.7 is a view of the structures of the membranous labyrinth. Correctly identify and label the following major areas of the labyrinth on the figure: membranous semicircular canals, saccule and utricle, and the cochlear duct. Next, correctly identify and label each of the receptor types shown in enlarged views (organ of Corti, crista ampullaris, and macula). Finally, using terms from the key choices, identify all receptor structures with leader lines. (Some of these terms may need to be used more than once.) Color the diagram as you wish.

Key Choices

A. Basilar membrane   E. Hair cells

B. Cochlear nerve fibers   F. Otoliths

C. Cupula   G. Tectorial membrane

D. Otolithic membrane   H. Vestibular nerve fibers

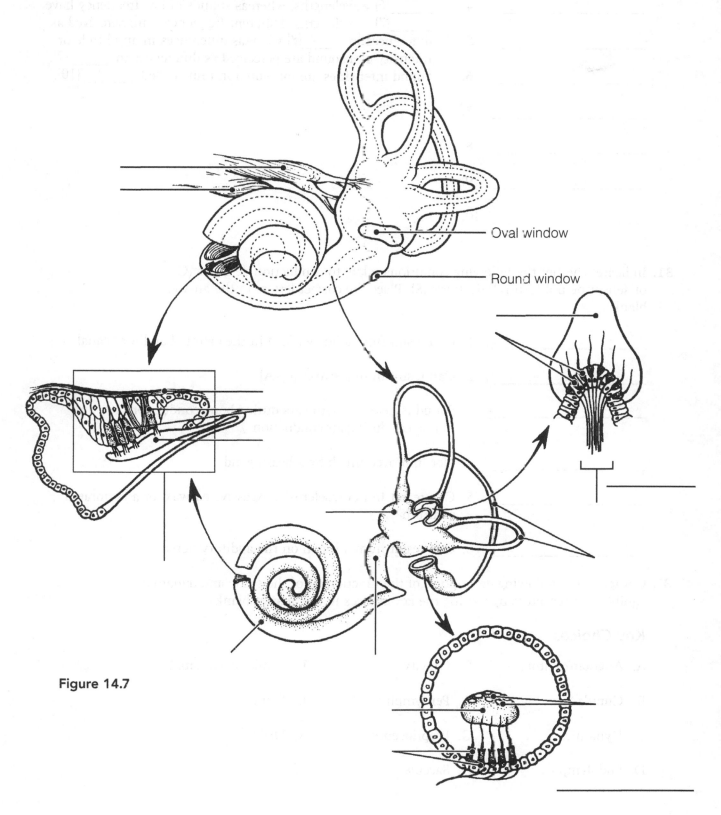

Oval window

Round window

Figure 14.7

30. Complete the following statements referring to the physics of sound.

_____ 1.

_____ 2.

_____ 3.

_____ 4.

_____ 5.

_____ 6.

_____ 7.

_____ 8.

_____ 9.

_____ 10.

1. The source of sound is a _____(1). In order for sound to be propagated, there must be a medium, and it must be _____(2) so that alternating regions of _____(3) and _____(4) can be produced. Sound waves are periodic, and the distance between successive peaks of a sound sine wave is referred to as the _____(5) of sound. As a rule, sounds of high frequency have _____(6) wavelengths, whereas sounds of low frequency have _____(7) wavelengths. Different frequencies are perceived as differences in _____(8) whereas differences in amplitude or intensity of a sound are perceived as differences in _____(9). Sound intensities are measured in units called _____(10).

31. Indicate whether the following conditions relate to conduction deafness (C) or sensorineural (central) deafness (S). Place the correct letters in the answer blanks.

_____ 1. Can result from a bug wedged in the external auditory canal

_____ 2. Can result from a stroke (CVA)

_____ 3. Sound is heard in both ears during bone conduction, but only in one ear during air conduction

_____ 4. Not improved much by a hearing aid

_____ 5. Can result from otosclerosis, excessive earwax, or a perforated eardrum

_____ 6. Can result from a lesion on the auditory nerve

32. Complete the following description of the functioning of the static and dynamic equilibrium receptors by writing the key choices in the answer blanks.

Key Choices

A. Angular/rotatory   E. Gravity   I. Semicircular canals

B. Cupula   F. Perilymph   J. Static

C. Dynamic   G. Proprioception   K. Utricle

D. Endolymph   H. Saccule   L. Vision

_____   1.   The receptors for _____(1) equilibrium are found in the crista
                             ampullaris of the _____(2). These receptors respond to changes
_____   2.   in _____(3) motion. When motion begins, the _____(4) fluid
                             lags behind and the _____(5) is bent, which excites the hair
_____   3.   cells. When the motion stops suddenly, the fluid flows in the
                             opposite direction and again stimulates the hair cells. The
_____   4.   receptors for _____(6) equilibrium are found in the maculae of
                             the _____(7) and _____(8). These receptors report on the posi-
_____   5.   tion of the head in space. Tiny stones found in a gel overlying
                             the hair cells roll in response to the pull of _____(9). As they
_____   6.   roll, the gel moves and tugs on the hair cells, exciting them.
                             Besides the equilibrium receptors of the inner ear, the senses of
_____   7.   _____(10) and _____(11) are also important in helping
                             maintain equilibrium.
_____   8.

_____   9.

_____   10.

_____   11.

33. Circle the term that does not belong in each of the following groupings.

1. Hammer   Anvil   Pinna   Stirrup

2. Tectorial membrane   Crista ampullaris   Semicircular canals   Cupula

3. Gravity   Angular motion   Sound waves   Rotation

4. Utricle   Saccule   Pharyngotympanic tube   Vestibule

5. Vestibular nerve   Optic nerve   Cochlear nerve   Vestibulocochlear nerve

6. Crista ampullaris   Maculae   Retina   Proprioceptors   Pressure receptors

7. Fast motility   Inner hair cells   Ear sounds   Outer hair cells

Transmission Lines:
Nerves and Their Structure and Repair

1. Name the four functional types of nerve fibers.

_____

_____

_____

_____

2. Figure 14.8 is a diagrammatic view of a section of a nerve wrapped in its connective tissue coverings. Select different colors to identify the following structures and use them to color the figure. Then, label these sheaths, indicated by leader lines on the figure.

◯ Endoneurium

◯ Perineurium

◯ Epineurium

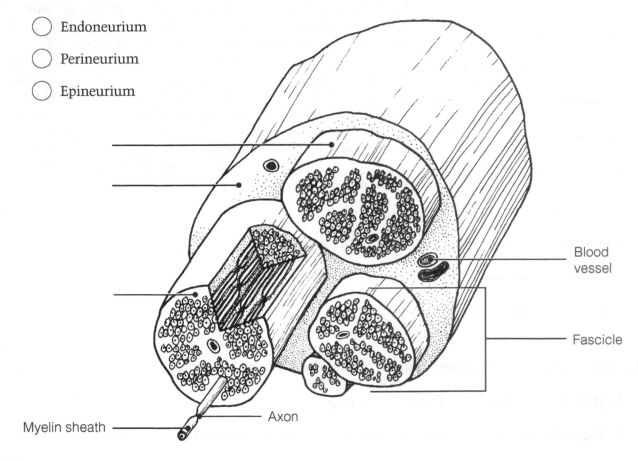

Blood vessel

Fascicle

Myelin sheath

Axon

Figure 14.8

3. Complete the following statements relating to regeneration of nervous tissue. Write the missing terms in the answer blanks.

_____ 1.

_____ 2.

_____ 3.

_____ 4.

_____ 5.

_____ 6.

_____ 7.

_____ 9.

Lost neurons cannot be replaced because mature neurons usually do not _____(1). An axon in the _____(2) nervous system can regenerate successfully if the injury is distal to the _____(3) which must remain intact. After the injured axon ends seal off, the axon and its myelin sheath distal to the injury _____(4). This debris is disposed of by _____(5). Channels, formed by _____(6) that align within the _____(7), guide growing axonal processes toward their original contacts.

Nerve fibers located in the _____(8) nervous system essentially never regenerate. Although the _____(9) cells clean up the degenerated neural debris, _____(10) are notably absent from the CNS, thus cleanup is slower. Additionally, the _____(11) that form the myelin sheath _____(12). Consequently no guiding channels are formed.

_____ 10.   _____ 11.   _____ 12.

4. Match the names of the cranial nerves listed in Column B with the appropriate descriptions in Column A by inserting the correct letters in the answer blanks.

Column A	Column B
_____ 1. The only nerve that originates from the forebrain	A. Accessory
_____ 2. The only cranial nerve that extends beyond the head and neck region	B. Abducens
_____ 3. The largest cranial nerve	C. Facial
_____ 4. Fibers arise from the sensory apparatus within the inner ear	D. Glossopharyngeal
_____ 5. Supplies somatic motor fibers to the lateral rectus muscle of the eye	E. Hypoglossal
_____ 6. Has five major branches; transmits sensory, motor, and autonomic impulses	F. Oculomotor
_____ 7. Cell bodies are located within their associated sense organs	G. Olfactory
_____ 8. Transmits sensory impulses from pressure receptors of the carotid artery	H. Optic
_____ 9. Mixed nerve formed from the union of a cranial root and a spinal root	I. Trigeminal
_____ 10. Innervates four of the muscles that move the eye and the iris	J. Trochlear
_____ 11. Supplies the superior oblique muscle of the eye	K. Vagus
_____ 12. Two nerves that supply the tongue muscles	L. Vestibulocochlear
_____ 13. Its *tract* is frequently misidentified as this nerve	
_____ 14. Serves muscles covering the facial skeleton	

5. Provide the name and number of the cranial nerves involved in each of the following activities, sensations, or disorders. Write your answers in the answer blanks.

_____   1. Hyperextending and flexing the neck

_____   2. Smelling freshly baked bread

_____   3. Constricting the pupils for reading

_____   4. Stimulates the mobility and secretory activity of the digestive tract

_____   5. Involved in frowning and puzzled looks

_____   6. Crunching an apple and chewing gum

_____   7. Tightrope walking and listening to music

_____   8. Gagging and swallowing; tasting bitter foods

_____   9. Involved in "rolling" the eyes (three nerves; provide numbers only)

_____ 10. Feeling a toothache

_____ 11. Watching tennis on TV

_____ 12. If this nerve is damaged, deafness results

_____ 13. Stick out your tongue!

_____ 14. Inflammation of this nerve may cause Bell's palsy

_____ 15. Damage to this nerve may cause anosmia

6. Match each of the cranial nerves listed in Column A to its terminal connection in the cerebral cortex (an item from Column B).

	Column A		Column B
_____	1. Oculomotor	A.	Frontal eye field
_____	2. Olfactory	B.	Hypothalamus
_____	3. Facial	C.	Parietal lobe
_____	4. Trigeminal	D.	Primary motor cortex
_____	5. Optic	E.	Occipital lobe
_____	6. Vagus	F.	Temporal lobe

7. The 12 pairs of cranial nerves are indicated by leader lines on Figure 14.9. First, label each by name and Roman numeral on the figure. Then, color each nerve with a different color.

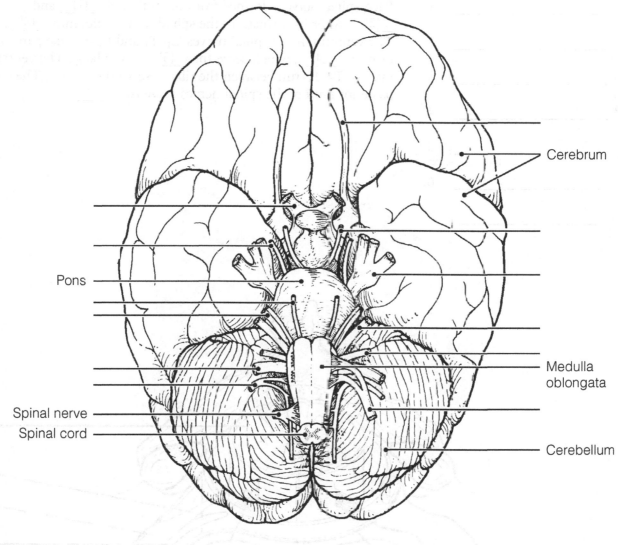

Figure 14.9

8. Name the five major motor branches of the facial nerve.

_____ , _____ , _____ ,

_____ , and _____ .

9. Identify all structures provided with leader lines in Figure 14.10. Color the diagram as you wish and then complete the following statements by inserting your responses in the answer blanks.

_____ 1.

_____ 2.

_____ 3.

_____ 4.

_____ 5.

_____ 6.

_____ 7.

1. Each spinal nerve is formed from the union of __(1)__ and __(2)__. After its formation, the spinal nerve splits into __(3)__.
2. The ventral rami of spinal nerves C_1–T_1 and L_1–S_4 take part in forming __(4)__, which serve the __(5)__ of the body. The ventral
3. rami of T_1–T_{12} run between the ribs to serve the __(6)__. The posterior rami of the spinal nerves serve the __(7)__.

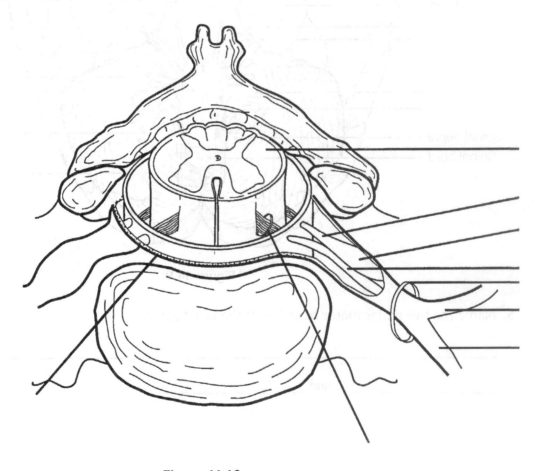

Figure 14.10

10. Referring to the distribution of spinal nerves, circle the term that does not belong in each of the following groupings.

1. Division of spinal nerve   Two rami   Meningeal branch   Two roots

2. Thoracic roots   Lumbar roots   Sacral roots   Cauda equina

3. Activation of skeletal muscles   Ventral root   Motor root   Afferent fibers

4. Anterior ramus   Motor function   Sensory function   Ventral root

5. Ventral ramus   Dorsal ramus   Division of spinal nerve   Two spinal roots

11. Name the major nerves that serve the following body parts. Insert your responses in the answer blanks.

_____ 1. Head, neck, shoulders (name plexus only)

_____ 2. Diaphragm

_____ 3. Hamstrings

_____ 4. Leg and foot (name two)

_____ 5. Most anterior forearm muscles

_____ 6. Flexor muscles of the arm

_____ 7. Abdominal wall (name plexus only)

_____ 8. Thigh flexors and knee extensors

_____ 9. Medial side of the hand

_____ 10. Plexus serving the upper limb

_____ 11. Large nerve composed of two nerves in a common sheath

_____ 12. Buttock, pelvis, lower limb (name plexus only)

_____ 13. Largest branch of the brachial plexus

_____ 14. Largest nerve of the lumbar plexus

_____ 15. Adductor muscles of the thigh

_____ 16. Gluteus maximus

12. Figure 14.11 is an anterior view of the principal nerves arising from the cords of the brachial plexus. Select five different colors and color the coding circles and the nerves listed below. Also, label each nerve by inserting its name at the appropriate leader line.

- ◯ Axillary nerve
- ◯ Musculocutaneous nerve
- ◯ Median nerve
- ◯ Radial nerve
- ◯ Ulnar nerve

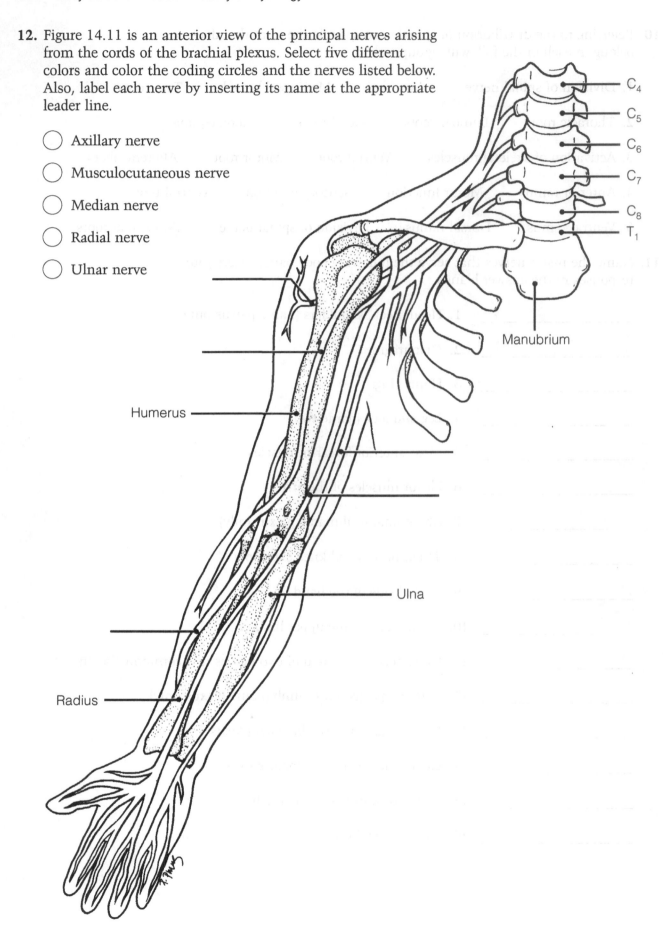

C_4

C_5

C_6

C_7

C_8

T_1

Manubrium

Humerus

Ulna

Radius

Figure 14.11

13. Figure 14.12 is a posterior view of the major nerves arising from the cords of the sacral plexus. Choose seven colors and color the coding circles and the nerves listed below. Then, identify each nerve by inserting its name at the appropriate leader line.

○ Common fibular nerve

○ Inferior gluteal nerve

○ Plantar nerve branches

○ Sciatic nerve

○ Superior gluteal nerve

○ Sural nerve

○ Tibial nerve

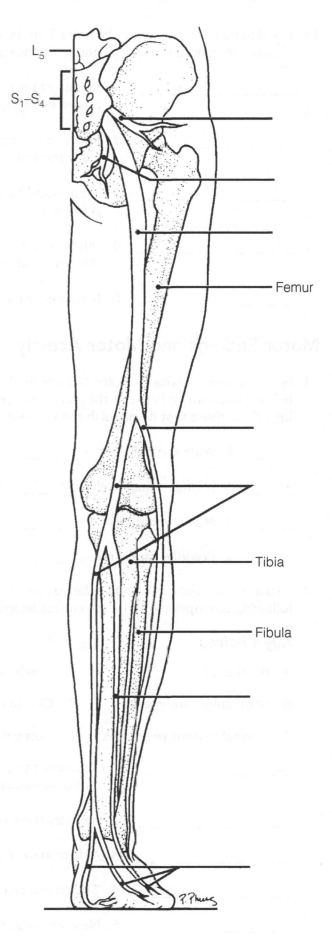

Figure 14.12

14. If a statement is true, write the letter T in the answer blank. If a statement is false, change the underlined word(s) and write the correct word(s) in the answer blank.

_____ 1. Inability to extend the hand at the wrist (wristdrop) can be caused by injury to the <u>median</u> nerve.

_____ 2. Injury to the <u>common fibular</u> nerve causes loss of foot and ankle movements (footdrop).

_____ 3. Thumb and little finger opposition is lost if the <u>axillary</u> nerve is injured.

_____ 4. Injury to the <u>radial</u> nerve causes loss of flexion of the fingers at the distal interphalangeal joints (clawhand).

_____ 5. Irritation of the <u>phrenic nerve</u> may cause hiccups.

Motor Endings and Motor Activity

1. Several characteristics of motor endings (both autonomic and somatic) are listed below. Differentiate between the autonomic and somatic motor endings by checking (✓) all those that distinguish the synapses en passant of autonomic fibers.

_____ 1. Wide synaptic cleft   _____ 5. Clustered boutons

_____ 2. Narrow synaptic cleft   _____ 6. Glycoprotein-rich basal lamina in synaptic cleft

_____ 3. May contain NE   _____ 7. Innervate skeletal muscle fibers

_____ 4. Beadlike varicosities   _____ 8. Innervate smooth muscle fibers and glands

2. Using the key choices, identify the structures, or associated structures, in the following descriptions. Write the correct letters in the answer blanks.

Key Choices

A. Basal nuclei   D. Cerebellum   G. Indirect (multineuronal) system

B. Brain stem motor areas   E. Command neurons   H. Direct (pyramidal) system

C. Central pattern generators   F. Cortical motor area   I. Spinal cord

_____ 1. Activates anterior horn neurons of a spinal cord segment during locomotion

_____ 2. Includes the reticular, red, and vestibular nuclei of the brain stem

_____ 3. Able to start, stop, or modify the central pattern generators

_____ 4. The crucial center for sensory-motor integration and control

_____ 5. Neurons located in the precentral gyri of the frontal lobes

_____ 6. May involve networks of spinal cord neurons arranged in reverberating circuits

_____ 7. Function as a liaison between various areas of the cerebral cortex and interact with brain stem "motor programs" areas

_____ 8. Precommand areas

3. Several neural structures play important roles in the hierarchy of motor control. In the flowchart shown in Figure 14.13, there are several blanks. First, fill in the names for the lowest, middle, and highest levels of the motor hierarchy (put terms inside the appropriate boxes). Then, next to the level terms (lowest, etc.), write the names of the brain regions that contribute to that level of the hierarchy. Also, identify the boxes representing motor output and sensory input. Finally, color the diagram as you like.

Interactions   **Control Level**   **Structures Involved**

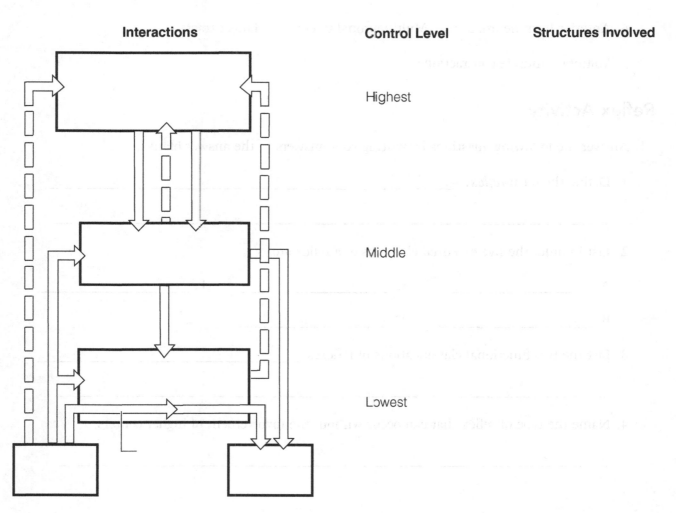

Highest

Middle

Lowest

Figure 14.13

4. Circle the term that does not belong in each of the following groupings.

    1. Fixed action pattern   Consciously considered actions   Complex motor behavior

       All-or-none sequence of motor actions

    2. Cerebral cortex   Pyramidal neurons   Conscious level   Command neurons

    3. Cerebellum   Rhythmic bursts of motor impulses   Inherited

       Central pattern generators

    4. Command neurons   Breathing rhythms   Interneurons   Precommand areas

    5. Reticular nuclei   Vestibular nuclei   Basal nuclei   Red nuclei

    6. Anterior horn neurons   Multineuronal tracts   Direct tracts

       Voluntary muscle contractions

Reflex Activity

1. Answer the following questions by writing your answers in the answer blanks.

    1. Define the term *reflex*. _____

       _____

    2. List in order the five essential elements of a reflex arc.

       A. _____   C. _____   E. _____

       B. _____   D. _____

    3. List the two functional classifications of reflexes. _____

       _____

    4. Name the type of reflex that can occur without the involvement of higher centers.

       _____

2. Using the key choices, identify the types of reflexes involved in each of the following situations.

Key Choices

A. Somatic reflex(es)   B. Autonomic reflex(es)

_____ 1. Patellar (knee-jerk) reflex   _____ 5. Flexor reflex

_____ 2. Pupillary light reflex   _____ 6. Regulation of blood pressure

_____ 3. Effectors are skeletal muscles   _____ 7. Salivary reflex

_____ 4. Effectors are smooth muscle   _____ 8. Clinical testing for spinal cord
            and glands   assessment

3. Complete the following statements by writing the missing terms in the answer blanks:

_____ 1.

_____ 2.

_____ 3.

_____ 4.

_____ 5.

_____ 6.

_____ 7.

_____ 8.

_____ 9.

_____ 10.

_____ 11.

Stretch reflexes are initiated by _____(1), which monitor changes in muscle length. Each consists of small _____(2) enclosed in a capsule. The nerve endings wrapped around these cells are of two types, responding to two different aspects of stretch: the _____(3) endings of the larger _____(4) are stimulated by amount and rate of stretch. The _____(5) endings of the small _____(6) respond only to degree of stretch. Motor innervation to these special muscle cells is via _____(7), which arise from small motor neurons. The large, contractile _____(8) are innervated by _____(9). These nerve fibers' cell bodies, known as _____(10), are excited in the stretch reflex; antagonists are inhibited via _____(11).

4. Some of the structural elements described in Exercise 3 are illustrated in Figure 14.14. Identify each of the numbered structures by matching it to the terms listed below the diagram.

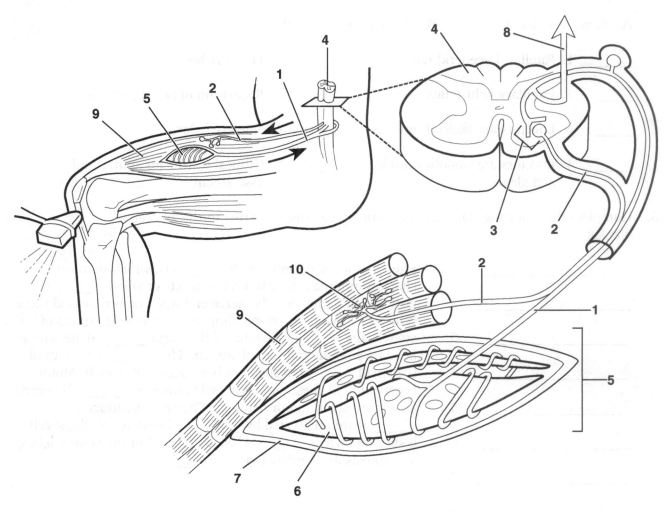

Figure 14.14

_____ Primary sensory afferent

_____ Alpha (α) motor neuron

_____ Spinal cord

_____ Synapse

_____ Muscle spindle

_____ Skeletal muscle (extrafusal fibers)

_____ Motor ending to extrafusal fiber

_____ Intrafusal fiber

_____ Receptor capsule

_____ Ascending fibers

5. The table below lists several reflex characteristics. Check (✓) each characteristic that relates to a stretch reflex, to a deep-tendon reflex, or to both reflexes.

Characteristic	Stretch	Deep tendon
1. Sensor is the muscle spindle		
2. Sensor is the Golgi tendon organ		
3. Alpha motor neuron innervates agonist muscle		
4. Contraction of agonist muscle is inhibited		
5. Agonist muscle contracts		
6. Contraction of antagonist muscle is inhibited		
7. Antagonist muscle is stimulated		
8. Neuron to antagonist muscle is inhibitory		
9. Type of innervation is reciprocal		
10. Helps ensure smooth onset and termination of muscle contraction		

6. Using the key choices, characterize the types of somatic spinal reflexes according to the descriptions listed below. Insert the letter that best matches each description in the corresponding answer blank.

Key Choices

A. Abdominal   C. Deep tendon   E. Stretch

B. Crossed extensor   D. Flexor   F. Superficial

_____ 1. Maintain normal muscle tone and body posture

_____ 2. Initiated by painful stimuli

_____ 3. Particularly important in maintaining balance

_____ 4. Polysynaptic

_____ 5. Initiated by proprioceptors

_____ 6. Monosynaptic and ipsilateral

_____ 7. Polysynaptic and both ipsilateral and contralateral

_____   8. Initiated by cutaneous stimulation

_____   9. Polysynaptic and ipsilateral

_____   10. Functioning of corticospinal tracts is required

_____   11. Protective and overrides the spinal pathways

_____   12. The patellar reflex (knee-jerk reflex)

_____   13. Plantar reflex

_____   14. Stimulation causes the umbilicus to move toward the stimulated site

THE INCREDIBLE JOURNEY

A Visualization Exercise for the Special Senses

You . . . see a discontinuous sea of glistening, white rock slabs . . .

1. Complete the narrative by inserting the missing words in the answer blanks.

_____   1.   Your present journey will take you through your host's inner ear to observe and record events documenting what you have

_____   2.   learned about how hearing and equilibrium receptors work.

_____   3.   This is a very tightly planned excursion. Your host has been instructed to move his head at specific intervals and will be

_____   4.   exposed to various sounds so that you can make specific observations. For this journey you are injected into the bony cavity

_____   5.   of the inner ear, the _____(1 , and are to make your way through its various chambers in a limited amount of time.

Your first observation is that you are in a warm sea of _____(2) in the vestibule. To your right are two large sacs, the _____(3) and _____(4). You swim over to one of these membranous sacs, cut a small semicircular opening in the wall, and wiggle through. Since you are able to see very little in the dim light, you set out to explore this area more fully. As you try to move, however, you find that your feet are embedded in a thick, gluelike substance. The best you manage is slow-motion movements through this _____(5).

_____ 6.   It is now time for your host's first scheduled head movement.
Suddenly your world tips sharply sideways. You hear a roar

_____ 7.   (rather like an avalanche) and look up to see a discontinuous
sea of glistening, white rock slabs sliding toward you. You pro-

_____ 8.   tect yourself from these _____(6) by ducking down between
the hair cells that are bending vigorously with the motion of

_____ 9.   the rocks. Now that you have seen and can document the operation of a(n) _____(7), a sense organ of _____(8) equilibrium,

_____ 10.   you quickly back out through the hole you made.

_____ 11.   Keeping in mind the schedule and the fact that it is nearly time
for your host to be exposed to tuning forks, you swim quickly

_____ 12.   to the right, where you see what looks like the opening of a
cave with tall seaweed waving gently in the current. Abruptly,

_____ 13.   as you enter the cave, you find that you are no longer in
control of your movements, but instead are swept along in a

_____ 14.   smooth undulating pattern through the winding passageway of
the cave, which you now know is the cavity of the _____(9).

_____ 15.   As you move up and down with the waves, you see hair cells of
the _____(10), the sense organ for _____(11), being vigorously

_____ 16.   disturbed below you. Flattening yourself against the chamber
wall to prevent being carried further by the waves, you wait for
the stimulus to stop. Meanwhile you are delighted by the elec-
trical activity of the hair cells below you. As they depolarize and send impulses along the
_____(12) nerve, the landscape appears to be alive with fireflies.

Now that you have witnessed the events for this particular sense receptor, you swim back
through the vestibule toward your final observation area at the other end of the bony chambers.
You recognize that your host is being stimulated again because of the change in fluid currents,
but since you are not close to any of the sensory receptors, you are not sure just what the stimulus is. Then, just before you, three dark openings appear, the _____(13). You swim into the middle opening and see a strange structure that looks like the brush end of an artist's paint brush;
you swim upward and establish yourself on the soft brushy top portion. This must be the
_____(14) of the _____(15), the sensory receptor for _____(16) equilibrium. As you rock back and
forth in the gentle currents, a sudden wave of fluid hits you. Clinging to the hairs as the fluid
thunders past you, you realize that there will soon be another such wave in the opposite
direction. You decide that you have seen enough of the special senses and head back for the
vestibule to leave your host once again.

CHALLENGING YOURSELF

At the Clinic

1. Brian is brought to the clinic by his parents, who noticed that his right eye does
not rotate laterally very well. The doctor explains that the nerve serving the lateral rectus muscle is not functioning correctly. What nerve is involved?

2. Mrs. Krikbaum comes to the clinic because of excruciating pain in the left side of her face whenever she drinks cold fluids. What nerve is likely to be inflamed and what name is given to this condition?

3. Nine children attending the same Happy-Time Day-care Center developed red, inflamed eyes and eyelids. What is the most likely cause and name of the condition? Would antibiotics be an appropriate treatment?

4. After brain surgery, Ray complains that the hospital food tastes unbearably repugnant. His ability to taste salt and sugar are normal, but he firmly maintains that the food is rotten and inedible. From what condition is he suffering, and why?

5. A blow to the neck has caused Yolanda to lose her voice. What nerve is affected and what would happen if the entire nerve were nonfunctional?

6. In John's checkup, one year after an accident severed his right accessory nerve, severe muscle atrophy was noted. What two prominent muscles have been affected?

7. Three-year-old Samantha is sobbing that her right arm is "gone" and the examination shows her to have little muscle strength in that limb. Questioning the parents reveals that her father had been swinging her by the arms. What part of the PNS has been damaged?

8. A man comes to the clinic for physical therapy after injuring his right elbow. The flexors of the forearm are weak, and he has great difficulty picking up objects with thumb and forefinger. What nerve has been damaged?

9. An infant girl is brought to the clinic with strabismus, and tests show that she can control both eyes independently. What noninvasive procedure will be tried before surgery?

10. Bernie Noyes, a man in his early 60s, comes to the clinic complaining of fuzzy vision. An eye examination reveals clouding of his lenses. What is his problem and what factors might have contributed to it?

11. Frita, a woman in her early 70s, was having problems chewing. She was asked to stick out her tongue. It deviated to the right and its right side was quite wasted. What nerve was injured?

12. Ted is a war veteran who was hit in the back by fragments of an exploding bomb. His skin is numb in the center of his buttocks and along the entire posterior side of a lower limb, but there is no motor problem at all. One of the following choices is the most likely site of his nerve injury. Choose and explain: (a) a few dorsal roots of the cauda equina; (b) spinal cord transection at C_6; (c) spinal cord transection at L_5; (d) femoral nerve transected in the lumbar region.

13. A 67-year-old woman was diagnosed as having advanced nasopharyngeal cancer with cranial infiltration. How would you test her for integrity of cranial nerves 9–11?

Stop and Think

1. When a PNS neuron's axon is cut, several structural changes occur in the cell body (particularly concerning the Nissl bodies [chromatophilic substance] and nucleoli). What are these changes and what is their significance to the repair process?

2. Follow the pathway from pricking your finger with a needle to saying "ouch."

3. Name exteroceptors that are not cutaneous receptors.

4. Name, in order, the cranial nerves involved in rolling your eyes to follow the second hand on a watch through one complete rotation. Do this separately for each eye.

5. Why are the cerebellum and basal nuclei called *"pre* command" areas?

6. Are the cords of nerve fibers forming the cauda equina truly spinal nerves?

7. What is the benefit of having the nerve supply of the diaphragm, which is located in the thoracic-lumbar area of the spinal cord, arise from cervical nerves?

8. How does accommodation of muscle spindles figure in the importance of stretch routines as a warm-up for exercise?

9. Use Hilton's law to deduce the nerves that innervate the ankle joint.

10. Dharma, a psychiatric nurse, prepares a bath for a patient and as the tub fills she continuously mixes the water with her hand. As she helps the patient into the tub, he cries out, "What's the matter with you—you're scalding me!" What important aspect of sensory receptor behavior has the nurse forgotten? Explain this phenomenon.

11. Dr. Omata noticed that her anatomy students always confused the glossopharyngeal (IX) and hypoglossal (XII) nerves because the two names have certain similarities. Thus, every year she made her class explain some basic differences between these two nerves. What would you tell her?

12. Adrian and Abdul, two anatomy students, were arguing about the facial nerve. Adrian said it innervates all the skin of the face, and that is why it is called the facial nerve. Abdul said the facial nerve does not innervate face skin at all. Who was more correct? Explain your choice.

13. As Craig stepped onto the sailboat, he smelled the salty sea air and felt the boat rocking beneath his feet. After a few minutes, the smell faded but he was aware of the rocking motion for the entire sail—four hours. What type of receptors are involved in smell and detection of motion? Why did the sensation of smell fade but the rather unpleasant sensation of rocking persist?

14. Why do stars "disappear" when you look directly at them?

15. What difference in the length of the organ of Corti of an elephant allows it to hear low-pitch sounds that are beyond the range of human hearing? What about a dog's ability to hear high-frequency sounds?

16. Name two special senses whose receptor cells are replaced throughout life and two whose receptor cells are never replaced.

COVERING ALL YOUR BASES

Multiple Choice

Select the best answer or answers from the choices given.

1. In an earthquake, which type of sensory receptor is most likely to sound the *first* alarm?

    A. Exteroceptor   C. Mechanoreceptor

    B. Visceroceptor   D. Proprioceptor

2. A cerebral cortical area *not* associated with a special sense is the:

    A. postcentral gyrus   C. temporal lobe

    B. occipital lobe   D. precentral gyrus

3. Examples of encapsulated nerve endings are:

    A. nociceptors   C. Pacinian corpuscles

    B. Merkel discs   D. muscle spindles

4. Structures that can be either exteroceptors or proprioceptors include:

   A. Meissner's corpuscle

   B. Krause's end bulb

   C. Pacinian corpuscle

   D. Ruffini's corpuscle

5. Which of the following are examples of graded potentials?

   A. Generator potential

   B. Action potential

   C. Receptor potential

   D. Synaptic potential

6. Which of the following would be found in the fovea centralis?

   A. Ganglion neurons   C. Cones

   B. Bipolar neurons   D. Rhodopsin

7. The vitreous humor:

   A. helps support the lens

   B. holds the retina in place

   C. contributes to intraocular pressure

   D. is constantly replenished

8. Refraction can be altered for near or far vision by the:

   A. cornea

   B. ciliary muscles

   C. vitreous humor

   D. neural layer of the retina

9. The near point of vision:

   A. occurs when the lens is at its maximum thickness

   B. gets closer with advancing age

   C. changes due to loss of lens elasticity

   D. occurs when the ciliary muscles are totally relaxed

10. Gustatory cells are:

    A. bipolar neurons

    B. multipolar neurons

    C. unipolar neurons

    D. specialized receptor cells

11. Cranial nerves that are part of the gustatory pathway include:

    A. trigeminal   C. hypoglossal

    B. facial   D. glossopharyngeal

12. Which of the following parasympathetic responses can be triggered reflexively by the activation of taste receptors?

    A. Coughing   C. Secretion of saliva

    B. Gagging   D. Secretion of gastric juice

13. The receptors for olfaction are:

    A. the ends of dendrites of bipolar neurons

    B. cilia

    C. specialized nonneural receptor cells

    D. olfactory hairs

14. Which cranial nerve controls contraction of the circular smooth muscle of the iris?

    A. Trigeminal   C. Oculomotor

    B. Facial   D. Abducens

15. Second-order neurons for olfaction are located in the:

    A. olfactory bulb

    B. olfactory epithelium

    C. uncus of limbic system

    D. primary olfactory cortex

16. Objects in the periphery of the visual field:

    A. stimulate cones

    B. cannot have their color determined

    C. can be seen in low light intensity

    D. appear fuzzy

17. Which of the following statements apply to rhodopsin?

    A. Rhodopsin consists of opsin and retinal.

    B. Rhodopsin is identical to the visual pigment in the cones.

    C. The concentration of rhodopsin increases in the rods during dark adaptation.

    D. A solution of rhodopsin looks reddish-purple but becomes colorless after illumination.

18. When moving from darkness to bright light:

   A. rhodopsin breakdown accelerates

   B. adaptation inhibits cones

   C. retinal sensitivity declines

   D. visual acuity increases

19. Excitation of a retinal bipolar cell:

   A. can result from excitation of its photo-receptor cells

   B. causes excitation of its ganglion cell

   C. always results from light striking its photoreceptor cells

   D. is modified by lateral inhibition

20. Depth perception is due to all of the following factors except which one(s)?

   A. The eyes are frontally located.

   B. There is total crossover of the optic nerve fibers at the optic chiasma.

   C. There is partial crossover of the optic nerve fibers at the optic chiasma.

   D. Each visual cortex receives input from both eyes.

21. Movement of the _____ membrane triggers bending of hairs of the hair cells in the spiral organ of Corti.

   A. tympanic

   B. tectorial

   C. basilar

   D. vestibular

22. Sounds entering the external auditory canal are eventually converted to nerve impulses via a chain of events including:

   A. vibration of the eardrum

   B. vibratory motion of the ossicles against the round window

   C. stimulation of hair cells in the organ of Corti

   D. resonance of the basilar membrane

23. In the cochlea:

   A. high-frequency sounds resonate close to the helicotrema

   B. low-frequency sounds resonate farther from the oval window than high-frequency sounds

   C. amplitude determines the intensity of movements of the basilar membrane

   D. sound signals are mechanically processed by the basilar membrane before reaching the receptor cells

24. Transmission of impulses from the sound receptors along the cochlear nerve includes which of the following "way stations"?

   A. Spiral ganglion

   B. Superior olivary nucleus

   C. Cochlear nuclei of the medulla

   D. Auditory cortex

25. When light strikes the lateral aspect of the left retina, activity increases in the:

   A. left optic tract

   B. superior colliculus

   C. pretectal nucleus

   D. right primary visual cortex

26. Sound localization is possible if:

   A. the sound source is in front of the head or slightly to the side; otherwise not

   B. there is a slight difference in the amplitude of the sound entering the two ears

   C. there is a slight difference in the time sound reaches the two ears

   D. the sound is originating at a point exactly equidistant between the ears

27. According to the place theory:

   A. a sound stimulus excites hair cells at a single site on the basilar membrane

   B. the fibers of the cochlear nerve all arise from the same site in the organ of Corti

   C. each frequency component of a sound excites hair cells at particular (and different sites) along the basilar membrane

   D. each sound is interpreted at a specific "place" in the auditory cortex

28. If the loudness of a (20 dB) sound is doubled, the resulting sound's pressure level is:

    A. 0 dB   C. 40 dB

    B. 22 dB   D. 10 dB

29. Which of the following structures is involved in static equilibrium?

    A. Maculae   C. Crista ampullaris

    B. Saccule   D. Otoliths

30. Which lies closest to the posterior pole of the eye?

    A. Cornea   C. Macula lutea

    B. Optic disc   D. Central artery

31. Which of the following are paired incorrectly?

    A. Cochlear duct—cupula

    B. Saccule—macula

    C. Ampulla—otoliths

    D. Semicircular duct—ampulla

32. The vestibular apparatus:

    A. responds to changes in linear acceleration

    B. responds to unchanging acceleratory stimuli

    C. does not usually contribute to conscious awareness of its activity

    D. is helpful, but not crucial, to maintaining balance

33. Taste receptor cells are stimulated by:

    A. chemicals binding to the nerve fibers supplying them

    B. chemicals binding to their microvilli

    C. stretching of their microvilli

    D. impulses from the sensory nerves supplying them

34. Which of the following could be found in a ganglion?

    A. Perikaryon of somatic afferent neuron

    B. Autonomic synapse

    C. Visceral efferent neuron

    D. Somatic interneuron

35. Axonal regeneration involves:

    A. disintegration of the proximal portion of the cut nerve fibers

    B. loss of the oligodendrocyte's myelin sheath

    C. proliferation of the oligodendrocytes

    D. maintenance of the neurilemma

36. Cranial nerves that have some function in vision include the:

    A. trochlear   C. abducens

    B. trigeminal   D. facial

37. Which nerve is tested by the corneal reflex?

    A. Optic

    B. Oculomotor

    C. Ophthalmic division of the trigeminal

    D. Abducens

38. Dependence on a respirator (artificial breathing machine) would result from spinal cord transection:

    A. between C_1 and C_2

    B. between C_2 and C_3

    C. between C_6 and C_7

    D. between C_7 and T_1

39. An inability to extend the leg would result from a loss of function of the:

    A. lateral femoral cutaneous nerve

    B. ilioinguinal nerve

    C. saphenous branch of femoral nerve

    D. femoral nerve

40. The gastrocnemius muscle is served by the:

    A. branches of the tibial nerve

    B. inferior gluteal

    C. deep branch of the common peroneal nerve

    D. superficial branch of common peroneal nerve

41. Which contains only motor fibers?

    A. Dorsal root   C. Ventral root

    B. Dorsal ramus   D. Ventral ramus

42. Which nerve would be blocked by anesthetics administered during childbirth?

    A. Superior gluteal   C. Obturator

    B. Inferior gluteal   D. Pudendal

43. Dermatomes on the posterior body surface are supplied by:

    A. cutaneous branches of dorsal rami of spinal nerves

    B. cutaneous branches of ventral rami of spinal nerves

    C. cutaneous branches of all cranial nerves

    D. cutaneous branch of cranial nerve V

44. After staying up too late the previous night (studying, no doubt), a college student dozed off in his eight o'clock anatomy and physiology lecture. As his head slowly drifted forward to his chest, he snapped it erect again. What type of reflex does this exemplify?

    A. Acquired reflex

    B. Autonomic reflex

    C. Deep tendon reflex

    D. Stretch reflex

Word Dissection

For each of the following word roots, fill in the literal meaning and give an example, using a word found in this chapter.

Word root	Translation	Example
1. ampulla	_____	_____
2. cer	_____	_____
3. cochlea	_____	_____
4. esthesi	_____	_____
5. fove	_____	_____
6. glauc	_____	_____
7. glosso	_____	_____
8. gust	_____	_____
9. kines	_____	_____
10. lut	_____	_____
11. macula	_____	_____
12. noci	_____	_____
13. olfact	_____	_____
14. papill	_____	_____
15. presby	_____	_____

Word root	Translation	Example
16. propri	_____	_____
17. puden	_____	_____
18. scler	_____	_____
19. tars	_____	_____
20. trema	_____	_____
21. tympan	_____	_____
22. vagus	_____	_____

15

THE AUTONOMIC NERVOUS SYSTEM

Student Objectives

When you have completed the exercises in this chapter, you will have accomplished the following objectives:

Introduction

1. Define the autonomic nervous system and explain its relationship to the peripheral nervous system.
2. Compare the somatic and autonomic nervous systems relative to effectors, efferent pathways, and neurotransmitters released.
3. Compare and contrast the general functions of the parasympathetic and sympathetic divisions.

ANS Anatomy

4. For the parasympathetic and sympathetic divisions, describe the site of CNS origin, locations of ganglia, and general fiber pathways.

ANS Physiology

5. Define *cholinergic* and *adrenergic fibers*, and list the different types of their receptors.
6. Describe the clinical importance of drugs that mimic or inhibit adrenergic or cholinergic effects.
7. State the effects of the parasympathetic and sympathetic divisions on the following organs: heart, blood vessels, gastrointestinal tract, lungs, adrenal medulla, and external genitalia.
8. Describe autonomic nervous system controls.

Homeostatic Imbalances of the ANS

9. Explain the relationship of some types of hypertension, Raynaud's disease, and the mass reflex reaction to disorders of autonomic functioning.

The autonomic nervous system (ANS) is the involuntary part of the efferent motor division of the peripheral nervous system (PNS). The ANS is structurally and functionally subdivided into sympathetic and parasympathetic divisions. The two divisions innervate cardiac muscle, smooth muscle, and glands in a coordinated and reciprocal manner to maintain homeostasis of the internal environment.

In Chapter 15, topics for study include structural and functional comparisons between the somatic and autonomic nervous systems and between the sympathetic and parasympathetic divisions. Also included are exercises on the anatomy and physiology of the ANS and impairments and developmental aspects of the ANS.

BUILDING THE FRAMEWORK

Introduction

1. Identify the following descriptions as characteristic of the somatic nervous system (use S), of the autonomic nervous system (use A), or of both systems (use S, A). Insert your letter responses in the answer blanks.

_____ 1. Has efferent motor fibers

_____ 2. Single axonal pathway extends from the CNS to each effector

_____ 3. Slower conduction of nerve impulses

_____ 4. Motor neuron cell bodies are located in the CNS

_____ 5. Typically thick, heavily myelinated motor fibers

_____ 6. Target organs are skeletal muscles

_____ 7. Has preganglionic and ganglionic neurons

_____ 8. Effectors are glands and involuntary muscles

_____ 9. Neural pathways are found in cranial and spinal nerves

_____ 10. One ganglion of each motor unit is located outside the CNS

_____ 11. Typically thin fibers with little or no myelination

_____ 12. Effect of neurotransmitter on target organ is always excitatory

_____ 13. Neurotransmitter at effector site is always acetylcholine

_____ 14. No ganglia are present

_____ 15. Neurotransmitter effect on target organ may be excitation or inhibition

_____ 16. Motor activities under control of higher brain centers

2. Identify, by color coding and coloring, the following structures in Figure 15.1, which depicts the major anatomical differences between the somatic and autonomic motor divisions of the PNS. Also identify by labeling all structures provided with leader lines.

○ Somatic motor neuron

○ ANS preganglionic neuron

○ ANS ganglionic neuron

○ Autonomic ganglion

○ Gray matter of spinal cord (CNS)

○ Effector of the somatic motor neuron

○ Effector of the autonomic motor neuron

○ Intrinsic ganglionic cell

○ Myelin sheath

○ White matter of spinal cord (CNS)

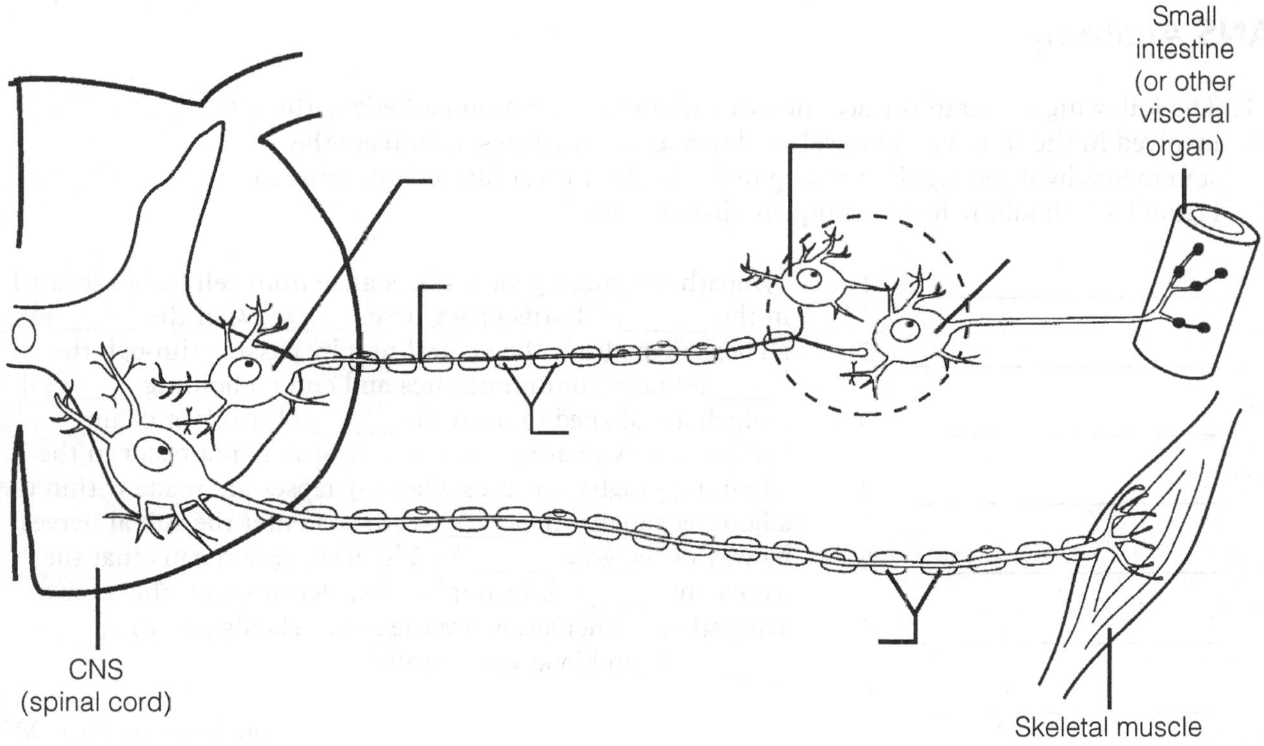

Figure 15.1

3. The following table lists general functions of the ANS. Use a check mark (✓) to show which division of the ANS is involved in each function.

Function	Sympathetic	Parasympathetic
1. Normally in control		
2. "Fight-or-flight" system		
3. More specific local control		
4. Causes a dry mouth, dilates bronchioles		
5. Constricts eye pupils, decreases heart rate		
6. Conserves body energy		
7. Causes increased blood glucose levels		
8. Causes increase in digestive tract mobility		
9. Arector pili muscles contract ("goose bumps")		

ANS Anatomy

1. The following paragraphs trace the sympathetic and parasympathetic pathways involved in the innervation of selected organs or structures. Complete the statements by inserting the missing terms in the answer blanks. Referring to Figure 15.2 should help you complete this exercise.

_____ 1.

_____ 2.

_____ 3.

_____ 4.

_____ 5.

_____ 6.

_____ 7.

_____ 8.

_____ 9.

_____ 10.

Sympathetic preganglionic fibers arise from cell bodies located in the _____(1) horns of segments _____(2) of the _____(3) . These fibers leave the ventral root by passing through the _____(4) rami communicantes and enter adjoining _____(5) , which are aligned to form the _____(6) trunk or chain. Synapses of sympathetic fibers may or may not occur in the adjoining ganglia. In cases where synapses are made within the adjoining ganglia, the _____(7) axons enter the spinal nerves by way of the gray _____(8). The term *gray* means that the axons are _____(9). Examples of structures with this type of sympathetic innervation are the sweat glands and the _____(10)in blood vessel walls.

(continues on page 332)

○ Sites of parasympathetic neurons in the CNS

○ Sites of sympathetic neurons in the CNS

○ Sympathetic fibers

○ Sympathetic trunk of paravertebral ganglia

○ Terminal ganglia

○ Boxes specifying organs that are provided only with sympathetic fibers

○ Parasympathetic fibers

○ Prevertebral ganglia

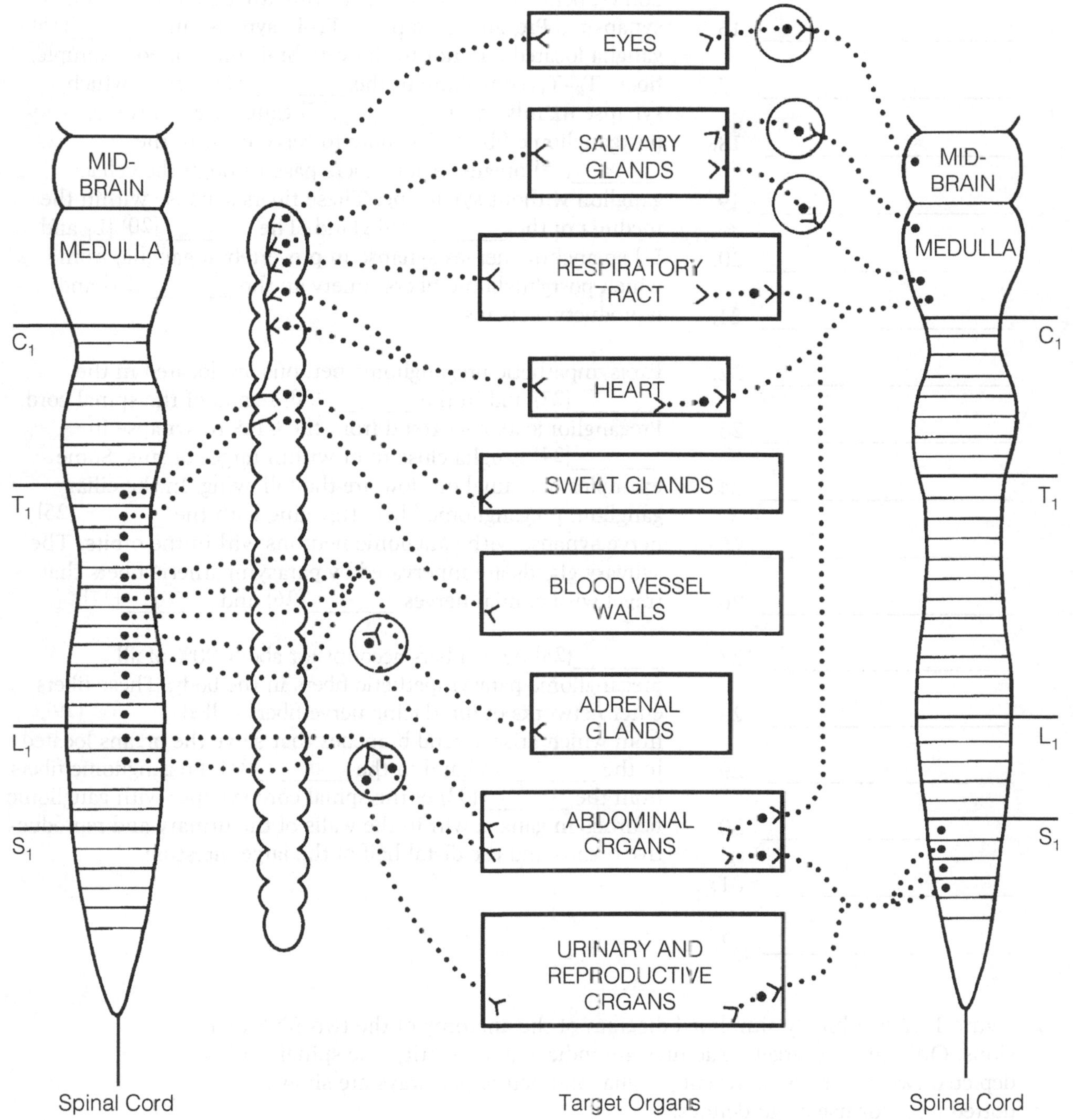

MID-BRAIN

MEDULLA

C₁

T₁

L₁

S₁

Spinal Cord

EYES

SALIVARY GLANDS

RESPIRATORY TRACT

HEART

SWEAT GLANDS

BLOOD VESSEL WALLS

ADRENAL GLANDS

ABDOMINAL ORGANS

URINARY AND REPRODUCTIVE ORGANS

Target Organs

MID-BRAIN

MEDULLA

C₁

T₁

L₁

S₁

Spinal Cord

A. _____ division   B. _____ division

Figure 15.2

_____ 11.
_____ 12.
_____ 13.
_____ 14.
_____ 15.
_____ 16.
_____ 17.
_____ 18.
_____ 19.
_____ 20.
_____ 21.
_____ 22.
_____ 23.
_____ 24.
_____ 25.
_____ 26.
_____ 27.
_____ 28.
_____ 29.
_____ 30.
_____ 31.
_____ 32.

11. Some preganglionic axons may travel within the sympathetic trunk to synapse in other than adjoining ganglia. For example, synapses within the superior _____(11) ganglion contribute fibers innervating the _____(12) of the eye, the _____(13) glands, the heart, and the respiratory tract organs. Though some fibers serve the heart, most of the postganglionic fibers issuing from the other two cervical ganglia innervate the _____(14).

Some fibers enter and leave the sympathetic chain without synapsing. Preganglionic fibers $T_5–L_2$ synapse in _____(15) ganglia located anterior to the vertebral column. For example, fibers $T_5–T_{12}$ contribute to the _____(16) nerves, which synapse mainly in the _____(17) ganglia. From there, postganglionic fibers distribute to serve most of the _____(18) organs. A few fibers pass through the celiac ganglion without synapsing. These fibers synapse within the medulla of the _____(19) gland. The _____(20) (L_1 and L_2) splanchnic nerves synapse in prevertebral ganglia, from which postganglionic fibers innervate the _____(21) and reproductive organs.

Parasympathetic preganglionic neurons are located in the _____(22) and in the _____(23) region of the spinal cord. Preganglionic axons extend from the CNS to synapse in _____(24) ganglia close to or within target organs. Some examples of cranial outflow are the following. In the ciliary ganglion, preganglionic fibers traveling with the _____(25) nerve synapse with ganglionic neurons within the orbits. The salivary glands are innervated by parasympathetic fibers that travel with cranial nerves _____(26) and _____(27).

_____(28) nerve fibers account for about 90% of all preganglionic parasympathetic fibers in the body. These fibers enter networks of interlacing nerve fibers called _____(29), from which arise several branches that serve the organs located in the _____(30) and in the _____(31). Preganglionic fibers from the _____(32) of the spinal cord synapse with ganglionic neurons in ganglia within the walls of the urinary and reproductive organs and the distal half of the large intestine.

2. Figure 15.2 is a highly simplified diagram of the anatomy of the two ANS divisions. Only certain target structures are indicated; for clarity, the spinal cord is depicted twice. Circles represent ganglia, and neural pathways are shown as dotted lines for use as guidelines.

Select eight colors; color the coding circles, structures, and specified boxes listed on the facing page. Use solid lines for preganglionic fibers and dashed lines for postganglionic fibers. Next, label each division in the answer blanks below the figure. Then, insert leader lines and label the four cranial nerves by number.

3. Characterize each of the following anatomical descriptions as it relates to the sympathetic division (use S), the parasympathetic division (use P), or to both divisions (use S, P). Write the correct letter answers in the answer blanks.

_____ 1. Short preganglionic and long postganglionic axons

_____ 2. Travel within cranial and sacral nerves

_____ 3. Called the thoracolumbar division

_____ 4. Long preganglionic and short postganglionic axons

_____ 5. No fibers in rami communicantes

_____ 6. Called the craniosacral division

_____ 7. Ganglia are close to the CNS

_____ 8. Minimal branching of preganglionic fibers

_____ 9. Terminal ganglia are close to or in the visceral organs served

_____ 10. Gray and white rami communicantes utilized

_____ 11. Extensive branching of preganglionic fibers

_____ 12. Nearly all fibers are accompanied by sensory afferent fibers

ANS Physiology

1. Define *cholinergic* fibers, and name the two types of cholinergic receptors below.

   1. Cholinergic fibers _____

   2. Cholinergic receptors _____

2. Define *adrenergic* fibers, and name the two major classes of adrenergic receptors.

   1. Adrenergic fibers _____

   2. Adrenergic receptors _____

3. Using the key choices, select which CNS centers control the autonomic activities listed below. Write the correct letters in the answer blanks.

Key Choices

A. Brain stem   B. Cerebral cortex   C. Hypothalamus   D. Spinal cord

_____   1. The main integration center of the ANS

_____   2. Exerts the most direct control over ANS functioning

_____   3. Coordinates blood pressure, water balance, and endocrine activity

_____   4. Integrates defecation and micturition reflexes

_____   5. Controls some autonomic functioning through meditation

_____   6. Regulates heart and respiration rates and gastrointestinal reflexes

_____   7. Awareness of autonomic functioning through biofeedback training

_____   8. Influences autonomic functioning via limbic system connections

4. The following table lists several physiological conditions. Use a check mark (✓) to show which autonomic division is involved for each condition.

Function	Sympathetic	Parasympathetic
1. All neurons secrete acetylcholine		
2. Controls secretions of catecholamines		
3. Control of reflexes that act in thermoregulation		
4. Accelerates metabolism		
5. Short-lived control of effectors		
6. Postganglionic neurons secrete NE		
7. Localized control of effectors; not diffuse		

5. Circle the term that does not belong in each of the following groupings. (*Note:* ACh = acetylcholine; NE = norepinephrine.)

1. Skeletal muscle contraction   Cholinergic receptors   ACh   NE

2. NE   Usually stimulatory   Nicotinic receptor   Adrenergic receptor

3. Beta receptor   Cardiac muscle   Heart rate slows   NE

4. Blood pressure control   Sympathetic tone   Parasympathetic tone

    Blood vessels partially constricted

5. Parasympathetic tone   Urinary tract   Digestive tract   Rapid heart rate

6. External genitalia   Sympathetic tone   Blood vessels dilate   Penis erection

Homeostatic Imbalances of the ANS

1. If a statement is true, write the letter T in the answer blank. If a statement is false, change the underlined word(s) and write the correct word(s) in the answer blank.

       _____   1. Most autonomic disorders reflect the abnormal control of <u>adrenal medulla</u> activity.

       _____   2. The cause of Raynaud's disease is thought to be intense <u>vasoconstriction</u> in response to exposure to cold.

       _____   3. To promote vasodilation in the patient with a severe case of Raynaud's disease, a <u>parasympathectomy</u> is performed.

       _____   4. Hypertension in the overly stressed patient can be controlled with <u>cholinergic</u> blocker medication.

CHALLENGING YOURSELF

At the Clinic

1. After surgery, patients are often temporarily unable to urinate, and bowel sounds are absent. What division of the ANS is affected by anesthesia?

2. Stress-induced stomach ulcers are due to excessive sympathetic stimulation. For example, one suspected cause of the ulcers is almost total lack of blood flow to the stomach wall. How is this related to sympathetic function?

3. Mrs. Griswold has been receiving treatment at the clinic for Raynaud's disease. Lately her symptoms have been getting more pronounced and severe, and her doctor determines that surgery is her only recourse. What surgical procedure will be performed, and what effect is it designed to produce?

4. Which is the more likely side effect of Mrs. Griswold's surgery—anhidrosis or hyperhidrosis—in the area of concern? (Hidrosis = sweating.)

5. Brian, a young man who was paralyzed from the waist down in an automobile accident, has seen considerable progress in the return of spinal cord reflexes. However, quite unexpectedly, he is brought to the ER because of profuse sweating and involuntary voiding. From what condition is Brian suffering? For what life-threatening complication will the clinical staff be alert?

6. John Ryder, a black male in his mid-40s, has hypertension for which no organic cause can be pinpointed. Which class of autonomic nervous system drugs will most likely be prescribed to manage his condition and why?

7. Roweena Gibson, a high-powered marketing executive, develops a stomach ulcer. She complains of a deep abdominal pain that she cannot quite locate, plus a pain in her abdominal wall. Exactly where on the abdominal wall is the superficial pain most likely to be located? (Doing a little research in Chapter 22 may be helpful here.)

8. Imagine that a mad scientist is seeking to invent a death ray that destroys a person's ciliary, sphenopalatine, and submandibular ganglia (and nothing else). List all the symptoms that would be apparent in the victim. Would the victim die, or would the scientist have to go back to the laboratory to try again?

Stop and Think

1. Can the autonomic nervous system function properly in the absence of visceral afferent input? Explain your response.

   Use the following information for questions 2–6: Stretch receptors in the bladder send impulses along visceral afferent nerve fibers to the sacral region of the spinal cord. Synapses with motor neurons there initiate impulses along visceral efferent fibers that stimulate contraction of the smooth muscle of the bladder wall and relaxation of the smooth muscle (involuntary) sphincter to allow urination.

2. What division of the autonomic nervous system is involved?

3. What sort of neuronal circuit does this exemplify?

4. What nerves carry the impulses?

5. How is urination inhibited consciously?

6. How would this pathway be affected by spinal cord transection above the sacral region?

7. Migraine headaches are caused by constriction followed by dilation of the vessels supplying the brain. The pain is associated with the dilation phase and is apparently related to the high rate of blood flow through these vessels. Some migraine sufferers seek relief through biofeedback, learning to trigger dilation of the vessels in the hand(s). How does this provide relief?

8. Trace the sympathetic pathway from the spinal cord to the iris of the eye, naming all associated structures, fiber types, and neurotransmitters.

9. Trace the parasympathetic pathway from the brain to the heart, naming all associated structures, fiber types, and neurotransmitters.

COVERING ALL YOUR BASES

Multiple Choice

Select the best answer or answers from the choices given.

1. Which of the following is true of the autonomic, but not the somatic, nervous system?

   A. Neurotransmitter is acetylcholine

   B. Axons are myelinated

   C. Effectors are muscle cells

   D. Has motor neurons located in ganglia

2. Examination of nerve fibers supplying the rectus femoris muscle reveals an assortment of type A fibers and type C fibers. The type A fibers are known to be somatic motor fibers supplying the skeletal muscle. Which of these is likely to be the function of the type C fibers?

   A. Parasympathetic innervation to the muscle spindles

   B. Sympathetic innervation to the muscle spindles

   C. Parasympathetic innervation to the blood vessels

   D. Sympathetic innervation to the blood vessels

3. Which best describes ANS control?

   A. Completely under control of the cerebral cortex

   B. Completely under control of the brain stem

   C. Entirely controls itself

   D. Major control by the hypothalamus and spinal reflexes

4. Which of the following disorders is (are) related specifically to sympathetic functions?

   A. Achalasia

   B. Raynaud's disease

   C. Orthostatic hypotension

   D. Hirschsprung's disease

5. Adrenal medulla development involves:

   A. neural crest cells

   B. nerve growth factor

   C. sympathetic preganglionic axons

   D. parasympathetic preganglionic axons

6. Orville said he had a heartache because he broke up with his girlfriend and put his hand over his heart on his anterior chest. Staci told him that if his heart really hurt, he could also be pointing somewhere else. Where?

   A. His left arm   C. His gluteal region

   B. His head   D. His abdomen

Use the following choices to respond to questions 7–25:

A. sympathetic division

B. parasympathetic division

C. both sympathetic and parasympathetic

D. neither sympathetic nor parasympathetic

_____ 7. Typically has long preganglionic and short postganglionic fibers

_____ 8. Some fibers utilize gray rami communicantes

_____ 9. Courses through spinal nerves

_____ 10. Has nicotinic receptors on its ganglionic neurons

_____ 11. Has nicotinic receptors on its target cells

_____ 12. Has splanchnic nerves

_____ 13. Courses through cranial nerves

_____ 14. Originates in cranial nerves

_____ 15. Effects enhanced by direct stimulation of a hormonal mechanism

_____ 16. Includes otic ganglion

_____ 17. Includes celiac ganglion

_____ 18. Contains cholinergic fibers

_____ 19. Stimulatory impulses from hypothalamus and/or medulla pass through the thoracic spinal cord to connect to preganglionic neurons

_____ 20. Hyperactivity of this division can lead to ischemia (loss of circulation) to various body parts and hypertension

_____ 21. Affected by beta blockers

_____ 22. Hypoactivity of this division would lead to decrease in metabolic rate

_____ 23. Stimulated by the RAS

_____ 24. Has widespread, long-lasting effects

_____ 25. Sets the tone for the heart

Word Dissection

For each of the following word roots, fill in the literal meaning and give an example, using a word found in this chapter.

Word root	Translation	Example
1. adren	_____	_____
2. chales	_____	_____
3. epinephr	_____	_____
4. mural	_____	_____
5. ortho	_____	_____
6. para	_____	_____
7. pathos	_____	_____
8. splanchn	_____	_____

16

THE ENDOCRINE SYSTEM

Student Objectives

When you have completed the exercises in this chapter, you will have accomplished the following objectives:

1. Indicate important differences between hormonal and neural controls of body functioning.

The Endocrine System: An Overview

2. List the major endocrine organs and describe their body locations.
3. Distinguish between circulating hormones and local hormones.

Hormones

4. Describe how hormones are classified chemically.
5. Describe the two major mechanisms by which hormones bring about their effects on their target tissues.
6. List three kinds of interactions that different hormones acting on the same target cell can have.
7. Explain how hormone release is regulated.

Major Endocrine Organs

8. Describe structural and functional relationships between the hypothalamus and the pituitary gland.
9. List and describe the chief effects of adenohypophyseal hormones.

10. Discuss the structure of the neurohypophysis, and describe the effects of the two hormones it releases.
11. Describe important effects of the two groups of hormones produced by the thyroid gland. Follow the process of thyroxine formation and release.
12. Indicate general functions of parathyroid hormone.
13. List hormones produced by the adrenal gland, and cite their physiological effects.
14. Compare and contrast the effects of the two major pancreatic hormones.
15. Describe the functional roles of hormones of the testes and ovaries.
16. Briefly describe the importance of thymic hormones in immunity.

Other Hormone-Producing Structures

17. Name a hormone produced by the heart, and localize enteroendocrine cells.
18. Briefly explain the hormonal functions of the placenta, kidney, skin, and adipose tissue.

The endocrine system is vital to homeostasis and plays an important role in regulating the activity of body cells. Acting through blood-borne chemical messengers called hormones, the endocrine system organs orchestrate cellular changes that lead to growth and development, reproductive capability, and the physiological homeostasis of many body systems.

Activities in this chapter concern the localization of the various endocrine organs in the body and explaining the general function of the various hormones and the results of their hypersecretion or hyposecretion.

BUILDING THE FRAMEWORK

The Endocrine System: An Overview

1. Complete the following statements by choosing answers from the key choices. Record the answers in the answer blanks.

Key Choices

A. Circulatory system   E. Metabolism   I. Nutrient

B. Electrolyte   F. More rapid   J. Reproduction

C. Growth and development   G. Nerve impulses   K. Slower and more prolonged

D. Hormones   H. Nervous system   L. Water

_____ 1.

_____ 2.

_____ 3.

_____ 4.

_____ 5.

_____ 6.

_____ 7.

_____ 8.

The endocrine system is a major controlling system in the body. Its means of control, however, is much _____(1) than that of the _____(2), the other major body system that acts to maintain homeostasis. Perhaps the reason for this is that the endocrine system uses chemical messengers, called _____(3), instead of _____(4). These chemical messengers enter the blood and are carried throughout the body by the activity of the _____(5) .

The endocrine system has several important functions: It helps maintain _____(6), _____(7), and _____(8) balance; regulates energy balance and _____(9); and prepares the body for childbearing or _____(10).

_____ 9.   _____ 10.

2. Figure 16.1 is a diagram of the various endocrine organs of the body. Next to each letter on the diagram, write the name of the endocrine-producing organ (or area). Then select different colors for each and color the illustration. To complete your identification of the hormone-producing organs, name the organs (not illustrated) described in J, K, and L.

J. Small glands that ride "horseback" on the thyroid

_____

K. Endocrine-producing organ present only in pregnant women

_____

L. B and C hang from the floor of this neuro-endocrine organ

Figure 16.1

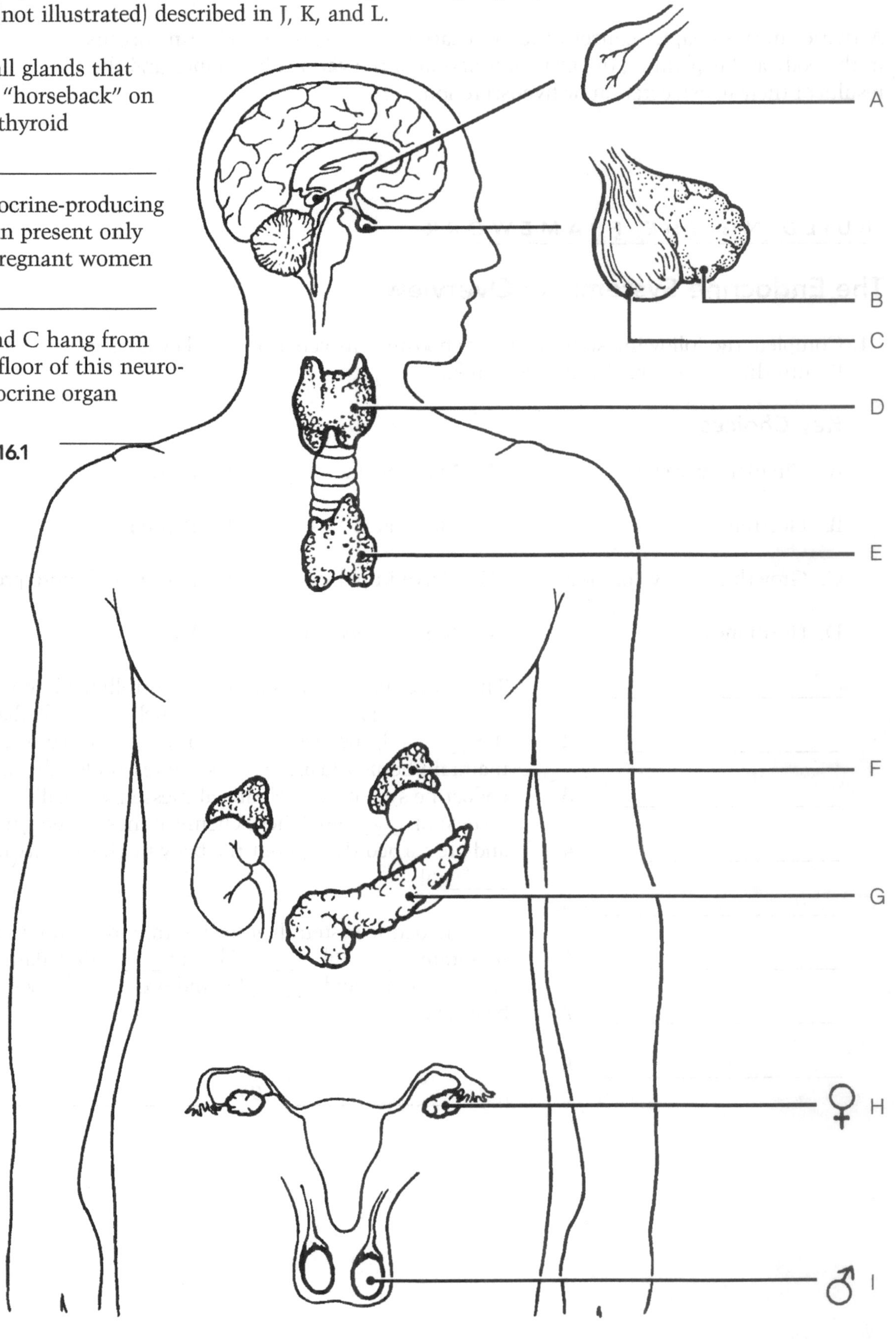

Hormones

1. Complete the following statements by choosing answers from the key choices.
Record the answers in the answer blanks.

Key Choices

A. Altering activity   F. Negative feedback   K. Steroid or amino acid-based

B. Anterior pituitary   G. Neural   L. Stimulating new or unusual activities

C. Hormonal   H. Neuroendocrine   M. Sugar or protein

D. Humoral   I. Receptors   N. Target cell(s)

E.   Hypothalamus J.   Releasing and
inhibiting factors (hormones)

_____ 1.

_____ 2.

_____ 3.

_____ 4.

_____ 5.

_____ 6.

_____ 7.

_____ 8.

_____ 9.

_____ 10.

_____ 11.

_____ 12.

_____ 13.

All cells do not respond to endocrine system stimulation. Only those that have the proper _____(1) on their cell membranes are activated by the chemical messengers. These responsive cells are called the _____(2) of the various endocrine glands.

Hormones promote homeostasis by _____(3) of body cells rather than by _____(4). Most hormones are _____(5) molecules. The various endocrine glands are prodded to release their hormones by nerve fibers (a _____(6) stimulus), by other hormones (a _____(7) stimulus), or by the presence of increased or decreased levels of various other substances in the blood (a _____(8) stimulus). The secretion of most hormones is regulated by a _____(9) system, in which increasing levels of that particular hormone "turn off" its stimulus. The _____(10) is called the master endocrine gland because it regulates so many other endocrine organs. However, it is in turn controlled by _____(11) secreted by the _____(12). The structure identified in item 12 above is also part of the brain, so it is appropriately called a _____(13) organ.

2. Differentiate clearly between a circulating hormone and a local hormone (autocrine or paracrine).

_____

_____

3. Indicate the major stimulus for release of each of the hormones listed below. Choose your response from the key choices.

Key Choices

A. Hormonal   B. Humoral   C. Neural

_____   1. Adrenocorticotropic hormone

_____   2. Parathyroid hormone

_____   3. Insulin

_____   4. Thyroxine and triiodothyronine

_____   5. Epinephrine

_____   6. Oxytocin and antidiuretic hormone

_____   7. Estrogen and progesterone

_____   8. Calcitonin

4. Complete the following description of a second-messenger system by writing the missing words in the answer blanks.

_____   1.

_____   2.

_____   3.

_____   4.

_____   5.

_____   6.

_____   7.

_____   8.

_____   9.

_____   10.

_____   11.   _____   12.

The cyclic AMP mechanism is a good example of a second-messenger system. In this mechanism, the hormone, acting as the _____(1) messenger, binds to target cell membrane receptors coupled to a signal transducer called _____(2). This signal transducer molecule, in turn, acts as an intermediary to activate the enzyme _____(3), which catalyzes the conversion of intracellular _____(4) to cyclic AMP. Cyclic AMP then acts as the _____(5) messenger to initiate a cascade of reactions in the target cell. Most of the subsequent events are mediated by the activation of enzymes called _____(6), which in turn activate or inactivate other enzymes by adding a _____(7) group to them. The sequence of events initiated by the second messenger depends on the _____(8). In addition to cyclic AMP, many other molecules are known to act as second messengers, including _____(9), _____(10), and _____(11). Additionally, the ion _____(12) can act intracellularly as a "third messenger" in certain cases.

5. Explain why the persistence of a hormone in the blood is so limited.

_____

_____

6. Match the terms or phrases in Column B with the descriptions in Column A.

Column A

_____ 1. _____ 2. _____ 3. The extent of target cell activation by hormone-receptor binding depends equally on these three factors

_____ 4. The mechanism by which most steroid-based hormones influence their target cells

_____ 5. _____ 6. _____ 7. _____ 8. Four ways hormones may alter cellular activity (depending on target cell type)

_____ 9. Target cell responds to continued high hormone levels by forming more receptors capable of binding the hormone

_____ 10. Reduced target cell response to continued high hormone levels in the blood

_____ 11. Period of persistence of a hormone in the bloodstream

Column B

A. Affinity of the receptor for the hormone

B. Change in membrane permeability and/or voltage

C. Direct gene activation

D. Down-regulation

E. Enzyme activation/inactivation

F. Half-life

G. Hormone blood levels

H. Initiation of secretory activity

I. Relative number of hormone receptors on the target cells

J. Second-messenger system

K. Synthesis of regulatory molecules such as enzymes

L. Up-regulation

7. Using the key choices listed, respond to the following questions concerning hormone interaction at target cells.

Key Choices

A. Antagonism   B. Permissiveness   C. Synergism

_____ 1. Another hormone must be present for a given hormone to exert its effects.

_____ 2. Combined effects of several different hormones acting on a target cell are amplified.

_____ 3. A hormone opposes or prevents the action of another hormone on a target cell.

Major Endocrine Organs

1. For each of the following hormones, indicate specifically its chemical nature by choosing from the key choices.

Key Choices

A. Steroid   B. Catecholamine   C. Peptide   D. Iodinated amino acid derivative

_____   1. Thyroxine   _____   3. Aldosterone

_____   2. Epinephrine   _____   4. Insulin

2. Figure 16.2 depicts the anatomical relationships between the hypothalamus and the anterior and posterior parts of the pituitary in a highly simplified way. First, identify each of the structures listed below by color coding and coloring them on the diagram. Then, on the appropriate lines write in the names of the hormones that influence each of the target organs shown at the bottom of the diagram. Color the target organ diagrams as you like.

◯ Hypothalamus   ◯ Anterior pituitary

◯ Sella turcica of the sphenoid bone   ◯ Posterior pituitary

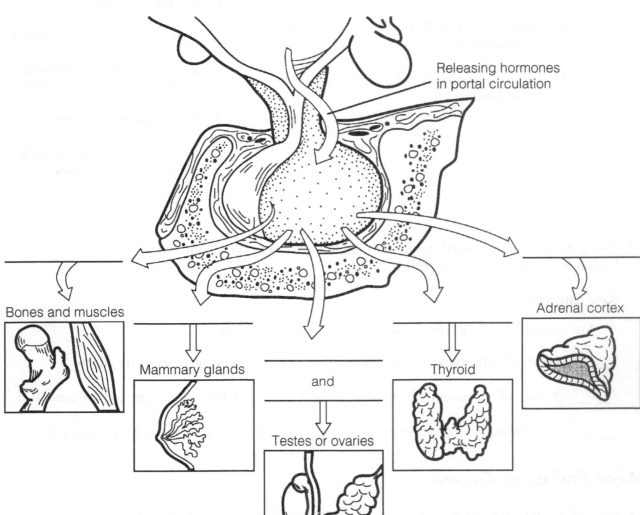

Figure 16.2

3. Indicate the organ (or organ part) producing or releasing each of the hormones listed below by inserting the appropriate answers from the key choices in the answer blanks.

Key Choices

A. Adrenal gland (cortex)   E. Ovaries   I. Placenta

B. Adrenal gland (medulla)   F. Pancreas   J. Testes

C. Anterior pituitary   G. Parathyroids   K. Thymus

D. Hypothalamus   H. Pineal   L. Thyroid

_____ 1. ACTH   _____ 12. Melatonin

_____ 2. ADH   _____ 13. MSH

_____ 3. Aldosterone   _____ 14. Oxytocin

_____ 4. Cortisone   _____ 15. Progesterone

_____ 5. Epinephrine   _____ 16. Prolactin

_____ 6. Estrogens   _____ 17. PTH

_____ 7. FSH   _____ 18. Testosterone

_____ 8. Glucagon   _____ 19. Thymosin

_____ 9. Growth   _____ 20. Thyrocalci-
                     hormone   tonin/calcitonin

_____ 10. Insulin   _____ 21. Thyroxine

_____ 11. LH   _____ 22. TSH

4. Name the hormone that best fits each of the following descriptions.

_____ 1. Basal metabolic hormone

_____ 2. "Programs" T lymphocytes

_____ 3. Most important hormone regulating the amount of calcium circulating in the blood; released when blood calcium levels drop

_____ 4. Helps protect the body during long-term stressful situations, such as extended illness and surgery

_____ 5. Short-term stress hormone; aids in the fight-or-flight response; increases blood pressure and heart rate, for example

_____ 6. Necessary if glucose is to be taken up by most body cells

_____ 7. _____ 8. Regulate the function of
                                                          another endocrine organ; four
_____ 9. _____ 10. tropic hormones

_____ 11. Acts antagonistically to insulin; produced by the same endo-
                              crine organ

_____ 12. Hypothalamic hormone important in regulating water balance

_____ 13. _____ 14. Anterior pituitary hormones
                                                           that regulate the ovarian cycle

_____ 15. _____ 16. Directly regulate the menstrual
                                                           or uterine cycle

_____ 17. Adrenal cortex hormone involved in regulating salt levels of
                              body fluids

_____ 18. _____ 19. Necessary for milk production
                                                           and ejection

5. Circle the term that does not belong in each of the following groupings.

1. Posterior lobe   Neurohypophysis   Nervous tissue   Anterior lobe

2. Posterior lobe   Adenohypophysis   Glandular tissue   Anterior lobe

3. Sympathomimetic amines   Norepinephrine   Epinephrine   Cortisol

4. Neurohormones   Hypophyseal portal system   Axonal transport

   Hypothalamic-hypophyseal tract

5. Growth hormone   Prolactin   Oxytocin   ACTH   Pro-opiomelanocortin

6. Calcitonin   Increases blood Ca^{2+} levels   Thyroid gland   Enhances Ca^{2+} deposit

7. Thyroxine   Increases BMR   Calorigenic effect   Depresses glucose uptake

   Enhances sympathetic nervous system activity

8. Glucocorticoids   Steroids   Aldosterone   Sex hormones   Thyroxine

6. Parathyroid hormone has multiorgan effects. Indicate its effects on the organs
listed below.

1. Kidneys _____

2. Intestine _____

3. Bones _____

7. Explain why antidiuretic hormone is also called vasopressin.

_____

_____

8. Growth hormone has numerous effects, both direct and indirect. Indicate the direct effects of GH by checking (✓) the appropriate choices. Circle the choices that indicate effects mediated indirectly by somatomedins.

_____ 1. Encourages lipolysis

_____ 2. Promotes amino acid uptake from the blood and protein synthesis

_____ 3. Promotes an increase in size and strength of the skeleton

_____ 4. Promotes elevated blood sugar levels

_____ 5. Stimulates cartilage synthesis

_____ 6. Prompts the liver to produce somatomedins

_____ 7. Promotes glucose sparing

_____ 8. Promotes cell division

_____ 9. Causes muscle cell growth

_____ 10. Inhibits glucose metabolism

_____ 11. Increases blood levels of fatty acids

9. Relative to thyroxine synthesis and release, put the following events in their correct time sequence by numbering them from 1 to 9. Event number 1 is already designated.

_____ 1. Within the Golgi apparatus, sugar molecules are attached to the thyroglobulin protein, and the glycolated molecules are packaged in membranous sacs.

_____ 2. Iodinated thyroglobulin is taken up into the follicle cells by endocytosis and combined with lysosomes.

_____ 3. T_3 and T_4 are cleaved out of the colloid by lysosomal enzymes.

_____ 4. Iodine is attached to tyrosine residues of the colloid, forming DIT and MIT.

_____ 5. T_4 and T_3 diffuse into the bloodstream.

__1__ 6. Thyroglobulin protein is synthesized on the ribosomes of the follicle cell.

_____ 7. Iodides are oxidized and transformed into iodine.

_____ 8. Thyroglobulin is discharged into the lumen of the follicle.

_____ 9. Enzymes in the colloid link DITs and MITs together to form T_4 and T_3.

10. List the cardinal symptoms of diabetes mellitus and provide the rationale for the occurrence of each symptom.

1. _____

_____

2. _____

_____

3. _____

_____

11. Compare the magnitude of the conditions in Column A with those immediately opposite in Column B. Circle the phrase indicating the condition that is always or usually greater. If the conditions are essentially always of the same magnitude, put an S on the dotted line between them.

Column A	Column B
1. Plasma levels of gonadotropins during . . . . childhood	Plasma levels of gonadotropins during puberty
2. Activity of T_3 at target cells	Activity of T_4 at target cells
3. Protein wasting and depressed immunity . . with high levels of glucocorticoids	Protein wasting and depressed immunity with low levels of glucocorticoids
4. Stimulation of aldosterone release by . . . . . elevated Na^+ levels in plasma	Stimulation of aldosterone release by elevated K^+ levels in plasma
5. Urine volume in a diabetes mellitus . . . . . . patient	Urine volume in a diabetes insipidus patient
6. Renin release by the kidneys when . . . . . . blood pressure is low	Renin release by the kidneys when blood pressure is elevated
7. Iodine atoms in a thyroxine molecule	Iodine atoms in a triiodothyronine molecule
8. Mineralocorticoid release by zona . . . . reticularis cells	Mineralocorticoid release by zona glomerulosa cells
9. PTH release when blood calcium levels . . . are high (above 11 mg/100 ml)	PTH release when blood calcium levels are low (below 9 mg/100 ml)
10. Hyperglycemia with high levels of . . . . insulin in plasma	Hyperglycemia with high levels of glucagon in plasma
11. ACTH release with high plasma levels . . . . of cortisol	ACTH release with low plasma levels of cortisol
12. Synthesis of insulin by beta cells of . . . . . . pancreatic islets	Synthesis of insulin by alpha cells of pancreatic islets

12. For each of the hormones listed below, indicate its effect on blood glucose, blood calcium, and/or blood pressure by using the key choices.

Key Choices

A. Increases blood glucose   D. Decreases blood calcium

B. Decreases blood glucose   E. Increases blood pressure

C. Increases blood calcium   F. Decreases blood pressure

_____ 1. Cortisol

_____ 2. Insulin

_____ 3. Parathormone

_____ 4. Aldosterone

_____ 5. Growth hormone

_____ 6. Antidiuretic hormone

_____ 7. Glucagon

_____ 8. Thyroxine

_____ 9. Epinephrine

_____ 10. Calcitonin

13. The structure of endocrine cells often allows recognition of the type of hormone product they secrete. Use the key choices to characterize the endocrine cells listed below.

Key Choices

A. Has a well-developed rough ER and secretory granules

B. Has a well-developed smooth ER; prominent lipid droplets

_____ 1. Interstitial cell of the testis

_____ 2. Chief cell in the parathyroid gland

_____ 3. Zona fasciculata cell

_____ 4. Parafollicular cells of the thyroid

_____ 5. Beta cell of a pancreatic islet

_____ 6. Any endocrine cell in the anterior pituitary

14. Concerning the histology of the pure endocrine glands, match each endocrine gland in Column B with the best approximation of its histology in Column A.

Column A

_____ 1. Spherical clusters of cells

_____ 2. Parallel cords of cells

_____ 3. Branching cords of cells

_____ 4. Follicles

_____ 5. Nervous tissue

Column B

A. Posterior pituitary

B. Zona glomerulosa of the adrenal cortex

C. Thyroid gland

D. Zona fasciculata of adrenal cortex

E. Parathyroid gland

15. Name the hormone that would be produced in *inadequate* amounts in each of the following conditions.

_____ 1. Maturation failure of reproductive organs

_____ 2. Tetany (death due to respiratory paralysis)

_____ 3. Polyuria without high blood glucose levels; causes dehydration and tremendous thirst

_____ 4. Goiter

_____ 5. Cretinism, a type of dwarfism in which the individual retains childlike proportions and is mentally retarded

_____ 6. Excessive thirst, high blood glucose levels, acidosis

_____ 7. Abnormally small stature, normal proportions, a "Tom Thumb"

_____ 8. Spontaneous abortion

_____ 9. Myxedema in the adult

16. Name the hormone that would be produced in *excessive* amounts in each of the following conditions.

_____ 1. Acromegaly in the adult

_____ 2. Bulging eyeballs, nervousness, increased pulse rate, weight loss (Graves' disease)

_____ 3. Demineralization of bones; spontaneous fractures

_____ 4. Cushing's syndrome: moon face, hypertension, edema

_____ 5. Abnormally large stature, relatively normal body proportions

_____ 6. Abnormal hairiness; masculinization

Other Hormone-Producing Structures

1. Besides the major endocrine organs, isolated clusters of cells produce hormones within body organs that are usually not associated with the endocrine system. A number of these hormones are listed in the table below. Complete the missing information on these hormones by filling in the blank spaces in the table.

Hormone	Chemical makeup	Source	Effects
Gastrin	Peptide		
Secretin		Duodenum	
Cholecystokinin	Peptide		
Erythropoietin		Kidney in response to hypoxia	
Cholecalciferol (vitamin D_3)		Skin; activated by kidneys	
Atrial natriuretic peptide (ANP)		Peptide	

A Visualization Exercise
for the Endocrine System

*. . . you notice charged particles, shooting
pell-mell out of the bone matrix . . .*

1. Complete the following narrative by writing the missing words in the
answer blanks.

_____ 1.
_____ 2.
_____ 3.
_____ 4.
_____ 5.
_____ 6.
_____ 7.
_____ 8.
_____ 9.

For this journey, you will be miniaturized and injected into a
vein of your host. Throughout the journey, you will be traveling
in the bloodstream. Your instructions are to record changes in
blood composition as you float along and to form some conclu-
sions as to why these changes are occurring (that is, which hormone is being released).

Bobbing gently along in the slowly moving blood, you realize
that there is a sugary taste to your environment; however, the
sweetness begins to decrease quite rapidly. As the glucose levels
of the blood have just decreased, obviously _____(1) has been
released by the _____(2) so that the cells can take up glucose.

A short while later, you notice that the depth of the blood in
the vein you are traveling in has diminished substantially. To
remedy this potentially serious situation, the _____(3) will
have to release more _____(4), so the kidney tubules will reabsorb more water. Within a few minutes the blood becomes
much deeper; you wonder if the body is psychic as well as wise.

As you circulate past the bones, you notice charged particles, shooting pell-mell out of the bone
matrix and jumping into the blood. You conclude that the _____(5) glands have just released
PTH because the _____(6) levels have increased in the blood. As you continue to move in the
bloodstream, the blood suddenly becomes sticky sweet, indicating that your host must be nervous
about something. Obviously, his _____(7) has released _____(8) to cause this sudden increase in
blood glucose.

Sometime later, you become conscious of a humming activity around you, and you sense that the
cells are very busy. Obviously your host's _____(9) levels are sufficient since his cells are
certainly not sluggish in their metabolic activities. You record this observation and prepare to end
this journey.

At the Clinic

1. Pete is very short for his chronological age of 8. What physical features will allow you to determine quickly whether to check GH or thyroxine levels?

2. A young girl is brought to the clinic by her father. He complains that his daughter fatigues easily and seems mentally sluggish. You notice a slight swelling in the anterior neck. What condition do you suspect? What are some possible causes and their treatments?

3. Lauralee, a middle-aged woman, comes to the clinic and explains in an agitated way that she is "very troubled" by excessive urine output and consequent thirst. What two hormones might be causing the problem and what urine tests will be done to identify the problem?

4. A 2-year-old boy is brought to the clinic by his anguished parents. He is developing sexually and shows an obsessive craving for salt. Blood tests reveal hyperglycemia. What endocrine gland is hypersecreting?

5. Lester, a 10-year-old, has been complaining of severe lower back pains. The nurse notices that he seems weak and a reflex check shows abnormal response. Kidney stones are soon diagnosed. What abnormality is causing these problems?

6. Bertha Wise, age 40, is troubled by swelling in her face and unusual fat deposition on her back and abdomen. She reports that she bruises easily. Blood tests show elevated glucose levels. What is your diagnosis and what glands might be causing the problem?

7. A middle-aged man comes to the clinic, complaining of extreme nervousness, insomnia, and weight loss. The nurse notices that his eyes bulge and his thyroid is enlarged. What is the man's hormonal imbalance and what are two likely causes?

8. Mr. Holdt brings his wife to the clinic, concerned about her nervousness, heart palpitations, and excessive sweating. Tests show hyperglycemia and hypertension. What hormones are probably being hypersecreted? What is the cause? What physical factors allow you to rule out thyroid problems?

9. Phyllis, a type-I diabetic, is rushed to the hospital. She had been regulating her diabetes extremely well, with no chronic problems, when her mother found her unconscious. Will blood tests reveal hypoglycemia or hyperglycemia? What probably happened?

10. A woman calls for an appointment at the clinic because she is not menstruating. She also reports that her breasts are producing milk, although she has never been pregnant. What hormone is being hypersecreted and what is the likely cause?

11. An accident victim who had not been wearing a seat belt received severe trauma to his forehead when he was thrown against the windshield. The physicians in the emergency room worried that his brain stem may have been driven inferiorly through the foramen magnum. To help assess this possibility, they quickly took a standard X ray of his head and searched for the position of the pineal gland. How could anyone expect to find a tiny, boneless gland like the pineal in an X ray?

Stop and Think

1. Compare and contrast protein and steroid hormones with regard to the following: (a) organelles involved in their manufacture; (b) ability to store the hormones within the cell; (c) rate of manufacture; (d) method of secretion; (e) means of transport in the bloodstream; (f) location of receptors in/on target cell; (g) use of second messenger; (h) relative time from attachment to receptor until effects appear; and (i) whether effects persist after the hormone is metabolized.

2. (a) Hypothalamic factors act both to stimulate and to inhibit the release of certain hormones. Name these hormones.

   (b) Blood levels of certain humoral factors are regulated both on the "up" and the "down" side by hormones. Name some such humoral factors.

3. What are enteroendocrine cells and why are they sometimes called paraneurons?

4. Would drug tolerance be due to up-regulation or down-regulation?

5. Why do the chemical structures of thyroxine and triiodothyronine require complexing with a large protein to allow long-term storage?

6. The brain is "informed" when we are in a stressful situation, and the hypothalamus responds to stressors by secreting a releasing hormone called corticotropin-releasing hormone. This hormone helps the body deal with the stress through a long sequence of events. Outline this entire sequence, starting with corticotropin-releasing hormone and ending with the release of cortisol. (Be sure to trace the hormones through the hypophyseal portal system and out of the pituitary gland.)

7. Joshua explained to his classmate Jennifer that the thyroid gland contains parathyroid cells in its follicles and the parathyroid cells secrete parathyroid hormone and calcitonin. Jennifer told him he was all mixed up. Can you correct Josh's mistakes?

8. When the carnival was scheduled to come to a small town, health professionals who felt that the sideshows were cruel and exploitive joined with the local consumer groups to enforce truth-in-advertising laws. They demanded that the fat man, the dwarf, the giant, and the bearded lady be billed as "people with endocrine system problems" (which of course removed all the sensationalism usually associated with these attractions). Identify the endocrine disorder in each case and explain how (or why) the disorder produced the characteristic features of these four showpeople.

Closer Connections: Checking the Systems—
Regulation and Integration of the Body

1. How does the central nervous system exert control over the endocrine system?

2. How does the endocrine system exert control over the nervous system?

3. Which of the two regulatory systems is designed to respond to rapid environmental changes?

4. Which system exerts a greater degree of control over the skeletal system? Over metabolism?

5. Explain the differences in control of the muscular system by the nervous system and the endocrine system.

COVERING ALL YOUR BASES

Multiple Choice

Select the best answer or answers from the choices given.

1. Relative to the cyclic AMP second-messenger system, which of the following is not accurate?

   A. The activating hormone interacts with a receptor site on the plasma membrane.

   B. Binding of the galvanizing hormone directly activates adenylate cyclase.

   C. Activated adenylate cyclase catalyzes the transformation of AMP to cyclic AMP.

   D. Cyclic AMP acts within the cell to alter cell function as is characteristic for that specific hormone.

2. Which of the following hormones is (are) released by neurons?

   A. Oxytocin   C. ADH

   B. Insulin   D. Cortisol

3. The paraventricular nucleus of the hypothalamus is named for its proximity to the:

   A. lateral ventricles   C. third ventricle

   B. cerebral aqueduct   D. fourth ventricle

4. Which of the following might be associated with a second-messenger system?

   A. Phosphatidyl inositol   C. Glucagon

   B. Corticosteroids   D. Calmodulin

5. ANP, the hormone secreted by the heart, has exactly the opposite function to this hormone secreted by the zona glomerulosa:

   A. epinephrine   C. aldosterone

   B. cortisol   D. testosterone

6. Hormones that act directly or indirectly to elevate blood glucose include:

   A. GH   C. insulin

   B. cortisol D. CRH

7. The release of which of the following hormones will be stimulated via the hypothalamic-hypophyseal tract?

   A. ACTH   C. ADH

   B. TSH   D. GH

8. Cells sensitive to the osmotic concentration of the blood include:

   A. chromaffin cells

   B. paraventricular neurons

   C. supraoptic neurons

   D. parafollicular cells

9. The gland derived from embryonic throat tissue known as Rathke's pouch is the:

   A. posterior pituitary   C. thyroid

   B. anterior pituitary   D. thymus

10. The primary capillary plexus is located in the:

    A. hypothalamus   C. posterior pituitary

    B. anterior pituitary   D. infundibulum

11. Pro-opiomelanocortin is the precursor of:

    A. cortisol   C. melatonin

    B corticotropin   D. opium

12. Which of the following are direct or indirect effects of growth hormone?

    A. Stimulates cells to take in amino acids

    B. Increases synthesis of chondroitin sulfate

    C. Increases blood levels of fatty acids

    D. Decreases utilization of glucose by most body cells

13. Which of the following are tropic hormones secreted by the anterior pituitary gland?

    A. LH   C. TSH

    B. ACTH   D. FSH

14. Hormones secreted by females include:

    A. estrogens   C. prolactin

    B. progesterone   D. testosterone

15. Smooth muscle contractions are stimulated by:

    A. testosterone   C. prolactin

    B. FSH   D. Oxytocin

16. Nerve input regulates the release of:

    A. oxytocin   C. melatonin

    B. epinephrine   D. cortisol

17. Hypertension may result from hypersecretion of:

    A. thyroxine   C. aldosterone

    B. cortisol   D. antidiuretic hormone

18. In initiating the secretion of stored thyroxine, which of these events occurs first?

    A. Production of thyroglobulin

    B. Discharge of thyroglobulin into follicle

    C. Attachment of iodine to thyroglobulin

    D. Lysosomal activity to cleave hormone from thyroglobulin

19. Hypothyroidism can cause:

    A. myxedema   C. cretinism

    B. Cushing's syndrome   D. exophthalmos

20. Calcitonin targets the:

    A. kidneys   C. bone

    B. liver   D. small intestine

21. Imbalances of which hormones will affect neural function?

    A. Thyroxine   C. Insulin

    B. Parathormone   D. Aldosterone

22. Hormones that regulate mineral levels include:

    A. calcitonin

    B. aldosterone

    C. atrial natriuretic peptide

    D. glucagon

23. Which of the following is given as a drug to reduce inflammation?

    A. Epinephrine   C. Aldosterone

    B. Cortisol   D. ADH

24. After menopause, steroids that maintain anabolism come from the:

    A. ovaries   C. anterior pituitary

    B. adrenal cortex   D. thyroid

25. Which is generally true of hormones?

    A. Exocrine glands produce them.

    B. They travel throughout the body in the blood.

    C. They affect only nonhormone-producing organs.

    D. All steroid hormones produce very similar physiological effects in the body.

26. The major endocrine organs of the body:

    A. tend to be very large organs

    B. are closely connected with each other

    C. all contribute to the same function (digestion)

    D. tend to lie near the midline of the body

27. Which type of cell secretes releasing hormones?

    A. Neuron   C. Chromaffin cell

    B. Parafollicular cell   D. Adenohypophysis cell

28. Of the following endocrine structures, which develops from the brain?

    A. Neurophyophysis   C. Thyroid gland

    B. Adenohypophysis   D. Thymus gland

Word Dissection

For each of the following word roots, fill in the literal meaning and give an example, using a word found in this chapter.

Word root	Translation	Example
1. adeno	_____	_____
2. crine	_____	_____
3. dips	_____	_____
4. diuresis	_____	_____
5. gon	_____	_____
6. hormon	_____	_____
7. humor	_____	_____
8. mell	_____	_____
9. toci	_____	_____
10. trop	_____	_____

25. **Which is generally true of hormones?**
    A. Exocrine glands produce them.
    B. They travel throughout the body in the blood.
    C. They affect only nonhormone-producing organs.
    D. All steroid hormones produce their physiological effect in the liver.

26. The major endocrine organs of the body
    A. tend to be very large organs.
    B. are loosely connected with each other.
    C. all respond to the same stimulus (pituitary).
    D. tend to lie near the midline of the body.

27. Which type of cell secretes releasing hormones?
    A. neuron
    B. parafollicular cell

    chromaffin cell
    adenohypophysis cell

28. Of the following endocrine structures, which develops in the brain?
    A. parathyroids
    B. adenohypophysis

    thyroid gland
    Thymus gland

Word Dissection

For each of the following word roots, fill in the literal translation and give an example using a word found in this chapter.

Word root	Translation	Example
1. adeno		
2. crine		
3. crips		
4. diuresis		
5. gona		
6. hormon		
7. humor		
8. melt		
9. trol		
10. trop		

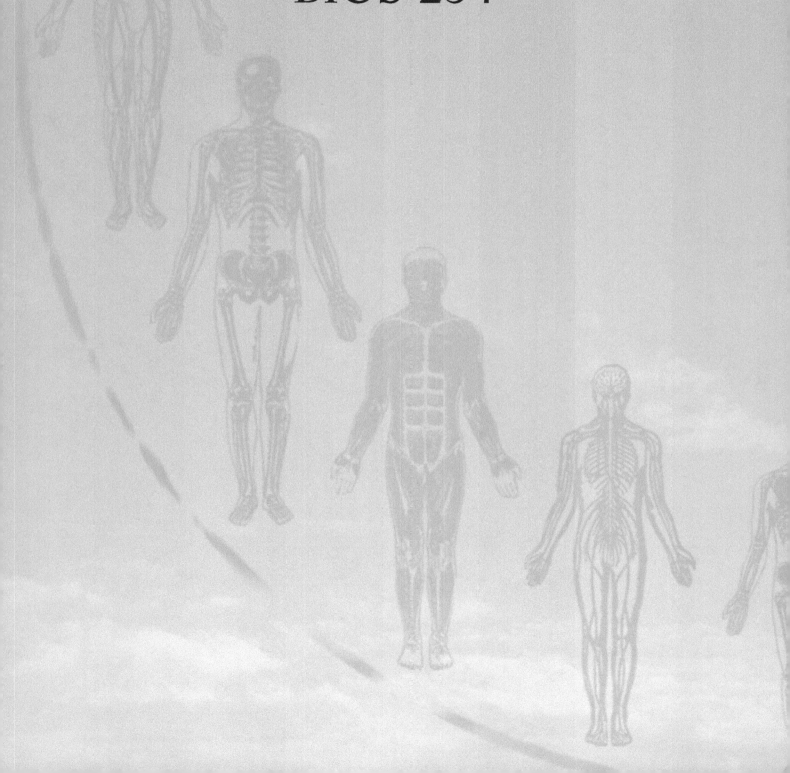

PART 2

BIOS 254

17

THE CARDIOVASCULAR SYSTEM: HEART

Student Objectives

When you have completed the exercises in this chapter, you will have accomplished the following objectives:

Heart Anatomy

1. Describe the size, shape, location, and orientation of the heart in the thorax.

2. Name the coverings of the heart.

3. Describe the structure and function of each of the three layers of the heart wall.

4. Describe the structure and functions of the four heart chambers. Name each chamber and provide the name and general route of its associated great vessel(s).

5. Trace the pathway of blood through the heart.

6. Name the major branches and describe the distribution of the coronary arteries.

7. Name the heart valves and describe their location, function, and mechanism of operation.

Properties of Cardiac Muscle Fibers

8. Describe the structural and functional properties of cardiac muscle, and explain how it differs from skeletal muscle.

9. Briefly describe the events of cardiac muscle cell contraction.

Heart Physiology

10. Name the components of the conduction system of the heart and trace the conduction pathway.

11. Draw a diagram of a normal electrocardiogram tracing; name the individual waves and intervals and indicate what each represents. Name some of the abnormalities that can be detected on an EGG tracing.

12. Describe the timing and events of the cardiac cycle.

13. Describe normal heart sounds and explain how heart murmurs differ.

14. Name and explain the effects of various factors regulating stroke volume and heart rate.

15. Explain the role of the autonomic nervous system in regulating cardiac output.

As part of the cardiovascular system, the heart has a single function—to pump the blood into the blood vessels so that it reaches the trillions of tissue cells of the body. Survival of tissue cells depends on constant access to oxygen and nutrients and removal of carbon dioxide and wastes. This critical homeostatic requirement is met by a continuous flow of blood. The heart is designed to maintain this continuous flow by pumping blood simultaneously through two circuits: the pulmonary circulation to the lungs and the systemic circulation to all body regions.

Topics for study in Chapter 17 include the microscopic and gross anatomy of the heart, the related events of the cardiac cycle, the regulation of cardiac output, malfunctions of the heart, and changes in the heart throughout life.

BUILDING THE FRAMEWORK

Heart Anatomy

1. Complete the following statements by writing the missing terms in the answer blanks.

_____ 1.

_____ 2.

_____ 3.

_____ 4.

_____ 5.

_____ 6.

_____ 7.

_____ 8.

_____ 9.

_____ 10.

_____ 11.

_____ 12.

_____ 13.

_____ 14.

_____ 15.

_____ 16.

The heart is a cone-shaped muscular organ located within the __(1)__ of the thorax. Its apex rests on the __(2)__ and its superior margin lies at the level of the __(3)__ rib. Approximately two-thirds of the heart mass is seen to the left of the __(4)__.

The heart is enclosed in a serosa sac called the pericardium. The loosely fitting double outer layer consists of the outermost __(5)__ pericardium, lined by the parietal layer of the serous pericardium. The inner __(6)__ pericardium, also called the __(7)__, is the outermost layer of the heart wall. The function of the fluid that fills the pericardial sac is to decrease __(8)__ during heart activity. The middle layer of the heart wall, called the __(9)__, is composed of __(10)__; it forms the bulk of the heart.

Connective tissue fibers that ramify throughout this layer construct the so-called __(11)__ of the heart. The membrane that lines the heart and also forms the valve flaps is the __(12)__. This layer is continuous with the __(13)__ linings of the blood vessels that enter and leave the heart. The heart has __(14)__ chambers. Relative to the roles of these chambers, the __(15)__ are the receiving chambers, whereas the __(16)__ are the discharging chambers.

2. Figure 17.1A is a transverse section through the thorax. Label the structures that have leader lines. Figure 17.1B is a highly schematic longitudinal section through the heart wall and pericardium. Select colors for each structure listed below; color the corresponding coding circles and the structure on the figure.

○ Fibrous pericardium   ○ Parietal layer of serous pericardium   ○ Endocardium

○ Myocardium   ○ Visceral layer of serous pericardium (epicardium)   ○ Diaphragm

○ Pericardial cavity

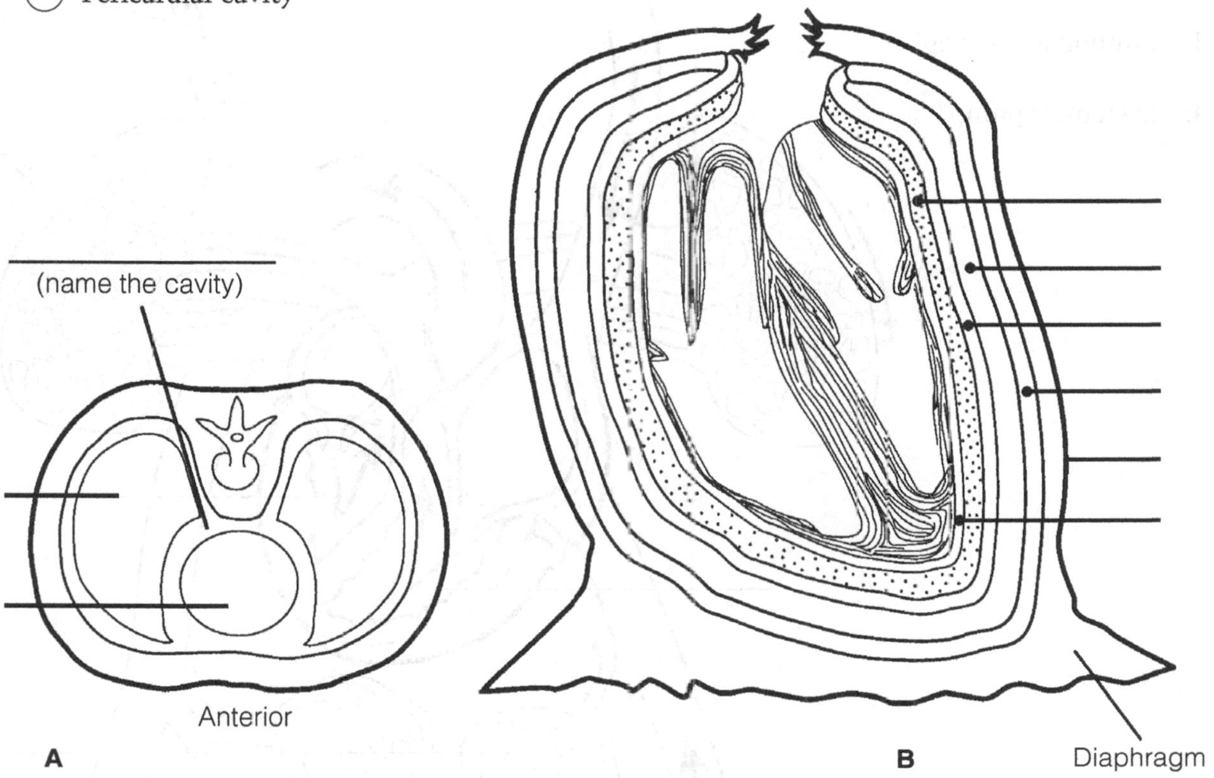

(name the cavity)

Anterior

A   **B**   Diaphragm

Figure 17.1

3. The heart is called a double pump because it serves two circulations. Trace the flow of blood through both pulmonary and systemic circulations by writing the missing terms in the answer blanks below. Then, identify the various regions of the circulation shown in Figure 17.2 by labeling them using the key choices. Color regions transporting O$_2$-poor blood blue and regions transporting O$_2$-rich blood red.

_____ 1.

_____ 2.

_____ 3.

_____ 4.

_____ 5.

_____ 6.

_____ 7.

From the atrium through the tricuspid valve to the __(1)__, through the __(2)__ valve to the pulmonary trunk to the right and left __(3)__, to the capillary beds of the __(4)__, to the __(5)__, to the __(6)__ of the heart through the __(7)__ valve, to the __(8)__ through the __(9)__ semilunar valve to the __(10)__, to the systemic arteries, to the __(11)__ of the body tissues, to the systemic veins, to the __(12)__ and __(13)__ which enter the right atrium of the heart.

_____ 8.   _____ 11.

_____ 9.   _____ 12.

_____ 10.   _____ 13.

Key Choices

A. Vessels serving head and upper limbs

B. Vessels serving body trunk and lower limbs

C. Vessels serving the viscera

D. Pulmonary circulation

E. Pulmonary "pump"

F. Systemic "pump"

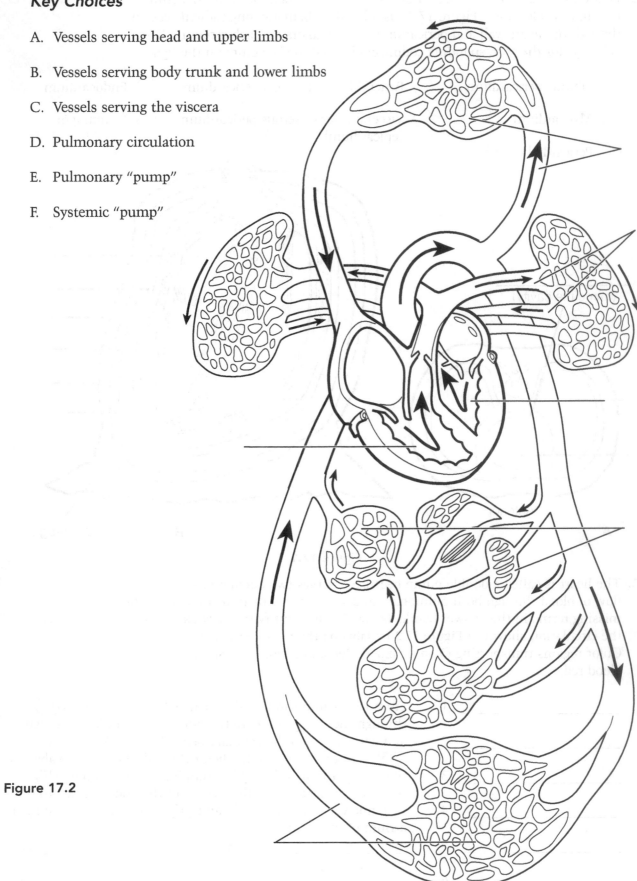

Figure 17.2

4. Figure 17.3 is an anterior view of the heart. Identify each numbered structure and write its name in the corresponding numbered answer blank. Then, select different colors for each structure with a coding circle and color the structures on the figure.

○ _____ 1.   ○ _____ 6.   ○ _____ 11.

○ _____ 2.   ○ _____ 7.   _____ 12.

○ _____ 3.   ○ _____ 8.   _____ 13.

○ _____ 4.   _____ 9.   _____ 14.

○ _____ 5.   _____ 10.   ○ _____ 15.

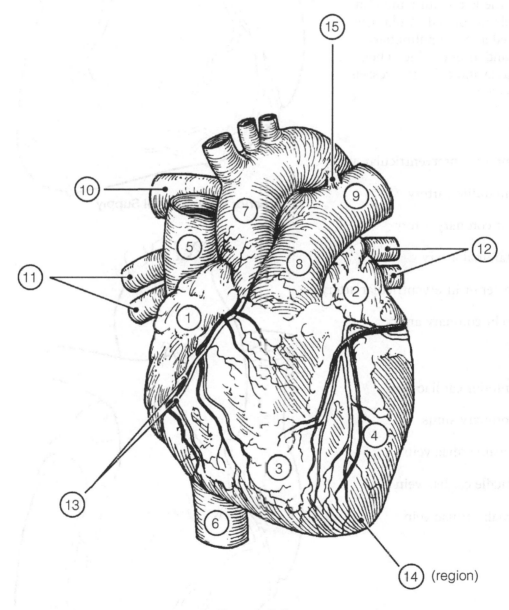

Figure 17.3

Blood Supply to the Heart: Coronary Circulation

1. Figure 17.4 shows the vascular supply of the myocardium. Part A shows the arterial supply; part B shows the venous drainage. In each case, the anterior view is shown and the vessels located posteriorly are depicted as dashed lines. Use a light color to color in the *right atrium* and the *left ventricle* in each diagram. (Leave the left atrium and right ventricle uncolored.) Color the aorta red and the pulmonary trunk and arteries blue. Then color code and color the vessels listed below.

Part A

○ Anterior interventricular artery

○ Circumflex artery

○ Left coronary artery

○ Marginal artery

○ Posterior interventricular artery

○ Right coronary artery

Part B

○ Anterior cardiac vein

○ Coronary sinus

○ Great cardiac vein

○ Middle cardiac vein

○ Small cardiac vein

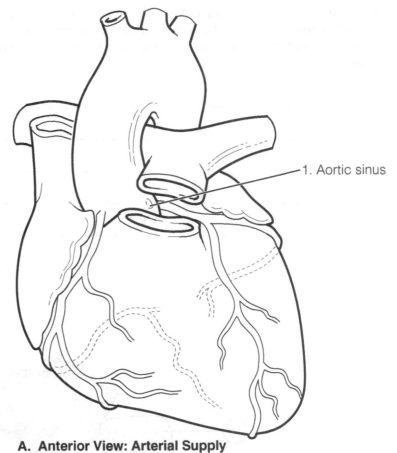

1. Aortic sinus

A. Anterior View: Arterial Supply

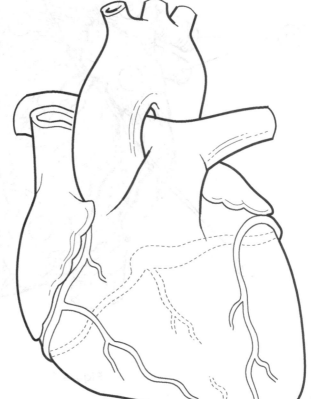

Figure 17.4

B. Anterior View: Venous Drainage

Properties of Cardiac Muscle Fibers

1. A number of characteristics peculiar to skeletal or cardiac muscle are listed below. Select which ones refer to each muscle type by writing S in the answer blanks preceding descriptions that apply to skeletal muscle and C in the answer blanks of those that identify characteristics of cardiac muscle.

   _____ 1. One centrally located nucleus

   _____ 2. More mitochondria per cell

   _____ 3. T tubules line up at the Z lines

   _____ 4. Uses fatty acids more effectively for ATP harvest

   _____ 5. Requires stimulation by the nervous system to contract

   _____ 6. Has a shorter refractory period

   _____ 7. Contains self-excitable cells

   _____ 8. Has well-developed terminal cisternae

   _____ 9. Wide T tubules

   _____ 10. More distinct myofibrils

   _____ 11. All-or-none law applies at the organ level

   _____ 12. Intercalated discs enhance intercellular electrical communication

2. Figure 17.5 is a schematic drawing of the microscopic structure of cardiac muscle. Using different colors, color the coding circles of the structures listed below and the corresponding structures on the figure. Then answer the questions that follow the figure. Write your answers in the answer blanks.

   ○ Nuclei (with nucleoli)   ○ Muscle fibers

   ○ Intercalated discs   ○ Striations

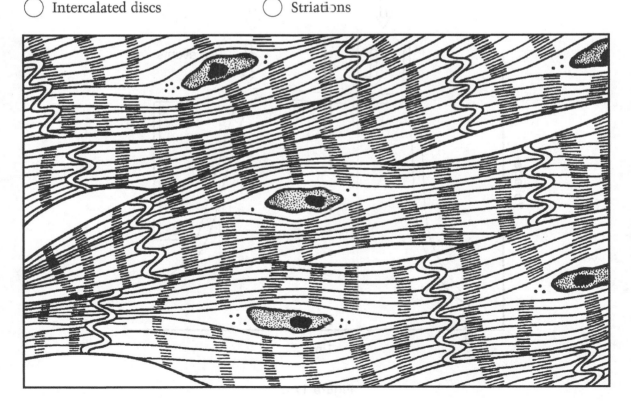

Figure 17.5

_____ 1. Name the loose connective tissue that fills the intercellular spaces.

_____ 2. What is the function during contraction of the desmosomes present in the intercalated discs? (*Note:* The desmosomes are not illustrated.)

_____ 3. What is the function of the gap junctions (not illustrated) also present in the intercalated discs?

_____ 4. What term describes the interdependent, interconnecting cardiac cells?

_____ 5. Which structures provide electrical coupling of cardiac cells?

3. On Figure 17.6, indicate (by adding labels) the following changes in membrane permeability and events of an action potential at their approximate point of occurrence. Also indicate by labeling a bracket: (1) the plateau, and (2) the period when Ca^{2+} is pumped out of the cell. Also color code and color the arrows and brackets.

○ ↑ Na^+ (Na^+ gates open)   ○ ↓ Ca^{2+} (Ca^{2+} gates close)

○ ↓ Na^+ (Na^+ gates close)   ○ ↑ K^+ (K^+ gates open)

○ ↑ Ca^{2+} (Ca^{2+} gates open)   ○ Plateau

○ Ca^{2+} pumped from cell

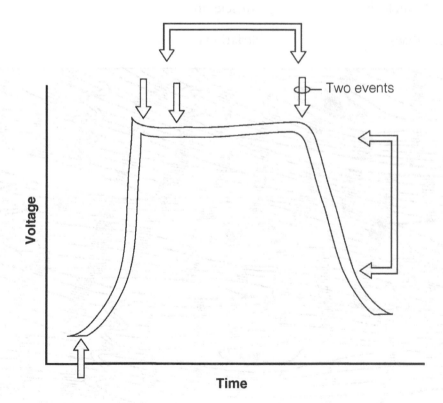

Figure 17.6

Heart Physiology

1. Complete the following statements concerning the cells of the nodal system of the heart. Write the missing terms in the answer blanks.

_____	1.
_____	2.
_____	3.
_____	4.
_____	5.
_____	6.
_____	7.
_____	8.
_____	9.

The nodal cells of the heart, unlike cardiac contractile muscle fibers, have an intrinsic ability to depolarize __(1)__. This reflects their unstable __(2)__, which drifts slowly toward the threshold for firing, that is, __(3)__. These spontaneously changing membrane potentials, called __(4)__, are probably due to reduced membrane permeability to __(5)__. However, __(6)__ permeability is unchanged and it continues to diffuse __(7)__ the cell at a slow rate. Ultimately, when threshold is reached, gated channels called __(8)__ open, allowing extracellular __(9)__ to rush into the cells and reverse the membrane potential.

2. Figure 17.7 is a diagram of the frontal section of the heart. Follow the instructions below to complete this exercise, which considers both anatomical and physiological aspects of the heart.

1. Draw arrows to indicate the direction of blood flow through the heart. Draw the pathway of the oxygen-rich blood with red arrows and trace the pathway of oxygen-poor blood with blue arrows.

2. Identify each of the elements of the intrinsic conduction system (numbers 1–5 on the figure) by writing the appropriate terms in the numbered answer blanks. Then, indicate with green arrows the pathway that impulses take through this system.

3. Identify each of the heart valves (numbers 6–9 on the figure) by writing the appropriate terms in the numbered answer blanks. Draw and identify by name the cordlike structures that anchor the flaps of the atrioventricular (AV) valves.

4. Use the numbers from the figure to identify structures (A–H).

_____ A. _____ B. Prevent backflow into the ventricles when the heart is relaxed

_____ C. _____ D. Prevent backflow into the atria when the ventricles are contracting

_____ E. AV valve with three flaps

_____ F. AV valve with two flaps

_____ G. The pacemaker of the Purkinje system

_____ H. The point in the Purkinje system where the impulse is temporarily delayed

_____ 1.

_____ 2.

_____ 3.

_____ 4.

_____ 5.

_____ 6.

_____ 7.

_____ 8.

_____ 9.

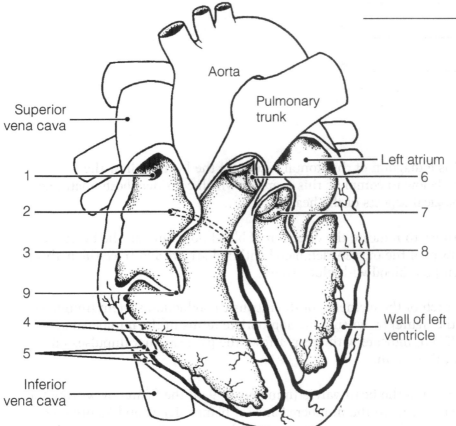

Figure 17.7

3. Respond to the questions below concerning the nodal system.

   1. What name is given to the rate set by the heart's pacemaker? _____

   2. What are the observed contraction rates of the different components
      of the intrinsic conduction system?

   SA node _____ beats/min   AV node _____ beats/min

   AV bundle _____ beats/min   Purkinje fibers _____ beats/min

   3. The intrinsic conduction system enforces a faster rate of impulse conduc-
      tion across the heart—at the rate of several meters per second in most
      parts of the conduction system. What would be the natural speed of
      impulse transmission across the heart in the absence of such a system?
      _____ m/s

   4. What is the total time for impulse conduction across the healthy heart,
      on average? _____ seconds

4. Part of an electrocardiogram is shown in Figure 17.8. On the figure, identify
the QRS complex, the P wave, and the T wave. Using a green pencil, bracket
the P-Q interval and the Q-T interval. Then, using a red pencil, bracket a
portion of the recording equivalent to the length of one cardiac cycle. Using a
blue pencil, bracket a portion of the recording in which the *ventricles* would
be in diastole.

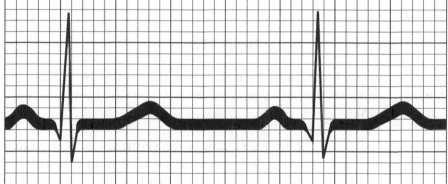

Figure 17.8

5. Examine the abnormal EGG tracings shown in Figure 17.9.

   _____   1. Which shows extra P waves?

   _____   2. Which shows tachycardia?

   _____   3. Which has an abnormal QRS complex?

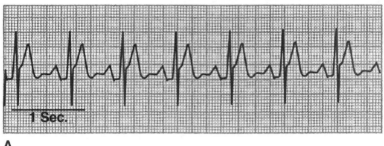

A

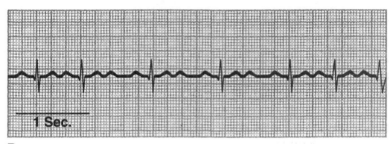

B

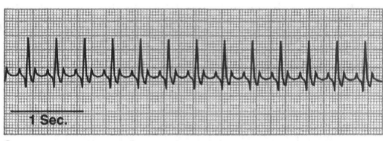

C

Figure 17.9

6. The events of one complete heartbeat are referred to as the cardiac cycle. Complete the following statements that describe these events by writing the missing terms in the answer blanks.

_____ 1.

_____ 2.

_____ 3.

_____ 4.

_____ 5.

_____ 6.

_____ 7.

_____ 8.

_____ 9.

The contraction of the ventricles is referred to as __(1)__ and the period of ventricular relaxation is called __(2)__. The monosyllables describing heart sounds during the cardiac cycle are __(3)__. The first heart sound is a result of closure of the __(4)__ valves; closure of the __(5)__ valves causes the second heart sound. The heart chambers that have just been filled when you hear the first heart sound are the __(6)__ and the chambers that have just emptied are the __(7)__. Immediately after the second heart sound, the __(8)__ are filling with blood and the __(9)__ are empty. Abnormal heart sounds, or __(10)__, usually indicate valve problems.

_____ 10.

7. The events of one cardiac cycle are graphed in Figure 17.10. First, identify the following by color:

○ ECG tracing   ○ Atrial pressure line

○ Aortic pressure line   ○ Ventricular pressure line

Then, identify by labeling the following:

- The P, QRS, and T waves of the ECG

- Points of opening and closing of the AV and semilunar valves

- Elastic recoil of the aorta

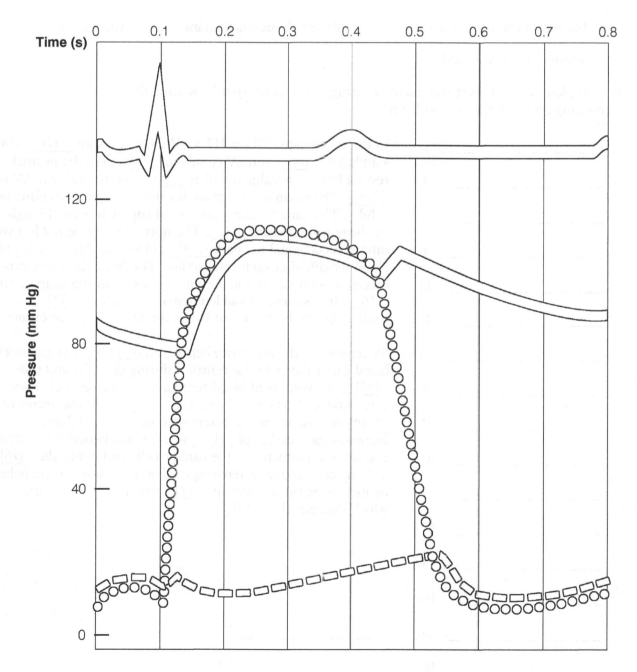

Figure 17.10

8. Circle the term that does not belong in each of the following groupings.

1. AV valves closed   AV valves open   Ventricular systole   Semilunar valves open

2. No P wave   SA node is pacemaker   AV node is pacemaker   Junctional rhythm

3. Ventricles fill   Ventricular systole   AV valves open   Late diastole

4. Early diastole   Semilunar valves open   Isovolumetric relaxation

   Ventricular pressure drops

5. Stenotic valve   Restricted blood flow   High-pitched heart sound

   Heart sound after valve closes

6. Isovolumetric ventricular systole   Blood volume unchanging   AV valve open

   Semilunar valve closed

9. Complete the following statements relating to cardiac output by writing the missing terms in the answer blanks.

_____ 1.

_____ 2.

_____ 3.

_____ 4.

_____ 5.

_____ 6.

_____ 7.

_____ 8.

_____ 9.

_____ 10.

_____ 11.

_____ 12.

_____ 13.

_____ 14.

_____ 15.   _____ 17.

_____ 16.   _____ 18.

In the relationship CO = HR × SV, CO stands for __(1)__, HR stands for __(2)__, and SV stands for __(3)__. For the normal resting heart, the value of HR is __(4)__ and the value of SV is __(5)__. The normal average adult cardiac output, therefore, is __(6)__. The time for the entire blood supply to pass through the body is once each __(7)__. The normal ventricle holds a volume of blood equal to about __(8)__, of which about __(9)__ of blood remain after each contraction. The heart, however, can exceed its normal cardiac output, a property of the heart called __(10)__. In response to sudden demands, such as __(11)__, cardiac reserve is about four times the normal cardiac output.

SV represents the difference between the __(12)__, the amount of blood that collects in the ventricle during diastole, and the __(13)__, the volume of blood remaining in the ventricle after contraction. SV is critically related to __(14)__, or the degree of stretch of cardiac muscle before it contracts. Stretching increases the number of __(15)__ interactions between the *actin* and myosin filaments in the cardiac cells and hence the __(16)__ of heart contraction. Stretching cardiac muscle is accomplished by increasing the amount of __(17)__ returned to the heart, which distends the __(18)__.

10. Stroke volume may be enhanced in two major ways: by increasing venous return and by enhancing contractility of heart muscle.

   1. Explain *contractility*. _____

   _____

   2. Name three factors, one neural and two hormonal, that enhance contractility.

   _____

   3. Explain how exercise increases venous return. _____

   _____

11. Check (✓) all factors that lead to an *increase* in cardiac output by influencing either heart rate or stroke volume.

   _____ 1. Epinephrine

   _____ 2. Thyroxine

   _____ 3. Hemorrhage

   _____ 4. Fear

   _____ 5. Exercise

   _____ 6. Fever

   _____ 7. Depression

   _____ 8. Anxiety

   _____ 9. Activation of the vasomotor center

   _____ 10. Activation of the cardio-acceleratory center

   _____ 11. Activation of the cardioinhibitory center

   _____ 12. Activation of the vagus nerves

   _____ 13. Low blood pressure

   _____ 14. High blood pressure

   _____ 15. Increased end diastolic volume

   _____ 16. Prolonged grief

   _____ 17. Acidosis

   _____ 18. Calcium channel blockers

   _____ 19. Atrial reflex

   _____ 20. Hyperkalemia

   _____ 21. Increased afterload

12. If a statement is true, write the letter T in the answer blank. If a statement is false, change the underlined word(s) and write the correct word(s) in the answer blank.

   _____ 1. Norepinephrine, released by <u>parasympathetic</u> fibers, stimulates the SA and AV nodes and the myocardium itself.

   _____ 2. The resting heart is said to exhibit "vagal tone," meaning that the heart rate slows under the influence of <u>acetylcholine</u>.

   _____ 3. Epinephrine secreted by the adrenal medulla <u>decreases</u> heart rate.

   _____ 4. <u>Low</u> levels of ionic calcium cause prolonged cardiac contractions.

_____   5. The resting heart rate is fastest in <u>adult</u> life.

_____   6. Because the heart of the highly trained athlete hypertrophies, its <u>stroke volume</u> decreases.

_____   7. In congestive heart failure, there is a marked rise in the end <u>diastolic</u> volume.

_____   8. If the <u>right</u> side of the heart fails, pulmonary congestion occurs.

_____   9. In <u>peripheral</u> congestion, the feet, ankles, and fingers become edematous.

_____   10. The pumping action of the healthy heart ordinarily maintains a balance between cardiac output and <u>venous return</u>.

_____   11. The <u>cardioacceleratory center</u> in the medulla gives rise to sympathetic nerves supplying the heart.

13. Match the terms in Column B with the statements in Column A. Place the correct letters in the answer blanks.

Column A

_____   1. Results from prolonged coronary blockage

_____   2. Abnormal pacemaker

_____   3. Allows backflow of blood

_____   4. Because of cardiac decompensa- tion, circulation is inadequate to meet tissue needs

_____   5. A slow heartbeat, that is, below 60 beats per minute

_____   6. A condition in which the heart is uncoordinated and useless as a pump

_____   7. A rapid heart rate, that is, over 100 beats per minute

_____   8. Damage to the AV node, totally or partially releasing the ventricles from the control of the SA node

_____   9. Chest pain, resulting from ischemia of the myocardium

_____   10. Result of initial failure of the left side of the heart

Column B

A. Angina pectoris

B. Bradycardia

C. Congestive heart failure

D. Ectopic focus

E. Fibrillation

F. Heart block

G. Incompetent valve

H. Myocardial infarction

I. Pulmonary congestion

J. Tachycardia

14. Match the ionic imbalances in Column B to the descriptions of their effects in Column A.

	Column A	Column B
_____	1. Depresses heart	A. Hypercalcemia
_____	2. Spastic contractions	B. Hyperkalemia
_____	3. Inhibits Ca^{2+} transport	C. Hypernatremia
_____	4. Lowers resting potential	D. Hypocalcemia
_____	5. Feeble contractions, abnormal rhythms	E. Hypokalemia

CHALLENGING YOURSELF

At the Clinic

1. Homer Fox, a patient with acute severe pericarditis, has a critically low stroke volume. What is the name for the condition causing the low stroke volume and how does it cause it?

2. An elderly man is brought to the clinic because he fatigues extremely easily. An examination reveals a heart murmur associated with the bicuspid valve during ventricular systole. What is the diagnosis? What is a possible treatment?

3. Jimmy is brought to the clinic complaining of a sore throat. His mother says he has had the sore throat for about a week. Culture of a throat swab is positive for strep, and the boy is put on antibiotics. A week later, the boy is admitted to the hospital after fainting several times. He is cyanotic. What is a likely diagnosis?

4. After a bout with bacterial endocarditis, scar tissue often stiffens the edges of the heart valves. What condition will this cause? How would this be picked up in a routine examination?

5. Mary Ghareeb, a woman in her late 50s, has come to the clinic because of chest pains whenever she begins to exert herself. What is her condition called?

6. After a fairly severe heart attack, the EGG reveals normal sinus rhythm, but only for the P wave. The QRS and T waves are no longer in synchrony with the P wave, and the ventricular contraction corresponds to junctional rhythm. What is the problem? What part of the heart is damaged?

7. Ms. Hamad, who is 73 years old, is admitted to the coronary care unit of a hospital with a diagnosis of left ventricular failure resulting from a myocardial infarction. Her heart rhythm is abnormal. Explain what a myocardial infarction is, how it is likely to have been caused, and why the heart rhythm is affected.

8. Mr. Trump, en route to the hospital ER by ambulance, is in fibrillation. What is his cardiac output likely to be? He arrives at the emergency entrance DOA (dead on arrival). His autopsy reveals a blockage of the posterior interventricular artery. What is the cause of death?

9. Excessive vagal stimulation can be caused by severe depression. How would this be reflected in a routine physical examination?

10. Mrs. Suffriti has swollen ankles and signs of degenerating organ functions. What is a likely diagnosis?

11. You are a young nursing student and are called upon to explain how each of the following tests or procedures might be helpful in evaluating a patient with heart disease: blood pressure measurement, determination of blood lipid and cholesterol levels, electrocardiogram, chest X ray. How would you respond?

12. Mr. Langley is telling his friend about his recent visit to his doctor for a checkup. During his story, he mentions that the EGG revealed that he had a defective mitral valve and a heart murmur. Mr. Langley apparently misunderstood some of what the doctor explained to him about his diagnosis process. What has he misunderstood?

Stop and Think

1. The major coronary vessels are on the surface of the heart. What is the advantage of that location?

2. Since the SA node is at the top of the atrial mass, the atria contract from the top down. How does this increase the efficiency of atrial contraction? Do the ventricles have a similar arrangement? If so, how does it work?

3. What parts of the body feel referred pain when there is a major myocardial infarction?

4. What is the purpose of prolonged contraction of the myocardium?

5. How long does it take for a hormone released from the anterior pituitary gland to reach its target organ in the body?

6. What is the functional difference between ventricular hypertrophy due to exercise and hypertrophy due to congestive heart failure?

7. How does hypothyroidism affect heart rate?

8. The foramen ovale has a flap that partially covers it, and a groove leads from the opening of the inferior vena cava (which carries freshly oxygenated blood from the umbilical vein) to the foramen ovale. Explain these structural features in terms of directing blood flow.

9. A less-than-respectable news tabloid announced that "Doctors show exercise shortens life. Life expectancy is programmed into a set number of heartbeats; the faster your heart beats, the sooner you die!" Even if this "theory" were true, what is wrong with the conclusion concerning exercise?

COVERING ALL YOUR BASES

Multiple Choice

Select the best answer or answers from the choices given.

1. A knife plunged into the sixth intercostal space will:

   A. pierce the aorta

   B. pierce the atria

   C. pierce the ventricles

   D. miss the heart completely

2. The innermost layer of the pericardial sac is the:

   A. epicardium

   B. fibrous pericardium

   C. parietal layer of the serous pericardium

   D. visceral layer of the serous pericardium

3. Which of the heart layers are vascularized?

   A. Myocardium

   B. Endothelium of endocardial layer

   C. Mesothelium of epicardium

   D. Connective tissue layers of both endocardium and epicardium

4. The fibrous skeleton of the heart:

   A. supports valves

   B. anchors vessels

   C. provides electrical insulation to separate the atrial mass from the ventricular mass

   D. anchors cardiac muscle fibers

5. Which of the following is associated with the right atrium?

   A. Fossa ovalis   C. Chordae tendineae

   B. Tricuspid valve   D. Pectinate muscle

6. A surface feature associated with the circumflex artery is the:

   A. right atrioventricular groove

   B. anterior interventricular sulcus

   C. left atrioventricular groove

   D. posterior interventricular sulcus

7. Atrioventricular valves are held closed by:

   A. papillary muscles

   B. trabeculae carneae

   C. pectinate muscles

   D. chordae tendineae

8. During atrial systole:

   A. the atrial pressure exceeds ventricular pressure

   B. 70% of ventricular filling occurs

   C. the AV valves are open

   D. valves prevent backflow into the great veins

9. Occlusion of which of the following arteries would damage primarily the right ventricle?

   A. Marginal artery

   B. Posterior interventricular artery

   C. Circumflex artery

   D. Anterior interventricular artery

10. A choking sensation in the chest is the result of:

    A. myocardial infarction

    B. death of cardiac cells

    C. temporary lack of oxygen to cardiac cells

    D. possibly spasms of the coronary arteries

11. Which feature(s) is/are greater in number/value/size or more developed in cardiac than in skeletal muscle?

    A. T tubule diameter

    B. Terminal cisternae

    C. Mitochondria

    D. Absolute refractory period

12. Which is/are characteristic of cardiac but not of skeletal muscle?

    A. Gap junctions

    B. All-or-none law

    C. Endomysium

    D. Branching fibers

13. Ca^{2+} slow channels are open in cardiac cells' plasma membranes during:

    A. depolarization   C. plateau

    B. repolarization   D. resting membrane potential

14. Which of the following depolarizes next after the AV node?

    A. Atrial myocardium

    B. Ventricular myocardium

    C. Bundle branches

    D. Purkinje fibers

15. Threshold in pacemaker cells is marked by:

    A. opening of Na^+ gates

    B. opening of Ca^{2+} slow channels

    C. opening of Ca^{2+} fast channels

    D. opening of K^+ gates

16. Freshly oxygenated blood is first received by the:

    A. right ventricle   C. right atrium

    B. left ventricle   D. left atrium

17. A heart rate of 30 bpm indicates that the _____ is functioning as an ectopic focus.

    A. AV node   C. Purkinje fibers

    B. bundle branches D. AV bundle

18. Stimulation of the cardiac plexus involves stimulation of the:

    A. baroreceptors in the great arteries

    B. cardioacceleratory center

    C. vagus nerve

    D. sympathetic chain

19. Atrial repolarization coincides in time with the:

    A. P wave   C. QRS wave

    B. T wave   D. P-Q interval

20. Soon after the onset of ventricular systole the:

    A. AV valves close

    B. semilunar valves open

    C. first heart sound is heard

    D. aortic pressure increases

21. Which of the following will occur first after the T wave?

    A. Increase in ventricular volume

    B. Decrease in atrial volume

    C. Closure of the semilunar valves

    D. Decrease in ventricular pressure

22. Given an end-diastolic volume of 150 ml, an end-systolic volume of 50 ml, and a heart rate of 60 bpm, the cardiac output is:

    A. 600 ml/min   C. 1200 ml/min

    B. 6 liters/min   D. 3 liters/min

23. The statement "strength of contraction increases intrinsically due to increased stretching of the heart wall" is best attributed to:

    A. contractility

    B. Frank-Starling law of the heart

    C. Bainbridge reflex

    D. aortic sinus reflex

24. An increase in cardiac output is triggered by:

    A. Bainbridge reflex

    B. stimulation of carotid sinus baroreceptors

    C. increase in vagal tone

    D. epinephrine

25. Which of the following ionic imbalances inhibits Ca^{2+} transport into cardiac cells and blocks contraction?

    A. Hyponatremia   D. Hyperkalemia

    B. Hypokalemia   E. Hypercalcemia

    C. Hypernatremia

26. Cardiovascular conditioning results in:

    A. ventricular hypertrophy

    B. bradycardia

    C. increase in SV

    D. increase in CO

27. Conditions known to be associated with congestive heart failure include:

    A. coronary atherosclerosis

    B. diastolic pressure chronically elevated

    C. successive sublethal infarcts

    D. decompensated heart

28. In heart failure, venous return is slowed. Edema results because:

    A. blood volume is increased

    B. venous pressure is increased

    C. osmotic pressure is increased

    D. none of the above

29. Which structures is/are fetal remnant(s) associated with a healthy adult heart?

    A. Foramen ovale

    B. Ligamentum arteriosum

    C. Interventricular septal opening

    D. Patent ductus arteriosus

30. Age-related changes in heart function include:

    A. decrease in cardiac reserve

    B. decrease in resting heart rate

    C. valvular sclerosis

    D. fibrosis of cardiac muscle

31. Which of the following terms refers to an unusually strong heartbeat, so that the person is aware of it?

    A. Extrasystole   C. Flutter

    B. Tamponade   D. Palpitation

32. The base of the heart is its _____ surface.

    A. diaphragmatic   C. arterier

    B. posterior   D. superior

33. The thickest layer of the heart wall is:

    A. endocardium   C. epicardium

    B. myocardium   D. fibrous pericardium

34. Conditions associated with the tetralogy of Fallot include:

    A. interventricular septal opening

    B. cyanosis

    C. aorta arising from both ventricles

    D. treatment with drugs rather than surgery

Word Dissection

For each of the following word roots, fill in the literal meaning and give an example, using a word found in this chapter.

Word root	Translation	Example
1. angina		
2. baro		
3. brady		
4. carneo		
5. cusp		
6. diastol		
7. dicro		
8. ectop		
9. intercal		
10. pectin		
11. sino		
12. stenos		
13. systol		
14. tachy		

18

THE CARDIOVASCULAR SYSTEM: BLOOD VESSELS AND CIRCULATION

Overview

Blood vessels form a closed system of ducts that transport blood and allow exchange of gases, nutrients, and wastes between the blood and the body cells. The general plan of the cardiovascular system includes the heart, arteries that carry blood away from the heart, capillaries that allow exchange of substances between blood and the cells, and veins that carry blood back to the heart. The pulmonary circuit carries deoxygenated blood from the right side of the heart to the lung capillaries where the blood is oxygenated. The systemic circuit carries the oxygenated blood from the left side of the heart to the systemic capillaries in all parts of the body. The cyclic nature of the system results in deoxygenated blood returning to the right atrium to continue the cycle of circulation.

Blood vessels in the muscles, the skin, the cerebral circulation, and the hepatic portal circulation are specifically adapted to serve the functions of organs and tissues in these important special areas of cardiovascular activity.

Chapter 18 describes the structure and functions of the blood vessels, the dynamics of the circulatory process, cardiovascular regulation, and patterns of cardiovascular response.

LEVEL 1   Review of Chapter Objectives

1. Distinguish among the types of blood vessels on the basis of their structure and function.

2. Describe how and where fluid and dissolved materials enter and leave the cardiovascular system.

3. Explain the mechanisms that regulate blood flow through arteries, capillaries, and veins.

4. Describe the factors that influence blood pressure and how blood pressure is regulated.

5. Discuss the mechanisms and various pressures involved in the movement of fluids between capillaries and interstitial spaces.

6. Describe how central and local control mechanisms interact to regulate blood flow and pressure in tissues.

7. Explain how the activities of the cardiac, vasomotor, and respiratory centers are coordinated to control the blood flow through the tissues.

8. Explain how the circulatory system responds to the demands of exercise, hemorrhaging, and shock.

9. Identify the principal blood vessels and the functional characteristics of the special circulation to the brain, heart, and lungs.

10. Describe three general functional patterns seen in the pulmonary and systemic circuits of the cardiovascular system.

11. Identify the major arteries and veins of the pulmonary circuit and the areas they serve.

12. Identify the major arteries and veins of the systemic circuit and the areas they serve.

13. Identify the differences between fetal and adult circulation patterns.

14. Describe the changes in the patterns of blood flow that occur at birth.

15. Discuss the effects of aging on the cardiovascular system.

[L1] Multiple Choice

Place the letter corresponding to the correct answer in the space provided.

OBJ. 1 _____ 1. The layer of vascular tissue that consists of an endothelial lining and an underlying layer of connective tissue dominated by elastic fibers is the:

    a. tunica interna

    b. tunica media

    c. tunica externa

    d. tunica adventitia

OBJ. 1 _____ 2. Smooth muscle fibers in arteries and veins are found in the:

    a. endothelial lining

    b. tunica externa

    c. tunica interna

    d. tunica media

OBJ. 1 _____ 3. One of the major characteristics of the arteries supplying peripheral tissues is that they are:

    a. elastic

    b. muscular

    c. rigid

    d. a, b, and c are correct

OBJ. 2 _____ 4. The only blood vessels whose walls permit exchange between the blood and the surrounding interstitial fluids are

    a. arterioles

    b. venules

    c. capillaries

    d. a, b, and c are correct

OBJ. 2 _____ 5. The *primary* route for substances entering or leaving a continuous capillary is:

    a. diffusion through gaps between adjacent endothelial cells

    b. crossing the endothelia of fenestrated capillaries

    c. bulk transport of moving vesicles

    d. active transport or secretion across the capillary wall

OBJ. 2 _____ 6. The unidirectional flow of blood in venules and medium-sized veins is maintained by:

    a. the muscular walls of the veins

    b. pressure from the left ventricle

    c. arterial pressure

    d. the presence of valves

OBJ. 3 _____ 7. The "specialized" arteries that are able to tolerate the pressure shock produced each time ventricular systole occurs and blood leaves the heart are:

    a. muscular arteries

    b. elastic arteries

    c. arterioles

    d. fenestrated arteries

OBJ. 3 _____ 8. Of the following blood vessels, the greatest resistance to blood flow occurs in the:

    a. veins

    b. capillaries

    c. venules

    d. arterioles

OBJ. 3 _____ 9. If the systolic pressure is 120 mm Hg and the diastolic pressure is 90 mm Hg, the mean arterial pressure (MAP) is:

    a. 30 mm Hg

    b. 210 mm Hg

    c. 100 mm Hg

    d. 80 mm Hg

OBJ. 3 _____ 10. The distinctive sounds of Korotkoff heard when taking the blood pressure are produced by:

    a. turbulences as blood flows past the constricted portion of the artery

    b. the contraction and relaxation of the ventricles

    c. the opening and closing of the atrioventricular valves

    d. a, b, and c are correct

OBJ. 3 _____ 11. When taking a blood pressure, the first sound picked up by the stethoscope as blood pulses through the artery is the:

    a. mean arterial pressure

    b. pulse pressure

    c. diastolic pressure

    d. peak systolic pressure

OBJ. 4 _____ 12. The most important determinant of vascular resistance is:

    a. a combination of neural and hormonal mechanisms

    b. differences in the length of the blood vessels

    c. friction between the blood and the vessel walls

    d. the diameter of the arterioles

OBJ. 4 _____ 13. Venous pressure is produced by:

    a. the skeletal muscle pump

    b. increasing sympathetic activity to the veins

    c. increasing respiratory movements

    d. a, b, and c are correct

OBJ. 4 _____ 14. From the following selections, choose the answer that correctly identifies all the factors that would increase blood pressure. (Note: CO = cardiac output; SV = stroke volume; VR = venous return; PR = peripheral resistance; BV = blood volume.)

    a. increasing CO, increasing SV, decreasing VR, decreasing PR, increasing BV

    b. increasing CO, increasing SV, increasing VR, increasing PR, increasing BV

    c. increasing CO, increasing SV, decreasing VR, increasing PR, decreasing BV

    d. increasing CO, decreasing SV, increasing VR, decreasing PR, increasing BV

OBJ. 5 _____ 15. The two major factors affecting blood flow rates are:

   a. diameter and length of blood vessels
   b. pressure and resistance
   c. neural and hormonal control mechanisms
   d. turbulence and viscosity

OBJ. 5 _____ 16. The formula F = P/R means: (Note: F = flow; P = pressure; R = resistance.)

   a. increasing P, decreasing R, increasing F
   b. decreasing P, increasing R, increasing F
   c. increasing P, increasing R, decreasing F
   d. decreasing P, decreasing R, increasing F

OBJ. 6 _____ 17. Atrial natriuretic peptide (ANP) reduces blood volume and pressure by:

   a. blocking release of ADH
   b. stimulating peripheral vasodilation
   c. increased water loss by kidneys
   d. a, b, and c are correct

OBJ. 6 _____ 18. The mechanisms that enhance short-term adjustments and direct long-term changes in cardiovascular performance are:

   a. autoregulatory
   b. neural adjustments
   c. endocrine secretions
   d. tissue perfusions

OBJ. 6 _____ 19. The regulatory mechanism(s) that cause immediate, localized homeostatic adjustments is (are):

   a. autoregulation
   b. endocrine regulations
   c. neural regulation
   d. all of the above

OBJ. 7 _____ 20. The central regulation of cardiac output primarily involves the activities of the:

   a. somatic nervous system
   b. autonomic nervous system
   c. central nervous system
   d. a, b, and c are correct

OBJ. 7 _____ 21. An increase in cardiac output normally occurs during:

   a. widespread sympathetic stimulation
   b. widespread parasympathetic stimulation
   c. the process of vasomotion
   d. stimulation of the vasomotor center

OBJ. 7 _____ 22. Stimulation of the vasomotor center in the medulla causes _____, and inhibition of the vasomotor center causes _____.

   a. vasodilation; vasoconstriction
   b. increasing diameter of arteriole; decreasing diameter of arteriole
   c. hyperemia; ischemia
   d. vasoconstriction; vasodilation

OBJ. 7 _____ 23. Hormonal regulation by vasopressin, epinephrine, angiotensin II, and norepinephrine results in:

    a. increasing peripheral vasodilation

    b. decreasing peripheral vasoconstriction

    c. increasing peripheral vasoconstriction

    d. a, b, and c are correct

OBJ. 8 _____ 24. The three primary interrelated changes that occur as exercise begins are:

    a. decreasing vasodilation, increasing venous return, increasing cardiac output

    b. increasing vasodilation, decreasing venous return, increasing cardiac output

    c. increasing vasodilation, increasing venous return, increasing cardiac output

    d. decreasing vasodilation, decreasing venous return, decreasing cardiac output

OBJ. 8 _____ 25. The only area of the body where the blood supply is unaffected while exercising at maximum levels is the:

    a. hepatic portal circulation

    b. pulmonary circulation

    c. brain

    d. peripheral circulation

OBJ. 9 _____ 26. The four large blood vessels, two from each lung, that empty into the left atrium, completing the pulmonary circuit, are the:

    a. venae cavae

    b. pulmonary arteries

    c. pulmonary veins

    d. subclavian veins

OBJ. 9 _____ 27. The blood vessels that provide blood to capillary networks that surround the alveoli in the lungs are:

    a. pulmonary arterioles

    b. fenestrated capillaries

    c. left and right pulmonary arteries

    d. left and right pulmonary veins

OBJ. 10 _____ 28. Other than near the heart, the peripheral distributions of arteries and veins on the left and right sides are:

    a. completely different

    b. large vessels that connect to the atria and ventricles

    c. generally identical on both sides

    d. different on the left but the same on the right

OBJ. 10 _____ 29. As the external iliac artery leaves the body trunk and enters the lower limb, it becomes the:

    a. lower tibial artery

    b. femoral artery

    c. anterior fibular artery

    d. lower abdominal aorta

OBJ. 10 _____ 30. The link between adjacent arteries or veins that reduces the impact of a temporary or permanent occlusion of a single blood vessel is:

    a. an arteriole

    b. a venule

    c. an anastomosis

    d. a cardiovascular bridge

OBJ. 11 _____ 31. The three elastic arteries that originate along the aortic arch and deliver blood to the head, neck, shoulders, and arms are the:

    a. axillary, R. common carotid, right subclavian

    b. R. dorsoscapular, R. thoracic, R. vertebral

    c. R. axillary, R. brachial, L. internal carotid

    d. brachiocephalic, L. common carotid, left subclavian

OBJ. 11 _____ 32. The large blood vessel that collects most of the venous blood from organs below the diaphragm is the:

    a. superior vena cava

    b. inferior vena cava

    c. hepatic portal vein

    d. superior mesenteric vein

OBJ. 11 _____ 33. The three blood vessels that provide blood to all of the digestive organs in the abdominopelvic cavity are the:

    a. thoracic aorta, abdominal aorta, superior phrenic artery

    b. intercostal, esophageal, and bronchial arteries

    c. celiac artery and the superior and inferior mesenteric arteries

    d. suprarenal, renal, and lumbar arteries

OBJ. 12 _____ 34. The diaphragm divides the descending aorta into:

    a. brachiocephalic and carotid arteries

    b. right and left common iliac arteries

    c. superior phrenic and suprarenal arteries

    d. superior thoracic aorta and inferior abdominal aorta

OBJ. 12 _____ 35. The three unpaired arteries originating from the abdominal aorta are the:

    a. L. gastric, splenic, and common hepatic arteries

    b. celiac trunk, superior-inferior mesenteric arteries

    c. bronchial, pericardial, and esophageal arteries

    d. mediastinal, intercostal, and phrenic arteries

OBJ. 12 _____ 36. Except for the cardiac veins, all the body's systemic veins drain into either the:

    a. superior or inferior vena cava

    b. internal or external jugular veins

    c. sigmoid or cavernous sinuses

    d. inferior or superior mesenteric veins

OBJ. 12 _____ 37. Blood from the tissues and organs of the head, neck, chest, shoulders, and upper limbs is delivered to the:

a. inferior vena cava

b. cavernous sinus

c. conus venosus

d. superior vena cava

OBJ. 12 _____ 38. Blood from the lower limbs, the pelvis, and the lower abdomen is delivered to the:

a. hepatic veins

b. hepatic portal system

c. external iliac veins

d. great saphenous veins

OBJ. 12 _____ 39. Blood leaving the capillaries supplied by the celiac, superior, and inferior mesenteric arteries flows into the:

a. hepatic portal system

b. inferior vena cava

c. superior vena cava

d. abdominal aorta

OBJ. 13 _____ 40. The nutritional and respiratory needs of a fetus are provided by:

a. the stomach and lungs of the fetus

b. the stomach and lungs of the mother

c. diffusion across the placenta

d. a, b, and c are correct

OBJ. 13 _____ 41. In early fetal life, the foramen ovale allows blood to flow freely from the:

a. right ventricle to the left ventricle

b. right atrium to the left atrium

c. right atrium to the left ventricle

d. left atrium to the right ventricle

OBJ. 14 _____ 42. In the adult, the ductus arteriosus persists as a fibrous cord called the:

a. fossa ovalis

b. ligamentum arteriosum

c. ductus venosus

d. umbilicus

OBJ. 14 _____ 43. A few seconds after birth, rising O_2 levels stimulate the constriction of the ductus arteriosus, isolating the:

a. ligamentum arteriosum and fossa ovalis

b. ductus venosus and ligamentum arteriosum

c. superior and inferior vena cava

d. pulmonary and aortic trunks

OBJ. 15 _____ 44. The primary effect of a decrease in the hematocrit of elderly individuals is:

a. thrombus formation in the blood vessels

b. a lowering of the oxygen-carrying capacity of the blood

c. a reduction in the maximum cardiac output

d. damage to ventricular cardiac muscle fibers

OBJ. 15 ____ 45. In the region of the heart, age-related progressive atherosclerosis causes:

       a. changes in activities of conducting cells

       b. a reduction in the elasticity of the fibrous skeleton

       c. restricted coronary circulation

       d. a reduction in maximum cardiac input

[L1] Completion

Using the terms below, complete the following statements.

foramen ovale	aortic arch	anastomoses
hydrostatic pressure	vasomotion	sphygmomanometer
autoregulation	shock	circulatory pressure
thoracoabdominal pump	vasoconstriction	total peripheral resistance
pulse pressure	central ischemic	hepatic portal system
arterioles	venules	precapillary sphincter
arteriosclerosis	fenestrated	femoral artery
osmotic pressure	viscosity	oxygen levels
right atrium	vasodilators	

OBJ. 1   1. The smallest vessels of the arterial system are the _____.

OBJ. 1   2. Blood flowing out of the capillary complex first enters small _____.

OBJ. 2   3. Capillaries that have an incomplete endothelial lining are _____ capillaries.

OBJ. 3   4. The entrance to each capillary is guarded by a band of smooth muscle, the _____.

OBJ. 3   5. The total peripheral resistance of the cardiovascular system reflects a combination of vascular resistance, turbulence and _____.

OBJ. 4   6. The difference between the systolic and diastolic pressures is the _____.

OBJ. 4   7. The instrument used to determine blood pressure is called a _____.

OBJ. 4   8. The pressure difference between the base of the ascending aorta and the entrance to the right atrium is the _____.

OBJ. 4   9. For circulation to occur, the circulatory pressure must be greater than the _____.

OBJ. 5   10. The blood flow within any one capillary occurs in a series of pulses called _____.

OBJ. 5   11. The force that pushes water molecules *out* of solution is _____.

OBJ. 5   12. A force that pulls water *into* a solution is _____.

OBJ. 6   13. The regulation of blood flow at the tissue level is called _____.

OBJ. 6   14. Decreased tissue oxygen levels or increased CO_2 levels are examples of local _____.

OBJ. 7

15. Stimulation of the vasomotor center in the medulla causes _____.

OBJ. 7

16. A rise in the respiratory rate accelerates venous return through the action of the _____.

OBJ. 8

17. An acute circulatory crisis marked by low blood pressure and inadequate peripheral blood flow is referred to as _____.

OBJ. 8

18. The reflex causing circulation to be reduced to an absolute minimum is called the _____ response.

OBJ. 9

19. Blood leaving the capillaries supplied by the celiac, superior, and inferior mesenteric arteries flows into the _____.

OBJ. 10

20. As the external iliac artery leaves the trunk and enters the lower limb it becomes the _____.

OBJ. 10

21. The structures between adjacent arteries or veins that reduce the impact of a temporary blockage of a single blood vessel are called _____.

OBJ. 11

22. The part of the vascular system that connects the ascending aorta with the caudally directed descending aorta is the _____.

OBJ. 12

23. The systemic circuit, which at any moment contains about 84 percent of the total blood volume, begins at the left ventricle and ends at the _____.

OBJ. 13

24. During fetal life, blood can flow freely from the right atrium to the left atrium due to the presence of the _____.

OBJ. 14

25. At birth, the constriction of the ductus arteriosus that isolates the pulmonary and aortic trunks is stimulated by rising _____.

OBJ. 15

26. Most of the age-related changes in the circulatory system are related to _____.

[L1]   Matching

Match the terms in column B with the terms in column A. Use letters for answers in the spaces provided.

Part I

	Column A	Column B
OBJ. 1 ____	1. tunica externa	A. changes in blood pressure
OBJ. 1 ____	2. vasa vasorum	B. preferred channel
OBJ. 2 ____	3. sinusoids	C. carotid bodies
OBJ. 3 ____	4. metarteriole	D. minimum blood pressure
OBJ. 3 ____	5. thoracoabdominal pump	E. fenestrated capillaries
		F. connected by tight junction
OBJ. 4 ____	6. systole	
OBJ. 4 ____	7. diastole	G. "vessels of vessels"
OBJ. 5 ____	8. continuous capillaries	H. hydrostatic force = osmotic force
OBJ. 5 ____	9. dynamic center	
OBJ. 6 ____	10. baroreceptors	I. connective tissue sheath
OBJ. 6 ____	11. mean arterial pressure	J. "peak" blood pressure
OBJ. 6 ____	12. atrial natriuretic peptide	K. vasodilation
OBJ. 7 ____	13. chemoreceptors	L. single value for blood pressure
		M. venous return

Part II

	Column A	Column B
OBJ. 7 ____	14. medulla	N. pulmonary circuit
OBJ. 8 ____	15. atrial reflex	O. carry deoxygenated blood
OBJ. 8 ____	16. rise in body temperature	P. foramen ovale
OBJ. 9 ____	17. circle of Willis	Q. carry oxygenated blood
OBJ. 10 ____	18. blood between heart and lungs	R. vasomotor center
		S. ruptured aneurysm
OBJ. 10 ____	19. blood to cells and tissues	T. increasing venous return
OBJ. 11 ____	20. pulmonary arteries	U. internal jugular vein
OBJ. 11 ____	21. pulmonary veins	V. ligamentum arteriosum
OBJ. 12 ____	22. carries O_2 blood to head	W. systemic circuit
OBJ. 12 ____	23. blood from skull	X. increased blood flow to skin
OBJ. 13 ____	24. blood flow to placenta	Y. umbilical arteries
OBJ. 13 ____	25. interatrial opening	Z. age-related change
OBJ. 14 ____	26. ductus arteriosus	AA. brain circulation
OBJ. 15 ____	27. decreased hematocrit	BB. carotid arteries
OBJ. 15 ____	28. massive blood loss	

[L1]   Drawing/Illustration Labeling

Identify each numbered structure by labeling the following figures:

OBJ. 11   **Figure 18.1   The Arterial System**

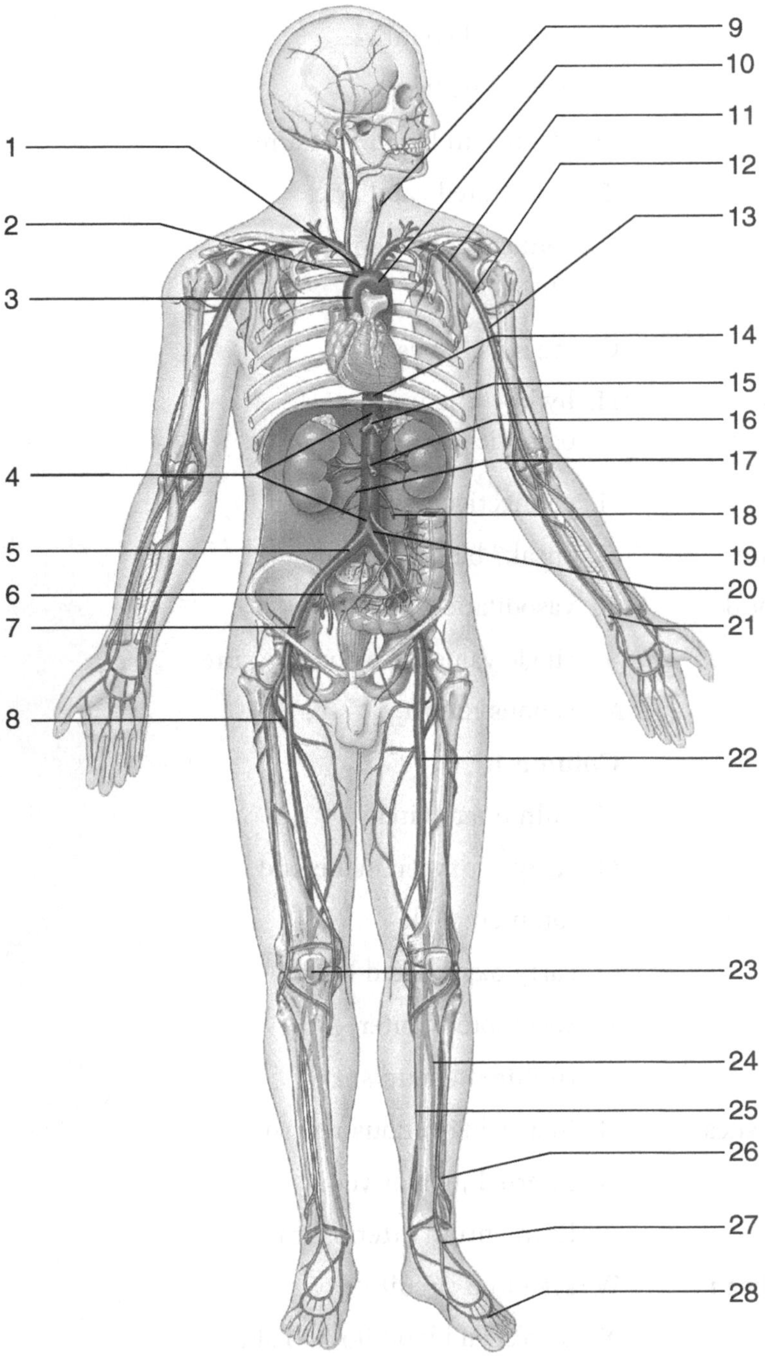

Arteries

1 _____
2 _____
3 _____
4 _____
5 _____
6 _____
7 _____
8 _____
9 _____
10 _____
11 _____
12 _____
13 _____
14 _____
15 _____
16 _____
17 _____
18 _____
19 _____
20 _____
21 _____
22 _____
23 _____
24 _____
25 _____
26 _____
27 _____
28 _____

OBJ. 11   **Figure 18.2   The Venous System**

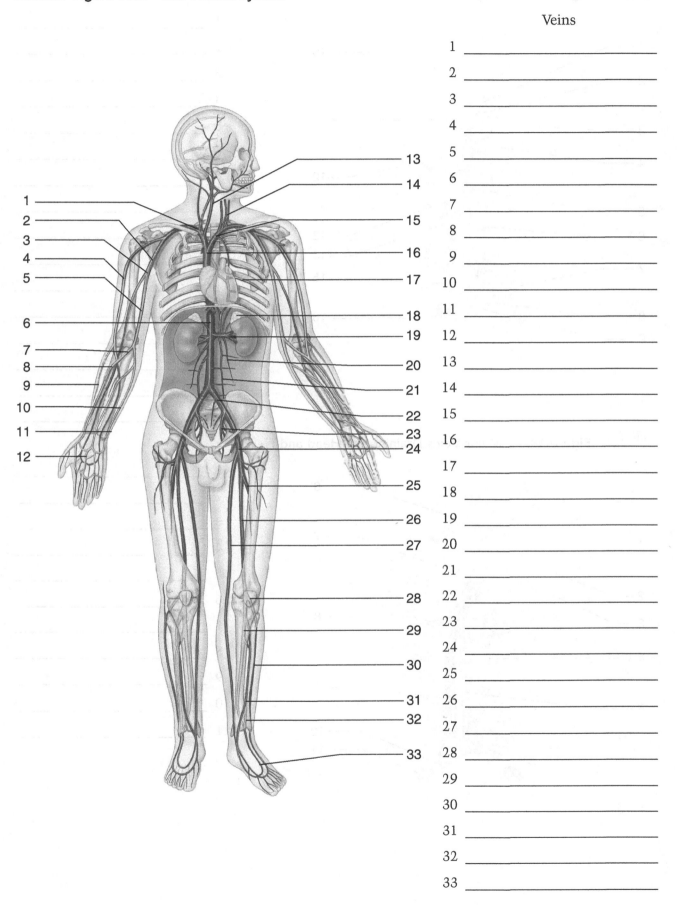

Veins

1 _____

2 _____

3 _____

4 _____

5 _____

6 _____

7 _____

8 _____

9 _____

10 _____

11 _____

12 _____

13 _____

14 _____

15 _____

16 _____

17 _____

18 _____

19 _____

20 _____

21 _____

22 _____

23 _____

24 _____

25 _____

26 _____

27 _____

28 _____

29 _____

30 _____

31 _____

32 _____

33 _____

OBJ. 11   **Figure 18.3   Major Arteries of the Head and Neck**

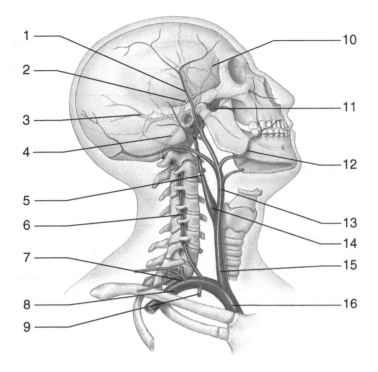

1 _____
2 _____
3 _____
4 _____
5 _____
6 _____
7 _____
8 _____
9 _____
10 _____
11 _____
12 _____
13 _____
14 _____
15 _____
16 _____

OBJ. 11   **Figure 18.4   Major Veins Draining the Head and Neck**

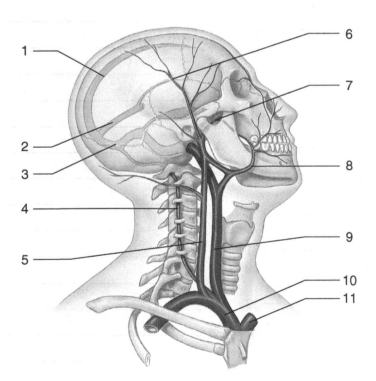

1 _____
2 _____
3 _____
4 _____
5 _____
6 _____
7 _____
8 _____
9 _____
10 _____
11 _____

LEVEL 2   Concept Synthesis

Concept Map I

Using the following terms, fill in the circled, numbered, blank spaces to complete the concept map. Follow the numbers to comply with the organization of the map.

Pulmonary arteries   Veins and venules   Systemic circuit
Arteries and arterioles   Pulmonary veins

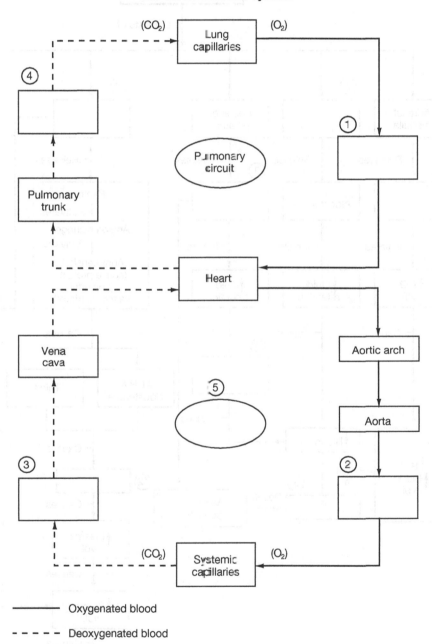

The cardiovascular system

Concept Map II

Using the following terms, fill in the circled, numbered, blank spaces to complete the concept map. Follow the numbers to comply with the organization of the map.

Erythropoietin   Increasing plasma volume Adrenal cortex
ADH (vasopressin) Epinephrine, norepinephrine Kidneys
Increasing fluid   Increasing blood pressure Atrial natriuretic factor

Endocrine system and cardiovascular regulation

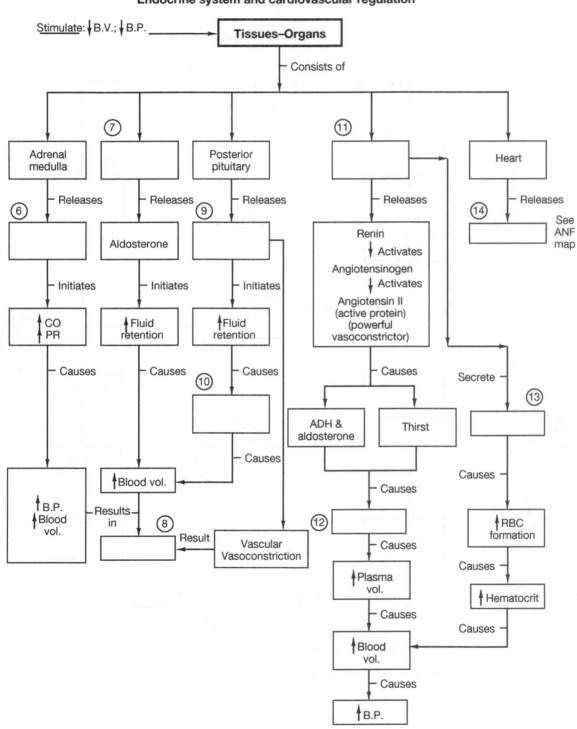

Concept Map III

Using the following terms, fill in the circled, numbered, blank spaces to complete the concept map. Follow the numbers to comply with the organization of the map.

Vasoconstriction   Vasomotor center   Hyperemia
Reactive   Epinephrine   Vasodilation
ADH (vasopressin)

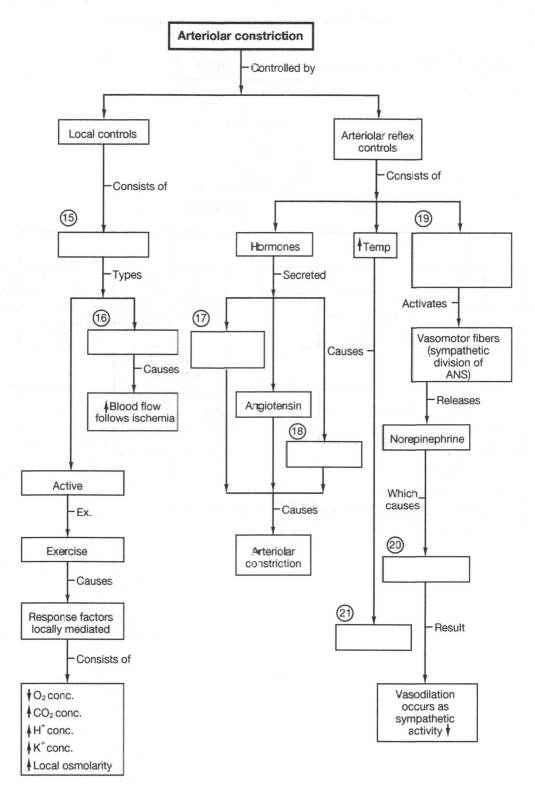

Concept Map IV

Using the following terms, fill in the circled, numbered, blank spaces to complete the concept map. Follow the numbers to comply with the organization of the map.

Decreasing blood pressure   Increasing H_2O loss by kidneys
Decreasing H_2O intake   Increasing blood flow (*l*/min.)

ANF effects on blood volume and blood pressure

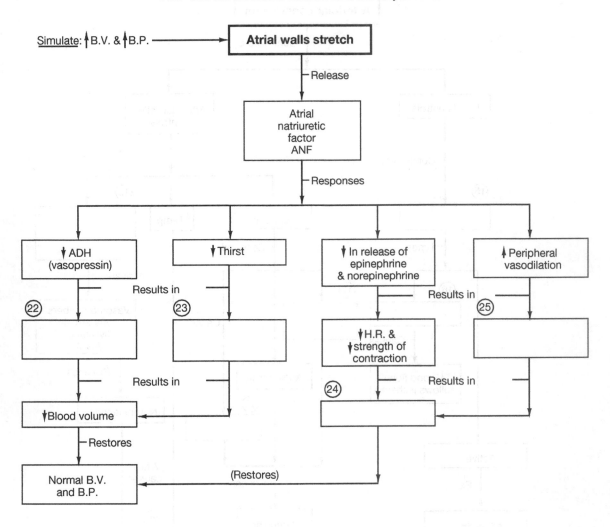

Concept Map V

Using the following terms, fill in the circled, numbered, blank spaces to complete the concept map. Follow the numbers to comply with the organization of the map.

L. subclavian artery   Superior mesenteric artery
L. common iliac artery   Thoracic aorta
Ascending aorta   R. gonadal artery
Celiac trunk   Brachiocephalic artery

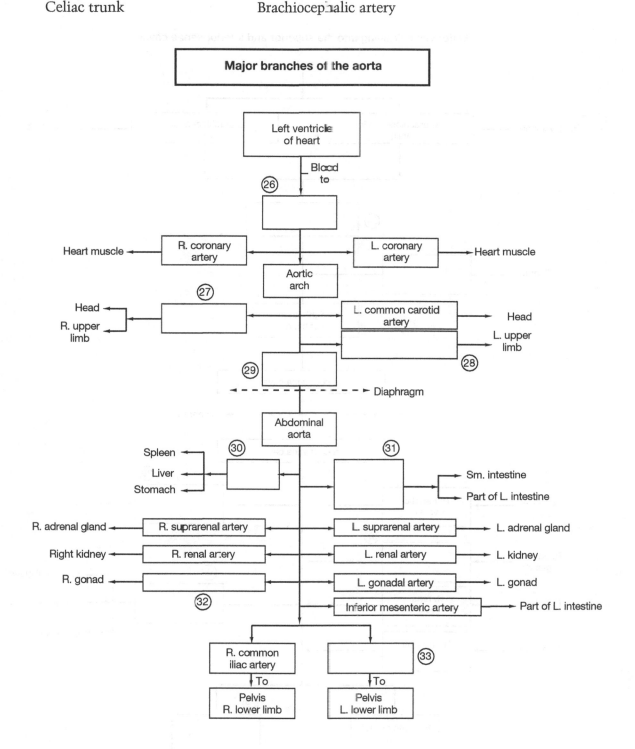

Concept Map VI

Using the following terms, fill in the circled, numbered, blank spaces to complete the concept map. Follow the numbers to comply with the organization of the map. (Note the direction of the arrows on this map.)

Azygous vein   L. common iliac vein   L. renal vein
L. hepatic veins   superior vena cava   R. suprarenal vein

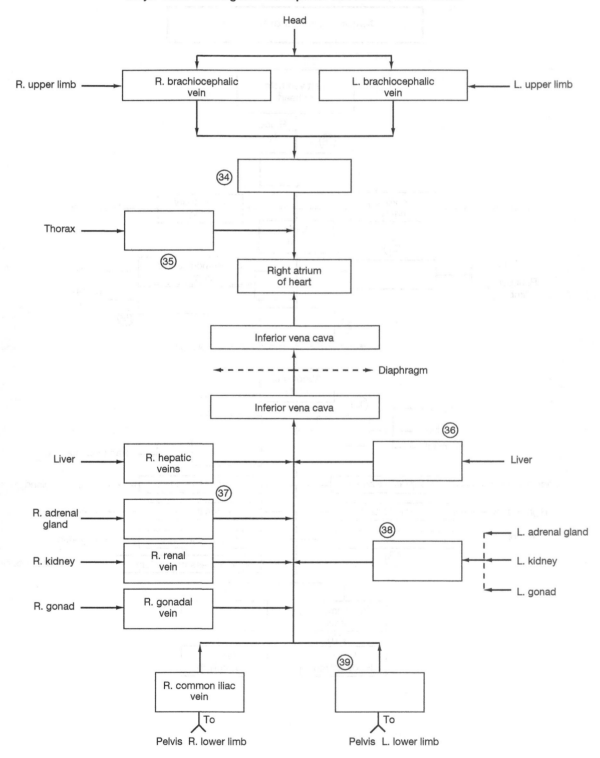

Major veins draining into the superior and inferior venae cavae

Body Trek

Using the terms below, fill in the blanks to complete a trek through the major arteries of the body.

lumbar	abdominal aorta	superior phrenic
intercostal	L. subclavian	common iliacs
brachiocephalic	aortic valve	inferior mesenteric
suprarenal	L. common carotid	celiac
renal	mediastinum	superior mesenteric
descending aorta	gonadal	inferior phrenic
thoracic aorta	aortic arch	

Robo has been "charged" and "programmed" to take an "aortic trek." The objective of the mission is to identify the regions and major arteries that branch off the aorta from its superior position in the thorax to its inferior location in the abdominopelvic region.

The micro-robot is catheterized directly into the left ventricle of the heart, via a technique devised exclusively for introducing high-tech devices directly into the heart. A ventricular contraction "swooshes" the robot through the (1) _____ into the (2) _____ , which curves across the superior surface of the heart, connecting the ascending aorta with the caudally directed (3) _____. The first artery branching off the aortic arch, the (4) _____ serves as a passageway for blood to arteries that serve the arms, neck, and head. As the robot continues its ascent, the (5) _____ and the (6) _____ arteries arise separately from the aortic arch, both supplying arterial blood to vessels that provide blood to regions that include the neck, head, shoulders, and arms. All of a sudden the robot is directed downward to begin its descent into the (7) _____ located within the (8) _____ and providing blood to the (9) _____ arteries that carry blood to the spinal cord and the body wall. Proceeding caudally, near the diaphragm, a pair of (10) _____ arteries deliver blood to the muscular diaphragm that separates the thoracic and abdominopelvic cavities. Leaving the thoracic aorta Robo continues trekking along the same circulatory pathway into the (11) _____, which descends posteriorly to the peritoneal cavity. The robot's "thermosensors" detect record high temperatures in the area, probably due to the cushion of adipose tissue surrounding the aorta in this region.

Just below the diaphragm, the (12) _____ arteries, which carry blood to the diaphragm, precede the (13) _____ artery, which supplies blood to arterial branches that circulate blood to the stomach, liver, spleen, and pancreas. Trekking downward, the (14) _____ arteries serving the adrenal glands and the (15) _____ arteries supplying the kidneys arise along the posteriolateral surface of the abdominal aorta behind the peritoneal lining. In the same region the (16) _____ arteries arise on the anterior surface of the abdominal aorta and branch into the connective tissue of the mesenteries. A pair of (17) _____ arteries supplying blood to the testicles in the male and the ovaries in the female are located slightly superior to the (18) _____ artery, which branches into the connective tissues of the mesenteries supplying blood to the last third of the large intestine, colon, and rectum.

On the final phase of the aortic trek, prior to the bifurcation of the aorta, small (19) _____ arteries begin on the posterior surface of the aorta and supply the spinal cord and the abdominal wall. Near the level of L4 the abdominal aorta divides to form a pair of muscular arteries, the (20) _____, which are the major blood suppliers to the pelvis and the legs.

As Robo completes the programmed mission, the message relayed to Mission Control reads, "Mission accomplished, please remove." Mission Control instructs the robot to continue its descent into the femoral artery where an arterial removal technique for high-tech gadgetry will facilitate Robo's exit and return to Mission Control for the next assignment.

COVERING ALL YOUR BASES

[L2]   Multiple Choice

Select the best answer or answers from the choices given.

1. In traveling from the heart to the peripheral capillaries, blood passes through:

   A. arteries, arterioles, and venules

   B. elastic arteries, muscular arteries, and arterioles

   C. veins, venules, and arterioles

   D. a, b, and c are correct

2. In general terms, blood flow (F) is directly proportional to:

   A. resistance

   B. increased viscosity

   C. peripheral resistance

   D. pressure

3. The goal of cardiovascular regulation is:

   A. to equalize the stroke volume with the cardiac output

   B. to increase pressure and reduce resistance

   C. to equalize the blood flow with the pressure differences

   D. maintenance of adequate blood flow through peripheral tissues and organs

4. Along the length of a typical capillary, blood pressure gradually falls from about:

   A. 120 to 80 mm Hg

   B. 75 to 50 mm Hg

   C. 30 to 18 mm Hg

   D. 15 to 5 mm Hg

5. In which of the following organs would you find *fenestrated* capillaries?

   A. kidneys

   B. liver

   C. endocrine glands

   D. both a and c

6. The *average* pressure in arteries is approximately:

   A. 120 mm Hg

   B. 100 mm Hg

   C. 140 mm Hg

   D. 80 mm Hg

7. The *average* pressure in veins is approximately:

   A. 2 mm Hg

   B. 10 mm Hg

   C. 15 mm Hg

   D. 80 mm Hg

8. When fluid moves across capillary membranes, the pressures forcing fluid *out* of the capillaries are:

   A. hydrostatic pressure; interstitial osmotic pressure

   B. interstitial fluid pressure; osmotic pressure of plasma

   C. hydrostatic pressure; interstitial fluid pressure

   D. interstitial osmotic pressure; osmotic pressure of plasma

9. The formula for resistance, $R = Ln/r^4$, where (L) is the length of the vessel, (n) is the viscosity of the blood, and (r) is the radius of the vessel, would confirm the following correct relationship:

   A. increasing radius, increasing friction, increasing flow

   B. decreasing radius, decreasing friction, decreasing flow

   C. increasing radius, decreasing friction, increasing flow

   D. decreasing radius, increasing friction, decreasing flow

10. Considering cardiac output (CO), mean arterial pressure (AP), and total peripheral resistance (PR), the relationship among flow, pressure, and resistance could be expressed as:

    A. $AP = CO \times PR$

    B. $CO = AP/PR$

    C. $CO/AP = 1/PR$

    D. a, b, and c are correct

11. To increase blood flow to an adjacent capillary, the local controls that operate are:

    A. decreasing O_2, increasing CO_2, decreasing pH

    B. increasing O_2, decreasing CO_2, decreasing pH

    C. increasing O_2, increasing CO_2, increasing pH

    D. decreasing O_2, decreasing CO_2, decreasing pH

12. The adrenergic fibers innervating arterioles are _____ fibers that release _____ and cause _____.

    A. parasympathetic; norepinephrine; vasodilation

    B. sympathetic; epinephrine; vasodilation

    C. sympathetic; norepinephrine; vasoconstriction

    D. parasympathetic; epinephrine; vasoconstriction

13. Two arteries formed by the bifurcation of the brachiocephalic artery are the:

    A. aorta, subclavian

    B. common iliac, common carotid

    C. jugular, carotid

    D. common carotid, subclavian

14. The artery that serves the posterior thigh is the:

    A. deep femoral

    B. common iliac

    C. internal iliac

    D. celiac

15. The _____ return blood to the heart and the _____ transport blood away from the heart.

    A. arteries; veins

    B. venules; arterioles

    C. veins; arteries

    D. arterioles; venules

16. The large vein that drains the thorax is the:

    A. superior vena cava

    B. internal jugular

    C. vertebral vein

    D. azygous vein

17. The veins that drain the head, neck, and upper extremities are the:

    A. jugulars

    B. brachiocephalics

    C. subclavian

    D. azygous

18. The veins that drain venous blood from the legs and the pelvis are:

    A. posterior tibials

    B. femorals

    C. great saphenous

    D. common iliacs

19. The vein that drains the knee region of the body is the:

    A. femoral   C. external iliacs

    B. popliteal   D. great saphenous

20. The large artery that serves the brain is the:

    A. internal carotid

    B. external carotid

    C. subclavian

    D. cephalic

21. The "link" between the subclavian and brachial artery is the:

    A. brachiocephalic

    B. vertebral

    C. cephalic

    D. axillary

22. The three arterial branches of the celiac trunk are the:

    A. splenic, pancreatic, mesenteric

    B. phrenic, intercostal, adrenolumbar

    C. L. gastric, splenic, hepatic

    D. brachial, ulnar, radial

23. The artery that supplies most of the small intestine and the first half of the large intestine is the:

    A. suprarenal artery

    B. superior mesenteric

    C. hepatic

    D. inferior mesenteric

24. The artery that supplies the pelvic organs is the:

    A. internal iliac artery

    B. external iliac artery

    C. common iliacs

    D. femoral artery

25. The subdivision(s) of the popliteal artery is (are):

    A. great saphenous artery

    B. anterior and posterior tibial arteries

    C. peroneal artery

    D. femoral and deep femoral arteries

[L2]   Completion

Using the terms below, complete the following statements.

radial	precapillary sphincters	aorta
mesoderm	great saphenous	circle of Willis
edema	reactive hyperemia	brachial
lumen	elastic rebound	venous return
veins	endothelium	recall of fluids

1. The anastomosis that encircles the infundibulum of the pituitary gland is the
   _____.

2. When the arteries absorb part of the energy provided by ventricular systole and give it back during ventricular diastole, the phenomenon is called _____.

3. When the blood volume increases at the expense of interstitial fluids, the process is referred to as _____.

4. The abnormal accumulation of interstitial fluid is called _____.

5. Rhythmic alterations in blood flow in capillary beds are controlled by
   _____.

6. The response in which tissue appears red in a given area is referred to as
   _____.

7. The lining of the lumen of blood vessels is comprised of a tissue layer called the
   _____.

8. The heart and blood vessels develop from the germ layer called the
   _____.

9. The blood vessels that contain valves are the _____.

10. Changes in thoracic pressure during breathing and the action of skeletal muscles serve to aid in _____.

11. The largest artery in the body is the _____.

12. The artery generally auscultated to determine the blood pressure in the arm is the _____ artery.

13. The artery generally used to take the pulse at the wrist is the _____ artery.

14. The longest vein in the body is the _____.

15. The central cavity through which blood flows in a blood vessel is referred to as the _____.

[L2]   Short Essay

Briefly answer the following questions in the spaces provided below.

1. What three distinct layers comprise the histological composition of typical arteries and veins?

2. List the types of blood vessels in the cardiovascular tree and briefly describe their anatomical associations (use arrows to show this relationship).

3. (a) What are sinusoids?

(b) Where are they found?

(c) Why are they important functionally?

4. Relative to gaseous exchange, what is the primary difference between the pulmonary circuit and the systemic circuit?

5. (a) What are the three primary sources of peripheral resistance?

(b) Which one can be adjusted by the nervous or endocrine system to regulate blood flow?

6. Symbolically summarize the relationship among blood pressure (BP), peripheral resistance (PR), and blood flow (F). State what the formula means.

7. Explain what is meant by: BP = 120 mm Hg/80 mm Hg

8. What is the mean arterial pressure (MAP) if the systolic pressure is 110 mm Hg and the diastolic pressure is 80 mm Hg?

9. What are the three important functions of continual movement of fluid from the plasma into tissues and lymphatic vessels?

10. What are the three primary factors that influence blood pressure and blood flow?

11. What three major baroreceptor populations enable the cardiovascular system to respond to alterations in blood pressure?

12. What hormones are responsible for long-term and short-term regulation of cardio-vascular performance?

13. What are the clinical signs and symptoms of age-related changes in the blood?

14. How does arteriosclerosis affect blood vessels?

LEVEL 3   Critical Thinking/Application

Using principles and concepts learned about blood vessels and circulation, answer the following questions. Write your answers on a separate sheet of paper.

1. Trace the circulatory pathway a drop of blood would take if it begins in the L. ventricle, travels down the left arm, and returns to the R. atrium. (Use arrows to indicate direction of flow.)

2. During a clinical experience, taking a pulse is one of the primary responsibilities of the clinician. What arteries in the body serve as locations for detecting a pulse?

3. Suppose you are lying down and quickly rise to a standing position. What causes dizziness or a loss of consciousness to occur as a result of standing up quickly?

4. While pedaling an exercycle, Mary periodically takes her pulse by applying pressure to the carotid artery in the upper neck. Why might this method give her an erroneous perception of her pulse rate while exercising?

5. Recent statistics show that approximately 30 to 35 percent of the adult American population is involved in some type of exercise program. What cardiovascular changes occur and what benefits result from exercising?

19

THE CARDIOVASCULAR SYSTEM: BLOOD

Student Objectives

When you have completed the exercises in this chapter, you will have accomplished the following objectives:

Overview of Blood Vessel Structure and Function

1. Describe the three layers that typically form the wall of a blood vessel and state the function of each.
2. Define *vasoconstriction* and *vasodilation*.
3. Compare and contrast the structure and function of the three types of arteries.
4. Describe the structure and function of veins and explain how veins differ from arteries.
5. Describe the structure and function of a capillary bed.

Physiology of Circulation

6. Define *blood flow, blood pressure,* and *resistance,* and explain the relationships between these factors.
7. List and explain the factors that influence blood pressure and describe how blood pressure is regulated.
8. Define *hypertension.* Describe its symptoms and its consequences.

9. Explain how blood flow is regulated in the body in general and in its specific organs.
10. Outline factors involved in capillary dynamics and explain the significance of each.
11. Define *circulatory shock.* Note several possible causes.

Circulatory Pathways: Blood Vessels of the Body

12. Trace the pathway of blood through the pulmonary circuit and state the importance of this special circulation.
13. Describe the general functions of the systemic circuit. Name and give the location of the major arteries and veins in the systemic circulation.
14. Describe the structure and special function of the hepatic portal system.

After leaving the heart, the blood is sent through a vast network of vessels that ultimately reach each cell, supplying oxygen and nutrients and removing wastes. Blood flows through an equally extensive vascular network back to the heart. In the adult human, the length of these circulatory pathways is about 60,000 miles. These are not passive tubular structures but dynamic structures that rapidly alter the blood flow in response to changing internal and external conditions.

The focus of Chapter 19 is on the vascular portion of the cardiovascular system. Topics include blood vessel structure and function, the physiology of circulation and blood pressure, the dynamics of the capillary bed, the anatomy of the pulmonary and systemic vasculature, and aspects of the development and diseases of blood vessels.

BUILDING THE FRAMEWORK

Overview of Blood Vessel Structure and Function

1. Assume someone has been injured in an automobile accident and is bleeding profusely. What pressure points could you compress to help stop the bleeding from the following areas?

   _____ 1. Thigh

   _____ 2. Forearm

   _____ 3. Calf

   _____ 4. Lower jaw

   _____ 5. Thumb

   _____ 6. Plantar surface of foot

   _____ 7. Temple

   _____ 8. Ankle

2. Select different colors for each of the three blood vessel tunics listed in the key choices and illustrated in Figure 19.1. (*Note:* Elastic laminae are *not* illustrated.) Color each tunic on the three diagrams and correctly identify each vessel type. Identify valves if appropriate. Write your answers in the blanks beneath the illustrations. In the additional blanks, list the structural details that allowed you to make the identifications. Then, using the key choices, identify the blood vessel tunics described in each of the following cases by writing the correct answers in the answer blanks.

Key Choices

◯ A. Tunica interna ◯ B. Tunica media ◯ C. Tunica externa

_____ 1. Single thin layer of endothelium associated with scant connective tissue

_____ 2. Bulky middle coat, containing smooth muscle and elastin

_____ 3. Provides a smooth surface to decrease resistance to blood flow

_____ 4. The only tunic of capillaries

_____ 5. Called the adventitia in some cases

_____ 6. The only tunic that plays an active role in blood pressure regulation

_____ 7. Supporting, protective coat

_____ 8. Forms venous valves

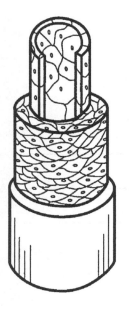 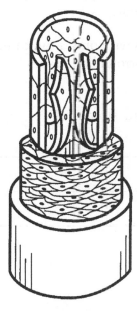 

Figure 19.1

A. _____   B. _____   C. _____

   _____   _____   _____

   _____   _____   _____

3. Match the terms pertaining to blood vessels in Column B to the appropriate descriptions in Column A.

Column A	Column B
_____ 1. Transport blood away from heart	A. Arteries
_____ 2. Largest arteries, low resistance	B. Arterioles
_____ 3. Arteries with thickest tunica media; active in vasoconstriction	C. Capillaries
	D. Continuous
_____ 4. Control blood flow into individual capillary beds	E. Elastic
_____ 5. Lumen is the size of red blood cells	F. Fenestrated
_____ 6. Capillary type with an uninterrupted lining	G. Muscular
_____ 7. Capillary type with numerous pores and gap junctions	H. Sinusoids
	I. Veins
_____ 8. Capillaries with large intercellular clefts and irregular lumen	J. Venous sinuses
_____ 9. Vessels formed when capillaries unite	K. Venules
_____ 10. Vessels with thin walls and large lumens that often appear collapsed in histologic preparations	
_____ 11. Veins with only a tunica intima; supported by surrounding tissues	

4. What is the importance of arterial anastomoses?

_____

_____

_____

5. Figure 19.2 shows diagrammatic views of the three types of capillaries. Below each diagram, write in the type of capillary shown. Then, identify all elements and structures that have leader lines. Finally, color code and color the following structures:

◯ Basal lamina   ◯ Endothelial cell(s)   ◯ Macrophage location (if present)

◯ Capillary lumen   ◯ Erythrocyte(s)

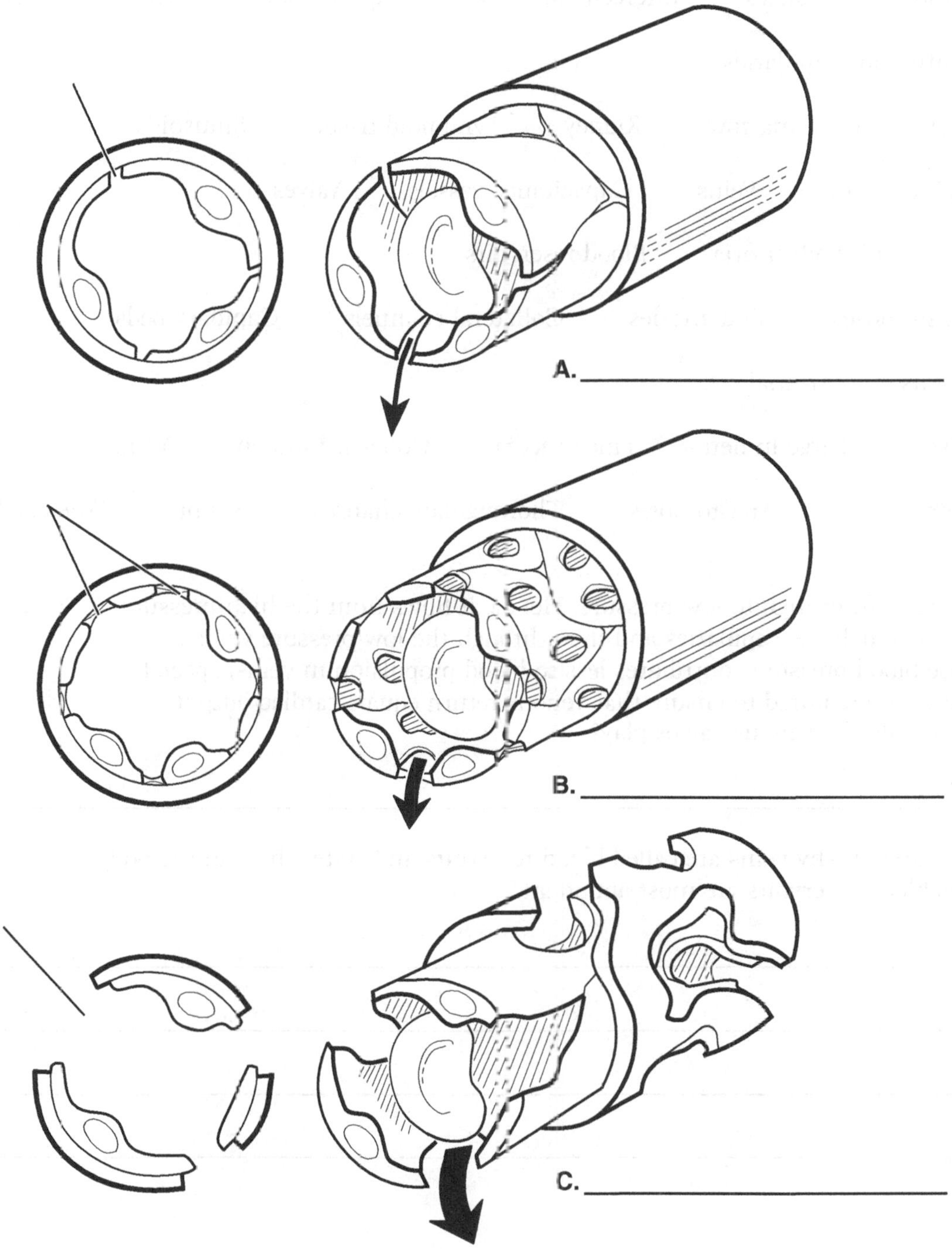

A. _____

B. _____

C. _____

Figure 19.2

6. Circle the term that does not belong in each of the following groupings.

1. Elastic   Conducting   Continuous flow   Muscular   Pulse

2. Distributing   Vasoconstriction   Muscular   Most arteries   Pressure points

3. Cornea   Heart   Cartilage   Epithelium   Tendons

4. Cytoplasmic vesicles   Intercellular clefts   Gap junctions   Tight junctions

   Continuous capillaries

5. Liver   Bone marrow   Kidney   Lymphoid tissue   Sinusoids

6. High pressure   Veins   Capacitance vessels   Valves

   Thick tunica adventitia   Blood reservoirs

7. Anastomoses   End arteries   Collateral channels   Capillary beds

   Venous   Arterial

8. Valves   Large lumen   Thick media   Collapsed lumen   Veins

9. Metarteriole   Anastomosis   Thoroughfare channel   Shunt   True capillaries

7. Blood flows from high to low pressure. Hence, it flows from the high-pressure arteries through the capillaries and then through the low-pressure veins. Because blood pressure contributes less to blood propulsion in veins, special measures are required to ensure that venous return equals cardiac output. What role do the venous valves play?

_____

8. Briefly explain why veins are called blood reservoirs and state where in the body venous blood reservoirs are most abundant.

_____

_____

_____

_____

Physiology of Circulation

1. Fill in the blanks in the flowcharts below indicating the relationships between the terms provided. The position of some elements in these schemes has already been indicated.

   1. difference in blood pressure   resistance   atherosclerosis

      blood viscosity   vessel length   hematocrit

      vasoconstriction

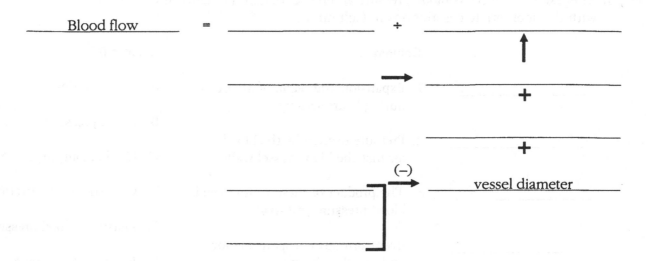

   2. cardiac output   peripheral resistance   polycythemia

      blood volume   heart beat   excessive salt intake

      vasoconstriction

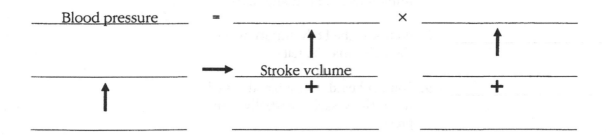

2. Briefly explain why blood flow in large, thick-walled arteries, such as the aorta and its branches, is fairly continuous and does not stop when the heart relaxes.

_____

_____

_____

_____

3. This exercise concerns blood pressure and pulse. Match the items in Column B with the appropriate descriptions in Column A.

Column A

_____ 1. Expansion and recoil of an artery during heart activity

_____ 2. Pressure exerted by the blood against the blood vessel walls

_____ 3. The product of these factors yields blood pressure (#3–#4)

_____ 4. Event primarily responsible for peripheral resistance

_____ 5. Blood pressure during heart contraction

_____ 6. Blood pressure during heart relaxation

_____ 7. Site where blood pressure determinations are normally made

_____ 8. Points at the body surface where the pulse may be felt

_____ 9. Sounds heard over a blood vessel when the vessel is partially compressed

Column B

A. Over arteries

B. Blood pressure

C. Cardiac output

D. Constriction of arterioles

E. Diastolic blood pressure

F. Peripheral resistance

G. Pressure points

H. Pulse

I. Sounds of Korotkoff

J. Systolic blood pressure

K. Over veins

4. What effects do the following factors have on blood pressure? Use I to indicate an increase in pressure and D to indicate a decrease in pressure.

_____ 1. Increased diameter of the arterioles

_____ 2. Increased blood viscosity

_____ 3. Increased cardiac output

_____ 4. Increased pulse rate

_____ 5. Anxiety, fear

_____ 6. Increased urine output

_____ 7. Sudden change in position from reclining to standing

_____ 8. Physical exercise

_____ 9. Physical training

_____ 10. Alcohol

_____ 11. Hemorrhage

_____ 12. Nicotine

_____ 13. Arteriosclerosis

_____ 14. Stimulation of arterial baroreceptors

_____ 15. Stimulation of carotid body chemoreceptors

_____ 16. Release of epinephrine from adrenal medulla

_____ 17. Secretion of atrial natriuretic peptide

_____ 18. Secretion of antidiuretic hormone

_____ 19. Release of endothelin

_____ 20. Secretion of NO

_____ 21. Renin/angiotensin mechanism

_____ 22. Secretion of aldosterone

_____ 23. Secretion of PDGF

5. Circle the term that does not belong in each of the following groupings.

1. Blood pressure   mm Hg   Cardiac output   Force of blood on vessel wall

2. Peripheral resistance   Friction   Arterioles   Blood flow

3. Low viscosity   High viscosity   Blood   Resistance to flow

4. Blood viscosity   Blood pressure   Vessel length   Vessel diameter

5. High blood pressure   Hemorrhage   Weak pulse   Low cardiac output

6. Resistance   Friction   Vasodilation   Vasoconstriction

7. High pressure   Vein   Artery   Spurting blood

8. Elastic arteries   Diastolic pressure   120 mm Hg   Auxiliary pumps

9. Cardiac cycle   Intermittent blood flow   Capillary bed   Precapillary sphincters

10. Muscular pump   Respiratory pump   Inactivity   Venous return

11. Hypotension   Sympathetic activity   Poor nutrition   Training

6. If a statement is true, write the letter T in the answer blank. If a statement is false, change the underlined word(s) and write the correct word(s) in the answer blank.

_____ 1. Renin, released by the kidneys, causes a <u>decrease</u> in blood pressure.

_____ 2. The decreasing efficiency of the sympathetic nervous system vasoconstrictor functioning due to aging leads to a type of hypotension called <u>sympathetic</u> hypotension.

_____ 3. Two body organs in which vasoconstriction rarely occurs are the heart and the <u>kidneys</u>.

_____ 4. A <u>sphygmomanometer</u> is used to take the apical pulse.

_____ 5. The pulmonary circuit is a <u>high</u>-pressure circulation.

_____ 6. Cold has a <u>vasodilating</u> effect.

_____ 7. <u>Thrombophlebitis</u> is called the silent killer.

_____ 8. The nervous system controls blood pressure and blood distribution by altering the diameters of the <u>venules</u>.

_____ 9. The vasomotor center for blood pressure control is located in the <u>left atrium</u>.

_____ 10. Pressoreceptors in the <u>large arteries</u> of the neck and thorax detect changes in blood pressure.

_____ 11. ANP, the hormone produced by the atria, causes a <u>rise</u> in blood volume and blood pressure.

_____ 12. The hormone vasopressin causes intense <u>vasodilation</u>.

_____ 13. Hypertension in obese people can be promoted by increased <u>viscosity of the blood</u>.

_____ 14. The velocity of blood flow is slowest in the <u>veins</u>.

_____ 15. The total cross-sectional area of the vascular bed is least in the <u>capillary bed</u>.

_____ 16. <u>Hypertension</u> is the local adjustment of blood flow to a given tissue at any particular time.

_____ 17. In active skeletal muscles, autoregulated vasodilation is promoted by an increase of <u>acetylcholine</u> in the area.

7. Figure 19.3 is a diagram of a capillary bed. Arrows indicate the direction of blood flow. Select five different colors and color the coding circles and their structures on the figure. Then answer the questions that follow by referring to Figure 19.3. Notice that questions 6–14 concern fluid flows at capillary beds and the forces (hydrostatic and osmotic pressures) that promote such fluid shifts.

⬭ Arteriole   ⬭ Thoroughfare channel   ⬭ Postcapillary venule

⬭ Precapillary sphincters   ⬭ True capillaries   ⬭ Metarteriole

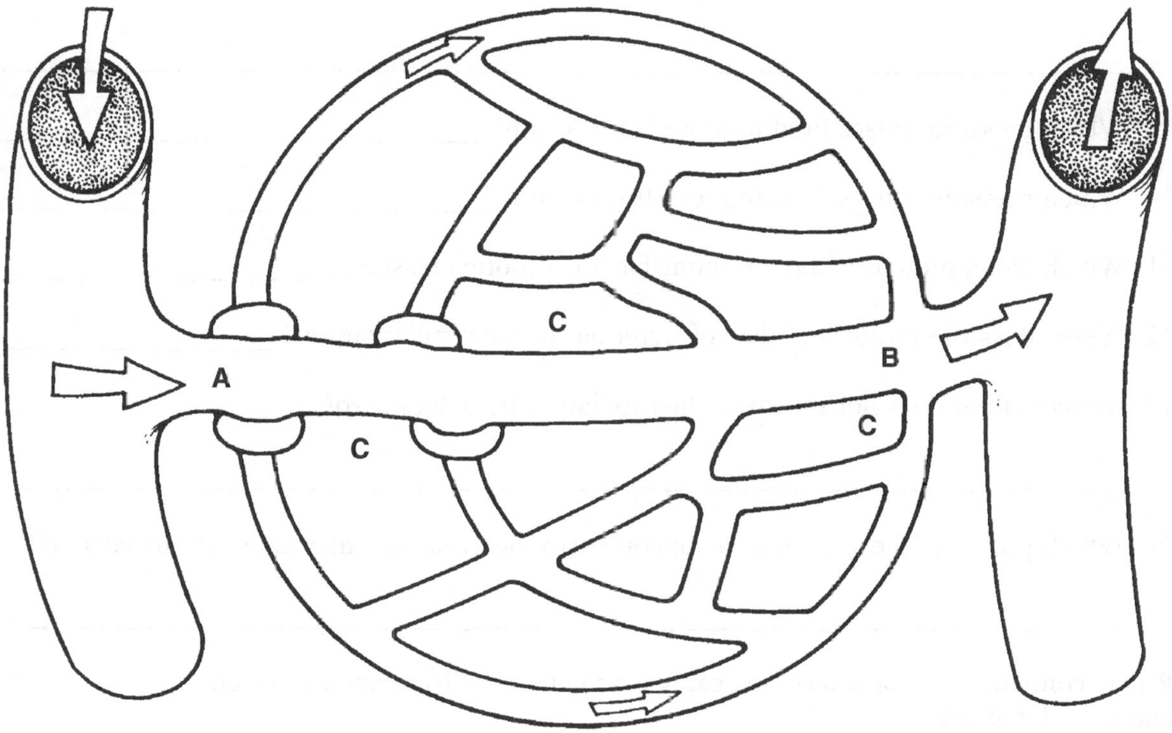

Figure 19.3

1. What is the liquid that surrounds tissue cells called?

_____

2. What drives the movement of soluble substances between tissue fluids and the blood?

_____

3. Which substances pass readily through the endothelial cell plasma membrane?

_____

4. Which substances move through fluid-filled capillary clefts?

_____

5. If the precapillary sphincters are contracted, by which route will the blood flow?

   _____

6. Under normal conditions, in which area does hydrostatic pressure predominate, A, B, or C?

   _____

7. Which area has the highest osmotic pressure? _____

8. Which pressure is in excess and causes fluids to move from A to C? (Be specific as to whether the force exists in the capillary or the interstitial space.)

   _____

9. Which pressure causes fluid to move from A to B? _____

10. Which pressure causes fluid to move from C to B? _____

11. Which blood protein is most responsible for osmotic pressure? _____

12. Where does the greater net flow of water out of the capillary occur? _____

13. If excess fluid does not return to the capillary, where does it go?

    _____

14. Which pressure in excess at B, as in congestive heart failure, may cause tissue edema?

    _____

8. Briefly compare the characteristics, causes, and effects of hypovolemic shock and vascular shock.

   _____

   _____

   _____

   _____

   _____

   _____

9. Choose the vessel type (arteries, capillaries, veins) with the indicated characteristic.

_____ 1. Highest total cross-sectional area

_____ 2. Highest velocity of blood flow

_____ 3. Lowest velocity of blood flow

_____ 4. Pulse pressure

_____ 5. Lowest blood pressure

10. Using the key choices, identify the special circulations described below.

Key Choices

A. Cerebral	C. Hepatic	E. Skeletal muscle
B. Coronary	D. Pulmonary	F. Skin

_____ 1. Blood flow increases markedly when the body temperature rises

_____ 2. The major autoregulatory stimulus is a drop in pH

_____ 3. Arteries characteristically have thin walls and large lumens

_____ 4. Vessels do not constrict but are compressed during systole

_____ 5. Receives constant blood flow whether the body is at rest or strenuously exercising

_____ 6. Vasodilation promoted by high oxygen levels

_____ 7. Capillary flow markedly sluggish; phagocytes present

_____ 8. Prolonged activity places extreme demands on cardiovascular system

_____ 9. Additional oxygen can be supplied only by increased blood flow

_____ 10. Much lower arterial pressure than that in systemic circulation

_____ 11. Large, atypical capillaries with fenestrations

_____ 12. Impermeable tight junctions in capillary endothelium

_____ 13. One of the most precise autoregulatory systems in the body

_____ 14. Venous blood empties into large dural sinuses rather than into veins

_____ 15. Abundance of superficial veins

_____ 16. During vigorous physical activity, receives up to two-thirds of total blood flow

_____ 17. Arterioles have receptors for both acetylcholine and epinephrine

Circulatory Pathways:
Blood Vessels of the Body

1. Figure 19.4 shows the pulmonary circuit. Identify all vessels that have leader lines. Color the vessels (and heart chambers) transporting oxygen-rich blood *red;* color those transporting carbon dioxide-rich blood *blue.*

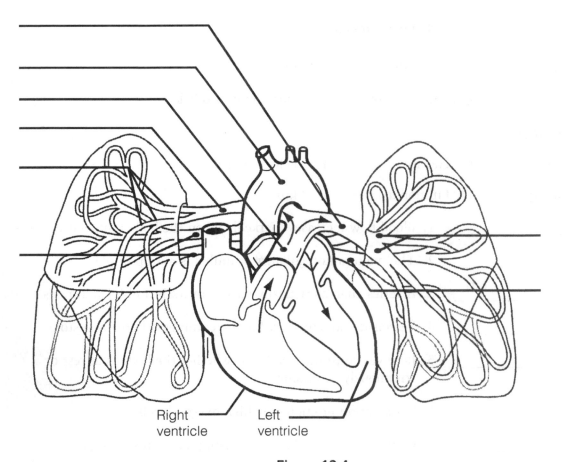

Right ventricle   Left ventricle

Figure 19.4

2. Figures 19.5 and 19.6 illustrate the locations of the major systemic arteries and veins of the body. These figures are highly simplified and will serve as a "warm-up" for the more detailed vascular diagrams to come. The arteries are shown in Figure 19.5. Color the arteries red, then identify those indicated by leader lines on the figure. The veins are shown in Figure 19.6. Color the veins blue, then identify each vein that has a leader line on the figure. Or, if you wish, color the individual vessels with different colors to help you to identify their extent.

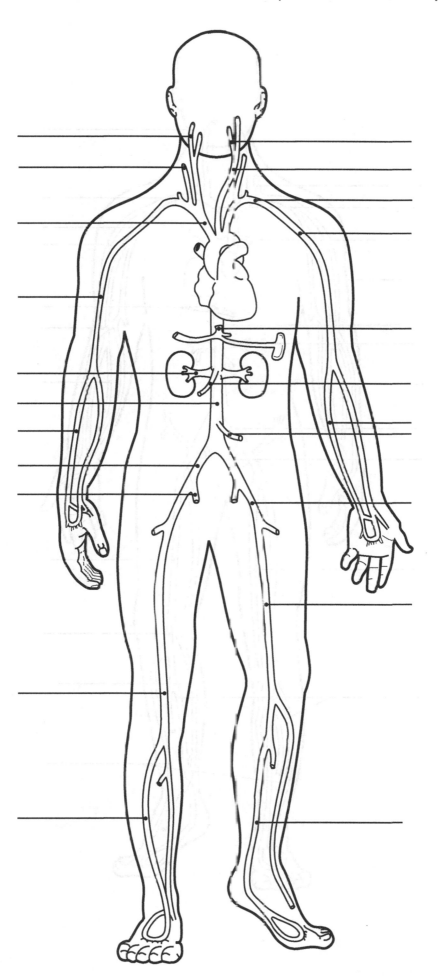

**Figure 19.5
Arteries**

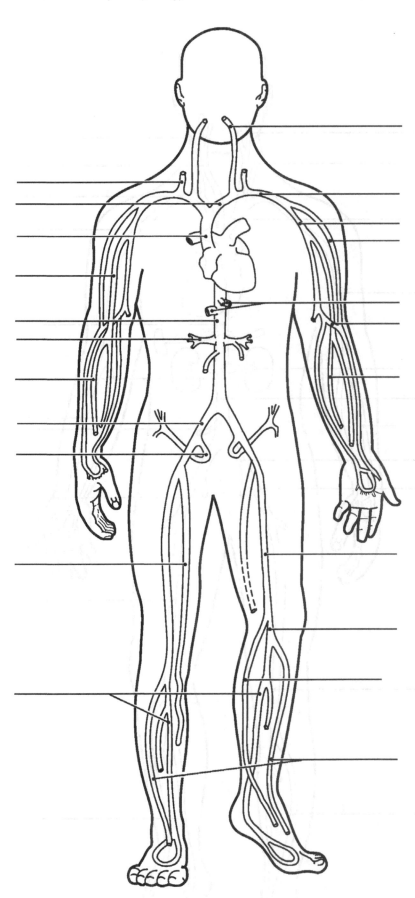

Figure 19.6
Veins

3. Figure 19.7 shows the major arteries of the head and neck. Note that the clavicle is omitted and that dashed lines represent deeper vessels. Color code and color the following vessels.

○ Brachiocephalic   ○ Internal thoracic   ○ Right common carotid

○ Costocervical trunk   ○ Lingual   ○ Right subclavian

○ External carotid   ○ Maxillary   ○ Superficial temporal

○ Facial   ○ Occipital   ○ Superior thyroid

○ Internal carotid   ○ Ophthalmic   ○ Thyrocervical trunk

○ Vertebral

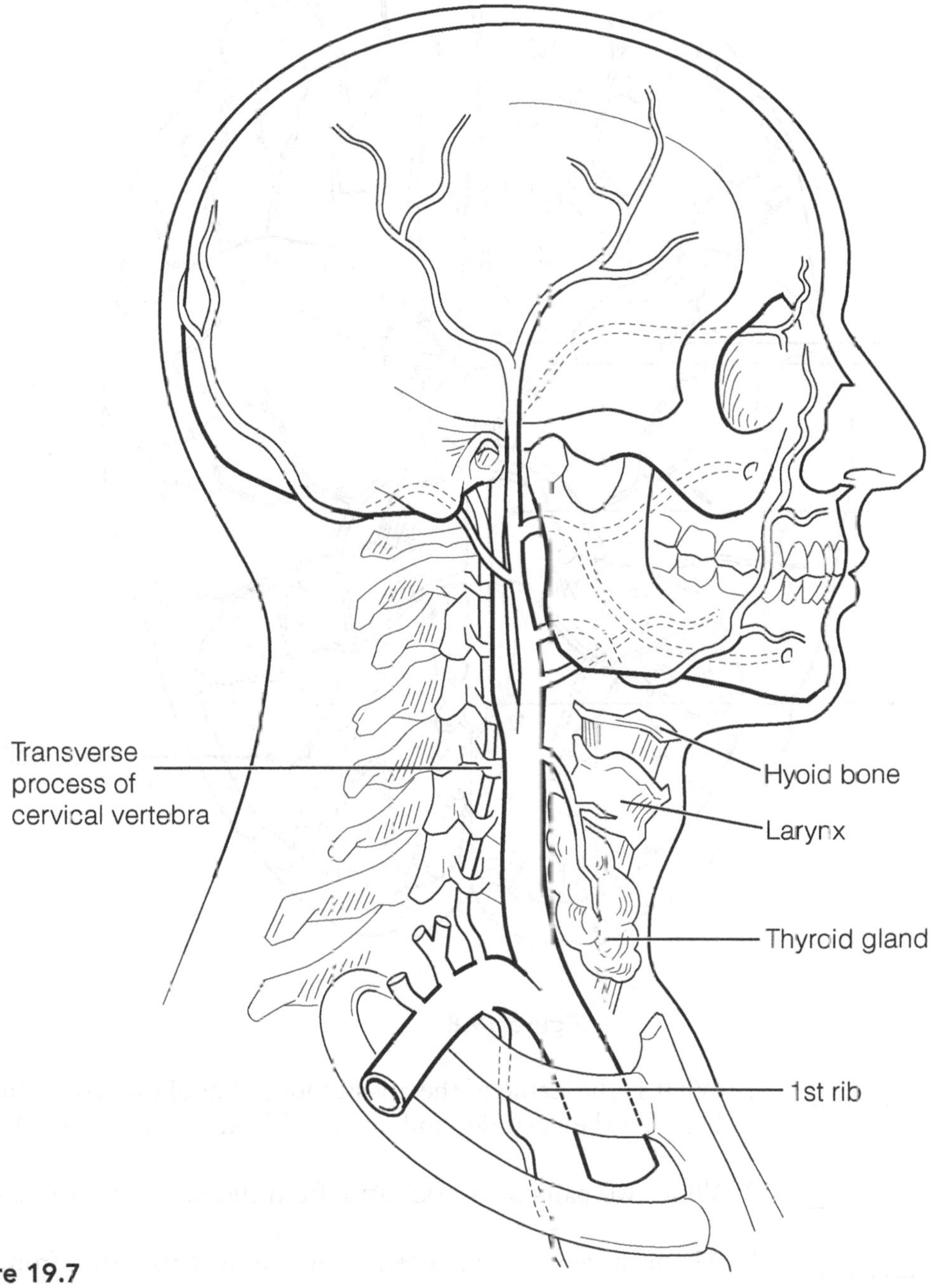

Transverse process of cervical vertebra

Hyoid bone

Larynx

Thyroid gland

1st rib

Figure 19.7
Arteries of the head and neck

4. Figure 19.8 illustrates the arterial circulation of the brain. Select different colors for the following structures, and color the diagram. Then respond to the questions following the diagram by choosing responses from the structures to be identified.

◯ A. Basilar artery   ◯ D. Middle cerebral arteries

◯ B. Communicating arteries   ◯ E. Posterior cerebral arteries

◯ C. Anterior cerebral arteries   ◯ F. Circle of Willis

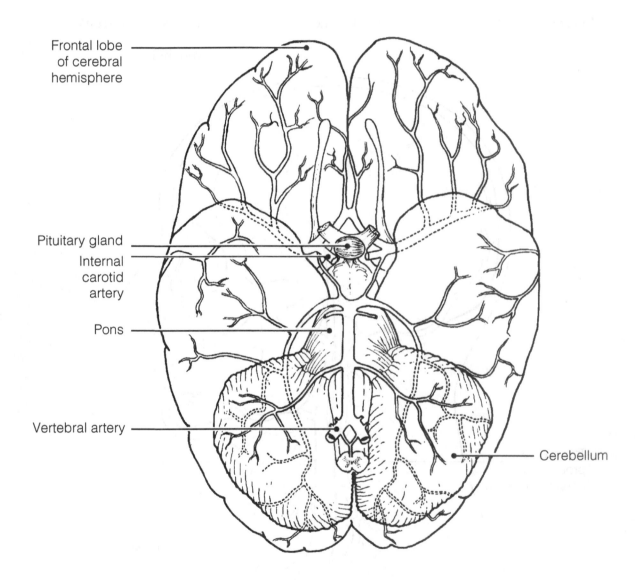

Figure 19.8

_____ 1. What is the name of the anastomosis that allows communication between the posterior and anterior blood supplies of the brain?

_____ 2. What two pairs of arteries arise from the internal carotid artery?

_____ 3. The posterior cerebral arteries serving the brain arise from what artery?

5. Using the key choices, identify the *arteries* in the following descriptions.

Key Choices

A. Anterior tibial	H. Coronary	O. Intercostals	V. Renal
B. Aorta	I. Deep femoral	P. Internal carotid	W. Subclavian
C. Brachial	J. Dorsalis pedis	Q. Internal iliac	X. Superior mesenteric
D. Brachiocephalic	K. External carotid	R. Fibular	
E. Celiac trunk	L. Femoral	S. Phrenic	Y. Vertebral
F. Common carotid	M. Hepatic	T. Posterior tibial	Z. Ulnar
G. Common iliac	N. Inferior mesenteric	U. Radial	

_____ 1. _____ 2. Two arteries formed by the division of the brachiocephalic artery

_____ 3. First branches off the ascending aorta; serve the heart

_____ 4. _____ 5. Two paired arteries serving the brain

_____ 6. Largest artery of the body

_____ 7. Arterial network on the dorsum of the foot

_____ 8. Serves the posterior thigh

_____ 9. Supplies the diaphragm

_____ 10. Splits to form the radial and ulnar arteries

_____ 11. Auscultated to determine blood pressure in the arm

_____ 12. Supplies the last half of the large intestine

_____ 13. Serves the pelvis

_____ 14. External iliac becomes this artery on entering the thigh

_____ 15. Major artery serving the arm

_____ 16. Supplies the small intestine and part of the large intestine

_____ 17. Terminal branches of the dorsal, or descending, aorta

_____ 18. Arterial trunk that has three major branches, which serve the liver, spleen, and stomach

_____ 19. Major artery serving the tissues external to the skull

_____ 20. _____ 21. _____ 22. Three arteries serving the leg

_____ 23. Artery generally used to feel the pulse at the wrist

6. Figure 19.9 shows the venous drainage of the head. Color code and color each of the drainage veins individually. Label each of the dural venous sinuses that has a leader line, but color all the dural sinuses yellow. Note that the clavicle has been omitted.

Dural venous sinuses

Cavernous sinus
Inferior sagittal sinus
Straight sinus
Superior sagittal sinus
Transverse sinus

Drainage veins

◯ Brachiocephalic   ◯ Ophthalmic

◯ External jugular   ◯ Subclavian

◯ Facial   ◯ Superficial temporal

◯ Internal jugular   ◯ Superior thyroid

◯ Middle thyroid   ◯ Vertebral

Sinuses:

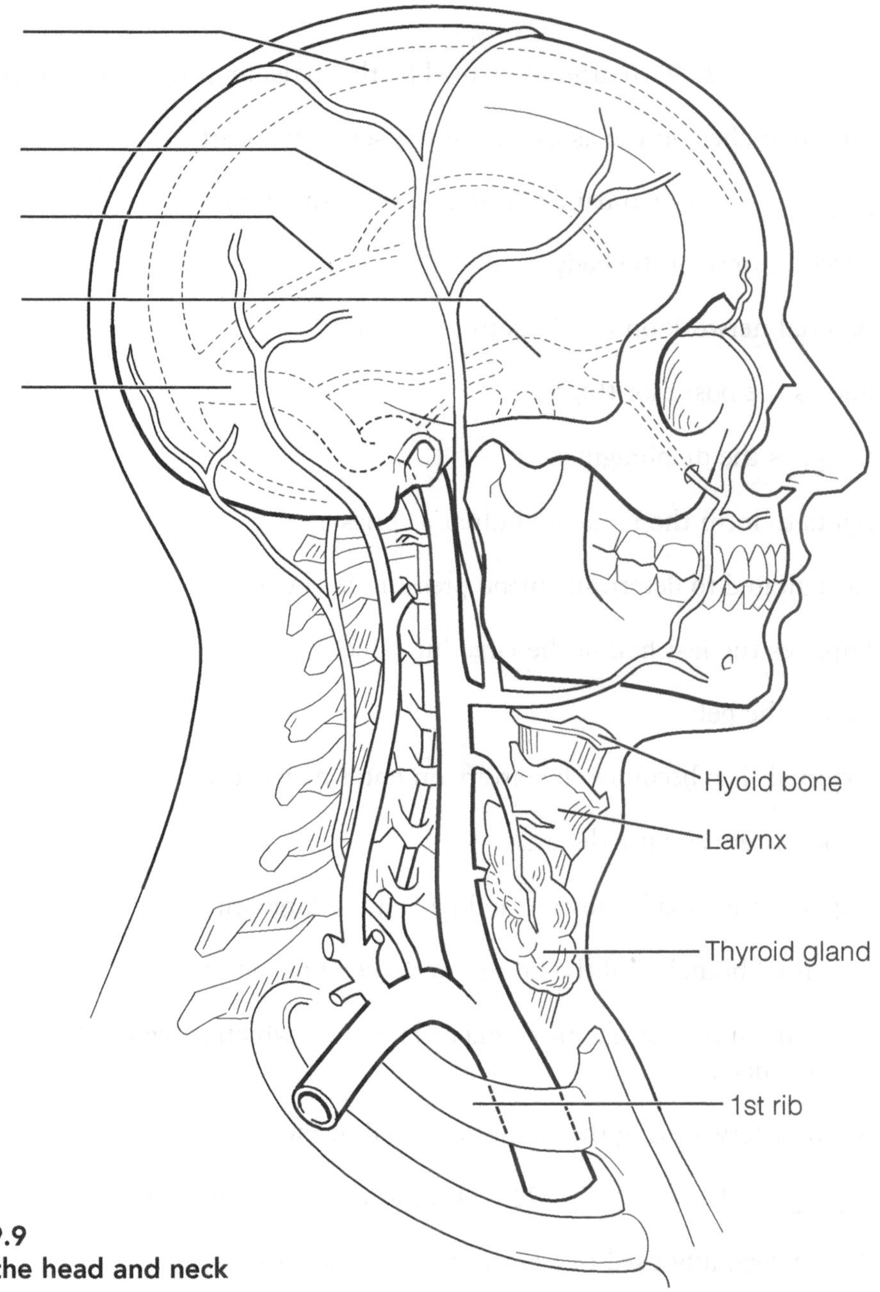

Hyoid bone

Larynx

Thyroid gland

1st rib

Figure 19.9
Veins of the head and neck

7. Figure 19.10 shows the arteries and veins of the upper limb. Using the key choices, identify each vessel provided with a leader line. (*Note:* In many cases, the same term will be used to identify both an artery and a deep vein.)

Key Choices

A. Axillary	H. Costocervical trunk	O. Subclavian
B. Basilic	I. Deep brachial	P. Subscapular
C. Brachial	J. Deep palmar arch	Q. Superficial palmar arch
D. Brachiocephalic	K. Digital	R. Thoracoacromial trunk
E. Cephalic	L. Median cubital	S. Thoracocervical trunk
F. Circumflex (anterior humeral)	M. Lateral thoracic	T. Thoracodorsal
G. Common interosseous	N. Radial	U. Ulnar

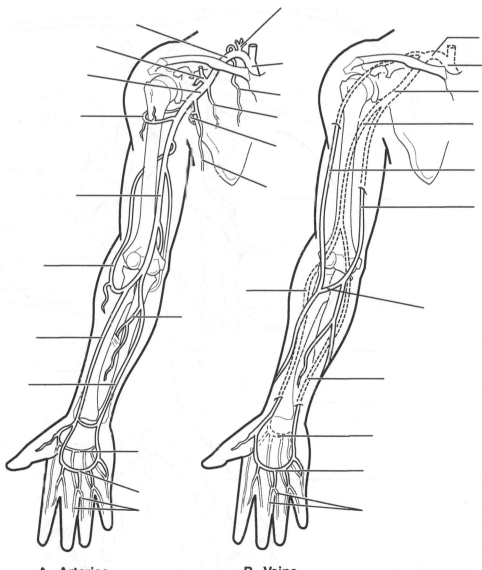

Figure 19.10   **A. Arteries**   **B. Veins**

8. The abdominal vasculature is depicted in Figure 19.11. Using the key choices, identify the following vessels by selecting the correct letters. Color the diagram as you wish.

Key Choices

A. Aorta

B. Celiac trunk

C. Common iliac arteries

D. Gonadal arteries

E. Hepatic veins

F. Inferior mesenteric artery

G. Inferior vena cava

H. Lumbar arteries

I. Median sacral artery

J. Superior mesenteric artery

K. Renal arteries

L. Renal veins

M. Left gonadal vein

N. Right gonadal vein

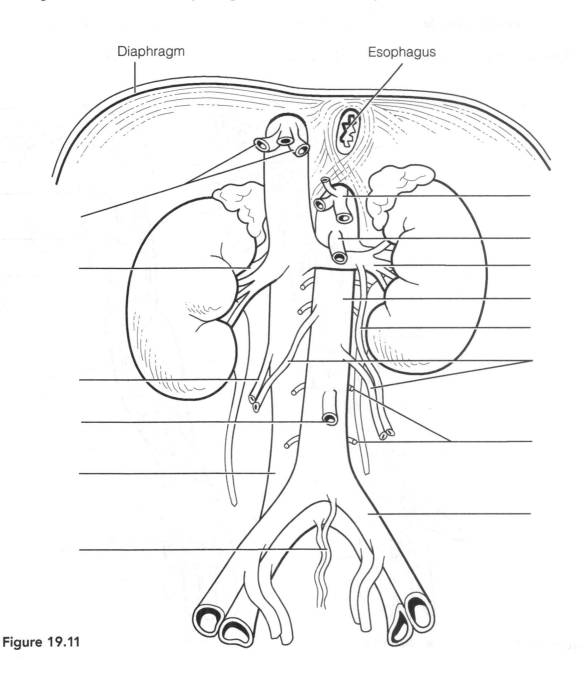

Figure 19.11

9. On Figure 19.12, identify the thoracic veins by choosing a letter from the key choices.

Key Choices

A. Accessory hemiazygos   E. External jugular   I. Left subclavian

B. Axillary   F. Inferior vena cava   J. Posterior intercostals

C. Azygos   G. Hemiazygos   K. Right subclavian

D. Brachiocephalic   H. Internal jugular   L. Superior vena cava

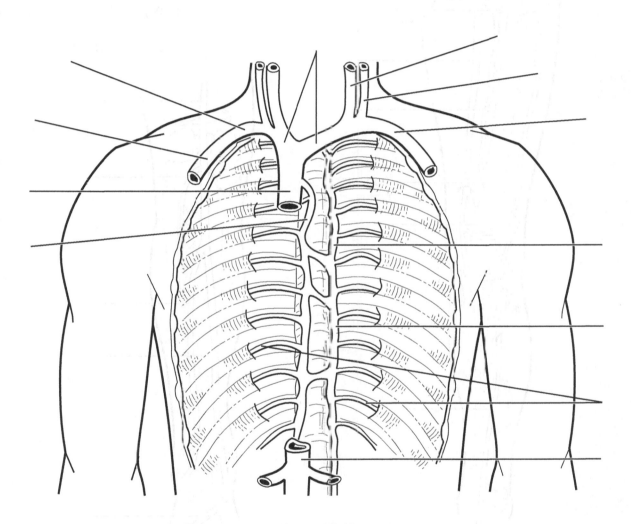

Figure 19.12

10. Figure 19.13, on the next page, illustrates the arterial supply of the right lower limb. Correctly identify all arteries that have leader lines by using   letters from the key choices. *Notice that the key choices continue onto the opposite page.*

Key Choices

A. Abdominal aorta   C. Common iliac   E. Digital   G. External iliac

B. Anterior tibial   D. Deep femoral   F. Dorsalis pedis   H. Femoral

I.   Internal iliac

J.   Lateral femoral circumflex

K.   Lateral plantar artery

L.   Medial plantar artery

M. Fibular

N. Plantar arch

O. Popliteal

P.   Posterior tibial

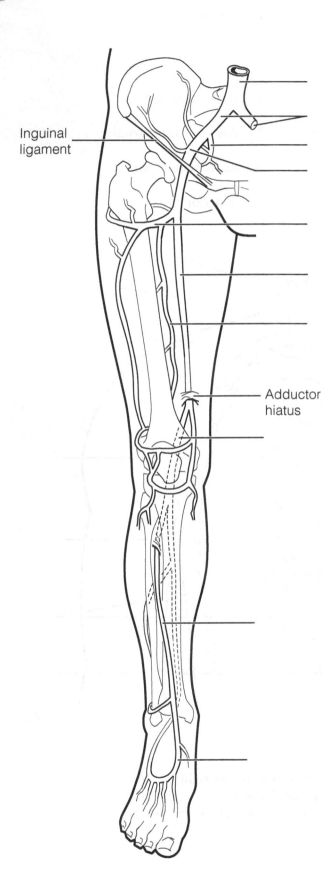

Inguinal ligament

Adductor hiatus

A. Arteries of the pelvis, thigh, and leg (anterior view)

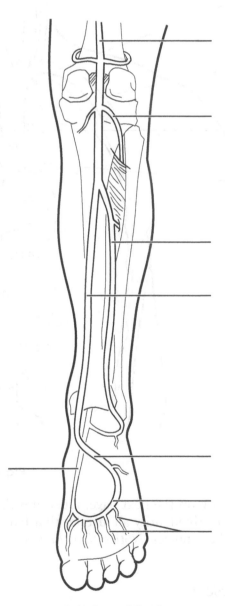

B. Arteries of the leg (posterior view)

Figure 19.13

11. Figure 19.14 is a diagram of the hepatic portal circulation. Select different colors for the structures listed below and color the structures on the illustration.

◯ Inferior mesenteric vein   ◯ Superior mesenteric vein

◯ Splenic vein   ◯ Gastric vein

◯ Hepatic portal vein

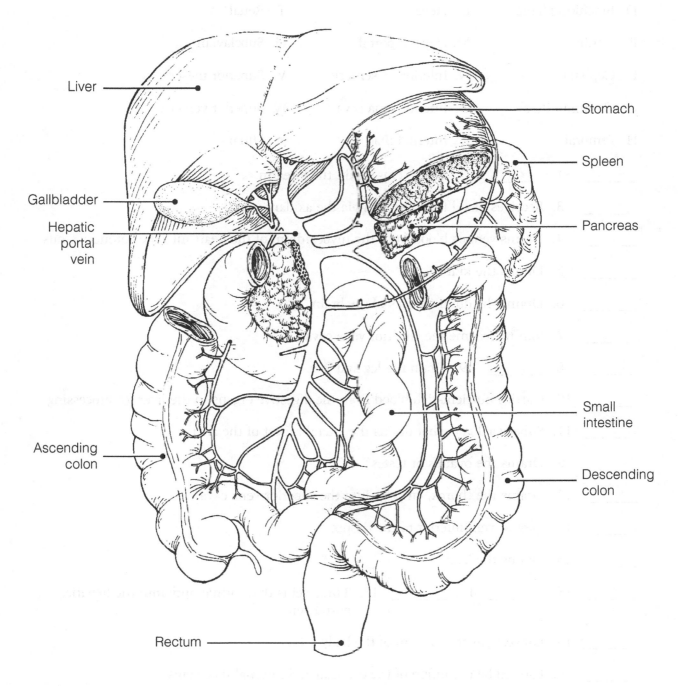

Liver

Gallbladder

Hepatic portal vein

Ascending colon

Rectum

Stomach

Spleen

Pancreas

Small intestine

Descending colon

Figure 19.14

12. Using the key choices, identify the veins in the following descriptions.

Key Choices

A. Anterior tibial	I. Gastric	Q. Internal jugular
B. Azygos	J. Gonadal	R. Posterior tibial
C. Basilic	K. Great saphenous	S. Radial
D. Brachiocephalic	L. Hepatic	T. Renal
E. Cardiac	M. Hepatic portal	U. Subclavian
F. Cephalic	N. Inferior mesenteric	V. Superior mesenteric
G. Common iliac	O. Inferior vena cava	W. Superior vena cava
H. Femoral	P. Internal iliac	X. Ulnar

_____ 1. _____ 2. Deep veins; drain the forearm

_____ 3. Receives blood from the arm via the axillary vein

_____ 4. Drains venous blood from the myocardium of the heart into the coronary sinus

_____ 5. Drains the kidney

_____ 6. Drains the dural sinuses of the brain

_____ 7. Join to become the superior vena cava (2)

_____ 8. _____ 9. Drain the leg and foot

_____ 10. Carries nutrient-rich blood from the digestive organs to the liver for processing

_____ 11. Superficial vein that drains the lateral aspect of the arm

_____ 12. Drains the ovaries or testes

_____ 13. Drains the thorax, empties into the superior vena cava

_____ 14. Largest vein inferior to the thorax

_____ 15. Drains the liver

_____ 16. _____ 17. _____ 18. Three veins that form/empty into the hepatic portal vein

_____ 19. Longest superficial vein of the body

_____ 20. Formed by the union of the external and internal iliac veins

_____ 21. Deep vein of the thigh

THE INCREDIBLE JOURNEY

A Visualization Exercise for the Cardiovascular System

All about you are huge white cords, hanging limply from two flaps of endothelial tissue . . .

1. Complete the following narrative by writing the missing terms in the answer blanks.

1. _____

2. _____

3. _____

4. _____

5. _____

6. _____

7. _____

8. _____

9. _____

10. _____

11. _____

12. _____

13. _____

Your journey starts in the pulmonary vein and includes a trip to part of the systemic circulation and a special circulation. You ready your equipment and prepare to be injected into your host.

Almost immediately after injection, you find yourself swept into a good-sized chamber, the __(1)__ . However, you do not stop in this chamber but continue to plunge downward into a larger chamber below. You land with a large splash and examine your surroundings. All about you are huge white cords, hanging limply from two flaps of endothelial tissue far above you. You report that you are sitting in the __(2)__ chamber of the heart, seeing the flaps of the __(3)__ valve above you. The valve is open, and its anchoring cords, the __(4)__ , are lax. Since this valve is open, you conclude that the heart is in the __(5)__ phase of the cardiac cycle.

Suddenly you notice that the chamber walls seem to be closing in. You hear a thundering boom, and the whole chamber vibrates as the valve slams shut above you. The cords, now rigid and strained, form a cage about you, and you feel extreme external pressure. Obviously, the heart is in a full-fledged __(6)__ . Then, high above on the right, the "roof" opens, and you are forced through this __(7)__ valve. A fraction of a second later, you hear another tremendous boom that sends shock waves through the whole area. Out of the corner of your eye, you see that the valve below you is closed, and it looks rather like a pie cut into three wedges.

As you are swept along in a huge artery, the __(8)__ , you pass several branch-off points, but continue to careen along straight down at a dizzying speed until you approach the __(9)__ artery feeding the small intestine. After entering this artery and passing through successively smaller and smaller subdivisions of it, you finally reach the capillary bed of the small intestine. You watch with fascination as nutrient molecules move into the blood through the single layer of __(10)__ cells forming the capillary wall. As you move to the opposite shore of the capillary bed, you enter a venule and begin to move superiorly once again. The venules draining the small intestine combine to form the __(11)__ vein, which in turn combines with the __(12)__ vein to form the hepatic portal vein that carries you into the liver. As you enter the liver, you are amazed at the activity there. Six-sided hepatic cells, responsible for storing glucose and making blood proteins, are literally grabbing __(13)__ out of the blood as it percolates slowly past them.

_____ 14.

_____ 15.

_____ 16.

_____ 17.

_____ 18.

_____ 19.

_____ 20.

_____ 21.

_____ 22.

Protective __(14)__ cells are removing bacteria from the slowly moving blood. Leaving the liver through the __(15)__ vein, you almost immediately enter the huge __(16)__, which returns blood from the lower part of the body to the __(17)__ of the heart. From here, you move consecutively through the right chambers of the heart into the __(18)__ artery, which carries you to the __(19)__.

You report that your surroundings are now relatively peaceful. You catch hold of a red blood cell and scramble aboard. As you sit cross-legged on its concave surface, you muse that it is just like riding in a big, soft rubber boat. Riding smoothly along, you enter vessels that become narrower and narrower. Your red blood cell slows down as it squeezes through the windings of tiny blood vessels. You conclude that you are located in the pulmonary __(20)__. You report hearing great whooshes of sound as your host breathes, and you can actually see large air-filled spaces! But your little red cell "boat" seems strangely agitated. Its contours change so often that you are almost thrown out.

You report that these contortions must be the result of the exchange of __(21)__ molecules because your "boat" is assuming a brilliant red color. This experience has left you breathless, so you poke your head between two thin endothelial cells for some fresh air. You then continue your journey, through increasingly wider vessels. After traveling through the left side of the heart again, you leave your host when you are aspirated out of the __(22)__ artery, which extends from the aorta to the axillary artery of the armpit.

CHALLENGING YOURSELF

At the Clinic

1. Mrs. Gray, age 50, is complaining of dull aching pains in her legs, which she claims have been getting progressively worse since the birth of her last child. (She is the mother of seven children.) During her physical examination, numerous varicosities are seen in both legs. How are varicosities recognized? What veins are most likely involved? What pathologic changes have occurred in these veins and what is the most likely causative factor in this patient's case? What instructions might be helpful to Mrs. Gray?

2. A routine scan on an elderly man reveals partial occlusion of the internal carotid artery, yet blood supply to his cerebrum is unimpaired. What are two possible causes of the occlusion? What compensatory mechanism is maintaining blood supply to the brain?

3. A patient with a bone marrow cancer is polycythemic. Will his blood pressure be high or low? Why?

4. Mrs. Baevich, an elderly, bedridden woman, has several "angry-looking" decubitus ulcers. During the past week, one of these has begun to hemorrhage very slowly. What will occur eventually if this situation is not properly attended to?

5. A blow to the base of the skull has sent an accident victim to the emergency room. Although there are no signs of hemorrhage, his blood pressure is critically low. What is a probable cause of his hypotension?

6. Mr. Grimaldi was previously diagnosed as having a posterior pituitary tumor that causes hypersecretion of ADH. He comes to the clinic regularly to have his blood pressure checked. Would you expect his BP to be chronically elevated or depressed? Why?

7. Renal (kidney) disease in a young man has resulted in blockage of the smaller arteries within the kidneys. Explain why this will lead to secondary hypertension.

8. A worried mother has brought Terry, her 11-year-old son, to the clinic after he complained of feeling dizzy and nauseous. No abnormalities are found during the examination. Upon questioning, however, Terry sheepishly admits that he was smoking with a friend, who had dared him to "take deep drags." Explain how this might have caused his dizziness.

9. Mrs. Shultz has died suddenly after what seemed to be a low-grade infection. A blood culture reveals that the infection had spread to the blood. What is this condition called and why was it fatal?

10. Progressive heart failure has resulted in insufficient circulation to sustain life. What type of circulatory shock does this exemplify?

11. Mr. Connors has just had a right femoral arterial graft and is resting quietly. Orders are given to palpate his popliteal and pedal (dorsalis pedis) pulses and to assess the color and temperature of his right leg four times daily. Why were these orders given?

12. Examination of Mr. Cummings, a man in his 60s, reveals a blood pressure of 140/120. What is his pulse pressure? Is it normal, high, or low? What does this indicate about the state of his elastic arteries?

13. A man in his 40s was diagnosed as hypertensive. Dietary changes and exercise have helped, but his blood pressure is still too high. Explain to him why his doctor recommended beta blocker and diuretic drugs to treat his condition.

14. Sidney received a small but deep cut from broken glass in the exact midline of the anterior side of his distal forearm. He worried that he would bleed to death because he had heard stories about people committing suicide by slashing their wrist. Judge if Sid's fear of death is justified and explain your reasoning.

Stop and Think

1. Why is the cardiovascular lining a simple squamous epithelium rather than a thicker layer?

2. Does vasoconstriction increase or decrease the supply of blood to the tissues beyond the vasoconstricted area? Explain your answer.

3. When an entire capillary bed is closed off due to arteriolar vasoconstriction, are the precapillary sphincters open or closed? What is the pattern of blood flow into the capillaries when the arteriole dilates? From this, explain why the face flushes when coming inside on a cold day.

4. Standing up quickly after being in a horizontal position can cause dizziness. Why is this more likely in a warm room than in a cool room?

5. Why shouldn't a pregnant woman sleep on her back late in pregnancy?

6. The dura mater reinforces the walls of the intracranial sinuses. What reinforces the wall of the coronary sinus?

7. Why is necrosis more common in areas supplied by end arteries?

8. What would trigger a change in blood vessel length in the body?

9. Assume there is a clot blocking the right internal carotid artery. Briefly describe another route that might be used to provide blood to the areas served by its branches.

10. Kwashiorkor results from a dietary deficiency in protein. Explain why this causes edema.

11. Describe the positive feedback mechanism between heart and vasomotor center that would be involved in untreated or irreversible circulatory shock.

12. Your friend, who knows very little about science, is reading a magazine article about a patient who had an "aneurysm at the base of his brain that suddenly grew much larger." The surgeons' first goal was to "keep it from rupturing" and the second goal was to "relieve the pressure on the brain stem and cranial nerves." The surgeons were able to "replace the aneurysm with a section of plastic tubing," so the patient recovered. Your friend asks you what all this means, and why the condition is life-threatening. What would you tell him?

13. Mr. Brown was distracted while trying to fell a large tree. His power saw whipped around and severed his right arm at the shoulder. Without a limb stump, applying a tourniquet is impossible. Where would you apply pressure to save Mr. Brown from fatal hemorrhage?

14. Freddy was looking for capillaries in his microscope slides of body organs. Although Freddy disagreed, Karl, his lab partner, kept insisting that a venule was a capillary. Finally, the teaching assistant said, "Look, here you see five erythrocytes lined up across the width of the lumen of this vessel so it cannot be a capillary." Explain the logic behind this statement and tell exactly how wide the vessel was (in micrometers).

Multiple Choice

Select the best answer or answers from the choices given.

1. Which of the following is/are part of the tunica interna?

    A. Simple squamous epithelium

    B. Basement membrane

    C. Loose connective tissue

    D. Smooth muscle

2. The tunica externa contains:

    A. nerves   C. lymphatics

    B. blood vessels   D. collagen

3. In comparing a parallel artery and vein, you would find that:

    A. the artery wall is thicker

    B. the artery diameter is greater

    C. the artery lumen is smaller

    D. the artery endothelium is thicker

4. Which vessels are conducting arteries?

    A. Brachiocephalic artery

    B. Common iliac artery

    C. Digital artery

    D. Arcuate artery (foot)

5. A pulse would be palpable in the:

    A. anterior cerebral artery

    B. hepatic portal vein

    C. muscular arteries

    D. inferior vena cava

6. Pulse pressure is increased by:

    A. an increase in diastolic pressure

    B. an increase in systolic pressure

    C. an equivalent increase in both systolic and diastolic pressures

    D. vasoconstriction

7. Vessels that do not have all three tunics include the:

    A. smallest arterioles   C. capillaries

    B. smallest venules   D. venous sinuses

8. Structures that are totally avascular are the:

    A. skin

    B. cornea

    C. articular surfaces of long bones

    D. joint capsules

9. Fenestrated capillaries occur in the:

    A. liver   C. cerebrum

    B. kidney   D. intestinal mucosa

10. Kupffer cells are:

    A. true capillary endothelium

    B. found throughout the body

    C. macrophages in the liver

    D. macrophages in the spleen

11. Which of the following is/are part of a capillary bed?

    A. Precapillary sphincter

    B. Metarteriole

    C. Thoroughfare channel

    D. Terminal arteriole

12. Which vessels actively supply blood to associated capillary networks when the body is primarily controlled by the parasympathetic division?

    A. Femoral artery

    B. Superior mesenteric artery

    C. Cerebral arteries

    D. Coronary arteries

13. Which of the following can function as a blood reservoir?

    A. Brachiocephalic artery

    B. Cerebral capillaries

    C. Dural sinuses

    D. Inferior vena cava

14. Collateral circulation occurs in the:

    A. joint capsules   C. kidney

    B. cerebrum   D. myocardium

15. Venous return to the right atrium is increased by:

    A. increasing depth of respiration

    B. vigorous walking

    C. an increase in ventricular contraction strength

    D. activation of angiotensin II

16. The single most important factor in blood pressure regulation is:

    A. feedback by baroreceptors

    B. renal compensatory mechanisms

    C. regulation of cardiac output

    D. short-term changes in blood vessel diameter

17. Blood volume is altered by:

    A. vasodilation

    B. edema

    C. increased salt intake

    D. polycythemia

18. Vasomotor fibers that secrete acetylcholine are (probably) found in:

    A. cerebral arteries   C. skin

    B. skeletal muscle   D. digestive organs

19. The vasomotor center is inhibited by:

    A. impulses from the carotid sinus baroreceptors

    B. impulses from the aortic sinus baro- receptors

    C. stimulation by carotid body chemo- receptors

    D. alcohol

20. Chemical factors that increase blood pressure include:

    A. endothelin   C. ADH

    B. NO   D. ANP

21. Which of the regulatory chemicals listed involve or target the kidneys?

    A. Angiotensin

    B. ADH

    C. Aldosterone

    D. ANP

22. Mechanisms to decrease systemic arterial blood pressure are invoked by:

    A. standing up

    B. public speaking

    C. losing weight

    D. moving to higher altitude

23. Which of the following interfere with contraction of the smooth muscle of precapil- lary sphincters?

    A. Adenosine

    B. Oxygen

    C. Lactic acid

    D. Potassium ions

24. Increase in blood flow to a capillary bed after its supply has been blocked is called:

    A. a myogenic response

    B. reactive hyperemia

    C. active hyperemia

    D. a cardiogenic response

25. An increase in which of the following results in increased filtration from capillaries to the interstitial space?

    A. Capillary hydrostatic pressure

    B. Interstitial fluid hydrostatic pressure

    C. Capillary osmotic pressure

    D. Duration of precapillary sphincter contraction

26. Vessels involved in the circulatory pathway to and from the brain are the:

    A. brachiocephalic artery

    B. subclavian artery

    C. internal jugular vein

    D. internal carotid artery

27. The fight-or-flight response results in the constriction of:

    A. renal arteries

    B. celiac trunk

    C. internal iliac arteries

    D. external iliac arteries

28. Prominent venous anastomoses are formed by the:

    A. azygos vein

    B. median cubital vein

    C. circle of Willis

    D. hepatic portal vein

29. An abnormal thickening of the capillary basement membrane associated with diabetes mellitus is called:

    A. phlebitis

    B. aneurysm

    C. microangiopathic lesion

    D. atheroma

30. Which of the following are associated with aging?

    A. Increasing blood pressure

    B. Weakening of venous valves

    C. Arteriosclerosis

    D. Stenosis of the ductus arteriosus

31. Based on the vessels named pulmonary trunk, thyrocervical trunk, and celiac trunk, the term *trunk* must refer to:

    A. a vessel in the heart wall

    B. a vein

    C. a capillary

    D. a large artery from which other arteries branch

32. Which of these vessels is bilaterally symmetrical (i.e., one vessel of the pair occurs on each side of the body)?

    A. Internal carotid artery

    B. Brachiocephalic artery

    C. Azygos vein

    D. Superior mesenteric vein

33. The deep femoral and deep brachial veins drain the:

    A. biceps brachii and hamstring muscles

    B. flexor muscles in the hand and leg

    C. quadriceps femoris and triceps brachii muscles

    D. intercostal muscles of the thorax

34. A stroke that occludes a posterior cerebral artery will most likely affect:

    A. hearing

    B. vision

    C. smell

    D. higher thought processes

35. Tracing the drainage of the *superficial* venous blood from the leg, we find that blood enters the greater saphenous vein, femoral vein, inferior vena cava, and right atrium. Which veins are missing from that sequence?

    A. Coronary sinus and superior vena cava

    B. Posterior tibial and popliteal

    C. Fibular (peroneal) and popliteal

    D. External and common iliacs

36. Tracing the drainage of venous blood from the small intestine, we find that blood enters the superior mesenteric vein, hepatic vein, inferior vena cava, and right atrium. Which vessels are missing from that sequence?

    A. Coronary sinus and left atrium

    B. Celiac and common hepatic veins

    C. Internal and common iliac veins

    D. Hepatic portal vein and liver sinusoids

Word Dissection

For each of the following word roots, fill in the literal meaning and give an example, using a word found in this chapter.

Word root	Translation	Example
1. anastomos	_____	_____
2. angio	_____	_____
3. aort	_____	_____
4. athera	_____	_____
5. auscult	_____	_____
6. azyg	_____	_____
7. capill	_____	_____
8. carot	_____	_____
9. celia	_____	_____
10. entero	_____	_____
11. epiplo	_____	_____
12. fenestr	_____	_____
13. jugul	_____	_____
14. ortho	_____	_____
15. phleb	_____	_____
16. saphen	_____	_____
17. septi	_____	_____
18. tunic	_____	_____
19. vaso	_____	_____
20. viscos	_____	_____

20

THE LYMPHATIC SYSTEM AND IMMUNITY

Overview

The lymphatic system includes lymphoid organs and tissues, a network of lymphatic vessels that contain a fluid called lymph, and a dominant population of individual cells, the lymphocytes. The cells, tissues, organs, and vessels containing lymph perform three major functions:

1. The lymphoid organs and tissues serve as operating sites for the phagocytes and cells of the immune system that provide the body with protection from pathogens.

2. The lymphatic vessels containing lymph help to maintain blood volume in the cardiovascular system and absorb fats and other substances from the digestive tract.

3. The lymphocytes are the "defensive specialists" that protect the body from pathogenic microorganisms, foreign tissue cells, and diseased or infected cells in the body that pose a threat to the normal cell population.

Chapter 20 provides exercises focusing on topics that include the organization of the lymphatic system, the body's defense mechanisms, patterns of immune response, and interactions between the lymphatic system and other physiological systems.

LEVEL 1   Review of Chapter Objectives

1. Explain the difference between nonspecific and specific defense and the role of lymphocytes in the immune response.

2. Identify the major components of the lymphatic system and explain their functions.

3. Discuss the importance of lymphocytes and describe their distribution in the body.

4. Describe the structure of the lymphoid tissues and organs and explain their functions.

5. List the body's nonspecific defenses and explain the function of each.

6. Describe the components and mechanisms of each nonspecific defense.

7. Define specific resistance and identify the forms and properties of immunity.

8. Distinguish between cell-mediated (cellular) immunity and antibody-mediated (humoral) immunity and identify the cells responsible for each.

9. Discuss the different types of T cells and the role played by each in the immune response.

10. Describe the mechanisms of T cell activation and the differentiation of the major classes of T cells.

11. Describe the mechanisms of B cell activation and the differentiation of plasma cells and memory B cells.

12. Describe the general structure of an antibody and discuss the types of antibodies in body fluids and secretions.

13. Explain the functions of antibodies and how they perform those functions.

14. Discuss the primary and secondary responses to antigen exposure.

15. Describe the origin, development, activation, and regulation of normal resistance.

16. Explain the origin of autoimmune disorders, immunodeficiency diseases, and allergies, and list important examples of each type of disorder.

17. Discuss the effects of stress on the immune function.

18. Discuss important hormones of the immune response and explain their significance.

19. Describe the effects of aging on the lymphatic system and the immune response.

[L1]   Multiple Choice

Place the letter corresponding to the correct answer in the space provided.

OBJ. 1 _____ 1. The primary responsibility(-ies) of the lymphocytes in the lymphatic system is (are) to respond to the presence of:

    a. invading pathogens

    b. abnormal body cells

    c. foreign particles

    d. a, b, and c are correct

OBJ. 1 _____ 2. The anatomical barriers and defense mechanisms that cannot distinguish one potential threat from another are called:

    a. the immune response

    b. specific defenses

    c. nonspecific defenses

    d. abnormal nontoxicity

OBJ. 2 _____ 3. The *major components* of the lymphatic system include:

    a. lymph nodes, lymph, lymphocytes

    b. spleen, thymus, tonsils

    c. thoracic duct, R. lymphatic duct, lymph nodes

    d. lymphatic vessels, lymph, lymphatic organs

OBJ. 2 _____ 4. Lymphatic *organs* found in the lymphatic system include:

    a. thoracic duct, R. lymphatic duct, lymph nodes

    b. lymphatic vessels, tonsils, lymph nodes

    c. spleen, thymus, lymph nodes

    d. a, b, and c are correct

OBJ. 2 _____ 5. The *primary* function of the lymphatic system is:

    a. transporting of nutrients and oxygen to tissues

    b. removal of carbon dioxide and waste products from tissues

    c. regulation of temperature, fluid, electrolytes, and pH balance

    d. production, maintenance, and distribution of lymphocytes

OBJ. 3 _____ 6. Lymphocytes that assist in the regulation and coordination of the immune response are:

    a. plasma cells

    b. helper T and suppressor T cells

    c. B cells

    d. NK and B cells

OBJ. 3 _____ 7. Normal lymphocyte populations are maintained through lymphopoiesis in the:

    a. bone marrow and lymphatic tissues

    b. lymph in the lymphatic tissues

    c. blood and the lymph

    d. spleen and liver

OBJ. 4 ____ 8. The largest collection of lymphoid tissue in the body is contained within the:

    a. adult spleen

    b. thymus gland

    c. tonsils

    d. lymphatic nodules

OBJ. 4 ____ 9. The reticular epithelial cells in the cortex of the thymus maintain the blood–thymus barrier and secrete the hormones that:

    a. form distinctive structures known as Hassall's Corpuscles

    b. cause the T cells to leave circulation via blood vessels

    c. stimulate stem cell divisions and T cell differentation

    d. cause the T cells to enter the circulation via blood vessels

OBJ. 5 ____ 10. Of the following selections, the one that includes only nonspecific defenses is:

    a. T- and B-cell activation, complement, inflammation, phagocytosis

    b. hair, skin, mucous membranes, antibodies

    c. hair, skin, complement, inflammation, phagocytosis

    d. antigens, antibodies, complement, macrophages

OBJ. 5 ____ 11. The protective categories that prevent the approach of, deny entrance to, or limit the spread of microorganisms or other environmental hazards are called:

    a. specific defenses

    b. nonspecific defenses

    c. specific immunity

    d. immunological surveillance

OBJ. 5 ____ 12. NK (natural killer) cells sensitive to the presence of abnormal cell membranes are primarily involved with:

    a. defenses against specific threats

    b. complex and time-consuming defense mechanisms

    c. phagocytic activity for defense

    d. immunological surveillance

OBJ. 6 ____ 13. A physical barrier such as the epithelial covering of the skin provides effective immunity due to its makeup, which includes:

    a. multiple layers

    b. a keratin coating

    c. a network of desmosomes that lock adjacent cells together

    d. a, b, and c are correct

OBJ. 6 ____ 14. The "first line" of cellular defense against pathogenic invasion is:

    a. interferon

    b. pathogens

    c. phagocytes

    d. complement system

OBJ. 6 _____ 15. NK cells contain the proteins perforin and protectin that provide a type of immunity called:

    a. immunological surveillance

    b. the inflammatory response

    c. the complement system

    d. phagocytosis

OBJ. 7 _____ 16. The four general characteristics of specific defenses include:

    a. specificity, versatility, memory, and tolerance

    b. innate, active, acquired, and passive

    c. accessibility, recognition, compatibility, and immunity

    d. a, b, and c are correct

OBJ. 7 _____ 17. The two major ways that the body "carries out" the immune response are:

    a. phagocytosis and the inflammatory response

    b. immunological surveillance and fever

    c. direct attack by T cells and attack by circulating antibodies

    d. physical barriers and the complement system

OBJ. 7 _____ 18. A *specific* defense mechanism is always activated by:

    a. an antigen

    b. an antibody

    c. inflammation

    d. fever

OBJ. 8 _____ 19. The type of immunity that develops as a result of natural exposure to an antigen in the environment is:

    a. naturally acquired immunity

    b. naturally innate immunity

    c. naturally acquired active immunity

    d. naturally acquired passive immunity

OBJ. 8 _____ 20. The fact that people are not subject to the same diseases as goldfish describes the presence of:

    a. active immunity

    b. passive immunity

    c. acquired immunity

    d. innate immunity

OBJ. 8 _____ 21. When an antigen appears, the immune response begins with:

    a. the presence of immunoglobulins in body fluids

    b. the release of endogenous pyrogens

    c. the activation of the complement system

    d. the activation of specific T cells and B cells

OBJ. 8 _____ 22. When the immune "recognition" system malfunctions, activated B cells begin to:

    a. manufacture antibodies against other cells and tissues

    b. activate cytotoxic T killer cells

    c. secrete lymphotoxins to destroy foreign antigens

    d. recall memory T cells to initiate the proper response

OBJ. 9   _____   23. T-cell activation leads to the formation of cytotoxic T cells and memory T cells that provide:

   a. humoral immunity

   b. cellular immunity

   c. phagocytosis and immunological surveillance

   d. stimulation of inflammation and fever

OBJ. 9   _____   24. Before an antigen can stimulate a lymphocyte, it must first be processed by a:

   a. macrophage

   b. NK cell

   c. cytotoxic T cell

   d. neutrophil

OBJ. 10   _____   25. Two different classes of CD8 T cells are activated by exposure to antigens bound to:

   a. antigen-presenting cells (APCs)

   b. Class I MHC proteins

   c. CD_4 receptor complex

   d. Class II MHC antigens

OBJ. 10   _____   26. The T cells that limit the degree of immune system activation from a single stimulus are:

   a. memory T_C cells

   b. suppressor T cells

   c. cytotoxic T cells

   d. CD_4 T cells

OBJ. 10   _____   27. Since each kind of B cell carries its own particular antibody molecule in its cell membrane, activation can only occur in the presence of a(n):

   a. immunosuppressive drug

   b. cytotoxic T cell

   c. corresponding antigen

   d. CD_3 receptor complex

OBJ. 11   _____   28. Activated B cells produce plasma cells that are specialized because they:

   a. synthesize and secrete antibodies

   b. produce helper T cells

   c. direct a physical and chemical attack

   d. a, b, and c are correct

OBJ. 12   _____   29. An active antibody is shaped like a(n):

   a. T

   b. A

   c. Y

   d. B

OBJ. 12   _____   30. The most important antibody action in the body is:

   a. alteration in the cell membrane to increase phagocytosis

   b. to attract macrophages and neutrophils to the infected areas

   c. activation of the complement systems

   d. cell lysis and the cell membrane digestion

OBJ. 13 _____ 31. Antibodies may promote inflammation through the stimulation of:
a. basophils and mast cells
b. plasma cells and memory B cells
c. suppressor T cells
d. cytotoxic T cells

OBJ. 14 _____ 32. The antigenic determinant site is the certain portion of the antigen's exposed surface where:
a. the foreign "body" attacks
b. phagocytosis occurs
c. the antibody attacks
d. the immune surveillance system is activated

OBJ. 14 _____ 33. In order for an antigenic molecule to be a complete antigen, it must:
a. be a large molecule
b. be immunogenic and reactive
c. contain a hapten and a small organic molecule
d. be subject to antibody activity

OBJ. 15 _____ 34. The ability to demonstrate an immune response upon exposure to an antigen is called:
a. anaphylaxis
b. passive immunity
c. immunosuppression
d. immunological competence

OBJ. 15 _____ 35. Fetal antibody production is uncommon because the developing fetus has:
a. cell-mediated immunity
b. natural passive immunity
c. antibody-mediated immunity
d. endogenous pyrogens

OBJ. 16 _____ 36. When an immune response mistakenly targets normal body cells and tissues, the result is:
a. immune system failure
b. the development of an allergy
c. depression of the inflammatory response
d. an autoimmune disorder

OBJ. 16 _____ 37. Cells of the immune system influence CNS and endocrine activity by:
a. secreting endorphins and thymic hormones
b. increasing circulating thyroid hormone levels during immune responses
c. stimulating cell and tissue metabolism
d. a, b, and c are correct

OBJ. 17 _____ 38. Depression of the immune system due to chronic stress may cause:
a. depression of the inflammatory response
b. a reduction in the activities and numbers of phagocytes in peripheral tissues
c. the inhibition of interleukin secretion
d. a, b, and c are correct

OBJ. 18 _____ 39. The effect(s) of tumor necrosis factor (TNF) in the body is (are) to:

    a. slow tumor growth and to kill sensitive tumor cells

    b. stimulate granulocyte production

    c. increase T-cell sensitivity to interleukins

    d. a, b, and c are correct

OBJ. 18 _____ 40. The major functions of interleukins in the immune system are to:

    a. increase T-cell sensitivity to antigens exposed on macrophage membranes

    b. stimulate B-cell activity, plasma-cell formation, and antibody production

    c. enhance nonspecific defenses

    d. a, b, and c are correct

OBJ. 19 _____ 41. With advancing age, B cells are less responsive, causing a:

    a. decrease in antigen exposure

    b. decreased antibody level after antigen exposure

    c. deactivation of T-cell production

    d. a, b, and c are correct

OBJ. 19 _____ 42. The tonsils are more susceptible to infection due to a:

    a. reduction in interleukin production

    b. depression of the inflammatory response

    c. decrease in the number of cytotoxic T cells

    d. phagocytic inactivity phase

[L1] Completion

Using the terms below, complete the following statements.

lymphokines	innate	immunological competence
helper T	haptens	plasma cells
diapedesis	active	lymph capillaries
lacteals	passive	cell-mediated
precipitation	monokines	immunodeficiency disease
lymphatic	neutralization	cytotoxic T cells
suppressor T	phagocytes	IgG
antibodies	immunity	lymphocytes
antigens	interferons	sensitization
costimulation	memory B cells	memory T cells
inflammation	thymic hormones	

OBJ. 1   1. The ability to resist infection and disease through the activation of specific defenses constitutes _____

OBJ. 1   2. The cells that provide a specific defense known as the immune response are the _____.

OBJ. 2   3. The special lymphatic vessels in the lining of the small intestines are the _____.

OBJ. 3   4. Lymphocytes that attack foreign cells or body cells infected by viruses are called _____ cells.

OBJ. 3   5. Plasma cells are responsible for the production and secretion of _____.

OBJ. 4   6. The lymphatic system begins in the tissues as _____.

OBJ. 5   7. Cells that represent the "first line" of cellular defense against pathogenic invasion are the _____.

OBJ. 5   8. The process during which macrophages move through adjacent endothelial cells of capillary walls is called _____.

OBJ. 6   9. The small proteins released by activated lymphocytes and macrophages and by tissue cells infected with viruses are called _____.

OBJ. 6   10. An immunization where antibodies are administered to fight infection or prevent disease is _____.

OBJ. 6   11. Cytotoxic T cells are responsible for the type of immunity referred to as _____.

OBJ. 7   12. Immunity that is present at birth and has no relation to previous exposure to the pathogen involved is _____.

OBJ. 8   13. Immunity that appears following exposure to an antigen as a consequence of the immune response is referred to as _____.

OBJ. 9   14. The types of cells that inhibit the responses of other T cells and B cells are called _____ cells.

OBJ. 9   15. Before B cells can respond to an antigen, they must receive a signal from _____ cells.

OBJ. 10   16. The vital secondary binding process that eventually confirms the "OK to activate" signal is called _____.

OBJ. 10   17. When an inactive cytotoxic T cell is activated and divides, it produces active T cells and _____.

OBJ. 11   18. When binding occurs and the B cell prepares to undergo activation, the process is called _____.

OBJ. 11   19. When an activated B cell divides, it ultimately produces daughter cells that differentiate into plasma cells and _____.

OBJ. 12   20. Antibodies are produced and secreted by _____.

OBJ. 13   21. When a direct attack by an antibody covers an antigen, its effect is _____.

OBJ. 13   22. The formation of insoluble immune complexes is called _____.

OBJ. 14   23. Small organic molecules that are not antigens by themselves are called _____.

OBJ. 14   24. The ability to demonstrate an immune response upon exposure to an antigen is called _____.

OBJ. 15   25. The only antibodies that cross the placenta from the maternal bloodstream are _____ antibodies.

OBJ. 16   26. When the immune system fails to develop normally or the immune response is blocked in some way, the condition is termed _____.

OBJ. 16   27. The system responsible for providing the body with specific defenses against infection is the _____ system.

OBJ. 17   28. When glucocorticoids reduce the permeability of capillaries, they reduce the possibility of _____.

OBJ. 18   29. Chemical messengers secreted by lymphocytes are called _____.

OBJ. 18   30. Chemical messengers released by active macrophages are called _____.

OBJ. 19   31. As a person advances in age, his/her T cells become less responsive to _____.

OBJ. 19   32. A decrease in cytotoxic T cells may be associated with a reduction in circulating levels of _____.

[L1]   Matching

Match the terms in column B with the terms in column A. Use letters for answers in the spaces provided.

Part I		Column A	Column B
OBJ. 1	_____	1. specific defense	A. thymus medullary cells
OBJ. 2	_____	2. fever's patch	B type II allergy
OBJ. 3	_____	3. macrophages	C active and passive
OBJ. 3	_____	4. microphages	D chemical messengers
OBJ. 4	_____	5. Hassall's corpuscles	E innate or acquired
OBJ. 5	_____	6. mast cells	F nonspecific immune response
OBJ. 6	_____	7. interferons	
OBJ. 7	_____	8. acquired immunity	G immune response
OBJ. 7	_____	9. specific immunity	H monocytes
OBJ. 8	_____	10. B cells	I lymph nodules in small intestine
OBJ. 8	_____	11. passive immunity	
OBJ. 8	_____	12. antigen contact	J transfer of antibodies
			K neutrophils and eosinophils
			L humoral immunity

PART II	Column A	Column B
OBJ. 9	_____ 13. cytotoxic T cells	M. resistance to viral infections
OBJ. 9	_____ 14. T lymphocytes	N. activation of T cells
OBJ. 10	_____ 15. memory T_C cells	O. type II allergy
OBJ. 11	_____ 16. endocytosis	P. activation of B cells
OBJ. 12	_____ 17. antibody	Q. lyse cells directly
OBJ. 13	_____ 18. bacteriophage	R. exposure to an antigen
OBJ. 13	_____ 19. opsonization	S. cell-mediated immunity
OBJ. 14	_____ 20. active immunity	T. coating of antibodies
OBJ. 15	_____ 21. IgG antibodies	U. enhances nonspecific defenses
OBJ. 16	_____ 22. cytotoxic reactions	
OBJ. 16	_____ 23. immune complex disorder	V. decrease in immunity
		W. two parallel pairs of polypeptide chains
OBJ. 17	_____ 24. glucocorticoids	
OBJ. 18	_____ 25. interleukins	X. accompany fetal-maternal Rh incompatibility
OBJ. 18	_____ 26. interferons	
OBJ. 18	_____ 27. lymphokines	Y. immediate response
OBJ. 19	_____ 28. decreased thymic hormones	Z. involution of thymus
		AA. anti-inflammatory effect
OBJ. 19	_____ 29. advancing age	BB. antigen presentation
		CC. agglutination

[L1]   Drawing/Illustration Labeling

Identify each numbered structure by labeling the following figures:

OBJ. 2   **Figure 20.1   The Lymphatic System**

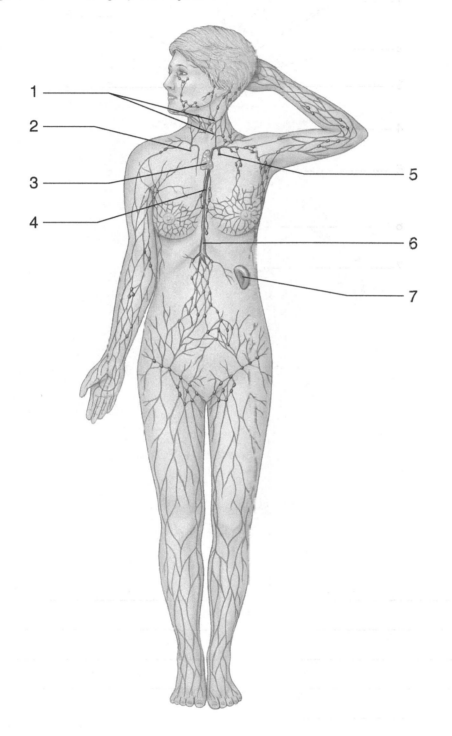

1 _____   5 _____

2 _____   6 _____

3 _____   7 _____

4 _____

OBJ. 2   **Figure 20.2   The Lymphatic Ducts**

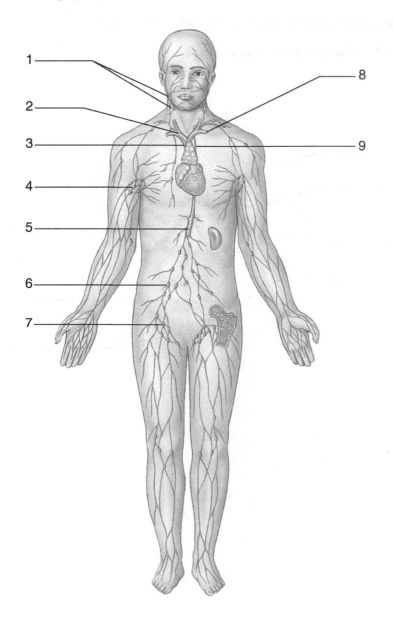

1 _____   6 _____

2 _____   7 _____

3 _____   8 _____

4 _____   9 _____

5 _____

OBJ. 5

Figure 20.3   Nonspecific Defenses

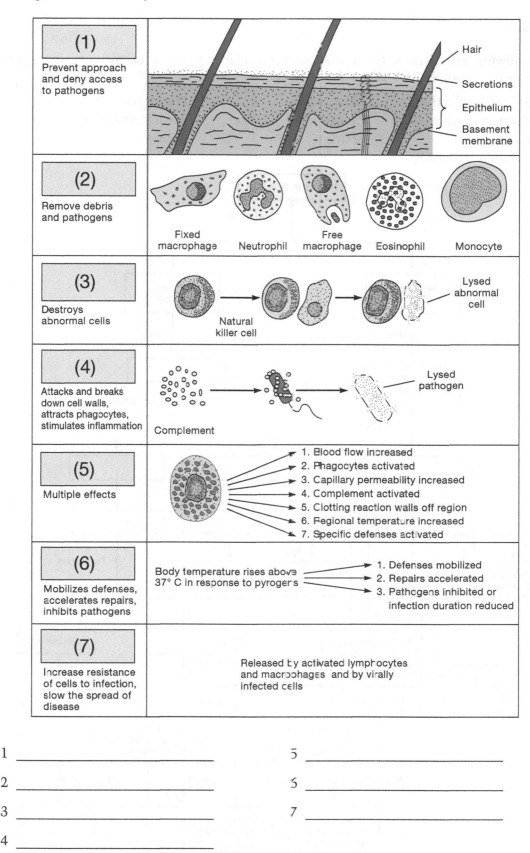

1 _____   5 _____

2 _____   6 _____

3 _____   7 _____

4 _____

LEVEL 2 Concept Synthesis

Concept Map I

Using the following terms, fill in the circled, numbered, blank spaces to complete the concept map. Follow the numbers to comply with the organization of the map.

Active immunization   Inflammation   Phagocytic cells
Transfer of antibodies   Passive immunization   Specific immunity
Acquired   Active   Innate
Nonspecific immunity

Concept Map II

Using the following terms, fill in the circled, numbered, blank spaces to complete the concept map. Follow the numbers to comply with the organization of the map.

Increasing vascular permeability	Tissue damaged	Phagocytosis of bacteria
	Tissue repaired	Bacteria not destroyed

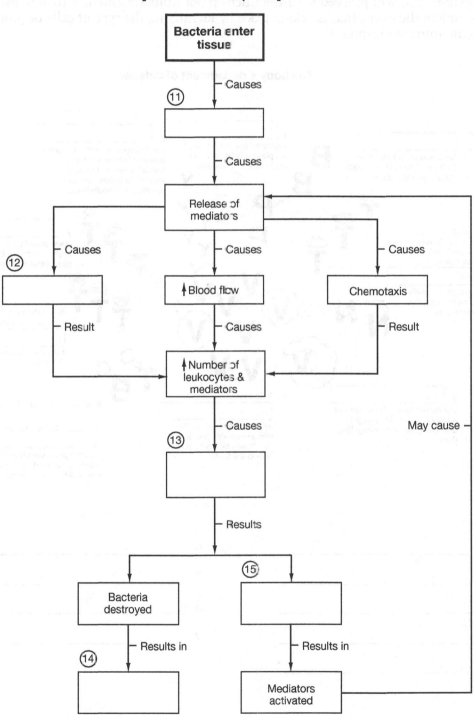

[Inflammation response]

Body Trek

Using the terms below, fill in the blanks to complete a trek through the body's department of defense.

killer T cells	viruses	B cells
antibodies	helper T cells	macrophages
natural killer cells	suppressor T cells	memory T and B cells

Robo has been programmed to guide you on a trek through the body's department of defense—the immune system. You will proceed with the micro-robot from statement 1 to statement 9. At each site you will complete the event that is taking place by identifying the type of cells or proteins participating in the specific immune response.

The body's department of defense

4 (the battle managers of the immune system) emit signals to B cells and killer T cells to join the attack.

5 (produced in bones) mature into plasma cells, which in turn produce antibodies.

6 are Y-shaped proteins designed specifically to recognize a particular viral or bacterial invader. Antibodies bind to the virus and neutralize it.

3 Stimulated by the release of interleukins from macrophages, helper T cells, and interferons, join the attack on virally infected cells. They also fight cancer cells.

7 wage chemical warfare on virally infected cells by firing lethal proteins at them.

8 As the body begins to conquer the viruses, help the immune system gear down. Otherwise, it might attack the body.

2 quickly recognize the viruses as a foreign threat. They begin destroying viruses by engulfing them.

1 The race is on; try to replicate before the immune system can gear up. Two have already taken over cells in the body.

9 As the viruses are being defeated, the body creates and that circulate permanently in the bloodstream, ensuring that next time, that particular virus will be swiftly conquered.

1 _____

2 _____

3 _____

4 _____

5 _____

6 _____

7 _____

8 _____

9 _____

COVERING ALL YOUR BASES

[L2]   Multiple Choice

Select the best answer or answers from the choices given.

1. The three different classes of lymphocytes in the blood are:

   A. cytotoxic cells, helper cells, suppressor cells

   B. T cells, B cells, NK cells

   C. plasma cells, B cells, cytotoxic cells

   D. antigens, antibodies, immunoglobulins

2. The primary effect(s) of complement activation include:

   A. destruction of target cell membranes

   B. stimulation of inflammation

   C. attraction of phagocytes and enhancement of phagocytosis

   D. a, b, and c are correct

3. Of the following selections, the one that *best* defines the lymphatic system is that it is:

   A. an integral part of the circulatory system

   B. a one-way route from the blood to the interstitial fluid

   C. a one-way route from the interstitial fluid to the blood

   D. closely related to and a part of the circulatory system

4. Tissue fluid enters the lymphatic system via the:

   A. thoracic duct

   B. lymph capillaries

   C. lymph nodes

   D. bloodstream

5. The larger lymphatic vessels contain valves.

   A. trueB.   false

6. Systemic evidence of the inflammatory response would include:

   A. redness and swelling

   B. fever and pain

   C. production of WBCs, fever

   D. swelling and fever

7. Chemical mediators of inflammation include:

   A. histamine, kinins, prostaglandins, leukotrienes

   B. epinephrine, norepinephrine, acetylcholine, histamine

   C. kinins, opsonins, epinephrine, leukotrienes

   D. a, b, and c are correct

8. T lymphocytes comprise approximately _____ percent of circulating lymphocytes.

   A. 5–10   C. 40–50

   B. 20–30   D. 70–80

9. B lymphocytes differentiate into:

   A. cytotoxic and suppressor cells

   B. helper and suppressor cells

   C. memory and helper cells

   D. memory and plasma cells

10. _____ cells may activate B cells while _____ cells inhibit the activity of B cells.

   A. Memory; plasma

   B. Macrophages; microphages

   C. Memory; cytotoxic

   D. Helper T; suppressor T

11. The primary response of T-cell differentiation in cell-mediated immunity is the production of _____ cells.

   A. helper T

   B. suppressor T

   C. cytotoxic T

   D. memory

12. The vaccination of antigenic materials into the body is called:

   A. naturally acquired active immunity

   B. induced active immunity

   C. naturally acquired passive immunity

   D. induced passive immunity

13. In passive immunity _____ are induced into the body by injection.

    A. antibodies

    B. antigens

    C. T and B cells

    D. lymphocytes

14. The lymphatic function of the white pulp of the spleen is:

    A. phagocytosis of abnormal blood cell components

    B. release of splenic hormones into lymphatic vessels

    C. initiation of immune responses by B cells and T cells

    D. to degrade foreign proteins and toxins released by bacteria

15. A person with type AB blood has:

    A. anti-A and anti-B antibodies

    B. only anti-O antibodies

    C. no antigens

    D. neither anti-A nor anti-B antibodies

16. The antibodies produced and secreted by B lymphocytes are soluble proteins called:

    A. lymphokines

    B. agglutinins

    C. immunoglobulins

    D. leukotrienes

17. The genes found in a region called the *major histocompatibility complex* are called:

    A. immunoglobulins (IgG)

    B. human leukocyte antigens (HLAs)

    C. autoantibodies

    D. alpha and gamma interferons

18. Memory B cells do not differentiate into plasma cells unless they:

    A. are initially subjected to a specific antigen

    B. are stimulated by active immunization

    C. are exposed to the same antigen a second time

    D. are stimulated by passive immunization

19. The three-dimensional "fit" between the variable segments of the antibody molecule and the corresponding antigenic determinant site is referred to as the:

    A. immunodeficiency complex

    B. antibody-antigen complex

    C. protein-complement complex

    D. a, b, and c are correct

20. One of the primary nonspecific effects that glucocorticoids have on the immune response is:

    A. inhibition of interleukin secretion

    B. increased release of T and B cells

    C. decreased activity of cytotoxic T cells

    D. depression of the inflammatory response

[L2] Completion

Using the terms below, complete the following statements.

cytokines	T cells	antigen	mast
pyrogens	Kupffer cells	interferon	IgM
NK cells	properdin	helper T cells	IgG
Langerhans cells	opsonins	microglia	

1. Approximately 80 percent of circulating lymphocytes are classified as _____.

2. Fixed macrophages inside the CNS are called _____.

3. Macrophages in and around the liver sinusoids are referred to as _____.

4. Macrophages that reside within the epithelia of the skin and digestive tract are _____.

5. A negative immune response leads to tolerance of the _____.

6. Hormones of the immune system released by tissue cells to coordinate local activities are classified as _____.

7. The complement factor involved in the alternative pathway in the complement system is _____.

8. Cells that play a pivotal role in the inflammatory process are called _____ cells.

9. Circulating proteins that can reset the body's "thermostat" and cause a rise in body temperature are referred to as _____.

10. Enhanced phagocytosis is accomplished by a group of proteins called _____.

11. Immunological surveillance involves specific lymphocytes called _____.

12. The protein that appears to slow cell division and is effective in the treatment of cancer is _____.

13. Antibodies that comprise approximately 80 percent of all antibodies in the body are _____.

14. Antibodies that occur naturally in blood plasma and are used to determine an individual's blood type are _____.

15. The human immunodeficiency virus (HIV) attacks _____ cells in humans.

[L2] Short Essay

Briefly answer the following questions in the spaces provided below.

1. What are the three primary organizational components of the lymphatic system?

2. What three major functions are performed by the lymphatic system?

3. What are the three different *classes* of lymphocytes found in the blood and where does each class originate?

4. What three kinds of T cells comprise 80 percent of the circulating lymphocyte population? What is each type basically responsible for?

5. What is the primary function of stimulated B cells and what are they ultimately responsible for?

6. What three lymphatic organs are important in the lymphatic system?

7. What are the six defenses that provide the body with a defensive capability known as *nonspecific immunity*?

8. What are the primary differences between the "recognition" mechanisms of NK (natural killer) cells and T and B cells?

9. What four primary effects result from complement activation?

10. What are the four general characteristics of specific defenses?

11. What is the primary difference between active and passive immunity?

12. What two primary mechanisms are involved in order for the body to reach its goal of the immune response?

13. What seven possible processes could result when the antibody-antigen complex is found to eliminate the threat posed by the antigen?

14. What five different classes of antibodies (immunoglobulins) are found in body fluids?

15. What are the four primary subgroups of the lymphokines and the monokines?

16. What is an autoimmune disorder and what happens in the body when it occurs?

LEVEL 3   Critical Thinking/Application

Using principles and concepts learned about the lymphatic system and immunity, answer the following questions. Write your answers on a separate sheet of paper.

1. Organ transplants are common surgical procedures in a number of hospitals throughout the United States. What happens if the donor and recipient are not compatible?

2. Via a diagram, draw a schematic model to illustrate your understanding of the immune system as a whole. (*Hint: Begin with the antigen and show the interactions that result in cell-mediated and antibody-mediated immunity.*)

3. Defensins are protein molecules found in neutrophils that form peptide spears that pierce the cell membranes of pathogenic microbes. How does the role of defensin fit into the mechanisms of immunity?

4. A common cop-out for a sudden or unexplainable pathogenic condition in the body is, "He has a virus." Since viruses do not conform to the prokaryotic or eukaryotic plan of organization, how can they be classified as infectious agents?

5. Why are NK cells effective in fighting viral infections?

6. We usually associate a fever with illness or disease. In what ways may a fever be beneficial?

7. Stress of some kind is an everyday reality in the life of most human beings throughout the world. How does stress contribute to the effectiveness of the immune response?

21

THE RESPIRATORY SYSTEM

Student Objectives

When you have completed the exercises in this chapter, you will have accomplished the following objectives:

Functional Anatomy of the Respiratory System

1. Identify the organs forming the respiratory passageway(s) in descending order until the alveoli are reached. Distinguish between conducting and respiratory zone structures.

2. List and describe several protective mechanisms of the respiratory system.

3. Describe the makeup of the respiratory membrane, and relate structure to function.

4. Describe the gross structure of the lungs and pleurae.

Mechanics of Breathing

5. Relate Boyle's law to the events of inspiration and expiration.

6. Explain the relative roles of the respiratory muscles and lung elasticity in producing the volume changes that cause air to flow into and out of the lungs.

7. Explain the functional importance of the partial vacuum that exists in the intrapleural space.

8. List several physical factors that influence pulmonary ventilation.

9. Explain and compare the various lung volumes and capacities. Indicate types of information that can be gained from pulmonary function tests.

10. Define *dead space*.

Gas Exchanges in the Body

11. State Dalton's law of partial pressures and Henry's law.

12. Describe how atmospheric and alveolar air differ in composition, and explain these differences.

13. Relate Dalton's and Henry's laws to events of external and internal respiration.

Transport of Respiratory Gases by Blood

14. Describe how oxygen is transported in the blood, and explain how oxygen loading and unloading is affected by temperature, pH, BPG, and P_{CO_2}.

15. Describe carbon dioxide transport in the blood.

Control of Respiration

16. Describe the neural controls of respiration.

17. Compare and contrast the influences of lung reflexes, volition, emotions, arterial pH, and arterial partial pressures of oxygen and carbon dioxide on respiratory rate and depth.

Respiratory Adjustments

18. Compare and contrast the hyperpnea of exercise with involuntary hyperventilation.

19. Describe the process and effects of acclimatization to high altitude.

Homeostatic Imbalances of the Respiratory System

20. Compare the causes and consequences of chronic bronchitis, emphysema, asthma, and lung cancer.

Body cells require an abundant and continuous supply of oxygen to carry out their activities. As cells use oxygen, they release carbon dioxide, a waste product the body must get rid of. The circulatory and respiratory systems obtain and deliver oxygen to body cells and eliminate carbon dioxide from the body. The respiratory system structures are responsible for gas exchange between the blood and the external environment (that is, external respiration). The respiratory system also plays an important role in maintaining the acid-base balance of the blood.

Questions and activities in Chapter 21 consider both the anatomy and the physiology of the respiratory system structures.

BUILDING THE FRAMEWORK

Functional Anatomy of the Respiratory System

1. What are the four main events of respiration?

_____

_____

_____

_____

2. The respiratory system is divisible into *conducting zone* and *respiratory zone* structures.

   1. Name the respiratory zone structures. _____

   _____

   2. What is their common function? _____

   3. Name the conducting zone structures. _____

   _____

   _____

3. Use the terms provided to complete the pathway of air to the primary bronchi. Some of the terms have already been filled in. The main pathway—through the upper respiratory organs—is the vertical pathway at the far left. To the right of the name of most of those organs are horizontal lines for listing the subdivisions of that organ or the structures over which air passes as it moves through that organ.

Adenoids	Internal nares	Nasopharynx	Trachea
Carina	Laryngopharynx	Nose	Vocal folds
Epiglottis	Larynx	Oropharynx	
External nares	Middle meatus	Pharynx	

Nose: _____ → _____ → _____

___: _____ → _____ → _____

_____

Larynx: _____ → _____

_____ → _____ → Primary bronchi

4. Figure 21.1 illustrates the skeletal framework of the nose. Identify the various bones and cartilages contributing to that framework by color coding and coloring them on the figure.

- ◯ Dense fibrous connective tissue
- ◯ Greater alar cartilages
- ◯ Lateral cartilage
- ◯ Lesser alar cartilages
- ◯ Maxillary bone (frontal process)
- ◯ Nasal bone
- ◯ Septal cartilage

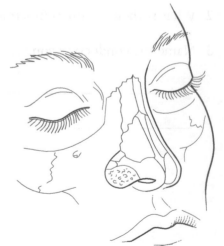

Figure 21.1

5. Figure 21.2 is a sagittal view of the upper respiratory structures. First, correctly identify all structures with leader lines on the figure. Then, select different colors for the structures listed below and color the coding circles and the corresponding structures on the figure.

◯ Nasal cavity   ◯ Larynx   ◯ Tongue

◯ Pharynx   ◯ Paranasal sinuses   ◯ Hard palate

◯ Trachea

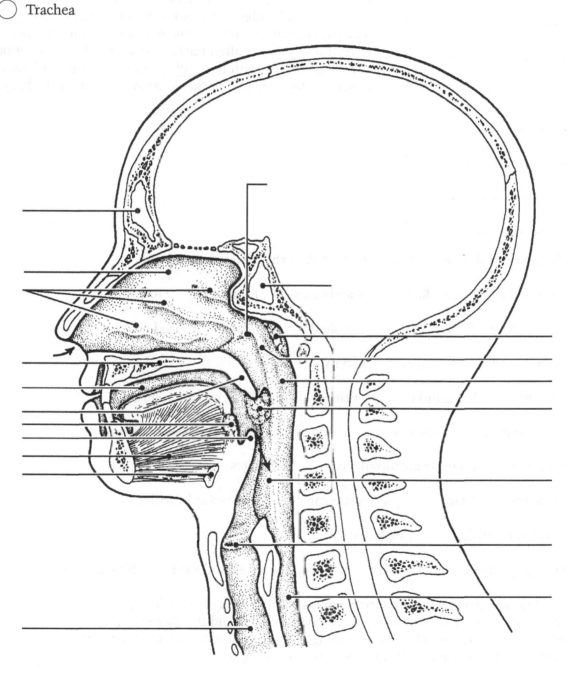

Figure 21.2

6. Complete the following statements concerning the nasal cavity and adjacent structures by inserting your answers in the answer blanks.

_____ 1.

_____ 2.

_____ 3.

_____ 4.

_____ 5.

_____ 6.

_____ 7.

_____ 8.

_____ 9.

_____ 10.

1. Air enters the nasal cavities of the respiratory system through the __(1)__ . The nasal cavity is divided by the midline __(2)__ .
2. The nasal cavity mucosa has several functions. Its major functions are to __(3)__ , __(4)__ , and __(5)__ the incoming air.
3. Mucous membrane-lined cavities called __(6)__ are found in several bones surrounding the nasal cavities. They make the skull less heavy and probably act as resonance chambers for __(7)__ . The passageway common to the digestive and respiratory systems, the __(8)__ , is often referred to as the throat; it connects the nasal cavities with the __(9)__ below. Clusters of lymphatic tissue, __(10)__ , are part of the defensive system of the body.

7. Circle the term that does not belong in each of the following groupings.

1. Sphenoidal   Maxillary   Mandibular   Ethmoid   Frontal

2. Nasal cavity   Trachea   Alveolus   Bronchus   Dead air

3. Apex   Base   Hilus   Larynx   Pleura

4. Sinusitis   Peritonitis   Pleurisy   Tonsillitis   Laryngitis

5. External nose   Nasal bones   Lateral cartilages   Nasal septum

6. Conchae   Increase air turbulence   Turbinates   Choanae

7. Cuneiform cartilage   Corniculate cartilage   Tracheal cartilage

   Arytenoid cartilage   Epiglottis

8. Laryngopharynx   Oropharynx   Transports air and food   Nasopharynx

8. Figure 21.3 is a diagram of the larynx and associated structures. Select a different color for each structure and color the coding circles and the corresponding structures on the figure. Identify, by adding a label and leader line, the laryngeal prominence. Then, answer the questions below the figure.

○ Hyoid bone   ○ Tracheal cartilages   ○ Thyrohyoid membrane

○ Cricoid cartilage   ○ Epiglottis   ○ Cricothyroid ligament

○ Thyroid cartilage   ○ Cricotracheal ligament

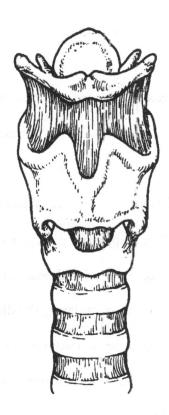

Figure 21.3

1. What are the three functions of the larynx? _____

_____

_____

_____

2. What cartilages, not illustrated, anchor the vocal cords internally?

_____

3. What type of cartilage forms the epiglottis? _____

4. What type of cartilage forms the other eight laryngeal cartilages? _____

5. Explain this difference. _____

_____

_____

6. What is the common name for the laryngeal prominence?

_____

9. Use the key choices to match the following definitions with the correct terms.

Key Choices

A. Alveoli	E. Esophagus	I. Phrenic nerve	M. Visceral pleura
B. Bronchioles	F. Glottis	J. Primary bronchi	N. Uvula
C. Conchae	G. Palate	K. Trachea	O. Vocal folds
D. Epiglottis	H. Parietal pleura	L. Vagus nerve	

_____ 1. Smallest respiratory passageways

_____ 2. Separates the oral and nasal cavities

_____ 3. Major nerve stimulating the diaphragm

_____ 4. Food passageway posterior to the trachea

_____ 5. Closes off the larynx during swallowing

_____ 6. Windpipe

_____ 7. Actual site of gas exchanges

_____ 8. Pleural layer covering the thorax walls

_____ 9. Autonomic nervous system nerve serving the thorax

_____ 10. Lumen of the larynx

_____ 11. Fleshy lobes in the nasal cavity that increase its surface area

_____ 12. Close the glottis during the Valsalva maneuver

_____ 13. Closes the nasopharynx during swallowing

_____ 14. The cilia of its mucosa beat upward toward the larynx

10. Complete the following statements by writing the missing terms in the answer blanks.

_____ 1.

_____ 2.

_____ 3.

_____ 4.

_____ 5.

_____ 6.

_____ 7.

_____ 8.

_____ 9.

Within the larynx are the __(1)__, which vibrate with exhaled air and allow an individual to __(2)__. Speech involves opening and closing the __(3)__. The __(4)__ muscles control the length of the true vocal cords by moving the __(5)__ cartilages. The tenser the vocal cords, the __(6)__ the pitch. To produce deep tones, the glottis is __(7)__. The greater the force of air rushing past the vocal cords, the __(8)__ the sound produced. Inflammation of the vocal cords is called __(9)__.

11. Figure 21.4 shows a cross section through the trachea. First, label the layers indicated by the leader lines. Next, color the following: mucosa (including the cilia, epithelium, lamina propria) light pink; area containing the submucosal seromucous glands—purple; hyaline cartilage ring—blue; trachealis muscle—orange; and adventitia—yellow. Then, respond to the questions following the figure.

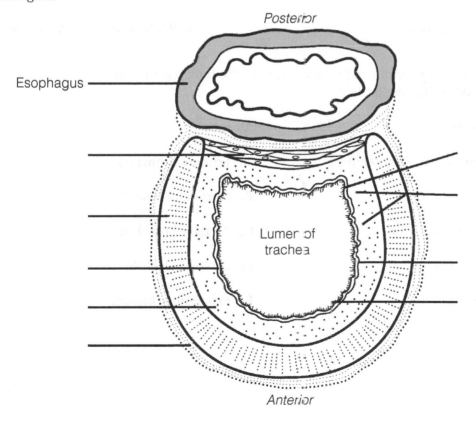

Figure 21.4

1. What important role is played by the cartilage rings that reinforce the trachea?

   _____

2. Of what importance is the fact that the cartilage rings are incomplete posteriorly?

   _____

3. What occurs when the trachealis muscle contracts and in what activities might this action

   be very helpful? _____

   _____

12. Using the key choices, match the proper type of lining epithelium with each respiratory structure listed below.

    Key Choices

    A. Stratified squamous   D. Stratified columnar

    B. Pseudostratified ciliated columnar   E. Simple cuboidal

    C. Simple squamous

    _____ 1. Nasal cavity   _____ 4. Trachea and primary bronchi

    _____ 2. Nasopharynx   _____ 5. Bronchioles

    _____ 3. Laryngopharynx   _____ 6. Walls of alveoli (type I cells)

13. Match the bronchus or bronchiole type (at right) with the lung region supplied by that specific type of air tube (at left).

    Lung region   **Air tube**

    _____ 1. Bronchopulmonary segment   A. Primary bronchus

    _____ 2. Lobule   B. Secondary bronchus

    _____ 3. Alveolar ducts and sacs   C. Tertiary bronchus

    _____ 4. Entire lung   D. Large bronchiole

    _____ 5. Lung lobe   E. Respiratory bronchiole

14. Figure 21.5 illustrates the gross anatomy of lower respiratory structures. Intact structures are shown on the left; isolated respiratory passages are shown on the right. Select a different color for each of the respiratory system structures listed below and color the coding circles and the corresponding structures on the figure. Then complete the figure by labeling the areas and structures with leader lines. Be sure to include the pleural space, mediastinum, apex of right lung, diaphragm, clavicle, and the base of the right lung.

○ Trachea   ○ Primary bronchi   ○ Visceral pleura

○ Larynx   ○ Secondary bronchi   ○ Parietal pleura

○ Intact lung   ○ Tertiary bronchi

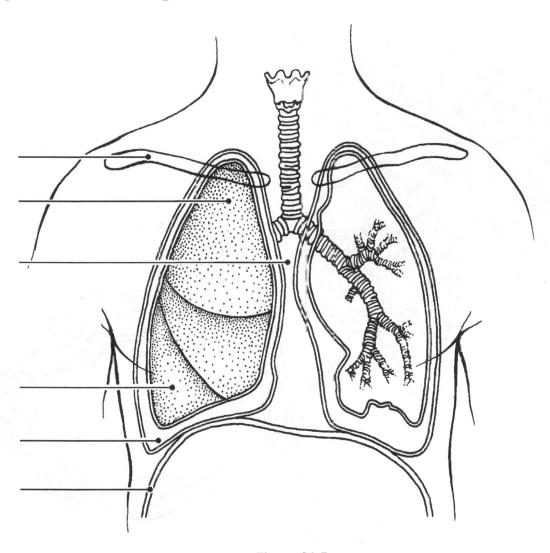

Figure 21.5

15. Figure 21.6 illustrates the microscopic structure of the respiratory unit of lung tissue. The external anatomy is shown in Figure 21.6A. Color the intact alveoli yellow, the pulmonary capillaries red, and the respiratory bronchioles green. Bracket and label an alveolar sac. Also label an alveolar duct.

A cross section through an alveolus is shown in Figure 21.6B. Color the alveolar epithelium yellow, the capillary endothelium pink, and the red blood cells in the capillary red. Also, label the alveolar chamber and color it blue. Finally, add the symbols for oxygen gas (O_2) and carbon dioxide gas (CO_2) in the sites where they would be in higher concentration and add arrows showing their direction of movement through the respiratory membrane.

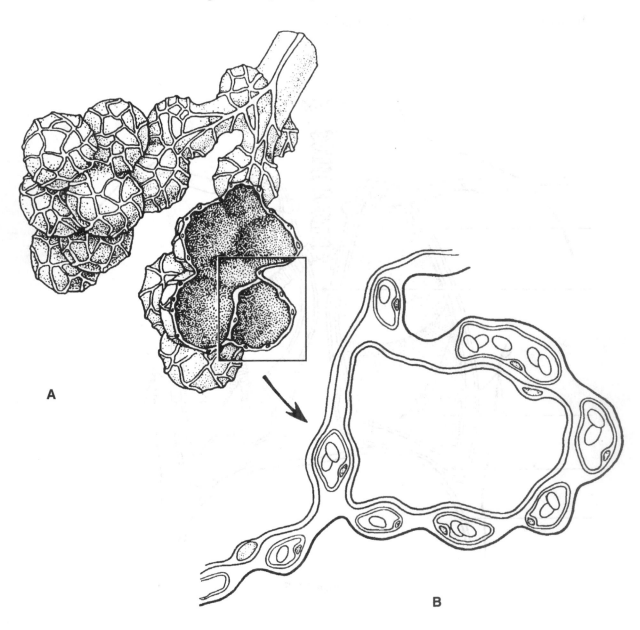

Figure 21.6

16. Complete the following paragraph on the alveolar cells and their roles by writing the missing terms in the answer blanks.

_____   1.

_____   2.

_____   3.

_____   4.

_____   5.

_____   6.

_____   7.

With the exception of the stroma of the lungs, which is ___(1)___ tissue, the lungs are mostly air spaces, of which the alveoli comprise the greatest part. The bulk of the alveolar walls are made up of squamous epithelial cells called ___(2)___ cells. Structurally, these cells are well suited for their ___(3)___ function. The cuboidal cells of the alveoli, called ___(4)___ cells, are much less numerous. These cells produce a fluid that coats the air-exposed surface of the alveolus and contains a lipid-based molecule called ___(5)___ that functions to ___(6)___ of the alveolar fluid. Although the pulmonary capillaries spiderweb over the alveolar surfaces, the nutritive blood supply of the lungs is provided by the ___7)___ arteries.

Mechanics of Breathing

1. Using the key choices, match the following facts about pressure with the correct terms.

Key Choices

A. Atmospheric pressure   B. Intrapulmonary pressure   C. Intrapleural pressure

_____ 1. Baring pneumothorax, this pressure is always lower than atmospheric pressure (that is, is negative pressure)

_____ 2. Pressure of air outside the body

_____ 3. As it decreases, air flows into the passageways of the lungs

_____ 4. As it increases over atmospheric pressure, air flows out of the lungs

_____ 5. If this pressure becomes equal to the atmospheric pressure, the lungs collapse

_____ 6. Rises well over atmospheric pressure during a forceful cough

_____ 7. Also known as the intra-alveolar pressure

2. Many changes occur within the lungs as the diaphragm (and external inter-costal muscles) contract and then relax. These changes cause air to flow into and out of the lungs. The activity of the diaphragm is given in the left column of the following table. Several changes in internal thoracic conditions are listed in the column heads to the right. Complete the table by checking (✓) the appropriate column to correctly identify the change that would be occurring in each case relative to the stated diaphragm activity.

Activity of diaphragm (↑ = increased) (↓ = decreased)	Changes in							
	Internal volume of thorax		Internal pressure in thorax		Size of lungs		Direction of air flow	
	↑	↓	↑	↓	↑	↓	Into lung	Out of lung
Contracted, moves downward								
Relaxed, moves superiorly								

3. Various factors that influence pulmonary ventilation are listed in the key choices. Select the appropriate key choices to match the following descriptions about the lungs.

Key Choices

A. Respiratory passageway resistance   C. Lung elasticity

B. Alveolar surface tension forces   D. Lung compliance

_____   1. The change in lung volume with a given change in transpulmonary pressure

_____   2. Gas flow changes inversely with this factor

_____   3. Essential for normal expiration

_____   4. Leads to RDS (respiratory distress syndrome) when surfactant is absent

_____   5. Diminished by age-related lung fibrosis and increasing rigidity of the thoracic cage

_____   6. Its loss is the major pathology in emphysema

_____   7. Reflects a state of tension at the surface of a liquid

_____   8. Dramatically increased by asthma

_____   9. Greatest in the medium-sized bronchi

4. During forced inspiration, accessory muscles are activated that raise the rib cage more vigorously than occurs during quiet inspiration.

    1. Name three such muscles. _____

    2. Although normal quiet expiration is largely passive due to lung recoil, when expiration must be more forceful (or the lungs are diseased), muscles that increase the abdominal pressure or depress the rib cage are enlisted. Provide two examples of muscles that cause abdominal

       pressure to rise. _____

    3. Provide two examples of muscles that depress the rib cage. _____

5. Figure 21.7 is a diagram showing respiratory volumes. Complete the figure by making the following additions.

    1. Bracket the volume representing the vital capacity and color it yellow; label it VC.

    2. Add green stripes to the area representing the inspiratory reserve volume and label it IRV.

    3. Add red stripes to the area representing the expiratory reserve volume and label it ERV.

    4. Identify and label the respiratory volume, which is *now* yellow. Color the residual volume blue and label it appropriately on the figure.

    5. Bracket and label the inspiratory capacity (IC).

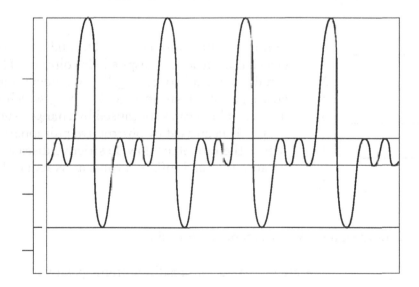

Figure 21.7

6. Check (✓) all factors that *decrease* the AVR.

    _____ 1. Shallow breathing   _____ 4. Slow breathing

    _____ 2. Deep breathing   _____ 5. Mucus in the respiratory passageways

    _____ 3. Rapid breathing

7. This exercise concerns respiratory volume or capacity measurements. Using the key choices, select the terms that identify the respiratory volumes described by inserting the appropriate answers in the answer blanks.

Key Choices

A. Dead space volume   D. Residual volume (RV)   G. Vital capacity (VC)

B. Expiratory reserve volume (ERV)   E. Tidal volume (TV)

C. Inspiratory reserve volume (IRV)   F. Total lung capacity (TLC)

_____ 1. Respiratory volume inhaled or exhaled during normal breathing

_____ 2. Air in respiratory passages that does not contribute to gas exchange

_____ 3. Total amount of exchangeable air

_____ 4. Gas volume that allows gas exchange to go on continuously

_____ 5. Amount of air that can still be exhaled (forcibly) after a normal exhalation

_____ 6. Sum of all lung volumes

8. Complete the following statements by writing the missing terms in the answer blanks.

_____ 1.

_____ 2.

_____ 3.

_____ 4.

_____ 5.

Pulmonary function tests can be conducted using a __(1)__, a device that measures respired air volumes. This type of test can distinguish between __(2)__, disorders that result from increased airway resistance, and __(3)__, which result from decreased lung capacity caused by changes such as tuberculosis. __(4)__ is decreased by obstructive pulmonary diseases, which reduce the rate of air flow. Restrictive diseases lower __(5)__, because the total inflation capacity is reduced.

9. Identify the three nonrespiratory movements described below.

_____ 1. Sudden inspiration, resulting from spasms of the diaphragm

_____ 2. A deep breath is taken, the glottis is closed, and air is forced out of the lungs against the glottis; clears the lower respiratory passageways

_____ 3. As just described, but clears the upper respiratory passageways

Gas Exchanges in the Body

1. This exercise describes some ideal gas laws that relate the physical properties of gases and their behavior in liquids. Match the key choices with the descriptions that follow.

Key Choices

A. Boyle's law   B. Dalton's law   C. Henry's law

_____   1. Describes the fact that each gas in a mixture exerts pressure according to its percentage in the mixture

_____   2. States that $P_1V_1 = P_2V_2$ when temperature is constant

_____   3. States that when gases are in contact with liquids, each gas will dissolve in proportion to its partial pressure and solubility in the liquid

2. What therapy is used to treat cases of carbon monoxide poisoning, gas gangrene, and tetanus? This therapy represents a clinical application of which of the ideal gas laws?

_____

_____

3. What are the mechanism and consequences of oxygen toxicity? _____

_____

_____

4. Match the key choices with the following descriptions.

Key Choices

A. External respiration   C. Inspiration   E. Pulmonary ventilation (breathing)

B. Expiration   D. Internal respiration

_____   1. Period of breathing when air enters the lungs

_____   2. Period of breathing when air leaves the lungs

_____   3. Alternate flushing of air into and out of the lungs

_____   4. Exchange of gases between alveolar air and pulmonary capillary blood

_____   5. Exchange of gases between blood and tissue cells

5. Rank the following body regions by numbering them in the proper sequence in each column to indicate the relative partial pressure of the gases named in each column heading. Indicate the area of lowest gas partial pressure by the number 1.

PO_2	PCO_2	PN_2	PH_2O
_____ 1. Alveoli	_____ 6. Alveoli	_____ 11. Alveoli	_____ 13. Alveoli
_____ 2. External atmosphere	_____ 7. External atmosphere	_____ 12. External atmosphere	_____ 14. External atmosphere
_____ 3. Arterial blood	_____ 8. Arterial blood		
_____ 4. Venous blood	_____ 9. Venous blood		
_____ 5. Tissue cells	_____ 10. Tissue cells		

6. Use the key choices to complete the following statements about gas exchanges in the body.

Key Choices

A. Active transport

B. Air of alveoli to capillary blood

C. Carbon dioxide-poor and oxygen-rich

D. Capillary blood to alveolar air

E. Capillary blood to tissue cells

F. Diffusion

G. Higher concentration

H. Lower concentration

I. Oxygen-poor and carbon dioxide-rich

J. Tissue cells to capillary blood

_____ 1.

_____ 2.

_____ 3.

_____ 4.

_____ 5.

_____ 6.

_____ 7.

_____ 8.

_____ 9.

All gas exchanges are made by __(1)__. When substances pass in this manner, they move from areas of their __(2)__ to areas of their __(3)__. Thus oxygen continually passes from the __(4)__ and then from the __(5)__. Conversely, carbon dioxide moves from the __(6)__ and from __(7)__. From there it passes out of the body during expiration. As a result of such exchanges, arterial blood tends to be relatively __(8)__, while venous blood is relatively __(9)__.

7. Circle the correct alternative in each of the following statements about alveolar airflow and blood flow coupling.

   1. When alveolar ventilation is inadequate, the PO_2 is low/high.

   2. Consequently, the pulmonary vessels dilate/constrict.

   3. Additionally, when alveolar ventilation is inadequate, the PCO_2 is low/high.

   4. Consequently, the bronchioles dilate/constrict.

Transport of Respiratory Gases by Blood

1. Complete the following paragraphs concerning gas transport in the blood by writing the missing terms in the answer blanks.

   _____ 1.

   _____ 2.

   _____ 3.

   _____ 4.

   _____ 5.

   _____ 6.

   _____ 7.

   _____ 8.

   _____ 9.

   _____ 10.

   _____ 11.

   _____ 12.

   Most oxygen is transported bound to __(1)__ inside the red blood cells. A very small amount is carried simply dissolved in __(2)__. Most carbon dioxide is carried in the form of __(3)__ in the plasma. The reaction in which CO_2 is converted to this chemical occurs more rapidly inside red blood cells than in plasma because the cells contain the enzyme __(4)__. After the chemical is generated, it diffuses into the plasma, and __(5)__ diffuse into the red blood cells. This exchange is called the __(6)__. Smaller amounts of carbon dioxide are transported dissolved in plasma and bound to hemoglobin as __(7)__.

   The amount of CO_2 carried in blood is greatly influenced by the degree of oxygenation of the blood, an effect called the __(8)__. In general, the lower the amount of oxygen in the blood, the __(9)__ CO_2 that can be transported. Conversely, as CO_2 enters the blood, it prompts oxygen to dissociate from __(10)__. This effect is called the __(11)__. Carbon monoxide poisoning is lethal because carbon monoxide competes with __(12)__ for binding sites.

2. List four factors that enhance O_2 loading onto hemoglobin.

   _____

3. What is the functional importance of the following facts?

   1. Hemoglobin is over 90% saturated with oxygen well before the blood has completed its route through the pulmonary capillaries.

   _____

   _____

2. Venous blood still has a hemoglobin saturation of over 70%.

_____

_____

_____

4. In the grid provided in Figure 21.8, plot the following points. Then draw a sigmoid curve to connect the points. Finally, answer the questions following the grid.

A. PO_2 = 100 mm Hg; saturation = 99%   D. PO_2 = 20 mm Hg; saturation = 35%

B. PO_2 = 70 mm Hg; saturation = 98%   E. PO_2 = 10 mm Hg; saturation = 10%

C. PO_2 = 40 mm Hg; saturation = 75%   F. PO_2 = 0 mm Hg; saturation = 0%

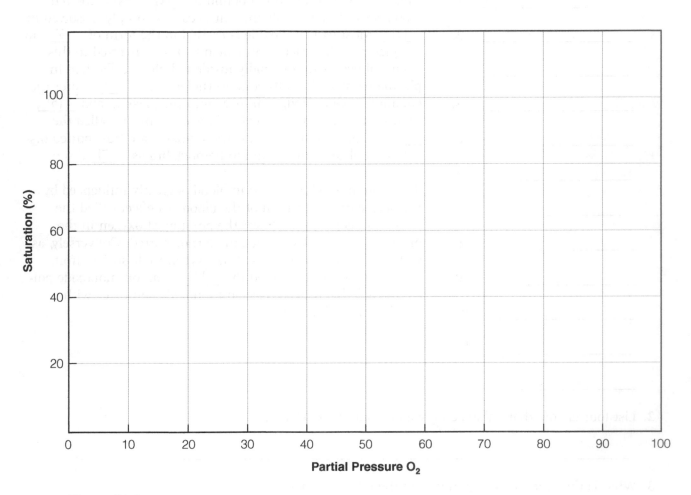

Figure 21.8

1. What is the curve just plotted called? _____

_____

2. What three factors will decrease the percent saturation of hemoglobin in the tissues?

_____

_____

5. Fetal hemoglobin (HbF) differs from that of an adult (HbA), as illustrated by the oxygen dissociation curve shown in Figure 21.9.

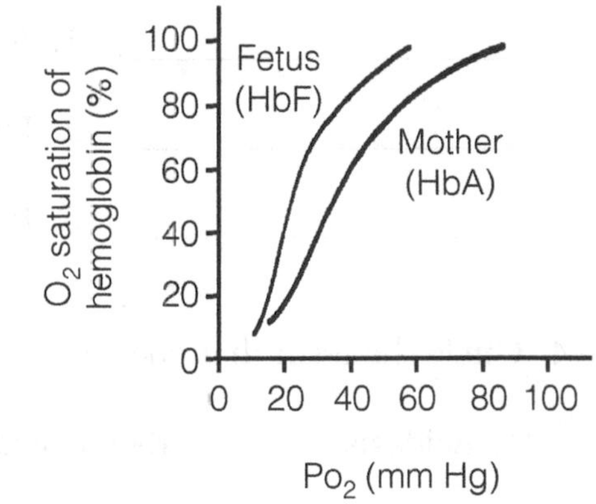

Figure 21.9

1. Explain what the differences in the graph mean or represent.

_____

2. Explain the difference in the two hemoglobins that accounts for the variation.

_____

Control of Respiration

1. There are several types of breathing controls. Match the structures in Column B with the descriptions in Column A.

Column A	Column B
_____ , _____ 1. Actual or hypothetical respiratory control centers in the pons	A. Apneustic center
_____ , _____ 2. Respiratory control centers in the medulla	B. Chemoreceptors in the aortic arch and carotid body
_____ 3. Respond to overinflation and underinflation of the lungs	
_____ 4. Respond to decreased oxygen levels in the blood	C. VRG
_____ 5. Also called the inspiratory center	D. DRG
_____ 6. Medullary area that contains approximately even numbers of neurons involved in inspiration and expiration	E. Pneumotaxic center
_____ 7. The breathing "rhythm" center	F. Stretch receptors in the lungs
_____ 8. Basically acts to inhibit the dorsal respiratory group (DRG)	

2. Why is it inadvisable to administer pure O_2 to a patient who suffers from pulmonary disease and retains CO_2?

_____

_____

3. For each of the following, designate whether it primarily affects the central chemoreceptors or the peripheral chemoreceptors:

_____   1. Arterial PO_2 below 60 mm Hg stimulates hyperventilation.

_____   2. Decrease in arterial pH stimulates hyperventilation.

_____   3. Increase in PCO_2 in the CSF causes increase in respiratory rate and depth.

4. Circle the term that does not belong in each of the following groupings.

1. Acidosis   ↑ Carbonic acid   ↓ pH   ↑ pH

2. Acidosis   Hyperventilation   Hypoventilation CO_2 buildup

3. Apnea   Cyanosis   ↑ Oxygen   ↑ Oxygen

4. ↓ Respiratory rate   Exercise   Anger   ↓ CO_2 in blood

5. N narcosis   The bends   N toxicity   Rapture of the deep

6. High altitude   ↓ PO_2 ↑ PCO_2 ↓ Atmospheric pressure

Respiratory Adjustments

1. Answer the following questions concerning respiratory adjustments during exercise:

1. What are two differences between hyperpnea and hyperventilation?

_____

_____

2. What are three neural factors that trigger the abrupt increase in ventilation during exercise?

_____

_____

2. List three adaptive responses to high-altitude living.

1. _____

2. _____

3. _____

Homeostatic Imbalances of the Respiratory System

1. Match the terms in Column B with the pathologic conditions described in Column A.

	Column A	Column B
_____	1. Lack or cessation of breathing	A. Apnea
_____	2. Normal breathing in terms of rate and depth	B. Asthma
		C. Chronic bronchitis
_____	3. Labored breathing, or "air hunger"	
_____	4. Chronic oxygen deficiency	D. Dyspnea
		E. Emphysema
_____	5. Condition characterized by fibrosis of the lungs and an increase in size of the alveolar chambers	F. Eupnea
		G. Hypoxia
_____	6. Condition characterized by increased mucus production, which clogs respiratory passageways and promotes coughing	H. Lung cancer
		I. Sleep apnea
_____	7. Respiratory passageways narrowed by bronchiolar spasms	J. Tuberculosis
_____	8. Together called COPD	
_____	9. Incidence strongly associated with cigarette smoking; has increased dramatically in women recently	
_____	10. Victims become barrel-chested because of air retention	
_____	11. Infection spread by airborne bacteria; a recent alarming increase in cases among drug users and HIV-infected people	
_____	12. Temporary cessation of breathing during sleep	

THE INCREDIBLE JOURNEY

A Visualization Exercise for the Respiratory System

You carefully begin to pick your way down, using cartilages as steps.

1. Complete the following narrative by writing the missing terms in the answer blanks.

_____ 1.

_____ 2.

_____ 3.

_____ 4.

_____ 5.

_____ 6.

_____ 7.

_____ 8.

Your journey through the respiratory system is to be on foot. To begin, you simply will walk into your host's external nares. You are miniaturized, and your host is sedated lightly to prevent sneezing during your initial observations in the nasal cavity and subsequent descent.

You begin your exploration of the nasal cavity in the right nostril. One of the first things you notice is that the chamber is very warm and humid. High above, you see three large, round lobes, the __(1)__ , which provide a large mucosal surface area for warming and moistening the entering air. As you walk toward the rear of this chamber, you see a large lumpy mass of lymphatic tissue, the __(2)__ in the __(3)__ , or first portion of the pharynx. As you peer down the pharynx, you realize that it will be next to impossible to maintain your footing during the next part of your journey—it is nearly straight down, and the __(4)__ secretions are like grease. You sit down and dig in your heels to get started. After a quick slide, you land abruptly on one of a pair of flat sheetlike structures that begins to vibrate rapidly, bouncing you up and down helplessly. You are also conscious of a rhythmic hum during this jostling, and you realize that you have landed on a __(5)__ . You pick yourself up and look over the superior edge of the __(6)__ , down into the seemingly endless esophagus behind. You chastise yourself for not remembering that the __(7)__ and respiratory pathways separate at this point. Hanging directly over your head is a leaflike __(8)__ cartilage. Normally, you would not have been able to get this far because it would have closed off this portion of the respiratory tract. With your host sedated, however, this protective reflex did not work.

_____ 9.   You carefully begin to pick your way down, using the cartilages as steps. When you reach the next respiratory organ, the __(9)__

_____ 10.   your descent becomes much easier, because the structure's C-shaped cartilages form a ladderlike supporting structure. As you

_____ 11.   climb down the cartilages, your face is stroked rhythmically by soft cellular extensions, or __(10)__. You remember that their

_____ 12.   function is to move mucus laden with bacteria or dust and other debris toward the __(11)__.

_____ 13.

You finally reach a point where the descending passageway

_____ 14.   splits into the two __(12)__, and since you want to control your progress (rather than slide downward), you choose the more

_____ 15.   horizontal __(13__ branch. If you remain in the superior portion of the lungs, your return trip will be less difficult because the

_____ 16.   passageways will be more horizontal than steeply vertical. The passageways get smaller and smaller, slowing your progress.

_____ 17.

As you are squeezing into one of the smallest of the respiratory

_____ 18.   passageways, a __(14)__, you see a bright spherical chamber ahead. You scramble into this __(15)__, pick yourself up, and sur-

_____ 19.   vey the area. Scattered here and there are lumps of a substance that looks suspiciously like coal, reminding you that your host

_____ 20.   is a smoker. As you stand there, a soft rustling wind seems to flow in and out of the chamber. You press your face against the transparent chamber wall and see disclike cells, __(16)__ passing

by in the capillaries on the other side. As you watch, they change from a somewhat bluish color to a bright __(17)__ color as they pick up __(18)__ and unload __(19)__.

You record your observations and then contact headquarters to let them know you are ready to begin your ascent. You begin your return trek, slipping and sliding as you travel. By the time you reach the inferior edge of the trachea, you are ready for a short break. As you rest on the mucosa, you begin to notice that the air is becoming close and very heavy. You pick yourself up quickly and begin to scramble up the trachea. Suddenly and without warning, you are hit by a huge wad of mucus and catapulted upward and out onto your host's freshly pressed handkerchief! Your host has assisted your exit with a __(20)__.

At the Clinic

1. Barbara is rushed to the emergency room after an auto accident. The 8th through 10th ribs on her left side have been fractured and have punctured the lung. What term is used to indicate lung collapse? Will both lungs collapse? Why or why not?

2. A young boy is diagnosed with cystic fibrosis. What effect will this have on his respiratory system?

3. Len LaBosco, a medical student, has recently moved to Mexico City for his internship. As he examines the lab report of his first patient, he notices that the RBC count is high. Why is this normal for this patient? (*Hint:* Mexico City is located on a high-altitude mesa.) What respiratory adjustments will Len have to make in his own breathing, minute ventilation, arterial PCO_2, and hemoglobin saturation level?

4. Why must patients be forced to cough when recovering from chest surgery?

5. A mother, obviously in a panic, brings her infant who is feverish, hyperventilating, and cyanotic to the clinic. The infant is quickly diagnosed with pneumonia. What aspect of pneumonia has caused the cyanosis?

6. After a long bout of bronchitis, Mrs. Dupee complains of a stabbing pain in her side with each breath. What is her condition?

7. A patient with congestive heart failure has cyanosis coupled with liver and kidney failure. What type of hypoxia is this?

8. The Kozloski family is taking a long auto trip. Michael, who has been riding in the back of a station wagon, complains of a throbbing headache. Then, a little later, he seems confused and his face is flushed. What is your diagnosis of Michael's problem?

9. A new mother checks on her sleeping infant, only to find that it has stopped breathing and is turning blue. The mother quickly picks up the baby and pats its back until it starts to breathe. What tragedy has been averted?

10. Roger Proulx, a rugged four-pack-a-day smoker, comes to the clinic because of painful muscle spasms. Blood tests reveal hypocalcemia and elevated levels of calcitonin. What type of lung cancer is suspected?

11. A young man visiting his father in the hospital hears the clinical staff refer to the patient in the next bed as a "pink puffer." He notes the patient's barrel-shaped chest and wonders what the man's problem is. What is the patient's diagnosis, and why is he called a "pink puffer"?

12. Joanne Willis, a long-time smoker, is complaining that she has developed a persistent cough. What is your first guess as to her condition? What has happened to her bronchial cilia?

13. Mrs. Jackson, an elderly matron has severe kyphosis (dowager's hump) of her spine. She is complaining of being breathless a lot and her vital capacity is below normal. What does her kyphosis have to do with her reduced vital capacity?

14. As a result of a stroke, the swallowing mechanism in an elderly woman is uncoordinated. What effects might this have on her respiratory system?

15. While diapering his 1-year-old boy (who puts almost everything in his mouth), Mr. Gregoire failed to find one of the small safety pins previously used. Two days later, his son developed a cough and became feverish. What probably had happened to the safety pin and where (anatomically) would you expect to find it?

16. Mr. and Ms. Rao took their sick 5-year-old daughter to the doctor. The girl was breathing entirely through her mouth, her voice sounded odd and whiny, and a puslike fluid was dripping from her nose. Which one of the four sets of tonsils was most likely infected in this child?

Stop and Think

1. When dogs pant, they inhale through the nose and exhale through the mouth. How does this provide a cooling mechanism?

2. Is the partial pressure of oxygen in expired air higher, lower, or the same as that of alveolar air? Explain your answer.

3. Consider the following: (a) Two girls in a high school cafeteria were giggling over lunch, and both accidentally sprayed milk out their nostrils at the same time. Explain in anatomical terms why swallowed fluids can sometimes come out the nose.

(b) A boy in the same cafeteria then stood on his head and showed he could drink milk upside down without any of it entering his nasal cavity or nose. What prevented the milk from flowing downward into his nose?

4. A surgeon had to remove three adjacent bronchopulmonary segments from the left lung of Mr. Krigbaum, a patient with tuberculosis. Almost half of the lung was removed, yet there was no severe bleeding, and relatively few blood vessels had to be cauterized (closed off). Why was the surgery so easy to perform?

5. The cilia lining the upper respiratory passages (superior to the larynx) beat inferiorly while the cilia lining the lower respiratory passages (larynx and below) beat superiorly. What is the functional "reason" for this difference?

6. What is the function of the abundant elastin fibers that occur in the stroma of the lung and around all respiratory tubes from the trachea through the respiratory tree?

7. A man was choking on a piece of meat and no one was around to offer help. He saw a horizontal railing in his house that ran just above the level of his navel. He hurled himself against the railing in an attempt to perform the Heimlich maneuver on himself. Use logic to deduce whether this was a wise move that might save the man's life.

8. Three terms that are easily confused are *choanae, conchae,* and *carina.* Define each of these, clarifying their differences.

COVERING ALL YOUR BASES

Multiple Choice

Select the best answer or answers from the choices given.

1. Structures that are part of the respiratory zone include:

   A. terminal bronchioles

   B. respiratory bronchioles

   C. tertiary bronchi

   D. alveolar ducts

2. Which of the following have a respiratory function?

   A. Olfactory mucosa   C. Vibrissae

   B. Adenoids   D. Auditory tubes

3. Which structures are associated with the production of speech?

   A. Cricoid cartilage

   B. Glottis

   C. Arytenoid cartilage

   D. Pharynx

4. The skeleton of the external nose consists of:

   A. cartilage and bone

   B. bone only

   C. hyaline cartilage only

   D. elastic cartilage only

5. Which of the following is not part of the conducting zone of the respiratory system?

   A. Pharynx   D. Secondary bronchioles

   B. Alveolar sac   E. Larynx

   C. Trachea

6. The mucus sheets that cover the inner surfaces of the nasal cavity and bronchi are secreted by which cells?

   A. Serous cells in tubuloacinar glands

   B. Mucous cells in tubuloacinar glands and epithelial goblet cells

   C. Ciliated cells

   D. Alveolar type II cells

7. Select the single false statement about the true vocal cords:

   A. They are the same as the vocal folds.

   B. They attach to the arytenoid cartilages via the vocal ligaments.

   C. Exhaled air flowing through the glottis vibrates them to produce sound.

   D. They are also called the vestibular folds.

8. The function of alveolar type I cells is:

   A. to produce surfactant

   B. to propel mucous sheets

   C. phagocytosis of dust particles

   D. to allow rapid diffusion of respiratory gases

9. An examination of a lobe of the lung reveals many branches off the main passageway. These branches are:

   A. primary bronchi

   B. secondary bronchi

   C. lobar bronchi

   D. segmental bronchi

10. Microscopic examination of lung tissue shows a relatively small passageway with nonciliated simple cuboidal epithelium, abundant elastic fibers, absence of cartilage, and some smooth muscle. What is the classification of this structure?

    A. Secondary bronchus

    B. Tertiary bronchus

    C. Respiratory bronchiole

    D. Terminal bronchiole

11. An alveolar sac:

    A. is an alveolus

    B. relates to an alveolus as a bunch of grapes relates to one grape

    C. is a huge, saclike alveolus in an emphysema patient

    D. is the same as an alveolar duct

12. The respiratory membrane (air-blood barrier) consists of:

    A. alveolar type I cell, basal laminae, endothelial cell

    B. air, connective tissue, lung

    C. type II cell, dust cell, type I cell

    D. pseudostratified epithelium, lamina propria, capillaries

13. Cells responsible for removing foreign particles from inspired air include:

    A. goblet cells   C. dust cells

    B. type II cells   D. ciliated cells

14. The root of the lung is at its:

    A. apex   C. hilus

    B. base   D. cardiac notch

15. Which of the following are characteristic of a bronchopulmonary segment?

    A. Removal causes collapse of adjacent segments

    B. Fed by a tertiary bronchus

    C. Supplied by its own branches of the pulmonary artery and vein

    D. Separated from other segments by its septum

16. During inspiration, intrapulmonary pressure is:

    A. greater than atmospheric pressure

    B. less than atmospheric pressure

    C. greater than intrapleural pressure

    D. less than intrapleural pressure

17. Lung collapse is prevented by:

    A. high surface tension of alveolar fluid

    B. high surface tension of pleural fluid

    C. high pressure in the pleural cavities

    D. high elasticity of lung tissue

18. Accessory muscles of inspiration include:

    A. external intercostals

    B. scalenes

    C. internal intercostals

    D. pectoralis major

19. The greatest resistance to gas flow occurs at the:

    A. terminal bronchioles

    B. alveolar ducts

    C. medium-sized bronchi

    D. respiratory bronchioles

20. Resistance is increased by:

    A. epinephrine

    B. parasympathetic stimulation

    C. inflammatory chemicals

    D. contraction of the trachealis muscle

21. Which of the following conditions will reduce lung compliance?

    A. Tuberculosis   C. IRDS

    B. Aging   D. Osteoporosis

22. Chemically, surfactant is classified as a:

    A. polar molecule

    B. hydrophobic molecule

    C. polysaccharide

    D. lipoprotein

23. Which of the following changes will accompany the loss of elasticity associated with aging?

    A. Increase in tidal volume

    B. Increase in inspiratory reserve volume

    C. Increase in residual volume

    D. Increase in vital capacity

24. What is the approximate alveolar ventilation rate in a 140-pound female with a tidal volume of 400 ml and a respiratory rate of 20 breaths per minute?

    A. 10,800 ml/min   C. 5200 ml/min

    B. 8000 ml/min   D. 2800 ml/mm

25. FEV is reduced but FVC is not affected in which disorder(s)?

    A. Asthma

    B. Tuberculosis

    C. Polio

    D. Cystic fibrosis

26. Disorders classified as COPDs include:

    A. pneumonia   C. bronchitis

    B. emphysema   D. sleep apnea

27. Considering an individual in good health, an increase in blood flow rate through the pulmonary capillaries so that blood is in the capillaries for about 0.5 sec instead of 0.75 sec:

    A. decreases the rate of oxygenation

    B. reduces oxygenation of the blood

    C. does not change the level of oxygen saturation of hemoglobin

    D. increases rate of diffusion of oxygen

28. Relatively high alveolar PO_2, coupled with low PCO_2 triggers:

    A. dilation of the supplying bronchiole

    B. constriction of the supplying bronchiole

    C. dilation of the supplying arteriole

    D. constriction of the supplying arteriole

29. In blood flowing through systemic veins of a person at rest:

    A. hemoglobin is about 75% saturated

    B. the blood is carrying about 20% vol oxygen

    C. the Bohr effect has reduced hemoglobin's affinity for oxygen

    D. on average, each hemoglobin molecule is carrying two oxygen molecules

30. Which of the following is (are) true concerning CO_2 transport in systemic venous blood in an exercising person?

    A. The level of bicarbonate ion is higher than resting values.

    B. Due to the Haldane effect, the amount of carbaminohemoglobin is increased.

    C. The pH of the blood is higher.

    D. The chloride shift is greater.

31. Stimulation of which of the following stimulates inspiration?

    A. Dorsal respiratory group

    B. Pneumotaxic area

    C. Lung stretch receptors

    D. Medullary chemoreceptors

32. The factor that has the greatest effect on the medullary chemoreceptors is:

    A. acute hypercapnia

    B. hypoxia

    C. chronic hypercapnia

    D. arterial pH

33. Which term refers to increase in depth, but not rate, of ventilation?

    A. Eupnea   C. Hyperpnea

    B. Dyspnea   D. Hyperventilation

34. Adjustment to high altitude involves:

    A. increase in minute respiratory volume

    B. hypersecretion of erythropoietin

    C. dyspnea

    D. increase in hemoglobin saturation

35. Compared to the interstitial fluid bathing active muscle fibers, blood in the arteries serving those fibers has a:

    A. higher PO_2

    B. higher PCO_2

    C. higher HCO_3^- content

    D. higher H^+ content

Word Dissection

For each of the following word roots, fill in the literal meaning and give an example, using a word found in this chapter.

Word root	Translation	Example
1. alveol		
2. bronch		
3. capn		
4. carin		
5. choan		
6. crico		
7. ectasis		
8. emphys		
9. flat		
10. nari		
11. nas		
12. pleur		
13. pne		
14. pneum		
15. pulmo		
16. respir		
17. spire		
18. trach		
19. ventus		
20. vestibul		
21. vibr		

22

THE DIGESTIVE SYSTEM

Student Objectives

When you have completed the exercises in this chapter, you will have accomplished the following objectives:

PART 1: OVERVIEW OF THE DIGESTIVE SYSTEM

1. Describe the function of the digestive system, and differentiate between organs of the alimentary canal and accessory digestive organs.

2. List and define briefly the major processes occurring during digestive system activity.

3. Describe the location and function of the peritoneum. Define *retroperitoneal* and name the retroperitoneal organs.

4. Describe the tissue composition and the general function of each of the four layers of the alimentary tube.

PART 2: FUNCTIONAL ANATOMY OF THE DIGESTIVE SYSTEM

5. Describe the anatomy and basic function of each organ and accessory organ of the alimentary canal.

6. Explain the dental formula and differentiate clearly between deciduous and permanent teeth.

7. Describe the composition and functions of saliva, and explain how salivation is regulated.

8. Describe the mechanisms of chewing and swallowing.

9. Identify structural modifications of the wall of the stomach and small intestine that enhance the digestive process in these regions.

10. Describe the composition of gastric juice, name the cell types responsible for secreting its components, and indicate the importance of each component in stomach activity.

11. Explain regulation of gastric secretion and stomach motility.

12. Describe the function of local intestinal hormones.

13. State the roles of bile and of pancreatic juice in digestion.

14. Describe how entry of pancreatic juice and bile into the small intestine is regulated.

15. List the major functions of the large intestine, and describe the regulation of defecation.

PART 3: PHYSIOLOGY OF CHEMICAL DIGESTION AND ABSORPTION

16. List the enzymes involved in chemical digestion; name the foodstuffs on which they act and the end-products of protein, fat, carbohydrate, and nucleic acid digestion.

17. Describe the process of absorption of digested foodstuffs that occurs in the small intestine.

The digestive system processes food so that it can be absorbed and utilized by the body's cells. The digestive organs are responsible for food ingestion, digestion, absorption, and elimination of undigested remains from the body. In one sense, the digestive tract can be viewed as a disassembly line in which food is carried from one stage of its breakdown process to the next by muscular activity, and its nutrients are made available en route to the cells of the body. In addition, the digestive system provides for one of life's greatest pleasures—eating.

Chapter 22 reviews the anatomy of the alimentary canal and accessory digestive organs, the processes of mechanical and enzymatic breakdown, and absorption mechanisms. Cellular metabolism (utilization of foodstuffs by body cells) is considered in Chapter 23.

BUILDING THE FRAMEWORK

PART 1: OVERVIEW OF THE DIGESTIVE SYSTEM

1. The organs of the alimentary canal form a continuous tube from the mouth to the anus. List the organs of the alimentary canal, including the specific regions of the small and large intestine, from proximal to distal, in the blanks below.

Mouth → (1) _____ → (2) _____ →

(3) _____ → small intestine: (4) _____ →

(5) _____ → (6) _____ → large intestine: cecum,

appendix, (7) _____ → (8) _____ →

(9) _____ → (10) _____ →

(11) _____ → (12) _____ → anus

2. List the accessory structures associated with the mouth and the duodenum of the small intestine; mark each with an I if it is located inside the tract and an O if it is located outside the tract.

Mouth: _____

Duodenum: _____

3. Figure 22.1 is a frontal view of the digestive system. First, identify all structures with leader lines. Then, select a different color for each of the following organs and color the coding circles and the corresponding structures on the figure.

○ Esophagus   ○ Colon   ○ Salivary glands   ○ Tongue

○ Liver   ○ Pancreas   ○ Small intestine   ○ Uvula

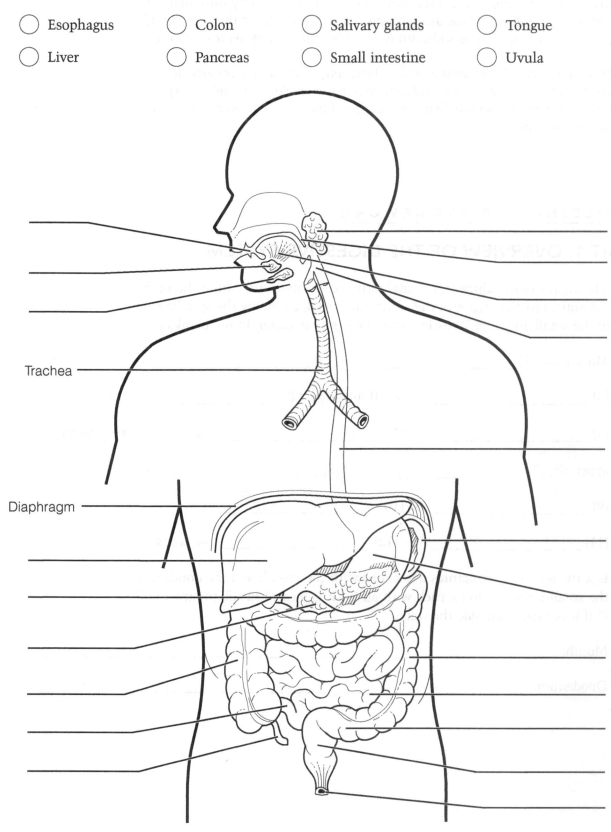

Trachea

Diaphragm

Figure 22.1

4. Match the descriptions in Column B with the appropriate terms referring to digestive processes in Column A.

Column A	Column B
_____ 1. Ingestion	A. Transport of nutrients from lumen to blood
_____ 2. Propulsion	B. Enzymatic breakdown
_____ 3. Mechanical digestion	C. Elimination of feces
_____ 4. Chemical digestion	D. Eating
_____ 5. Absorption	E. Chewing
_____ 6. Defecation	F. Churning
	G. Includes swallowing
	H. Segmentation and peristalsis

5. Relative to neural controls of digestive activity, answer the following questions in the spaces provided:

1. What are three stimuli that elicit a response from sensors in the wall

   of the tract organs? _____

   _____

2. What are the two primary nerve plexuses regulating digestive function?

   _____

3. What are some differences between long and short reflexes?

   _____

   _____

   _____

6. Fill in the blanks below:

_____ 1.

_____ 2.

_____ 3.

_____ 4.

    1. The body's most extensive serous membrane is the __(1)__ . Connecting its visceral and parietal layers is a double serous
    2. sheet called __(2)__ , which provides a route for blood vessels, lymphatics, and nerves. Organs behind the parietal layer are
    3. called __(3)__ ; those within this area are called __(4)__ .

7. Various types of glands secrete substances into the alimentary tube. Match the glands listed in Column B with the functions and locations described in Column A.

Column A

Column B

_____ 1. Mucus-producing glands located in the submucosa of the small intestine

A. Duodenal glands

_____ 2. Secretory product contains amylase, a starch-digesting enzyme

B. Gastric glands

C. Liver

_____ 3. Sends a variety of enzymes in bicarbonate-rich fluid into the small intestine

D. Pancreas

E. Salivary glands

_____ 4. Produces bile, which is transported to the duodenum via the bile duct

_____ 5. Produce hydrochloric acid and pepsinogen

8. Using the key choices, match the terms with the descriptions of digestive system organs that follow by inserting the appropriate answers in the answer blanks.

Key Choices

A. Anal canal	H. Ileocecal valve	O. Pharynx	V. Tongue
B. Appendix	I. Lesser omentum	P. Plicae circulares	W. Vestibule
C. Colon	J. Mesentery	Q. Pyloric valve	X. Villi
D. Esophagus	K. Microvilli	R. Rugae	Y. Visceral peritoneum
E. Greater omentum	L. Oral cavity	S. Small intestine	
F Hard palate	M. Parietal peritoneum	T. Soft palate	
G. Haustra	N. Peyer's patches	U. Stomach	

_____ 1. Connects the small intestine to the posterior abdominal wall; looks like lacy curtains

_____ 2. Projections of the intestinal mucosa that increase the surface area

_____ 3. Large collections of lymph nodules found in the submucosa of the small intestine

_____ 4. Folds of the small intestine wall

_____ 5. Two anatomical regions involved in the mechanical breakdown of food

_____ 6. Mixes food in the mouth and initiates swallowing

_____ 7. Common passage for food and air

_____ 8. Three peritoneal modifications

_____ 9. A food chute; has no digestive or absorptive role

_____ 10. Folds of the stomach mucosa and submucosa

_____ 11. Saclike outpocketing of the large intestine wall

_____ 12. Projections of the plasma membrane of a cell that increase the cell's surface area

_____ 13. Prevents food from moving back into the small intestine once it has entered the large intestine

_____ 14. Responsible for most food and water absorption

_____ 15. Primarily involved in water absorption and feces formation

_____ 16. Cul-de-sac between the teeth and lips or cheeks

_____ 17. Blind-ended tube hanging from the cecum

_____ 18. Organ in which protein digestion begins

_____ 19. Membrane that runs from the lesser curvature of the stomach to the liver

_____ 20. Organ into which the stomach empties

_____ 21. Sphincter controlling the movement of food from the stomach into the duodenum

_____ 22. The uvula hangs from its posterior edge

_____ 23. Receives pancreatic juice and bile

_____ 24. Serosa of the abdominal cavity wall

_____ 25. Major site of vitamin (K, B) formation by bacteria

_____ 26. Region, containing two sphincters, through which feces are expelled from the body

_____ 27. Anteriosuperior boundary of the oral cavity; supported by bone

_____ 28. Extends as a double fold from the greater curvature of the stomach; very fat-laden

_____ 29. Superiorly, its muscle is striated; inferiorly, it is smooth

9. The walls of the alimentary canal have four typical layers, as illustrated in Figure 22.2. Identify each layer by placing its correct name in the answer blank before the appropriate description. Select different colors for each layer and color the coding circles and corresponding structures on the figure. Finally, assume the figure shows a cross-sectional view of the small intestine, and label the three structures with leader lines.

_____ ◯ 1. The secretory and absorptive layer

_____ ◯ 2. Layer composed of at least two muscle layers

_____ ◯ 3. Connective tissue layer, containing blood, lymph vessels, and nerves

_____ ◯ 4. Outermost layer of the wall; visceral peritoneum

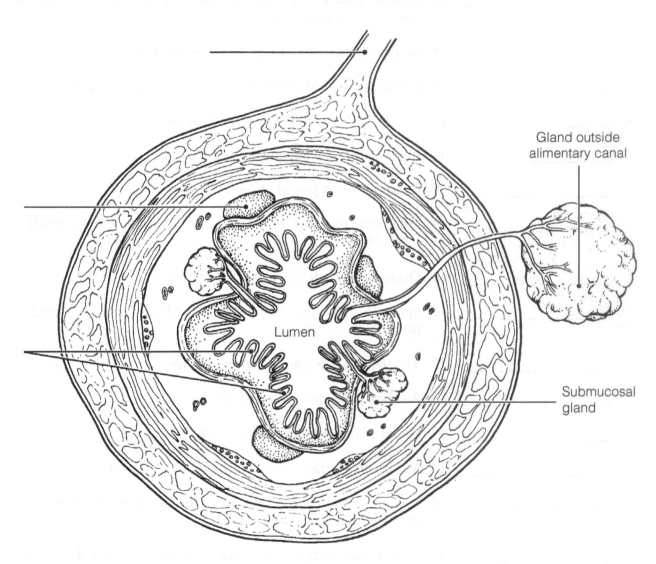

Figure 22.2

PART 2: FUNCTIONAL ANATOMY OF THE DIGESTIVE SYSTEM

1. Figure 22.3 illustrates oral cavity structures. First, identify all structures with leader lines. Then, color the structure that attaches the tongue to the floor of the mouth red, color the portions of the roof of the mouth unsupported by bone blue, color the structures that are essentially masses of lymphatic tissue yellow, and color the structure that contains the bulk of the taste buds pink.

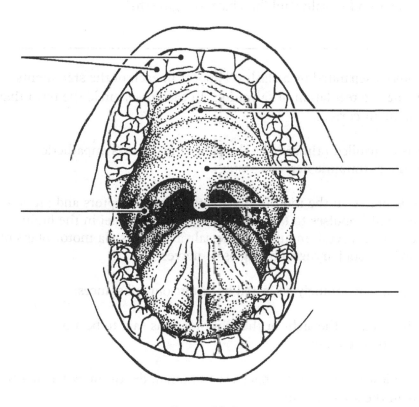

Figure 22.3

2. Answer the following questions concerning the salivary glands and saliva in the spaces provided:

   1. What are four functions of saliva? _____

   _____

   _____

   2. What are the three main pairs of salivary glands, and in what part of the

   oral cavity do the ducts of each gland open? _____

   _____

   _____

3. What are the two main cell types found in salivary glands, and what

   are their secretions? _____

   _____

   _____

4. What enzyme found in saliva inhibits bacterial growth?

   _____

3. Alternative choices separated by a slash (/) appear in each of the statements below concerning the regulation of salivation. In each case, circle the term that makes the statement correct.

   1. Salivation is controlled primarily by the parasympathetic/sympathetic division of the autonomic nervous system.

   2. When food is placed in the mouth, it activates chemoreceptors and presso-receptors to send impulses to the salivatory/gustatory nuclei in the brain stem, which in turn send impulses to the salivary glands via motor fibers of the facial and glossopharyngeal/hypoglossal nerves.

   3. Chemoreceptors are strongly activated by bitter/sour substances.

   4. Salivation induced by the sight or thought of food is said to be a(n) conditioned/intrinsic reflex.

4. Complete the following statements referring to human dentition by writing the missing terms in the answer blanks.

   _____ 1.   The first set of teeth, called the __(1)__ teeth, begin to appear around the age of __(2)__ and usually have begun to be replaced

   _____ 2.   by the age of __(3)__. The __(4)__ teeth are more numerous; that is, there are __(5)__ teeth in the second set as opposed to a total

   _____ 3.   of __(6)__ teeth in the first set. If an adult has a full set of teeth, you can expect to find two __(7)__, one __(8)__, two __(9)__, and

   _____ 4.   three __(10)__ in one side of each jaw. The most posterior molars in each jaw are commonly called __(11)__ teeth.

   _____ 5.

   _____ 6.

   _____ 7.

   _____ 8.

   _____ 9.

   _____ 10.

   _____ 11.

5. Using the key choices, identify each tooth area described below and label the tooth in Figure 22.4. Then select different colors to represent the key structures with coding circles and color them on the figure. Finally, add labels to the figure to identify the crown, gingiva, and root of the tooth.

Key Choices

○ A. Cementum   ○ C. Enamel   ○ E. Pulp

○ B. Dentin   ○ D. Periodontal membrane

_____ 1. Material covering the tooth root

_____ 2. Hardest substance in the body; covers tooth crown

_____ 3. Attaches the tooth to bone and surrounding alveolar structures

_____ 4. Forms the bulk of tooth structure; similar to bone

_____ 5. A collection of blood vessels, nerves, and lymphatics

_____ 6. Cells that produce this substance degenerate after tooth eruption

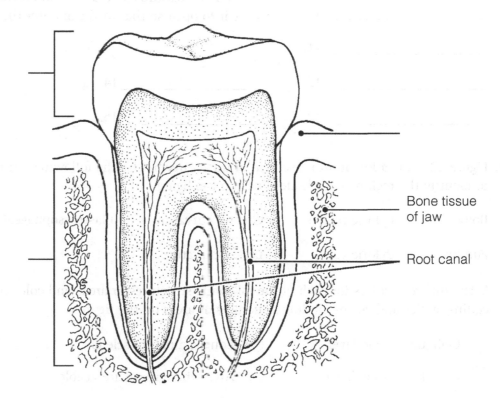

Bone tissue of jaw

Root canal

Figure 22.4

6. Complete the following statements that describe mechanisms of food mixing and movement from the mouth to the stomach. Insert your responses in the answer blanks.

_____ 1.

_____ 2.

_____ 3.

_____ 4.

_____ 5.

_____ 6.

_____ 7.

_____ 8.

_____ 9.

_____ 10.

_____ 11.

_____ 12.   _____ 14.

_____ 13.   _____ 15.

Common pathways for food and air are the __(1)__ , which connects to the mouth, and __(2)__ , which connects to the larynx. Epithelium in this region is __(3)__ , which provides good protection from friction. Three bands of skeletal muscle, the __(4)__ , propel food into the __(5)__ . Entrance to the stomach is guarded by the __(6)__ .

Swallowing, or __(7)__ , occurs in two major phases, the __(8)__ and __(9)__ . During the initial voluntary phase, the __(10)__ is used to push the food into the throat and the __(11)__ rises to close off the nasal passageways. As food is moved involuntarily through the pharynx, the __(12)__ rises to ensure that its passageway is covered by the __(13)__ so that ingested substances do not enter respiratory passages. It is possible to swallow water while standing on your head because the water is carried along the esophagus involuntarily by the process of __(14)__ . The pressure exerted by food on the __(15)__ valve causes it to open so that food can enter the stomach.

7. Figure 22.5A is a longitudinal section of the stomach. Use the following terms to identify the regions with leader lines on the figure.

Body	Pyloric region	Greater curvature	Gastroesophageal valve
Fundus	Pyloric valve	Lesser curvature	

Select different colors for each of the following structures or areas and color the coding circles and corresponding structures or areas on the figure.

◯ Oblique muscle layer   ◯ Longitudinal muscle layer   ◯ Serosa

◯ Circular muscle layer   ◯ Area where rugae are visible

Figure 22.5B shows two types of secretory cells found in gastric glands. Identify the third type, called *chief (or zymogenic) cells*, by choosing a few cells deep in the glands and labeling them appropriately. Then, color the hydrochloric acid–secreting cells red, color the cells that produce mucus yellow, and color those that produce protein-digesting enzymes blue.

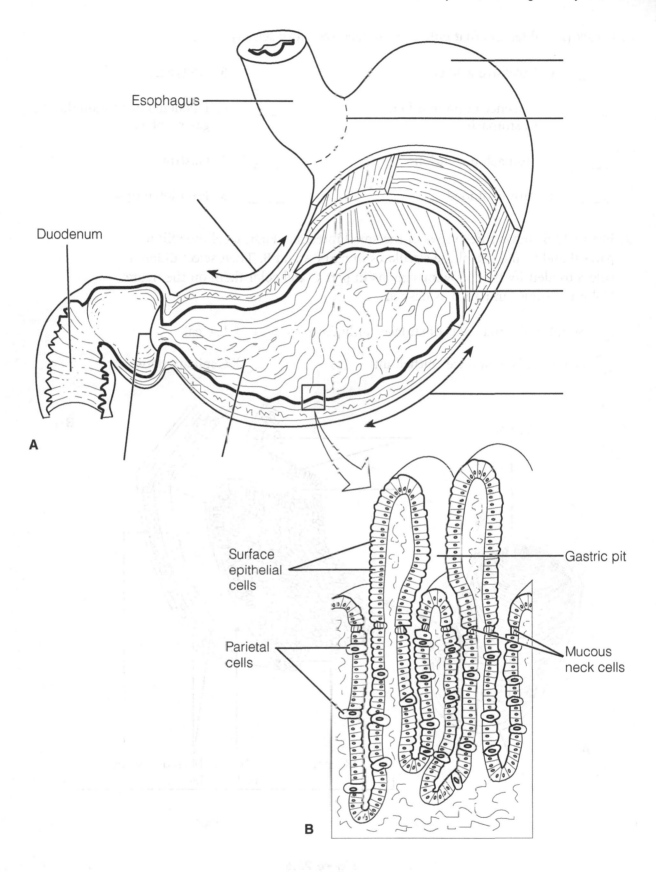

Esophagus

Duodenum

A

Surface
epithelial
cells

Gastric pit

Parietal
cells

Mucous
neck cells

B

Figure 22.5

8. Check (✓) all factors that enhance stomach secretory activity.

_____ 1. Excessive acidity

_____ 2. Presence of protein foods in stomach

_____ 3. Stomach distention

_____ 4. Aroma of food

_____ 5. Acetylcholine

_____ 6. Duodenal distention during gastric phase

_____ 7. Gastrin

_____ 8. Emotional upset

9. Figure 22.6 shows three views of the small intestine. First, label the villi in parts B and C and the plicae circulares in parts A and B. Then select different colors to identify the following regions in part C and color them on the figure. Color the tunics in part B as desired.

◯ Simple columnar cells of surface epithelium

◯ Goblet cells of surface epithelium

◯ Lacteal

◯ Capillary network

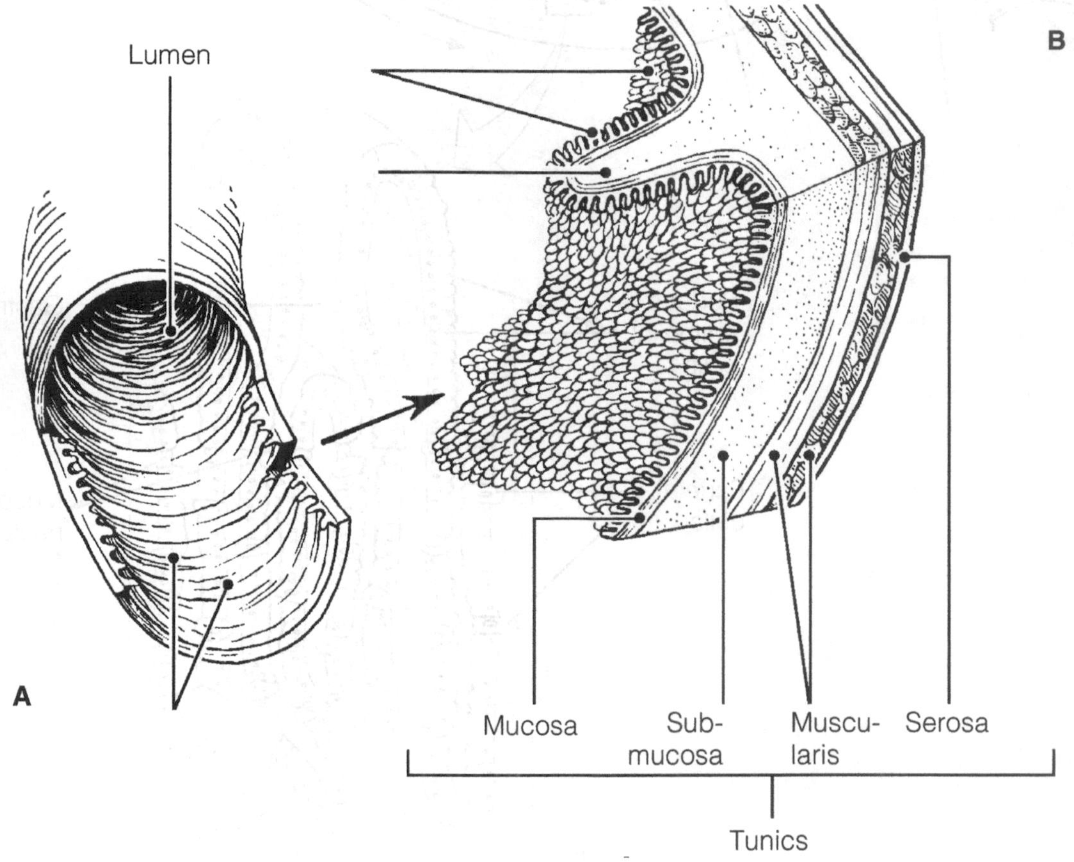

Figure 22.6

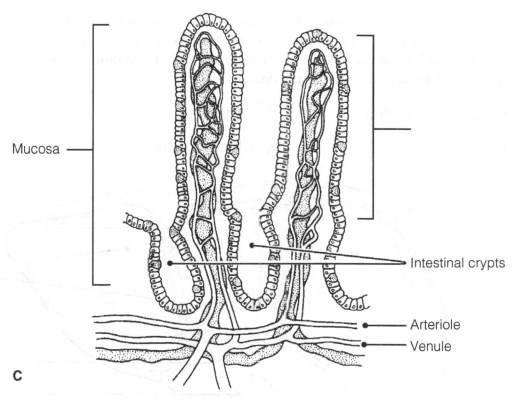

Mucosa

Intestinal crypts

Arteriole

Venule

C

Figure 22.6 (continued)

10. Match the mesenteries in Column B with their descriptions in Column A.

Column A	Column B
_____ 1. Lies closely apposed to serous lining of anterior abdominal cavity	A. Falciform ligament
_____ 2. Divides liver into lobes	B. Mesentery proper
_____ 3. Fan-shaped intestinal membrane	C. Mesocolon
_____ 4. Attaches part of large intestine to body wall	D. Greater omentum

11. Circle the term that does not belong in each of the following groupings.

1. HCl secretion   Acetylcholine   Histamine   Secretin   Gastrin

2. Gastric emptying   Slowed by fats   Enterogastrone   Solid foods

3. Cephalic phase   Reflex phase   Intestinal phase   Psychological stimuli

4. Saliva   IgA   Lysozyme   HCl   Growth factor

5. Local reflexes   Vagovagal reflexes   Parasympathetic   Sympathetic

6. Pacemaker cells   Small intestine   Esophagus   Stomach

7. Stomach absorption   Lipid-soluble drugs   Salts   Aspirin   Alcohol

12. Three accessory organs are illustrated in Figure 22.7. Identify each of the three organs, their ducts, and the ligament with leader lines on the figure. Then select different colors for the following structures and color the coding circles and the corresponding structures on the figure.

◯ Common hepatic duct   ◯ Bile duct

◯ Cystic duct   ◯ Pancreatic duct

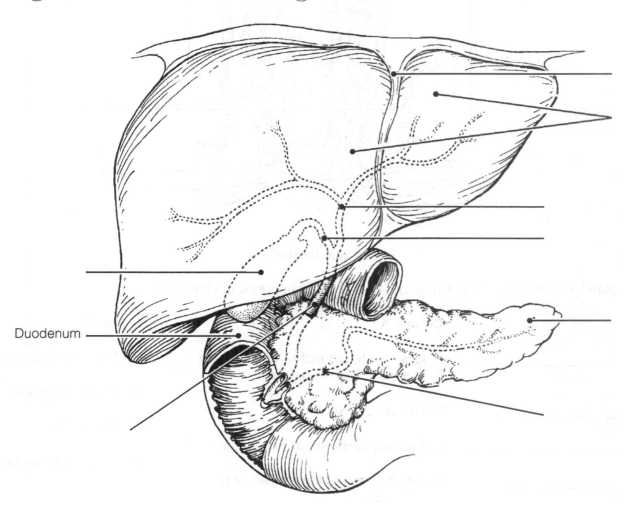

Duodenum

Figure 22.7

13. List the three major vessels of the portal triad: _____, _____,

and _____. Describe the location of the triads relative to the liver lobules.

_____

_____

14. Hormonal stimuli are important in digestive activities that occur in the stomach and small intestine. Using the key choices, identify the hormones that function as described in the following statements.

Key Choices

A. Cholecystokinin   B. Gastrin   C. Secretin   D. Somatostatin

_____ 1. These two hormones stimulate the pancreas to release its secretions.

_____ 2. This hormone stimulates increased production of gastric juice.

_____ 3. This hormone causes the gallbladder to release stored bile.

_____ 4. This hormone causes the liver to increase its output of bile.

_____ 5. These hormones inhibit gastric mobility and secretory activity.

15. This exercise concerns some aspects of food breakdown in the digestive tract. Using the key choices, select the appropriate terms to complete the following statements.

Key Choices

A. Bicarbonate-rich fluid   D. HCl (hydrochloric acid)   G. Mucus

B. Chewing   E. Hormonal stimulus   H. Psychological stimulus

C. Churning   F. Mechanical stimulus

_____ 1. The means of mechanical food breakdown in the mouth is __(1)__.

_____ 2. The fact that the mere thought of a relished food can make your mouth water is an example of __(2)__.

_____ 3. Many people chew gum to increase saliva formation when their mouth is dry. This type of stimulus is a __(3)__.

_____ 4. Since living cells of the stomach (and everywhere) are largely protein, it is amazing that they are not digested by the activity of stomach enzymes. The most important means of stomach protection is the __(4)__ it produces.

_____ 5. The third layer of smooth muscle found in the stomach wall allows mixing and mechanical breakdown by __(5)__.

_____ 6. The small intestine is protected from the corrosive action of HCl in chyme by __(6)__, which is ducted in from the pancreas.

16. Figure 22.8 shows a view of the large intestine. First, label a haustrum, the ileocecal valve, the external anal sphincter, the hepatic and splenic flexures, and the transverse mesocolon. Then, select different colors to identify the following parts in the figure:

◯ Anal canal	◯ Appendix	◯ Ascending colon
◯ Cecum	◯ Rectum	◯ Descending colon
◯ Sigmoid colon	◯ Teniae coli	◯ Transverse colon

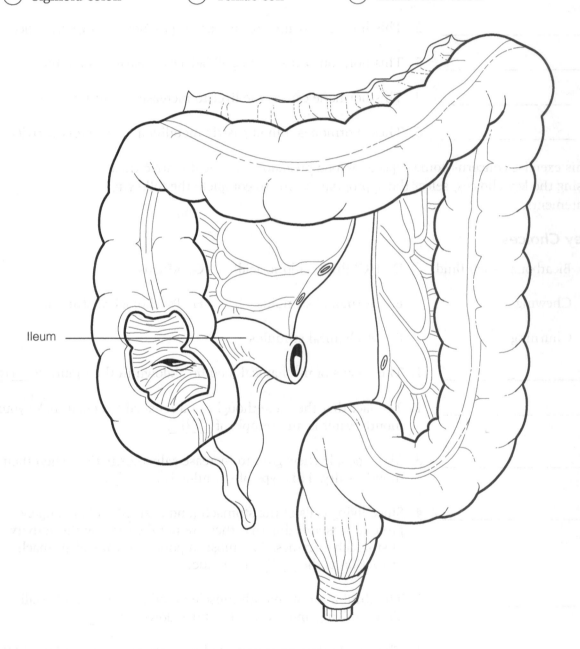

Ileum

Figure 22.8

17. Complete the paragraph relating to digestive system mobility by writing the missing terms in the answer blanks.

_____ 1.

_____ 2.

_____ 3.

_____ 4.

_____ 5.

_____ 6.

_____ 7.

_____ 8.

The two major types of movements that occur in the small intestine are __(1)__ and __(2)__. One of these movements, __(3)__, acts to continually mix the food with digestive juices and, strangely, also plays the major role in propelling foods along the tract. Another type of movement seen only in the large intestine, __(4)__, occurs infrequently and acts to move feces over relatively long distances toward the anus. The presence of feces in the __(5)__ excites stretch receptors so that the __(6)__ reflex is initiated. Irritation of the gastrointestinal tract by drugs or bacteria might stimulate the __(7)__ center in the medulla, causing __(8)__, which is essentially a reverse peristalsis.

18. Identify the following pathological conditions using the key choices.

Key Choices

A. Ankyloglossia   C. Constipation   E. Gallstones   G. Hiatal hernia   I. Peritonitis

B. Appendicitis   D. Diarrhea   F. Gingivitis   H. Jaundice   J. Ulcer

_____ 1. Inflammation of the abdominal serosa

_____ 2. Condition that may lead to reflux of acidic gastric juice into the esophagus causing heartburn due to esophagitis

_____ 3. Usually indicates liver problems or blockage of the biliary ducts

_____ 4. An erosion of the stomach or duodenal mucosa

_____ 5. Passage of watery stools

_____ 6. Causes severe epigastric pain; associated with prolonged storage of bile in the gallbladder

_____ 7. Inability to pass feces; often a result of poor bowel habits

_____ 8. Inflammation of the gums

_____ 9. Person is "tongue tied" because of a short lingual frenulum

PART 3: PHYSIOLOGY OF CHEMICAL DIGESTION AND ABSORPTION

1. Various types of foods are ingested in the diet and broken down to their building blocks. Use the key choices to complete the following statements. For some questions, more than one term is correct.

Key Choices

A. Amino acids	E. Fatty acids	H. Glucose	K. Meat/fish
B. Bread/pasta	F. Fructose	I. Lactose	L. Starch
C. Cheese/cream	G. Galactose	J. Maltose	M. Sucrose
D. Cellulose			

_____ 1. Examples of dietary carbohydrates

_____ 2. The three common simple sugars in our diet

_____ 3. The most important of the simple sugars; referred to as "blood sugar"

_____ 4. Disaccharides

_____ 5. The only important *digestible* polysaccharide

_____ 6. An indigestible polysaccharide that aids elimination because it adds bulk to the diet

_____ 7. Protein-rich foods include these two food groups

_____ 8. Protein foods must be broken down to these units before they can be absorbed

_____ 9. Fats are broken down to these building blocks and glycerol

2. Dietary substances capable of being absorbed are listed below. If the substance is *most often* absorbed from the digestive tract by active transport processes, write A in the blank. If it is usually absorbed passively (by diffusion or osmosis), write P in the blank. In addition, circle the substance that is *most likely* to be absorbed into a lacteal rather than into the capillary bed of the villus.

_____ 1. Water　　　_____ 3. Simple sugars　　　_____ 5. Electrolytes

_____ 2. Amino acids　　　_____ 4. Fatty acids

3. This exercise concerns chemical food breakdown and absorption in the digestive tract. Using the key choices, select the appropriate terms to complete the statements.

Key Choices

A. Amino acids

B. Bile

C. Brush border enzymes

D. Capillary

E. Fatty acids

F. Glycerol

G. HCl

H. Intrinsic factor

I. Lacteal

J. Lipases

K. Monosaccharides

L. Monoglycerides

M. Nucleic acids

N. Pepsin

O. Proteases

P. Rennin

Q. Salivary amylase

R. Vitamin D

_____ 1. Starch digestion begins in the mouth when __(1)__ is ducted in by the salivary glands.

_____ 2. Protein foods are largely acted on in the stomach by __(2)__.

_____ 3. A milk-coagulating enzyme found in children but not usually in adults is __(3)__.

_____ 4. Intestinal enzymes are called __(4)__.

_____ 5. For the stomach protein-digesting enzymes to become active, __(5)__ is needed.

_____ 6. A nonenzyme substance that emulsifies fats is __(6)__.

_____ 7. Trypsin, chymotrypsin, aminopeptidase, and dipeptidase are all __(7)__.

_____ 8. Chylomicrons are the products that ultimately enter the __(8)__ when fats are being digested and absorbed.

_____ 9. Unlike most other foodstuffs, __(9)__ are broken down even further than their building blocks. The enzyme(s) involved in the final

_____ 10. steps of that breakdown process is/are __(10)__.

_____ 11. Required for calcium absorption is __(11)__.

_____ 12. _____ 13. Transport for (12–14) is active and often coupled to the Na$^+$ pump.

_____ 14.

4. Circle the term that does not belong in each of the following groupings.

   1. Trypsin   Dextrinase   Maltase   Aminopeptidase   Intestinal enzymes

   2. Micelles   Accelerate lipid absorption   Bile salts   Chylomicrons

   3. Ferritin   Mucosal iron barrier   Lost during hemorrhage   Iron storage

   4. Dextrinase   Glucoamylase   Maltase   Nuclease   Amylase

   5. Hydrolysis   Bond splitting   Removal of water   pH specific

   6. Chymotrypsin   Alkaline pH   Pepsin   Trypsin   Dipeptidase

   7. Vitamin A   Vitamin C   Passively absorbed   Vitamin B_{12} Vitamin D

5. Fill in the table below with the specific information indicated in the headings:

Enzyme	Substrate	Product	Secreted by	Active in
Salivary amylase				
Pepsin				
Trypsin				
Dipeptidase				
Pancreatic amylase				
Lipase				
Maltase				
Carboxypeptidase				
Nuclease				

THE INCREDIBLE JOURNEY

A Visualization Exercise for the Digestive System

. . . the passage beneath you opens, and you fall into a huge chamber with mountainous folds.

1. Complete the following narrative by writing the missing terms in the answer blanks.

_____ 1.

_____ 2.

_____ 3.

_____ 4.

_____ 5.

_____ 6.

_____ 7.

_____ 8.

_____ 9.

_____ 10.

In this journey, you are to travel through the digestive tract as far as the appendix and then await further instructions. You are miniaturized as usual and provided with a wetsuit to protect you from being digested during your travels. You have a very easy entry into your host's open mouth. You look around and notice the glistening pink lining, or __(1)__ , and the perfectly cared-for teeth. Within a few seconds, the lips part and you find yourself surrounded by bread. You quickly retreat to the safety of the __(2)__ between the teeth and the cheek to prevent getting chewed. From there you watch with fascination as a number of openings squirt fluid into the chamber, and the __(3)__ heaves and rolls, mixing the bread with the fluid. As the bread begins to disappear, you decide that the fluid contains the enzyme __4)__ .

You then walk toward the back of the oral cavity, and suddenly you find yourself being carried along by a squeezing motion of the walls around you. The name given to this propelling motion is __(5)__ . As you are carried helplessly downward, you see two openings, the __(6)__ and the __(7)__ , below you. Just as you are about to straddle the solid area between them to stop your descent, the structure to your left moves quickly upward, and a trapdoorlike organ, the __(8)__ , flaps over the anterior opening. Down you go into the dark, yawning posterior opening seeing nothing. Then the passage beneath you opens, and you fall into a huge chamber with mountainous folds. Obviously, you have reached the __(9)__ . The folds are very slippery, and you conclude that it must be the __(10)__ coat that you read about earlier. As you survey your surroundings, juices begin to gurgle into the chamber from pits in the "floor," and your face begins to sting and smart. You cannot

_____ 11.   seem to escape this caustic fluid, and you conclude that it must
be very dangerous to your skin since it contains __(11)__ and

_____ 12.   __(12)__. You reach down and scoop up some of the slippery substance from the folds and smear it on your face, confident that

_____ 13.   if it can protect this organ it can protect you as well! Relieved,
you begin to slide toward the organ's far exit and squeeze

_____ 14.   through the tight __(13)__ valve into the next organ. In the dim
light, you see lumps of cellulose lying at your feet and large fat

_____ 15.   globules dancing lightly about. A few seconds later, your observations are interrupted by a wave of fluid pouring into the

_____ 16.   chamber from an opening high in the wall above you. The large
fat globules begin to fall apart, and you decide that this enzyme

_____ 17.   flood has to contain __(14)__ and the opening must be the duct
from the __(15)__. As you move quickly away to escape the del-

uge, you lose your footing and find yourself on a rollercoaster ride—twisting, coiling, turning, and
diving through the lumen of this active organ. As you move, you are stroked by velvety, fingerlike
projections of the wall, the __(16)__. Abruptly your ride comes to a halt as you are catapulted
through the __(17)__ valve and fall into the appendix. Headquarters informs you that you are at
the end of your journey. Your exit now depends on your own ingenuity and your sympathy for
your host.

CHALLENGING YOURSELF

At the Clinic

1. A young boy is brought to the clinic wincing with pain whenever he opens his
   mouth. His parents believe he dislocated his jaw, which is obviously swollen on
   the left side. Luckily, the clinic has seen a number of similar cases in the past
   week, so the diagnosis is quick. What is the diagnosis?

2. Marv comments to his doctor at the clinic that he gets a "full," very uncomfort-
   able feeling in his chest after every meal, as if the food were lodged there instead
   of traveling to his stomach. The doctor states that the description fits the condition called achalasia, in which the valve between the esophagus and stomach fails
   to open. What valve is involved?

3. Mr. Ashe, a man in his mid-60s, comes to the clinic complaining of heartburn. Questioning by the clinic staff reveals that the severity of his attacks increases when he lies down after eating a heavy meal. The man is about 50 pounds overweight. What is your diagnosis? Without treatment, what conditions might develop?

4. A young woman is put through an extensive battery of tests to determine the cause of her "stomach pains." She is diagnosed with gastric ulcers. An antihistamine drug is prescribed and she is sent home. What is the mechanism of her medication? What life-threatening problems can result from a poorly managed ulcer? Why did the clinic doctor warn the woman not to take aspirin?

5. Continuing from the previous question, the woman's ulcer got worse. She started complaining of back pain. The physician discovered that the back pain occurred because the pancreas was now damaged. Use logic to deduce how a perforating gastric ulcer could come to damage the pancreas.

6. An elderly man, found unconscious in the alley behind a local restaurant, is brought to the clinic in a patrol car. His abdomen is distended, his skin and scleras are yellow, and he reeks of alcohol. What do you surmise is the cause of his condition and what terms are used to describe the various aspects of his appearance?

7. Duncan, an inquisitive 8-year-old, saw his grandfather's dentures soaking overnight in a glass. He asked his grandfather how his teeth had fallen out. Reconstruct the kind of story the man is likely to have told.

8. A feverish 12-year-old girl named Kelly is brought to the clinic complaining of pain in the lower right abdominal quadrant. According to her parents, for the past week she has been eating poorly and often vomits when she does eat. What condition do you suspect? What treatment will she need? What complication will occur if treatment is given too late?

9. Eva, a woman in her 50s, complains of bloating, cramping, and diarrhea when she drinks milk. What is the cause of her complaint and what is a solution?

10. Mr. Erickson complains of diarrhea after eating and relates that it is most pronounced when he eats starches. Subsequent dietary variations reveal intolerance to wheat and other grains, but no problem with rice. What condition do you suspect?

11. A 21-year-old man with severe appendicitis did not seek treatment in time and died a week after his abdominal pain and fever began. Explain why appendicitis can quickly lead to death.

12. Pancreatitis often results from a gallstone. Another major cause of pancreatitis is chronic alcoholism, which can lead to precipitation of protein in the pancreatic duct. Why do you think such protein precipitation can result in problems?

Stop and Think

1. How do the following terms relate to the function of the smooth muscle of the digestive system? gap junction, stress-relaxation response, nonstriated

2. What happens to salivary amylase in the stomach? Pepsin in the duodenum?

3. How would the release of histamine by gastric enteroendocrine cells improve the *absorption* of nutrients?

4. Which would be more effective: a single "megadose" of calcium supplement once a day or a smaller supplement with each meal?

5. Trace the digestion and absorption of fats from their entrance into the duodenum to their arrival at the liver.

6. Clients are instructed not to eat before having blood tests run. How would a lab technician know if someone "cheated" and ate a fatty meal a few hours before having his blood drawn?

7. Why does liver impairment result in edema?

8. The location of the rapidly dividing, undifferentiated epithelial cells differs in the stomach and intestine. (a) Compare the locations of these cells in the two digestive organs. (b) What is the basic function of these dividing cells?

9. Bianca went on a trip to the Bahamas during spring vacation and did not study enough for her anatomy test that was scheduled early in the following week. On the test, she mixed up the following pairs of structures: (a) serous cells and serous membranes, (b) caries and canaliculi (bile canaliculi), (c) anal canal and anus, (d) diverticulosis and diverticulitis, (e) hepatic vein and hepatic portal vein. Can you help her by defining and differentiating all these sound-alike structures?

10. Name three organelles that are abundant in hepatocytes and explain how each of these organelles contributes to liver functions.

COVERING ALL YOUR BASES

Multiple Choice

Select the best answer or answers from the choices given.

1. Which of the following terms are synonyms?

    A. Gastrointestinal tract

    B. Digestive system

    C. Digestive tract

    D. Alimentary canal

2. A digestive organ that is not part of the alimentary canal is the:

    A. stomach   D. large intestine

    B. liver   E. pharynx

    C. small intestine

3. An organ that is not covered by a visceral peritoneum is the:

    A. stomach   C. thoracic esophagus

    B. jejunum   D. transverse colon

4. The GI tube layer responsible for the actions of segmentation and peristalsis is:

    A. serosa   C. muscularis externa

    B. mucosa   D. submucosa

5. The nerve plexus that stimulates secretion of digestive juices is the:

    A. submucosal plexus

    B. myenteric plexus

    C. subserous plexus

    D. local plexuses

6. Organs that are partly or wholly retroperitoneal include:

    A. stomach   C. duodenum

    B. pancreas   D. colon

7. Which of the following are part of the splanchnic circulation?

    A. Hepatic artery

    B. Hepatic vein

    C. Hepatic portal vein

    D. Splenic artery

8. Which alimentary canal tunic has the greatest abundance of lymph nodules?

    A. Mucosa   C. Serosa

    B. Muscularis   D. Submucosa

9. Proteins secreted in saliva include:

   A. mucin C. lysozyme

   B. amylase D. IgA

10. Which of these tissue types is most cellular?

    A. Enamel C. Dentin

    B. Pulp D. Cementum

11. The closure of which valve is assisted by the diaphragm?

    A. Ileocecal

    B. Pyloric

    C. Gastroesophageal

    D. Upper esophageal

12. Stratified squamous epithelium lines the:

    A. cardia of stomach C. anal canal

    B. esophagus D. rectum

13. Smooth muscle is found in the:

    A. tongue

    B. pharynx

    C. esophagus

    D. external anal sphincter

14. Rugae in the stomach encompass which tunics?

    A. Mucosa C. Serosa

    B. Muscularis D. Submucosa

15. Where in the stomach do the strongest peristaltic waves occur?

    A. Body C. Fundus

    B. Cardia D. Pylorus

16. The greater omentum:

    A. contains lymph nodes

    B. covers most of the anterior peritoneal cavity

    C. contains fat deposits

    D. attaches to the liver

17. Carbonic anhydrate is contained in:

    A. parietal cells of gastric glands

    B. chief cells of gastric glands

    C. pancreatic acini cells

    D. pancreatic duct cells

18. Sometimes the only treatment for chronic ileitis is surgical removal. What functions will be lost?

    A. Vitamin B_{12} absorption

    B. Absorption of calcium and iron

    C. Normal resistance to bacterial infection

    D. Enterohepatic circulation

19. Which statement is true about the peritoneal cavity?

    A. It is the same thing as the abdomino-pelvic cavity.

    B. This large cavity is filled with air.

    C. Like the pleural and pericardial cavities, it is a potential space containing serous fluid.

    D. It contains the pancreas and all the duodenum.

20. Which of these organs lies in the right hypochondriac region of the abdomen?

    A. Stomach C. Cecum

    B. Spleen D. Liver

21. Which phases of gastric secretion depend (at least in part) on the vagus nerve?

    A. Cephalic

    B. Gastric

    C. Intestinal (stimulatory)

    D. Intestinal (inhibitory)

22. Which of the following is/are classified as enterogastrone(s)?

    A. Gastrin C. CCK

    B. GIP D. Secretin

23. After gastrectomy, it will be necessary to supplement:
    A. pepsin
    B. vitamin B_{12}
    C. gastrin
    D. intrinsic factor

24. Villi:
    A. are composed of both mucosa and submucosa
    B. contain lacteals
    C. can contract to increase circulation of lymph
    D. are largest in the duodenum

25. Brush border enzymes include:
    A. dipeptidase
    B. lactase
    C. enterokinase
    D. lipase

26. The portal triads include:
    A. branch of the hepatic artery
    B. central vein
    C. branch of the hepatic portal vein
    D. bile duct

27. Which of the following are in greater abundance in the hepatic vein than in the hepatic portal vein?
    A. Urea
    B. Aging RBCs
    C. Plasma proteins
    D. Fat-soluble vitamins

28. Jaundice may be a result of:
    A. hepatitis
    B. blockage of enterohepatic circulation
    C. biliary calculi in the common bile duct
    D. removal of the gallbladder

29. Release of CCK leads to:
    A. contraction of smooth muscle in the duodenal papilla
    B. increased activity of hepatocytes
    C. activity of the muscularis of the gallbladder
    D. exocytosis of zymogenic granules in pancreatic acini

30. The pH of chyme entering the duodenum is adjusted by:
    A. bile
    B. intestinal juice
    C. secretions from pancreatic acini
    D. secretions from pancreatic ducts

31. Peristalsis in the small intestine begins:
    A. with the cephalic phase of stomach activity
    B. when chyme enters the duodenum
    C. when CCK is released
    D. when most nutrients have been absorbed

32. Relaxation of the ileocecal sphincter is triggered by:
    A. gastrin
    B. enterogastrones
    C. presence of bile salts in the blood
    D. gastroileal reflex

33. Relaxation of the teniae coli would result in loss of:
    A. haustra
    B. splenic and hepatic flexures
    C. rectal valves
    D. anal columns

34. Diverticulitis is associated with:
    A. too much bulk in the diet
    B. too little bulk in the diet
    C. gluten intolerance
    D. lactose intolerance

35. Which of the following are associated with the complete digestion of starch?
    A. Maltose
    B. Sucrose
    C. Amylase
    D. Oligosaccharides

36. Which of the following are tied to sodium transport?
    A. Glucose
    B. Fructose
    C. Galactose
    D. Amino acids

37. Endocytosis of proteins in newborns accounts for:

    A. absorption of casein

    B. absorption of antibodies

    C. some food allergies

    D. absorption of butterfat

38. Cell organelles in the intestinal epithelium that are directly involved in lipid digestion and absorption include:

    A. smooth ER   C. secretory vesicles

    B. Golgi apparatus   D. lysosomes

39. Excess iron is stored primarily in the:

    A. liver

    B. bone marrow

    C. duodenal epithelium

    D. blood

40. Which of the following correctly describes the flow of blood through the classical liver lobule and beyond? (More than one choice is correct.)

    A. Portal vein branch to sinusoids to central vein to hepatic vein to inferior vena cava

    B. Porta hepatis to hepatic vein to portal vein

    C. Portal vein branch to central vein to hepatic vein to sinusoids

    D. Hepatic artery branch to sinusoids to central vein to hepatic vein

41. Difficult swallowing is called:

    A. ascites   C. ileus

    B. dysphagia   D. stenosis

42. A digestive organ that has a head, neck, body, and tail is the:

    A. pancreas   C. greater omentum

    B. gallbladder   D. stomach

43. The hepatopancreatic ampulla lies in the wall of the:

    A. liver   C. duodendum

    B. pancreas   D. stomach

44. Two structures that produce alkaline secretions that neutralize the acidic stomach chyme as it enters the duodendum are:

    A. intestinal flora and pancreatic acinar cells

    B. gastric glands and gastric pits

    C. lining epithelium of the intestine and Paneth cells

    D. pancreatic ducts and duodenal glands

45. A 3-year-old girl was rewarded with a hug because she was now completely toilet trained. Which muscle had she learned to control?

    A. Levator ani

    B. Internal anal sphincter

    C. Internal and external obliques

    D. External anal sphincter

46. Which cell type fits this description? It occurs in the stomach mucosa, contains abundant mitochondria and many microvilli, and pumps hydrogen ions.

    A. Absorptive cell   C. Goblet cell

    B. Parietal cell   D. Mucous neck cell

47. The only feature in this list that is shared by both the large and small intestines is:

    A. intestinal crypts   D. teniae coli

    B. Peyer's patches   E. haustra

    C. circular folds   F. intestinal villi

Word Dissection

For each of the following word roots, fill in the literal meaning and give an example, using a word found in this chapter.

Word root	Translation	Example
1. aliment		
2. cec		
3. chole		
4. chyme		
5. decid		
6. duoden		
7. enter		
8. epiplo		
9. eso		
10. falci		
11. fec		
12. fren		
13. gaster		
14. gest		
15. glut		
16. haustr		
17. hiat		
18. ile		
19. jejun		
20. micell		
21. oligo		
22. oment		
23. otid		

Word root	Translation	Example
24. pep	_____	_____
25. plic	_____	_____
26. proct	_____	_____
27. pylor	_____	_____
28. ruga	_____	_____
29. sorb	_____	_____
30. splanch	_____	_____
31. stalsis	_____	_____
32. teni	_____	_____

23

NUTRITION, METABOLISM, AND BODY THERMOGENESIS

Student Objectives

When you have completed the exercises in this chapter, you will have accomplished the following objectives:

Nutrition

1. Define *nutrient, essential nutrient,* and *calorie.*
2. List the six major nutrient categories. Note important sources and main cellular uses of each.
3. Distinguish between nutritionally complete and incomplete proteins.
4. Define *nitrogen balance* and indicate possible causes of positive and negative nitrogen balance.
5. Distinguish between fat-and water-soluble vitamins, and list the vitamins in each group.
6. For each vitamin, list important sources, body functions, and consequences of its deficit or excess.
7. List minerals essential for health; note important dietary sources and describe how each is used.

Metabolism

8. Define *metabolism.* Explain how catabolism and anabolism differ.
9. Define *oxidation* and *reduction* and note the importance of these reactions in metabolism. Indicate the role of coenzymes used in cellular oxidation reactions.
10. Explain the difference between substrate-level phosphorylation and oxidative phosphorylation.
11. Follow the oxidation of glucose in body cells. Summarize the important events and products of glycolysis, the Krebs cycle, and electron transport.
12. Define *glycogenesis, glycogenolysis,* and *gluconeogenesis.*

13. Describe the process by which fatty acids are oxidized for energy.
14. Define *ketone bodies,* and indicate the stimulus for their formation.
15. Describe how amino acids are metabolized for energy.
16. Describe the need for protein synthesis in body cells.
17. Explain the concept of amino acid or carbohydrate–fat pools and describe pathways by which substances in these pools can be interconverted.
18. List important events of absorptive and postabsorptive states, and explain how these events are regulated.
19. Describe several metabolic functions of the liver.
20. Differentiate between LDLs and HDLs relative to their structures and major roles in the body.

Energy Balance

21. Explain what is meant by body energy balance.
22. Describe some current theories of food intake regulation.
23. Define *basal metabolic rate* and *total metabolic rate.* Name factors that influence each.
24. Describe how body temperature is regulated, and indicate the common mechanisms regulating heat production/retention and heat loss from the body.

In this chapter you will complete the studies of digestion and absorption presented in Chapter 22 by examining in detail the nature of nutrients and the roles they play in meeting the body's various needs. The breakdown products resulting from digestion of large nutrient molecules enter the cells. In cells, metabolic pathways may lead to the extraction of energy, the synthesis of new or larger molecules, or the interchange of parts of molecules. Unusable residues of molecules are eliminated as waste.

Subjects for study and review in Chapter 23 include nutrition, metabolism, control of the absorptive and postabsorptive states, the role of the liver, the regulation of body temperature, and important developmental aspects of metabolism.

BUILDING THE FRAMEWORK

Nutrition

1. Respond to the following questions by writing your answers in the answer blanks.

   1. Name the six categories of nutrients._____

   _____

   2. What is meant by the term *essential nutrients*? _____

   _____

   3. Define the unit used to measure the energy value of foods._____

   _____

   4. Which carbohydrate is used by cells as the major ready source of energy? _____

   5. Which two types of cells rely almost entirely for their energy needs on the carbohydrate

      named in question 4? _____

   6. What is meant by the term *empty calories*? _____

   _____

   7. Name the major dietary source of cholesterol. _____

   8. Which fatty acid(s) cannot be synthesized by the liver and must be ingested as a lipid?

   _____

9. Define *complete protein*. _____

_____

_____

10. What is meant by the term *nitrogen balance*? _____

_____

_____

11. Name the two major uses of proteins synthesized in the body. _____

_____

12. What is the function of most vitamins in the body? _____

_____

13. Which organ chemically processes nearly every category of nutrient? _____

14. Which two minerals account for most of the weight of the body's minerals?

_____

15. Which food category makes foods more tender or creamy and makes us feel full and

satisfied? _____

2. Several descriptive statements concerning vitamins and the consequences
of their excess and deficit appear below. Use the key choices to correctly
identify each vitamin considered.

Key Choices

A. Vitamin A	E. Vitamin B_{12}	H. Vitamin E	K. Folic acid
B. Vitamin B_1	F. Vitamin C	I. Vitamin K	L. Niacin
C. Vitamin B_2	G. Vitamin D	J. Biotin	M. Pantothenic acid
D. Vitamin B_6			

_____ 1. Most is synthesized in the colon by resident bacteria; essential for the liver's synthesis of clotting proteins.

_____ 2. The most complex vitamin; contains cobalt; an essential coenzyme for DNA synthesis and production of choline.

_____ 3. Also called pyridoxine; involved in amino acid metabolism; excess causes neurological defects (loss of sensation, etc.).

_____ 4. Part of coenzyme cocarboxylase; deficit results in beriberi.

_____ 5. Chemically related to sex hormones

_____ 6. Best extrinsic source is fortified milk; also made in the skin from cholesterol; deficit results in rickets in children and osteomalacia in adults.

_____ 7. _____ 8. _____ 9. _____ 10. Fat-soluble vitamins.

_____ 11. Functions in the body in the form of coenzyme A; essential for oxidation reactions and fat synthesis.

_____ 12. Part of the coenzyme NAD required for many metabolic reactions; deficit results in pellagra.

_____ 13. Found in large amounts in citrus fruits, strawberries, and tomatoes; essential for connective tissue matrix synthesis, blood clotting.

_____ 14. The vitamin of vision; required for photopigment synthesis; deficit results in night blindness, clouding of cornea.

_____ 15. Part of the coenzyme FAD; named for its similarity to ribose sugar; deficit causes cheilosis.

_____ 16. Required for erythropoiesis; deficit causes macrocytic anemia.

_____ 17. _____ 18. _____ 19. Act as antioxidants to disarm free radicals in the body.

3. Match the minerals listed in the key choices to the appropriate descriptions. (*Note:* Not all of the trace minerals have been considered.)

Key Choices

A. Calcium	C. Iodine	E. Magnesium	G. Potassium	I. Sulfur
B. Chlorine	D. Iron	F. Phosphorus	H. Sodium	J. Zinc

_____ 1. Required for normal growth, wound healing, taste, and smell

_____ 2. Concentrates in the thyroid gland; essential for T_3 and T_4 synthesis

_____ 3. Essential component of many proteins (e.g., insulin) as part of -S–S- bonds; found in virtually all of the denser connective tissues as part of the ground substance

_____ 4. In the anion part of the calcium salts found in bone

_____ 5. Principal intracellular cation; excesses result in muscle weakness and cardiac abnormalities

_____ 6. The most abundant cation in extracellular fluid; a major factor in determining fluid shifts in the body; excesses lead to hypertension in some cases

_____ 7. Its ion is the major extracellular anion

_____ 8. An essential component of hemoglobin and some cytochromes; excesses cause liver damage

_____ 9. Part of coenzymes that act in hydrolysis of ATP; excesses lead to diarrhea

4. Circle the term that does not belong in each of the following groupings.

1. Neutral fats   Triglycerides   Trisaccharides   Triacylglycerols

2. Meats   Eggs   Milk   Nuts   Fish

3. Mineral-rich foods   Vegetables   Fats   Milk   Legumes

4. Coenzymes B_2 Niacin   Vitamin C   Biotin

5. K^+ Osmotic pressure of blood Na^+ Cl^-

6. Stored for long-term use   Amino acids   Triacylglycerols   Glycogen

7. Vitamin D   Must be ingested   Ultraviolet radiation   Skin

8. Copper   Iron   Hemoglobin synthesis   Zinc

9. 0.8 g/kg of body weight   About 2 oz   About 16 oz

    Minimum daily requirement of protein

10. Catabolic hormones   Anabolic hormones   Sex hormones   Pituitary growth hormones

5. Using the key choices, identify the foodstuffs used by cells in the following descriptions of cellular functions.

Key Choices

A. Carbohydrates   B. Fats   C. Proteins

_____ 1. The most-used substance for producing the energy-rich ATP

_____ 2. Important in building myelin sheaths and cell membranes

_____ 3. Tend to be conserved by cells

_____ 4. The second most important food source for making cellular energy

_____ 5. Form insulating deposits around body organs and beneath the skin

_____ 6. Used to make the bulk of structural and functional cell substances such as collagen, enzymes, and hemoglobin

_____ 7. Building blocks are amino acids

_____ 8. One of their building blocks, glycerol, is a sugar alcohol

Metabolism

1. Complete the following statements, which provide an overview of the metabolism of energy-containing nutrients, by writing the missing words in the answer blanks.

_____ 1.

_____ 2.

_____ 3.

_____ 4.

_____ 5.

_____ 6.

_____ 7.

_____ 8.

_____ 9.

_____ 10.

The general term for all chemical reactions necessary to maintain life is __(1)__ . The breakdown of complex molecules to simpler ones is called __(2)__ , and the reverse process, the synthesis of larger molecules from smaller ones, is called __(3)__ . The term that means the extraction of energy from nutrient molecules is __(4)__ . The chemical form of energy that cells generally use to drive their activities is __(5)__ .

There are three states in the metabolism of energy-containing nutrients. Stage 1 occurs in the __(6)__ , where large nutrient molecules are broken down to their absorbable forms (monomers). In Stage 2, the blood transports these monomers to tissue cells, where the monomers undergo catabolic or anabolic reactions in the cytoplasm of the cells.

Stage 3 occurs in the __(7)__ of cells, where generation of ATP requires the gas __(8)__ and where __(9)__ and __(10)__ gas are formed as the final waste products.

_____ 11.

_____ 12.

_____ 13.

_____ 14.

_____ 15.

_____ 16.

Reactions that generate ATP are called oxidation reactions. In most cases, the substrate molecules (the substance oxidized) lose __(11)__ and also __(12)__ . Reactions in which substrate molecules gain energy by the addition of hydrogen atoms and electrons are called __(13)__ reactions. Since the enzymes regulating the oxidation-reduction (OR) reactions cannot accept (bind) hydrogen atoms removed during oxidation, molecules called __(14)__ are required. The abbreviations for two of the most important coenzymes in Stage 3 are __(15)__ and __(16)__ .

2. Figure 23.1 is a simplified, highly schematic diagram of the major catabolic pathways taken by one glucose molecule entering a typical cell. Only the organelles involved with these reactions are included, and only *types* of molecules (*not quantities*) are shown. Dashed arrows indicate two or more steps in a series of reactions, and open arrows indicate the movement of molecules.

Using the key choices, complete the diagram by inserting the correct symbols or words in the empty boxes on the diagram. Also color code and color each box provided with a color-coding circle. Then, referring to Figure 23.1, complete the statements that follow by inserting your answers in the answer blanks.

Key Choices

○ Acetyl CoA (Acetyl coenzyme A)

○ ADP (Adenosine diphosphate)

○ CO_2 (Carbon dioxide)

○ $FADH_2$ (Reduced FAD)

○ Glucose-6-phosphate

○ H_2O (Water)

○ Krebs cycle

○ NADH + H$^+$ (Reduced NAD)

○ O_2 (Oxygen)

○ Pi (Inorganic phosphate)

○ Pyruvic acid

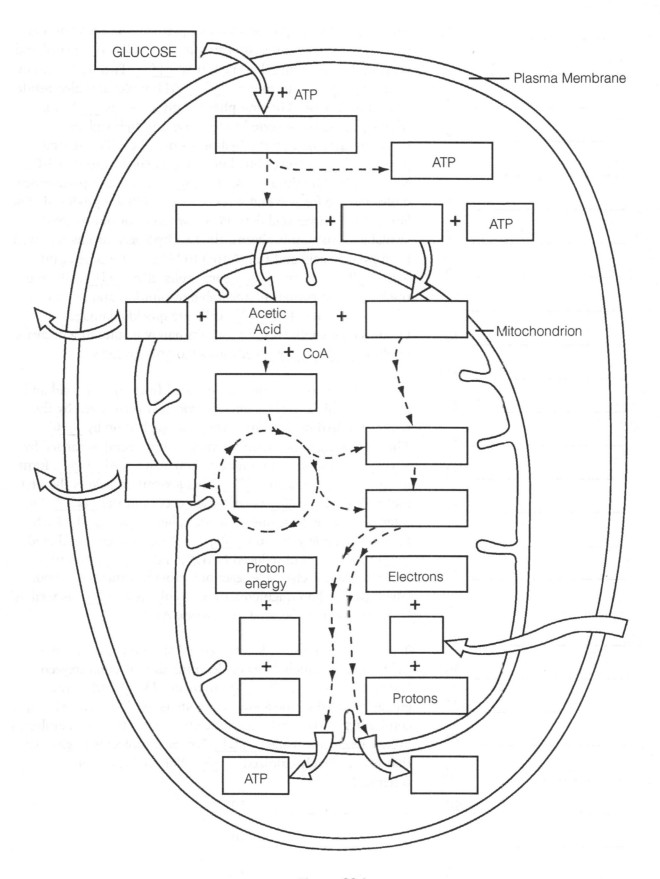

Figure 23.1

_____ 1.

_____ 2.

_____ 3.

_____ 4.

_____ 5.

_____ 6.

_____ 7.

_____ 8.

_____ 9.

_____ 10.

_____ 11.

_____ 12.

_____ 13.

_____ 14.

_____ 15.

_____ 16.

_____ 17.

_____ 18.

_____ 19.

_____ 20.

_____ 21.

_____ 22.

_____ 23.

_____ 24.

_____ 25.

_____ 26.

_____ 27.

_____ 28.

1. The catabolism of glucose into two pyruvic acid molecules is called __(1)__. This process occurs in the __(2)__ of the cell and is anaerobic, meaning that oxygen is __(3)__. Two molecules of reduced __(4)__ a net gain of __(5)__ ATP molecules also result from this process. The first phase of glycolysis is __(6)__, in which glucose is converted to fructose-1,6-diphosphate, reactions energized by the hydrolysis of 2 ATP. The second phase, __(7)__, involves breaking the 6-C sugar into two 3-C compounds. The third phase is __(8)__, in which 2 pyruvic acid molecules are formed and 4 ATP (2 net ATP) are produced. The fate of the pyruvic acid depends on whether or not oxygen is available. If oxygen is absent, the two hydrogen atoms removed from pyruvic acid and transferred to NAD^+ combine again with __(9)__ to form __(10)__. Some cells, like __(11)__ cells, routinely undergo periods of anaerobic respiration and are not adversely affected, but __(12)__ cells are quickly damaged. Prolonged anaerobic respiration ultimately results in a decrease in blood __(13)__. __(14)__ cells undergo only glycolysis.

If oxygen is present, carbon is removed from pyruvic acid and leaves the cell as __(15)__, and pyruvic acid is oxidized by the removal of hydrogen atoms, which are picked up by __(16)__. The remaining two-carbon fragment (acetic acid) is carried by __(17)__ to combine with a four-carbon acid called __(18)__, forming the six-carbon acid __(19)__. This six-carbon acid is the first molecule of the __(20)__ cycle, which occurs in the __(21)__. The intermediate acids of this cycle are called __(22)__ acids. Each turn of the cycle generates __(23)__ molecules of carbon dioxide, __(24)__ molecules of reduced NAD^+, and __(25)__ molecules of reduced FAD. Krebs cycle reactions provide a metabolic pool, where two-carbon fragments from __(26)__ and __(27)__ as well as from glucose may be used to generate ATP.

The final reactions of glucose catabolism are those of the __(28)__ chain, which delivers electrons to molecular oxygen. Oxygen combines with __(29)__ to form __(30)__. Part of the energy released in the above reactions is used to form ATP by combining __(31)__ with inorganic phosphate (Pi). The combined overall reaction is called __(32)__. For each molecule of glucose that is completely oxidized, __(33)__ ATP molecules are generated.

_____ 29.

_____ 30.

_____ 31.

_____ 32.

_____ 33.

3. Figure 23.2 is a simplified diagram of a cross section of part of a mitochondrion. First, label the intermembrane space and the mitochondrial matrix on the appropriate lines on the diagram. (*Note:* The structures labeled EC [1–4] represent enzyme complexes.) Next, select two colors and color the coding circles and the circles on the diagram that represent the electrically charged particles listed below. Remember that the *types* of particles are indicated, *not* the quantities of each. Then, referring to Figure 23.2, complete the statements that follow by inserting your answers in the answer blanks.

○ Electrons (Color the appropriate circles and insert e⁻ in each.)

○ Protons (Color the appropriate circles and insert H^+ in each.)

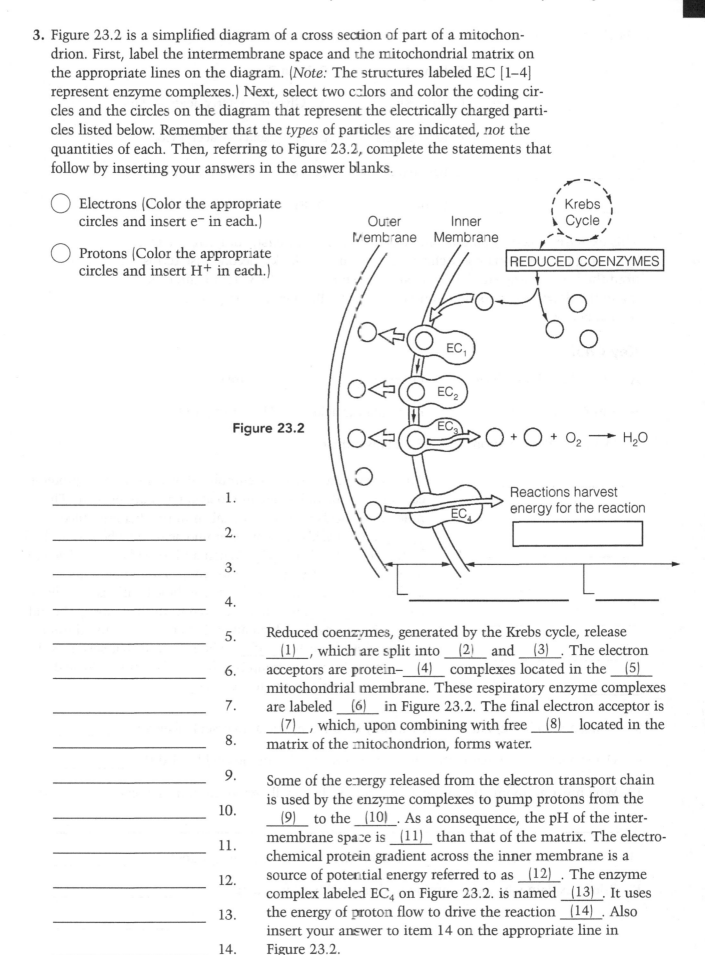

Figure 23.2

_____ 1.

_____ 2.

_____ 3.

_____ 4.

_____ 5.

_____ 6.

_____ 7.

_____ 8.

_____ 9.

_____ 10.

_____ 11.

_____ 12.

_____ 13.

_____ 14.

Reduced coenzymes, generated by the Krebs cycle, release __(1)__, which are split into __(2)__ and __(3)__. The electron acceptors are protein–__(4)__ complexes located in the __(5)__ mitochondrial membrane. These respiratory enzyme complexes are labeled __(6)__ in Figure 23.2. The final electron acceptor is __(7)__, which, upon combining with free __(8)__ located in the matrix of the mitochondrion, forms water.

Some of the energy released from the electron transport chain is used by the enzyme complexes to pump protons from the __(9)__ to the __(10)__. As a consequence, the pH of the intermembrane space is __(11)__ than that of the matrix. The electrochemical proton gradient across the inner membrane is a source of potential energy referred to as __(12)__. The enzyme complex labeled EC_4 on Figure 23.2. is named __(13)__. It uses the energy of proton flow to drive the reaction __(14)__. Also insert your answer to item 14 on the appropriate line in Figure 23.2.

4. Match the metabolic reactions in Column B to the terms in Column A.

	Column A	Column B
_____	1. Lipolysis	A. Glycerol + fatty acids → fats
_____	2. Ketogenesis	B. Fatty acids → acetyl CoA
_____	3. Beta oxidation	C. Fats → glycerol + fatty acids
_____	4. Lipogenesis	D. Fatty acids → ketone bodies

5. This exercise considers protein/amino acid metabolism. First, complete the text by writing the appropriate key choices in the answer blanks. Second, use terms from the key to complete the flowcharts shown in Figure 23.3. Third, after filling in the flowchart, respond to questions 8–12 following the completion section below.

Key Choices

A. Alpha ketoglutaric acid   D. Essential   G. Urea

B. Ammonia (NH_3)   E. Glutamic acid   H. Water (H_2O)

C. Oxidative deamination   F. Transamination

_____ 1.

_____ 2.

_____ 3.

_____ 4.

_____ 5.

_____ 6.

_____ 7.

Amino acids are actively accumulated by cells because proteins cannot be made unless all amino acid types are present. The nine amino acids that *must* be taken in the diet are called __(1)__ amino acids. The other amino acids may be synthesized by the process called __(2)__. When amino acids are oxidized to form cellular energy, their amino groups are removed and liberated as __(3)__. In the liver, this is combined with carbon dioxide to form __(4)__, which is removed from the body by the kidneys. The process by which an amine group is removed from an amino acid is called __(5)__. The keto acid that serves as the acceptor of the amine group is __(6)__. When this keto acid accepts the amine group, it becomes __(7)__.

8. Using a key choice, identify the pathway followed by the amino acid labeled I. _____

9. Using a key choice, name the pathway followed by the amino acid labeled II. _____

10. Why must ammonia (from the amine groups) be rapidly removed from the blood?

_____

11. What is the general term for amino acids that lose their amine groups? _____

12. Briefly explain why excess amino acids are oxidized for energy. _____

_____

_____

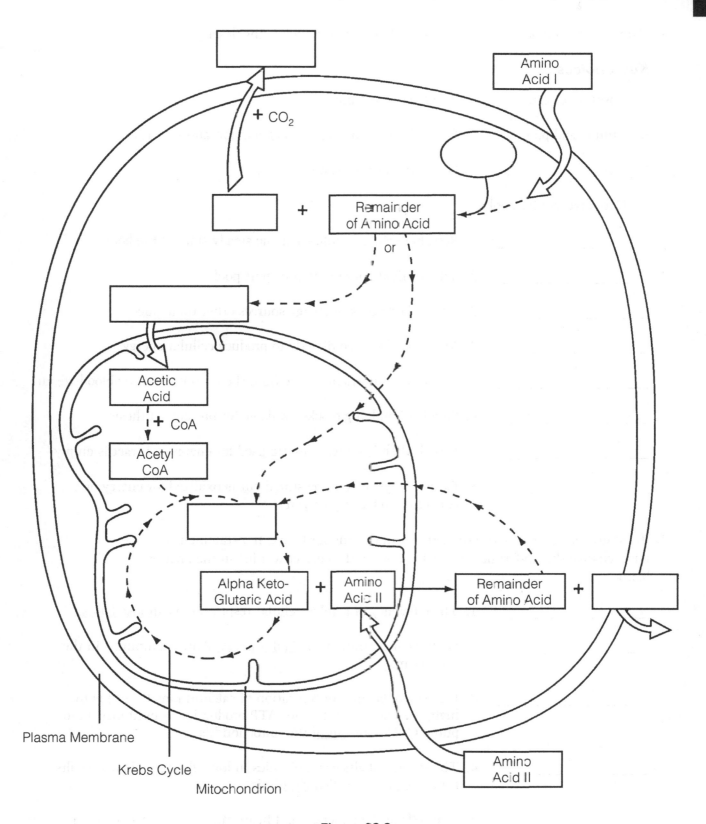

Figure 23.3

6. Using the key choices, select the terms that match the following descriptions.

Key Choices

A. Absorptive state   E. Glucose sparing

B. Amino acid pool   F. Molecular turnover (by degradation and synthesis)

C. Blood   G. Postabsorptive state

D. Carbohydrate-fat pool

_____   1. Results in the catabolic-anabolic steady state of the body

_____   2. The nutrient-containing transport pool

_____   3. Use by body cells of energy sources other than glucose

_____   4. Molecules oxidized directly to produce cellular energy

_____   5. Period when nutrients move from the GI tract into the bloodstream

_____   6. Supply of building blocks available for protein synthesis

_____   7. Period when body reserves are used for energy; GI tract is empty

_____   8. Excess supply cannot be stored but is oxidized for energy or converted to fat or glycogen

7. If a statement is true, write the letter T in the answer blank. If a statement is false, change the underlined word(s) and write the correct word(s) in the answer blank.

_____   1. The efficiency of aerobic cellular respiration is <u>almost 100%</u>.

_____   2. Higher concentrations of <u>ADP than ATP</u> are maintained in the cytoplasm.

_____   3. If the cytoplasmic concentration of calcium ions (Ca^{2+}) is too high, the gradient energy for ATP production is used instead to pump Ca^{2+} ions <u>out of</u> the mitochondria.

_____   4. The storage of glucose molecules in long glycogen chains results from the process called <u>glycolysis</u>.

_____   5. The cells of the <u>pancreas and heart muscle</u> are most active in glycogen synthesis.

8. Circle the term that does not belong in each of the following groupings pertaining to triglyceride (fat) metabolism.

   1. 9 kcal/g   Glucose   Fat   Most concentrated form of energy

   2. Chylomicrons   Transported in lymph   Hydrolyzed in plasma

      Hydrolyzed in mitochondria

   3. Cytoplasm   Beta oxidation   Two-carbon fragments   Mitochondria

   4. Triglyceride synthesis   Lipogenesis   ATP deficit   Excess ATP

   5. High dietary carbohydrates   Glucose conversion to fat   Condensation of acetyl

      CoA molecules   Low blood sugar level

9. If a statement about the *absorptive* state is true, write the letter T in the answer blank. If a statement is false, change the underlined word(s) and write the correct word(s) in the answer blank.

   _____ 1. Major metabolic events are <u>catabolic</u>.

   _____ 2. The major energy fuel is <u>glucose</u>.

   _____ 3. Excess glucose is stored in muscle cells as <u>glucagon</u> or in adipose cells as fat.

   _____ 4. The major energy source of skeletal muscle cells is <u>glucose</u>.

   _____ 5. In a balanced diet, most amino acids pass through the liver to other cells, where they are used for <u>the generation of ATP</u>.

   _____ 6. The hormone most in control of the events of the absorptive state is <u>insulin</u>.

   _____ 7. <u>The sympathetic nervous system</u> signals the pancreatic beta cells to secrete insulin.

   _____ 8. Insulin stimulates the <u>active transport</u> of glucose into tissue cells.

   _____ 9. Insulin inhibits lipolysis and <u>glycogenesis</u>.

   _____ 10. Most amino acids in the hepatic portal blood remain in the blood for uptake by <u>hepatocytes</u>.

   _____ 11. Amino acids move into tissue cells by <u>active transport</u>.

10. Respond to the following questions about the *postabsorptive* state by writing your answers in the answer blanks.

1. What is the homeostatic range of blood glucose levels? Give units.

   _____

2. Why must blood glucose be maintained at least at the lower levels?

   _____

3. Name four sources of glucose in order from the most to the least available when blood glucose levels are falling. Include the tissues of origin and the name of the metabolic process involved.

   _____

   _____

   _____

   _____

4. Briefly explain the indirect metabolic pathway by which skeletal muscle cells help maintain blood glucose levels.

   _____

   _____

   _____

5. Trace the metabolic pathway by which lipolysis produces blood glucose.

   _____

   _____

   _____

   _____

6. How are tissue proteins used as a source of blood glucose?

   _____

   _____

7. During the period of glucose sparing, which energy source is available

   to organs other than the brain? _____

8. After four or five days of fasting, accompanied by low blood glucose levels, the brain begins to use a different energy source. What is this energy source?

   _____

9. Name the two major hormones controlling events of the postabsorptive state.

   _____

10. Name the origin and targets of glucagon.

    _____

11. Name two humoral factors that stimulate the release of glucagon.

    _____

    _____

12. Why is the release of glucagon important when blood levels of amino acids rise (as after a high-protein, low-carbohydrate meal)?

    _____

    _____

13. Briefly describe the role of the sympathetic nervous system. _____

    _____

    _____

11. Complete the table below, which indicates the effects of several hormones on the characteristics indicated at the top of each column. Use an up arrow (↑) to indicate an increase in a particular value or a down arrow (↓) to indicate a decrease. No response is required in the boxes with XXX.

Hormone	Blood glucose	Blood amino acids	Glycogenolysis	Lipogenesis	Protein synthesis
Insulin					
Glucagon		XXX			XXX
Epinephrine		XXX			XXX
Growth hormone					
Thyroxine		XXX			

12. The liver has many functions in addition to its digestive function. Complete the following statements that elaborate on the liver's function by inserting the correct terms in the answer blanks.

_____ 1.

_____ 2.

_____ 3.

_____ 4.

_____ 5.

_____ 6.

_____ 7.

_____ 8.

_____ 9.

_____ 10.

_____ 11.

_____ 12.

_____ 13.

_____ 14.

_____ 15.

_____ 16.

_____ 17.

_____ 18.

_____ 19.

_____ 20.

_____ 21.

_____ 22.

_____ 23.

_____ 24.

_____ 25.

_____ 26.

_____ 27.

The liver is the most important metabolic organ in the body. In its metabolic role, the liver uses amino acids from the nutrient-rich hepatic portal blood to make many blood proteins such as __(1)__ , which helps to hold water in the bloodstream, and __(2)__ , which prevent blood loss when blood vessels are damaged. The liver also makes a steroid substance that is released to the blood. This steroid, __(3)__ , has been implicated in high blood pressure and heart disease. Additionally, the liver acts to maintain homeostatic blood glucose levels. It removes glucose from the blood when blood levels are high, a condition called __(4)__ , and stores it as __(5)__ . Then, when blood glucose levels are low, a condition called __(6)__ , liver cells break down the stored carbohydrate and release glucose to the blood once again. This latter process is termed __(7)__ . When the liver makes glucose from noncarbohydrate substances such as fats or proteins, the process is termed __(8)__ . In addition to its processing of amino acids and sugars, the liver plays an important role in the processing of fats. Other functions of the liver include the __(9)__ of drugs and alcohol, and its __(10)__ cells protect the body by ingesting bacteria and other debris.

The liver forms small complexes called __(11)__ , which are needed to transport fatty acids, fats, and cholesterol in the blood because lipids are __(12)__ in a watery medium. The higher the lipid content of the lipoprotein, the __(13)__ is its density. Thus, low-density lipoproteins (LDLs) have a __(14)__ lipid content. __(15)__ are lipoproteins that transport dietary lipids from the GI tract. The liver produces VLDLs (very low density lipoproteins) to transport __(16)__ to adipose tissue.

After releasing their cargo, VLDL residues convert to LDLs, which are rich in __(17)__ . The function of LDLs is transport of cholesterol to peripheral tissues, where cells use it to construct their plasma __(18)__ or to synthesize __(19)__ . The function of HDLs (high-density lipoproteins) is transport of cholesterol to the __(20)__ , where it is degraded and secreted as __(21)__ , which are eventually excreted.

High levels of cholesterol in the plasma are of concern because of the risk of __(22)__ . The type of dietary fatty acid affects cholesterol levels. __(23)__ fatty acids promote excretion of cholesterol. When cholesterol levels in plasma are measured, high levels of __(24)__ DLs indicate that the fate of the transported cholesterol is catabolism to bile salts.

Two other important functions of the liver are the storage of vitamins (such as vitamins __(25)__) and of the metal __(26)__ (as ferritin) and the processing of bilirubin, which results from the breakdown of __(27)__ cells.

Energy Balance

1. Circle the term that does not belong in each of the following groupings.

1. BMR   TMR   Rest   Postabsorptive state

2. Thyroxine   Iodine   ↓ Metabolic rate   ↑ Metabolic rate

3. Obese person   ↓ Metabolic rate   Women   Child

4. 4 kcal/gram   Fats   Carbohydrates   Proteins

5. ↑ TMR   Fasting   Muscle activity   Ingestion of protein

6. Body's core   Lowest temperature   Heat loss surface   Body's shell

7. Radiation   Evaporation   Vasoconstriction   Conduction

2. Using the key choices, select the factor regulating food intake that best fits the following conditions. Also state whether hunger is depressed (use ↓), or stimulated (use ↑), or both (use ↑ ↓) by each condition described. Insert your letter answers and the arrows in the answer blanks.

Key Choices

A. Body temperature   C. Nutrient signals related to total energy stores

B. Hormones   D. Psychological factors   E. Hypothalamic peptides

_____ 1. Rise in plasma glucose levels

_____ 2. Ingestion, digestion, and liver activities increase

_____ 3. Secretions of insulin or cholecystokinin

_____ 4. Low plasma levels of amino acids

_____ 5. The sight, taste, smell, or thought of food

_____ 6. Secretions of glucagon or epinephrine

_____ 7. Increasing amounts of fatty acids and glycerol in the blood

_____ 8. Release of leptin, GLP, or serotonin

3. Respond to the following by writing your answers in the answer blanks.

1. Briefly explain cell metabolism in terms of the first law of thermodynamics (energy can neither be created nor destroyed).

_____

_____

_____

2. Nearly all the energy derived from food is eventually converted to _____

3. How does the balance between energy input and energy output affect body weight?

_____

_____

4. Using the key choices, select the terms that match the following descriptions pertaining to body temperature regulation. Insert the appropriate answers in the answer blanks.

Key Choices

A. Blood   D. Heat   G. Hypothermia   J. Pyrogens

B. Vasoconstriction in skin   E. Hyperthermia   H. Perspiration   K. Shivering

C. Frostbite   F. Hypothalamus   I. Radiation

_____ 1. By-product of cell metabolism

_____ 2. Means of conserving or increasing body heat

_____ 3. Medium that distributes heat to all body tissues

_____ 4. Site of the body's thermostat

_____ 5. Chemicals released by injured tissue cells and macrophages that cause resetting of the thermostat

_____ 6. Death of cells deprived of oxygen and nutrients, resulting from withdrawal of blood from the skin circulation

_____ 7. Means of liberating excess body heat

_____ 8. Extremely low body temperature

_____ 9. Fever

_____ 10. Cause release of hypothalamic prostaglandins

5. If a statement about the regulation of body temperature is true, write the letter T in the answer blank. If a statement is false, change the underlined word(s) and write the correct word(s) in the answer blank.

_____   1. One of the most important ways the body regulates temperature is by changing <u>visceral organ</u> activity.

_____   2. The homeostatic range of body temperature is from 35.6°C (96°F) to <u>43°C (110°F)</u>.

_____   3. With each 1°C rise in body temperature, the rate of enzymatic catalysis increases by <u>1%</u>.

_____   4. When the body temperature exceeds the homeostatic range, <u>carbohydrates</u> begin to break down.

_____   5. Convulsions occur when the body temperature reaches <u>41°C (106°F)</u>.

_____   6. The cessation of all thermoregulatory mechanisms may lead to <u>heat exhaustion</u>.

CHALLENGING YOURSELF

At the Clinic

1. Mary Maroon comes to the clinic to get information on a vegetarian diet. What problems may arise when people make uninformed decisions on what to eat for a vegetarian diet? What combination of vegetable foods will provide Mary with all the essential amino acids?

2. A group of new parents is meeting to learn about good nutrition for their children. The topic is "empty calories." What does the term mean and what are some foods with empty calories?

3. Mrs. Piercecci, a woman in her mid-40s, complains of extreme fatigue and faintness about four hours after each meal. What hormone might be deficient and what condition is indicated?

4. Zena, a teenager, has gone to the sports clinic for the past 2 years to have her fat content checked. This year, her percent body fat is up and tissue protein has not increased. Questioning reveals that Zena has been on crash diets four times since the last checkup, only to regain the weight (and more) each time. She also admits sheepishly that she "detests" exercise. How does cyclic dieting, accompanied by lack of exercise, cause an increase in fat and a decrease in protein?

5. Benny, a 6-year-old child who is allergic to milk, has extremely bowed legs. What condition do you suspect and what is the connection to not drinking milk?

6. An anorexic girl shows high levels of acetone in her blood. What is this condition called and what has caused it?

7. There has been a record heat wave lately, and many elderly people are coming to the clinic complaining that they "feel poorly." In most cases, their skin is cool and clammy, and their blood pressure is low. What is their problem? What can be done to alleviate it?

8. During the same period, Bert Winchester, a construction worker, is rushed in unconscious. His skin is hot and dry, and his co-workers say that he suddenly keeled over on the job. What is Bert's condition and how should it be handled?

9. The mother of a 1-year-old confides in the pediatrician (somewhat proudly) that she has started her child on skim milk to head off any future problems with atherosclerosis. Why is this not a good practice?

10. A blood test shows cholesterol levels at about 280 mg/100 ml. What is this condition called? What cholesterol level is safe? What are some complications of high cholesterol?

11. Mrs. Rodriguez has a bleeding ulcer and has lost her appetite. She appears pale and lethargic when she comes in for a physical. She proves to be anemic and her RBCs are large and pale. What mineral supplements should be ordered?

12. Mr. Hodges, pretty much a recluse, unexpectedly appears at the clinic seeking help with a change he has experienced. He has been losing weight, his skin is full of bruises, and his gums are bleeding. However, what really "drove" him to the clinic is a sore that won't heal. What is his problem called? What vitamin deficiency causes it? What dietary changes would you suggest?

Stop and Think

1. Amino acids must be metabolized; they cannot be stored. What would be the osmotic and acid-base effects of accumulating amino acids?

2. What would be the diffusion and osmotic effects of failing to turn glucose into glycogen and adipose tissue for storage?

3. What is the *specific* mechanism by which oxygen starvation causes death?

4. Does urea production increase or decrease when essential amino acids are lacking in the diet? Explain your answer.

5. What is the difference in the effect on blood glucose of a meal of simple sugars versus a meal of an equal amount of complex carbohydrates?

6. Does loss of mental function accompany the deterioration associated with diabetes mellitus? Why or why not?

7. What would happen to blood clotting if excess omega-3 fatty acids were ingested?

8. Why is the factor for calculating BMR higher for males than it is for females?

9. Why might PKU sufferers have poor vision?

10. What supplements would you suggest for someone taking diuretics?

11. What is the metabolic link between diabetes mellitus and arteriosclerosis?

12. Does hypothyroidism result in hyperthermia or hypothermia? Explain.

13. Why do we feel hot when we exercise vigorously?

14. As indicated in Figure 23.4 concerning the Krebs cycle, succinic acid is converted to fumaric acid. This conversion process involves the liberation of H^+, a detail not shown in the figure. During a laboratory exercise dealing with this reaction, you are working with a suspension of bean-cell mitochondria and a blue dye that loses its color as it absorbs hydrogen ions. You know from previous enzyme experiments that the higher the concentration of the substrate (succinic acid in this case), the more rapidly the reaction proceeds (the faster the dye will decolor). Your experimental tubes contain three different succinic acid concentrations—0.1 mg/L, 0.2 mg/L, and 0.3 mg/L. Which of the graphs shown—A, B, or C—represents the expected results and why?

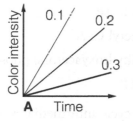 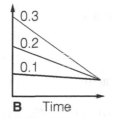 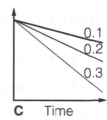

Figure 23.4

15. The body easily converts excess carbohydrates into fats. However, it needs input from dietary proteins to convert carbohydrates or fats alone into proteins. What do proteins in the diet contribute?

COVERING ALL YOUR BASES

Multiple Choice

Select the best answer or answers from the choices given.

1. Which of the following are "essential" nutrients?

   A. Glucose

   B. Linoleic acid

   C. Cholesterol

   D. Leucine

2. Which factors will work to promote (and allow) protein synthesis?

   A. Presence of all 20 amino acids

   B. Sufficiency of caloric intake

   C. Negative nitrogen balance

   D. Secretion of anabolic hormones

3. Which of the listed vitamins is not found in plant foods?

   A. Folic acid

   B. Biotin

   C. Cyanocobalamin (B_{12})

   D. Pantothenic acid

4. Deficiency of which of these vitamins results in anemia?

   A. Thiamin

   B. Riboflavin

   C. Biotin

   D. Folic acid

5. Vitamins that act as coenzymes in the Krebs cycle include:

   A. riboflavin

   B. niacin

   C. biotin

   D. pantothenic acid

6. Absorption of which of the following minerals parallels absorption of calcium?

   A. Zinc

   B. Magnesium

   C. Iron

   D. Copper

7. Components of the electron transport system include:

   A. cobalt

   B. copper

   C. iron

   D. zinc

8. Substrate-level phosphorylation occurs during:

   A. glycolysis

   B. beta-oxidation

   C. Krebs cycle

   D. electron transport

9. Which processes occur in the mitochondria?

   A. Glycogenesis

   B. Gluconeogenesis

   C. Beta-oxidation

   D. Formation of acetyl CoA

10. The chemiosmotic process involves:

    A. buildup of hydrogen ion concentration

    B. electron transport

    C. oxidation and reduction

    D. ATP synthase

11. Which of the following molecules has the highest energy content?

    A. Glucose

    B. Acetyl CoA

    C. Dihydroxyacetone phosphate

    D. ATP

12. Krebs cycle intermediates include:

    A. glutamic acid

    B. pantothenic acid

    C. succinic acid

    D. fumaric acid

13. Chemicals that can be used for gluconeogenesis include:

    A. amino acids

    B. glycerol

    C. fatty acids

    D. alpha ketoglutaric acid

14. Ingestion of saturated fatty acids (as opposed to equal quantities of polyunsaturated fatty acids) is followed by:

    A. increased cholesterol formation

    B. increased cholesterol excretion

    C. increased production of chylomicrons

    D. increased formation of bile salts

15. Which events occur during the absorptive state?

    A. Use of amino acids as a major source of energy

    B. Lipogenesis

    C. Beta oxidation

    D. Increased uptake of glucose by skeletal muscles

16. Hormones that act to decrease blood glucose level include:

    A. insulin

    B. glucagon

    C. epinephrine

    D. growth hormone

17. During the postabsorptive state:

    A. glycogenesis occurs in the liver

    B. fatty acids are used for fuel

    C. amino acids are converted to glucose

    D. lipolysis occurs in adipose tissue

18. Which processes contribute to gluconeogenesis?

    A. Conversion of pyruvic acid to glucose by skeletal muscle

    B. Release of lactic acid by skeletal muscle

    C. Formation of glucose from triglycerides in adipose tissue

    D. Release of glycerol from adipose tissue

19. Only the liver functions to:

    A. store iron

    B. form urea

    C. produce plasma proteins

    D. form ketone bodies

20. Which transport particles carry cholesterol destined for excretion from the body?

    A. HDL   C. LDL

    B. Chylomicron   D. VLDL

21. Transport of triglycerides from the liver to adipose tissue is the function of:

    A. LDL   C. VLDL

    B. HDL   D. all lipoproteins

22. Glucose (or its metabolites) can be converted to:

    A. glycogen

    B. triglycerides

    C. nonessential amino acids

    D. starch

23. Basal metabolic rate:

    A. is the lowest metabolic rate of the body

    B. is the metabolic rate during sleep

    C. is measured as kcal per square meter of skin per hour

    D. increases with age

24. Body temperature is higher:

    A. in children than in adults

    B. in cases of hyperthyroidism

    C. after eating

    D. when sleeping

25. Which of the following types of heat transfer involves heat loss in the form of infrared waves?

    A. Conduction   C. Evaporation

    B. Convection   D. Radiation

26. Body temperature increases:
    A. during chemical thermogenesis
    B. when pyrogens are released
    C. when sweating and flushing occur
    D. with heat exhaustion

27. PKU is the result of inability to metabolize:
    A. tyrosine   C. ketone bodies
    B. melanin   D. phenylalanine

Word Dissection

For each of the following word roots, fill in the literal meaning and give an example, using a word found in this chapter.

Word root	Translation	Example
1. acet		
2. calor		
3. flav		
4. gluco		
5. kilo		
6. lecith		
7. linol		
8. nutri		
9. pyro		

24

THE URINARY SYSTEM

Overview

As you have learned in previous chapters, the body's cells break down the food we eat, release energy from it, and produce chemical by-products that collect in the bloodstream. The kidneys, playing a crucial homeostatic role, cleanse the blood of these waste products and excess water by forming urine, which is then transferred to the urinary bladder and eventually removed from the body via urination. The kidneys receive more blood from the heart than any other organ of the body. They handle 1 ½ quarts of blood every minute through a complex blood circulation housed in an organ 4 inches high, 2 inches wide, 1 inch thick, and weighing 5 to 6 ounces.

In addition to the kidneys, which produce the urine, the urinary system consists of the ureters, urinary bladder, and urethra, components that are responsible for transport, storage, and conduction of the urine to the exterior.

The activities for Chapter 24 focus on the structural and functional organization of the urinary system, the major regulatory mechanisms that control urine formation and modification, and urine transport, storage, and elimination.

LEVEL 1   Review of Chapter Objectives

1. Identify the components of the urinary system and describe the functions it performs.

2. Describe the location and structural features of the kidney.

3. Identify the major blood vessels associated with each kidney and trace the path of blood flow through a kidney.

4. Describe the structures of the nephron and outline the processes involved in the formation of urine.

5. Discuss the major functions of each portion of the nephron and collecting system.

6. Identify and describe the major factors responsible for the production of urine.

7. Describe the normal characteristics, composition, and solute concentrations of a representative urine sample.

8. List and describe the factors that influence filtration pressure and the rate of filtrate formation.

9. Identify the types of transport mechanisms found along the nephron and discuss the reabsorptive or secretory functions of each segment of the nephron and collecting system.

10. Explain the role of countercurrent multiplication in the formation of a concentration gradient in the medulla.

11. Describe how antidiuretic hormone and aldosterone levels influence the volume and concentration of urine.

12. Describe the structures and functions of the ureters, urinary bladder, and urethra.

13. Discuss the voluntary and involuntary regulation of urination and describe the micturition reflex.

[L1]   Multiple Choice

Place the letter corresponding to the correct answer in the space provided.

OBJ. 1 _____ 1. Urine leaving the kidneys travels along the following sequential pathway to the exterior.

    a. ureters, urinary bladder, urethra

    b. urethra, urinary bladder, ureters

    c. urinary bladder, ureters, urethra

    d. urinary bladder, urethra, ureters

OBJ. 1 _____ 2. Which organ or structure does not belong to the urinary system?

    a. urethra

    b. gallbladder

    c. kidneys

    d. ureters

OBJ. 1 _____ 3. The openings of the urethra and the two ureters mark an area on the internal surface of the urinary bladder called the:

    a. internal urethral sphincter

    b. external urethral sphincter

    c. trigone

    d. renal sinus

OBJ. 1 _____ 4. The initial factor that determines if urine production occurs is:

    a. secretion

    b. absorption

    c. sympathetic activation

    d. filtration

OBJ. 1 _____ 5. Along with the urinary system, the other systems of the body that affect the composition of body fluids are:

    a. nervous, endocrine, and cardiovascular

    b. lymphatic, cardiovascular, and respiratory

    c. integumentary, respiratory, and digestive

    d. muscular, digestive, and lymphatic

OBJ. 2 _____ 6. Seen in section, the kidney is divided into:

    a. renal columns and renal pelves

    b. an outer cortex and an inner medulla

    c. major and minor calyces

    d. a renal tubule and renal corpuscle

OBJ. 2 _____ 7. The basic functional unit in the kidney is the:

    a. glomerulus

    b. loop of Henle

    c. Bowman's capsule

    d. nephron

OBJ. 2 _____ 8. The three concentric layers of connective tissue that protect and anchor the kidneys are the:

   a. hilus, renal sinus, renal corpuscle

   b. cortex, medulla, papillae

   c. renal capsule, adipose capsule, renal fascia

   d. major calyces, minor calyces, renal pyramids

OBJ. 3 _____ 9. Dilation of the afferent arteriole and glomerular capillaries and constriction of the efferent arteriole causes:

   a. elevation of glomerular blood pressure to normal levels

   b. a decrease in glomerular blood pressure

   c. a decrease in the glomerular filtration rate

   d. an increase in the secretion of renin and erythropoietin

OBJ. 3 _____ 10. Blood supply to the proximal and distal convoluted tubules of the nephron is provided by the:

   a. peritubular capillaries

   b. afferent arterioles

   c. segmental veins

   d. interlobular veins

OBJ. 3 _____ 11. In a nephron, the long tubular passageway through which the filtrate passes includes:

   a. collecting tubule, collecting duct, papillary duct

   b. renal corpuscle, renal tubule, renal pelvis

   c. proximal and distal convoluted tubules and loop of Henle

   d. loop of Henle, collecting and papillary duct

OBJ. 4 _____ 12. The primary site of regulating water, sodium, and potassium ion loss in the nephron is the:

   a. distal convoluted tubule

   b. loop of Henle and collecting duct

   c. proximal convoluted tubule

   d. glomerulus

OBJ. 4 _____ 13. The three processes involved in urine formation are:

   a. diffusion, osmosis, and filtration

   b. cotransport, countertransport, and facilitated diffusion

   c. regulation, elimination, and micturition

   d. filtration, reabsorption, and secretion

OBJ. 4 _____ 14. The primary site for secretion of substances into the filtrate is the:

   a. renal corpuscle

   b. loop of Henle

   c. distal convoluted tubule

   d. proximal convoluted tubule

OBJ. 5 _____ 15. The filtration of plasma that generates approximately 180 liters/day of filtrate occurs in the:

    a. loop of Henle

    b. proximal convoluted tubule

    c. renal corpuscle

    d. distal convoluted tubule

OBJ. 5 _____ 16. Approximately 60–70 percent of the water is reabsorbed in the:

    a. renal corpuscle

    b. proximal convoluted tubule

    c. distal convoluted tubule

    d. collecting duct

OBJ. 5 _____ 17. The portion of the renal segment that is under ADH and aldosterone stimulation is the:

    a. proximal convoluted tubule

    b. loop of Henle

    c. vasa recta

    d. distal convoluted tubule

OBJ. 6 _____ 18. The three distinct basic processes of urine formation are:

    a. filtration, reabsorption, secretion

    b. diffusion, osmosis, cotransport

    c. countertransport, cotransport, carrier-mediated transport

    d. a, b, and c are correct

OBJ. 6 _____ 19. The location and orientation of the carrier proteins determine whether a particular substance is reabsorbed or secreted in:

    a. active transport

    b. cotransport

    c. countertransport

    d. all of the above

OBJ. 7 _____ 20. The three primary waste products found in a representative urine sample are:

    a. ions, metabolites, nitrogenous wastes

    b. urea, creatinine, uric acid

    c. glucose, lipids, proteins

    d. sodium, potassium, chloride

OBJ. 7 _____ 21. The average pH for normal urine is about:

    a. 5.0

    b. 6.0

    c. 7.0

    d. 8.0

OBJ. 8 _____ 22. The glomerular filtration rate is regulated by:

    a. autoregulation

    b. hormonal regulation

    c. autonomic regulation

    d. a, b, and c are correct

OBJ. 8 _____ 23. The pressure that represents the resistance to flow along the nephron and conducting system is the:

  a. blood colloid osmotic pressure (BCOP)

  b. glomerular hydrostatic pressure (GHP)

  c. capsular hydrostatic pressure (CHP)

  d. capsular colloid osmotic pressure (CCOP)

OBJ. 9 _____ 24. The mechanism important in the reabsorption of glucose and amino acids when their concentrations in the filtrate are relatively high is:

  a. active transport

  b. facilitated transport

  c. cotransport

  d. countertransport

OBJ. 9 _____ 25. Countertransport resembles cotransport in all respects except:

  a. calcium ions are exchanged for sodium ions

  b. chloride ions are exchanged for bicarbonate ions

  c. the two transported ions move in opposite directions

  d. a, b, and c are correct

OBJ. 9 _____ 26. The primary site of nutrient reabsorption in the nephron is the:

  a. proximal convoluted tubule

  b. distal convoluted tubule

  c. loop of Henle

  d. renal corpuscle

OBJ. 10 _____ 27. In countercurrent multiplication the *countercurrent* refers to the fact that an exchange occurs between:

  a. sodium ions and chloride ions

  b. fluids moving in opposite directions

  c. potassium and chloride ions

  d. solute concentrations in the loop of Henle

OBJ. 10 _____ 28. The result of the countercurrent multiplication mechanism is:

  a. decreased solute concentration in the descending limb of loop of Henle

  b. decreased transport of sodium and chloride in the ascending limb of loop of Henle

  c. increased solute concentration in the descending limb of loop of Henle

  d. osmotic flow of water from peritubular fluid into the descending limb of loop of Henle

OBJ. 11 _____ 29. When antidiuretic hormone levels rise, the distal convoluted tubule becomes:

  a. less permeable to water; reabsorption of water decreases

  b. more permeable to water; water reabsorption increases

  c. less permeable to water; reabsorption of water increases

  d. more permeable to water; water reabsorption decreases

OBJ. 11 _____ 30. The results of the effect of aldosterone along the DCT, the collecting tubule, and the collecting duct are:

    a. increased conservation of sodium ions and water

    b. increased sodium ion excretion

    c. decreased sodium ion reabsorption in the DCT

    d. increased sodium ion and water excretion

OBJ. 12 _____ 31. When urine leaves the kidney, it travels to the urinary bladder via the:

    a. urethra

    b. ureters

    c. renal hilus

    d. renal calyces

OBJ. 12 _____ 32. The expanded, funnel-shaped upper end of the ureter in the kidney is the:

    a. renal pelvis

    b. urethra

    c. renal hilus

    d. renal calyces

OBJ. 12 _____ 33. Contraction of the muscular bladder forces the urine out of the body through the:

    a. ureter

    b. urethra

    c. penis

    d. a, b, and c are correct

OBJ. 13 _____ 34. During the micturition reflex, increased afferent fiber activity in the pelvic nerves facilitates:

    a. parasympathetic motor neurons in the sacral spinal cord

    b. sympathetic sensory neurons in the sacral spinal cord

    c. the action of stretch receptors in the wall of the bladder

    d. urine ejection due to internal and external sphincter contractions

OBJ. 13 _____ 35. Urine reaches the urinary bladder by the:

    a. action of stretch receptors in the bladder wall

    b. fluid pressures in the renal pelvis

    c. peristaltic contractions of the ureters

    d. sustained contractions and relaxation of the urinary bladder

[L1] Completion

Using the terms below, complete the following statements.

cerebral cortex	urethra	micturition reflex
composition	rugae	concentration
secretion	filtrate	parathyroid hormone
glomerulus	neck	loop of Henle
renal threshold	antidiuretic hormone	internal sphincter
kidneys	interlobar veins	countertransport
countercurrent	glomerular hydrostatic	ureters
multiplication	glomerular filtration	nephrons

OBJ. 1 1. The excretory functions of the urinary system are performed by the _____.

OBJ. 1 2. Urine leaving the kidneys flows through paired tubes called _____.

OBJ. 1 3. The structure that carries urine from the urinary bladder to the exterior of the body is the _____.

OBJ. 2 4. The renal corpuscle contains a capillary knot referred to as the _____.

OBJ. 2 5. Urine production begins in microscopic, tubular structures called _____.

OBJ. 3 6. In a mirror image of arterial distribution, the interlobular veins deliver blood to arcuate veins that empty into _____.

OBJ. 4 7. The outflow across the walls of the glomerulus produces a protein-free solution known as the _____.

OBJ. 5 8. The creation of the concentration gradient in the medulla occurs in the _____.

OBJ. 6 9. The primary method of excretion for some compounds, including many drugs, is the process of _____.

OBJ. 7 10. The plasma concentration at which a specific component or ion will begin appearing in the urine is called the _____.

OBJ. 7 11. The filtration, absorption, and secretion activities of the nephrons reflect the urine's _____.

OBJ. 7 12. The osmotic movement of water across the walls of the tubules and collecting ducts determines the urine's _____.

OBJ. 8 13. The pressure that tends to drive water and solute molecules across the glomerular wall is the _____ pressure.

OBJ. 8 14. The vital first step essential to all other kidney functions is _____.

OBJ. 9 15. The hormone that stimulates carrier proteins to reduce the urinary loss of calcium ions is _____.

OBJ. 9 16. To keep intracellular calcium concentrations low, most cells in the body use sodium-calcium _____.

OBJ. 10 17. The mechanism that operates efficiently to reabsorb solutes and water before the tubular fluid reaches the DCT and collecting system is _____.

OBJ. 11 18. Passive reabsorption of water from urine in the collecting system is regulated by circulating levels of _____.

OBJ. 12 19. The muscular ring that provides involuntary control over the discharge of urine from the urinary bladder is the _____.

OBJ. 12 20. In a relaxed condition, the epithelium of the urinary bladder forms a series of prominent folds called _____.

OBJ. 12 21. The area surrounding the urethral entrance of the urinary bladder is the

_____.

OBJ. 13 22. The process of urination is coordinated by the _____.

OBJ. 13 23. We become consciously aware of the fluid pressure in the urinary bladder because of sensations relayed to the _____.

[L1] Matching

Match the terms in column B with the terms in column A. Use letters for answers in the spaces provided.

Part I

	Column A	Column B
OBJ. 1	____ 1. micturition	A. blood to kidney
OBJ. 1	____ 2. urinary bladder	B. ADH stimulation
OBJ. 2	____ 3. renal capsule	C. blood colloid osmotic pressure
OBJ. 2	____ 4. renal medulla	D. glucose in urine
OBJ. 3	____ 5. renal artery	E. active transport
OBJ. 3	____ 6. renal vein	F. urine storage
OBJ. 4	____ 7. glomerular epithelium	G. fibrous tunic
OBJ. 5	____ 8. collecting system	H blood from kidney
OBJ. 6	____ 9. carrier-mediated	I. elimination of urine
OBJ. 7	____ 10. glycosuria	J. podocytes
OBJ. 8	____ 11. opposes filtration	K. renal pyramids

Part II

	Column A	Column B
OBJ. 9	____ 12. countertransport	L. voluntary control
OBJ. 9	____ 13. reabsorption processes	M. urge to urinate
OBJ. 10	____ 14. loop of Henle	N. sodium-bicarbonate ion exchange
OBJ. 11	____ 15. aldosterone	O. detrusor muscle
OBJ. 12	____ 16. urinary bladder	P. urachus
OBJ. 12	____ 17. middle umbilical ligament	Q. ion pump—K+ channels
OBJ. 13	____ 18. internal sphincter	R. countercurrent multiplication
OBJ. 13	____ 19. external sphincter	S. involuntary control
OBJ. 13	____ 20. 200 ml. of urine in bladder	T. role of sodium ion

[L1]   Drawing/Illustration Labeling

Identify each numbered structure by labeling the following figures:

OBJ. 1   **Figure 24.1   Components of the Urinary System**

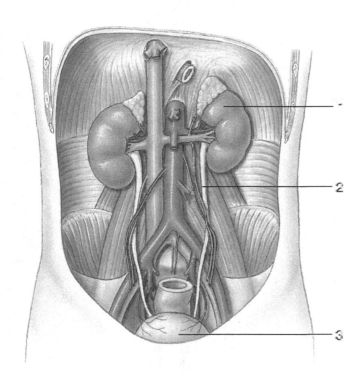

1 _____

2 _____

3 _____

OBJ. 2   **Figure 24.2   Sectional Anatomy of the Kidney**

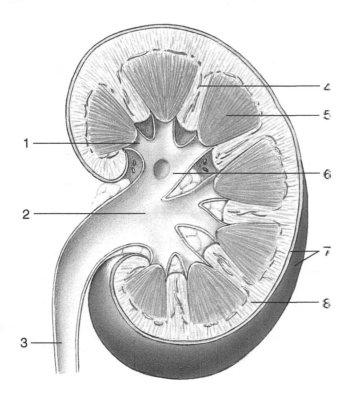

1 _____

2 _____

3 _____

4 _____

5 _____

6 _____

7 _____

8 _____

OBJ. 4   **Figure 24.3   Structure of a Typical Nephron Including Circulation**

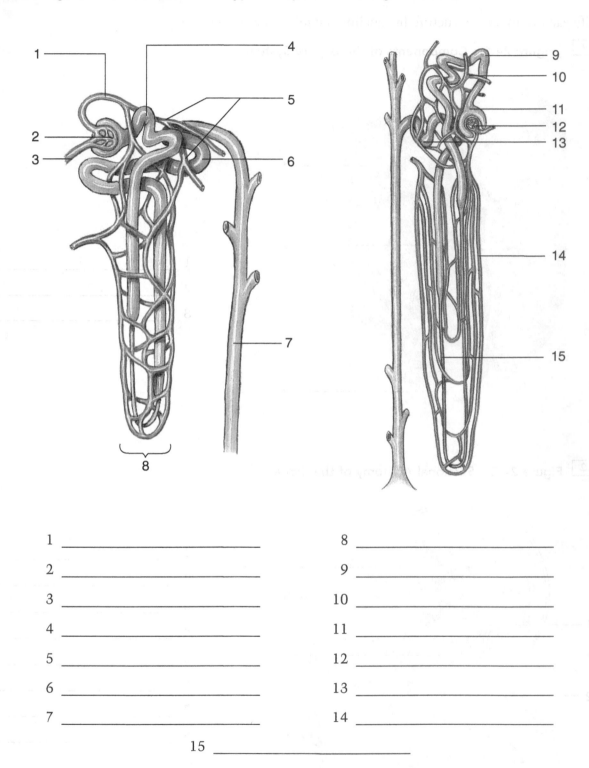

1 _____   8 _____

2 _____   9 _____

3 _____   10 _____

4 _____   11 _____

5 _____   12 _____

6 _____   13 _____

7 _____   14 _____

15 _____

LEVEL 2   Concept Synthesis

Concept Map I

Using the following terms, fill in the circled, numbered, blank spaces to complete the concept map. Follow the numbers to comply with the organization of the map.

Renal sinus   Urinary bladder   Medulla
Ureters   Minor calyces   Nephrons
Glomerulus   Proximal convoluted   Collecting tubules
                       tubule

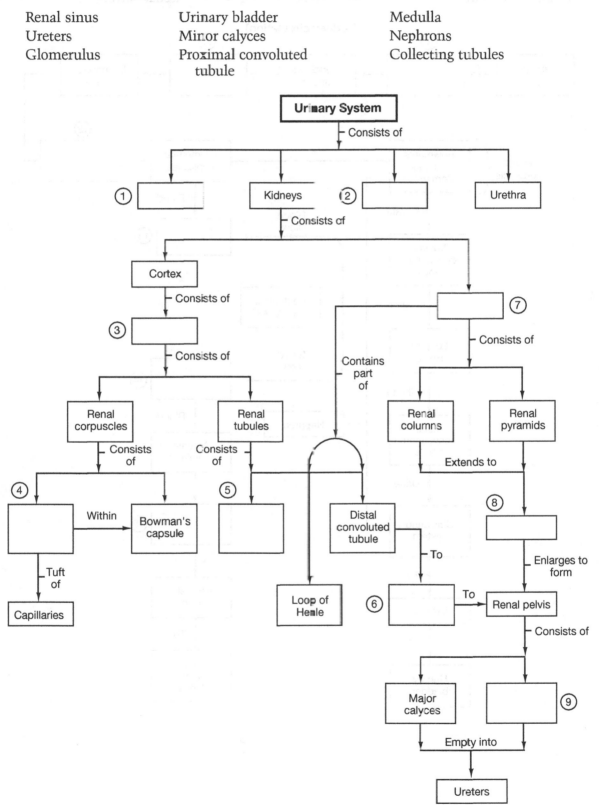

Concept Map II

Using the following terms, fill in the circled, numbered, blank spaces to complete the concept map. Follow the numbers to comply with the organization of the map.

Efferent artery   Afferent artery   Interlobar vein
Interlobular vein   Renal artery   Arcuate artery

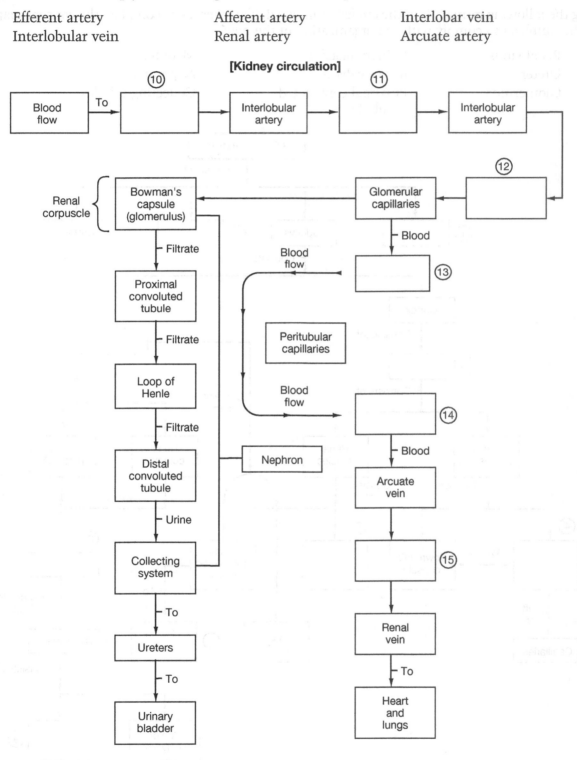

[Kidney circulation]

Concept Map III

Using the following terms, fill in the circled, numbered, blank spaces to complete the concept map. Follow the numbers to comply with the organization of the map.

Adrenal cortex $\downarrow Na^+$ excretion $\downarrow H_2O$ excretion
liver $\downarrow$ plasma volume $\uparrow Na^+$ reabsorption
angiotensin I   Renin

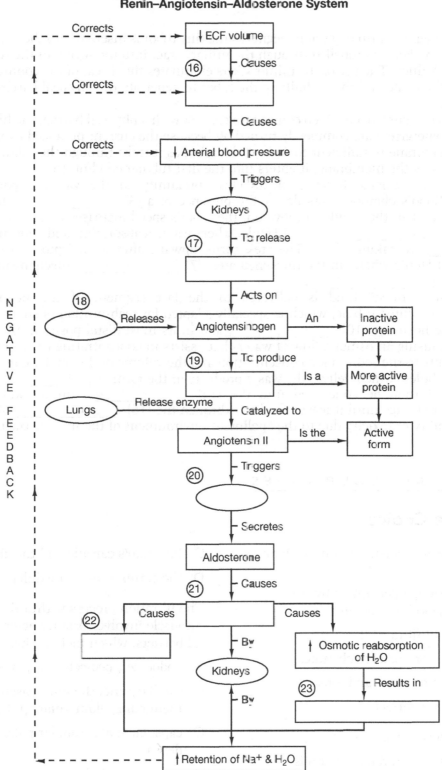

Renin–Angiotensin–Aldosterone System

Body Trek

Using the terms below, fill in the blanks to complete the trek through the urinary system.

aldosterone	protein-free	ions
ascending limb	active transport	ADH
glomerulus	urine	urinary bladder
collecting	proximal	descending limb
urethra	filtrate	ureters
distal		

Robo's trek through the urinary system begins as the tiny robot is inserted into the urethra and with the aid of two mini-rockets is propelled through the urinary tract into the region of the renal corpuscle in the cortex of the kidney. The use of the mini-rockets eliminates the threat of the countercurrent flow of the filtrate and the urine and the inability of the robot to penetrate the physical barriers imposed in the capsular space.

Rocket shutdown occurs just as Robo comes into contact with a physical barrier, the filtration membrane. The robot's energizers are completely turned off because the current produced by the fluid coming through the membrane is sufficient to "carry" the robot as it treks through the tubular system.

As the fluid crosses the membrane, it enters into the first tubular conduit, the (1) _____ convoluted tubule, identifiable because of its close proximity to the vascular pole of the (2) _____. Robo's chemosensors detect the presence of a (3) _____ filtrate in this area. Using the current in the tubule to move on, the robot's speed increases because of a sharp turn and descent into the (4) _____ of Henle, where water reabsorption and concentration of the (5) _____ are taking place. The trek turns upward after a "hairpin" turn into the (6) _____ of Henle where, in the thickened area, (7) _____ mechanisms are causing the reabsorption of (8) _____.

The somewhat "refined" fluid is delivered to the last segment of the nephron, the (9) _____ convoluted tubule, which is specially adapted for reabsorption of sodium ions due to the influence of the hormone (10) _____, and in its most distal position, the effect of (11) _____, causing an osmotic flow of water that assists in concentrating the filtrate.

Final adjustments to the sodium ion concentration and the volume of the fluid are made in the (12) _____ tubules, which deliver the waste products in the form of (13) _____ to the renal pelvis. It will then be conducted into the (14) _____ on its way to the (15) _____ for storage until it leaves the body through the (16) _____—Robo's way of escaping the possibility of toxicity due to the "polluted" environment of the urinary tract.

COVERING ALL YOUR BASES

[L2] Multiple Choice

Select the best answer or answers from the choices given.

1. The vital function(s) performed by the nephrons in the kidneys is (are):

   A. production of filtrate

   B. reabsorption of organic substrates

   C. reabsorption of water and ions

   D. a, b, and c are correct

2. The renal corpuscle consists of:

   A. renal columns and renal pyramids

   B. major and minor calyces

   C. Bowman's capsule and the glomerulus

   D. the cortex and the medulla

3. The filtration process within the renal corpuscle involves passage across three physical barriers, which include the:

   A. podocytes, pedicels, slit pores

   B. capillary endothelium, basement membrane, glomerular epithelium

   C. capsular space, tubular pole, macula densa

   D. collecting tubules, collecting ducts, papillary ducts

4. The thin segments in the loop of Henle are:

   A. relatively impermeable to water; freely permeable to ions and other solutes

   B. freely permeable to water, ions, and other solutes

   C. relatively impermeable to water, ions, and other solutes

   D. freely permeable to water; relatively impermeable to ions and other solutes

5. The thick segments in the loop of Henle contain:

   A. ADH-regulated permeability

   B. an aldosterone-regulated pump

   C. transport mechanisms that pump materials out of the filtrate

   D. diffusion mechanisms for getting rid of excess water

6. The collecting system in the kidney is responsible for:

   A. active secretion and reabsorption of sodium ions

   B. absorption of nutrients, plasma proteins, and ions from the filtrate

   C. creation of the medullary concentration gradient

   D. making final adjustments to the sodium ion concentration and volume of urine

7. Blood reaches the vascular pole of each glomerulus through a(n):

   A. efferent arteriole

   B. afferent arteriole

   C. renal artery

   D. arcuate arteries

8. Sympathetic innervation into the kidney is responsible for:

   A. regulation of glomerular blood flow and pressure

   B. stimulation of renin release

   C. direct stimulation of water and sodium ion reabsorption

   D. a, b, and c are correct

9. When plasma glucose concentrations are higher than the renal threshold, glucose concentrations in the filtrate exceed the tubular maximum (T_m) and:

   A. glucose is transported across the membrane by countertransport

   B. the glucose is filtered out at the glomerulus

   C. glucose appears in the urine

   D. the individual has eaten excessive amounts of sweets

10. The outward pressure forcing water and solute molecules across the glomerulus wall is the:

    A. capsular hydrostatic pressure

    B. glomerular hydrostatic pressure

    C. blood osmotic pressure

    D. filtration pressure

11. The opposing forces of the filtration pressure at the glomerulus are the:

    A. glomerular hydrostatic pressure and blood osmotic pressure

    B. capsular hydrostatic pressure and glomerular hydrostatic pressure

    C. blood pressure and glomerular filtration rate

    D. capsular hydrostatic pressure and blood osmotic pressure

12. The amount of filtrate produced in the kidneys each minute is the:

    A. glomerular filtration rate

    B. glomerular hydrostatic pressure

    C. capsular hydrostatic pressure

    D. osmotic gradient

13. Inadequate ADH secretion results in the inability to reclaim the water entering the filtrate, causing:

    A. glycosuria

    B. dehydration

    C. anuria

    D. dysuria

14. Under normal circumstances virtually all the glucose, amino acids, and other nutrients are reabsorbed before the filtrate leaves the:

    A. distal convoluted tubule

    B. glomerulus

    C. collecting ducts

    D. proximal convoluted tubule

15. Aldosterone stimulates ion pumps along the distal convoluted tubule (DCT), the collecting tubule, and the collecting duct, causing a(n):

    A. increase in the number of sodium ions lost in the urine

    B. decrease in the concentration of the filtrate

    C. reduction in the number of sodium ions lost in the urine

    D. countercurrent multiplication

16. The high osmotic concentrations found in the kidney medulla are primarily due to:

    A. presence of sodium ions, chloride ions, and urea

    B. presence of excessive amounts of water

    C. hydrogen and ammonium ions

    D. a, b, and c are correct

17. The hormones that affect the glomerular filtration rate (GFR) by regulating blood pressure and volume are:

    A. aldosterone, epinephrine, oxytocin

    B. insulin, glucagon, glucocorticoids

    C. renin, erythropoietin, ADH

    D. a, b, and c are correct

18. Angiotensin II is a potent hormone that:

    A. causes constriction of the efferent arteriole at the nephron

    B. triggers the release of ADH in the CNS

    C. stimulates secretion of aldosterone by the adrenal cortex and epinephrine by the adrenal medulla

    D. a, b, and c are correct

19. Sympathetic innervation of the afferent arterioles causes a(n):

    A. decrease in GFR and slowing of filtrate production

    B. increase in GFR and an increase in filtrate production

    C. decrease in GFR and an increase in filtrate production

    D. increase in GFR and a slowing of filtrate production

20. During periods of strenuous exercise, sympathetic activation causes the blood flow to:

    A. decrease to skin and skeletal muscles; increase to kidneys

    B. cause an increase in GFR

    C. increase to skin and skeletal muscles; decrease to kidneys

    D. be shunted toward the kidneys

[L2]   Completion

Using the terms below, complete the following statements.

aldosterone	vasa recta	angiotensin II
filtration	diabetes insipidus	osmotic gradient
macula densa	renin	glomerular filtration rate
secretion	transport maximum	cortical
retroperitoneal	reabsorption	glomerular filtration

1. The kidneys lie between the muscles of the dorsal body wall and the peritoneal lining in a position referred to as _____.

2. The amount of filtrate produced in the kidneys each minute is the _____.

3. The process responsible for concentrating the filtrate as it travels through the collecting system toward the renal pelvis is the _____.

4. When all available carrier proteins are occupied at one time, the saturation concentration is called the _____.

5. The region in the distal convoluted tubule (DCT) where the tubule cells adjacent to the tubular pole are taller and contain clustered nuclei is called the _____.

6. Approximately 85 percent of the nephrons in a kidney are called _____ nephrons.

7. A capillary that accompanies the loop of Henle into the medulla is termed the _____.

8. When hydrostatic pressure forces water across a membrane, the process is referred to as _____.

9. The removal of water and solute molecules from the filtrate is termed _____.

10. Transport of solutes across the tubular epithelium and into the filtrate is _____.

11. The vital first step essential to all kidney function is _____.

12. The ion pump and the potassium ion channels are controlled by the hormone _____.

13. When a person produces relatively large quantities of dilute urine, the condition is termed _____.

14. The hormone that causes a brief but powerful vasoconstriction in peripheral capillary beds is _____.

15. Sympathetic activation stimulates the juxtaglomerular apparatus to release _____.

[L2]   Short Essay

Briefly answer the following questions in the spaces provided below.

1. What are six essential functions of the urinary system?

2. Trace the pathway of a drop of urine from the time it leaves the kidney until it is urinated from the body. (Use arrows to show direction.)

3. What three concentric layers of connective tissue protect and anchor the kidneys?

4. Trace the pathway of a drop of filtrate from the time it goes through the filtration membrane in the glomerulus until it enters the collecting tubules as concentrated urine. (Use arrows to indicate direction of flow.)

5. What vital functions of the kidneys are performed by the nephrons?

6. (a) What three physical barriers are involved with passage of materials during the filtration process?

   (b) Cite one structural characteristic of each barrier.

7. What two hormones are secreted by the juxtaglomerular apparatus?

8. What known functions result from sympathetic innervation into the kidneys?

9. What are the three processes involved in urine formation?

10. Write a formula to show the following relationship and define each component of the formula:

    The *filtration pressure* (P$_f$) at the glomerulus is the difference between the blood pressure and the opposing capsular and osmotic pressures.

11. Why does hydrogen ion secretion accelerate during starvation?

12. What three basic concepts describe the mechanism of countercurrent multiplication?

13. What three control mechanisms are involved with regulation of the glomerular filtration rate (GFR)?

14. What four hormones affect urine production? Describe the role of each one.

LEVEL 3   Critical Thinking/Application

Using principles and concepts learned about the urinary system, answer the following questions. Write your answers on a separate sheet of paper.

1. I. O. Yew spends an evening with the boys at the local tavern. During the course of the night he makes numerous trips to the rest room to urinate. In addition to drinking an excessive amount of fluid, what effect does the consumption of alcohol have on the urinary system to cause urination?

2. Lori C. has had a series of laboratory tests, including a CBC, lipid profile series, and a urinalysis. The urinalysis revealed the presence of an abnormal amount of plasma proteins and white blood cells. (a) What is your diagnosis? (b) What effect does her condition have on her urine output?

3. On an anatomy and physiology examination your instructor asks the following question:

   What is the *principal function* associated with each of the following components of the nephron?

   (a) renal corpuscle

   (b) proximal convoluted tubule

   (c) distal convoluted tubule

   (d) loop of Henle and collecting system

4. (a) Given the following information, determine the effective filtration pressure (EFP) at the glomerulus:

glomerular blood hydrostatic pressure	G_{hp}	60 mm Hg
capsular hydrostatic pressure	C_{hp}	18 mm Hg
glomerular blood osmotic pressure	OP_b	32 mm Hg
capsular osmotic pressure	C_{op}	5 mm Hg

   (b) How does the effective filtration pressure affect the GFR?

   (c) What are the implications of an effective filtration pressure (EFP) of 15 mm Hg?

5. Cindy F. is a marathon runner who, from time to time, experiences acute kidney dysfunction during the event. Laboratory tests have shown elevated serum concentrations of K^+, lowered serum concentrations of Na^+, and a decrease in the GFR. At one time she experienced renal failure. Explain why these symptoms and conditions may occur while running a marathon.

25

FLUID, ELECTROLYTE, AND ACID–BASE BALANCE

Overview

In many of the previous chapters we examined the various organ systems, focusing on the structural components and the functional activities necessary to *support* life. This chapter details the roles the organ systems play in *maintaining* life in the billions of individual cells in the body. Early in the study of anatomy and physiology we established that the cell is the basic unit of structure and function of all living things, no matter how complex the organism is as a whole. The last few chapters concentrated on the necessity of meeting the nutrient needs of cells and getting rid of waste products that might interfere with normal cell functions. To meet the nutrient needs of cells, substances must move in; and to get rid of wastes, materials must move out. The result is a constant movement of materials into and out of the cells.

Both the external environment (interstitial fluid) and the internal environment of the cell (intracellular fluid) comprise an "exchange system" operating within controlled and changing surroundings, producing a dynamic equilibrium by which homeostasis is maintained.

Chapter 25 considers the mechanics and dynamics of fluid balance, electrolyte balance, acid–base balance, and the interrelationships of functional patterns that operate in the body to support and maintain a constant state of equilibrium.

LEVEL 1   Review of Chapter Objectives

1. Explain what is meant by the terms "fluid balance," "electrolyte balance," and "acid–base balance," and discuss their importance for homeostasis.

2. Compare the composition of the intracellular and extracellular fluids.

3. Explain the basic concepts involved in the regulation of fluids and electrolytes.

4. Identify the hormones that play important roles in regulating fluid and electrolyte balance and describe their effects.

5. Describe the movement of fluid that takes place within the ECF, between the ECF and the ICF, and between the ECF and the environment.

6. Discuss the mechanisms by which sodium, potassium, calcium, and chloride ion concentrations are regulated to maintain electrolyte balance.

7. Explain the buffering systems that balance the pH of the intracellular and extracellular fluid.

8. Describe the compensatory mechanisms involved in the maintenance of acid–base balance.

9. Identify the most frequent threats to acid–base balance.

10. Explain how the body responds when the pH of body fluids varies outside normal limits.

11. Describe the effects of aging on fluid, electrolyte, and acid–base balance.

[L1]   Multiple Choice

Place the letter corresponding to the correct answer in the space provided.

OBJ. 1   _____   1. When the amount of water you gain each day is equal to the amount you lose to the enviroment, you are in:

    a. electrolyte balance

    b. fluid balance

    c. acid–base balance

    d. dynamic equilibrium

OBJ. 1   _____   2. When the production of hydrogen ions in your body is precisely offset by their loss, you are in:

    a. electrolyte balance

    b. osmotic equilibrium

    c. fluid balance

    d. acid–base balance

OBJ. 1   _____   3. Electrolyte balance primarily involves balancing the rates of absorption across the digestive tract with rates of loss at the:

    a. heart and lungs

    b. kidneys and sweat glands

    c. stomach and liver

    d. pancreas and gallbladder

OBJ. 2   _____   4. Nearly two-thirds of the total body water content is:

    a. extracellular fluid (ECF)

    b. intracellular fluid (ICF)

    c. tissue fluid

    d. interstitial fluid (IF)

OBJ. 2   _____   5. Extracellular fluids in the body consist of:

    a. interstitial fluid, blood plasma, lymph

    b. cerebrospinal fluid, synovial fluid, serous fluids

    c. aqueous humor, perilymph, endolymph

    d. a, b, and c are correct

OBJ. 2   _____   6. The principal ions in the extracellular fluid (ECF) are:

    a. sodium, chloride, and bicarbonate

    b. potassium, magnesium, and phosphate

    c. phosphate, sulfate, and magnesium

    d. potassium, ammonium, and chloride

OBJ. 3   _____   7. If the ECF is *hypertonic* with respect to the ICF, water will move:

    a. from the ECF into the cell until osmotic equilibrium is restored

    b. from the cells into the ECF until osmotic equilibrium is restored

    c. in both directions until osmotic equilibrium is restored

    d. in response to the pressure of carrier molecules

OBJ. 3 _____ 8. When water is lost but electrolytes are retained, the osmolarity of the ECF rises and osmosis then moves water:

    a. out of the ECF and into the ICF until isotonicity is reached

    b. back and forth between the ICF and the ECF

    c. out of the ICF and into the ECF until isotonicity is reached

    d. directly into the blood plasma until equilibrium is reached

OBJ. 3 _____ 9. When pure water is consumed, the extracellular fluid becomes:

    a. hypotonic with respect to the ICF

    b. hypertonic with respect to the ICF

    c. isotonic with respect to the ICF

    d. the ICF and the ECF are in equilibrium

OBJ. 4 _____ 10. Physiological adjustments affecting fluid and electrolyte balance are mediated primarily by:

    a. antidiuretic hormone (ADH)

    b. aldosterone

    c. atrial natriuretic peptide (ANP)

    d. a, b, and c are correct

OBJ. 4 _____ 11. The two important effects of increased release of ADH are:

    a. increased rate of sodium absorption and decreased thirst

    b. reduction of urinary water losses and stimulation of the thirst center

    c. decrease in the plasma volume and elimination of the source of stimulation

    d. decrease in plasma osmolarity and alteration of composition of tissue fluid

OBJ. 4 _____ 12. Secretion of aldosterone occurs in response to:

    a. a fall in plasma volume at the juxtaglomerular apparatus

    b. a fall in blood pressure at the juxtaglomerular apparatus

    c. potassium ion concentrations

    d. a, b, and c are correct

OBJ. 4 _____ 13. Atrial natriuretic peptide hormone:

    a. reduces thirst

    b. blocks the release of ADH

    c. blocks the release of aldosterone

    d. a, b, and c are correct

OBJ. 4 _____ 14. The major contributors to the osmolarities of the ECF and the ICF are:

    a. ADH and aldosterone

    b. sodium and potassium

    c. renin and angiotensin

    d. chloride and bicarbonate

OBJ. 5 _____ 15. The force that tends to push water out of the plasma and into the interstitial fluid is the:

    a. net hydrostatic pressure

    b. colloid osmotic pressure

    c. total peripheral resistance

    d. mean arterial pressure

OBJ. 5 _____ 16. The exchange between plasma and interstitial fluid is determined by the relationship between the:

    a. total peripheral resistance and mean arterial pressure

    b. fluid balance and acid–base balance

    c. net hydrostatic and net colloid osmotic pressures

    d. none of the above

OBJ. 6 _____ 17. The concentration of potassium in the ECF is controlled by adjustments in the rate of active secretion:

    a. in the proximal convoluted tubule of the nephron

    b. in the loop of Henle

    c. along the distal convoluted tubule of the nephron

    d. along the collecting tubules

OBJ. 6 _____ 18. The activity that occurs in the body to maintain calcium homeostasis occurs primarily in the:

    a. bone

    b. digestive tract

    c. kidneys

    d. a, b, and c are correct

OBJ. 7 _____ 19. The hemoglobin buffer system helps prevent drastic alterations in pH when:

    a. the plasma P_{CO_2} is rising or falling

    b. there is an increase in hemoglobin production

    c. there is a decrease in RBC production

    d. the plasma P_{CO_2} is constant

OBJ. 7 _____ 20. The primary role of the carbonic acid–bicarbonate buffer system is in preventing pH changes caused by:

    a. rising or falling P_{CO_2}

    b. organic acid and fixed acids in the ECF

    c. increased production of sulfuric acid and phosphoric acid

    d. a, b, and c are correct

OBJ. 7 _____ 21. Pulmonary and renal mechanisms support the buffer systems by:

    a. secreting or generating hydrogen ions

    b. controlling the excretion of acids and bases

    c. generating additional buffers when necessary

    d. a, b, and c are correct

OBJ. 7 _____ 22. The lungs contribute to pH regulation by their effects on the:

    a. hemoglobin buffer system

    b. phosphate buffer system

    c. carbonic acid–bicarbonate buffer system

    d. protein buffer system

OBJ. 7 _____ 23. Increasing or decreasing the rate of respiration can have a profound effect on the buffering capacity of body fluids by:

    a. lowering or raising the Po_2

    b. lowering or raising the Pco_2

    c. increasing the production of lactic acid

    d. a, b, and c are correct

OBJ. 8 _____ 24. The renal response to acidosis is limited to:

    a. reabsorption of H^+ and secretion of HCO_3^-

    b. reabsorption of H^+ and HCO_3^-

    c. secretion of H^+ and generation or reabsorption of HCO_3^-

    d. secretion of H^+ and HCO_3^-

OBJ. 8 _____ 25. When carbon dioxide concentrations rise, additional hydrogen ions and bicarbonate ions are excreted and the:

    a. pH goes up

    b. pH goes down

    c. pH remains the same

    d. pH is not affected

OBJ. 9 _____ 26. Disorders that have the potential for disrupting pH balance in the body include:

    a. emphysema, renal failure

    b. neural damage, CNS disease

    c. heart failure, hypotension

    d. a, b, and c are correct

OBJ. 9 _____ 27. Respiratory alkalosis develops when respiratory activity:

    a. raises plasma Pco_2 to above-normal levels

    b. lowers plasma Pco_2 to below-normal levels

    c. decreases plasma Po_2 to below-normal levels

    d. when Pco_2 levels are not affected

OBJ. 9 _____ 28. The most frequent cause of metabolic acidosis is:

    a. production of a large number of fixed or organic acids

    b. a severe bicarbonate loss

    c. an impaired ability to excrete hydrogen ions at the kidneys

    d. generation of large quantities of ketone bodies

OBJ. 10 _____ 29. A mismatch between carbon dioxide generation in peripheral tissues and carbon dioxide excretion at the lungs is a:

    a. metabolic acid–base disorder

    b. condition known as ketoacidosis

    c. respiratory acid–base disorder

    d. severe bicarbonate loss

OBJ. 10 _____ 30. The major cause(s) of metabolic acidosis is (are):

    a. production of a large number of fixed or organic acids

    b. impaired ability to excrete H^- at the kidneys

    c. a severe bicarbonate loss

    d. a, b, and c are correct

OBJ. 10 _____ 31. When bicarbonate ions interact with hydrogen ions in solution forming carbonic acid (H_2CO_3), the resulting condition is:

    a. metabolic alkalosis

    b. metabolic acidosis

    c. hypoventilation

    d. hypercapnia

OBJ. 11 _____ 32. As a result of the aging process, the ability to regulate pH through renal compensation is due to:

    a. a reduction in the number of functional nephrons

    b. increased glomerular filtration

    c. increased ability to concentrate urine

    d. a reduction in the rate of insensible perspiration

OBJ. 11 _____ 33. The risk of respiratory acidosis in the elderly is increased due to:

    a. a reduction in the number of nephrons

    b. a reduction in vital capacity

    c. increased insensible perspiration

    d. a decrease in ADH and aldosterone sensitivity

[L1]   Completion

Using the terms below, complete the following statements.

respiratory compensation	fluid	skeletal mass
osmoreceptors	hypotonic	alkalosis
acidosis	hypertonic	fluid shift
aldosterone	renal compensation	electrolyte
antidiuretic hormone	kidneys	calcium
buffers	hemoglobin	edema
hypercapnia	colloid osmotic pressure	net hydrostatic pressure

OBJ. 1   1. When there is neither a net gain nor a net loss of any ion in the body fluid, an _____ balance exists.

OBJ. 1   2. When the amount of water gained each day is equal to the amount lost to the environment, a person is in _____ balance.

OBJ. 2   3. Water movement between the ECF and the ICF is termed a _____.

OBJ. 3   4. Osmotic concentrations of the plasma are monitored by special cells in the hypothalamus called _____.

OBJ. 3   5. If the ECF becomes more concentrated with respect to the ICF, the ECF is _____.

OBJ. 3   6. If the ECF becomes more dilute with respect to the ICF, the ECF is _____.

OBJ. 4   7. The rate of sodium absorption along the DCT (distal convoluted tubule) and collecting system of the kidneys is regulated by the secretion of _____.

OBJ. 4   8. The hormone that stimulates water conservation at the kidneys and the thirst center to promote the drinking of fluids is _____.

OBJ. 5

9. The movement of abnormal amounts of water from plasma into interstitial fluid is called _____.

OBJ. 5

10. The force that tends to push water out of the plasma and into the interstitial fluid is the _____.

OBJ. 5

11. The force that tends to draw water out of the interstitial fluid and into the plasma is the _____.

OBJ. 6

12. The most important site of sodium ion regulation is the _____.

OBJ. 6

13. Calcitonin from the C cells of the thyroid gland promotes a loss of _____.

OBJ. 7

14. Dissolved compounds that can provide or remove hydrogen ions and thereby stabilize the pH of a solution are _____.

OBJ. 7

15. The only intracellular buffer system that can have an immediate effect on the pH of the CSF is the _____ buffer system.

OBJ. 8

16. A change in the respiratory rate that helps stabilize pH is called _____.

OBJ. 8

17. A change in the rates of hydrogen ion and bicarbonate ion secretion or absorption in response to changes in plasma pH is called _____.

OBJ. 9

18. When the pH in the body falls below 7.35, the condition is called _____.

OBJ. 9

19. When the pH in the body increases above 7.45, the condition is called _____.

OBJ. 10

20. A low plasma pH due to an elevated plasma P_{CO_2} is called _____.

OBJ. 11

21. Many people over age sixty experience a net loss in their body mineral content due to decreased muscle mass and _____.

[L1]   Matching

Match the terms in column B with the terms in column A. Use letters for answers in the spaces provided.

Part I		Column A	Column B
OBJ. 1	_____	1. fluid balance	A. H_2O moves cells into ECF
OBJ. 2	_____	2. tissue fluid	B. dominant cation—ECF
OBJ. 2	_____	3. fluid compartments	C. concentration of dissolved solutes
OBJ. 2	_____	4. potassium	
OBJ. 2	_____	5. sodium	D. dominant cation—ICF
OBJ. 3	_____	6. key components of ECF	E. ICF and ECF
OBJ. 3	_____	7. osmolarity	F. posterior pituitary gland
OBJ. 4	_____	8. cardiac muscle fiber	G. hyponatremia
OBJ. 4	_____	9. antidiuretic hormone	H. plasma, cerebrospinal fluid
OBJ. 5	_____	10. hypertonic	I. water gain-water loss
OBJ. 5	_____	11. overhydration	J. atrial natriuretic peptide
			K. interstitial fluid

Part II		Column A	Column B
OBJ. 6	_____	12. ADH secretion decrease	L. buffers pH of ICF
OBJ. 6	_____	13. increased venous return	M. hyperventilation
OBJ. 7	_____	14. phosphate buffer system	N. buffers pH of ECF
			O. respiratory acidosis
OBJ. 7	_____	15. carbonic acid– bicarbonate buffer	P. water loss at kidneys increases
OBJ. 8	_____	16. balancing H^+ gains/losses	Q. release of ANP
OBJ. 8	_____	17. decreased P_{CO^2}	R. pH increases
OBJ. 9	_____	18. starvation	S. ↓ renal compensation
OBJ. 10	_____	19. hypocapnia	T. ketoacidosis
OBJ. 10	_____	20. hypercapnia	U. maintenance of acid–base balance
OBJ. 11	_____	21. aging effect	

[L1]   Drawing/Illustration Labeling

Using the terms and figures below, fill in each numbered box to complete the information regarding pH.

Figure 25.1   The pH Scale

alkalosis   pH 6.80   pH 7.80

acidosis   pH 7.35   pH 7.45

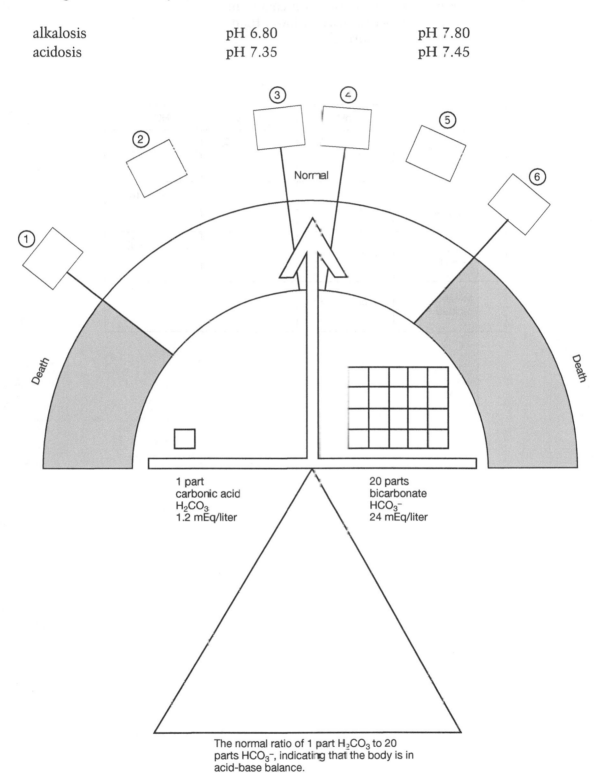

Normal

Death

Death

1 part
carbonic acid
H_2CO_3
1.2 mEq/liter

20 parts
bicarbonate
HCO_3^-
24 mEq/liter

The normal ratio of 1 part H_2CO_3 to 20
parts HCO_3^-, indicating that the body is in
acid-base balance.

OBJ. 9   **Figure 25.2   Relationships among pH, Pco$_2$, and HCO$_3^-$**

Using arrows and the letter N (normal), fill in the chart below to show the relationships among pH, Pco$_2$, and HCO$_3^-$. (Assume no compensation.)

Key: ↑ — increased or higher than
↓ — decreased or lower than
N — normal

	pH		Pco$_2$	HCO$_3^-$
Respiratory acidosis	7.35	①	⑤	⑨
Metabolic acidosis	7.35	②	⑥	⑩
Respiratory acidosis	7.45	③	⑦	⑪
Metabolic acidosis	7.45	④	⑧	⑫

LEVEL 2   Concept Synthesis

Concept Map I

Using the following terms, fill in the circled, numbered, blank spaces to complete the concept map. Follow the numbers to comply with the organization of the map.

↑ H₂O retention at kidneys   ↓ Volume of body H₂O
Aldosterone secretion by adrenal cortex

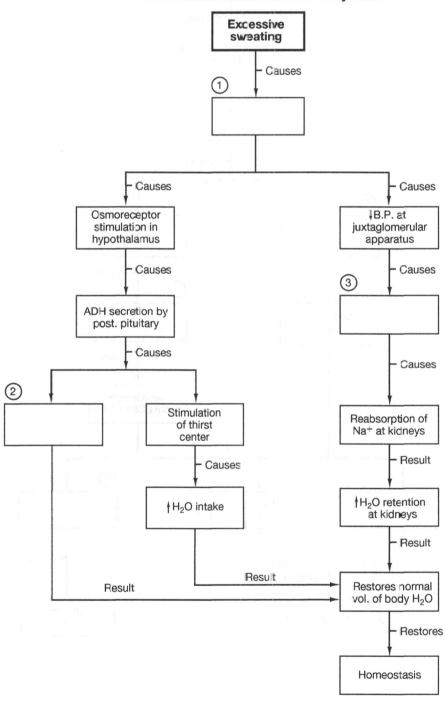

Homeostasis of total volume of body water

Concept Map II

Using the following terms, fill in the circled, numbered, blank spaces to complete the concept map. Follow the numbers to comply with the organization of the map.

$\downarrow$ ECF volume $\downarrow$ pH
$\uparrow$ ICF volume   ECF hypotonic to ICF

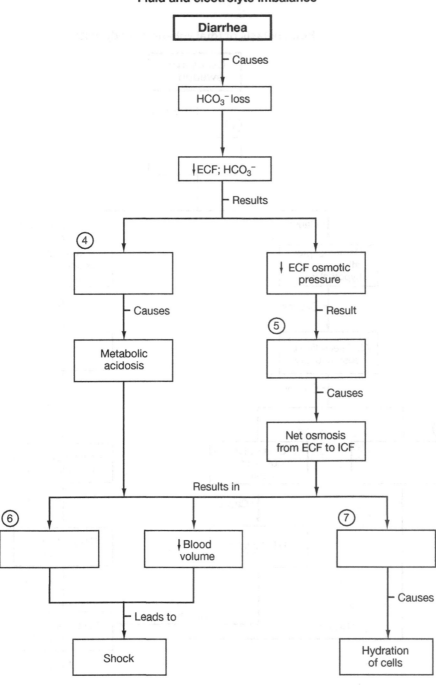

Fluid and electrolyte imbalance

Concept Map III

Using the following terms, fill in the circled, numbered, blank spaces to complete the concept map. Follow the numbers to comply with the organization of the map.

↑ Blood pH   ↑ Depth of breathing   ↑ Blood CO_2
Hyperventilation   Normal blood pH

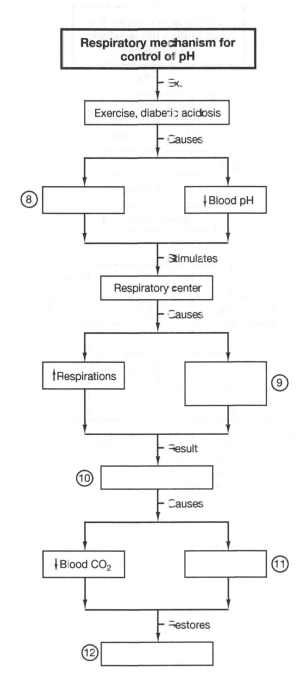

Concept Map IV

Using the following terms, fill in the circled, numbered, blank spaces to complete the concept map. Follow the numbers to comply with the organization of the map.

HCO$_3^-$ ↑ Blood pH   ↓ Blood pH

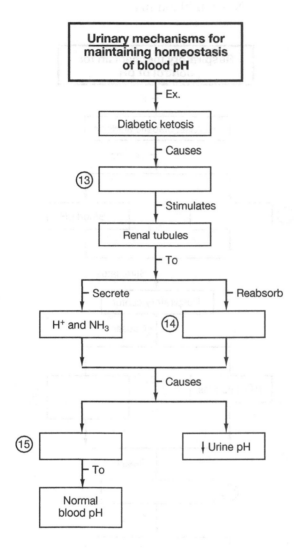

Concept Map V

Using the following terms, fill in the circled, numbered, blank spaces to complete the concept map. Follow the numbers to comply with the organization of the map.

↑ Plasma volume   ↓ H₂O loss
↑ ANP release   ↓ ADH release
↑ H₂O loss   ↓ B.P. at kidneys
↑ Aldosterone release   ↓ Aldosterone release

Homeostasis Fluid volume regulation—sodium ion concentrations

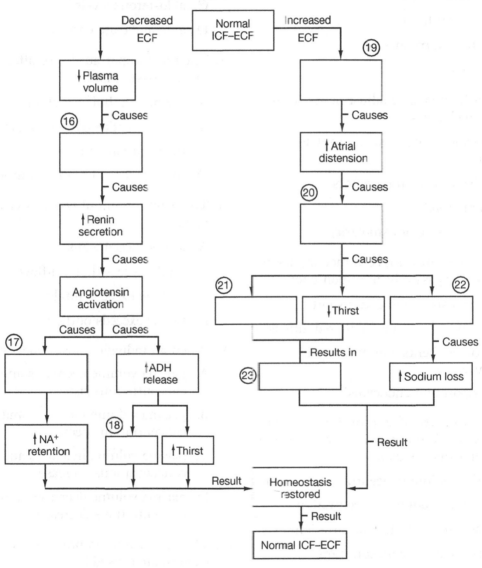

COVERING ALL YOUR BASES

[L2] Multiple Choice

Select the best answer or answers from the choices given.

1. All of the homeostatic mechanisms that monitor and adjust the composition of body fluids respond to changes in the:

   A. intracellular fluid

   B. extracellular fluid

   C. regulatory hormones

   D. fluid balance

2. Important homeostatic adjustments occur in response to changes in:

   A. cell receptors that respond to ICF volumes

   B. hypothalamic osmoreceptors

   C. hormone levels

   D. plasma volume or osmolarity

3. All water transport across cell membranes and epithelia occur passively, in response to:

   A. active transport and cotransport

   B. countertransport and facilitated diffusion

   C. osmotic gradients and hydrostatic pressure

   D. cotransport and endocytosis

4. Whenever the rate of sodium intake or output changes, there is a corresponding gain or loss of water that tends to:

   A. keep the sodium concentration constant

   B. increase the sodium concentration

   C. decrease the sodium concentration

   D. alter the sodium concentration

5. Angiotensin II produces a coordinated elevation in the extracellular fluid volume by:

   A. stimulating thirst

   B. causing the release of ADH

   C. triggering the secretion of aldosterone

   D. a, b, and c are correct

6. The rate of tubular secretion of potassium ions changes in response to:

   A. alterations in the potassium ion concentration in the ECF

   B. changes in pH

   C. aldosterone levels

   D. a, b, and c are correct

7. The most important factor affecting the pH in body tissues is:

   A. the protein buffer system

   B. carbon dioxide concentration

   C. the bicarbonate reserve

   D. the presence of ammonium ions

8. The body content of water or electrolytes will rise if:

   A. losses exceed gains

   B. intake is less than outflow

   C. outflow exceeds intake

   D. intake exceeds outflow

9. When an individual loses body water:

   A. plasma volume decreases and electrolyte concentrations rise

   B. plasma volume increases and electrolyte concentrations decrease

   C. plasma volume increases and electrolyte concentrations increase

   D. plasma volume decreases and electrolyte concentrations decrease

10. The most common problems with electrolyte balance are caused by:

    A. shifts of the bicarbonate ion

    B. an imbalance between sodium gains and losses

    C. an imbalance between chloride gains and losses

    D. a, b, and c are correct

11. Sodium ions enter the ECF by crossing the digestive epithelium via:

    A. diffusion

    B. active transport

    C. diffusion and active transport

    D. facilitated diffusion

12. Deviations outside of the normal pH range due to changes in hydrogen ion concentrations:

    A. disrupt the stability of cell membranes

    B. alter protein structure

    C. change the activities of important enzymes

    D. a, b, and c are correct

13. When the Pco_2 increases and additional hydrogen ions and bicarbonate ions are released into the plasma, the:

    A. pH goes up; ↑ alkalinity

    B. pH goes down; ↑ acidity

    C. pH goes up; ↓ acidity

    D. pH is not affected

14. Important examples of organic acids found in the body are:

    A. sulfuric acid and phosphoric acid

    B. hydrochloric acid and carbonic acid

    C. lactic acid and ketone bodies

    D. a, b, and c are correct

15. In a protein buffer system, if the pH increases, the carboxyl group (COOH) of the amino acid dissociates and releases:

    A. a hydroxyl ion

    B. a molecule of carbon monoxide

    C. a hydrogen ion

    D. a molecule of carbon dioxide

16. Normal pH values are limited to the range between:

    A. 7.35 to 7.45

    B. 6.8 to 7.0

    C. 6.0 to 8.0

    D. 6.35 to 8.35

17. Under normal circumstances, during respiratory acidosis the chemoreceptors monitoring the Pco_2 of the plasma and CSF will eliminate the problem by calling for:

    A. a decrease in the breathing rate

    B. a decrease in pulmonary ventilation rates

    C. an increase in pulmonary ventilation rates

    D. breathing into a small paper bag

18. When a normal pulmonary response does not reverse respiratory acidosis, the kidneys respond by:

    A. increasing the reabsorption of hydrogen ions

    B. increasing the rate of hydrogen ion secretion into the filtrate

    C. decreasing the rate of hydrogen ion secretion into the filtrate

    D. increased loss of bicarbonate ions

19. Chronic diarrhea causes a severe loss of bicarbonate ions resulting in:

    A. respiratory acidosis

    B. respiratory alkalosis

    C. metabolic acidosis

    D. metabolic alkalosis

20. Compensation for metabolic alkalosis involves:

    A. ↑ pulmonary ventilation; ↑ loss of bicarbonates in the urine

    B. ↑ pulmonary ventilation; ↓ loss of bicarbonates in the urine

    C. ↓ pulmonary ventilation; ↓ loss of bicarbonates in the urine

    D. ↓ pulmonary ventilation; ↑ loss of bicarbonates in the urine

[L2]   Completion

Using the terms below, complete the following statements.

buffer system	organic acids	fixed acids
lactic acidosis	hypoventilation	angiotensin II
volatile acid	kidneys	respiratory acidosis
alkaline tide	ketoacidosis	hyperventilation

1. The most important sites of sodium ion regulation are the _____.

2. Renin release by kidney cells initiates a chain of events leading to the activation of _____.

3. An acid that can leave solution and enter the atmosphere is referred to as a _____.

4. Acids that remain in body fluids until excreted at the kidneys are called _____.

5. Acid participants in or by-products of cellular metabolism are referred to as _____.

6. A combination of a weak acid and its dissociation products comprise a _____.

7. When the respiratory system is unable to eliminate normal amounts of CO_2 generated by peripheral tissues, the result is the development of _____.

8. The usual cause of respiratory acidosis is _____.

9. Physical or psychological stresses or conscious effort may produce an increased respiratory rate referred to as _____.

10. Severe exercise or prolonged oxygen starvation of cells may develop into _____.

11. Generation of large quantities of ketone bodies during the postabsorptive state results in a condition known as _____.

12. An influx of large numbers of bicarbonate ions into the ECF due to secretion of HCl by the gastric mucosa is known as the _____.

[L2]   Short Essay

Briefly answer the following questions in the spaces provided below.

1. What three different, interrelated types of homeostasis are involved in the maintenance of normal volume and composition in the ECF and the ICF?

2. What three primary hormones mediate physiological adjustments that affect fluid and electrolyte balance?

3. What two major effects does ADH have on maintaining homeostatic volumes of water in the body?

4. What three adjustments control the rate of tubular secretion of potassium ions along the DCT of the nephron?

5. What two primary steps are involved in the regulation of sodium ion concentrations?

6. Write the chemical equation to show how CO_2 interacts with H_2O in solution to form molecules of carbonic acid. Continue the equation to show the dissociation of carbonic acid molecules to produce hydrogen ions and bicarbonate ions.

7. (a) What three *chemical* buffer systems represent the first line of defense against pH shift?

   (b) What two *physiological* buffers represent the second line of defense against pH shift?

8. How do pulmonary and renal mechanisms support the chemical buffer systems?

9. What is the difference between hypercapnia and hypocapnia?

10. What are the three major causes of metabolic acidosis?

LEVEL 3   Critical Thinking/Application

Using principles and concepts learned in Chapter 25, answer the following questions. Write your answers on a separate sheet of paper. Some of the questions in this section will require the following information for your reference.

Normal arterial blood gas values:

pH: 7.35–7.45
Pco_2: 35 to 45 mm Hg
Po_2: 80 to 100 mm Hg
HCO_3^-: 22 to 26 mEq/liter

1. A comatose teenager is taken to the nearby hospital emergency room by the local rescue squad. His friends reported that he had taken some drug with a large quantity of alcohol. His arterial blood gas (ABG) studies reveal: pH 7.17; Pco_2 73 mm Hg; HCO_3^- 26 mEq/liter.

    Identify the teenager's condition and explain what the clinical values reveal.

2. A 62-year-old woman has been vomiting and experiencing anorexia for several days. After being admitted to the hospital, her ABG studies are reported as follows: pH 7.65; Pco_2 52 mm Hg; HCO_3^- 55 mEq/liter.

    Identify the woman's condition and explain what the clinical values reveal.

3. After analyzing the ABG values below, identify the condition in each one of the following four cases.

    (a) pH 7.30; Pco_2 37 mm Hg; HCO_3^- 16 mEq/liter

    (b) pH 7.52; Pco_2 32 mm Hg; HCO_3^- 25 mEq/liter

    (c) pH 7.36; Pco_2 67 mm Hg; HCO_3^- 23 mEq/liter

    (d) pH 7.58; Pco_2 43 mm Hg; HCO_3^- 42 mEq/liter

4. Tom S. has just completed his first marathon. For a few days following the event, he experiences symptoms related to dehydration due to excessive fluid and salt losses and a decrease in his ECF volume. What physiological processes must take place to restore his body to normal ECF and ICF values? (Use arrows to indicate the progression of processes that take place to restore homeostasis.)

26

THE REPRODUCTIVE SYSTEM

Overview

The structures and functions of the reproductive system are notably different from any other organ system in the human body. The other systems of the body are functional at birth or shortly thereafter; however, the reproductive system does not become functional until it is acted on by hormones during puberty.

Most of the other body systems function to support and maintain the individual, but the reproductive system is specialized to ensure survival, not of the individual but of the species.

Even though major differences exist between the reproductive organs of the male and female, both are pri-

marily concerned with propagation of the species and passing genetic material from one generation to another. In addition, the reproductive system produces hormones that allow for the development of secondary sex characteristics.

This chapter provides a series of exercises that will assist you in reviewing and reinforcing your understanding of the anatomy and physiology of the male and female reproductive systems, the effects of male and female hormones, and changes that occur during the aging process.

LEVEL 1   Review of Chapter Objectives

1. Specify the principal components of the human reproductive system, and summarize their functions.
2. Describe the components of the male reproductive system.
3. Outline the processes of meiosis and spermatogenesis in the testes.
4. Explain the roles played by the male reproductive tract and accessory glands in the functional maturation, nourishment, storage, and transport of spermatozoa.
5. Specify the normal composition of semen.
6. Summarize the hormonal mechanisms that regulate male reproductive functions.
7. Describe the components of the female reproductive system.

8. Outline the processes of meiosis and oogenesis in the ovary.
9. Identify the phases and events of the ovarian and uterine cycles.
10. Describe the structure, histology, and functions of the vagina.
11. Summarize the anatomical, physiological, and hormonal aspects of the female reproductive cycle.
12. Discuss the physiology of sexual intercourse as it affects the reproductive systems of males and females.
13. Describe the changes in the reproductive system that occur with aging.

[L1]   Multiple Choice

Place the letter corresponding to the correct answer in the space provided.

OBJ. 1 _____ 1. The systems involved in an adequate sperm count, correct pH and nutrients, and erection and ejaculation are:
   a. reproductive and digestive
   b. endocrine and nervous
   c. cardiovascular and urinary
   d. a, b, and c are correct

OBJ. 1 _____ 2. The reproductive organs that produce gametes and hormones are the:
   a. accessory glands
   b. gonads
   c. vagina and penis
   d. a, b, and c are correct

OBJ. 2 _____ 3. In the male the important function(s) of the epididymis is (are):
   a. monitors and adjusts the composition of the tubular fluid
   b. acts as a recycling center for damaged spermatozoa
   c. the site of physical maturation of spermatozoa
   d. a, b, and c are correct

OBJ. 2 _____ 4. Beginning inferior to the urinary bladder, sperm travel to the exterior through the urethral regions that include the:
   a. membranous urethra, prostatic urethra, penile urethra
   b. prostatic urethra, penile urethra, membranous urethra
   c. prostatic urethra, membranous urethra, penile urethra
   d. penile urethra, prostatic urethra, membranous urethra

OBJ. 2 _____ 5. The external genitalia of the male includes the:
   a. scrotum and penis
   b. urethra and bulbourethral glands
   c. raphe and dartos
   d. prepuce and glans

OBJ. 2 _____ 6. The three masses of erectile tissue that comprise the body of the penis are:
   a. two cylindrical corpora cavernosa and a slender corpus spongiosum
   b. two slender corpora spongiosa and a cylindrical corpus cavernosum
   c. preputial glands, a corpus cavernosum, and a corpus spongiosum
   d. two corpora cavernosa and a preputial gland

OBJ. 3 _____ 7. In the process of spermatogenesis, the developmental sequence includes:
   a. spermatids, spermatozoon, spermatogonia, spermatocytes
   b. spermatogonia, spermatocytes, spermatids, spermatozoon
   c. spermatocytes, spermatogonia, spermatids, spermatozoon
   d. spermatogonia, spermatids, spermatocytes, spermatozoon

OBJ. 3 _____ 8. An individual spermatozoan completes its development in the seminiferous tubules and its physical maturation in the epididymis in approximately:

    a. 2 weeks

    b. 3 weeks

    c. 5 weeks

    d. 8 weeks

OBJ. 4 _____ 9. In the male, sperm cells, before leaving the body, travel from the testes to the:

    a. ductus deferens → epididymis → urethra → ejaculatory duct

    b. ejaculatory duct → epididymis → ductus deferens → urethra

    c. epididymis → ductus deferens → ejaculatory duct → urethra

    d. epididymis → ejaculatory duct → ductus deferens → urethra

OBJ. 4 _____ 10. The accessory organs in the male that secrete into the ejaculatory ducts and the urethra are:

    a. epididymis, seminal vesicles, vas deferens

    b. prostate gland, inguinal canals, raphe

    c. adrenal glands, bulbourethral glands, seminal glands

    d. seminal vesicles, prostate gland, bulbourethral glands

OBJ. 5 _____ 11. Semen, the volume of fluid called the ejaculate, contains:

    a. spermatozoa, seminalplasmin, and enzymes

    b. alkaline and acid secretions and sperm

    c. mucus, sperm, and enzymes

    d. spermatozoa, seminal fluid, and enzymes

OBJ. 5 _____ 12. The correct average characteristics and composition of semen include:

    a. vol., 3.4 ml; specific gravity, 1.028; pH, 7.19; sperm count, 20–600 million/ml

    b. vol., 1.2 ml; specific gravity, 0.050; pH, 7.50; sperm count, 10–100 million/ml

    c. vol., 4.5 ml; specific gravity, 2.010; pH, 6.90; sperm count, 5–10 million/ml

    d. vol., 0.5 ml; specific gravity, 3.010; pH, 7.0; sperm count, 2–4 million/ml

OBJ. 6 _____ 13. The hormone synthesized in the hypothalamus that initiates release of pituitary hormones is:

    a. FSH (follicle-stimulating hormone)

    b. ICSH (interstitial cell-stimulating hormone)

    c. LH (luteinizing hormone)

    d. GnRH (gonadotropin-releasing hormone)

OBJ. 6 _____ 14. The hormone that promotes spermatogenesis along the seminiferous tubules is:

    a. ICSH

    b. FSH

    c. GnRH

    d. LH

OBJ. 6 _____ 15. In the male, between the ages of 50 and 60 circulating _____ levels begin to decline, coupled with increases in circulating levels of _____ .

    a. FSH and LH; testosterone

    b. FSH; testosterone and LH

    c. testosterone; FSH and LH

    d. a, b, and c are correct

OBJ. 7 _____ 16. The function of the uterus in the female is to:

    a. ciliate the sperm into the uterine tube for possible fertilization

    b. provide ovum transport via peristaltic contractions of the uterine wall

    c. provide mechanical protection and nutritional support to the developing embryo

    d. encounter spermatozoa during the first 12–24 hours of its passage

OBJ. 7 _____ 17. In the female, after leaving the ovaries, the ovum travels in the uterine tubes to the uterus via:

    a. ampulla → infundibulum → isthmus → intramural portion

    b. infundibulum → ampulla → isthmus → intramural portion

    c. isthmus → ampulla → infundibulum → intramural portion

    d. intramural portion → ampulla → isthmus → infundibulum

OBJ. 7 _____ 18. Starting at the superior end, the uterus in the female is divided into:

    a. body, isthmus, cervix

    b. isthmus, body, cervix

    c. body, cervix, isthmus

    d. cervix, body, isthmus

OBJ. 7 _____ 19. Ovum transport in the uterine tubes presumably involves a combination of:

    a. flagellar locomotion and ciliary movement

    b. active transport and ciliary movement

    c. ciliary movement and peristaltic contractions

    d. movement in uterine fluid and flagellar locomotion

OBJ. 7 _____ 20. The outer limits of the vulva are established by the:

    a. vestibule and the labia minora

    b. mons pubis and labia majora

    c. lesser and greater vestibular glands

    d. prepuce and vestibule

OBJ. 7 _____ 21. Engorgement of the erectile tissues of the clitoris and increased secretion of the greater vestibular glands involve neural activity that includes:

    a. somatic motor neurons

    b. sympathetic activation

    c. parasympathetic activation

    d. a, b, and c are correct

OBJ. 8   _____ 22. The ovarian cycle begins as activated follicles develop into:

    a. ova

    b. primary follicles

    c. Graafian follicles

    d. primordial follicles

OBJ. 8   _____ 23. The process of oogenesis produces three nonfunctional polar bodies that eventually disintegrate and:

    a. a primordial follicle

    b. a granulosa cell

    c. one functional ovum

    d. a zona pellucida

OBJ. 9   _____ 24. The proper sequence that describes the ovarian cycle involves the formation of:

    a. primary follicles, secondary follicles, tertiary follicles, ovulation, and formation and destruction of the corpus luteum

    b. primary follicles, secondary follicles, tertiary follicles, corpus luteum, and ovulation

    c. corpus luteum; primary, secondary, and tertiary follicles; and ovulation

    d. primary and tertiary follicles, secondary follicles, ovulation, and formation and destruction of the corpus luteum

OBJ. 9   _____ 25. Under normal circumstances, in a 28-day cycle, ovulation occurs on _____, and the menses begins on _____.

    a. day 1; day 14

    b. day 28; day 14

    c. day 14; day 1

    d. day 6; day 14

OBJ. 10   _____ 26. The reproductive function(s) of the vagina is (are):

    a. passageway for the elimination of menstrual fluids

    b. receives the penis during coitus

    c. forms the lower portion of the birth canal during childbirth

    d. a, b, and c are correct

OBJ. 11   _____ 27. Whether or not fertilization occurs the final destination of the ovum is the:

    a. myometrium

    b. endometrium

    c. serosa

    d. placenta

OBJ. 11   _____ 28. Hormones produced by the placenta include:

    a. estrogen and progesterone

    b. relaxin and human placental lactogen

    c. human chorionic gonadotrophin (HCG)

    d. a, b, and c are correct

OBJ. 11 _____ 29. The two hormones that help prepare the mammary glands for milk production are:

    a. prolactin and human placental lactogen

    b. colostrum and relaxin

    c. human chorionic gonadotrophin and estrogen

    d. estrogen and progesterone

OBJ. 12 _____ 30. Peristaltic contractions of the ampulla, pushing fluid and spermatozoa into the prostatic urethra, is called:

    a. emission

    b. ejaculation

    c. detumescence

    d. subsidence

OBJ. 12 _____ 31. In the male, erotic thoughts and stimulation of sensory nerves in the genital region lead to an increase in parasympathetic outflow over the pelvic nerves, which in turn leads to :

    a. emission and ejaculation

    b. erection of the penis

    c. orgasm and detumescence

    d. sexual dysfunction or impotence

OBJ. 13 _____ 32. Menopause is accompanied by a sharp and sustained rise in the production of _____ while circulating concentrations of _____ decline.

    a. estrogen and progesterone; GnRH, FSH, LH

    b. GnRH, FSH, LH; estrogen and progesterone

    c. LH, estrogen; progesterone, GnRH, and FSH

    d. FSH, LH, progesterone; estrogen and GnRH

[L1] Completion

Using the terms below, complete the following statements.

menopause	fertilization	ICSH
ovaries	implantation	testes
placenta	cardiovascular	digestive
ovulation	progesterone	oogenesis
seminiferous tubules	Graafian	ductus deferens
Bartholin's	gonads	fructose
spermiogenesis	prostate gland	spermatids
infundibulum		

OBJ. 1   1. The fusion of a sperm contributed by the father and an egg, or ovum, from the mother is called _____.

OBJ. 1   2. In the male and the female, the reproductive organs that produce gametes and hormones are the _____.

OBJ. 2   3. Sperm production occurs within the slender, tightly coiled _____.

OBJ. 2   4. The male gonads are the _____.

OBJ. 3 5. The physical transformation of a spermatid to a spermatozoon is called
_____.

OBJ. 3 6. The process of meiosis in the male produces undifferentiated male gametes called
_____.

OBJ. 4 7. After passing along the tail of the epididymis the spermatozoa arrive at the
_____.

OBJ. 4 8. The major systems involved in providing nutrients and the proper pH for semen are
the urinary and _____ systems.

OBJ. 5 9. Thirty percent of the secretions in a typical sample of seminal fluid is contributed
by the _____.

OBJ. 5 10. The primary energy source for the mobilization of sperm is _____.

OBJ. 6 11. A peptide hormone that causes the secretion of androgens by the interstitial cells of
the testes is _____.

OBJ. 7 12. The female gonads are the _____.

OBJ. 8 13. By the tenth day of the ovarian cycle, the mature tertiary follicle is called the
_____ follicle.

OBJ. 9 14. Egg release from the ovary into the uterine tube is called _____.

OBJ. 9 15. After ovulation the ovum passes from the ovary into the expanded funnel called the
_____.

OBJ. 9 16. When the blastocyst contacts the endometrial wall, erodes the epithelium, and buries
itself in the endometrium, the process is known as _____.

OBJ. 9 17. Ovum production, which occurs on a monthly basis as part of the ovarian cycle, is
referred to as _____.

OBJ. 10 18. The mucous glands that discharge secretions into the vestibule near the vaginal
entrance are known as _____ glands.

OBJ. 11 19. The principal hormone that prepares the uterus for pregnancy is _____.

OBJ. 11 20. Support for embryonic and fetal development occurs in a special organ called the
_____.

OBJ. 12 21. The major systems involved in the process of erection are the nervous and
_____.

OBJ. 13 22. In females, the time that ovulation and menstruation cease is referred to as
_____.

[L1]   Matching

Match the terms in column B with the terms in column A. Use letters for answers in the spaces provided.

Part I	Column A	Column B
OBJ. 1	_____ 1. gametes	A. sperm production
OBJ. 1	_____ 2. external genitalia	B. produce alkaline secretion
OBJ. 1	_____ 3. FSH, LH, ICSH	C. anterior pituitary
OBJ. 2	_____ 4. sustentacular cells	D. hormone—male secondary
OBJ. 2	_____ 5. interstitial cells	sex characteristics
OBJ. 3	_____ 6. seminiferous tubules	E. cells of Leydig
OBJ. 3	_____ 7. puberty in male	F. perineal structures
OBJ. 4	_____ 8. prostate glands	G. Sertoli cells
OBJ. 5	_____ 9. seminal plasmin	H. fallopian tubes
OBJ. 6	_____ 10. testosterone	I. spermatogenesis
OBJ. 7	_____ 11. oviducts	J. reproductive cells
		K. antibiotic enzyme in
		semen

Part II	Column A	Column B
OBJ. 8	_____ 12. ovaries	L. follicular degeneration
OBJ. 8	_____ 13. puberty in female	M. indicates pregnancy
OBJ. 8	_____ 14. immature eggs	N. egg production
OBJ. 9	_____ 15. atresia	O. milk ejection
OBJ. 10	_____ 16. vaginal folds	P. menarche
		Q. zygote
OBJ. 11	_____ 17. human chorionic	R. rugae
	hormone	S. cessation of ovulation
OBJ. 11	_____ 18. oxytocin	and menstruation
OBJ. 12	_____ 19. fertilized egg	T. oocytes
OBJ. 12	_____ 20. detumescence	U. reduced estrogen
OBJ. 13	_____ 21. menopause	concentrations
OBJ. 13	_____ 22. osteoporosis	V. subsidence of erection

[L1]   Drawing/Illustration Labeling

Identify each numbered structure by labeling the following figures:

OBJ. 2   **Figure 26.1   Male Reproductive Organs**

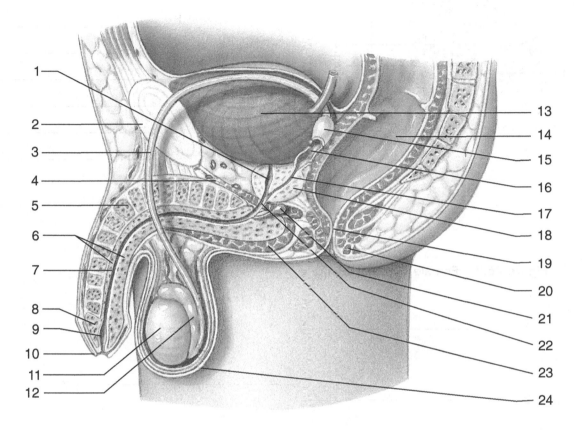

1 _____   13 _____

2 _____   14 _____

3 _____   15 _____

4 _____   15 _____

5 _____   17 _____

6 _____   13 _____

7 _____   19 _____

8 _____   2) _____

9 _____   21 _____

10 _____   22 _____

11 _____   23 _____

12 _____   24 _____

OBJ. 2   **Figure 26.2   The Testes**

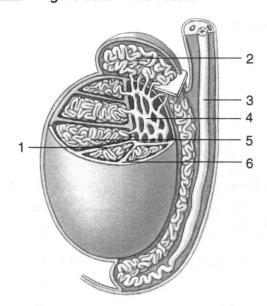

1 _____

2 _____

3 _____

4 _____

5 _____

6 _____

OBJ. 7   **Figure 26.3   Female External Genitalia**

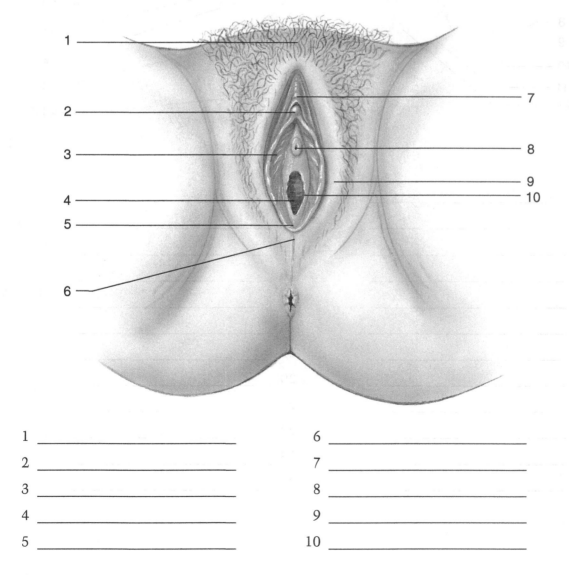

1 _____   6 _____

2 _____   7 _____

3 _____   8 _____

4 _____   9 _____

5 _____   10 _____

OBJ. 7   **Figure 26.4   Female Reproductive Organs (sagittal section)**

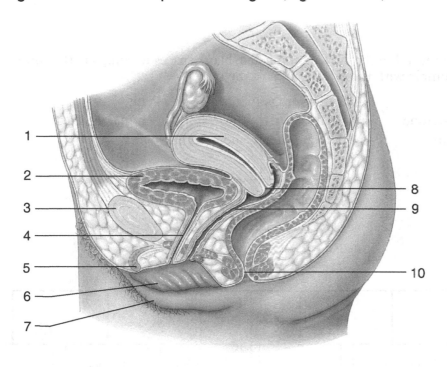

1 _____   6 _____

2 _____   7 _____

3 _____   8 _____

4 _____   9 _____

5 _____   10 _____

OBJ. 7   **Figure 26.5   Female Reproductive Organs (frontal section)**

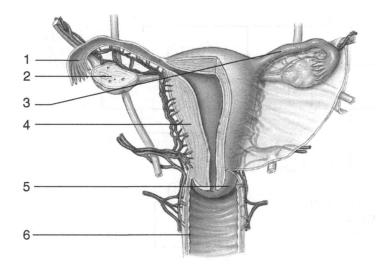

1 _____

2 _____

3 _____

4 _____

5 _____

6 _____

LEVEL 2   Concept Synthesis

Concept Map I

Using the following terms, fill in the circled, numbered, blank spaces to complete the concept map. Follow the numbers to comply with the organization of the map.

Urethra   Seminiferous tubules   Penis
Produce testosterone   FSH   Seminal vesicles
Ductus deferens   Bulbourethral glands

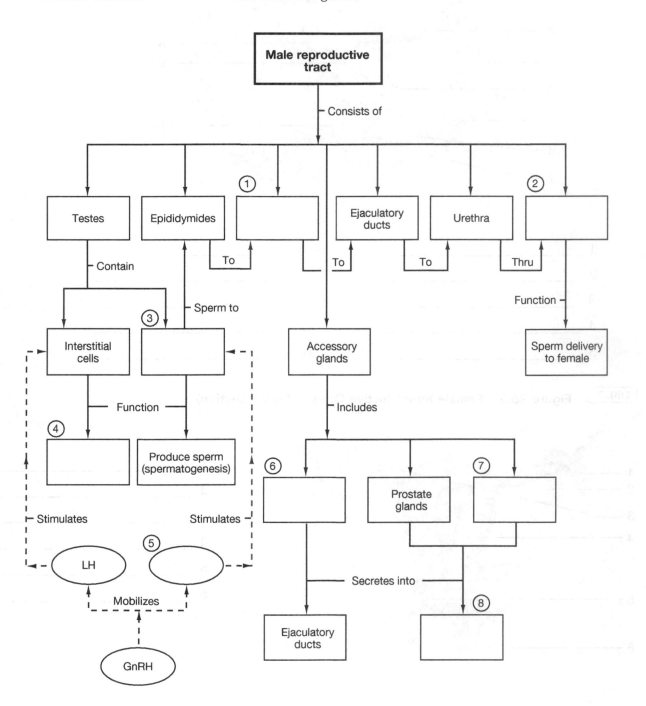

Concept Map II

Using the following terms, fill in the circled, numbered, blank spaces to complete the concept map. Follow the numbers to comply with the organization of the map.

External urinary meatus   Shaft   Crus
Corpora spongiosum   Prepuce   Frenulum

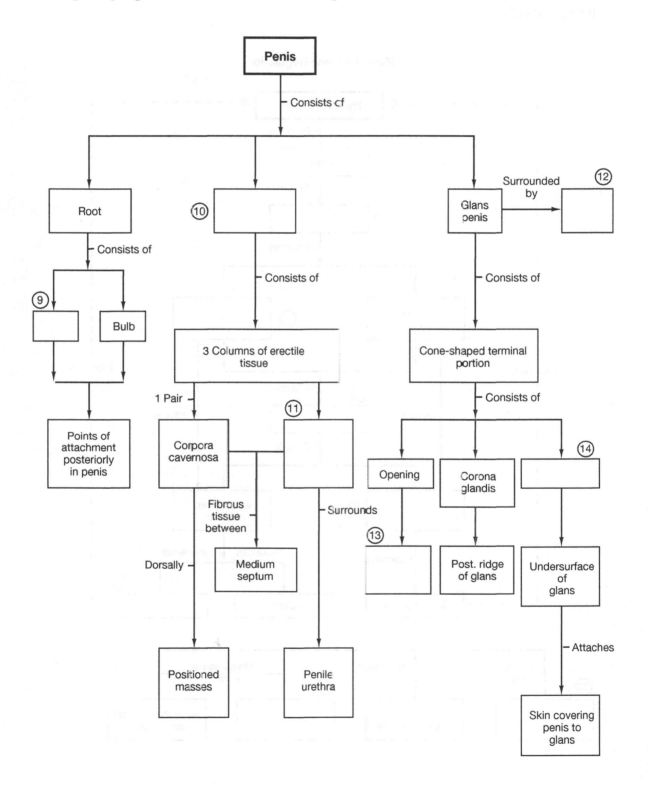

Concept Map III

Using the following terms, fill in the circled, numbered, blank spaces to complete the concept map. Follow the numbers to comply with the organization of the map.

Inhibin   Testes   Male secondary sex characteristics
FSH   CNS   Anterior pituitary
Interstitial cells

Male Hormone Regulation

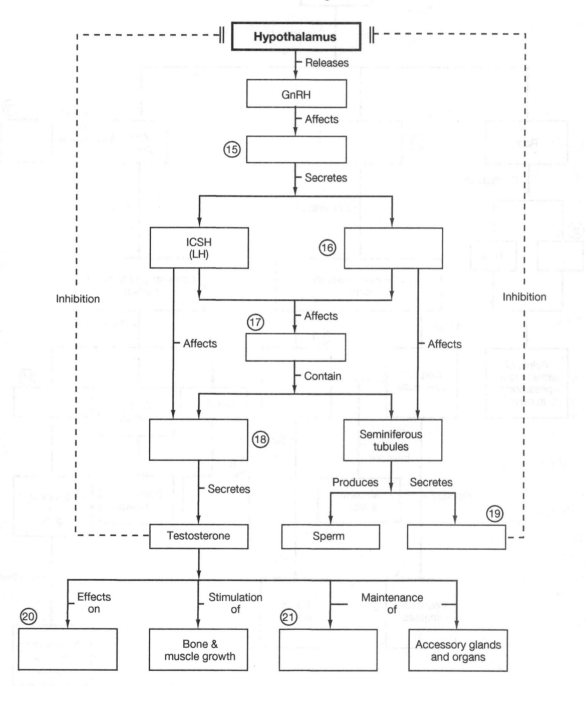

Concept Map IV

Using the following terms, fill in the circled, numbered, blank spaces to complete the concept map. Follow the numbers to comply with the organization of the map.

nutrients   supports fetal development   endometrium
vulva   granulosa and thecal cells   clitoris
vagina   uterine tubes   labis majora and minora
follicles

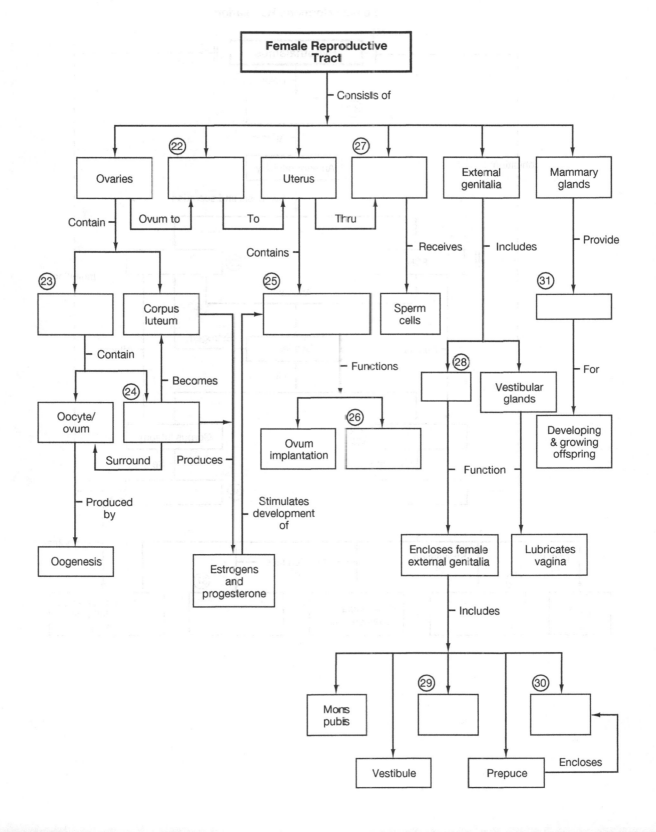

Concept Map V

Using the following terms, fill in the circled, numbered, blank spaces to complete the concept map. Follow the numbers to comply with the organization of the map.

Bone and muscle growth	Follicles	GnRH
Accessory glands and organs	Progesterone	LH

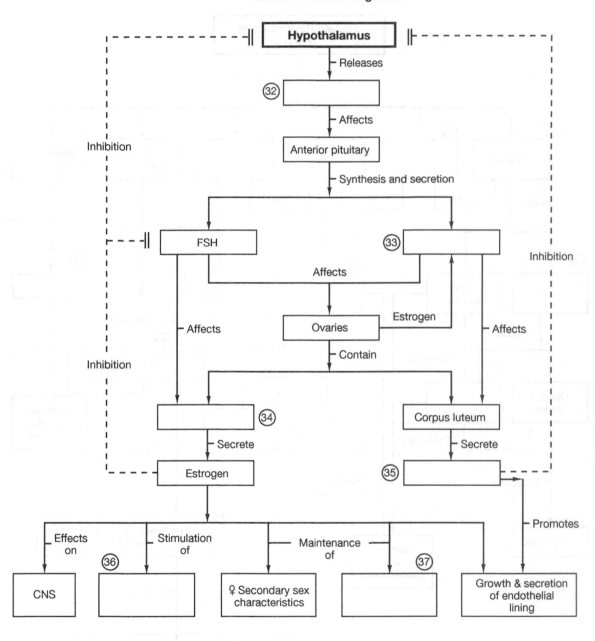

Female Hormone Regulation

Concept Map VI

Using the following terms, fill in the circled, numbered, blank spaces to complete the concept map. Follow the numbers to comply with the organization of the map.

Placenta   Ovary   Anterior pituitary
Relaxin   Progesterone   Mammary gland development

Hormones During Pregnancy

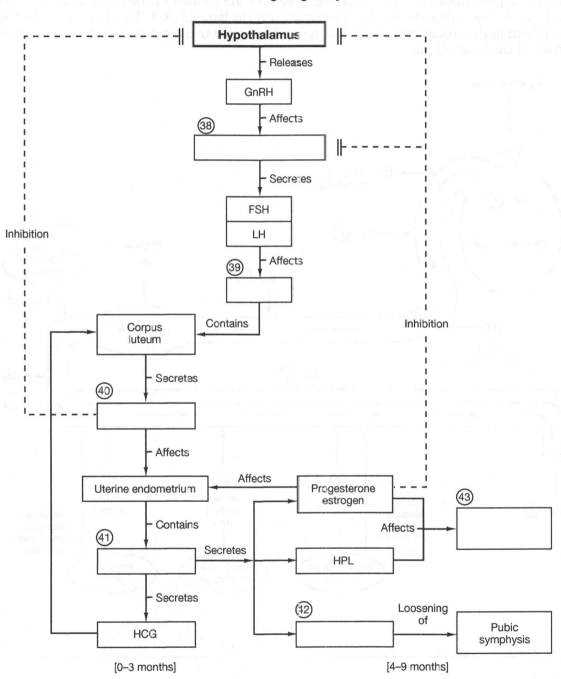

Body Trek

Using the terms below, identify the numbered locations on the trek map through the reproductive system of the male.

penile urethra   external urethral meatus   ejaculatory duct

ductus deferens   seminiferous tubules and   urethra

body of epididymis   rete testis

For the trek through the male reproductive system you will follow the path Robo takes as the micro-robot follows a population of sperm from the time they are formed in the testes until they leave the body of the male. You will assist the robot by identifying the lettered (A–L) locations along the route and recording them in the spaces provided below. If you need assistance from Robo, refer to the Answer Key in the back of the Study Guide.

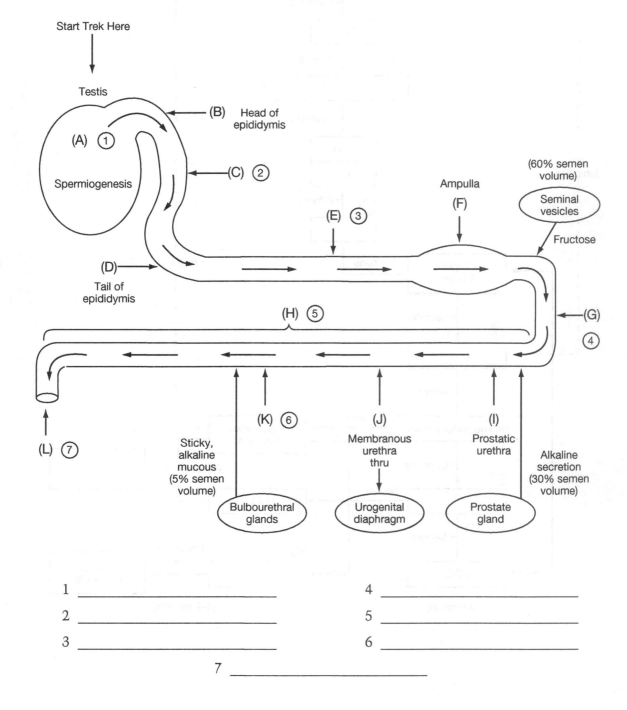

1 _____   4 _____

2 _____   5 _____

3 _____   6 _____

7 _____

COVERING ALL YOUR BASES

[L2]   Multiple Choice

Select the best answer or answers from the choices given.

1. The part of the endometrium that undergoes cyclical changes in response to sexual hormone levels is the:

   A. functional zone

   B. basilar zone

   C. serosa

   D. muscular myometrium

2. In a 28-day cycle, estrogen levels peak at:

   A. day 1

   B. day 7

   C. day 14

   D. day 28

3. The rupture of the follicular wall and ovulation are caused by:

   A. a sudden surge in LH (luteinizing hormone) concentration

   B. a sudden surge in the secretion of estrogen

   C. an increase in the production of progesterone

   D. increased production and release of GnRH (gonadotrophin-releasing hormone)

4. The body of the spermatic cord is a structure that includes:

   A. epididymis, ductus deferens, blood vessels, and nerves

   B. vas deferens, prostate gland, blood vessels, and urethra

   C. ductus deferens, blood vessels, nerves, and lymphatics

   D. a, b, and c are correct

5. The function(s) of the sustentacular cells (Sertoli cells) in the male is (are):

   A. maintenance of the blood–testis barrier

   B. support of spermiogenesis

   C. secretion of inhibin and androgen-binding protein

   D. a, b, and c are correct

5. The tail of the sperm has the unique distinction of being the:

   A. only flagellum in the body that contains chromosomes

   B. only flagellum in the human body

   C. only flagellum in the body that contains mitochondria

   D. only flagellum in the body that contains centrioles

7. The function(s) of the prostate gland is (are):

   A. to produce acid and alkaline secretions

   B. to produce alkaline secretions and a compound with antibiotic properties

   C. to secrete a thick, sticky, alkaline mucus for lubrication

   D. to secrete seminal fluid with a distinctive ionic and nutrient composition

8. Powerful, rhythmic contractions in the ischiocavernosus and bulbocavernosus muscles of the pelvic floor result in:

   A. erection

   B. emission

   C. ejaculation

   D. a, b, and c are correct

9. The process of erection involves complex neural processes that include:

A. increased sympathetic outflow over the pelvic nerves

B. increased parasympathetic outflow over the pelvic nerves

C. decreased parasympathetic outflow over the pelvic nerves

D. somatic motor neurons in the upper sacral segments of the spinal cord

10. Impotence, a common male sexual dysfunction, is:

A. the inability to produce sufficient sperm for fertilization

B. the term used to describe male infertility

C. the inability of the male to ejaculate

D. the inability to achieve or maintain an erection

11. The ovaries, uterine tubes, and uterus are enclosed within an extensive mesentery known as the:

A. rectouterine pouch

B. suspensory ligament

C. ovarian ligament

D. broad ligament

12. If fertilization is to occur, the ovum must encounter spermatozoa during the first:

A. 2–4 hours of its passage

B. 6–8 hours of its passage

C. 12–24 hours of its passage

D. 30–36 hours of its passage

13. The three pairs of suspensory ligaments that stabilize the position of the uterus and limit its range of movement are:

A. broad, ovarian, suspensory

B. uterosacral, round, lateral

C. anteflexure, retroflexure, tunica albuginea

D. endometrium, myometrium, serosa

14. The histological composition of the uterine wall consists of the:

A. body, isthmus, cervix

B. mucosa, epithelial lining, lamina propria

C. mucosa, functional zone, basilar layer

D. endometrium, myometrium, serosa

15. The hormone that acts to reduce the rate of GnRH and FSH production by the anterior pituitary is:

A. inhibin

B. LH

C. ICSH

D. testosterone

16. The three sequential stages of the menstrual cycle include:

A. menses, luteal phase, postovulatory phase

B. menses, follicular phase, preovulatory phase

C. menses, proliferative phase, follicular phase

D. menses, proliferative phase, secretory phase

17. At the time of ovulation, basal body temperature:

A. declines sharply

B. increases sharply

C. stays the same

D. is one-half a degree Fahrenheit lower than normal

18. The seminal vesicles:

A. store semen

B. secrete a fructose-rich mucoid substance

C. conduct spermatozoa into the epididymis

D. secrete a thin watery fluid

19. A recently marketed drug is said to "remind the pituitary" to produce gonadotropins, FSH, and LH. This drug might be useful as:

A. a male contraceptive

B. a female contraceptive

C. both a male and female contraceptive

D. a fertility drug

[L2] Completion

Using the terms below, complete the following statements.

cervical os	ampulla	inguinal canals
detumescence	androgens	smegma
raphe	prepuce	fimbriae
hymen	tunica albuginea	rete testis
zona pellucida	ejaculation	corona radiata
clitoris	acrosomal sac	corpus luteum
cremaster	corpus albicans	menopause
menses	mesovarium	fornix

1. The interstitial cells are responsible for the production of male sex hormones, which are called _____.

2. The narrow canals linking the scrotal chambers with the peritoneal cavity are called the _____.

3. The scrotum is divided into two separate chambers, and the boundary between the two is marked by a raised thickening in the scrotal surface known as the _____.

4. The layer of skeletal muscle that contracts and tenses the scrotum, pulling the testes closer to the body, is the _____ muscle.

5. Semen is expelled from the body by a process called _____.

6. The maze of interconnected passageways within the mediastinum of the seminiferous tubules is known as the _____.

7. The tip of the sperm containing an enzyme that plays a role in fertilization is the _____.

8. The fold of skin that surrounds the tip of the penis is the _____.

9. Preputial glands in the skin of the neck and the inner surface of the prepuce secrete a waxy material known as _____.

10. Subsidence of erection mediated by the sympathetic nervous system is referred to as _____.

11. The last menstrual cycle of the female is known as _____.

12. Microvilli are present in the *space* between the developing oocyte and the innermost follicular cells called the _____.

13. Follicular cells surrounding the oocyte prior to ovulation are known as the _____.

14. Degenerated follicular cells proliferate to create an endocrine structure known as the _____.

15. A knot of pale scar tissue produced by fibroblasts invading a degenerated corpus luteum is called a _____.

16. The thickened fold of mesentery that supports and stabilizes the position of each ovary is the _____.

17. The thickened mesothelium that overlies a layer of dense connective tissue covering the exposed surfaces of each ovary is the _____.

18. The fingerlike projections on the infundibulum that extend into the pelvic cavity are called _____.

19. The uterine cavity opens into the vagina at the _____.

20. The shallow recess surrounding the cervical protrusion is known as the _____.

21. Prior to sexual activity, the thin epithelial fold that partially or completely blocks the entrance to the vagina is the _____.

22. The female equivalent of the penis derived from the same embryonic structure is the _____.

23. The period marked by the wholesale destruction of the functional zone of the endometrium is the _____.

24. Just before it reaches the prostate and seminal vesicles, the ductus deferens becomes enlarged, and the expanded portion is known as the _____.

[L2]   Short Essay

Briefly answer the following questions in the spaces provided below.

1. What are the four important functions of the sustentacular cells (Sertoli cells) in the testes?

2. What are the three important functions of the epididymis?

3. (a) What three glands secrete their products into the male reproductive tract?

    (b) What are the four primary functions of these glands?

4. What is the difference between seminal fluid and semen?

5. What is the difference between emission and ejaculation?

6. What are the five primary functions of testosterone in the male?

7. What are the three reproductive functions of the vagina?

8. What are the three phases of female sexual function and what occurs in each phase?

9. What are the five steps involved in the ovarian cycle?

10. What are the five primary functions of the estrogens?

11. What are the three stages of the menstrual cycle?

12. What hormones are secreted by the placenta?

13. What is colostrum and what are its major contributions to the infant?

LEVEL 3   Critical Thinking/Application

Using principles and concepts learned about the reproductive system, answer the following questions. Write your answers on a separate sheet of paper.

1. I. M. Hurt was struck in the abdomen with a baseball bat while playing in a young men's baseball league. As a result, his testes ascend into the abdominopelvic region quite frequently, causing sharp pains. He has been informed by his urologist that he is sterile due to his unfortunate accident.

   (a) Why does his condition cause sterility?

   (b) What primary factors are necessary for fertility in males?

2. A 19-year-old female has been accused by her brothers of looking and acting like a male. They make fun of her because she has a low-pitched voice, growth of hair on her face, and they tease her about her small breast size. Physiologically speaking, what is her problem related to?

3. A contraceptive pill "tricks the brain" into thinking you are pregnant. What does this mean?

4. Sexually transmitted diseases in males do not result in inflammation of the peritoneum (peritonitis) as they sometimes do in females. Why?

27

DEVELOPMENT AND INHERITANCE

Overview

It is difficult to imagine that today there is a single cell that 38 weeks from now, if fertilized, will develop into a complex organism with over 200 million cells organized into tissues, organs, and organ systems— so it is the miracle of life!

The previous chapter considered the male and female reproductive tracts that lead to the bridge of life that spans the generations through which gametes are transported and by which both gametes and developing offspring are housed and serviced.

A new life begins in the tubes of these systems, and it is here that new genetic combinations, similar to the parents, yet different, are made and nourished until they emerge from the female tract to take up life on their own— at first highly dependent on extrinsic support but growing independent with physical maturation.

All of these events occur as a result of the complex, unified process of development—an orderly sequence of progressive changes that begin at fertilization and have profound effects on the individual for a lifetime.

Chapter 27 highlights the major aspects of development and development processes, regulatory mechanisms, and how developmental patterns can be modified for the good or ill of the individual. Appropriately, the chapter concludes by addressing the topic of death and dying.

LEVEL 1   Review of Chapter Objectives

1. Explain the relationship between differentiation and development, and specify the various stages of development.
2. Describe the process of fertilization.
3. Explain how developmental processes are regulated.
4. List the three prenatal periods and describe the major events associated with each.
5. Explain how the germ layers participate in the formation of extraembryonic membranes.
6. Discuss the importance of the placenta as an endocrine organ.
7. Describe the interplay between the maternal organ systems and the developing fetus.
8. Discuss the structural and functional changes in the uterus during gestation.
9. List and discuss the events that occur during labor and delivery.
10. Identify the features and functions associated with the various life stages.
11. Relate basic principles of genetics to the inheritance of human traits.

[L1] Multiple Choice

Place the letter corresponding to the correct answer in the space provided.

OBJ. 1 _____ 1. The creation of different types of cells during the processes of development is called:
- a. fertilization
- b. differentiation
- c. maturity
- d. implantation

OBJ. 1 _____ 2. The gradual modification of anatomical structures during development occurs during the period from:
- a. conception to birth
- b. birth to maturity
- c. birth to adolescence
- d. fertilization to maturity

OBJ. 1 _____ 3. Fetal development begins at the start of the:
- a. birth process
- b. second month after fertilization
- c. ninth week after fertilization
- d. process of fertilization

OBJ. 1 _____ 4. The stage of development that commences at birth and continues to maturity is the:
- a. postnatal period
- b. prenatal period
- c. embryological period
- d. childhood period

OBJ. 2 _____ 5. The normal male genotype is _____, and the normal female genotype is _____.
- a. XX; XY
- b. X; Y
- c. XY; XX
- d. Y; X

OBJ. 2 _____ 6. Normal fertilization occurs in the:
- a. lower part of the uterine tube
- b. upper one-third of the uterine tube
- c. upper part of the uterus
- d. antrum of a tertiary follicle

OBJ. 2 _____ 7. Sterility in males may result from a sperm count of less than:
- a. 20 million sperm/m*l*
- b. 40 million sperm/m*l*
- c. 60 million sperm/m*l*
- d. 100 million sperm/m*l*

OBJ. 2 _____ 8. Fertilization is completed with the:
  a. formation of a gamete containing 23 chromosomes
  b. formation of the male and female pronuclei
  c. completion of the meiotic process
  d. formation of a zygote containing 46 chromosomes

OBJ. 3 _____ 9. Alterations in genetic activity during development occur as a result of:
  a. the maturation of the sperm and ovum
  b. the chromosome complement in the nucleus of the cell
  c. differences in the cytoplasmic composition of individual cells
  d. conception

OBJ. 3 _____ 10. As development proceeds, the differentiation of other embryonic cells is affected by small zygotic cells that:
  a. produce the initial stages of implantation
  b. release RNAs, polypeptides, and small proteins
  c. are involved with the placental process
  d. produce the three germ layers during gastrulation

OBJ. 4 _____ 11. The most dangerous period in prenatal or postnatal life is the:
  a. first trimester
  b. second trimester
  c. third trimester
  d. expulsion stage

OBJ. 4 _____ 12. The four general processes that occur during the first trimester include:
  a. dilation, expulsion, placental, labor
  b. blastocyst, blastomere, morula, trophoblast
  c. cleavage, implantation, placentation, embryogenesis
  d. yolk sac, amnion, allantois, chorion

OBJ. 4 _____ 13. Organs and organ systems complete most of their development during the:
  a. first trimester
  b. second trimester
  c. third trimester
  d. time of placentation

OBJ. 5 _____ 14. Germ-layer formation results from the process of:
  a. embryogenesis
  b. organogenesis
  c. gastrulation
  d. parturition

OBJ. 5 _____ 15. The extraembryonic membranes that develop from the endoderm and mesoderm are:
  a. amnion and chorion
  b. yolk sac and allantois
  c. allantois and chorion
  d. yolk sac and amnion

OBJ. 5 _____ 16. The chorion develops from the:

a. endoderm and mesoderm

b. ectoderm and mesoderm

c. trophoblast and endoderm

d. mesoderm and trophoblast

OBJ. 6 _____ 17. Blood flows to and from the placenta via:

a. paired umbilical veins and a single umbilical artery

b. paired umbilical arteries and a single umbilical vein

c. a single umbilical artery and a single umbilical vein

d. two umbilical arteries and two umbilical veins

OBJ. 6 _____ 18. The hormone(s) produced by the placenta include(s):

a. human chorionic gonadotrophin hormone

b. estrogen, progesterone

c. relaxin, human placental lactogen

d. a, b, and c are correct

OBJ. 6 _____ 19. Throughout embryonic and fetal development metabolic wastes generated by the fetus are eliminated by transfer to the:

a. maternal circulation

b. amniotic fluid

c. chorion

d. allantois

OBJ. 7 _____ 20. During gestation, the mother's lungs deliver extra oxygen and remove excess carbon dioxide generated by the fetus requiring:

a. increased maternal respiratory rate and decreased tidal volume

b. decreased maternal respiratory rate and increased tidal volume

c. increased maternal respiratory rate and tidal volume

d. decreased maternal respiratory rate and tidal volume

OBJ. 7 _____ 21. The umbilical cord or umbilical stalk contains:

a. the amnion, allantois, and chorion

b. paired umbilical arteries and the amnion

c. a single umbilical vein and the chorion

d. the allantois, blood vessels, and yolk stalk

OBJ. 8 _____ 22. The stretching of the myometrium during gestation is associated with a gradual increase in the:

a. increased size of the developing fetus

b. excessive secretion of progesterone

c. rates of spontaneous smooth muscle contractions

d. amount of fluid in the uterus

OBJ. 8 _____ 23. Prostaglandins in the endometrium:

a. stimulate smooth muscle contractions

b. cause the mammary glands to begin secretory activity

c. cause an increase in the maternal blood volume

d. initiate the process of organogenesis

OBJ. 8 _____ 24. During gestation the primary major compensatory adjustment(s) is (are):
   a. increased respiratory rate and tidal volume
   b. increased maternal requirements for nutrients
   c. increased glomerular filtration rate
   d. all of the above

OBJ. 9 _____ 25. The sequential stages of labor include:
   a. dilation, expulsion, placental
   b. fertilization, cleavage, implantation
   c. fertilization, implantation, placental
   d. expulsion, placental, birth

OBJ. 9 _____ 26. When a woman's water breaks, it occurs late in the:
   a. expulsion stage
   b. placental state
   c. dilation stage
   d. neonatal period

OBJ. 10 _____ 27. The sequential stages that identify the features and functions associated with the human experience are:
   a. neonatal, childhood, infancy, maturity
   b. neonatal, postnatal, childbirth, adolescence
   c. infancy, childhood, adolescence, maturity
   d. prenatal, neonatal, postnatal, infancy

OBJ. 10 _____ 28. The systems that were relatively nonfunctional during the fetus's prenatal period that must become functional at birth are the:
   a. circulatory, muscular, skeletal
   b. integumentary, reproductive, nervous
   c. endocrine, nervous, circulatory
   d. respiratory, digestive, excretory

OBJ. 11 _____ 29. The normal chromosome complement of a typical somatic, or body, cell is:
   a. 23
   b. N or haploid
   c. 46
   d. 92

OBJ. 11 _____ 30. Gametes are different from ordinary somatic cells because:
   a. they contain only half the normal number of chromosomes
   b. they contain the full complement of chromosomes
   c. the chromosome number doubles in gametes
   d. gametes are diploid, or 2N

OBJ. 11 _____ 31. During gamete formation, meiosis splits the chromosome pairs, producing:
   a. diploid gametes
   b. haploid gametes
   c. gametes with a full chromosome complement
   d. duplicate gametes

OBJ. 11 _____ 32. The first meiotic division:
  a. results in the separation of the duplicate chromosomes
  b. yields four functional spermatids in the male
  c. produces one functional ovum in the female
  d. reduces the number of chromosomes from 46 to 23

OBJ. 11 _____ 33. Spermatogenesis produces:
  a. four functional spermatids for every primary spermatocyte undergoing meiosis
  b. functional spermatozoan with the diploid number of chromosomes
  c. secondary spermatocytes with the 2N number of chromosomes
  d. a, b, and c are correct

OBJ. 11 _____ 34. Oogenesis produces:
  a. an oogonium with the haploid number of chromosomes
  b. one functional ovum and three nonfunctional polar bodies
  c. a secondary oocyte with the diploid number of chromosomes
  d. a, b, and c are correct

OBJ. 11 _____ 35. If an allele is *dominant*, it will be expressed in the phenotype:
  a. if both alleles agree on the outcome of the phenotype
  b. by the use of lowercase abbreviations
  c. regardless of any conflicting instructions carried by the other allele
  d. by the use of capitalized abbreviations

OBJ. 11 _____ 36. If a female X chromosome of an allelic pair contains sex-linked character for color blindness, the individual would be:
  a. normal
  b. color blind
  c. color blind in one eye
  d. a, b, or c could occur

[L1] Completion

Using the terms below, complete the following statements.

childhood	thalidomide	placenta
capacitation	gametogenesis	autosomal
meiosis	polyspermy	induction
expulsion	infancy	heterozygous
chorion	second trimester	development
homozygous	true labor	gonadotropin
fertilization	parturition	embryological development
first trimester		

OBJ. 1   1. The gradual modification of anatomical structures during the period from fertilization to maturity is called _____.

OBJ. 1   2. The events that occur during the first two months after fertilization comprise _____.

OBJ. 2   3. One chromosome in each pair is contributed by the sperm and the other by the egg at _____.

OBJ. 2   4. Sperm cannot fertilize an egg until they have undergone an activation in the vagina called _____.

OBJ. 2   5. The process of fertilization by more than one sperm that produces a nonfunctional zygote is known as _____.

OBJ. 3   6. As development proceeds, the chemical interplay among developing cells is called _____.

OBJ. 3   7. During the 1960s the drug prescribed for women in early pregnancy that interfered with the induction process responsible for limb development was _____.

OBJ. 4   8. The time during prenatal development when the fetus begins to look distinctively human is referred to as the _____.

OBJ. 4   9. The period of time during which the rudiments of all the major organ systems appear is referred to as the _____.

OBJ. 5   10. The extraembryonic membrane formed from the mesoderm and trophoblast is the _____.

OBJ. 6   11. The placental hormone present in blood or urine samples that provides a reliable indication of pregnancy is _____.

OBJ. 7   12. The vital link between maternal and embryonic systems that support the fetus during development is the _____.

OBJ. 8   13. When the biochemical and mechanical factors reach the point of no return in the uterus, it indicates the beginning of _____.

OBJ. 9   14. The goal of labor is _____.

OBJ. 9   15. The stage in which contractions reach maximum intensity is the _____ stage.

OBJ. 10   16. The life stage characterized by events that occur prior to puberty is called _____.

OBJ. 10   17. The life stage that follows the neonatal period and continues to 2 years of age is referred to as _____.

OBJ. 11   18. The special form of cell division leading to the production of sperm or eggs is _____.

OBJ. 11   19. The formation of gametes is called _____.

OBJ. 11   20. Chromosomes with genes that affect only somatic characteristics are referred to as _____ chromosomes.

OBJ. 11   21. If both chromosomes of a homologous pair carry the same allele of a particular gene, the individual is _____ for that trait.

OBJ. 11   22. When an individual has two different alleles carrying different instructions, the individual is _____ for that trait.

[L1] Matching

Match the terms in column B with the terms in column A. Use letters for answers in the spaces provided.

Part I	Column A	Column B
OBJ. 1 ____	1. conception	A. cellular chemical interplay
OBJ. 1 ____	2. cell specialization	B. differentiation
OBJ. 2 ____	3. fertilization	C. prenatal development
OBJ. 2 ____	4. amphimixis	D. milk production
OBJ. 2 ____	5. N	E. pronuclei fusion
OBJ. 3 ____	6. induction	F. fetus looks human
OBJ. 3 ____	7. acrosin	G. fertilization
OBJ. 4 ____	8. gestation	H. zygote formation
OBJ. 4 ____	9. second trimester	I. mesoderm and trophoblast
OBJ. 5 ____	10. chorion	J. supports developing fetus
OBJ. 5 ____	11. amnion	K. proteolytic enzyme
OBJ. 6 ____	12. human placental lactogen	L. gamete
		M. mesoderm and ectoderm
OBJ. 7 ____	13. maternal organ systems	

Part II	Column A	Column B
OBJ. 8 ____	14. prostaglandin	N. reductional division
OBJ. 8 ____	15. relaxin	O. somatic cell
OBJ. 9 ____	16. parturition	P. visible characteristics
OBJ. 9 ____	17. true labor	Q. chromosomes and component genes
OBJ. 10 ____	18. neonate	
OBJ. 10 ____	19. adolescence	R. begins at puberty
OBJ. 11 ____	20. 2N	S. forcible expulsion of the fetus
OBJ. 11 ____	21. meiosis I	T. newborn infant
OBJ. 11 ____	22. meiosis II	U. positive feedback
OBJ. 11 ____	23. phenotype	V. equational division
OBJ. 11 ____	24. genotype	W. softens symphysis pubis
		X. stimulates smooth muscle contractions

[L1]   Drawing/Illustration Labeling

Identify each numbered structure by labeling the following figures.

OBJ. 1   **Figure 27.1   Spermatogenesis**

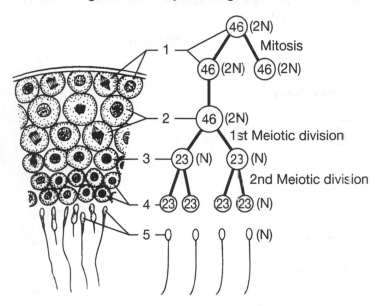

1 _____

2 _____

3 _____

4 _____

5 _____

OBJ. 1   **Figure 27.2   Oogenesis**

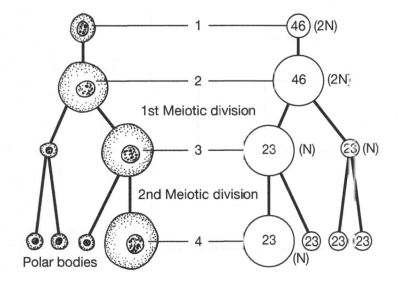

1 _____

2 _____

3 _____

4 _____

LEVEL 2   Concept Synthesis

Concept Map I

Using the following terms, fill in the circled, numbered, blank spaces to complete the concept map. Follow the numbers to comply with the organization of the map.

↑ Prostaglandin production   Relaxin   Estrogen
Positive feedback   Parturition

Interacting Factors – Labor and Delivery

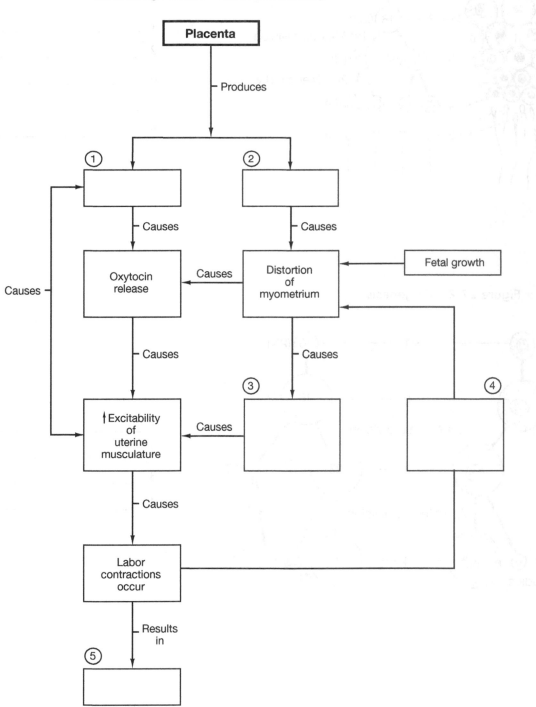

Concept Map II

Using the following terms, fill in the circled, numbered, blank spaces to complete the concept map. Follow the numbers to comply with the organization of the map.

Oxytocin	Prolactin	↑ milk secretion
Posterior pituitary	Milk ejection	Anterior pituitary

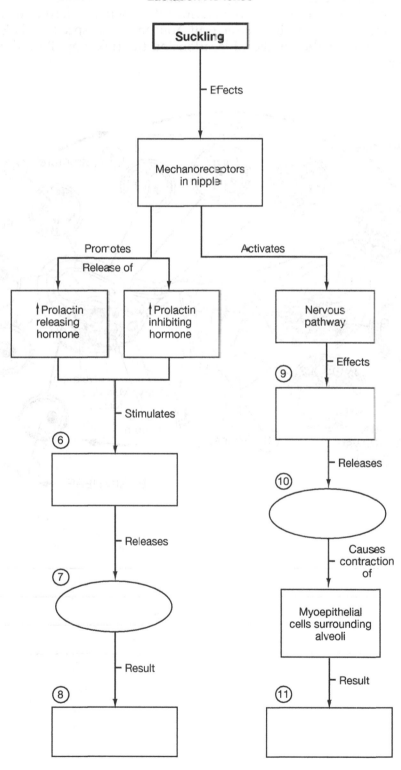

Lactation Reflexes

Body Trek

Using the terms below, identify the numbered locations on the trek map through the female reproductive tract.

early blastocyst	morula	2-cell stage
fertilization	implantation	8-cell stage
secondary oocyte	zygote	

For the trek through the female reproductive system, follow the path Robo takes as the tiny robot follows a developing ovum from the ovary into the uterine tube where it is fertilized and undergoes cleavage until implantation takes place in the uterine wall. Your task is to specify Robo's location by identifying structures or processes at the numbered locations on the trek map. Record your answers in the spaces below the map.

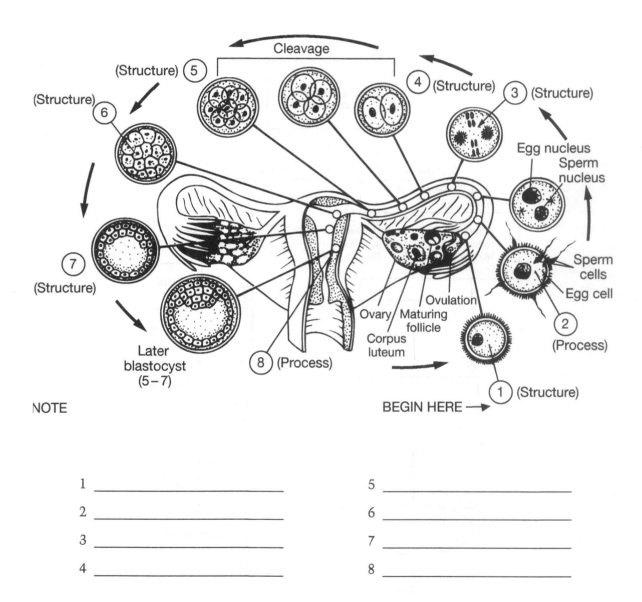

1 _____   5 _____

2 _____   6 _____

3 _____   7 _____

4 _____   8 _____

COVERING ALL YOUR BASES

[L2] Multiple Choice

Select the best answer or answers from the choices given.

1. In the male, the completion of metaphase II, anaphase II, and telophase II produces:

   A. four gametes, each containing 46 chromosomes

   B. four gametes, each containing 23 chromosomes

   C. one gamete containing 46 chromosomes

   D. one gamete containing 23 chromosomes

2. The primary function of the spermatozoa is to:

   A. nourish and program the ovum

   B. support the development of the ovum

   C. carry paternal chromosomes to the site of fertilization

   D. a, b, and c are correct

3. For a given trait, if the possibilities are indicated by *AA*, the individual is:

   A. homozygous recessive

   B. heterozygous dominant

   C. heterozygous recessive

   D. homozygous dominant

4. For a given trait, if the possibilities are indicated by *Aa*, the individual is:

   A. homozygous dominant

   B. homozygous recessive

   C. heterozygous

   D. homozygous

5. For a given trait, if the possibilities are indicated by *aa*, the individual is:

   A. homozygous recessive

   B. homozygous dominant

   C. homozygous

   D. heterozygous

6. If albinism is a recessive trait and an albino mother and a normal father with the genotype *AA* have an offspring, the child will:

   A. be an albino

   B. have normal coloration

   C. have abnormal pigmentation

   D. have blue eyes due to lack of pigmentation

7. During oocyte activation the process that is important in preventing penetration by more than one sperm is the:

   A. process of amphimixis

   B. process of capacitation

   C. process of monospermy

   D. cortical reaction

3. The sequential developmental stages that occur during cleavage include:

   A. blastocyst → blastomeres → trophoblast → morula

   B. blastomeres → morula → blastocyst → trophoblast

   C. yolk sac → amnion → allantois → chorion

   D. amnion → allantois → chorion → yolk sac

9. The zygote arrives in the uterine cavity as a:

   A. morula

   B. blastocyst

   C. trophoblast

   D. chorion

10. During implantation the inner cell mass of the blastocyst separates from the trophoblast, creating a fluid-filled chamber called the:

   A. blastodisk

   B. blastocoele

   C. allantois

   D. amniotic cavity

11. The formation of extraembryonic membranes occurs in the correct sequential steps, which include:

    A. blastomeres, morula, blastocyst, trophoblast

    B. amnion, allantois, chorion, yolk sac

    C. yolk sac, amnion, allantois, chorion

    D. blastocyst, trophoblast, amnion, chorion

12. In the event of "fraternal" or dizygotic twins:

    A. the blastomeres separate early during cleavage

    B. the inner cell mass splits prior to gastrulation

    C. two separate eggs are ovulated and fertilized

    D. a, b, and c are correct

13. The enzyme hyaluronidase is necessary to:

    A. induce labor

    B. permit fertilization

    C. promote gamete formation

    D. support the process of gastrulation

14. The important and complex development event(s) that occur during the first trimester is (are):

    A. cleavage

    B. implantation and placentation

    C. embryogenesis

    D. a, b, and c are correct

15. Exchange between the embryonic and maternal circulations occur by diffusion across the syncytial and cellular trophoblast layers via:

    A. the umbilicus

    B. the allantois

    C. the chorionic blood vessels

    D. the yolk sac

16. Karyotyping is the determination of:

    A. an individual's chromosome complement

    B. the life stages of an individual

    C. the stages of prenatal development

    D. an individual's stage of labor

17. Colostrum, produced and secreted by the mammary glands, contains proteins that help the infant:

    A. activate the digestive system to become fully functional

    B. get adequate amounts of fat to help control body temperature

    C. to initiate the milk let-down reflex

    D. ward off infections until its own immune system becomes fully functional

18. During fertilization, the process of *cortical reaction* is important in:

    A. ensuring the fusion of the sperm nucleus with the egg nucleus

    B. preventing penetration by additional sperm

    C. producing a condition known as polyspermy

    D. helping the sperm penetrate the corona radiata

19. Embryogenesis is the process that establishes the foundation for:

    A. the formation of the blastocyst

    B. implantation to occur

    C. the formation of the placenta

    D. all the major organ systems

20. An ectopic pregnancy refers to:

    A. implantation occurring within the endometrium

    B. implantation occurring somewhere other than within the uterus

    C. the formation of a gestational neoplasm

    D. the formation of extraembryonic membranes in the uterus

[L2] Completion

Using the terms below, complete the following statements.

cleavage	oogenesis	synapsis
alleles	chromatids	spermiogenesis
tetrad	X-linked	differentiation
inheritance	chorion	hyaluronidase
activation	spermatogenesis	simple inheritance
corona radiata	genetics	polygenic inheritance

1. Transfer of genetically determined characteristics from generation to generation refers to _____.

2. The study of the mechanisms responsible for inheritance is called _____.

3. Attached duplicate, doubled chromosomes resulting from the first meiotic division are called _____.

4. When corresponding maternal and paternal chromosomes pair off, the event is known as _____.

5. Paired, duplicated chromosomes visible at the start of meiosis form a combination of four chromatids called a _____.

6. The process of sperm formation is termed _____.

7. The process of ovum production is called _____.

8. Spermatids are transformed into sperm through the process of _____.

9. The various forms of any one gene are called _____.

10. Characteristics carried by genes on the X chromosome that affect somatic structures are termed _____.

11. Phenotypic characters determined by interactions between a single pair of alleles are known as _____.

12. Interactions between alleles on several genes involve _____.

13. When the oocyte leaves the ovary, it is surrounded by a layer of follicle cells, the _____.

14. The enzyme in the acrosomal cap of sperm that is used to break down the follicular cells surrounding the oocyte is _____.

15. The sequence of cell division that begins immediately after fertilization and ends at the first contact with the uterine wall is called _____.

16. The fetal contribution to the placenta is the _____.

17. The creation of different cell types during development is called _____.

18. Conditions inside the oocyte resulting from the sperm entering the ooplasm initiate _____.

[L2] Short Essay

Briefly answer the following questions in the spaces provided below.

1. What is the primary difference between simple inheritance and polygenic inheritance?

2. What does the term *capacitation* refer to?

3. What are the four general processes that occur during the first trimester?

4. What three germ layers result from the process of gastrulation?

5. (a) What are the four extraembryonic membranes that are formed from the three germ layers?

   (b) From which given layer(s) does each membrane originate?

6. What are the major compensatory adjustments necessary in the maternal systems to support the developing fetus?

7. What three major factors oppose the inhibitory effect of progesterone on the uterine smooth muscle?

8. What primary factors interact to produce labor contractions in the uterine wall?

9. What are the three stages of labor?

10. What are the identifiable life stages that comprise postnatal development of distinctive characteristics and abilities?

11. What is an Apgar rating and for what is it used?

12. What three events interact to promote increased hormone production and sexual maturation at adolescence?

13. What four processes are involved with aging that influence the genetic programming of individual cells?

LEVEL 3   Critical Thinking/Application

Using principles and concepts learned about development and inheritance, answer the following questions. Write your answers on a separate sheet of paper.

1. A common form of color blindness is associated with the presence of a dominant or recessive gene on the X chromosome. Normal color vision is determined by the presence of a dominant gene (C), and color blindness results from the presence of the recessive gene (c). Suppose a heterozygous normal female marries a normal male. Is it possible for any of their children to be color blind? Show the possibilities by using a Punnett square.

2. Albinism (aa) is inherited as a homozygous recessive trait. If a homozygous-recessive mother and a heterozygous father decide to have children, what are the possibilities of their offspring inheriting albinism? Use a Punnett square to show the possibilities.

3. Tongue rolling is inherited as a dominant trait. Even though a mother and father are tongue rollers (T), show how it would be possible to bear children who do not have the ability to roll the tongue. Use a Punnett square to show the possibilities.

4. Sharon S. has been married for two years and is pregnant with her first child. She has lived in the Harrisburg, Pennsylvania area all her life. During the nuclear power disaster at Three Mile Island she was exposed to radiation. Her gynecologist has advised her to have amniocentesis to determine whether her exposure to radiation has had any ill effects on the developing fetus. As a friend, would you encourage or discourage her from having the procedure? Why?

APPENDIX

ANSWERS

Part 1 BIOS 250
Chapter 1 An Introduction to Anatomy and Physiology

[L1] Multiple Choice

1. D 2. B 3. C 4. C 5. D 6. C 7. D 8. A 9. D 10. C 11. D 12. C 13. A 14. D 15. D
16. C 17. D 18. B 19. B 20. C 21. D 22. A

[L1] Completion

1. histologist 2. embryology 3. physiology 4. tissues 5. molecules 6. organs 7. urinary 8. digestive
9. integumentary 10. regulation 11. equilibrium 12. autoregulation 13. positive feedback 14. endocrine
15. liver 16. medial 17. distal 18. transverse 19. pericardial 20. mediastinum 21. peritoneal

[L1] Matching

1. F 2. D 3. G 4. A 5. B 6. E 7. C 8. J 9. N 10. L 11. I 12. H 13. O 14. M 15. K

[L1] Drawing/Illustration Labeling

Figure 1.1 Planes of the Body
1. frontal (coronal) 2. transverse 3. midsagittal

Figure 1.2 Human Body Orientation and Direction
1. superior (cephalad) 2. posterior (dorsal) 3. inferior (caudal) 4. anterior (ventral) 5. proximal 6. distal

Figure 1.3 Regional Body References
1. occipital 2. deltoid 3. scapular 4. lumbar 5. gluteal 6. popliteal 7. sural 8. axillary 9. brachial
10. abdominal 11. femoral 12. orbital 13. buccal 14. cervical 15. thorax 16. antecubital 17. umbilical 18. pubic 19. palmar 20. patellar

Figure 1.4 Body Cavities—Sagittal View
1. ventral cavity 2. thoracic cavity 3. diaphragm 4. abdominal cavity 5. pelvic cavity 6. cranial cavity
7. dorsal cavity 8. spinal cavity

Figure 1.5 Body Cavities—Anterior View
1. left pleural cavity 2. pericardial cavity 3. right pleural cavity 4. diaphragm 5. abdominal cavity

[L2] Concept Maps

I Anatomy

1. macroscopic anatomy 2. regional anatomy 3. structure of organ systems 4. surgical anatomy 5. embryology 6. cytology 7. tissues

II Physiology

8. functions of anatomical structures

9. functions of living cells

10. histophysiology

11. specific organ systems

12. pathological physiology

13. body function response to changes in atmospheric pressure

14. exercise physiology

15. body function response to athletics

III Body Cavities

16. cranial cavity 17. spinal cord 18. two pleural cavities 19. heart 20. abdominopelvic cavity 21. pelvic cavity

IV Clinical Technology

22. radiologist 23. high-energy radiation 24. angiogram 25. CT scans 26. radio waves 27. echogram

[L2]   Body Trek

1. subatomic particles   2. atoms   3. molecules   4. organelles   5. cells   6. tissues   7. organs   8. systems
9. organisms

[L2]   Multiple Choice

1. D   2. A   3. C   4. C   5. A   6. B   7. B   8. C   9. D   10. B   11. D   12. A   13. B   14. C   15. D

[L2]   Completion

1. adaptability   2. cardiovascular   3. lymphatic   4. extrinsic regulation   5. nervous   6. knee   7. appendicitis
8. elbow   9. stethoscope   10. sternum

[L2]   Short Essay

1. Any one of the following might be listed: responsiveness, adaptability, growth, reproduction, movement, absorption, respiration, excretion, digestion, circulation

2. Subatomic particles ↔ atoms ↔ molecules ↔ organelle ↔ cell(s) ↔ tissue(s) ↔ organ(s) ↔ system(s) ↔ organism

3. Homeostatic regulation refers to adjustments in physiological systems that are responsible for the preservation of homeostasis (the steady state).

4. In negative feedback a variation outside of normal limits triggers an automatic response that corrects the situation. In positive feedback the initial stimulus produces a response that exaggerates the stimulus.

5. ventral, dorsal, cranial (cephalic), caudal

6. A sagittal section separates right and left portions. A transverse or horizontal section separates superior and inferior portions of the body.

7. (a) dorsal cavity (b) ventral cavity (c) thoracic cavity (d) abdominopelvic cavity

8.

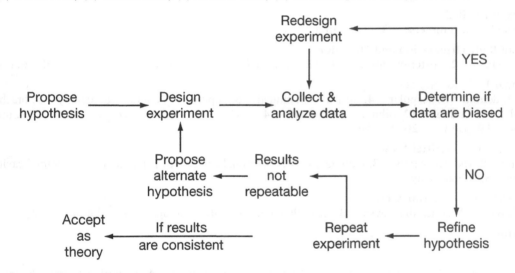

[L3]   Critical Thinking/Application

1. Since there is a lung in each compartment, if one lung is diseased or infected the other lung may remain functional. Also, if one lung is traumatized due to injury, the other one may be spared and function sufficiently to save the life of the injured person.

2. Stretching of the uterus by the developing embryo stimulates the start of contractions. Contractions push the baby toward the opening of the uterus, causing additional stretching, which initiates more contractions. The cycle continues until the baby is delivered and the stretching stimulation is eliminated.

3. pericardial, mediastinal, abdominal, pelvic

4. Extrinsic regulation. The nervous and endocrine systems can control or adjust the activities of many different systems simultaneously. This usually causes more extensive and potentially more effective adjustments in system activities.

5. No adverse effects have been attributed to the sound waves, and fetal development can be monitored without a significant risk of birth defects. Ultrasound machines are relatively inexpensive and portable.

6. Barium is very *radiodense*, and the contours of the gastric and intestinal lining can be seen against the white of the barium solution.

7. At no. 1 on the graph there will be *increased blood flow to the skin* and *increased sweating* if the body temperature rises above 99° F. The *body surface cools* and the *temperature declines*. If the temperature falls below 98° F there is *a decrease in blood flow to the skin* and *shivering* occurs. These activities help to *conserve body heat* and the body temperature rises.

Chapter 2 The Chemical Level of Organization

[L1]   Multiple Choice

1. D   2. B   3. C   4. B   5. A   6. C   7. C   8. D   9. D   10. A   11. C   12. A   13. D   14. D   15. B
16. C   17. B   18. C   19. B   20. A   21. C   22. B   23. D   24. B   25. C

[L1]   Completion

1. protons   2. mass number   3. covalent bonds   4. ionic bond   5. H_2 6. cation   7. decomposition
8. exergonic, endergonic   9. catalysts   10. organic   11. inorganic   12. solvent, solute   13. water   14. acidic
15. buffers   16. salt   17. carbonic acid   18. glucose   19. dehydration synthesis   20. prostaglandins

[L1]   Matching

1. C   2. E   3. F   4. B   5. A   6. E   7. H   8. D   9. N   10. O   11. I   12. M   13. L   14. K   15. J

[L1]   Drawing/Illustration Labeling

Figure 2.1   Diagram of an Atom
1. nucleus   2. orbital (shell)   3. electron   4. protons and neutrons

Figure 2.2   Identification of Types of Bonds
1. nonpolar covalent bond   2. polar covalent bond   3. ionic bond

Figure 2.3   Identification of Organic Molecules
1. monosaccharide   2. disaccharide   3. polysaccharide   4. saturated fatty acid   5. polyunsaturated fatty acid
6. amino acid   7. cholesterol   8. DNA

[L2]   Concept Maps

I Carbohydrates

1. monosaccharides   2. glucose   3. disaccharide   4. sucrose   5. complex carbohydrates   6. glycogen   7. bulk, fiber

II Lipids

8. saturated   9. glyceride   10. diglyceride (Di)   11. glycerol + 3 fatty acids   12. local hormones   13.
phospholipid   14. carbohydrates + diglyceride   15. steroids

III Proteins

16. amino acids   17. amino group   18. – COOH   19. variable group   20. structural proteins   21. elastin
22. enzymes   23. primary   24. alpha helix   25. globular proteins   26. quaternary

IV Nucleic Acids

27. deoxyribose nucleic acid   28. deoxyribose   29. purines   30. thymine   31. ribonucleic acid   32. N bases
33. ribose   34. pyrimidines   35. adenine

[L2]   Body Trek

1. electrons   2. orbitals   3. nucleus   4. protons   5. neutrons   6. deuterium   7. isotope   8. oxygen   9. six
10. eight   11. double covalent bond   12. molecule   13. oxygen gas   14. polar covalent   15. negatively
16. water   17. 66   18. zero   19. 100   20. heat capacity   21. lowering   22. solvent   23. hydrophilic
24. organic acids   25. glucose   26. monosaccharide   27. glycogen   28. dehydration synthesis   29. hydrolysis
30. DNA   31. RNA   32. polypeptide   33. protein   34. phosphorylation   35. ATP

[L2]   Multiple Choice

1. A   2. B   3. D   4. D   5. A   6. A   7. C   8. A   9. D   10. C   11. B   12. D   13. C   14. B   15. D
16. D   17. B   18. D   19. A   20. C   21. C   22. A   23. D   24. B

[L2]   Completion

1. alpha particles   2. mole   3. molecule   4. ions   5. ionic bond   6. molecular weight   7. inorganic
compounds   8. hydrophobic   9. alkaline   10. nucleic acids   11. isomers   12. hydrolysis   13. dehydration
synthesis   14. saturated   15. peptide bond

[L2]   Short Essay

1.

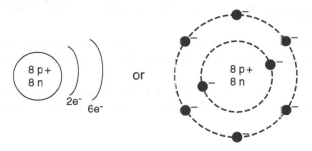

2. (a) hydrolysis   (b) dehydration synthesis

3. Their outer energy levels contain the maximum number of electrons and they will not react with one another nor combine with atoms of other elements.

4. The oxygen atom has a much stronger attraction for the shared electrons than do the hydrogen atoms, so the electrons spend most of this time in the vicinity of the oxygen nucleus. Because the oxygen atom has two extra electrons part of the time, it develops a slight negative charge. The hydrogens develop a slight positive charge because their electrons are away part of the time.

5. $6 \times 12 = $ 72

   $12 \times 1 = $ 12

   $6 \times 16 = $ $\underline{96}$

   MW =   180

6. 1. molecular structure, 2. freezing point 0° C; boiling point 100° C, 3. capacity to absorb and distribute heat, 4. heat absorbed during evaporation, 5. solvent properties, 6. 66 percent total body weight

7. *carbohydrates*, ex. glucose; *lipids*, ex. steroids; *proteins*, ex. enzymes; *nucleic acid*, ex. DNA

8. In a saturated fatty acid each carbon atom in the hydrocarbon tail has four single covalent bonds. If some of the carbon-to-carbon bonds are double covalent bonds, the fatty acid is unsaturated.

9. 1. adenine nucleotide

   2. thymine nucleotide

   3. cytosine nucleotide

   4. guanine nucleotide

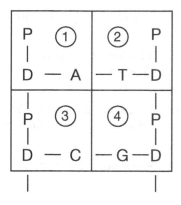

10. adenine, ribose, 3 phosphates

[L3]   Critical Thinking/Application

1. AB + CD → AD + CB or

   AB + CD → AC + BD

2. Baking soda is sodium bicarbonate ($NaHCO_3$). In solution sodium bicarbonate reversibly dissociates into a sodium ion (Na+) and a bicarbonate ion (HCO_3^-) [NaHCO ↔ NA^+ + HCO_3^-].   The bicarbonate ion will remove an excess hydrogen ion (H^+) from the solution and form a weak acid, carbonic acid [H^+ + HCO_3^- ↔ H_2CO_3].

3. $C_6H_{12}O_6 + C_6H_{12}O_6 ↔ C_{12}H_{22}O_{11} + H_2O$

4. Carbohydrates are an immediate source of energy and can be metabolized quickly. Those not immediately metabolized may be stored as glycogen or excesses may be stored as fat.

5. Cannabinol, the active ingredient in marijuana, is a lipid-soluble molecule; therefore, it slowly diffuses out of the body's lipids after administration has ceased.

6. A, D, E, and K are fat-soluble vitamins and are stored in the fats of our bodies. Excessive levels of these vitamins may cause toxicity to such vital organs as the liver and the brain.

7. The RDA for fat intake per day is 30 percent of the total caloric intake. Fats are necessary for good health. They are involved in many body functions and serve as energy reserves, provide insulation, cushion delicate organs, and are essential structural components of all cells.

8. Proteins perform a variety of essential functions in the human body. In addition to providing tissue growth and repair, some are involved as transport proteins, buffers, enzymes, antibodies, hormones, and other physiological processes.

Chapter 3 Cells: The Living Units

BUILDING THE FRAMEWORK

Overview of the Cellular Basis of Life

1. 1. A cell is the basic structural and functional unit; an organism's activity is dependent on cellular activity; biochemical activity determines and is determined by subcellular structure; continuity of life is based on cell reproduction.   2. cubelike, tilelike, disk-shaped, spherical, branching, cylindrical   3. plasma membrane, cytoplasm, nucleus   4. A model that describes a cell in terms of common features/functions that all cells share.

The Plasma Membrane: Structure and Functions

1.

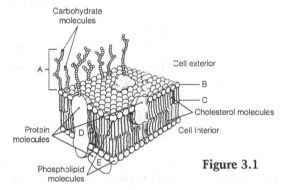

Figure 3.1

1. fluid mosaic model   2. to stabilize the plasma membrane by wedging between the phospholipid "tails"
3. glycocalyx   4. C   5. hydrophobic   6. D: integral; E peripheral

2.

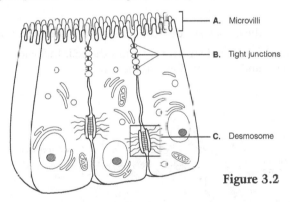

Figure 3.2

1. Microvilli increase the surface area of the plasma membrane.   2. Microvilli are found on cells involved in secretion and/or absorption.   3. actin   4. the glycocalyx and tongue-in-groove folding of adjacent plasma membranes   5. tight junction   6. desmosome   7. desmosome   8. gap junction   9. connexons

3.

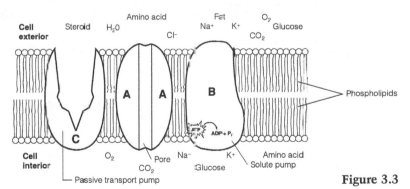

Figure 3.3

Arrow for Na^+ should be red and shown leaving the cell; those for glucose, Cl^-, O_2, fat, and steroids (except cholesterol which enters by receptor-mediated endocytosis) should be blue and entering the cell. CO_2 (blue arrow) should be leaving the cell and moving into the extracellular fluid. Amino acids and K^+ (red arrows) should be entering the cell. Water (H_2O) moves passively (blue arrows) through the membrane (in or out) depending on local osmotic conditions.
1. fat, steroid, O_2, CO_2 2. glucose   3. H_2O, (probably) Cl^- 4. Na^+, K^+, amino acid

4. l. A, F, G, H   2. B, C   3. E   4. B, C   5. I   6. F, G, H   7. I   8. A, D, F, G, H   9. F   10. D   11. A

5. 1. A. hypertonic B. isotonic C. hypotonic   2. A. crenated B. normal (discoid) C. spherical, some hemolyzed
3. same solute concentration inside and outside the cell   4. Water is moving by osmosis into the cell from the
site of higher water concentration (cell exterior) to the site of lower water concentration (cell interior).   5. Tonicity
deals with the effect of nonpenetrating solutes on the movement of water into or out of cells; osmolarity is a
measure of the total solute concentration, both penetrating and nonpenetrating solutes.

6.

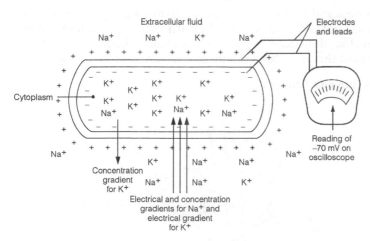

Figure 3.5

7.

1. Communication between adjacent cells   2. Impermeable junction   3. Impermeable intercellular space
4. High extracellular K^+ concentration   5. Protein anions move out of cell   6. More K^+ pumped out than Na^+
carried in   7. Carbohydrate chains on cytoplasmic side of membrane   8. Nonselective   9. Exocytosis   10.
CAMs   11. NO   12. Phospholipids   13. SNAREs

The Cytoplasm

1. The unstructured gel-like part of the cytoplasm that contains biological molecules in solution.

2. Organelles: the highly structured functional structures within the cell. Inclusions: stored nutrients, crystals of
various types, secretory granules, and waste products in the cell.

3.

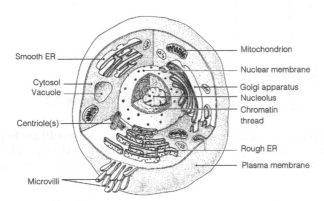

Figure 3.6

4.

Cell structure	Location	Function
Plasma membrane	External boundary of the cell	Confines cell contents; regulates entry and exit of materials
Lysosome	Scattered in cytoplasm	Digests ingested materials and worn-out organelles
Mitochondria	Scattered throughout the cell	Controls release of energy from foods; forms ATP
Microvilli	Projections of the plasma membrane	Increase the membrane surface area
Golgi apparatus	Near the nucleus (in the cytoplasm)	Packages proteins to be exported from the cell; packages lysosomal enzymes
Centrioles	Two rod-shaped bodies near the nucleus	"Spin" the mitotic spindle
Smooth ER	In the cytoplasm	Site of steroid synthesis and lipid metabolism
Rough ER	In the cytoplasm	Transports proteins (made on its ribosomes) to other sites in the cell; site of membrane lipid synthesis
Ribosomes	Attached to membranes or scattered in the cytoplasm	Synthesize proteins
Cilia	Extensions of cell to exterior	Act collectively to move substances across cell surface in one direction
Microtubules	Internal structure of centrioles; part of the cytoskeleton	Important in cell shape; suspend organelles
Peroxisomes	Throughout cytoplasm	Detoxify alcohol and free radicals accumulating from normal metabolism
Microfilaments	Throughout cytoplasm; part of cytoskeleton	Contractile protein (actin); moves cell or cell parts; core of microvilli
Intermediate filaments	Part of cytoskeleton	Act as internal "guy wires"; help form desmosomes
Inclusions	Dispersed in the cytoplasm	Provide nutrients; represent cell waste products, etc.

5. 1. Centrioles   2. Cilia   3. Smooth ER   4. Vitamin A storage   5. Mitochondria   6. Ribosomes   7. Lysosomes

6. 1. microtubules   2. intermediate filaments   3. microtubules   4. microfilaments   5. intermediate filaments
6. microtubules

7. 1. B   2. F   3. D   4. E   5. C, H   6. G   7. A

8. The nuclear and plasma membranes and essentially all organelles except mitochondria and cytoskeletal elements make up the endomembrane system. The components of this system act together to synthesize, store, and export cell products and to degrade or detoxify ingested or harmful substances.

The Nucleus

1.

Nuclear structure	General location/appearance	Function
Nucleus	Usually in center of the cell; oval or spherical	Storehouse of genetic information; directs cellular activities
Nucleolus	Dark spherical body in the nucleus	Storehouse and assembly site for ribosomes
Chromatin	Dispersed in the nucleus; threadlike	Contains genetic material (DNA); coils during mitosis
Nuclear membrane	Encloses nuclear contents; double membrane penetrated by pores	Regulates entry/exit of substances to and from the nucleus

2. 1. Histone proteins   2. The components are believed to play a role in regulating DNA function by exposing or not exposing certain DNA fragments.

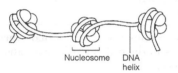

Nucleosome   DNA helix

Figure 3.7

Cell Growth and Reproduction

1. The cell life cycle consists of interphase and the mitotic phase, during which the cell divides.

Phase of interphase	Important events
G_1	Cell grows rapidly and is active in its normal metabolic activities. Centrioles begin replicating.
S	Cell growth continues. DNA is replicated, new histone proteins are made, and chromatin is assembled.
G_2	Brief phase when remaining enzymes (or other proteins) needed for cell division are synthesized; centriole replication completed.

2.

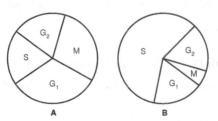

Figure 3.8

3. 1. MPF (maturation promoting factor or M-phase promoting factor)   2. Cdk (a kinase enzyme)   3. Cyclin

4. 1. C   2. A   3. D   4. D   5. B   6. C   7. C   8. E   9. B, C   10. C   11. E   12. A, B   13. E   14. A

5. Figure 3.9: A. Prophase   B. Anaphase   C. Telophase   D. Metaphase

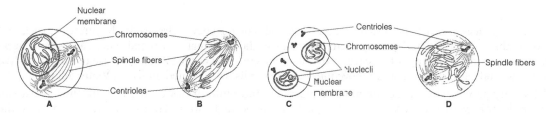

Figure 3.9

Figure 3.10: A. Prophase   B. Metaphase   C. Anaphase (early)   D. Prophase   E. Telophase   F. Anaphase (late)

6. 1. P   2. K   3. O   4. T   5. C   6. B   7. E   8. F   9. V   10. S   11. Q   12. M   13. U   14. L   15. N
16. H   17. I   18. R

7. 1. transcription   2. translation   3. DNA   4. anticodon triplet   5. One or more segments of a DNA strand that programs one polypeptide chain (or one tRNA or rRNA)

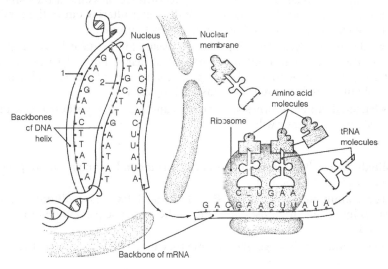

Figure 3.11

8. 1. nucleus   2. cytoplasm   3. coiled   4. centromeres   5. binucleate cell   6. spindle   7. interphase

Extracellular Materials

1. 1. Body fluids: e.g., blood plasma, interstitial fluid, cerebrospinal fluid, eye humors. Important in transport in body and as solvents.

2. Cellular secretions: e.g., saliva, gastric juice, mucus, tears. Important as lubricants and some aid the digestive process.

3. Extracellular matrix: e.g., glycoprotein intercellular "glue," and the matrix (ground substance and fibers) secreted by connective tissue cells. Important in binding cells together and providing strong structures (bones, cartilages, etc.) that can support or protect other body organs.

The Incredible Journey

1. 1. cytosol   2. nucleus   3. mitochondrion   4. ATP   5. ribosomes   6. rough endoplasmic reticulum
7. nuclear pores   8. chromatin   9. DNA   10. nucleoli   11. Golgi apparatus   12. lysosome (or peroxisome)

CHALLENGING YOURSELF

At the Clinic

1. Normally, lactose (a disaccharide) is digested to monosaccharides by the enzyme lactase in the intestine. Lactase deficiency prevents this digestion. Consequently, lactose remains in the intestinal lumen and acts as an osmotic agent to attract water and prevent its absorption. Hence, diarrhea (or watery feces) occurs. Adding lactase to milk hydrolyzes lactose to glucose and galactose, which can move into intestinal cells by facilitated diffusion. Water follows.

2. Increased capillary permeability causes more blood plasma to filter into the tissue spaces from the bloodstream. On a small scale, this causes the localized swelling (edema) associated with inflammation. In anaphylaxis, the systemic reaction causes so *much* fluid to leave the bloodstream that there is insufficient blood volume (fluid) to maintain circulation to the vital organs.

3. LDL is removed from the circulation by receptor-mediated endocytosis.

4. Glucose is reclaimed from the forming urine by carrier molecules in the plasma membranes of cells forming the tubules of the kidneys. If too much glucose is present, the carrier molecules are *saturated*. Hence, some glucose will not be reabsorbed and returned to the blood, but instead will be lost to the body in urine.

5. In blood stasis, the filtration pressure at the capillaries increases. Albumin (being a small protein) can be forced into the interstitial fluid under such conditions, increasing its osmotic pressure. If the osmotic pressure of the interstitial fluid exceeds that of the blood plasma, more of the water filtering out of the capillary will *remain* in the tissue spaces. This increase in interstitial fluid volume leads to edema.

6. Lysosomal destruction releases acid hydrolases into the cytoplasm, killing the cell. When the cell lyses, inflammation is triggered. Hydrocortisone is an anti-inflammatory steroid that stabilizes lysosomal membranes. Since hydrocortisone is a steroid, it is soluble in an oil base rather than a water base. Steroids can diffuse through the lipid bilayer of cell membranes, so they can be administered topically.

7. Streptomycin inhibits bacterial protein synthesis. If the cells are unable to synthesize new proteins (many of which would be essential enzymes), they will die.

Stop and Think

1. Because the phospholipids orient themselves so that polar-to-polar and nonpolar-to-nonpolar regions are aligned, any gaps in the membrane are quickly sealed.

2. The molecular weights are ammonium hydroxide, 35; sulfuric acid, 98. Since sulfuric acid is about three times the weight of ammonium hydroxide, it diffuses at about 1/3 the rate. The precipitate forms about 1/4 of a meter from the sulfuric acid end.

3. Skin cells lose their desmosomes as they age. By the time they reach the free surface, they are no longer tightly bound to each other.

4. Conjugation (attachment) of the lipid product to a non–lipid-soluble substance, such as protein, will trap the product.

5. The plasma membrane folds (microvilli); the internal membranes are folded (ER and Golgi apparatus); the inner membranes of mitochondria are folded (cristae).

6. Since mitochondria contain DNA and RNA, mitochondrial ribosomes could be expected to, and do indeed, exist. Mitochondrial nucleic acids and ribosomes are extremely similar to those of bacteria.

7. Avascular tissues rely on the diffusion of nutrients from surrounding fluids. Since this is not as efficient or effective as a vascular supply, these tissues do not get very thick. An exception is the epidermis of the skin, which is quite thick, but cells in the skin layers farthest from the underlying blood vessels are dead.

8. A: This cell secretes a protein product, as evidenced by large amounts of rough ER, Golgi apparatus, and secretory vesicles near the cell apex.   B: The cell secretes a lipid or steroid product, as evidenced by the lipid droplets surrounded by the abundant smooth ER.

9. 1. Fructose will diffuse into the cell.   2. Glucose will diffuse out of the cell.   3. Water enters the cell by diffusing along its concentration gradient.   4. The cell swells due to water entry.

10. 1.

		2. After deletion:	
DNA:	TAC GCA TCA CIT TTG ATC	DNA:	TAG ATC
mRNA:	AUG CGU AGU GAA AAC UAG	mRNA:	AUC UAG
amino acids:	Met Arg Ser Glu Asn Stop	amino acids:	none; a nonsense message

COVERING ALL YOUR BASES

Multiple Choice

1. E   2. C   3. B   4. A   5. C, D   6. C   7. B   8. B, D   9. B   10. C   11. C   12. A, D
13. A, B, C, D   14. C   15. E   16. D, E   17. C   18. A   19. E   20. B   21. D   22. C   23. D
24. C   25. A   26. A   27. A, B, C   28. A   29. A

Word Dissection

	Word root	Translation	Example		Word root	Translation	Example
1.	chondri	lump	mitochondria	13.	osmo	pushing	osmosis
2.	chrom	color	chromosome	14.	permea	pass through	permeable
3.	crist	crest	cristae	15.	phag	eat	phagocyte
4.	cyto	cell	cytology	16.	philo	love	hydrophilic
5.	desm	bond	desmosome	17.	phobo	fear	hydrophobic
6.	dia	through	dialysis	18.	pin	drink	pinocytosis
7.	dys	bad	dysplasia	19.	plasm	to be molded	cytoplasm
8.	flagell	whip	flagellum	20.	telo	end	telophase
9.	meta	between	metaphase	21.	tono	tension	isotonic
10.	mito	thread	mitosis, mitochondria	22.	troph	nourish	atrophy
11.	nucle	little nut	nucleus	23.	villus	hair	microvilli
12.	onco	a mass	oncogene				

Chapter 4 Tissues

BUILDING THE FRAMEWORK

Overview of Body Tissues

1. 1. Areolar   2. Cell   3. Elastic fibers   4. Bones   5. Nervous   6. Blood   7. Vascular   8. Keratin   9. Vascular

2. A. simple squamous epithelium   B. simple cuboidal epithelium   C. cardiac muscle   D. dense regular connective tissue   E. bone   F. skeletal muscle   G. nervous tissue   H. hyaline cartilage   I. smooth muscle tissue   J. adipose (fat) tissue   K. stratified squamous epithelium   L. areolar connective tissue
The noncellular areas of D, E, H, J, and L are matrix.

3. 1. B   2. C   3. D   4. A   5. B   6. D   7. C   8. B   9. A   10. A   11. C   12. A   13. D

Epithelial Tissue

1. protection, absorption, filtration, excretion, secretion, and sensory reception

2. cellularity, specialized contacts (junctions), polarity, avascularity, regeneration, supported by connective tissue

3. 1. B   2. F   3. A   4. D   5. G   6. K   7. H   8. J   9. I   10. L

4. A=1; C=2; E=3; D=4; B=5

5. B=1; D=2; C=3; A=4

6.
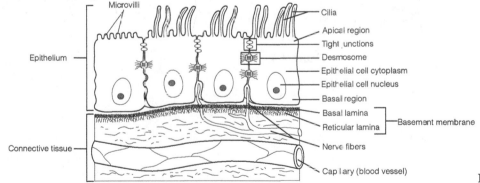

Figure 4.2

7. 1. simple alveolar gland   2. simple tubular gland   3. tubuloalveolar gland   4. compound gland

8. 1. T   2. glandular cells secrete their product   3. merocrine   4. merocrine   5. T   6. repair their damage   7. merocrine   8. T

9. 1. B   2. A   3. A   4. B   5. C   6. B

10. 1. epithelial   2. goblet cells   3. mucin   4.–6. duct (from epithelium), secretory unit, and supportive connective tissue   7. branching   8. tubular

Connective Tissue

1. 1. C   2. A   3. D   4. J   5. B   6. H   7. A   8. H   9. J   10. G   11. K   12. I   13. E   14. L   15. F

2.

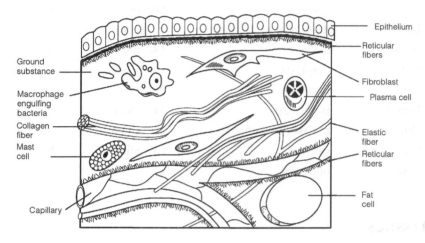

Figure 4.3

3. B=1; C=2; A=3

4. 1. H   2. E   3. C   4. F   5. L   6. G   7. E   8. B   9. D   10. E   11. A   12. I   13. K

Covering and Lining Membranes

1. In each case, the visceral layer of the serosa covers the external surface of the organ, and the parietal layer lines the body cavity walls.

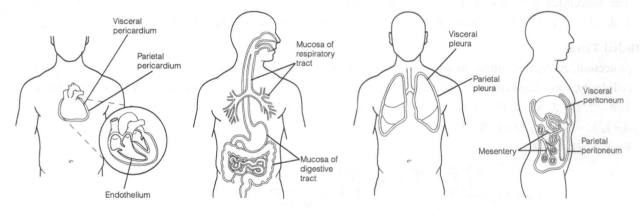

Figure 4.4

2.

Membrane	Tissue type (epithelial/connective)	Common locations	Functions
Mucous	Epithelial sheet with underlying connective tissue lamina propria	Lines respiratory, digestive, and reproductive tracts	Protection, lubrication, secretion, absorption
Serous	Epithelial sheet (mesothelium), scant areolar connective tissue	Lines internal ventral cavities and covers their organs	Lubrication for decreased friction during organ movements
Cutaneous	Epithelial (stratified squamous, keratinized) underlain by dense fibrous connective tissue dermis	Covers the body exterior; is the skin	Protection from external insults; protection from water loss

Nervous Tissue

1. The neuron has long cytoplasmic extensions that promote its ability to transmit impulses long distances within the body.
2. Conduct

Muscle Tissue

1. Skeletal: 1, 3, 5, 6, 7, 11, 13   Cardiac: 2, 3, 4 (typically), 10, 12, 14, 15   Smooth: 2, 4, 7, 8, 9, 14

Tissue Repair

1. 1. inflammation 2. clotting proteins 3. granulation 4. T 5. regeneration 6. T 7. collagen 8. T 9. T 10. bacteria-inhibiting 11. fibrosis

CHALLENGING YOURSELF

At the Clinic

1. Individual adipocytes easily lose and gain cell volume by losing or accumulating more fat.
2. Microglia are the macrophages of the brain. Their abundance is indicative of phagocytic activity to remove dead cells and any infectious organisms present.
3. Cartilage is avascular, and tendons are poorly vascularized. The more ample the blood supply, the quicker tissue heals.
4. Hypersecretion of serous fluid and its accumulation in the pleural space displaces lung volume. Because the lungs are not able to expand fully, respiration is more difficult. Additionally, when there is more fluid in the tissue spaces, diffusion of nutrients to the tissue cells (from the bloodstream) takes much longer and can impair tissue health and viability.
5. The peritoneum will be inflamed and infected. Since the peritoneum encloses so many richly vascularized organs, a spreading peritoneal infection can be life-threatening.

Stop and Think

1. Simple epithelium is thinner than the diameter of the smallest vessel and must overlie all other tissues. Stratified epithelium forms the protective covering of deeper tissues. If blood vessels were within the epithelial layer, protection of the vessels would be reduced. Cartilage undergoes severe compression, which could damage vessels. Tendons are designed to withstand a strong pull; vessels would weaken the structure of tendons and would be at risk for rupture during extreme tension.
2. By virtue of their elongated shape, columnar cells share more adjacent membrane with neighboring cells. This means more surface area for desmosomes and tongue-in-groove folds, both of which help bind cells together and reduce the chance of their separation.

3. Microvilli are found on virtually all simple cuboidal and simple columnar epithelia. The increase in surface area contributed by the microvilli offsets the decrease in transport rate by the thicker layers. Ciliated tissue can include all three types of simple epithelium but is found predominantly as simple columnar and pseudostratified.

4. Endocrine glands, like exocrine glands, are derived from the surface epithelium. In embryonic stages, these glands grow down from the surface, but eventually they lose their surface connection.

5. A basal lamina is only part of the basement membrane, which consists of epithelial cell secretions (the basal lamina) plus connective tissue fibers (the reticular lamina). A mucous membrane is an epithelial membrane composed of an epithelial sheet and underlying connective tissue. A sheet of mucus is a layer of secreted mucus (a cell product).

6. Large arteries must be able to expand in more than one direction; hence, they have irregularly arranged elastic connective tissue.

7. A bone shaft, like a skeletal cartilage, is surrounded by a sheet of dense irregular connective tissue.

8. Skeletal muscle cells are quite large compared to other muscle types. Typically, the multinucleate condition indicates that the demands for protein synthesis could not be handled by a single nucleus.

COVERING ALL YOUR BASES

Multiple Choice

1. B   2. D   3. A   4. B   5. C   6. B   7. D, E   8. C   9. A   10. D   11. B   12. A, C, D   13. C   14. D   15. B   16. D   17. A   18. B   19. C   20. B   21. E   22. B, C, D   23. C   24. C   25. B, E   26. A, B, D, E   27. A, B, C, D, E   28. A   29. A, B, D

Word Dissection

	Word root	Translation	Example		Word root	Translation	Example
1.	ap	tip	apical, apocrine	11.	hormon	excite	hormone
2.	areola	space	areolar connective	12.	hyal	glass	hyaline, hyaluronic
3.	basal	foundation	basal lamina				
4.	blast	forming	fibroblast	13.	lamina	thin plate	reticular lamina
5.	chyme	juice	mesenchyme	14.	mero	part	merocrine
6.	crine	separate	endocrine	15.	meso	middle	mesoderm, mesothelium
7.	endo	within	endoderm, endothelium				
8.	epi	upon, over	epithelium	16.	retic	network	reticular tissue
9.	glia	glue	neuroglia, microglia	17.	sero	watery fluid	serous, serosa
10.	holo	whole	holocrine	18.	squam	a scale	squamous
				19.	strat	layer	stratified

Chapter 5 The Integumentary System

BUILDING THE FRAMEWORK

The Skin

1. 1. stratified squamous epithelium   2. dense irregular connective tissue

2. 1. They are increasingly farther from the blood supply in the dermis.   2. They are increasingly laden with (water-insoluble) keratin and surrounded by glycolipids, which hinder their ability to receive nutrients by diffusion.

3. 1. lines of cleavage   2. striae   3. flexure lines   4. wrinkles

4.

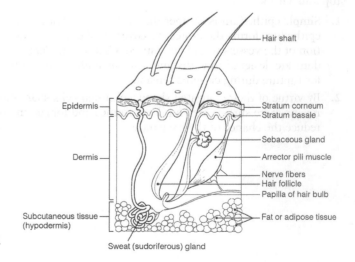

Figure 5.1

5. 1. D   2. B, D   3. F   4. I   5. A   6. B   7. I   8. H   9. I   10. J   11. A   12. A   13. C   14. B   15. I   16. B

6. 1. Keratin   2. Wart   3. Stratum basale   4. Keratinocytes   5. Arrector pili   6. Elastin   7. Melanocytes
8. Lamellated granules   9. Fibroblast

7. 1. C   2. A   3. C   4. B   5. C   6. A   7. B

8. 1. A   2. E   3. D   4. C   5. B

Appendages of the Skin

1. The papilla contains blood vessels that nourish the growth zone of the hair. The sebaceous gland secretes sebum into the follicle. The arrector pili muscle pulls the follicle into an upright position during cold or fright. The bulb is the actively growing region of the hair. See diagram B for localization of the dermal and epidermal root sheaths.

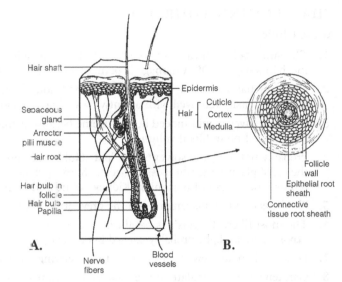

Figure 5.2

2. 1. Poor nutrition   2. Keratin   3. Stratum corneum   4. Eccrine glands   5. Vellus hair   6. Desquamation
7. Growth phase

3. Alopecia

4. Genetic factors; emotional trauma; some drugs (chemotherapy agents); ringworm infection

5. 1. cuticle   2. The stratum germinativum is thicker here, preventing the rosy cast of blood from flushing through

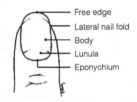

6. 1. A   2. B, C   3. B   4. C (B)   5. A   6. A   7. A, B   8. A   9. B   10. C

Functions of the Integumentary System

1. 1. B   2. M   3. C   4. M (C)   5. C   6. C

2. All *but* water-soluble substances

3. It depresses immune response by inhibiting the activity of macrophages that aid in the immune response.

4. Sweat glands are regulated by the sympathetic division of the nervous system. When it is hot, blood vessels in the skin become flushed with warm blood, allowing heat to radiate from the skin surface, and perspiration output increases. Evaporation of sweat from the body surface removes large amounts of body heat.

5. 1. nervous   2.–5. cold, heat, deep pressure, and light pressure   6. cholesterol   7. epidermis   8. ultraviolet
9. calcium

Homeostatic Imbalances of Skin

1. Loss of body fluids containing proteins and essential electrolytes, which can lead to dehydration, shock, and renal shutdown

2. 1. C   2. B   3. A   4. B   5. C   6. C

3. It allows the estimation of the extent of burns so that fluid volume replacement can be correctly calculated.

4. 1. squamous cell carcinoma   2. basal cell carcinoma   3. malignant melanoma

5. Pigmented areas that are Asymmetric, have irregular Borders, exhibit several Colors, and have a Diameter greater than 6 mm are likely to be cancerous.

The Incredible Journey

1. 1. collagen   2. elastin   3. dermis   4. phagocyte (macrophage)   5. connective tissue root   6. epidermis
   7. stratum basale   8. melanin   9. keratin   10. squamous (stratum corneum) cells

CHALLENGING YOURSELF

At the Clinic

1. The sun's radiation can cause damage to DNA, in spite of the protection afforded by melanin. Without repair mechanisms, the DNA damage is permanent, and the effects are cumulative.

2. The baby has seborrhea, or cradle cap, a condition of overactive sebaceous glands. It is not serious; the oily deposit is easily removed with attentive washing and soon stops forming.

3. Systemic hives would indeed be worrisome because it might indicate a possibly life-threatening plasma loss and correlated drop in blood volume.

4. Probably not. Organic solvents are lipid-soluble and thus can pass through the skin by dissolving in the lipids of the cells' plasma membranes. Hence, a shower (which would wash away substances soluble in water) will not remove the danger of poisoning. Kidney failure and brain damage can result from poisoning by organic solvents.

5. Fluid/electrolyte replacement and the prevention of massive infection.

6. The most likely diagnosis is basal cell carcinoma, because it causes ulcers and is slow to metastasize. Years of exposure to sunlight probably caused his cancer.

7. Because there are fewer connections to underlying tissues, wounds to the face tend to gape more.

8. Carotene can accumulate in the stratum corneum and the hypodermis, giving the skin an orange cast. Awareness of diet is particularly important in very young children who tend to go on "food jags," refusing all but one food, to determine whether "liked" foods are high in carotene.

9. The drugs used to treat cancer exert their major cell-killing effects on rapidly dividing cells. Like cancer cells, the hair follicles are targets of these drugs, which accounts for the children's baldness.

10. Healing is much cleaner and faster when the incision is made along or parallel to a cleavage line (which represents a separation between adjacent muscle bundles).

Stop and Think

1. The term "membrane" refers to the sheetlike *structure* of the skin; all epithelial membranes are at least simple organs. The term "organ" means there are at least *two types of tissue* in a structure's composition, and at least simple functions can be performed.

2. The undulating folds (formed by the dermal papillae) at the surface between the epidermis and the dermis increase the surface area at the site of their union. Increased surface area provides more space for capillary networks (increasing the area for diffusion of nutrients to and wastes from the avascular epidermis) and is more secure, making it harder for the epidermis to tear away from the dermis.

3. There is very little hypodermal tissue underlying the skin of the shins. Consequently, the skin is quite securely and tightly fastened to the underlying structure (bone) there.

4. The stratum corneum is so far removed from the underlying blood supply in the dermis that diffusion of nutrients is insufficient to keep the cells alive. Also, the accumulation of glycolipids in the intercellular spaces retards diffusion of water-soluble nutrients. The accumulated keratin within the cells inhibits life functions. In terms of benefit, bacterial or other infections cannot become established easily in the dead, water-insoluble layer. Dead cells provide a much more effective mechanical barrier than living cells.

5. The nerve endings located closest to the surface are the most sensitive to light touch. Merkel discs, in the epidermis, are very responsive to light touch; root hair plexuses, although not as close, are stimulated by the movement of hairs on the skin, which project from the surface.

6. When skin peels as a result of sunburn damage, the deeper layers of the stratum corneum, which still maintain their desmosomal connections, detach. The desmosomes hold the cells together within the layers.

7. Unless there is a protein deficiency, additional dietary protein will not increase protein utilization by hair- and nail-forming cells.

8. The apocrine sweat glands, associated with axillary and pubic hair follicles, appear to secrete chemicals that act as sexually important signals.

9. Because of the waterproofing substance in the epidermis (both in and between the cells), the skin is relatively impermeable to water entry.

COVERING ALL YOUR BASES

Multiple Choice

1. B, D   2. D   3. B   4. A   5. D   6. D   7. A   8. D   9. C   10. D, E   11. E   12. A, B, D   13. A, B
14. A, B   15. B   16. A, C, D   17. D   18. C   19. A, B, D   20. B, C, D   21. B   22. A, D, E   23. B, C, D
24. C   25. C   26. D   27. A, C, D   28. B, C, D, E

Word Dissection

	Word root	Translation	Example		Word root	Translation	Example
1.	arrect	upright	arrector pili	15.	lanu	wool, down	lanugo
2.	carot	carrot	carotene	16.	lunul	crescent	lunula
3.	case	cheese	vernix caseosa	17.	medull	marrow	medulla
4.	cere	wax	cerumen	18.	melan	black	melanin
5.	corn	horn, horny	stratum corneum	19.	pall	pale	pallor
6.	cort	bark, shell	cortex	20.	papilla	nipple	dermal papillae
7.	cutic	skin	cutaneous, cuticle	21.	pili	hair	arrector pili
8.	cyan	blue	cyanosis	22.	plex	network	plexus
9.	derm	skin	dermis, epidermis	23.	rrhea	flow	seborrhea
10.	folli	a bag	follicle	24.	seb	grease	sebaceous gland
11.	hemato	blood	hematoma	25.	spin	spine, thorn	stratum spinosum
12.	hirsut	hairy	hirsutism	26.	sudor	sweat	sudoriferous
13.	jaune	yellow	jaundice	27.	tegm	cover	integument
14.	kera	horn	keratin	28.	vell	fleece, wool	vellus

Chapter 6   Bones and Skeletal Tissues

BUILDING THE FRAMEWORK

Skeletal Cartilages

1. 1. C   2. A   3. C   4. B   5. A   6. C   7. C   8. B

2. 1. T   2. F   3. T   4. F   5. F   6. T   7. F

3. Although collagen fibers form cartilage's supporting framework, its proteoglycons and hyalouronic acid attract and organize huge amounts of water, which becomes the main component of cartilage. This water "saves space" for bone development and is responsible for cartilage's resilience throughout life.

Functions of the Bones

1. 1. They support the body by providing a rigid skeletal framework.   2. They protect the brain, spinal cord, lungs, and other internal organs.   3. They act as levers and provide attachments for muscles in movement.   4. They serve as a reservoir for fat and minerals.   5. They are the sites of formation of blood cells.

Classification of Bones

1. 1. S   2. F   3. L   4. L   5. F   6. L   7. L   8. F   9. l

Bone Structure

1.

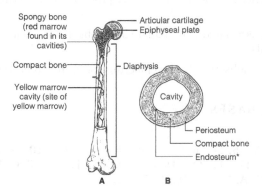

Figure 6.1

2. 1. C   2. A   3. C, D   4. A   5. E   6. B   7. B

3. 1. internal layer of spongy bone   2. endosteum

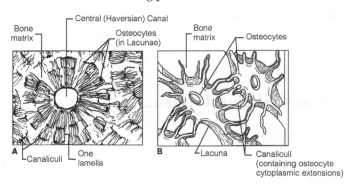

Figure 6. 2

4. 1. B   2. C   3. A   4. E   5. D Matrix is the nonliving part of bone shown as unlabeled white space on the figure.

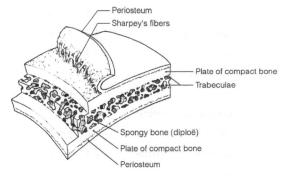

Figure 6.3

5. 1. P   2. P   3. O   4. O   5. P   6. O   7. P   8. P   9. P   10. D   11. P   12. O

6. 1. Collagen   2. Yellow marrow   3. Osteoclasts   4. Marrow cavity   5. Periosteum   6. Perichondrium
   7. Lamellar

Bone Development

1. If arranged in the correct sequence, the listed elements would be numbered: 1, 4, 2, 3, 5, 6 (note: events 2 and 3 may occur simultaneously).

2. 1. intramembranous   2. cartilage   3. T   4. calcium salts   5. T   6. mesenchymal cells or osteoblasts   7. T
   8. secondary   9. hyaline cartilage   10. endosteal   11. T

3. 1. mesenchymal cells   2. ossification center   3. osteoblasts   4. osteoid   5. mineralization   6. bone matrix
   7. woven   8. mesenchyme   9. periosteum   10. diploë

4. 1. chondroblasts   2. enlarging cartilage cells (chondrocytes)   3. B   4. C   5. osteoblasts   6. bone

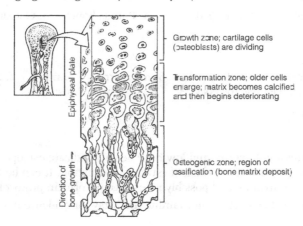

Growth zone; cartilage cells (osteoblasts) are dividing

Transformation zone; older cells enlarge; matrix becomes calcified and then begins deteriorating

Osteogenic zone; region of ossification (bone matrix deposit)

Figure 6. 4

Bone Homeostasis: Remodeling and Repair

1. 1. G   2. F   3. A   4. H   5. D   6. B   7. E   8. C

2. 1. Bone resorption   2. Calcium salts   3. Hypocalcemia   4. Blood calcium levels   5. Growth in length

3. Because the points of maximal compression and tension are on opposing sides of the shaft, they cancel each other out, so there is essentially no stress in the middle (center) of the shaft. Consequently, the shaft can contain spongy (rather than compact) bone in its center.

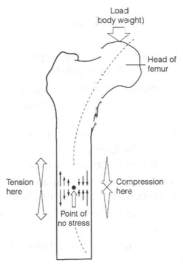

Load (body weight)

Head of femur

Tension here

Compression here

Point of no stress

Figure 6.5

4. 1. H   2. A   3. I   4. F   5. C   6. D   7. G   8. E   9 H   10. I   11. B

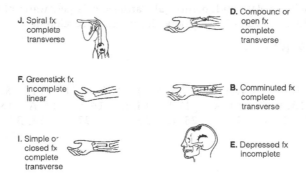

J. Spiral fx complete transverse

D. Compound or open fx complete transverse

F. Greenstick fx incomplete linear

B. Comminuted fx complete transverse

I. Simple or closed fx complete transverse

E. Depressed fx incomplete

Figure 6 6

5. 1. T   2. T   3. phagocytes (macrophages)   4. fibroblasts   5. periosteum   6. T   7. spongy

Homeostatic Imbalances of Bone

1. 1. Osteoporosis   2. Osteomalacia   3. Paget's disease   4. Porous bones   5. Osteomalacia
   6. Calcified epiphyseal discs

The Incredible Journey

1. 1. femur   2. spongy   3. stress   4. red blood cells   5. red marrow   6. nerve   7. central (Haversian)
   8. compact   9. canaliculi   10. lacunae (osteocytes)   11. matrix   12. osteoclast

CHALLENGING YOURSELF

At the Clinic

1. The woman's vertebral compression fractures and low bone density indicate osteoporosis. This condition in post-menopausal women is at least partially due to lack of estrogen production. It can be treated with supplements of calcium and vitamin D, proper nutrition, and possibly an estrogen-progestin protocol or fluoride and etidronate.

2. Infection can spread to the bone. The doctor will examine the X ray for evidence of osteomyelitis, which is notoriously difficult to manage.

3. The curving of the line indicates a spiral fracture.

4. The woman is suffering from hypercalcemia, which is causing metastatic calcification (i.e., calcium salt deposits in soft tissues of the body).

5. The doctor will check for hypersecretion of growth hormone.

6. Paget's disease can cause abnormal thickening of bone such as that experienced by Egil.

7. The epiphyseal plate remains the same thickness during the growth period because as cartilage on the distal epiphyseal plate face is formed, that on the proximal face is replaced by bone.

Stop and Think

1. The blood vessels determine the pattern for the development of the lamellae, so blood vessels in the osteon region appear first.

2. Bone tissue is too rigid for interstitial growth; there is only appositional growth after ossification. Before ossification, growth can occur in membrane or in cartilage templates.

3. Long bones tend to be arranged and to articulate end to end. Even if two long bones are side by side, they still articulate most prominently at their ends. Short bones are arranged and articulate side to side as well as end to end.

4. The medullary cavity's diameter must increase to keep pace with the appositional growth of the surrounding bone collar. Osteoclasts will remove the bone on the interior of the collar to widen the cavity. Likewise, osteoclasts are active on the internal surfaces of cranial bones to broaden their curvatures to accommodate the expanding brain.

5. Bone tissue is highly vascular. Fibrous tissue is poorly vascularized, and cartilage is avascular. In fact, the vascularization of the template is part of the process that triggers ossification.

6. The bone will heal faster because bone is vascularized and has an excellent nutrient delivery system (canaliculi). Cartilage lacks both of these characteristics.

7. Yes, he has cause to worry. The boy is about to enter his puberty-adolescence growth spurt, and interference with the growth plate (epiphyseal plate) is probable.

8. According to Wolff's law, growth of a bone is a response to the amount of compression and tension placed on it, and a bone will grow in the direction necessary to best respond to the stresses applied.

9. Signs of healing of the bone at the surgical incision (usually a hole in the skull) indicate that the patient lived at least for a while.

10. The high water content helps explain both points. (a) Cartilage is largely water plus resilient ground substance and fibers (no calcium salts). (b) Water "saves room" for bones to develop in.

COVERING ALL YOUR BASES

Multiple Choice

1. A, B, C   2. A, B, D   3. A, D   4. A, B, D   5. A, D   6. A, C, D   7. D   8. C   9. A, B, C, E   10. A, B
11. A, B, C, D   12. A   13. B, D   14. A, C, D, E   15. D   16. C   17. A   18. A, C   19. A, D   20. B, E
21. A   22. A, B, C, D, E   23. C   24. C   25. D   26. B, C   27. C   28. B

Word Dissection

	Word root	Translation	Example		Word root	Translation	Example
1.	call	hardened	callus	7.	myel	marrow	osteomyelitis
2.	cancel	latticework	cancellous bone	8.	physis	growth	diaphysis
3.	clast	break	osteoclast	9.	poie	make	hematopoiesis
4.	fract	break	fracture	10.	soma	body	somatomedin
5.	lamell	small plate	lamellar bone	11.	trab	beam	trabeculae
6.	malac	soft	osteomalacia				

Chapter 7 The Axial Skeleton

[L1] Multiple Choice

1. B 2. D 3. C 4. A 5. B 6. D 7. C 8. A 9. D 10. C 11. C 12. A 13. D 14. B 15. D
16. B 17. C 18. C 19. B 20. A 21. D 22. C 23. B 24. C 25. C 26. A 27. B 28. A 29. D
30. B 31. D 32. B

[L1] Completion

1. axial 2. muscles 3. cranium 4. foramen magnum 5. inferior concha 6. paranasal 7. mucus
8. fontanels 9. "soft spot" 10. compensation 11. centrum 12. cervical 13. costal 14. capitulum
15. floating 16. xiphoid process

[L1] Matching

1. H 2. G 3. A 4. F 5. D 6. E 7. C 8. B 9. N 10. O 11. P 12. K 13. L 14. M 15. J 16. I

[L1] Drawing/Illustration Labeling

Figure 7.1 Bones of the Axial Skeleton
1. cranium 2. face (maxilla) 3. hyoid 4. sternum (manubrium) 5. ribs 6. vertebral column 7. sacrum

Figure 7.2 Anterior View of the Skull
1. coronal suture 2. parietal bone 3. frontal bone 4. nasal bone 5. lacrimal bone 6. zygomatic bone
7. infraorbital foramen 8. alveolar margins 9. mental foramen 10. temporal bone 11. ethmoid bone
12. ethmoid bone 13. vomer 14. maxilla 15. mandible

Figure 7.3 Lateral View of the Skull
1. coronal suture 2. frontal bone 3. nasal bone 4. zygomatic process of temporal bone 5. zygomatic bone
6. maxilla 7. mandibular condyle 8. mandible 9. parietal bone 10. squamous suture 11. temporal bone
12. lambdoidal suture 13. external auditory canal 14. occipital bone 15. mastoid process 16. styloid
process

Figure 7.4 Inferior View of the Skull
1. sphenoid bone 2. vomer 3. styloid process 4. foramen magnum 5. occipital bone 6. palatine process
(maxillae) 7. maxilla 8. zygomatic process of temporal bone 9. carotid canal 10. jugular foramen
11. occipital condyle 12. inferior nuchal line 13. superior nuchal line

Figure 7.5 Paranasal Sinuses
1. frontal sinus 2. ethmoid sinus 3. sphenoid sinus 4. maxillary sinus

Figure 7.6 Fetal Skull—Lateral View
1. sphenoidal fontanel 2. anterior fontanel 3. posterior fontanel 4. mastoid fontanel

Figure 7.7 Fetal Skull—Superior View
1. anterior fontanel 2. posterior fontanel

Figure 7.8 The Vertebral Column
1. cervical vertebrae 2. thoracic vertebrae 3. lumbar vertebrae 4. sacrum 5. coccyx 6. intervertebral discs

Figure 7.9 The Ribs
1. sternum 2. manubrium 3. body of sternum 4. xiphoid process 5. vertebrochondral ribs 6. floating ribs
7. vertebrosternal ribs (true ribs) 8. false ribs 9. costal cartilage

[L2] Concept Map

I Skeleton—Axial Division

1. skull 2. mandible 3. lacrimal 4. occipital 5. temporal 6. sutures 7. coronal 8. hyoid 9. vertebral
column 10. thoracic 11. sacral 12. floating ribs 13. sternum 14. xiphoid process

[L2] Body Trek

1. axial   2. skull   3. cranium   4. ribs   5. sternum   6. vertebrae   7. zygomatic   8. nasal   9. lacrimal
10. mandible   11. occipital   12. sphenoid   13. parietal   14. sutures   15. sagittal   16. hyoid   17. cervical
18. thoracic   19. lumbar   20. sacrum   21. true   22. false   23. floating   24. manubrium   25. xiphoid
process

[L2] Multiple Choice

1. C   2. A   3. A   4. D   5. C   6. B   7. C   8. A   9. D   10. B   11. B

[L2] Completion

1. pharyngotympanic   2. metopic   3. tears   4. auditory ossicles   5. alveolar processes   6. mental foramina
7. compensation   8. kyphosis   9. lordosis   10. scoliosis

[L2] Short Essay

1. 1.   create a framework that supports and protects organ systems in the dorsal and ventral body cavities.

   2.   provide a surface area for attachment of muscles that adjust the positions of the head, neck, and trunk.

   3.   performs respiratory movements.

   4.   stabilize or position elements of the appendicular system.

2. A. *Paired bones*: parietal, temporal

   B. *Unpaired bones*: occipital, frontal, sphenoid, ethmoid

3. A. *Paired bones*: zygomatic, maxilla, nasal, palatine, lacrimal, inferior nasal concha

   B. *Unpaired bones*: mandible, vomer

4. The auditory ossicles consist of three (3) tiny bones on each side of the skull that are enclosed by the temporal bone. The hyoid bone lies below the skull suspended by the stylohyoid ligaments.

5. Craniostenosis is premature closure of one or more fontanels, which results in unusual distortions of the skull.

6. The thoracic and sacral curves are called primary curves because they begin to appear late in fetal development. They accommodate the thoracic and abdominopelvic viscera.

   The lumbar and cervical curves are called secondary curves because they do not appear until several months after birth. They help position the body weight over the legs.

7. *Kyphosis*: normal thoracic curvature becomes exaggerated, producing "roundback" appearance.

   Lordosis: exaggerated lumbar curvature produces "swayback" appearance.

   Scoliosis: abnormal lateral curvature.

8. The *true* ribs reach the anterior body wall and are connected to the sternum by separate cartilaginous extensions. The *false* ribs do not attach directly to the sternum.

[L3] Critical Thinking/Application

1. Vision, hearing, balance, olfaction (smell), and gustation (taste).

2. TMJ is temporomandibular joint syndrome. It occurs in the joint where the *mandible* articulates with the *temporal* bone. The mandibular condyle fits into the mandibular fossa of the temporal bone. The condition generally involves pain around the joint and its associated muscles, a noticeable clicking within the joint, and usually a pronounced malocclusion of the lower jaw.

3. The crooked nose may be a result of a deviated septum, a condition in which the nasal septum has a bend in it, most often at the junction between the bony and cartilaginous portions of the septum. Septal deviation often blocks drainage of one or more sinuses, producing chronic bouts of infection and inflammation.

4. During whiplash the movement of the head resembles the cracking of a whip. The head is relatively massive, and it sits on top of the cervical vertebrae. Small muscles articulate with the bones and can produce significant effects by tipping the balance one way or another. If the body suddenly changes position, the balancing muscles are not strong enough to stabilize the head. As a result, a partial or complete dislocation of the cervical vertebrae can occur, with injury to muscles and ligaments and potential injury to the spinal cord.

5. A plausible explanation would be that the child has scoliosis, a condition in which the hips are abnormally tilted sideways, making one of the lower limbs shorter than the other.

6. When the gelatinous interior (nucleus pulposus) of the disc leaks through the fibrous outer portion (annulus fibrosis) of the disc, the affected disc balloons out from between the bony parts of the vertebrae. If the bulging or herniated area is large enough, it may press on a nerve, causing severe or incapacitating pain. Usually, the sciatic nerve is affected. Sciatica is generally located in the lumbar region and can radiate over the buttock, rear thigh, and calf, and can extend into the foot.

Chapter 8 The Appendicular Skeleton

[L1] Multiple Choice

1. C 2. A 3. B 4. A 5. B 6. C 7. B 8. C 9. B 10. A 11. C 12. D 13. D 14. C 15. D
16. C 17. C 18. D 19. D

[L1] Completion

1. acromion 2. clavicle 3. pectoral girdle 4. glenoid fossa 5. styloid 6. wrist 7. coxae 8. pubic
symphysis 9. malleolus 10. acetabulum 11. knee 12. childbearing 13. teeth 14. pelvis 15. age

[L1] Matching

1. F 2. J 3. G 4. A 5. C 6. L 7. D 8. E 9. K 10. B 11. H 12. I

[L1] Drawing/Illustration Labeling

Figure 8.1 Appendicular Skeleton
1. scapula 2. humerus 3. ulna 4. radius 5. carpals 6. metacarpals 7. phalanges 8. femur 9. fibula
10. clavicle 11. ilium 12. pubis 13. ischium 14. patella 15. tibia 16. tarsals 17. metatarsals
18. phalanges

Figure 8.2 The Scapula
1. coracoid process 2. glenoid fossa 3. axillary border 4. inferior angle 5. acromion 6. coracoid process
7. superior border 8. spine 9. body 10. medial border

Figure 8.3 The Humerus
1. greater tubercle 2. lesser tubercle 3. deltoid tuberosity 4. lateral epicondyle 5. capitulum 6. head
7. coronoid fossa 8. medial epicondyle 9. greater tubercle 10. radial groove 11. olecranon fossa
12. lateral epicondyle

Figure 8.4 The Radius and Ulna
1. olecranon 2. ulna 3. ulnar head 4. head of radius 5. radius 6. styloid process of radius 7. trochlear
notch 8. coronoid process 9. ulna 10. styloid process of ulna

Figure 8.5 Bones of the Wrist and Hand
1. phalanges 2. carpals 3. distal 4. middle 5. proximal 6. hamate 7. pisiform 8. triangular
9. lunate 10. ulna 11. metacarpals 12. trapezoid 13. trapezium 14. scaphoid 15. capitate 16. radius

Figure 8.6 The Pelvis (anterior view)
1. acetabulum 2. pubic symphysis 3. obturator foramen 4. iliac crest 5. sacroiliac joint 6. ilium
7. pubis 8. ischium

Figure 8.7 The Pelvis (lateral view)
1. greater sciatic notch 2. ischial spine 3. lesser sciatic notch 4. ischial tuberosity 5. anterior superior iliac
spine 6. anterior inferior iliac spine 7. inferior iliac notch 8. ischial ramus

Figure 8.8 The Femur (anterior and posterior views)
1. greater trochanter 2. neck 3. lateral epicondyle 4. lateral condyle 5. head 6. lesser trochanter
7. medial epicondyle 8. medial condyle 9. trochanteric crest 10. gluteal tuberosity 11. linea aspera
12. lateral condyle 13. lateral epicondyle

Figure 8.9 The Tibia and Fibula
1. lateral condyle 2. head of the fibula 3. lateral malleolus 4. medial condyle 5. tibial tuberosity 6. anterior crest 7. medial malleolus

Figure 8.10 Bones of the Ankle and Foot
1. medial cuneiform 2. intermediate cuneiform 3. navicular 4. talus 5. distal 6. middle 7. proximal
8. lateral cuneiform 9. cuboid 10. calcaneus 11. phalanges 12. metatarsals 13. tarsals

[L2] Concept Map

I Skeleton—Appendicular Division

1. pectoral girdle 2. humerus 3. radius 4. metacarpals 5. ischium 6. femur 7. fibula 8. tarsals
9. phalanges

[L2] Body Trek

1. clavicle 2. pectoral 3. ball and socket 4. scapula 5. humerus 6. radius 7. ulna 8. brachium
9. hinge 10. carpals 11. metacarpals 12. finger bones 13. ilium 14. ischium 15. pubis 16. acetabulum
17. pelvic 18. femur 19. shoulder 20. fibula 21. tibia 22. patella 23. knee 24. elbow 25. tarsals
26. metatarsals 27. phalanges

[L2] Multiple Choice

1. C 2. A 3. A 4. D 5. D 6. B 7. A 8. B 9. D 10. D 11. D 12. C 13. C 14. B

[L2]   Completion

1. clavicle   2. scapula   3. ulna   4. metacarpals   5. bursae   6. bursitis   7. acetabulum   8. ilium   9. pelvis   10. femur   11. fibula   12. calcaneus   13. thumb   14. hallux   15. arthroscopy

[L2]   Short Essay

1. Provides control over the immediate environment; changes your position in space, and makes you an active, mobile person.

2. Bones of the arms and legs and the supporting elements that connect the limbs to the trunk.

3. Pectoral girdle: scapula, clavicle

   Pelvic girdle: ilium, ischium, pubis

4. Both have long shafts and styloid processes for support of the wrist. The radius has a radial tuberosity and the ulna has a prominent olecranon process for muscle attachments. Both the radius and the ulna articulate proximally with the humerus and distally with the carpal bones.

5. The knee joint and elbow joint are both hinge joints.

6. The tibia is the massive, weight-bearing bone of the lower leg.

   The fibula is the long narrow bone lateral to the tibia that is more important for muscle attachment than for support. The tibia articulates proximally with the femur and distally with the talus.

7. The shoulder and hip joints are both ball-and-socket joints.

8. The articulations of the carpals and tarsals are gliding diarthroses, which permit a limited gliding motion.

9. Muscle contractions can occur only when the extracellular concentration of calcium remains within relatively narrow limits. Most of the body's calcium is tied up in the skeleton.

[L3]   Critical Thinking/Application

1. The bones and ligaments that form the walls of the carpal tunnel do not stretch; therefore, any trauma or activity that applies pressure against the nerves or blood vessels passing through the tunnel will cause a fluid buildup (edema) or connective tissue deposition within the carpal tunnel, resulting in the described symptoms.

2. Doctors explained that the cause of death was fat embolism syndrome. Fatty droplets from the yellow marrow of the fractured bone got into the bloodstream and eventually passed through the heart to the lungs. The droplets triggered immune mechanisms in the lungs, filling the lungs with fluid and blocking the lungs' ability to take in oxygen. Hemorrhaging occurred and physicians were unable to save him.

3. The female pelvis has a wide oval pelvic inlet and widely spaced ischial spines that are ideal for delivery. The pelvic outlet is broader and more shallow in the female. The male pelvis has a heart-shaped pelvic inlet and the ischial spines are closer together. The pelvic outlet is deeper and narrower in the male.

4. Gout is a metabolic disorder in which there is an increase in uric acid in the body with precipitation of monosodium urate crystals in the kidneys and joint capsules. The presence of uric acid crystals in the joints can lead to an inflammatory response in the joints. Usually the great toe and other foot and leg joints are affected, and kidney damage from crystal formation occurs in more advanced cases.

5. A bunion is a common pressure-related bursitis. Bunions form over the base of the great toe as a result of the friction and distortion of the joint caused by tight shoes, especially those with pointed toes. There is chronic inflammation of the region, and as the wall of the bursa thickens, fluid builds up in the surrounding tissues. The result is a firm, tender nodule.

6. All three are conditions of bursitis, which indicate the occupations associated with them. "Housemaid's knee," which accompanies prolonged kneeling, affects the bursa, which lies between the patella and the skin. "Weaver's bottom" is produced by pressure on the posterior and inferior tip of the pelvic girdle and can result from prolonged sitting on hard surfaces. "Student's elbow" is a form of bursitis resulting from constant and excessive pressure on the elbows. A student propping his head above a desk while studying can trigger this condition.

Chapter 9 Joints and Articulations

BUILDING THE FRAMEWORK

Classification of Joints

1. 1. To bind bones together and permit movement 2. The type of material binding the bones; whether a joint cavity is present; degree of movement permitted 3. Fibrous: synarthroses, immovable; cartilaginous: amphiarthroses, slightly movable; synovial: diarthroses, freely movable

Fibrous, Cartilaginous, and Synovial Joints

1. 1. A; 5 2. C 3. B; 1, 2, 4, and 6 4. B; 2 and 6 5. C 6. C 7. A; 3 8. A; 3 9. C 10. C 11. B; 6 12. C 13. A; 5 14. C 15. B; 1 16. A; 5 17. B; 6 18. B; 4

2. Synovial. Synovial joints are ideal where mobility and flexibility are the goals. Most joints of the axial skeleton provide immobility (or at most slight mobility) because the bones of the axial skeleton typically *protect* or *support* internal (often fragile) organs.

3.
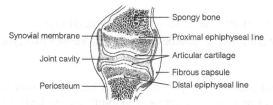

Figure 9.1

4. 1. A 2. C, D 3. B 4. B 5. C, D
5. 1. I 2. A 3. P 4. J 5. C 6. F 7. Q 8. E 9. K 10. N 11. A, B, C, E, H, I, L
6. 1. A, C, E 2. G 3. D, I 4. N 5. J 6. M 7. F 8. K 9. B, L 10. H
7. 1. B 2. E 3. E 4. E 5. A 6. B 7. E 8. F 9. C 10. D 11. C, D 12. B, F 13. A 14. E
8. 1. Multiaxial joint 2. Saddle joint 3. Tibiofibular joints 4. Multiaxial joint 5. Elbow joint 6. Amphiarthrotic 7. Bursae 8. Condyloid joint 9. Biaxial joint
9. 1. D 2. C 3. A 4. B
10. A. hip joint B. knee joint

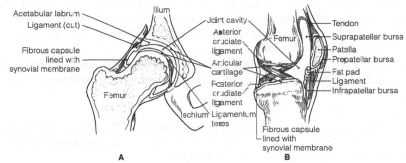

Figure 9.3

Homeostatic Imbalances of Joints

1. 1. dislocation 2. T 3. osteoarthritis 4. bursae 5. acute 6. vascularized 7. rheumatoid 8. gouty 9. T 10. synovial membrane 11. rheumatoid 12. menisci 13. reduce friction 14. osteoarthritis 15. synovial

2. Ligaments and tendons (injured during sprains) are poorly vascularized and cartilages are avascular. Hence, these structures heal slowly and often poorly.

The Incredible Journey

1. 1. meniscus   2. femur   3. tibia   4. joint cavity   5. synovial fluid   6. lubricate   7. condyles   8. anterior cruciate   9. patella   10. bursa   11. lateral (outer)   12. tibia   13. ligament   14. blood supply   15. meniscus

CHALLENGING YOURSELF

At the Clinic

1. Jenny's elbow has been dislocated.
2. The temporomandibular joint is the source of his problem.
3. Because the clavicles brace the scapulae, without clavicles the scapulae are extremely movable and the shoulders appear droopy. Although the condition is not serious, it reduces the shoulders' resistance to stress.
4. The rotator cuff consists of ligaments that are the main reinforcers of the shallow shoulder joint. Its rupture reduces outward movements, such as abduction.
5. The ligamentum teres contains a blood vessel that supplies the head of the femur. The femoral head ordinarily also receives nourishment from vessels reaching it from the diaphysis, but a fracture would cut off that blood supply.
6. Bertha's clavicle fractured.
7. Typically a "torn cartilage" is an articular disc, which is fibrocartilage.
8. Rheumatoid arthritis, fairly common in middle-aged women, causes this type of deformity.

Stop and Think

1. Diarthrotic joints in the axial skeleton: temporomandibular joint, atlanto-occipital joint, atlantoaxial joint, intervertebral joints (between articular processes), vertebrocostal joints, sternoclavicular joints (which include one axial bone, the sternum, and one appendicular bone, the clavicle), and sacroiliac joint (which also includes an appendicular bone).
2. Pronation and supination involve not only rotation at the proximal radioulnar joint (a diarthrotic joint) but also crossing of the shafts of the radius and the ulna (an amphiarthrotic syndesmosis). The wrist bones are not involved.
3. Interdigitation and interlocking increase the articulating surface area between adjoining bones. Such an increased area of attachment means more ligament between the bones, increasing the resistance to movement at the joints. Further, the interlocking of bony regions prevents separation of the bones.
4. The periosteum is a dense irregular connective tissue, and ligaments are dense regular connective tissue. Microscopic examination would reveal a transition from collagenous fibers, which are in different orientations to those arranged in parallel bundles.
5. The synovial membrane, which lines the joint cavity, is composed of loose connective tissue only. Hence, it is not an epithelial membrane.
6. The purpose of menisci is to more securely seat the bones within the joint and to absorb shock. Although such activities are uncommon, the jaw (temporomandibular) joint can withstand great pressure when you bite the cap off a glass bottle or hang by your teeth in a circus act. The sternoclavicular joint absorbs shock from your entire arm when you use your hand to break a fall.
7. Chronic slumping forward stretches the posterior intervertebral ligaments; once stretched, ligaments do not resume their original length. Eventually, the overextended ligaments are unable to hold the vertebral column in an erect position.
8. The knee joint flexes posteriorly.
9. The head is able to move in a manner similar to circumduction, but the term more accurately applies to movement at a single joint. Circular movement of the head involves the atlanto-occipital and atlantoaxial joints, as well as amphiarthrotic movements of the cervical vertebrae.
10. A typical hinge joint has a single articulation with a convex condyle fitting into a concave fossa. The knee joint has a double condylar articulation, with tibial (concave) condyles replacing the fossa. The doubling of the condyloid joints prevents movement in the frontal plane (abduction and adduction).

COVERING ALL YOUR BASES

Multiple Choice

1. E and possibly D   2. B, D   3. A   4. A, B, C, D   5. A, B, D   6. A, B   7. B, D   8. A, B, D   9. D
10. A, B, C, D   11. C   12. D   13. A, B   14. A, B   15. C   16. D   17. A   18. B, D   19. C   20. B, C, D
21. A, B, C, D   22. D   23. B   24. B   25. A, D   26. B   27. D

Word Dissection

	Word root	Translation	Example		Word root	Translation	Example
1.	ab	away	abduction	10.	gompho	nail	gomphosis
2.	ad	toward	adduction	11.	labr	lip	glenoid labrum
3.	amphi	between	amphiarthrosis	12.	luxa	dislocate	luxation
4.	ankyl	crooked	ankylosis	13.	menisc	crescent	meniscus
5.	arthro	joint	arthritis	14.	ovi	egg	synovial
6.	artic	joint	articulation	15.	pron	bent forward	pronation
7.	burs	purse	bursa	16.	rheum	flux	rheumatism
8.	cruci	cross	cruciate ligament	17.	spondyl	vertebra	spondylitis
9.	duct	lead, draw	abduction	18.	supine	lying on the back	supination

Chapter 10 Muscle Tissue

[L1] Multiple Choice

1. D   2. D   3. D   4. C   5. B   6. D   7. C   8. A   9. B   10. A   11. D   12. D   13. D   14. C   15. C
16. C   17. A   18. D   19. D   20. C   21. A   22. B   23. D   24. B   25. A   26. D   27. B   28. B   29. D
30. B   31. C   32. C   33. A   34. A   35. D

[L1] Completion

1. contraction   2. epimysium   3. fascicles   4. tendon   5. sarcolemma   6. T tubules   7. sarcomeres
8. cross-bridges   9. Z lines   10. action potential   11. recruitment   12. troponin   13. tension   14. complete
tetanus   15. incomplete tetanus   16. motor unit   17. skeletal muscle   18. treppe   19. twitch   20. ATP
21. lactic acid   22. glycolysis   23. white muscles   24. red muscles   25. oxygen debt   26. endurance
27. pacemaker   28. plasticity   29. smooth muscle   30 sphincter

[L1] Matching

1. J   2. E   3. R   4. Q   5. L   6. A   7. C   8. K   9. H   10. N   11. B   12. M   13. O   14. G   15. F
16. D   17. I   18. P

[L1] Drawing/Illustration Labeling

Figure 10.1   Organization of Skeletal Muscles
1. sarcolemma   2. sarcoplasm   3. myofibril   4. nucleus   5. muscle fiber   6. muscle fasciculus   7. muscle
fibers   8. endomysium   9. perimysium   10. endomysium   11. blood vessels   12. epimysium   13. muscle
fasciculus   14. body of muscle   15. tendon   16. bone

Figure 10.2   The Histological Organization of Skeletal Muscles
1. myofibril   2. mitochondrion   3. muscle fiber   4. nucleus   5. sarcoplasmic reticulum   6. T tubules
7. sarcomere   8. thin filament (actin)   9. thick filament (myosin)

Figure 10.3   Types of Muscle Tissue
1. smooth   2. cardiac   3. skeletal

Figure 10.4   Structure of a Sarcomere
1. sarcomere   2. Z line   3. H zone   4. Z line   5. I band   6. A band   7. myosin (thick filaments)   8. actin
(thin filaments)

Figure 10.5   Neuromuscular Junction
1. nerve impulse   2. neurilemma   3. sarcolemma   4. neuron (axon)   5. vesicle containing acetylcholine
6. synaptic cleft

[L2] Concept Maps

I Muscle Tissue

1. heart   2. striated   3. smooth   4. involuntary   5. nonstriated   6. bones   7. multi-nucleated

II Muscle

8. muscle bundles (fascicles)   9. myofibrils   10. sarcomeres   11. actin   12. Z lines   13. thick filaments
14. H zone

III Muscle Contraction

15. release of Ca^{++} from sacs of sarcoplasmic reticulum

16. cross-bridging (heads of myosin attach to turned-on thin filaments)

17. shortening, i.e., contraction of myofibrils and muscle fibers they comprise

18. energy + ADP + phosphate

[L2]   Body Trek

1. epimysium   2. perimysium   3. fascicles   4. endomysium   5. satellite   6. sarcolemma   7. T tubules
8. nuclei   9. myofibrils   10. myofilaments   11. actin   12. myosin   13. sarcomeres   14. Z line   15. I band
16. A band   17. thick   18. sliding filament   19. contraction

[L2]   Multiple Choice

1. A   2. B   3. B   4. C   5. D   6. C   7. B   8. B   9. D   10. D   11. C   12. A   13. B   14. C   15. C
16. A   17. A   18. A   19. C   20. C

[L2]   Completion

1. satellite   2. myoblasts   3. muscle tone   4. rigor   5. absolute refractory period   6. fatigue   7. A bands
8. motor unit   9. tetanus   10. isotonic

[L2]   Short Essay

1. (a) produce skeletal movement

   (b) maintain posture and body position

   (c) support soft tissues

   (d) guard entrances and exits

   (e) maintain body temperature

2. (a) an outer *epimysium*, (b) a central *perimysium*, and (c) an inner *endomysium*.

3.

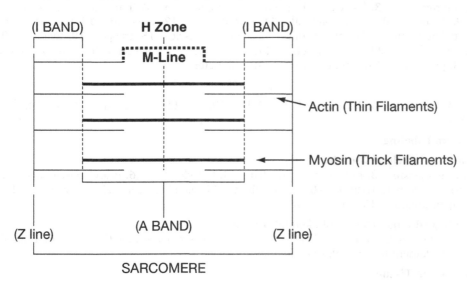

4. (a) active site exposure

   (b) cross-bridge attachment

   (c) pivoting

   (d) cross-bridging detachment

   (e) myosin activation

5. (a) release of acetylcholine

   (b) depolarization of the motor end plate

   (c) generation of an action potential

   (d) conduction of an action potential

   (e) release of calcium ions

6. A—twitch; B—incomplete tetanus; C—complete tetanus

7. *Isometric* contraction—tension rises to a maximum but the length of the muscle remains constant.

   Isotonic contraction—tension in the muscle builds until it exceeds the amount of resistance and the muscle shortens. As the muscle shortens, the tension in the muscle remains constant, at a value that just exceeds the applied resistance.

8. When fatigue occurs and the oxygen supply to muscles is depleted, aerobic respiration ceases owing to the decreased oxygen supply. Anaerobic glycolysis supplies the needed energy for a short period of time. The amount of oxygen needed to restore normal pre-exertion conditions is the oxygen debt.

9. Fast fiber muscles produce powerful contractions, which use ATP in massive amounts. Prolonged activity is primarily supported by anaerobic glycolysis, and fast fibers fatigue rapidly. Slow fibers are specialized to enable them to continue contracting for extended periods. The specializations include an extensive network of capillaries so supplies of O_2 are available, and the presence of myoglobin, which binds O_2 molecules and which results in the buildup of O_2 reserves. These factors improve mitochondrial performance.

[L3]   Critical Thinking/Application

1. Alcohol is a drug that interferes with the release of acetylcholine at the neuromuscular junction. When acetylcholine is not released, action potentials in the muscle cell membrane are prohibited and the release of calcium ions necessary to begin the contractile process does not occur.

2. Training to improve *aerobic* endurance usually involves sustained low levels of muscular activity. Jogging, distance swimming, biking, and other cardiovascular activities that do not require peak tension production are appropriate for developing aerobic endurance. Training to develop *anaerobic* endurance involves frequent, brief, intensive workouts. Activities might include running sprints; fast, short-distance swimming; pole vaulting; or other exercises requiring peak tension production in a short period of time.

3. *Rigor mortis* occurs several hours after death. It is caused by the lack of ATP in muscles to sustain the contractile process or to allow the cross-bridge to release. The muscles remain stiff until degeneration occurs. *Physiological contracture* occurs in the living individual as a result of a lack of ATP in muscle fibers. The lack of available energy does not allow cross-bridging to occur and prohibits the release of previously formed cross-bridges, resulting in physiological contracture.

4. This diet probably lacks dietary calcium and vitamin D. The resulting condition is hypocalcemia, a lower-than-normal concentration of calcium ions in blood or extracellular fluid. Because of the decreased number of calcium ions, sodium ion channels open and the sodium ions diffuse into the cell, causing depolarization of the cell membranes to threshold and initiate action potentials. Spontaneous reactions of nerves and muscles result in nervousness and muscle spasms.

5. Both attack motor neurons in the nervous system. The Botulinus toxin prevents the release of acetylcholine by the motor neuron, producing a severe and potentially fatal paralysis. The poliovirus attacks and kills motor neurons in the spinal cord and brain. The infection causes degeneration of the motor neurons and atrophy of the muscles they innervate.

Chapter 11   The Muscular System

BUILDING THE FRAMEWORK

Muscle Mechanics: The Importance of Leverage and Fascicle Arrangement

1. 1. muscles   2. bones   3. the muscle inserts   4. joint

2. Circle: fast, moves a small load over a large distance, requires minimal shortening, and muscle force greater than the load.

3.

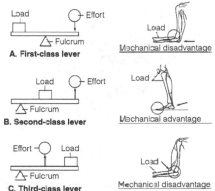

Figure 11.1

4. The brachialis, which is inserted closer to the fulcrum (elbow) than the load, is structured for mechanical disadvantage; the brachioradialis, which is inserted far from the elbow, works by mechanical advantage but is a weak elbow flexor at best.

5. 1. Bipennate; C   2. Circular; D   3. Parallel; A   4. Convergent; B. Examples of A include the biceps and triceps brachii of the arm, nearly all forearm muscles, and the rectus abdominis. Examples of B are the pectoralis major and minor. Examples of C include the rectus femoris and the flexor hallucis longus. Examples of D are the orbicularis oris and oculi muscles. Consult muscle tables for more examples.

Interactions of Skeletal Muscles in the Body

1. 1. B   2. C   3. A   4. D

Naming Skeletal Muscles

1. 1. A, F   2. D   3. G   4. A, F   5. B, C   6. A   7. B, C   8. C, F   9. C, E   10. D

Major Skeletal Muscles of the Body

1. 1. E   2. G   3. A   4. F   5. C   6. B   7. H

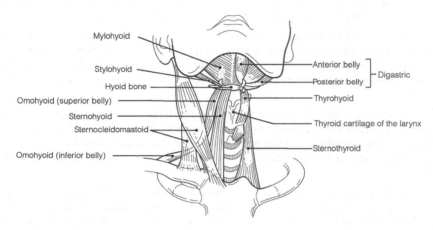

Figure 11.3

2. 1. E   2. C   3. H   4. F   5. B   6. D   7. G

3. 1. zygomatic   2. buccinator   3. orbicularis oculi   4. frontalis   5. orbicularis oris   6. masseter   7. temporalis 8. splenius   9. sternocleidomastoid   10. pterygoid

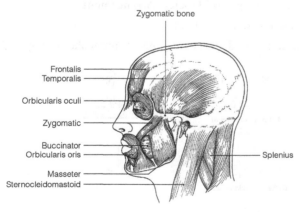

Figure 11.4

4. They work as a group during swallowing to propel a food bolus to the esophagus.

5. 1. rectus abdominis   2. pectoralis major   3. deltoid   4. external oblique   5. sternocleidomastoid   6. serratus anterior   7. rectus abdominis, external oblique, internal oblique, transversus abdominis   8. linea alba   9. transversus abdominis   10. external intercostals   11. diaphragm   12. pectoralis minor

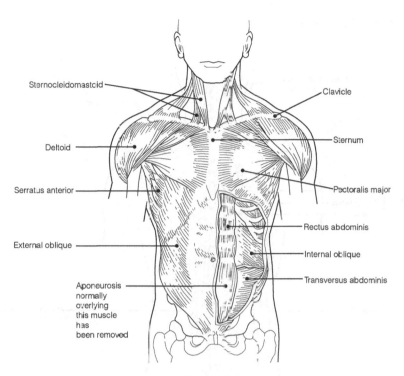

Figure 11.5

6. Muscles in the ventral leg either dorsiflex the ankle or extend the toes, movements that do not work against gravity. By contrast, posterior calf muscles plantar flex the ankle against the pull of gravity.

7. 1. trapezius   2. latissimus dorsi   3. deltoid   4. erector spinae   5. quadratus lumborum   6. rhomboids
   7. levator scapulae   8. teres major   9. supraspinatus   10. infraspinatus   11. teres minor

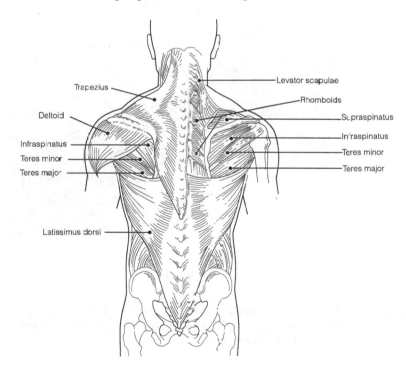

Figure 11.6

8. 1. C   2. D   3. B   4. A
9. 1. B, E   2. C, F   3. A, D, G   4. F   5. A   6. E   7. D

10. 1. C 2. A 3. B 4. D 5. F 6. E

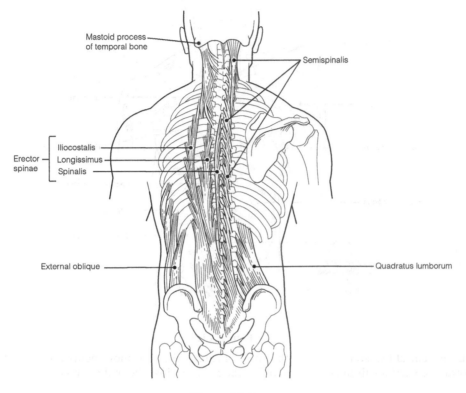

Figure 11.7

11. 1. H 2. K 3. G 4. E, F 5. I 6. A 7. C 8. D 9. L 10. J

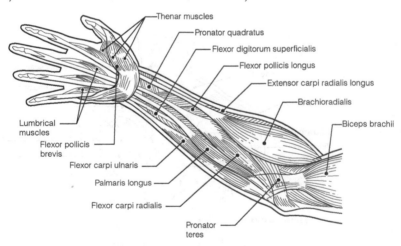

Figure 11.8

12. 1. flexor carpi ulnaris 2. extensor digitorum 3. biceps brachii 4. brachioradialis 5. triceps brachii 6. anconeus 7. brachialis 8. extensor carpi radialis brevis 9. extensor carpi radialis longus 10. abductor pollicis longus 11. extensor pollicis brevis 12. deltoid

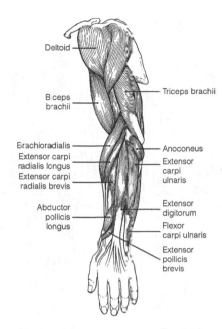

Figure 11.9

13. 1. iliopsoas   2. gluteus maximus   3. triceps surae   4. tibialis anterior   5. adductors   6. quadriceps
7. hamstrings   8. gluteus medius   9. gracilis   10. tensor fasciae latae   11. extensor digitorum longus
12. fibularis longus   13. tibialis posterior

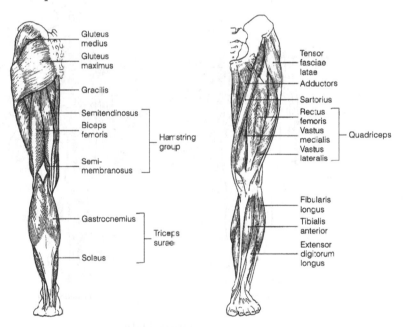

Figure 11.10

14. 1. deltoid   2. gluteus maximus or medius   3. vasti   4. quadriceps   5. calcaneal or Achilles   6. proximal
7. forearm   8. anterior   9. posteriorly   10. knee   11. flex

15. 1. iliopsoas, rectus femoris, (adductors longus and brevis)   2. quadriceps   3. tibialis anterior (extensor
digitorum longus, fibularis tertius, extensor hallucis longus)

16. 1. D   2. F   3. C   4. A   5. H   6. G   7. B

17. 1. E   2. D   3. F   4. A   5. G   6. C   7. B

18. 1. Biceps femoris   2. Antagonists   3. Gluteus minimus   4. Vastus medialis   5. Supraspinatus   6. Fibularis
longus   7. Teres major

19. 1. 4   2. 5   3. 17   4. 16   5. 7   6. 6   7. 20   8. 14   9. 19   10. 12   11. 11   12. 10   13. 22   14. 1
15. 2   16. 3   17. 15   18. 21   19. 13   20. 9   21. 18   22. 8

20. 1. 1   2. 2   3. 5   4. 9   5. 7   6. 4   7. 6   8. 3   9. 8   10. 10   11. 11

21.

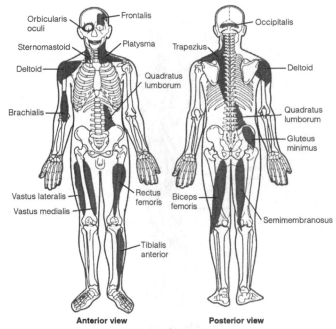

Figure 11.13

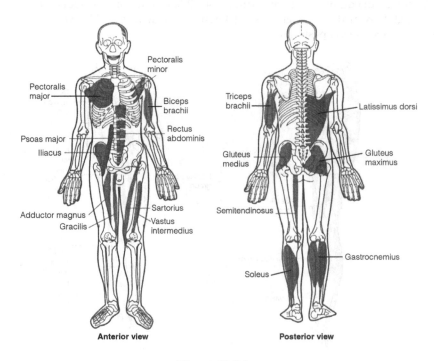

Figure 11.14

CHALLENGING YOURSELF

At the Clinic

1. The facial nerve, which innervates the muscles of the face.
2. When we are in the fully bent-over (hip flexed) position, the erector spinae are relaxed. When that movement is reversed, they are totally inactive, leaving the gluteus maximus and hamstring muscles to initiate the action. Thus sudden or improper lifting techniques are likely to injure both back ligaments and the erector spinae, causing the latter to go into painful spasms.
3. The phrenic nerve innervates the diaphragm; the intercostal nerves supply the intercostal muscles. Paralysis of these essential breathing muscles is fatal.
4. The unilateral weakening of the abdominal wall will result in scoliosis because the stronger contraction of the muscles of the opposite side will pull the spine out of alignment.
5. The rectus abdominis is a narrow, medially placed muscle that does not extend completely across the iliac regions. No, if the incision was made as described, the rectus abdominus was not cut.

6. The muscle of the urogenital diaphragm, which surrounds the vaginal opening, through which uterine prolapse would occur, is the deep transverse perineus. Lateral to the vagina is the pubococcygeus of the levator ani (part of the pelvic diaphragm).

7. The deltoid and the pectoralis major have broad origins on the inferior border of the clavicle. The sternocleidomastoid inserts on the medial superior border of the clavicle; the trapezius inserts on the lateral third of the clavicle. An arm sling inhibits use of these clavicle-moving muscles.

8. Tendons attaching at the anterior wrist are involved in wrist and finger flexion. Malcolm will lose his ability to make a fist and grasp a baseball.

9. The hamstrings can be strained (pulled) when the hip is flexed and the knee is vigorously extended at the same time.

10. The latissimus dorsi and the trapezius, which together cover most of the superficial surface of the back, are receiving most of the massage therapist's attention.

11. Gluteus maximus—action prevented is lateral rotation of the thigh; gluteus medius and minimus—actions prevented are thigh abduction and medial rotation.

Stop and Think

1. Very few muscles don't attach to bone at least at one end. The muscles in the tongue (intrinsic tongue muscles), which change the shape of the tongue, are among those few. Sphincter muscles, such as the orbicularis muscles of the face, the sphincter ani, and the sphincter urethrae, cause constriction of an opening. Muscles of facial expression mostly originate on bone but insert on fascia or skin; consequently, they alter the position of the soft tissues of the face.

2. With the help of fixators, an insertion can be the immovable end and the origin can be moved in selected cases. For example, the trapezius originates on the occipital bone and inserts on the scapula, but fixing the scapula will allow the trapezius to assist in extension of the head. Chin-ups give another example: the forearm is fixed when grasping a chin-up bar, so the bones of origin (the shoulder girdle)—and the body along with them—are moved.

3. Muscles pull bones toward their origin as they contract: muscles originating on the front of the body pull bones anteriorly (usually flexion); muscles on the back pull bones posteriorly (usually extension); laterally placed muscles abduct (or, with the foot, evert); medially located muscles adduct (or invert the foot). Muscles *usually* move the bone beyond (distal to) their bellies: the muscles on the thorax move the arm; the muscles of the arm move the forearm; the muscles of the forearm move the wrist and fingers. Likewise, the muscles of the hip move the thigh, the muscles of the thigh move the leg, and so on.

4. The latissimus dorsi inserts on the anterior surface of the humerus, getting there via its medial side. In rotation, the latissimus pulls the anterior surface of the humerus toward the body—this is medial rotation.

5. The tendon of the tibialis anterior is extensive, starting at the distal third of the tibia and continuing around the medial side of the ankle, finally inserting on the plantar surface of the foot. Because it inserts on the bottom of the foot, it can pull the sole of the foot medially (inversion). Likewise, on the lateral side, the fibularis longus inserts on the plantar surface, so it can pull the sole laterally (eversion).

6. The dorsal muscles of the lower limb are extensor muscles that act against the pull of gravity. Flexion at lower limb joints is assisted by gravity.

Closer Connections: Checking the Systems—Covering, Support, and Movement

1. The "tummy tuck," by reducing the abdominal musculature's girth, forces the abdominal contents into a smaller space. This increases abdominal pressure, which puts pressure on the vertebral column, forcing the vertebrae farther apart. As a result, compression of the intervertebral discs is lessened, which in turn reduces pressure on the nerves.

2. The need of the muscles for calcium is most crucial. Calcium plays an active role in muscle contraction but is fairly inert in bone tissue. Bones will give up calcium to the point of being excessively soft in order to maintain proper calcium levels for muscle contraction and other vital body functions (secretion of hormones and neurotransmitters, blood clotting, etc.).

3. Collagen is a component of connective tissue. In the integumentary system, it is in the dermis. In the skeletal system, which is composed almost entirely of connective tissue, collagen is found in the extracellular matrix of bone, as well as in hyaline cartilage, fibrocartilage, and the dense fibrous periosteum. In the muscular system, collagen fibers are found in the deep fascia and the deeper layers of connective tissue within and around individual muscles.

4. The greatest rate of mitosis in the systems in this unit is found in the epidermis of the skin. Least mitotically active in this group are mature skeletal muscle cells, which do not divide once full growth is achieved.

5. Homeostasis of body temperature is maintained by the skin (its thermoreceptors monitoring external environmental temperature, as well as sweating, flushing, turning blue) and by the activity of the muscular system (shivering).

6. The integumentary system has several lines of defense that protect the body not only from infection but also from excessive fluid and ion loss. The skeletal system contains bones that encase and protect vital organs.

COVERING ALL YOUR BASES
Multiple Choice

1. A 2. B 3. B, D 4. A, B, C, D 5. A, B, C 6. B, C, D 7. A, D 8. B, C 9. A, C, D 10. A, C, D
11. A, B 12. A, B 13. C 14. D 15. A, B, C, E 16. A, B, C, D 17. B, D 18. B 19. A, B, D 20. C
21. B, C 22. B, D 23. A, B 24. B, C, D 25. A, B, C, D 26. D 27. D 28. D 29. B 30. A, B, C, D

Word Dissection

	Word root	Translation	Example		Word root	Translation	Example
1.	agon	contest	agonist, antagonist	6.	glossus	tongue	genioglossus
2.	brevis	short	peroneus brevis	7.	pectus	chest, breast	pectoralis major
3.	ceps	head, origin	biceps brachii	8.	perone	fibula	peroneus longus
4.	cleido	clavicle	sternocleidomastoid	9.	rectus	straight	rectus abdominis
5.	gaster	belly	gastrocnemius				

Chapter 12 Neural Tissue

[L1] Multiple Choice

1. A 2. C 3. D 4. C 5. C 6. D 7. B 8. D 9. A 10. B 11. D 12. C 13. D 14. B 15. C
16. D 17. C 18. C 19. A 20. B 21. B 22. B 23. D 24. B 25. D 26. B 27. A 28. D 29. A
30. C 31. C 32. D 33. A

[L1] Completion

1. autonomic nervous system 2. collaterals 3. afferent 4. microglia 5. electrochemical gradient 6. threshold 7. saltatory 8. electrical 9. skeletal muscle fiber 10. cholinergic 11. adrenergic 12. neuromodulators 13. temporal summation 14. spatial summation 15. proprioceptors 16. divergence 17. IPSP

[L1] Matching

1. H 2. F 3. D 4. C 5. I 6. G 7. A 8. E 9. B 10. Q 11. L 12. O 13. J 14. S 15. R
16. M 17. K 18. N 19. P

[L1] Drawing/Illustration Labeling

Figure 12.1 Structure and Classification of Neurons
1. dendritic spines 2. dendrite 3. soma (cell body) 4. axon hillock 5. soma 6. nucleus 7. nucleus of Schwann cell 8. axon 9. Schwann cell 10. nodes of Ranvier 11. axolemma 12. telodendria 13. motor neuron 14. sensory neuron

Figure 12.2 Neuron Classification (based on structure)
1. multipolar neuron 2. unipolar neuron 3. anaxonic 4. bipolar neuron

Figure 12.3 Organization of Neuronal Pools
1. convergence 2. parallel processing 3. serial processing 4. reverberation 5. divergence

[L2] Concept Maps

I Neural Tissue

1. Schwann cells 2. Astrocytes 3. Microglia 4. transmit nerve impulses 5. surround peripheral ganglia 6. central nervous system

II Organization of Nervous System

6. brain 7. motor system 8. somatic nervous system 9. sympathetic nervous system 10. smooth muscle 11. peripheral nervous system 12. afferent division

[L2] Multiple Choice

1. C 2. D 3. A 4. B 5. A 6. C 7. D 8. D 9. A 10. B 11. A 12. C 13. D 14. B 15. B
16. C 17. D 18. A

[L2] Completion

1. perikaryon 2. ganglia 3. current 4. voltage 5. gated 6. hyperpolarization 7. nerve impulse 8. stroke 9. preganglionic fibers 10. postganglionic fibers 11. association 12. convergence 13. parallel 14. nuclei 15. tracts

[L2]   Short Essay

1. (a) providing sensation of the internal and external environments

    (b) integrating sensory information

    (c) coordinating voluntary and involuntary activities

    (d) regulating or controlling peripheral structures and systems

2. CNS consists of the brain and the spinal cord.

    PNS consists of the somatic nervous system and the autonomic nervous system.

3. astrocytes, oligodendrocytes, microglia, ependymal cells

4. *Neurons* are responsible for information transfer and processing in the nervous system.

    Neuroglia are specialized cells that provide support throughout the nervous system.

5. (a) activation of sodium channels and membrane depolarization

    (b) sodium channel inactivation

    (c) potassium channel activation

    (d) return to normal permeability

6. A node of Ranvier represents an area along the axon where there is an absence of myelin. Because ions can cross the membrane only at the nodes, only a node can respond to a depolarizing stimulus. Action potentials appear to "leap" or "jump" from node to node, a process called *saltatory conduction*. The process conducts nerve impulses along an axon five to seven times faster than continuous conduction.

7. In an adrenergic synapse at the postsynaptic membrane surface, norepinephrine activates an enzyme, adenyl cyclase, that catalyzes the conversion of ATP to cyclic AMP (cAMP) on the inner surface of the membrane. cAMP then activates cytoplasmic enzymes that open ion channels and produce depolarization. The cAMP is called a *second messenger*.

8. An EPSP is a depolarization produced by the arrival of a neurotransmitter at the postsynaptic membrane. A typical EPSP produces a depolarization of around 0.5 mV, much less than the 15–20 mV depolarization needed to bring the axon hillock to threshold.

    An IPSP is a transient hyperpolarization of the postsynaptic membrane. A hyperpolarized membrane is inhibited because a larger-than-usual depolarization stimulus must be provided to bring the membrane potential to threshold.

9. (a) sensory neurons—carry nerve impulses to the CNS

    (b) motor neurons—carry nerve impulses from CNS to PNS

    (c) association neurons—situated between sensory and motor neurons within the brain and spinal cord

10. *Divergence* is the spread of information from one neuron to several neurons, or from one neuronal pool to multiple pools.

    Convergence—several neurons synapse on the same postsynaptic neuron.

[L3]   Critical Thinking/Application

1. The combination of coffee and cigarette has a strong stimulatory effect, making the person appear to be "nervous" or "jumpy" or feeling like he or she is "on edge." The caffeine in the coffee lowers the threshold at the axon hillock, making the neurons more sensitive to depolarizing stimuli. Nicotine stimulates ACh (acetylcholine) receptors by binding to the ACh receptor sites.

2. In myelinated fibers, saltatory conduction transmits nerve impulses at rates over 300 mph, allowing the impulses to reach the neuromuscular junctions fast enough to initiate muscle contraction and promote normal movements. In unmyelinated fibers, continuous conduction transmits impulses at rates of approximately 2 mph. The impulses do not reach the peripheral neuromuscular junctions fast enough to initiate muscle contractions, which promote normal movements. Eventually the muscles atrophy because of a lack of adequate activity involving contraction.

3. Microglia do not develop in neural tissue; they are phagocytic WBC that have migrated across capillary walls in the neural tissue of the CNS. They engulf cellular debris, waste products, and pathogens. In times of infection or injury their numbers increase dramatically, as other phagocytic cells are attracted to the damaged area.

4. Acetylcholine is released at synapses in the central and peripheral nervous systems, and in most cases ACh produces a depolarization in the postsynaptic membrane. The ACh released at neuromuscular junctions in the heart produces a transient hyperpolarization of the membrane, moving the transmembrane potential farther from threshold.

5. A subthreshold membrane potential is referred to as an excitatory postsynaptic potential (EPSP), and the membrane is said to be *facilitated*. EPSPs may combine to reach threshold and initiate an action potential in two ways: (a) by spatial summation, during which several presynaptic neurons simultaneously release neurotransmitter to a single postsynaptic neuron; and (b) by temporal summation, during which the EPSPs result from the rapid and successive discharges of neurotransmitter from the same presynaptic knob.

Chapter 13 The Central Nervous System

BUILDING THE FRAMEWORK

The Brain

1.

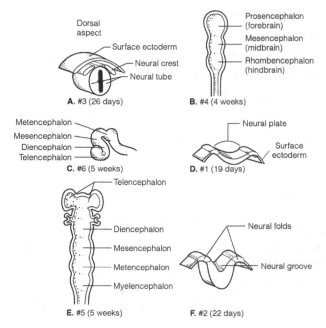

Figure 13.1

2. 1. D   2. L   3. F   4. C   5. K   6. B   7. E   8. A   9. I   10. H   11. J   12. G   Areas B and C should be striped.

3.

Secondary brain vesicle	Adult brain structures	Neural canal regions
Telencephalon	Cerebral hemispheres (cortex, white matter, basal nuclei)	Lateral ventricles; superior portion of third ventricle
Diencephalon	Diencephalon (thalamus, hypothalamus, epithalamus)	Most of third ventricle
Mesencephalon	Brain stem: midbrain	Cerebral aqueduct
Metencephalon	Brain stem: pons; cerebellum	Fourth ventricle
Myelencephalon	Brain stem: medulla oblongata	Fourth ventricle

4.

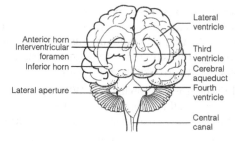

Figure 13.3

5.

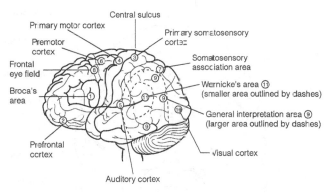

Figure 13.4

6. 1. G   2. W   3. W   4. W   5. W   6. G   7. G   8. W

7. 1. postcentral   2. temporal   3. frontal   4. Broca's   5. left   6. T   7. precentral   8. premotor   9. fingertips
10. somatosensory association area   11. occipital   12. T   13. prefrontal   14. T   15. affective   16. language
17. right

8. 1. B, C, D, F   2. H   3. A   4. I   5. B   6. G   7. E   8. D   9. F

9. 1. L   2. N   3. Q   4. O   5. B   6. F   7. A   8. D   9. M   10. I   11. K   12. G   13. P   14. H   15. J
16. C   17. E   Figure 12.5: Brain stem areas O, J, and K should be colored blue. The gray dotted areas contain
cerebrospinal fluid and should be colored yellow.

10.

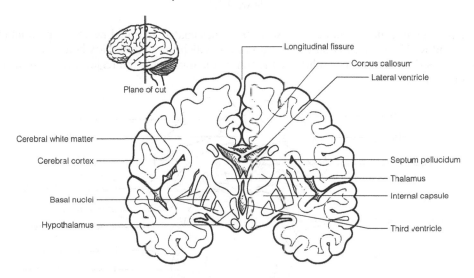

Figure 13.6

11. 1. hypothalamus   2. pons   3. cerebellum   4. thalamus   5. medulla oblongata   6. cerebral peduncle
7. pineal body   8. pons   9. corpora quadrigemina

12.

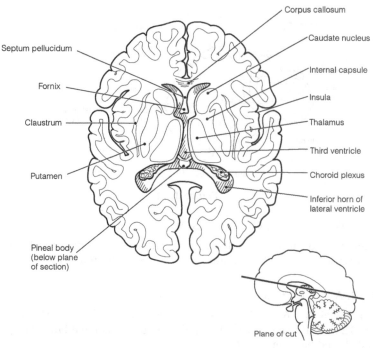

Figure 13.7

13. The cranial nerves include all named nerves (except those designated as spinal nerves). The midbrain is the area including C, I, and K. The diencephalon is the region from which the mammillary bodies and the infundibulum project. The pons is the enlarged region between K and A; the medulla is the region from A to just below D where the spinal cord begins.

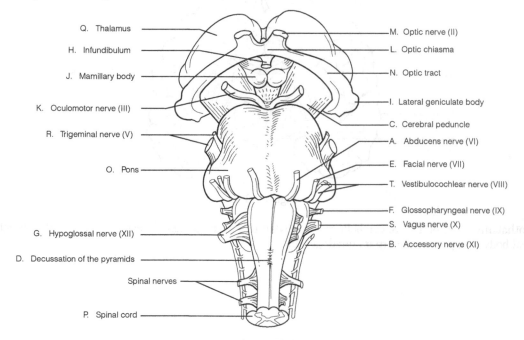

Figure 13.8

14. 1. Cerebral peduncles   2. Pineal gland   3. Pons   4. Paralysis   5. Speech disorder   6. Motor impairment   7. Association fibers   8. Internal capsule   9. Caudate nucleus   10. Parietal lobe

15. 1. 5   2. 2   3. 5   4. 1   5. 3   6. 4

16. 1. R   2. R   3. L   4. L   5. L   6. R   7. L   8. R   9. R   10. L   11. R   12. L   13. R   14. L

Higher Mental Functions

1. 1. A   2. D   3. A   4. C   5. C   6. B
2. 1. electroencephalogram (EEC)   2. frequencies   3. Hz (hertz or cycles per second)   4. amplitude   5. sleep   6. cerebral cortical function   7. epilepsy   8. grand mal   9. brain death
3. 1. 24   2. coma   3. brain stem   4. hypothalamus   5. increase   6. T   7. NREM   8. acetylcholine   9. REM   10. T   11. narcolepsy
4. Consciousness encompasses perception of sensations, initiation of voluntary movement and higher mental processing. It is evidence of holistic information-processing by the brain. Consciousness involves large areas of simultaneous cerebral cortical activity, is superimposed on other types of neural activity, and is totally interconnected throughout the cerebrum.
5. alertness, drowsiness, stupor, coma
6. 1. S   2. S   3. L   4. L   5. S   6. L
7. 1. An alert, aroused state of consciousness.   2. Repetition or rehearsal of facts or skills.   3. Association of new information with stored information.   4. Time for chemical or structural changes to occur.
8. 1. Fact memory: the learning of precise, detailed information; related to conscious thoughts when consolidation into long term memory is associated with already learned facts.   2. Skill memory: the learning of specific motor activities; not usually related to conscious thoughts; best acquired by practice and remembered in repeated performance.
9. 1. subcortical structures   2. basal forebrain   3. a more lasting memory   4. amygdala   5. anterograde amnesia   6. yes   7. no   8. throughout the cerebral cortex   9. corpus striatum

Protection of the Brain

1.

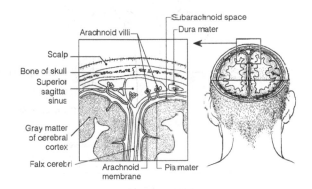

Figure 13.9

2. 1. pia mater   2. arachnoid villi   3. dura mater   4. subarachnoid space   5. subarachnoid space   6. superior sagittal sinus   7. falx cerebri
3. 1. blood plasma   2. hydrogen ions (H^+)   3. choroid plexuses   4. ventricle   5. ependymal   6. cerebral aqueduct   7. central canal   8. subarachnoid space   9. fourth ventricle   10. arachnoid villi   11. hydrocephalus   12. brain damage
4. 1. tight junctions   2. oxygen   3. potassium   4. hypothalamus   5. lipid-soluble   6. T
5. 1. E   2. F   3. D   4. G   5. B   6. C   7. I   8. A   9. H

The Spinal Cord

1. 1. C   2. A   3. F   4. D   5. E   6. B
2.

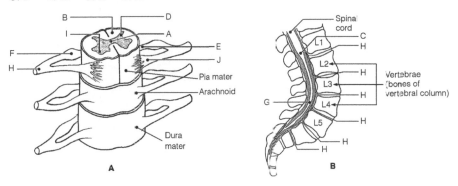

Figure 13.10

3. 1. foramen magnum   2. lumbar   3. lumbar tap or puncture   4. 31   5. 8   6. 12   7. 5   8. 5   9. cauda equina

4. 1. SS   2. VS   3. VM   4. SM   5. VS   6. SS   7. VM

5. The pathway could be accurately identified by the process of elimination. It continues all the way to the somato-sensory cortex, so it is not the spinocerebellar pathway. It ascends in the *lateral* white column, so it is not either the fasciculus cuneatus or gracilis, which are dorsal column pathways (and constitute the *specific* system). Circle the junctions (synapses) between the first- and second-order neurons and between the second- and third-order neurons.

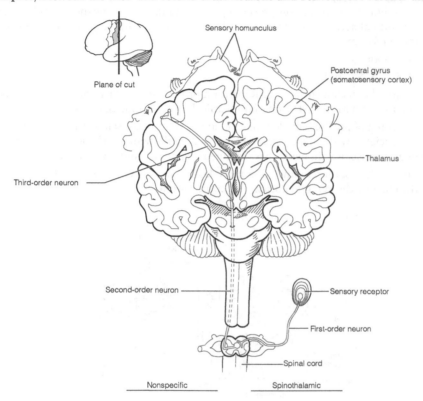

Figure 13.11

6. 1. meningeal   2. epidural   3. cerebrospinal fluid   4. anterior median fissure   5. white   6. gray commissure   7. anterior   8. lateral   9. sensory   10. motor   11. neural crest

7.

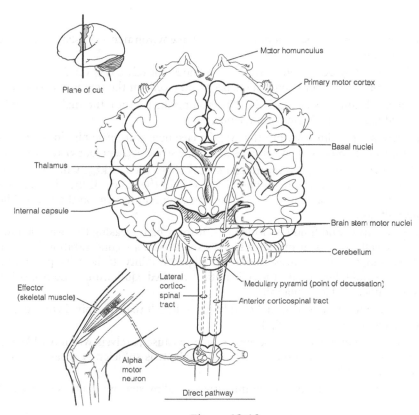

Figure 13.12

8. 1. E   2. G   3. C   4. I   5. D   6. H   7. F   8. B

Diagnostic Procedures for Assessing CNS Dysfunction

1. 1. pneumoencephalogram   2. T   3. cerebral angiogram   4. PET scan   5. above

THE INCREDIBLE JOURNEY

1. 1. cerebellum   2. medulla oblongata   3. hypothalamus   4. memories   5. temporal   6. a motor speech area
7. reasoning   8. frontal   9. vagus   10. dura mater   11. subarachnoid space   12. fourth

CHALLENGING YOURSELF

At the Clinic

1. The cerebellum.
2. Meningitis; by examining a sample of CSF for the presence of microbes.
3. The RAS of the reticular formation of the brain stem.
4. Somatosensory cortex.
5. Broca's area and adjacent regions of the motor cortex.
6. Left motor cortex.
7. Parkinson's disease.
8. Decreases.
9. Epilepsy; the condition will probably resolve itself without treatment.
10. Temporal-lobe epilepsy.
11. Intracranial hemorrhage.
12. Upper motor neuron damage will leave spinal reflexes intact (spastic paralysis), which will maintain the muscle mass.
13. Parkinson's disease; levodopa or perhaps a transplant of dopamine-secreting tissue.
14. Four hours of sleep is not abnormal for an elderly person A sleeping aid will reduce slow-wave (restorative) sleep, which compounds the problem.
15. Retrograde amnesia; this does not affect skill memory.

Stop and Think

1. Humans rely primarily on vision for assessment of the external environment; consequently, much of the cerebral cortex is devoted to this sense.

2. Short-term memory is affected by ECT. Long-term memory does not rely solely on the continuation of electrical output; rather, it is based on physical or chemical changes to the cells in the memory pathway.

3. Yes. All tracts from the cerebrum pass as projection fibers alongside (or into) the thalamus, and from there to the midbrain, pons, and medulla—all the brain stem regions.

4. The primary cortex receives input directly from the eye; damage here will cause blindness. Damage to the association cortex will cause inability to process visual images and make sense of them, but visual sensations will still occur.

5. Yes. If blockage of CSF flow is internal, the ventricular spaces above the blockage will enlarge, making the brain larger and more hollow and putting pressure on neural tissue from the inside. If the blockage is in the arachnoid villi, CSF will accumulate in the subarachnoid space, putting external pressure on the brain. The skull will enlarge, but the brain will not.

6. Since mannitol causes crenation and fluid loss from cells, it must be increasing the osmotic pressure of the solution bathing (outside) the cells; that is, it increases blood's solute osmotic concentration in comparison to that of the cells of the capillary wall. Osmosis hinges on differential permeability. If the cells' plasma membranes were permeable to mannitol, it would diffuse into the cells until it reached equilibrium, and osmosis would not occur. Thus, the cells must be impermeable to mannitol.

7. The correct choice is (c); the injury was at spinal cord level L_3. Recall that the spinal cord levels are several segments superior to vertebral levels (L_3 cf. T_{12}).

8. The spinal cord is so narrow that any damage severe enough to cause paralysis will most likely affect both sides of the cord. In the brain, motor control of the two sides of the body is sufficiently separated so that unilateral damage and paralysis are more likely.

9. The posterior side of the spinal cord carries predominantly ascending sensory tracts, so damage here would likely cause paresthesia.

10. The primary somatosensory cortex is being stimulated, so (c) is the most appropriate response.

COVERING ALL YOUR BASES

Multiple Choice

1. B 2. A 3. B 4. C, D 5. B 6. A 7. A, B, C, D 8. C 9. B, C 10. B, C, D 11. C 12. B, C
13. C 14. A, C 15. A, C 16. A, C, D 17. A, B, C 18. A, B, C, D 19. D 20. A, B, D 21. B, D
22. A, B, C 23. A, C 24. C 25. B 26. D 27. A, B, D 28. D 29. B 30. B 31. D 32. A, B, C, D
33. A, C, D 34. D 35. D 36. A, B, C, D 37. B, C, D 38. A, B, C, D 39. A, B, C, D 40. A

Word Dissection

	Word root	Translation	Example		Word root	Translation	Example
1.	campo	sea animal	hippocampus	10.	hippo	horse	hippocampus
2.	collicul	little hill	superior colliculi	11.	infundib	funnel	infundibulum
3.	commis	united	commissure	12.	isch	suppress	ischemia
4.	cope	cut	syncope	13.	lemnisc	ribbon	medial lemniscus
5.	enceph	within the head	mesencephalon	14.	nigr	black	substantia nigra
6.	epilep	laying hold of	epilepsy	15.	rhin	nose	rhinencephalon
7.	falx	sickle	falx cerebri	16.	rostr	snout	rostral
8.	forn	arch	fornix	17.	uncul	little	homunculus
9.	gyro	turn, twist	gyrus	18.	uncus	hook	uncus (olfactory)

Chapter 14 The Peripheral Nervous System

BUILDING THE FRAMEWORK

1. 1. sensory 2. afferent 3. motor 4. efferent 5. somatic 6. autonomic 7. somatic motor
   8. autonomic motor

2. 1. receptor → 2. sensory nerve fiber → 3. ventral ramus of spinal nerve → 4. spinal nerve → 5. dorsal root of spinal nerve → 6. motor nerve fiber → 7. spinal nerve → 8. ventral ramus of spinal nerve → 9. effector

Sensory Receptors and Sensation

1. 1. sensation 2. perception 3. electrical energy 4. permeability 5. graded 6. threshold 7. action
   8. anterolateral 9. lemniscal 10. anterolateral (nonspecific) 11. thalamus

2. 1. primary sensory cortex 2. frequency 3. nonspecific 4. T 5. thalamus 6. specific 7. first-order 8. T

3. 1. C, 2   2. B, 1   3. A, 5 (3)   4. A, 4   5. A, 2   6. A, 3   7. B, 2   8. B, 2   9. A, 1

4. 1. Tendon stretch   2. Numerous in muscle   3. Light touch   4. Thermoreceptor   5. Muscle spindle
6. Nociceptors   7. Merkel discs   8. Interoceptor   9. Free dendritic endings

5.

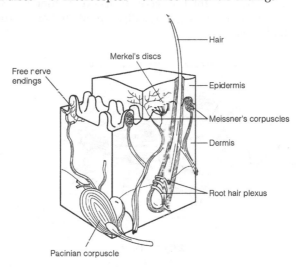

Figure 14.1

6. 1. A, F   2. A, F   3. B, E, F, G   4. B, E, G   5. C, D, H   6. A   7. C, D

7. 1. chemoreception   2. bitter   3. olfactory   4. roof   5. limbic   6. thalamus

8.

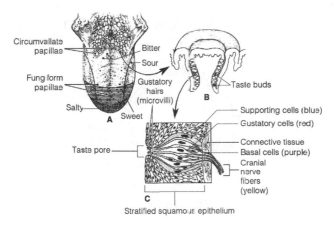

Figure 14.2

9. 1. They play a role as local integrator cells—they refine, amplify, and relay the signal.   2. glomeruli   3. granule
cells; olfactory adaptation   4. amygdala, hypothalamus, and other limbic system structures

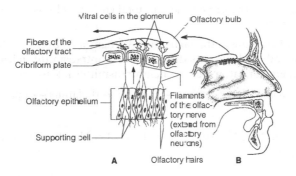

Figure 14.3

10. 1. Musky   2. Epithelial cell   3. Yellow-tinged epithelium   4. Olfactory nerve   5. Four receptor types
6. Metal ions   7. H$^+$ 8. Anosmia

11. 1. extrinsic   2. eyelids   3. tarsal or Meibomian   4. chalazion

12. 1. 2   2. 4   3. 3   4. 1

13. 1. Superior rectus turns eye superiorly.   2. Inferior rectus turns eye inferiorly.   3. Superior oblique turns eye inferiorly and laterally.   4. Lateral rectus turns eye laterally.   5. Medial rectus turns eye medially.   6. Inferior oblique turns eye superiorly and laterally.

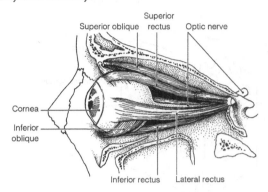

Figure 14.4

14. 1. Vitreous humor   2. Iris   3. Far vision   4. Mechanoreceptors   5. Iris   6. Pigmented retina   7. Pigmented layer   8. Macula lutea   9. Richly vascular   10. Inner segment   11. Tarsal plate

15. 1. In distant vision the ciliary muscle is relaxed, the lens convexity is decreased, and the degree of light refraction is decreased.   2. In close vision the ciliary muscle is contracted, the lens convexity is increased, and the degree of light refraction is increased.

16. 1. L   2. A   3. K   4. I   5. D   6. C   7. B   8. J   9. M   10. C   11. D   12. G   13. F   14.–17. E, H, M, A   18. E   19. G

17.

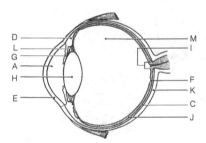

Figure 14.5

18. During reading, all intrinsic muscles and the extrinsic medial recti are contracted. Distant vision does not require accommodation and relaxes these muscles.

19. 1. E   2. F   3. D   4. A   5. C

20. 1. L   2. A   3. F   4. H   5. K   6. D   7. I   8. C   9. G   10. E   11. B   12. J

21. 1. 3   2. blue   3. green   4. red   5. at the same time   6. total color blindness   7. males   8. rods   9. fovea centralis   10. retinal periphery

22. 1. opsin; rhodopsin   2. all-*trans*; bleaching of the pigment   3. vitamin A; liver   4. Na$^+$; leaks into outer segments, causing depolarization and local currents that lead to neurotransmitter release.   5. Membrane becomes impermeable to N$^+$; hyperpolarization occurs; neurotransmitter release stops.

23. Retina → optic nerve → optic chiasma → optic tract → synapse in thalamus → optic radiation → optic cortex.

24. Check 1, 2, 3, 4, 11, 12

25. 1.–3. E, I, M   4.–6. C, K, N   7.–9. A, F, L   10. K, N   11. B   12. M   13. C   14. B   15.–16. K, N   17. G   18. D   19. H   20. L

26.

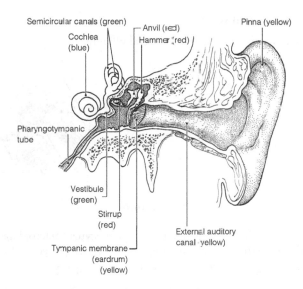

Figure 14.6

27. Eardrum → hammer → anvil → stirrup → oval window → perilymph → membrane → endolymph → hair cells.

28. 1. C 2. F 3. E 4. D 5. B 6. G 7. I 8. J 9. A

29.

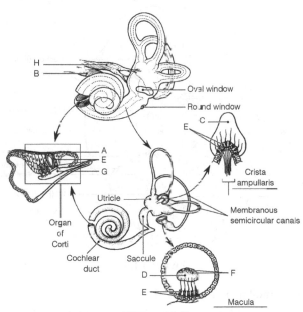

Figure 14.7

30. 1. vibrating object 2. elastic 3–4. compression and rarefaction 5. wavelength 6. short 7. long 8. pitch
9. loudness 10. decibels

31. 1. C 2. S 3. C 4. S 5. C 6. S

32. 1. C 2. I 3. A 4. D 5. B 6. J 7. H 8. K 9. E 10. G 11. L

33. 1. Pinna 2. Tectorial membrane 3. Sound waves 4. Pharyngotympanic tube 5. Optic nerve 6. Retina
7. Inner hair cells

Transmission Lines: Nerves and Associated Ganglia

1. somatic afferent, somatic efferent, visceral afferent, visceral efferent

2.

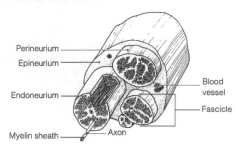

Figure 14.8

3. 1. divide   2. peripheral   3. cell body   4. degenerate   5. phagocytes (macrophages)   6. Schwann cells   7. endoneurium   8. central   9. astrocytes and microglia   10. macrophages   11. oligodendrocytes   12. die

4. 1. H   2. K   3. I   4. L   5. B   6. C   7. G, H, L   8. D   9. A   10. F   11. J   12. D, E   13. G   14. C

5. 1. Accessory (XI)   2. Olfactory (I)   3. Oculomotor (III)   4. Vagus (X)   5. Facial (VII)   6. Trigeminal (V)   7. Vestibulocochlear (VIII)   8. Glossopharyngeal (IX)   9. III, IV, VI   10. Trigeminal (V)   11. Optic (II)   12. Vestibulocochlear (VIII)   13. Hypoglossal (XII)   14. Facial (VII)   15. Olfactory (I)

6. 1. A   2. F   3. D   4. C   5. E   6. B

7.

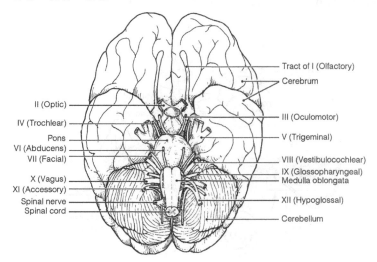

Figure 14.9

8. Temporal, zygomatic, buccal, mandibular, and cervical.

9. 1. dorsal   2. ventral roots   3. rami   4. plexuses   5. limbs   6. thorax   7. posterior trunk

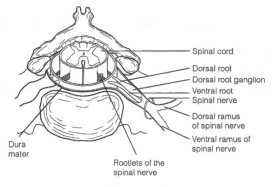

Figure 14.10

10. 1. Two roots   2. Thoracic roots   3. Afferent fibers   4. Ventral root   5. Two spinal roots

11. 1. cervical plexus 2. phrenic nerve 3. sciatic nerve (tibial division) 4. fibular, tibial 5. median 6. musculocutaneous 7. lumbar plexus 8. femoral 9. ulnar 10. brachial plexus 11. sciatic nerve 12. sacral plexus 13. radial nerve 14. femoral nerve 15. obturator nerve 16. inferior gluteal

12.

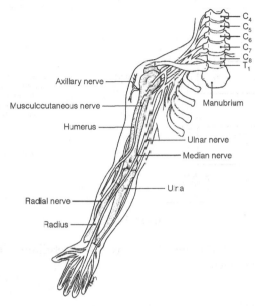

Figure 14.11

13.

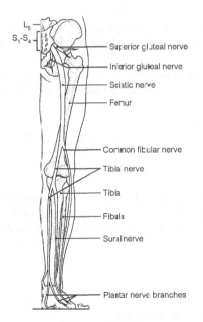

Figure 14.12

14. 1. radial 2. T 3. median 4. ulnar 5. T

Motor Endings and Motor Activity

1. Check 1, 3, 4, 8

2. 1. C 2. B, G 3. E 4. D 5. H 6. C 7. A 8. A, D

3.

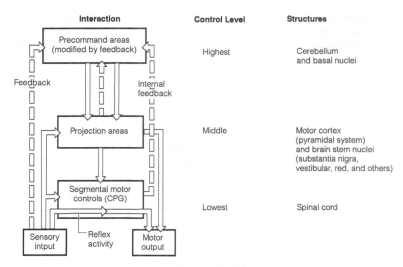

Figure 14.13

4. 1. Consciously considered actions   2. Command neurons   3. Cerebellum   4. Precommand areas
5. Basal nuclei   6. Multineuronal tracts

Reflex Activity

1. 1. A rapid, involuntary, predictable response to a stimulus.   2. receptor, sensory neuron, integration center,
motor neuron, effector   3. somatic reflexes and autonomic reflexes   4. spinal reflex

2. 1. A   2. B   3. A   4. B   5. A   6. B   7. B   8. A

3. 1. muscle spindles   2. intrafusal fibers   3. primary sensory   4. type Ia fibers   5. secondary sensory
6. type II fibers   7. gamma efferent fibers   8. extrafusal fibers   9. alpha efferent fibers   10. alpha motor
neurons   11. reciprocal inhibition

4. 1. primary sensory afferent   2. alpha motor neuron   3. synapse   4. spinal cord   5. muscle spindle
6. intrafusal fiber   7. capsule of the receptor   8. ascending fibers   9. skeletal muscle (extrafusal fibers)
10. motor ending to extrafusal fiber

5. Stretch: 1, 3, 5, 6, 8, 9   Deep tendon: 2, 3, 4, 7, 9, 10

6. 1. E   2. D   3. B   4. A, B, C, D, F   5. C, E   6. E   7. B   8. A, F   9. A, C, D, F   10. A, F   11. D   12. E
13. F   14. A

The Incredible Journey

1. 1. bony labyrinth   2. perilymph   3. saccule   4. utricle   5. (gel) otolithic membrane   6. otoliths   7. macula
8. static   9. cochlear duct   10. organ of Corti   11. hearing   12. cochlear division of cranial nerve VIII
13. semicircular canals   14. cupula   15. crista ampullaris   16. dynamic

CHALLENGING YOURSELF

At the Clinic

1. Abducens.

2. Trigeminal nerve; trigeminal neuralgia (tic douloureux).

3. Pinkeye (infectious conjunctivitis); yes, because infectious conjunctivitis is caused by a bacterial infection.

4. Uncinate fit; irritation of the olfactory pathway sometimes follows brain surgery.

5. Vagus; complete vagal paralysis results in death.

6. Trapezius, sternocleidomastoid.

7. Brachial plexus.

8. Median nerve.

9. Patching the strong eye to force the weaker eye muscles to become stronger.

10. Cataract; UV radiation, smoking.

11. The right hypoglossal nerve (cranial XII).

12. Spinal cord transection at L_5 (c). The posterior femoral cutaneous nerve, which arises from ventral rami S_1–S_3,
provides the sensory supply in the areas described. The motor nerves for those areas also receive fibers from the
ventral rami of L_4 and L_5, explaining his lack of motor problems.

13. Check the gag and swallowing reflexes (IX and X) and for weakness in the sternocleidomastoid and trapezius
muscles (XI).

Stop and Think

1. Nissl bodies are composed of rough ER and ribosomes. Since most of the protein synthesis will be devoted to synthesizing the internal proteins needed for repair and replacement of the damaged axon, the ribosomes will predominantly be free, rather than attached. The ribosomes of the Nissl bodies will separate from the ER membrane, and the characteristic appearance of the Nissl body will be lost until repair is nearly complete. The nucleolus functions in ribosome assembly, so as the demand for ribosomes increases, nucleolar function and appearance will become more significant. The accumulation of raw materials for protein synthesis may increase the osmotic pressure of the cell, causing it to attract water and take on a swollen appearance.

2. Pricking the finger excites the nonspecific pathway for pain, beginning with the dendritic endings of a first-order neuron, a nociceptor, in the finger. This neuron synapses with the second-order neuron in the spinal cord, and the axon of the second-order neuron (after crossing over in the spinal cord) ascends in the anterolateral pathway through the lateral spinothalamic tract. Synapse with third-order neurons occurs in thalamic nuclei, but there are many synapses with nuclei of the reticular formation as well. Pain is perceived, and the cortex is aroused as processing at the perceptual level occurs. The somatosensory cortex pinpoints the sensation; the sensory association area perceives the sensation as undesirable. Integrative input to the prefrontal area sends signals to the motor speech area, which directs the primary motor cortex to activate the muscles of speech to say "ouch."

3. Exteroceptors that are not cutaneous receptors include the chemoreceptors of the tongue and nasal mucosa, the photoreceptors of the eyes, and the mechanoreceptors of the inner ear. These all monitor changes in the external environment, so they are classified as exteroceptors.

4. Starting from twelve o'clock, for the right eye: lateral movement (abducens), inferior movement, medial movement (oculomotor), superior movement (oculomotor, trochlear). For the left eye: oculomotor for medial and inferior movements, abducens for lateral movement, oculomotor and trochlear for superior movement.

5. The precommand areas *ready* the primary motor cortex for action, but the actual command (nerve impulse) to the muscles is issued by the motor cortex.

6. No. The bundle of "nerves" in the cauda equina really consists of dorsal and ventral roots, which don't merge into the spinal nerve until after exiting the vertebral column.

7. The origin of the phrenic nerve so high up the spinal cord means that the distance between brain and phrenic is short. This decreases the likelihood of spinal cord damage above the phrenic nerve, since there isn't much spinal cord above that nerve's origin.

8. Initially, as muscle spindles are stretched, the reflex sends impulses back to contract the muscle. With prolonged stretching, accommodation decreases the vigor of the stretch reflex somewhat, and the muscle can relax and stretch more, reducing the risk of tearing muscle tissue during exercise.

9. The nerves serving the ankle joint are those serving the muscles that cause movement at the ankle joint—the posterior femoral cutaneous, common fibular, and tibial.

10. The nurse has forgotten the phenomenon of adaptation, a condition in which sensory receptor transmission declines or stops when the stimulus is unchanging. She has had her hand in the water while filling the tub, and the thermoreceptors in *her* skin have accommodated to the hot water.

11. Use word roots to help you remember. Glossopharyngeal means tongue-pharynx, and that nerve serves those regions. Hypoglossal means "below the tongue," and this nerve serves the small muscles that move the tongue.

12. Abdul was more correct. The facial nerve is almost entirely a motor nerve.

13. Smell receptors are chemoreceptors that respond to chemicals in solution and adapt quickly when the stimulus is unchanging. Motion receptors of the inner ear are mechanoreceptors involved in the sense of balance. Loss of balance can have dire consequences here. These receptors, like all proprioceptors, do not adapt.

14. Starlight is too dim to excite cones. Light from objects in the center of the visual field strikes the fovea centralis, which contains only cones, not rods.

15. In elephants, the spiral organ of Corti is elongated at the helicotrema end to increase the sensitivity to low-frequency sound. In dogs, the proximal end of the spiral organ is stiffer than it is in humans, so higher frequencies are required to excite the hair cells at that end.

16. The taste buds and olfactory epithelium can replace their receptor cells; the retina of the eye and the cochlea of the ear cannot.

COVERING ALL YOUR BASES

Multiple Choice

 1. C **2.** D **3.** C, D **4.** C, D **5.** A, C, D **6.** C **7.** A, B, C **8.** B **9.** A, C **10.** D **11.** B, D
12. B, C, D **13.** A, B, D **14.** C **15.** A **16.** B, C, D **17.** A, C, D **18.** A, C, D **19.** A, B, D **20.** B
21. C **22.** A, C, D **23.** B, C, D **24.** A, B, C, D **25.** A **26.** B, C **27.** C **28.** C **29.** A, B, D **30.** C
31. A, C **32.** A, C, D **33.** B **34.** A, B, C **35.** D **36.** A, C **37.** C **38.** A, B **39.** D **40.** A **41.** C
42. D **43.** A **44.** D

Word Dissection

	Word root	Translation	Example		Word root	Translation	Example
1.	ampulla	flask	crista ampullaris	12.	noci	harmful	nociceptors
2.	cer	wax	ceruminous gland	13.	olfact	smell	olfactory cell
3.	cochlea	snail shell	cochlear duct	14.	papill	nipple	fungiform papilla
4.	esthesi	sensation	kinesthetic	15.	presby	old	presbycusis
5.	fove	small pit	fovea centralis	16.	propri	one's own	proprioceptors
6.	glauc	gray	glaucoma	17.	puden	shameful	pudendal nerve
7.	glosso	tongue	glossopharyngeal	18.	scler	hard	sclera of eye
8.	gust	taste	gustatory hair	19.	tars	flat	tarsal plate
9.	kines	movement	kinesthetic	20.	trema	hole	helicotrema
10.	lut	yellow	macula lutea	21.	tympan	drum	tympanic membrane
11.	macula	spot	macula lutea	22.	vagus	wanderer	vagus nerve

Chapter 15 The Autonomic Nervous System

BUILDING THE FRAMEWORK

Introduction

1. 1. S, A 2. S 3. A 4. S, A 5. S 6. S 7. A 8. A 9. S, A 10. A 11. A 12. S 13. 5 14. 5
15. A 16. S, A

2.

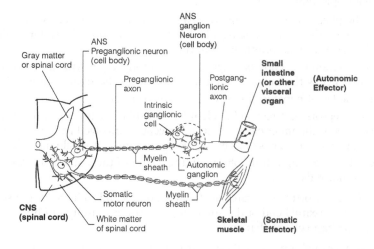

Figure 15.1

3. Sympathetic: 2, 4, 7, 9   Parasympathetic: 1, 3, 5, 6, 8

ANS Anatomy

1. 1. lateral   2. T_1–L_2 3. spinal cord   4. white (myelinated)   5. paravertebral ganglia   6. sympathetic   7. postganglionic   8. rami communicantes   9. unmyelinated   10. smooth muscle   11. cervical   12. pupil (iris)   13. salivary   14. skin   15. prevertebral (collateral)   16. thoracic splanchnic   17. celiac and superior mesenteric   18. abdominal   19. adrenal   20. lumbar   21. urinary   22. brain stem   23. sacral   24. terminal   25. oculomotor (III)   26. VII (facial)   27. IX (glossopharyngeal)   28. vagus (X)   29. plexuses   30. thorax   31. abdomen   32. sacral region

2.

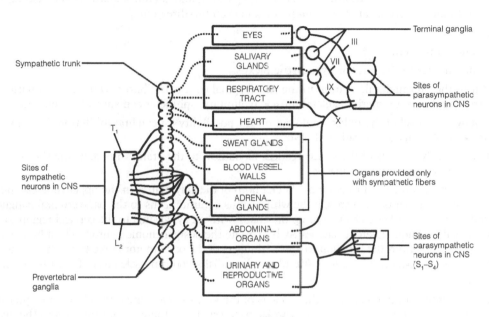

Figure 15.2

3. 1.S   2. P   3. S   4. P   5. P   6. P   7. S   8. P   9. P   10. S   11. S   12. S, P

ANS Physiology

1. 1. Fibers that release acetylcholine   2. Nicotinic and muscarinic receptors

2. 1. Fibers that release norepinephrine   2. Alpha and beta adrenergic receptors

3. 1.C   2. A   3. C   4. D   5. B   6. A   7. B   8. B

4. Sympathetic: 2, 3, 4, 6   Parasympathetic: 1, 5, 7

5. 1. NE   2. Nicotinic receptor   3. Heart rate slows   4. Parasympathetic tone   5. Rapid heart rate   6. Sympathetic tone

Homeostatic Imbalances of the ANS

1. 1. smooth muscle   2. T   3. sympathectomy   4. adrenergic

CHALLENGING YOURSELF

At the Clinic

1. Parasympathetic.

2. The sympathetic division causes vasoconstriction of vessels supplying the digestive organs. Stress-induced overstimulation of sympathetic nerves can cause an almost total shutdown of blood supply to the stomach. Lack of blood leads to tissue death and necrosis, which causes the ulcers.

3. A sympathectomy will be performed. It will result in dilation of the distal blood vessels as their vasoconstrictor fibers are cut.

4. Sweating is stimulated by sympathetic nerves; after they are cut, anhidrosis will result.

5. The condition is mass reflex reaction or autonomic hyperreflexia. The staff will watch for hypertension-induced cerebrovascular accident.

6. Antiadrenergic drugs (such as phentolamine) that interfere with the activity of the sympathetic vasomotor fibers.

7. Epigastric region.

8. Back to the laboratory for our mad scientist. His victim would suffer from vision problems (unable to control iris and ciliary muscle regulating the lens), have dry eyes, dry mouth, and dry nasal mucosa. Hardly fatal.

Stop and Think

1. No. Without sensory feedback to inform the CNS of the physical and chemical status of the viscera, the motor output of the autonomic nerves can be inappropriate and even life-threatening.

2. Parasympathetic.

3. Spinal reflex, autonomic reflex.

4. Pelvic splanchnic nerves to the inferior hypogastric plexus.

5. Cerebral input to the preganglionic neuron in the sacral spinal cord is inhibitory; cerebral stimulation of motor neurons controlling the more inferior skeletal muscle (voluntary) sphincter can shut off urine flow.

6. Transection above the level of the reflex would cut off the possibility for cerebral inhibition. Voiding would become entirely involuntary and totally reflexive.

7. Shunting of blood to the vessels of the hands reduces blood flow to the brain, thus reducing the vessel distension that causes the pain of a migraine headache.

8. The cholinergic preganglionic axon runs from a lateral horn of the gray matter in the upper thoracic spinal cord to the ventral root of the spinal nerve, through the white ramus communicans to the paravertebral ganglion of the thoracic region of the sympathetic chain, and up the chain (without synapsing) to the cervical region to synapse in the superior cervical ganglion. There it releases ACh to excite the postganglionic neuron. The adrenergic postganglionic axon runs from the ganglion to join with fibers of the oculomotor nerve to reach the iris of the eye. Release of NE at the neuroeffector junctions stimulates the radial smooth muscle layer of the iris, which results in dilation of the pupil.

9. From the cardiac center in the medulla to the nucleus of the vagus nerve, where the cholinergic preganglionic axon leaves in the vagus nerve and runs to the cardiac plexuses. From there it continues on to the heart itself, ending at an intramural ganglion, where ACh is released. ACh excites the postganglionic neurons, whose cholinergic postganglionic axons travel to the target cells, where they release ACh to inhibit cardiac function.

COVERING ALL YOUR BASES

Multiple Choice

1. D 2. D 3. D 4. B, C 5. A, B, C 6. A 7. B 8. A 9. A 10. C 11. D 12. C 13. C 14. B 15. A 16. B 17. A 18. C 19. C 20. A 21. A 22. A 23. A 24. A 25. B

Word Dissection

	Word root	Translation	Example		Word root	Translation	Example
1.	adren	toward the kidney	adrenaline	5.	ortho	straight	orthostatic
2.	chales	relaxed	achalasia	6.	para	beside	parasympathetic
3.	epinephr	upon the kidney	epinephrine	7.	pathos	feeling	sympathetic
4.	mural	wall	intramural ganglia	8.	splanchn	organ	splanchnic nerve

Chapter 16 The Endocrine System

BUILDING THE FRAMEWORK

The Endocrine System: An Overview

1. 1. K   2. H   3. D   4. G   5. A   6.–8. B, I, L   9. E   10. J
2. Figure 16.1: A. Pineal   B. Anterior pituitary   C. Posterior pituitary   D. Thyroid   E. Thymus   F. Adrenal gland   G. Pancreas   H. Ovary   I. Testis   J. Parathyroids   K. Placenta   L. Hypothalamus

Hormones

1. 1. I   2. N   3. A   4. L   5. K   6. G   7. C   8. D   9. F   10. B   11. J   12. E   13. H
2. A circulating hormone enters the bloodstream or lymph and often affects distant body targets. A local hormone, like a circulating hormone, is released into the interstitial fluid but it exerts its effects nearby on cells in the local area.
3. 1. A   2. B   3. B   4. A   5. C   6. C   7. A   8. B
4. 1. first   2. a G protein   3. adenylate cyclase   4. ATP   5. second   6. protein kinases   7. phosphate   8. target cell type   9.–11. diacylglycerol, inositol triphosphate, cyclic GMP   12. Ca^{2+}
5. Hormones are inactivated by enzymes in their target cells as well as by liver and kidney enzymes.
6. 1.–3. A, G, I   4. C   5.–8. B, E, H, K   9. L   10. D   11. F
7. 1. B   2. C   3. A

Major Endocrine Organs

1. 1. D   2. B   3. A   4. C
2.

Figure 15.2

3. 1. C   2. D   3. A   4. A   5. B   6 E, I (A)   7. C   8 F   9. C   10. F   11. C   12. H   13. C   14. D   15. E, I (A)   16. C   17. G   18. J (A)   19. K   20. L   21. L   22. C
4. 1. thyroxine/T_3 2. thymosin   3. PTH   4. cortisone (glucocorticoids)   5. epinephrine   6. insulin   7.–10. TSH, FSH, ACTH, LH   11. glucagon   12. ADH   13. FSH   14. LH   15. estrogens   16. progesterone   17. aldosterone   18. prolactin   19. oxytocin
5. 1. Anterior lobe   2. Posterior lobe   3. Cortisol   4. Hypophyseal portal system   5. Oxytocin   6. Increases blood Ca^{2+} levels   7. Depresses glucose uptake   8. Thyroxine
6. 1. Kidneys: Causes retention of Ca^{2+} and enhances excretion of PO_4^{3-}. Promotes activation of vitamin D.   2. Intestine: Causes increased absorption of Ca^{2+} from foodstuffs.   3. Bones: Causes enhanced release of Ca^{2+} from bone matrix.
7. In high amounts, it promotes blood vessel constriction, increasing blood pressure (it has a pressor effect).
8. Check 1, 4, 6, 7, 10, 11.   Circle 2, 3, 5, 8, 9.
9. 1. 2   2. 7   3. 8   4. 5   5. 9   6. 1   7. 4   8. 3   9. 6
10. 1. Polyuria—high sugar content in kidney filtrate (acts as an osmotic diuretic and) causes large amounts of water to be lost in the urine.   2. Polydipsia—thirst due to large volumes of urine excreted.   3. Polyphagia—hunger because blood sugar cannot be used as a body fuel even though its levels are high.

11. 1. B   2. A   3. A   4. B   5. B   6. A   7. A   8. B   9. B   10. B   11. B   12. A

12. 1. A, E   2. B   3. C   4. E   5. A   6. E   7. A   8. B, E   9. A, E   10. D

13. 1. B   2. A   3. B   4. A   5. A   6. A

14. 1. B   2. D   3. E   4. C   5. A

15. 1. estrogens/testosterone   2. PTH   3. ADH   4. thyroxine   5. thyroxine   6. insulin   7. growth hormone   8. estrogens/progesterone   9. thyroxine

16. 1. growth hormone   2. thyroxine   3. PTH   4. glucocorticoids   5. growth hormone   6. androgens

Other Hormone-Producing Structures

1.

Hormone	Chemical makeup	Source	Effects
Gastrin	Peptide	Stomach	Stimulates stomach glands to secrete HCl
Secretin	Peptide	Duodenum	Stimulates the pancreas to secrete HCO_3^--rich juice and the liver to release more bile; inhibits stomach glands
Cholecystokinin	Peptide	Duodenum	Stimulates the pancreas to secrete enzyme-rich juice and the gallbladder to contract; relaxes sphincter of Oddi
Erythropoietin	Glycoprotein	Kidney in response to hypoxia	Stimulates production of red blood cells by bone marrow
Cholecalciferol (vitamin D_3)	Steroid	Skin; activated by kidneys	Enhances intestinal absorption of calcium
Atrial natriuretic peptide (ANP)	Peptide	Heart atrial cells	Inhibits Na^+ reabsorption by kidneys; inhibits renin and aldosterone release

The Incredible Journey

1. 1. insulin   2. pancreas   3. hypothalamus   4. ADH   5. parathyroid   6. calcium   7. adrenal medulla   8. epinephrine   9. T_3/T_4

CHALLENGING YOURSELF

At the Clinic

1. Pituitary dwarfs (deficient in GH) are short in stature but have fairly normal proportions; cretins (deficient in thyroxine) retain childlike body proportions and have thick necks and protruding tongues.

2. Hypothyroidism; iodine deficiency (treated by dietary iodine supplement) or thyroid cell burnout (treated by hormonal supplement).

3. Hypersecretion of ADH causes diabetes insipidus, and insufficiency of insulin (or lack of response to insulin) causes diabetes mellitus. Both involve polyuria and consequent polydipsia. Glucose in the urine will indicate diabetes mellitus. (More complicated tests are used to diagnose diabetes insipidus.)

4. Adrenal cortex.

5. Hyperparathyroidism (resulting in hypercalcemia and undesirable calcium salt deposit), probably from a parathyroid tumor.

6. Cushing's syndrome, most likely caused by tumor; anterior pituitary (hypersecretion of ACTH) or adrenal cortex (hypersecretion of cortisol).

7. Hyperthyroidism; anterior pituitary tumor (hypersecretion of TSH) or thyroid tumor (hypersecretion of thyroxine).

8. Epinephrine and norepinephrine; pheochromocytoma, a tumor of the chromaffin cells of the adrenal medulla; exophthalmos and goiter would not be present.

9. Hypoglycemia; overdose of insulin.

10. Prolactin; tumor of the adenohypophysis.

11. Lying between the pinealocytes in the gland are grains of calcium salts. This "pineal sand," like the calcium salts of bone, is radiopaque.

Stop and Think

1. *Protein hormones* — *Steroid hormones*

   (a) rough ER, Golgi apparatus, secretory vesicles — smooth ER

   (b) storage in secretory vesicles — no storage

   (c) manufactured constantly — manufactured only as needed

   (d) secretion by exocytosis — leaves cell by diffusion through lipid bilayer

   (e) most (but not all) transported dissolved in plasma — transport may require a protein transport molecule

   (f) receptors on plasma membrane — receptors in cytoplasm or nucleus

   (g) second messenger used — no second messenger

   (h) immediate activation — lag time for protein synthesis to occur

   (i) effects end as soon as hormone is metabolized — effects prolonged after hormone is metabolized

2. (a) Growth hormone, TSH, ACTH, prolactin, FSH, LH.
   (b) Calcium, glucose, sodium, and potassium blood levels.
3. Hormone-producing cells located in organs of the digestive tract. They are called paraneurons because many of their hormones are identical to neurotransmitters released by neurons.
4. Down-regulation.
5. These hormones are lipid soluble; they must be "tied down" to prevent their escape through the plasma membrane.
6. Corticotropin-releasing hormone secreted by hypothalamus → capillaries of the hypophyseal portal system → anterior pituitary gland → release of ACTH by anterior pituitary → general circulation to zone fasciculata of the adrenal cortex → glucocorticoids (cortisol, etc.) released.
7. The thyroid gland contains thyroid follicles surrounded by soft connective tissue. The follicular cells of the follicles produce the thyroglobulin colloid from which T_3 and T_4 are split. At the external aspects of the follicles are *parafollicular* (C) cells that produce calcitonin, a completely different hormone. Usually structurally associated with the thyroid gland are the tiny parathyroid glands, which look completely different histologically. The parathyroid cells produce PTH, a calcitonin antagonist.
8. For the giant, GH is being secreted in excess by the anterior pituitary, resulting in extraordinary height. For the dwarf, GH is deficient, resulting in very small stature but normal body proportions. For the fat man, T_3 and T_4 are not being adequately produced, resulting in depressed metabolism and leading to obesity (myxedema). The bearded lady has a tumor of her adrenal cortex (androgen-secreting area) leading to hirsutism.

Closer Connections: Checking the Systems—Regulation and Integration of the Body

1. The CNS influences hormonal fluctuations through the hypothalamus, which not only synthesizes its own hormones (ADH and oxytocin) but also regulates release of anterior pituitary hormones.
2. The endocrine system includes hormones, such as thyroxine, that maintain the general health of nerve tissue and mineral-regulating hormones that maintain the proper balance of ions of sodium, calcium, and potassium required for optimal neural function. Additionally, certain hormones (T_3 and T_4) are required for normal growth and maturation of the nervous system.
3. Nervous system.
4. Endocrine system on both counts.
5. The nervous system elicits rapid responses from skeletal muscles; the endocrine system maintains the metabolism and general health of the muscle tissue and enhances its growth in mass during puberty. Both systems (sympathetic nervous system and catecholamines of the adrenal medulla) help ensure the muscles have an adequate blood supply during their activity when demands for O_2 and nutrients increase.

COVERING ALL YOUR BASES

Multiple Choice

1. B, C   2. A, C   3. C   4. A, C, D   5. C   6. A, B, D   7. C   8. C   9. B   10. D   11. B   12. A, B, C, D
13. A, B, C, D   14. A, B, C, D   15. D   16. A, B, C   17. A, B, C, D   18. D   19. A, C   20. C
21. A, B, C, D   22. A, B, C   23. B   24. B   25. B   26. D   27. A   28. A

Word Dissection

Word root	Translation	Example	Word root	Translation	Example
1. adeno	gland	adenohypophysis	5. hormon	excite	hormonal
2. crine	separate	endocrine	7. humor	fluid	humoral control
3. dips	thirst, dry	polydipsia	3. mell	honey	diabetes mellitus
4. diure	urinate	diuretic	9. toci	birth	oxytocin
5. gon	seed, offspring	gonad	10. trop	turn, change	tropic hormone

Part 2 BIOS 254
Chapter 17 The Cardiovascular System: Heart

BUILDING THE FRAMEWORK

Heart Anatomy

1. 1. mediastinum   2. diaphragm   3. second   4. midsternal line   5. fibrous   6. visceral   7. epicardium   8. friction   9. myocardium   10. cardiac muscle   11. fibrous skeleton   12. endocardium   13. endothelial   14. 4   15. atria   16. ventricles

2.

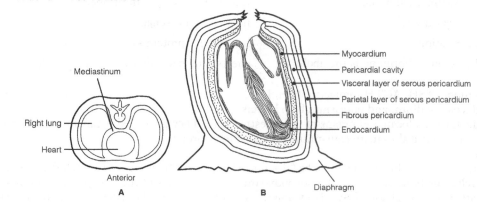

Figure 17.1

3. 1. right ventricle   2. pulmonary semilunar valve   3. pulmonary arteries   4. lungs   5. right and left pulmonary veins   6. left atrium   7. mitral (bicuspid)   8. left ventricle   9. aortic   10. aorta   11. capillary beds   12. superior vena cava   13. inferior vena cava

In Figure 17.2, the white areas represent regions transporting O_2-rich blood. The gray vessels transport O_2-poor blood.

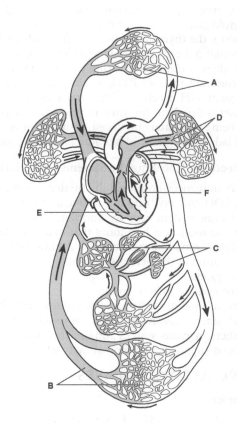

Figure 17.2

4. Figure 17.3: 1. right atrium   2. left atrium   3. right ventricle   4. left ventricle   5. superior vena cava   6. inferior vena cava   7. aorta   8. pulmonary trunk   9. left pulmonary artery   10. right pulmonary artery   11. right pulmonary veins   12. left pulmonary veins   13. vessels of coronary circulation   14. apex of heart   15. ligamentum arteriosum

Blood Supply to the Heart: Coronary Circulation

1.

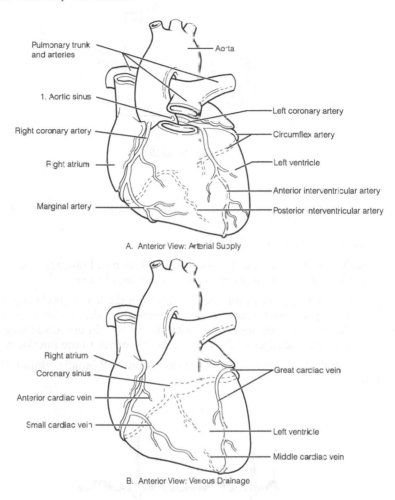

A. Anterior View: Arterial Supply

B. Anterior View: Venous Drainage

Figure 17.4

Properties of Cardiac Muscle Fibers

1. 1. C   2. C   3. C   4. C   5. S   6. S   7. C   8. S   9. C   10. S   11. C   12. C

2.

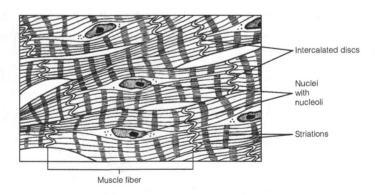

Figure 17.5

1. endomysium   2. prevent separation of adjacent cells   3. allow impulse (ions) to pass from cell to cell
4. functional syncytium   5. gap junctions

3.

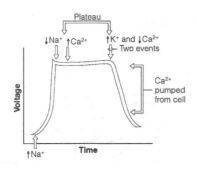

Figure 17.6

Heart Physiology

1. 1. spontaneously   2. resting membrane potential   3. action potential generation   4. pacemaker potentials   5. K⁺   6. Na⁺   7. into   8. fast Ca²⁺   9. Ca²⁺

2. A. 6   B. 7   C. 8   D. 9   E. 9   F. 8   G. 1   H. 2

   1. SA node   2. AV node   3. AV bundle or bundle of His   4. bundle branches   5. Purkinje fibers   6. pulmonary valve   7. aortic valve   8. mitral (bicuspid) valve   9. tricuspid valve

   Figure 17.7: Red arrows should be drawn from the left atrium to the left ventricle and out the aorta. Blue arrows should be drawn from the superior and inferior vena cavae into the right atrium, then into the right ventricle and out the pulmonary trunk. Green arrows should be drawn from 1 to 5 in numerical order. The cords, called chordae tendineae, should run from the edges of the flaps of the AV valves to the inferior ventricular walls.

3. 1. sinus rhythm   2. SA node 70–80 beats/mm; AV node 50/mm; AV bundle 30/mm; Purkinje fibers 30/mm   3. 0.3–0.5 m/s   4. 0.22

4.

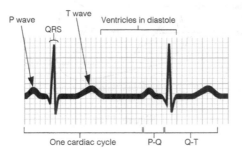

Figure 17.8

5. Figure 17.9: 1. B has extra P waves   2. C shows tachycardia   3. A has an abnormal QRS complex

6. 1. systole   2. diastole   3. lub-dup   4. atrioventricular   5. semilunar   6. ventricles   7. atria   8. atria   9. ventricles   10. murmurs

7.

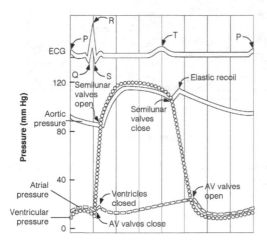

Figure 17.10

8. 1. AV valves open   2. SA node is pacemaker   3. Ventricular systole   4. Semilunar valves open   5. Heart sound after valve closes   6. AV valve open

9. 1. cardiac output   2. heart rate   3. stroke volume   4. 75 beats per minute   5. 70 ml per beat   6. 5250 ml per minute   7. minute   8. 120 ml   9. 50 ml   10. cardiac reserve   11. running, climbing, or any aerobic activity   12. end diastolic volume (EDV)   13. end systolic volume (ESV)   14. preload   15. cross–bridge   16. force   17. venous blood   18. ventricles

10. 1. Increased force of heart beat that is independent of EDV.   2. Sympathetic nervous system activation; thyroxine; epinephrine.   3. Exercise enhances the effectiveness of the respiratory and skeletal muscle "pumps" and activates the sympathetic nervous system.

11. Check 1, 2, 4, 5, 6, 8, 9, 10, 13, 15, 19

12. 1. sympathetic   2. T   3. increases   4. high   5. fetal   6. resting heart rate   7. systolic   8. left   9. T   10. T   11. T

13. 1.H   2. D   3. G   4. C   5. B   6. E   7. J   8. F   9. A   10. I

14. 1. D   2. A   3. C   4. B   5. E

CHALLENGING YOURSELF

At the Clinic

1. Cardiac tamponade; compression of the heart by excess pericardial fluid reduces the space for ventricular activity and impairs ventricular filling.

2. Mitral valve prolapse; valve replacement.

3. Myocarditis caused by the strep infection.

4. Valvular stenosis; heart murmur will be high-pitched during systole.

5. Angina pectoris.

6. Complete heart block; conduction pathway between SA node and AV node is damaged.

7. An MI is an area of dead cardiac muscle that may have been replaced by scar tissue. A clot lodged in a coronary vessel is the usual cause. Since part of the conduction pathway is obliterated by an MI, it takes longer to depolarize the heart and disturb its rhythm.

8. Zero; myocardial infarction. The posterior interventricular artery supplies much of the left ventricle, the systemic pump.

9. Bradycardia, which results from excessive vagal stimulation of the heart, can be determined by taking pulse.

10. Peripheral congestion due to right heart failure.

11. BP measurement: A high blood pressure may hint that the patient has hypertensive heart disease; when BP is chronically elevated, the heart has to work harder. Blood lipid and cholesterol levels: High levels of triglycerides and cholesterol are risk factors for coronary heart disease. Electrocardiogram: Will indicate if the pacing and electrical events of the heart are abnormal. Chest X ray: Will reveal if the heart is enlarged or abnormally located in the thorax.

12. A defective valve would be detected during auscultation. Since the valve flaps are not electrically excitable, an ECG does not reveal a valvular problem.

Stop and Think

1. They will not be compressed when the ventricles contract, as are the vessels within the myocardium.

2. Contraction from the top down is like squeezing a tube of toothpaste from the bottom up. The blood is moved in the direction of the outflow at the AV valves. Ventricles contract from the bottom up, due to the arrangement of the conduction system, from apex up the lateral walls. This also moves blood toward the valves but, in this case, against the pull of gravity.

3. Referred pain from damage to the heart is felt in the left chest and radiates down the medial side of the left arm to the fifth digit in severe cases.

4. Prolonged contraction of the myocardium allows sufficient tension to build to overcome the inertia of the blood and actually move the fluid out of the chambers.

5. It takes about one minute, the time it takes for the entire blood volume to circulate through the heart/body.

6. With exercise, blood flow to the myocardium is maintained and expanded, and the heart becomes stronger and more efficient. With CHP, myocardial blood flow is diminished, and the heart weakens. A healthy heart attains sufficient ventricular pressure to provide sufficient stroke volume with a reduced heart rate. The weakened, congested heart is thin-walled and flabby and cannot exert sufficient force to eject much blood during ventricular systole, hence heart rate often increases.

7. Hypothyroidism leads to reduced heart rate.

8. The flap over the foramen ovale acts as a valve, preventing backflow from the left atrium to the right atrium. The groove channels blood from the inferior vena cava to the left atrium (via the foramen ovale), providing the systemic circulation with most of the freshly oxygenated blood.

9. Exercise increases heart rate only during the period of increased activity; during rest (which is most of the time), the heart rate decreases as a result of regular exercise. If the resting heart rate drops from 80 to 60 bpm, and one hour of exercise a day causes heart rate to be elevated to 180 bpm, the net change in number of heart beats per day can be calculated as follows:

Sedentary: 80 bpm x 60 mm/hr x 24 hr/day = 115, 200 beats/day

Exerciser: 60 bpm x 60 mm/hr x 23 hr/day +
180 bpm x 60 mm/hr x 1 hr/day = 93, 600 beats/day

As you can see, an "exerciser" gains, not loses, time.

COVERING ALL YOUR BASES

Multiple Choice

1. D   2. A, D   3. A, D   4. A, B, C, D   5. A, B, D   6. C   7. A, D   8. A, C   9. A   10. C, D   11. A, C, D   12. A, D   13. C   14. C   15. C   16. D   17. C   18. B, D   19. C   20. A, C   21. D   22. B   23. B   24. A, D   25. C   26. A, B, C   27. A, B, C, D   28. B   29. B   30. A, C, D   31. D   32. B   33. B   34. A, B, C

WORD DISSECTION

	Word root	Translation	Example		Word root	Translation	Example
1.	angina	choked	angina pectoris	8.	ectop	displaced	ectopic focus
2.	baro	pressure	baroreceptor	9.	intercal	insert	intercalated disc
3.	brady	slow	bradycardia	10.	pectin	comb	pectinate muscle
4.	carneo	flesh	trabeculae carneae	11.	sino	hollow	sinoatrial node
5.	cusp	pointed	tricuspid valve	12.	stenos	narrow	mitral stenosis
6.	diastol	stand apart	diastole	13.	systol	contract	systole
7.	dicro	forked	dicrotic notch	14.	tachy	fast	tachycardia

Chapter 18 The Cardiovascular System: Blood Vessels and Circulation

[L1] Multiple Choice

1. A   2. D   3. B   4. C   5. A   6. D   7. B   8. D   9. C   10. A   11. D   12. C   13. D   14. B   15. B   16. A   17. D   18. C   19. A   20. B   21. A   22. D   23. A   24. C   25. C   26. C   27. A   28. C   29. B   30. C   31. D   32. B   33. C   34. D   35. B   36. A   37. D   38. C   39. A   40. C   41. B   42. B   43. D   44. B   45. C

[L1] Completion

1. arterioles   2. venules   3. fenestrated   4. precapillary sphincter   5. viscosity   6. pulse pressure   7. sphygmomanometer   8. circulatory pressure   9. total peripheral resistance   10. vasomotion   11. hydrostatic pressure   12. osmotic pressure   13. autoregulation   14. vasodilators   15. vasoconstriction   16. thoracoabdominal pump   17. shock   18. central ischemic   19. hepatic portal system   20. femoral artery   21. anastomoses   22. aortic arch   23. right atrium   24. foramen ovale   25. oxygen levels   26. arteriosclerosis

[L1] Matching

1. I   2. G   3. E   4. B   5. M   6. J   7. D   8. F   9. H   10. A   11. L   12. K   13. C   14. R   15. T   16. X   17. AA   18. N   19. W   20. O   21. Q   22. BB   23. U   24. Y   25. P   26. V   27. Z   28. S

[L1] Drawing/Illustration Labeling

Figure 18.1 The Arterial System

1. brachiocephalic   2. aortic arch   3. ascending aorta   4. abdominal aorta   5. common iliac   6. internal iliac   7. external iliac   8. deep femoral   9. common carotid   10. descending aorta   11. subclavian   12. axillary   13. brachial   14. thoracic aorta   15. celiac   16. renal   17. superior mesenteric   18. gonadal   19. radial   20. inferior mesenteric   21. ulnar   22. femoral   23. popliteal   24. anterior tibial   25. posterior tibial   26. peroneal   27. dorsalis pedis   28. plantar anastomoses

Figure 18.2 The Venous System

1. subclavian   2. axillary   3. brachial   4. cephalic   5. basilic   6. inferior vena cava   7. median cubital   8. accessory cephalic   9. cephalic   10. median antebrachial   11. basilic   12. palmar venous network   13. internal jugular   14. external jugular   15. brachiocephalic   16. superior vena cava   17. intercostals   18. left suprarenal   19. renal   20. gonadal   21. lumbar   22. common iliac   23. internal iliac   24. external iliac   25. deep femoral   26. femoral   27. great saphenous   28. popliteal   29. posterior tibial   30. small saphenous   31. anterior tibial   32. peroneal   33. plantar venous network

Figure 18.3 Major Arteries of the Head and Neck

1. superficial temporal artery   2. circle of Willis   3. posterior cerebral arteries   4. basilar artery   5. internal carotid artery   6. vertebral artery   7. thyrocervical trunk   8. subclavian artery   9. internal thoracic artery   10. anterior cerebral arteries   11. maxillary artery   12. facial artery   13. external carotid artery   14. carotid sinus   15. common carotid artery   16. brachiocephalic artery

Figure 18.4 Major Veins Draining the Head and Neck

1. superior sagittal sinus   2. straight sinus   3. transverse sinus   4. vertebral vein   5. external jugular vein   6. temporal vein   7. maxillary vein   8. facial vein   9. internal jugular vein   10. brachiocephalic vein   11. internal thoracic vein

[L2] Concept Maps

I The Cardiovascular System

1. pulmonary veins   2. arteries and arterioles   3. veins and venules   4. pulmonary arteries   5. systemic circuit

II Endocrine System and Cardiovascular Regulation

6. epinephrine, norepinephrine   7. adrenal cortex   8. increasing blood pressure   9. ADH (vasopressin)   10. increasing plasma volume   11. kidneys   12. increasing fluid   13. erythropoietin   14. atrial natriuretic factor

III Arteriolar Constriction

15. hyperemia   16. reactive   17. ADH (vasopressin)   18. epinephrine   19. vasomotor center   20. vasoconstriction   21. vasodilation

IV ANF Effects on Blood Volume and Blood Pressure

22. increasing H_2O loss by kidneys   23. decreasing H_2O intake   24. decreasing blood pressure   25. increasing blood flow (l/min)

V Major Branches of the Aorta

26. ascending aorta   27. brachiocephalic artery   28. L. subclavian artery   29. thoracic artery   30. celiac trunk   31. superior mesenteric artery   32. R. gonadal artery   33. L. common iliac artery

VI Major Veins Draining into the Superior and Inferior Venae Cavae

34. superior vena cava   35. azygous vein   36. L. hepatic veins   37. R. suprarenal vein   38. L. renal vein   39. L. common iliac vein

[L2] Body Trek

1. aortic valve   2. aortic arch   3. descending aorta   4. brachiocephalic   5. L. common carotid   6. L. subclavian   7. thoracic aorta   8. mediastinum   9. intercostal   10. superior phrenic   11. abdominal aorta   12. inferior phrenic   13. celiac   14. suprarenal   15. renal   16. superior mesenteric   17. gonadal   18. inferior mesenteric   19. lumbar   20. common iliacs

[L2] Multiple Choice

1. B   2. D   3. D   4. C   5. D   6. B   7. C   8. A   9. C   10. D   11. A   12. C   13. D   14. A   15. C   16. D   17. B   18. D   19. B   20. A   21. D   22. C   23. B   24. A   25. B

[L2] COMPLETION

1. circle of Willis   2. elastic rebound   3. recall of fluids   4. edema   5. precapillary sphincters   6. reactive hyperemia   7. endothelium   8. mesoderm   9. veins   10. venous return   11. aorta   12. brachial   13. radial   14. great saphenous   15. lumen

[L2] SHORT ESSAY

1. tunica interna, tunica media, tunica externa

2. heart → arteries → arterioles → capillaries (gas exchange area) → venules → veins → heart

3. (a) Sinusoids are specialized fenestrated capillaries.

   (b) They are found in the liver, bone marrow, and the adrenal glands.

   (c) They form fattened, irregular passageways, so blood flows through the tissues slowly maximizing time for absorption and secretion and molecular exchange.

4. In the pulmonary circuit, oxygen stores are replenished, carbon dioxide is excreted, and the "reoxygenated" blood is returned to the heart for distribution in the systemic circuit.

The systemic circuit supplies the capillary beds in all parts of the body with oxygenated blood, and returns deoxygenated blood to the heart of the pulmonary circuit for removal of carbon dioxide.

5. (a) vascular resistance, viscosity, turbulence

(b) Only vascular resistance can be adjusted by the nervous and endocrine systems.

6. $F = \dfrac{BP}{PR}$

Flow is directly proportional to the blood pressure and inversely proportional to peripheral resistance; i.e., increasing pressure, increasing flow; decreasing pressure, decreasing flow; increasing PR, decreasing flow; decreasing PR, increasing flow.

7. $\dfrac{120 \text{ mm Hg}}{80 \text{ mm Hg}}$ is a "normal" blood pressure reading.

The top number, 120 mm Hg, is the *systolic* pressure, i.e., the peak blood pressure measured during ventricular systole.

The bottom number, 80 mm Hg, is the *diastolic* pressure, i.e., the minimum blood pressure at the end of ventricular diastole.

8. MAP = 1/3 pulse pressure (p.p.) + diastolic pressure

Therefore, p.p. = 110 mm Hg – 80 mm Hg = 30 mm Hg

MAP = 1/3 (.30) = 10 + 80 mm Hg

MAP = 90 mm Hg

9. (a) Distributes nutrients, hormones, and dissolved gases throughout tissues.

(b) Transports insoluble lipids and tissue proteins that cannot enter circulation by crossing capillary linings.

(c) Speeds removal of hormones and carries bacterial toxins and other chemical stimuli to cells of the immune system.

10. Cardiac output, blood volume, peripheral resistance.

11. Aortic baroreceptors, carotid sinus baroreceptors, atrial baroreceptors.

12. Epinephrine and norepinephrine, ADH, angiotensin II, erythropoietin, and atrial natriuretic peptide.

13. Decreasing hematocrit, venous thrombosus, pulmonary embolism, increasing pulmonary blood pressure, pooling of blood in the veins, edema.

14. Arteries lose their elasticity, the amount of smooth muscle they contain decreases, and they become stiff and relatively inflexible.

[L3] Critical Thinking/Application

1. L. ventricle → aortic arch → L. subclavian artery → axillary artery → brachial artery → radial and ulnar arteries → palm and wrist arterial anastomoses → digital arteries → digital veins → palm and wrist venous anastomoses → cephalic and basilic veins → radius and ulnar veins → brachial vein → axillary vein → L. subclavian vein → brachiocephalic vein → superior vena cava → R. atrium

2. (a) superficial temporal artery

(b) common carotid artery

(c) facial artery

(d) axillary artery

(e) brachial artery

(f) femoral artery

(g) popliteal artery

(h) dorsalis pedis artery

3. When a person rises rapidly from a lying position, a drop in blood pressure in the neck and thoracic regions occurs because of the pull of gravity on the blood. Owing to the sudden decrease in blood pressure, the blood flow to the brain is reduced enough to cause dizziness or loss of consciousness.

4. By applying pressure on the carotid artery at frequent intervals during exercise, the pressure to the region of the carotid sinus may be sufficient to stimulate the baroreceptors. The increased action potentials from the baroreceptors initiate reflexes in parasympathetic impulses to the heart, causing a decrease in the heart rate.

5. During exercise the following changes and benefits occur:

   (a) increased blood flow to tissues, supplying O_2 and nutrients, removing wastes

   (b) increased blood flow to skin—thermoregulatory—gets rid of excess heat in the body

   (c) increased venous return due to skeletal muscle movement and the thoracoabdominal pump

   (d) decreased oxygen tension resulting from increased muscular activity

   (e) increased blood pressure

   (f) increased skeletal blood vessel dilation

   (g) increased sympathetic stimulation to the heart—increased cardiac output

   (h) increased sympathetic innervation—this causes vasoconstriction in blood vessels of skin and viscera, shunting blood to skeletal muscles

   (i) increased vasodilation of capillaries because of presence of CO_2, K^+, and lactic acid

Chapter 19 The Cardiovascular System: Blood

BUILDING THE FRAMEWORK

Overview of Blood Vessel Structure and Function

1. 1. femoral artery   2. brachial artery   3. popliteal artery   4. facial artery   5. radial artery   6. posterior tibial artery   7. temporal artery   8. dorsalis pedis

2. 1. A   2. B   3. A   4. A   5. C   6. B   7. C   8. A
   A. artery; relatively thick media; small round lumen   B. vein; (relatively) thin media; and large lumen; valves
   C. capillary; single layer of endothelium

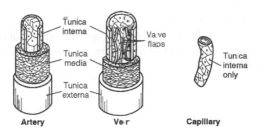

Figure 19.1

3. 1. A   2. E   3. G   4. B   5. C   6. D   7. F   8. H   9. K   10. I   11. J

4. Arterial anastomoses provide alternate pathways for blood to reach a given organ. If one branch is blocked, an alternate branch can still supply the organ.

5.

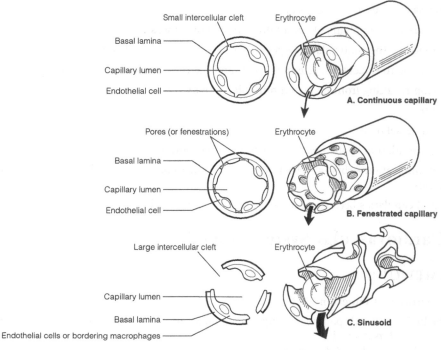

Figure 19.2

6. 1. Muscular   2. Pressure points   3. Heart   4. Gap junctions   5. Kidney   6. High pressure   7. End arteries   8. Thick media   9. True capillaries

7. The venous valves prevent backflow of blood.

8. Veins have large lumens and thin walls and can hold large volumes of blood. At any time, up to 65% of total blood volume can be contained in veins. These reservoirs are most abundant in the skin and visceral organs (particularly the digestive viscera).

Physiology of Circulation

1. 1. Blood Flow = difference in blood pressure ÷ resistance

hematocrit ⟶ blood viscosity
+
vessel length
+
atherosclerosis ⟶ (−) vessel diameter
vasoconstriction

2. Blood pressure = cardiac output × peripheral resistance

blood volume ⟶ stroke volume   vasoconstriction
+   +
excessive   heart rate   polycythemia
salt intake

2. When the heart contracts, blood is forced into the large arteries, stretching the elastic tissue in the artery walls. During diastole, the artery walls recoil against the blood, maintaining continuous pressure and blood flow.

3. 1. H   2. B   3. C   4. D   5. J   6. E   7. A   8. G (A)   9. I

4. 1. D   2. I   3. I   4. I   5. I   6. D   7. D   8. I   9. D   10. D   11. D   12. I   13. I   14. D   15. I   16. I   17. D   18. I   19. I   20. D   21. I   22. I   23. I

5. 1. Cardiac output   2. Blood flow   3. Low viscosity   4. Blood pressure   5. High blood pressure   6. Vasodilation   7. Vein   8. 120 mm Hg   9. Cardiac cycle   10. Inactivity   11. Sympathetic activity

6. 1. increase   2. orthostatic   3. brain   4. stethoscope   5. low   6. vasoconstricting   7. hypertension   8. arterioles   9. medulla/brain   10. T   11. reduction   12. vasoconstriction   13. blood vessel length   14. capillaries   15. arterial system   16. autoregulation   17. T

7. 1. interstitial fluid   2. concentration gradient (via diffusion)   3. fat-soluble substances like fats and gases   4. water and water-soluble substances like sugars and amino acids   5. through the metarteriole-thoroughfare channels   6. A   7. capillary blood   8. capillary hydrostatic (blood) pressure (Hp$_c$)   9. blood pressure   10. capillary colloid osmotic pressure (Op$_c$)   11. albumin   12. at the arterial end   13. It is picked up by lymphatic vessels for return to the bloodstream.   14. capillary hydrostatic (blood) pressure

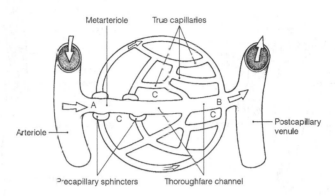

Figure 19.3

8. Hypovolemic shock is a decrease in total blood volume, as from acute hemorrhage. Increased heart rate and vaso-constriction result. In vascular shock, blood volume is normal, but pronounced vasodilation expands the vascular bed, resistance decreases, and blood pressure falls. A common cause of vascular shock is bacterial infection.

9. 1. capillaries   2. arteries   3. capillaries   4. arteries   5 veins

10. 1. F   2. A   3. D   4. B   5. A   6. D   7. C   8. E   9. B   10. D   11. C   12. A   13. A   14. A   15. F   16. E   17. E

Circulatory Pathways: Blood Vessels of the Body

1. The right atrium and ventricle and all vessels with "pulmonary" in their name should be colored blue; the left atrium and ventricle and the aortic arch and lobar arteries should be colored red.

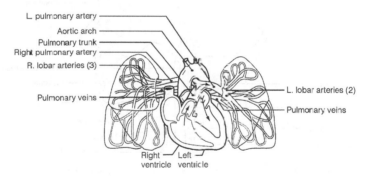

Figure 19.4

2.

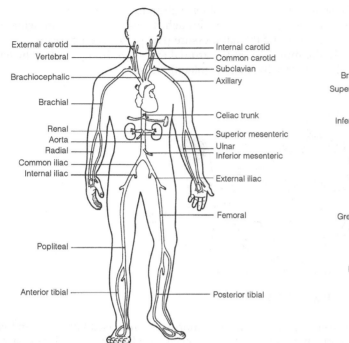

Figure 19.5 Arteries

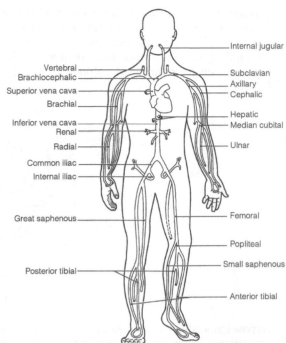

Figure 19.6 Veins

3.

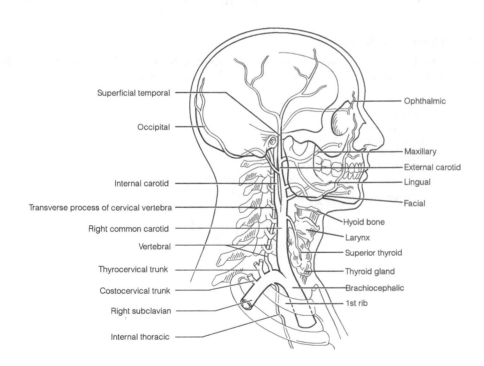

Figure 19.7 Arteries of the head and neck

4. 1. F 2. C, D 3. A The circle of Willis consists of the communicating arteries and those parts of the cerebral arteries that complete the arterial anastomosis around the pituitary.

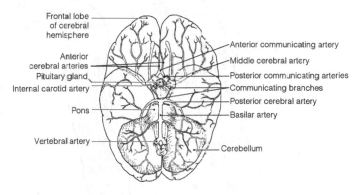

Figure 19.8

5. 1. F 2. W 3. H 4. P 5. Y 6. B 7. J 8. I 9. S 10. C 11. C 12. N 13. Q 14. L 15. C
16. X 17. G 18. E 19. K 20.–22. A, R, T 23. U

6.

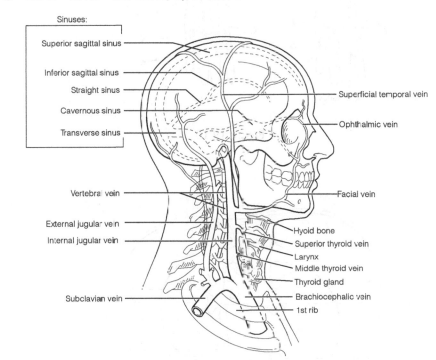

Figure 19.9 Veins of the head and neck

7.

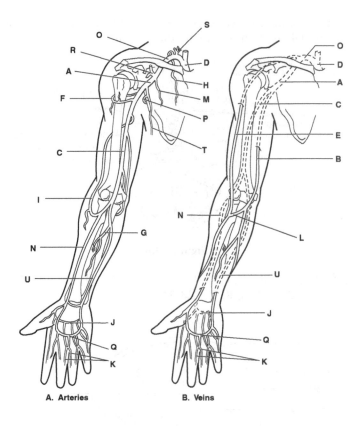

A. Arteries   B. Veins

Figure 19.10

8.

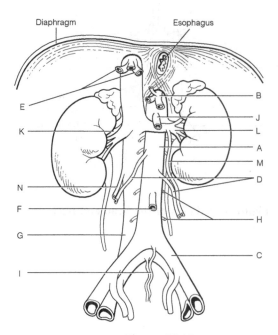

Figure 19.11

9.

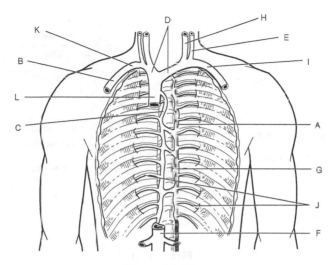

Figure 19.12

10.

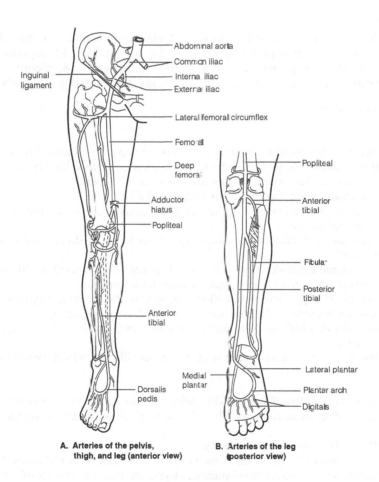

Figure 19.13

11.

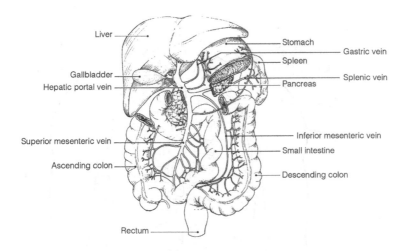

Figure 19.14

12. 1. S 2. X 3. U 4. E 5. T 6. Q 7. D 8. A 9. R 10. M 11. F 12. J 13. B 14. O 15. L
16.–18. I, N, V 19. K 20. G 21. H

The Incredible Journey

1. 1. left atrium 2. left ventricle 3. mitral (bicuspid) 4. chordae tendineae 5. diastole 6. systole/contraction
7. aortic semilunar 8. aorta 9. superior mesenteric 10. endothelial 11. superior mesenteric vein
12. splenic 13. nutrients 14. phagocytic (van Kupffer) 15. hepatic 16. inferior vena cava 17. right
atrium 18. pulmonary 19. lungs 20. capillaries 21. gas (O_2 and CO_2) 22. subclavian

CHALLENGING YOURSELF

At the Clinic

1. The veins, particularly the superficial saphenous veins, become very prominent and tortuous. Typically it is due
to failure of the venous valves. The problem here is the restriction of blood flow by her enlarged uterus during her
many pregnancies. Elevate the legs whenever possible; avoid standing still.
2. Thrombosis, atherosclerosis; arterial anastomosis (circle of Willis).
3. High; polycythemia increases blood viscosity (thus peripheral resistance), which increases blood pressure.
4. Hypovolemic shock due to blood loss.
5. Loss of vasomotor tone due to damage to the vasomotor center in the medulla could cause extreme vasodilation,
resulting in vascular shock.
6. Chronically elevated; chronic hypersecretion of ADH will trigger vasoconstriction (due to the vasopressin effect)
and excessive water retention, both of which increase peripheral resistance.
7. Occlusion of the renal blood supply will reduce blood pressure in the kidneys, triggering the release of renin,
which in turn precipitates activation of angiotensin, a powerful vasoconstrictor.
8. Nicotine is a vasoconstrictor; a high dose of nicotine in a body not accustomed to it can reduce blood flow to the
brain and cause dizziness.
9. Septicemia; blood-borne bacterial toxins trigger widespread vasodilation, which causes blood pressure to plummet
(vascular shock).
10. Cardiogenic shock.
11. The dorsalis pedis pulse is the most distal palpable pulse. Chances are if his popliteal and pedal pulses are strong,
his right limb is getting adequate circulation. Also, the skin will be warm and *non*cyanotic if the blood supply is
adequate.
12. Pulse pressure = 20 mm Hg; low; loss of elasticity.
13. Beta blockers prevent the effect of epinephrine, which constricts the arterioles and raises the blood pressure. Diuretics increase urine output, which reduces blood volume. Hence, the treatment will result in lower blood pressure.
14. His fears are unfounded because there is no artery in the exact middle of the anterior forearm. Most likely the
median vein of the forearm has been cut, but it is still a fairly small superficial vein and venous bleeding is much
slower than arterial bleeding.

Stop and Think

1. A thin layer is sufficient to withstand the frictional forces of the blood. A thicker layer would reduce the size of the lumen and require more nutrients to maintain it.
2. Decrease; vasoconstriction increases resistance, which decreases blood flow.
3. Open; all true capillaries will be flushed with blood. In the face exposed to cold, the capillary networks are closed off. The cells deplete oxygen and nutrients, and waste products build up. Precapillary sphincters relax, but no blood flows to the capillaries since the supplying arteriole is closed off. In warm air, the arterioles vasodilate, and blood flows into all the capillaries.
4. In a warm room, the skin capillaries are flushed with blood, which helps lose heat from the body. Rerouting blood to the head takes longer in this circumstance than in a cold room, in which many skin capillary beds are being bypassed by the metarteriole-thoroughfare channel shunts.
5. Pressure of the fetus on the inferior vena cava will reduce the return of blood from the lower torso and lower limbs.
6. Pericardial sac.
7. Organs supplied by end arteries have no collateral circulation. If the supplying end artery is blocked, no other circulatory route is available.
8. Formation of new tissues (adipose, muscle).
9. Vertebral arteries to basilar artery to posterior cerebral artery to posterior communicating artery to R. internal carotid artery beyond the blockage (hopefully).
10. Reduced plasma proteins (particularly albumin) will reduce the osmotic pressure of the blood. Consequently, less fluid will be drawn back at the venous end of capillaries, and edema will result.
11. Decreased cardiac output would reduce blood pressure to the brain. If compensatory mechanisms are inadequate to maintain blood supply to the vasomotor center, vasomotor tone will be reduced. The resulting vasodilation will cause vascular shock, which will reduce venous return to the heart. This will lead to even lower cardiac output, which will further diminish blood delivery to the vasomotor center.
12. An aneurysm is a ballooned-out and weakened area in a blood vessel. The primary problem in all cases is that it might rupture and cause a fatal stroke. The second problem in the patient discussed here is that the enlarged vessel is pressing on brain tissue and nerves. Since neural tissue is very fragile, it is susceptible to irreversible damage from physical trauma as well as from deprivation of a blood supply (another possible consequence of the compression of nervous tissue). Surgery was done to replace the weakened region of the vessel with inert plastic tubing.
13. There is no "great choice" to make here. Try to compress the subclavian artery that runs just deep to the clavicle by forcing your fingers inferiorly just posterior to the clavicular midline and lateral to the sternocleidomastoid muscle. Blockage of the subclavian artery would prevent the blood from reaching the axilla.
14. Erythrocytes are 7–8 μm in diameter, thus five of them side by side would measure a lumen diameter of 35–40 μm (the approximate size of the observed vessel). Since the average capillary is 8–10 μm, one erythrocyte would just about fill a capillary's entire lumen. Hence, the vessel is most likely a postcapillary venule.

COVERING ALL YOUR BASES

Multiple Choice

1. A, B, C 2. A, B, C, D 3. A, C 4. A, B 5. C 6. B 7. A, B, C, D 8. B, C 9. B, D 10. C 11. A, B, C
12. B, C, D 13. C, D 14. A, B, D 15. A, B, C, D 16. D 17. B, C, D 18. B 19. A, B, D 20. A, C
21. A, B, C, D 22. C 23. A, C, D 24. B 25. A 26. A, B, C, D 27. A, B, C 28. A, B 29. C
30. A, B, C 31. D 32. A 33. C 34. B 35. D 36. D

WORD DISSECTION

	Word root	Translation	Example		Word root	Translation	Example
1.	anastomos	coming together	anastomoses	11.	epiplo	membrane	epiploic artery
2.	angio	vessel	angiogram	12.	fenestr	window	fenestrated capillary
3.	aort	great artery	aorta	13.	jugul	throat	jugular vein
4.	athera	gruel	atherosclerosis	14.	ortho	straight	orthostatic hypotension
5.	auscult	listen	auscultation				
6.	azyg	unpaired	azygos vein	15.	phleb	vein	phlebitis
7.	capill	hair	capillary	16.	saphen	clear, apparent	great saphenous vein
8.	carot	stupor	carotid artery	17.	septi	rotten	septicemia
9.	celia	abdominal	celiac artery	18.	tunic	covering	tunica externa
10.	entero	intestine	mesenteric arteries	19.	vaso	vessel	vasodilation
				20.	viscos	sticky	viscosity

Chapter 20 The Lymphatic System and Immunity

[L1] Multiple Choice

1. D 2. C 3. D 4. C 5. D 6. B 7. A 8. A 9. C 10. C 11. B 12. D 13. D 14. C 15. A
16. A 17. C 18. A 19. C 20. D 21. D 22. A 23. B 24. A 25. B 26. B 27. C 28. A
29. C 30. C 31. A 32. C 33. B 34. D 35. B 36. D 37. D 38. D 39. D 40. D 41. B 42. C

[L1] Completion

1. immunity 2. lymphocytes 3. lacteals 4. cytotoxic T cells 5. antibodies 6. lymph capillaries
7. phagocytes 8. diapedesis 9. interferons 10. passive 11. cell-mediated 12. innate 13. active
14. suppressor T 15. helper T 16. costimulation 17. memory T cells 18. sensitization 19. memory
B cells 20. plasma cells 21. neutralization 22. precipitation 23. haptens 24. immunological competence
25. IgG 26. immunodeficiency disease 27. lymphatic 28. inflammation 29. lymphokines 30. monokines 31. antigens 32. thymic hormones

[L1] Matching

1. G 2. I 3. H 4. K 5. A 6. F 7. D 8. C 9. E 10. L 11. J 12. B 13. Q 14. S 15. Y
16. BB 17. W 18. CC 19. T 20. R 21. X 22. N 23. O 24. AA 25. U 26. M 27. P 28. Z
29. V

[L1] Drawing/Illustration Labeling

Figure 22.1 The Lymphatic System
1. cervical lymph nodes 2. R. lymphatic ducts 3. thymus 4. thoracic duct 5. L. lymphatic duct
6. cisterna chyli 7. spleen

Figure 22.2 The Lymphatic Ducts
1. cervical nodes 2. R. lymphatic duct 3. superior vena cava 4. axillary nodes 5. cisterna chyli 6. para-
aortic nodes 7. inguinal nodes 8. L. subclavian vein 9. thoracic duct

Figure 22.3 Nonspecific Defenses
1. physical barriers 2. phagocytes 3. immunological surveillance 4. complement system 5. inflammatory
response 6. fever 7. interferon

[L2] Concept Maps

I Immune System
1. nonspecific immunity 2. phagocytic cells 3. inflammation 4. specific immunity 5. innate 6. acquired
7. active 8. active immunization 9. transfer of antibodies via placenta 10. passive immunization

II Inflammation Response
11. tissue damage 12. increasing vascular permeability 13. phagocytosis of bacteria 14. tissue repaired
15. bacteria not destroyed

[L2] Body Trek

1. viruses 2. macrophages 3. natural killer cells 4. helper T cells 5. B cells 6. antibodies 7. killer
T cells 8. suppressor T cells 9. memory T and B cells

[L2] Multiple Choice

1. B 2. D 3. C 4. B 5. A 6. C 7. A 8. D 9. D 10. D 11. C 12. B 13. A 14. C 15. D
16. C 17. B 18. C 19. B 20. D

[L2] Completion

1. T cells 2. microglia 3. Kupffer cells 4. Langerhans cells 5. antigen 6. cytokines 7. properdin
8. mast 9. pyrogens 10. opsonins 11. NK cells 12. interferon 13. IgG 14. IgM 15. helper T

[L2] Short Essay

1. (a) lymphatic vessels

   (b) lymph

   (c) lymphatic organs

2. (a) production, maintenance, and distribution of lymphocytes

   (b) maintenance of normal blood volume

   (c) elimination of local variations in the composition of the interstitial fluid

3. (a) T cells (thymus)

   (b) B cells (bone marrow)

    (c) NK cells—natural killer (bone marrow)

4. (a) Cytotoxic T cells—cell-mediated immunity

    (b) Helper T cells—release lymphokines that coordinate specific and nonspecific defenses

    (c) Suppressor T cells—depress responses of other T cells and B cells

5. Stimulated B cells differentiate into plasma cells that are responsible for production and secretion of antibodies. B cells are said to be responsible for humoral immunity.

6. (a) lymph nodes

    (b) thymus

    (c) spleen

7. (a) physical barriers

    (b) phagocytes

    (c) immunological surveillance

    (d) complement system

    (e) inflammatory response

    (f) fever

8. NK (natural killer) cells are sensitive to the presence of abnormal cell membranes and respond immediately. When the NK cell makes contact with an abnormal cell, it releases secretory vesicles that contain proteins called perforins. The perforins create a network of pores in the target cell membrane, releasing free passage of intracellular materials necessary for homeostasis, thus causing the cell to disintegrate.

T cells and B cells provide defenses against specific threats and their activation requires a relatively complex and time-consuming sequence of events.

9. (a) destruction of target cell membranes

    (b) stimulation of inflammation

    (c) attraction of phagocytes

    (d) enhancement of phagocytosis

10. (a) specificity

    (b) versatility

    (c) memory

    (d) tolerance

11. Active immunity appears following exposure to an antigen as a consequence of the immune response.

Passive immunity is produced by transfer of antibodies from another individual.

12. (a) direct attack by activated T cells (cellular immunity)

    (b) attack by circulating antibodies released by plasma cells derived from activated B cells (humoral immunity)

13. (a) neutralization

    (b) agglutination and precipitation

    (c) activation of complement

    (d) attraction of phagocytes

    (e) opsonization

    (f) stimulation of inflammation

    (g) prevention of bacterial and viral adhesion

14. (a) IgG (b) IgE (c) IgD (d) IgM (e) IgA

15. (a) interleukins

    (b) interferons

    (c) tumor necrosis factor

    (d) chemicals that regulate phagocytic activity

16. Autoimmune disorders develop when the immune response mistakenly targets normal body cells and tissues. When the immune recognition system malfunctions, activated B cells begin to manufacture antibodies against other cells and tissues.

[L3] Critical Thinking/Application

1. Tissue transplants normally contain protein molecules called human lymphocyte antigen (HLA) genes that are foreign to the recipient. These antigens trigger the recipient's immune responses, activating the cellular and humoral mediated responses that may act to destroy the donated tissue.

2.

```
                        ┌────────── Specific antigen ──────────┐
                        ▼                                       ▼
                 T lymphocytes                           B lymphocytes
                        │          (Mitosis)                    │
                        ▼                                       ▼
            ┌──── Daughter cells ────┐           ┌──── Daughter cells ────┐
            ▼                        ▼           ▼                        ▼
      Memory T cells        Activated T cells ──Helper──▶ Plasma cells    Memory B cells
                                   │             "T"          │
                                   ▼                          ▼
                              Lymphokines              Immunoglobulins
                                   │                          │
                                   ▼                          ▼
                             Cell mediated            Antibody mediated
                             immunity via             immunity via
                             cytotoxic T-cells        antibodies
```

3. Neutrophils are leukocytes that comprise 50 to 70 percent of the circulating WBC population. Neutrophils are highly mobile and are usually the first white blood cells to arrive at an injury site. They are very active phagocytes specializing in attacking and digesting bacteria. Because their "weaponry" includes defenses and they are phagocytic specialists, they can segregate the microbe in a tiny fat-covered sac that merges with a pocket of defensins. The defensins pierce the membranes of the microbe, killing it by causing the intracellular components to leak out of the intruding microbe. Defensins provide additional weaponry for the body's immunological surveillance system similar to the NK cells and the action of perforins.

4. They are classified as infectious agents because they can enter cells and replicate themselves. Viruses contain a core of nucleic acid (DNA or RNA) surrounded by a protein coat. When a virus infects a cell, its nucleic acid enters the nucleus of the host and takes over the cell's metabolic machinery. The viral DNA replicates, forms new viruses, and causes the host's cell membrane to rupture or lyse, causing a disruption in normal cell function.

5. Viruses reproduce inside living cells, beyond the reach of lymphocytes. Infected cells incorporate viral antigens into their cell membranes. NK cells recognize these infected cells as abnormal. By destroying virally infected cells, NK cells slow or prevent the spread of viral infection.

6. High body temperatures may inhibit some viruses and bacteria, or may speed up their reproductive rates so that the disease runs its course more rapidly. The body's metabolic processes are accelerated, which may help mobilize tissue defenses and speed the repair process.

7. During times of stress the body responds by increasing the activity of the adrenal glands, which may cause a decrease in the inflammatory response, reduce the activities and numbers of phagocytes in peripheral tissues, and inhibit interleukin secretion. "Stress reduction" may cause a decrease in the adrenal gland secretions and maintain homeostatic control of the immune response.

Chapter 21 The Respiratory System

BUILDING THE FRAMEWORK

Functional Anatomy of the Respiratory System

1. pulmonary ventilation, external respiration, transport of respiratory gases, and internal respiration

2. 1. respiratory bronchioles, alveolar ducts, and alveoli   2. gas exchange   3. nasal cavity, pharynx, larynx, trachea, bronchi, and all of their branches except those of the respiratory zone

3. Nose: external nares → middle meatus → internal nares

    ↓

    Pharynx: nasopharynx → adenoids → oropharynx → laryngopharynx

    ↓

    Larynx: epiglottis → vocal folds

    ↓

    Trachea: → carina → primary bronchi

4.

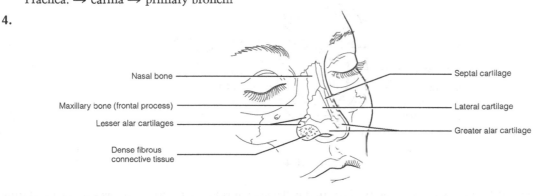

Nasal bone

Maxillary bone (frontal process)

Lesser alar cartilages

Dense fibrous connective tissue

Septal cartilage

Lateral cartilage

Greater alar cartilage

Figure 21.1

5. Note that the frontal and sphenoidal sinuses should be colored with the same color. Likewise, the subdivisions of the pharynx (the nasopharynx, oropharynx, and laryngopharynx) should be identified visually with a single color.

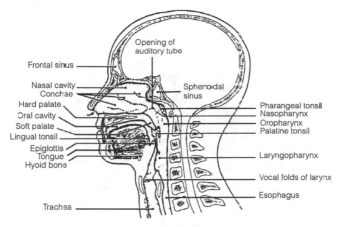

Opening of auditory tube

Frontal sinus

Nasal cavity

Conchae

Hard palate

Oral cavity

Soft palate

Lingual tonsil

Epiglottis

Tongue

Hyoid bone

Trachea

Sphenoidal sinus

Pharangeal tonsil

Nasopharynx

Oropharynx

Palatine tonsil

Laryngopharynx

Vocal folds of larynx

Esophagus

Figure 21.2

6. 1. external nares   2. nasal septum   3.–5. (in any order) warm; moisten; trap debris in   6. paranasal sinuses   7. speech   8. pharynx   9. larynx   10. tonsils

7. 1. Mandibular   2. Alveolus   3. Larynx   4. Peritonitis   5. Nasal septum   6. Choanae   7. Tracheal cartilage   8. Nasopharynx

8. 1. Provides a patent airway; serves as a switching mechanism to route food into the posterior esophagus; voice production location (contains vocal cords).   2. arytenoid cartilages   3. elastic   4. hyaline   5. The epiglottis has to be flexible to be able to flap over the glottis during swallowing. The more rigid hyaline cartilages support the walls of the larynx.   6. Adam's apple

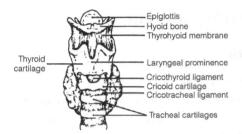

Figure 21.3

9.   1.B   2.G   3.I   4.E   5.D   6.K   7.A   8.H   9.L   10.F   11.C   12.O   13.N   14.K

10.   1. vocal folds (true vocal cords)   2. speak   3. glottis   4. intrinsic laryngeal   5. arytenoid   6. higher   7. wide   8. louder   9. laryngitis

11.

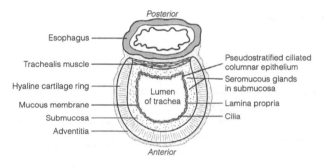

Figure 21.4

1. The C-shaped cartilage rings prevent the trachea from collapsing during the pressure changes occurring during breathing.   2. Allows the esophagus to expand anteriorly when we swallow food or fluids.   3. It constricts the tracheal lumen, causing air to be expelled with more force—coughing, yelling.

12.   1.B   2.B   3.A   4.B   5.E   6.C

13.   1.C   2.D   3.E   4.A   5.B

14.

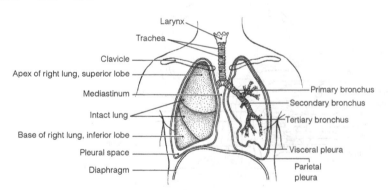

Figure 21.5

15.

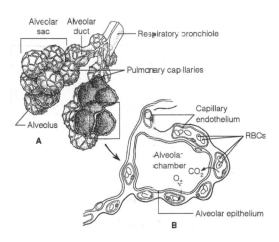

Figure 21.6

16. 1. elastic connective   2. type I   3. gas exchange   4. type II   5. surfactant   6. decrease the surface tension   7. bronchial

Mechanics of Breathing

1. 1. C   2. A   3. B   4. B   5. C   6. B   7. B

2. When the diaphragm is contracted, the internal volume of the thorax increases, the internal pressure in the thorax decreases, the size of the lungs increases, and the direction of air flow is into the lungs. When the diaphragm is relaxed, the internal volume of the thorax decreases, the internal pressure in the thorax increases, the size of the lungs decreases, and the direction of air flow is out of the lungs.

3. 1. D   2. A   3. C   4. B   5. D   6. C   7. B   8. A   9. A

4. 1. scalenes, sternocleidomastoids, pectorals   2. obliques and transversus muscles   3. internal intercostals and latissimus dorsi

5.

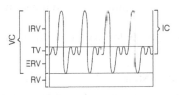

Figure 21.7

6. Check 1, 3, 5.

7. 1. E   2. A   3. G   4. D   5. B   6. F

8. 1. spirometer   2. obstructive pulmonary disease   3. restrictive disorders   4. FEV or forced expiratory volume   5. FVC or forced vital capacity

9. 1. hiccup   2. cough   3. sneeze

Gas Exchanges in the Body

1. 1. B   2. A   3. C

2. Hyperbaric oxygen; Henry's law.

3. Mechanism: generation of free radicals; consequences: CNS disturbances, coma, death.

4. 1. C   2. B   3. E   4. A   5. D

5. 1. 4   2. 5   3. 3   4. 2   5. 1   6. 2   7. 1   8. 3   9. 4   10. 5   11. 1   12. 2   13. 2   14. 1

6. 1. F   2. G   3. H   4. B   5. E   6. J   7. D   8. C   9. I

7. 1. low   2. constrict   3. high   4. dilate

Transport of Respiratory Gases by Blood

1. 1. hemoglobin   2. plasma   3. bicarbonate ion   4. carbonic anhydrase   5. chloride ions   6. chloride shift   7. carbamino Hb   8. Haldane effect   9. more   10. hemoglobin   11. Bohr effect   12. oxygen

2. high P_{O_2} of blood; low temperature; alkalosis; low levels of 2,3-BPG

3. 1. Hb can still be nearly completely saturated at lower atmospheric P_{O_2} or in those with respiratory disease.
2. Much more oxygen can be unloaded to the tissues without requiring cardiovascular or respiratory system adjustments to meet increased tissue demands.

4. 1. oxygen-hemoglobin dissociation curve   2. lower pH; higher temperature, increase in BPG

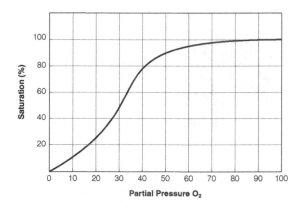

Figure 21.8

5. 1. HbF saturation is greater at a lower Po_2.   2. Po_2 levels are always lower in umbilical (and fetal) blood, and HbF has a greater affinity for O_2 than does HbA.

Control of Respiration

1. 1. A, E   2. C, D   3. F   4. B   5. D   6. C   7. D   8. E
2. In healthy people, rising CO_2 levels provide the respiratory drive by stimulating medullary centers. In people who retain CO_2, declining O_2 levels provide the respiratory drive; therefore, administering pure oxygen would result in apnea.
3. 1. peripheral   2. peripheral   3. central
4. 1. ↑ pH   2. Hyperventilation   3. ↑ Oxygen   4. ↓ CO_2 in blood   5. N toxicity   6. ↑ Pco_2

Respiratory Adjustments

1. 1. Hyperpnea increases depth of ventilation but not necessarily the rate of ventilation; hyperventilation is deep, and typically rapid, ventilation. Hyperpnea does not lead to significant changes in blood levels of O_2 and CO_2 whereas hyperventilation may result in hypocapnia.   2. Psychic stimuli, cortical motor activation, and proprioceptors.
2. 1. Hyperventilation.   2. Hemoglobin's affinity for oxygen declines so that more oxygen is unloaded to the tissues.   3. Enhanced erythropoiesis.

Homeostatic Imbalances of the Respiratory System

1. 1. A   2. F   3. D   4. G   5. E   6. C   7. B   8. C, E   9. H   10. E   11. J   12. I

The Incredible Journey

1. 1. nasal conchae   2. pharyngeal tonsil   3. nasopharynx   4. mucous   5. vocal fold   6. larynx   7. digestive   8. epiglottis   9. trachea   10. cilia   11. oral cavity   12. primary bronchi   13. left   14. bronchiole   15. alveolus   16. red blood cells   17. red   18. oxygen   19. carbon dioxide   20. cough

CHALLENGING YOURSELF

At the Clinic

1. Atelectasis; the lungs are contained in separate pleural sacs, so only the left lung will collapse.
2. The mucus secreted in the conducting zone will be abnormally thick and difficult to clear. Consequently, the respiratory passageways tend to become blocked and infection is more easily established.
3. The lower oxygen pressure of high altitudes prompts renal secretion of erythropoietin, leading to accelerated RBC production. Len will notice that he will begin to hyperventilate. His minute ventilation will increase by about 2–3 L/min. His arterial Pco_2 will be lower than the normal 40 mm Hg, and his hemoglobin saturation will be only about 67%.
4. Chest surgery causes painful breathing, and many patients try not to cough because the pain can be intense. However, coughing is necessary to clear mucus; if allowed to accumulate, mucus can cause blockage and increase the risk of infection.
5. Inflammation in the alveoli causes fluid to accumulate in the air spaces, which increases the apparent thickness of the respiratory membrane and reduces the lungs' ability to oxygenate the blood.
6. Pleurisy.
7. Stagnant hypoxia.
8. Michael most likely is suffering from carbon monoxide poisoning.
9. Sudden infant death syndrome.

10. Small cell (oat cell) carcinoma.
11. Emphysema; although ventilation is difficult, oxygenation is sufficient, and cyanosis does not occur until late in the disease progress.
12. Chronic bronchitis; smoking inhibits ciliary action.
13. Kyphosis is an exaggerated thoracic curvature which reduces the ability to inflate the lungs fully.
14. Failure of the epiglottis and soft palate to close the respiratory channels completely during swallowing. The former will place the patient at risk for aspiration pneumonia.
15. The baby most likely swallowed the safety pin (babies put everything in their mouths). It is probably in the R. primary bronchus, which is larger in diameter and runs more vertically.
16. Pharyngeal tonsils.

Stop and Think

1. When air is inhaled through the nose, it is warmed by the nasal mucosa. Exhaling through the mouth expels the warmed air, resulting in heat loss.
2. Expired air has a higher partial pressure of oxygen than does alveolar air. Expired air is a mixture of (fresh) air from the dead air space and oxygen-depleted air from the alveoli.
3. a. Normally, during swallowing, the soft palate reflects superiorly to seal the nasopharynx and prevent food or drink from entering the nasal cavity. During giggling, however, this sealing mechanism sometimes fails to operate (because giggling demands that air be forced out of the nostrils), and swallowed fluids may enter the nasal cavity, then exit through the nostrils.
   b. Even though standing on his head, the boy made certain that he swallowed carefully, so that his soft palate correctly sealed the entrance to his nasal cavity. Then, his swallowing muscles directed the milk, against gravity, through his esophagus to the stomach.
4. Because each bronchopulmonary segment is isolated by connective tissue septa and has its own vascular supply.
5. Those in the upper passageways move mucus toward the *esophagus* to be swallowed; those in the lower passageways do *likewise* but in the opposite direction, which prevents mucus from "pooling" in the lungs.
6. The elastin is responsible for the natural elasticity of the lungs, which allows them to recoil passively during expiration.
7. It could be if he was hitting the right spot (just inferior to the rib cage) with a vigorous upward thrust, which would rapidly propel the air out of his lungs upward through the respiratory passageways. (Of course, he might also break a few ribs or rupture his spleen or liver in the process.)
8. The choanae constitute the funnel-shaped junction between the nasal cavities and nasopharynx. The conchae are the mucosa-covered projections protruding medially from the lateral walls of the nasal cavities. The carina is the shield-shaped cartilage at the anteroinferior aspect of the trachea (junction with primary bronchi).

COVERING ALL YOUR BASES

Multiple Choice

1. B, D   2. C   3. B, C, D   4. A   5. B   6. B   7. D   8. D   9. D   10. B   11. B   12. A   13. A, C, D   14. C   15. B, C, D   16. B, C   17. B   18. B, D   19. C   20. B, C, D   21. A, B, C   22. D   23. C   24. C   25. A, D   26. B, C   27. C   28. B, C   29. A, C   30. A, B, D   31. A, D   32. A   33. C   34. A, B   35. A

Word Dissection

	Word root	Translation	Example		Word root	Translation	Example
1.	alveol	cavity	alveolus	12.	pleur	side; rib	pleura
2.	bronch	windpipe	bronchus	13.	pne	breath	eupnea, apnea
3.	capn	smoke	hypercapnia	14.	pneum	air, lungs	pneumothorax
4.	carin	keel	carina	15.	pulmo	lung	pulmonary
5.	choan	funnel	choanae	16.	respir	breathe	respiration
6.	crico	ring	cricoid cartilage	17.	spire	breathe	inspiration
7.	ectasis	dilation	atelectasis	18.	trach	rough	trachea
8.	emphys	inflate	emphysema	19.	ventus	wind	ventilation
9.	flat	blow, blown	inflation	20.	vestibul	porch	vestibule
10.	nari	nostril	nares	21.	vibr	shake, vibrate	vibrissae
11.	nas	nose	nasal				

Chapter 22 The Digestive System

BUILDING THE FRAMEWORK

PART 1: OVERVIEW OF THE DIGESTIVE SYSTEM

1. 1. pharynx   2. esophagus   3. stomach   4. duodenum   5. jejunum   6. ileum   7. ascending colon   8. transverse colon   9. descending colon   10. sigmoid colon   11. rectum   12. anal canal

2. Mouth: (I) teeth, tongue; (O) salivary glands and ducts.
    Duodenum: (O) liver, gall bladder, bile ducts, pancreas.

3. The salivary glands include the sublingual, submandibular, and parotid glands.

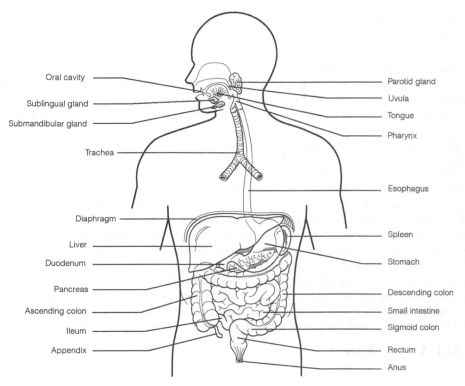

Oral cavity
Sublingual gland
Submandibular gland
Trachea
Diaphragm
Liver
Duodenum
Pancreas
Ascending colon
Ileum
Appendix

Parotid gland
Uvula
Tongue
Pharynx
Esophagus
Spleen
Stomach
Descending colon
Small intestine
Sigmoid colon
Rectum
Anus

Figure 22.1

4. 1. D   2. G, H   3. E, F, H   4. B   5. A   6. C

5. 1. stretch, osmolarity/pH, and presence of substrates and end products of digestion   2. submucosal plexus and myenteric plexus   3. long reflexes involve CNS centers and extrinsic autonomic nerves and can involve long regions of the tract; short reflexes involve only local (enteric) plexuses, and are very limited in their range

6. 1. peritoneum   2. mesentery   3. retroperitoneal organs   4. intraperitoneal or peritoneal organs

7. 1. A   2. D, E   3. D   4. C   5. B

8. 1. J   2. X   3. N   4. P   5. L, U   6. V   7. O   8. E, I, J   9. D   10. R   11. G   12. K   13. H   14. S   15. C   16. W   17. B   18. U   19. I   20. S   21. Q   22. T   23. S   24. M   25. C   26. A   27. F   28. E   29. D

9. 1. mucosa   2. muscularis externa   3. submucosa   4. serosa

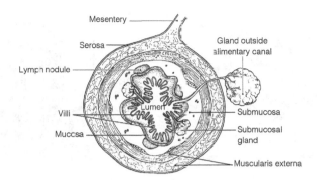

Figure 22.2

PART 2: FUNCTIONAL ANATOMY OF THE DIGESTIVE SYSTEM

1.

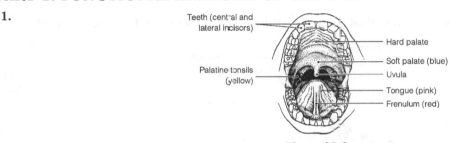

Figure 22 3

2. 1. Cleans the mouth, dissolves chemicals for tasting, moistens and compacts food, contains starch-digesting enzymes that begin the chemical digestion of starch.   2. Parotid glands, open next to second upper molar; submandibular glands, open at base of lingual frenulum; sublingual glands, open along floor of mouth   3. Serous cells secrete watery, enzyme-containing fluid: mucous cells secrete mucus   4. Lysozyme

3. Circle: 1. parasympathetic   2. salivatory; glossopharyngeal   3. sour   4. conditioned

4. 1. deciduous   2. 6 months   3. 6 years   4. permanent   5. 32   6. 20   7. incisors   8. canine (eyetooth)   9. premolars (bicuspids)   10. molars   11. wisdom

5. 1. A   2. C   3. D   4. B   5. E   6. C

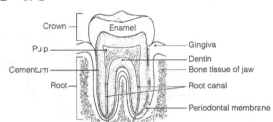

Figure 22.4

6. 1. oropharynx   2. laryngopharynx   3. stratified squamous   4. pharyngeal constrictor muscles   5. esophagus   6. gastroesophageal sphincter (valve)   7. deglutition   8. buccal   9. pharyngeal-esophageal   10. tongue   11. uvula   12. larynx   13. epiglottis   14. peristalsis   15. gastroesophageal

7. On part B, the HCl-secreting parietal cells should be colored red, the mucous neck cells yellow, and the cells identified as chief cells (which produce protein-digesting enzymes) blue.

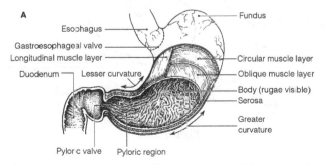

Figure 22.5

8. Check 2, 3, 4, 5, 7.

9.

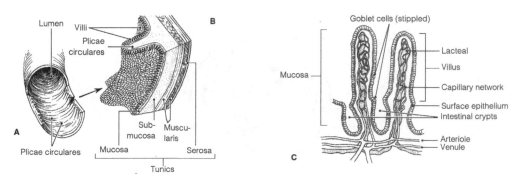

Figure 22.6

10. 1. D   2. A   3. B   4. C

11. 1. Secretin   2. Gastric emptying   3. Intestinal phase   4. HCl   5. Sympathetic   6. Esophagus   7. Salts

12.

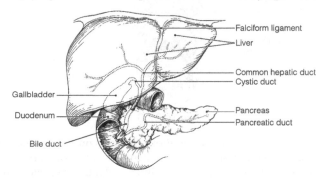

Figure 22.7

13. Branches of hepatic artery, hepatic vein, and bile duct. Located at the lobule periphery in the surrounding connective tissue.

14. 1. A, C   2. B   3. A   4. C   5. A, C, D

15. 1. B   2. H   3. F   4. G   5. C   6. A

16.

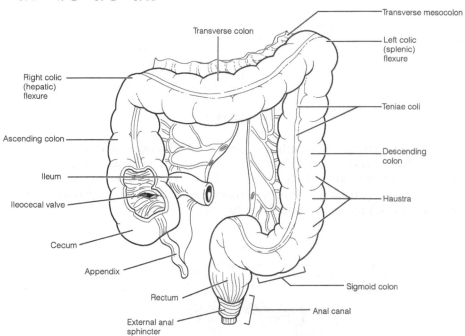

Figure 22.8

17. 1. peristalsis   2. segmentation   3. segmentation   4. mass movements   5. rectum   6. defecation   7. emetic   8. vomiting

18. 1. I   2. G   3. H   4. J   5. D   6. E   7. C   8. F   9. A

PART 3: PHYSIOLOGY OF CHEMICAL DIGESTION AND ABSORPTION

1. 1. B, D, F, G, H, I, J, L, M   2. F, G, H   3. H   4. I, J, M   5. L   6. D   7. C, K   8. A   9. E

2. 1. P   2. A   3. A   4. P   5. A. Circle 4, Fatty acids.

3. 1. Q   2. N   3. P   4. C   5. G   6. B   7. O   8. I   9. M   10. C   11. R   12.–14. A, F, K

4. 1. Trypsin   2. Chylomicrons   3. Lost during hemorrhage   4. Nuclease   5. Removal of water   6. Pepsin
7. Vitamin B$_{12}$

5.

Enzyme	Substrate	Product	Secreted by	Active In
Salivary amylase	Starch	Maltose and oligosaccharides	Salivary glands	Mouth
Pepsin	Protein	Polypeptides	Gastric glands	Stomach
Trypsin	Protein, peptides, amino acids	Dipeptides, small peptides	Pancreas	Small intestine
Dipeptidase	Dipeptides	Amino acids	Not secreted; brush border enzyme	Small intestine
Pancreatic amylase	Starch, oligosaccharides	Maltose	Pancreas	Small intestine
Lipase	Triglycerides	Monoglycerides, fatty acids, glycerol	Pancreas	Small intestine
Maltase	Maltose	Glucose	Not secreted; brush border enzyme	Small intestine
Carboxy-peptidase	Polypeptide	Amino acids	Not secreted; brush border enzyme	Small intestine
Nuclease	Nucleic acids	Nucleotides	Pancreas	Small intestine

The Incredible Journey

1. 1. mucosa   2. vestibule   3. tongue   4. salivary amylase   5. peristalsis   6. esophagus   7. larynx   8. epiglottis   9. stomach   10. mucus   11. pepsin   12. hydrochloric acid   13. pyloric   14. lipase   15. pancreas   16. villi   17. ileocecal

CHALLENGING YOURSELF

At the Clinic

1. Mumps.
2. Gastroesophageal sphincter.
3. Heartburn due to a hiatal hernia; esophagitis and esophageal ulcers.
4. Histamine is one of the chemical stimuli for HCl secretion; thus an antihistamine drug will inhibit HCl secretion; perforation, peritonitis, and massive hemorrhage. She was told not to take aspirin because it can cause stomach bleeding.
5. Leakage of HCl and pepsin from perforating gastric ulcer will literally erode and digest away any other tissues with which these chemicals come into contact.
6. Probably alcoholic cirrhosis; ascites (distended abdomen); jaundice (yellow skin).
7. Gramps probably told Duncan that germs "ate away" at the roots of his teeth so the teeth fell out. He concluded with the warning "So brush 3 times a day!"
8. Appendicitis; surgical removal; burst appendix with life-threatening peritonitis.
9. Lack of lactase (lactose intolerance); addition of lactase to milk.
10. Gluten enteropathy (adult celiac disease).
11. Appendicitis is caused by bacterial infection. If untreated, bacterial overgrowth may cause the appendix to rupture, resulting in fecal contamination of the peritoneal cavity.
12. The precipitated proteins may block the pancreatic ducts. Some of the proenzymes will be activated in the ducts over time, and these in turn will cause the pancreas to produce more digestive enzymes, causing digestion of the ducts.

Stop and Think

1. *Gap junctions* provide a continuous contraction along the digestive tract (peristalsis) because each muscle cell stimulates the next. The *stress-relaxation reflex* is important when mass peristalsis delivers fecal material to the rectum at an inconvenient moment. After stretching, the rectal smooth muscle will relax to accommodate to the increased mass. Because smooth muscle is *nonstriated*, it can stretch considerably without losing its ability to contract.

2. Salivary amylase is denatured by the acidity of the stomach; since it is a protein, it is digested along with dietary proteins. In the duodenum, pepsin is inactivated by the relatively high pH there and will be digested along with other proteins in the intestinal lumen.

3. Since histamine increases blood flow and capillary permeability, it might enhance the blood's ability to pick up nutrients from the digestive epithelium.

4. Since virtually all calcium is absorbed in the duodenum, a massive load of calcium can saturate the calcium transport mechanism. Smaller, more frequent doses will decrease likelihood of saturation and result in better absorption of the entire daily dose.

5. Fats are *emulsified* by bile salts. Digestion of triglycerides typically involves hydrolysis of two of the three fatty acids by *pancreatic lipase*, resulting in monoglycerides and free fatty acids. Bile salts form *micelles* that transport fat end products to the intestinal epithelium. *Absorption* occurs passively through the phospholipid bilayer. Triglycerides are re-formed in the epithelial cells and packaged with other lipids into protein-coated *chylomicrons*, which enter the *lacteals* to circulate from the lymphatic system to the general circulation. Entrance to the liver is via the hepatic artery of the systemic arterial system.

6. Examination of the plasma would quickly reveal the presence of chylomicrons, which give the plasma a milky-white appearance.

7. The liver manufactures albumin, which is essential in maintaining the osmotic balance of the blood. An albumin deficiency reduces the blood's osmotic pressure, and fluid is retained in the tissue spaces.

8. (a) In the stomach, these cells are found at the junctions of the gastric pits with the gastric glands. In the small intestine, they are at the base of the intestinal glands (crypts). (b) Their common function is to replace the epithelial cells (exposed to the harsh conditions of the digestive tract) as they die and slough off.

9. (a) Serous (gland) cells produce a watery enzyme-rich secretion; serous membranes produce a lubricating fluid within the ventral body cavity. (h) Caries are cavities (decayed areas) in teeth; (bile) canaliculi are tiny canals in the liver that carry bile. (c) Anal canal is the last portion of the tubular alimentary canal; runs from the rectum to the anus (external opening). (d) Diverticulosis is a condition in which the (weakened) walls of the large intestine pouch out; diverticulitis is inflammation of these diverticuli. (e) Hepatic vein drains venous blood from the liver; hepatic portal vein brings nutrient-rich venous blood to the liver from the digestive viscera.

10. Rough ER and Golgi apparatus: Liver makes tremendous amounts of proteins for export. Smooth ER: Liver is an important site of fat metabolism and cholesterol synthesis and breakdown. Peroxisomes: Liver is an important detoxifying organ.

COVERING ALL YOUR BASES

Multiple Choice

1. A, C, D   2. B   3. C   4. C   5. A   6. B, C, D   7. A, B, C, D   8. D   9. A, B, C, D   10. B   11. C
12. B, C   13. C   14. A, D   15. D   16. A, B, C   17. A, D   18. A, C, D   19. A, C   20. D   21. A, B
22. B, C, D   23. B   24. B, C, D   25. A, B, C   26. A, C, D   27. A, C   28. A, C   29. C, D   30. A, B, D
31. D   32. A, D   33. A   34. B   35. A, C, D   36. A, C, D   37. B, C   38. A, B, C   39. C   40. A, D
41. B   42. A   43. C   44. D   45. D   46. B   47. A

Word Dissection

	Word root	Translation	Example		Word root	Translation	Example
1.	aliment	nourish	alimentary canal	17.	hiat	gap	hiatal hernia
2.	cec	blind	cecum	18.	ile	intestine	ileum
3.	chole	bile	cholecystokinin	19.	jejun	hungry	jejunum
4.	chyme	juice	chyme	20.	micell	a little crumb	micelle
5.	decid	falling off	deciduous teeth	21.	oligo	few	oligosaccharides
6.	duoden	twelve each	duodenum	22.	oment	fat skin	greater omentum
7.	enter	intestine	mesentery	23.	otid	ear	parotid gland
8.	epiplo	thin membrane	epiploic appendages	24.	pep	digest	pepsin
9.	eso	within, inward	esophagus	25.	plic	fold	plicae circulares
10.	falci	sickle	falciform ligament	26.	proct	anus, rectum	proctodeum
11.	fec	dregs	feces	27.	pylor	gatekeeper	pylorus
12.	fren	bridle	lingual frenulum	28.	ruga	wrinkle	rugae
13.	gaster	stomach	gastric juice	29.	sorb	suck in	absorb
14.	gest	carry	digestion	30.	splanch	the viscera	splanchnic circ.
15.	glut	swallow	deglutition	31.	stalsis	constriction	peristalsis
16.	haustr	draw up	haustra	32.	teni	ribbon	tenia coli

Chapter 23 Nutrition, Metabolism, and Body Thermogenesis

BUILDING THE FRAMEWORK

Nutrition

1. 1. carbohydrates, lipids, proteins, vitamins, minerals, water   2. Molecules the body cannot make and must ingest.   3. 1 kcal = the heat necessary to raise the temperature of 1 kg of water by 1° centigrade.   4. glucose   5. brain cells and red blood cells   6. Carbohydrate foods that provide energy sources but no other nutrients.   7. egg yolk   8. linoleic acid (ingested as lecithin) and (possibly) linolenic acid   9. A protein containing all the different kinds of amino acids required by the body.   10. The amount of nitrogen ingested in proteins equals the amount of nitrogen excreted in urine or feces (rate of protein synthesis equals rate of protein degradation and loss).   11. structural and functional uses   12. Most vitamins function as coenzymes.   13. liver   14. calcium and phosphorous   15. Fats (lipids)

2. 1. I   2. E   3. D   4. B   5. H   6. G   7.–10. A, G, H, I   11. M   12. L   13. F   14. A   15. C   16. K   17.–19. A, F, H

3. 1. J   2. C   3. I   4. F   5. G   6. H   7. B   8. D   9. E

4. 1. Trisaccharides   2. Nuts   3. Fats   4. Vitamin C   5. K^+ 6. Amino acids   7. Must be ingested   8. Zinc   9. About 16 oz   10. Catabolic hormones

5. 1. A   2. B   3. C   4. B   5. B   6. C   7. C   8. B

Metabolism

1. 1. metabolism   2. catabolism   3. anabolism   4. cellular respiration   5. ATP   6. GI tract   7. mitochondria   8. oxygen   9. water   10. carbon dioxide   11. hydrogen atoms   12. electrons   13. reduction   14. coenzymes   15. NAD^+ 16. FAD

2. 1. glycolysis   2. cytoplasm   3. not used   4. NAD^+ 5. two   6. sugar activation   7. sugar cleavage   8. sugar oxidation   9. pyruvic acid   10. lactic acid   11. skeletal muscle   12. brain   13. pH   14. red blood   15. carbon dioxide   16. NAD^+ 17. coenzyme A   18. oxaloacetic acid   19. citric acid   20. Krebs   21. mitochondrion   22. keto   23. two   24. three   25. one   26. fatty acids   27. amino acids   28. electron transport   29. protons and electrons   30. water   31. ADP   32. oxidative phosphorylation   33. approximately 36

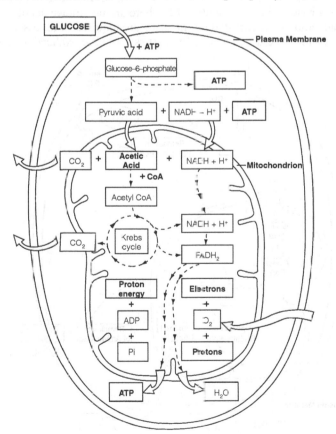

Figure 23.1

3. 1. hydrogen atoms   2. electrons   3. protons   4. metal   5. inner   6. EC_1, EC_2, and EC_3 7. oxygen
8. protons   9. mitochondrial matrix   10. intermembrane space   11. lower   12. proton motive force
13. ATP synthase   14. ADP + $P_i \rightarrow$ ATP

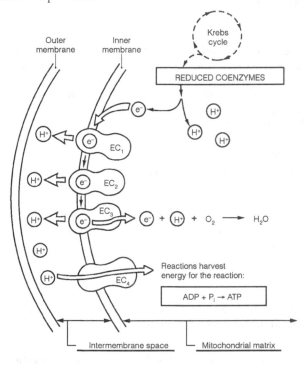

Figure 23.2

4. 1. C   2. D   3. B   4. A

5. 1. D   2. F   3. B   4. G   5. C   6. A   7. E   8. C   9. F   10. Ammonia is toxic to body cells; also blood pH
may rise because it acts as a base.   11. Keto acids   12. There are no storage depots for amino acids in the body.
Proteins continually degrade and newly ingested amino acids are required. If an essential amino acid is not consumed, the remaining ones cannot be used for protein synthesis and are oxidized for energy.

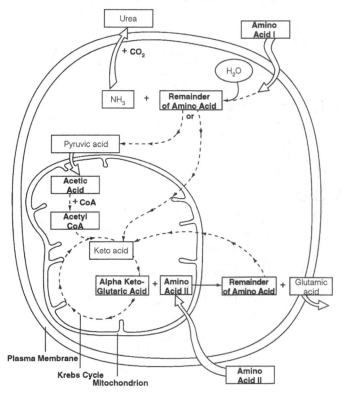

Figure 23.3

6. 1. F   2. C   3. E   4. D   5. A   6. B   7. G   8. B

7. 1. 40% or less   2. ATP than ADP   3. into   4. glycogenesis   5. liver and skeletal muscle

8. 1. Glucose   2. Hydrolyzed in mitochondria   3. Cytoplasm   4. ATP deficit   5. Low blood sugar level

9. 1. anabolic   2. T   3. glycogen   4. triglycerides   5. protein synthesis   6. T   7. rising blood glucose levels   8. facilitated diffusion   9. glycogenolysis and gluconeogenesis   10. other body cells   11. T

10. 1. 80–100 mg glucose per 100 ml blood   2. The brain prefers glucose as its energy source.   3. The liver, by glycogenolysis; skeletal muscle, by glycogenolysis; adipose tissue and liver, by lipolysis; tissue cells, by protein catabolism.   4. Skeletal muscle cells cannot dephosphorylate glucose, but they can produce pyruvic acid or lactic acid. The liver reconverts these to glucose, which is released to the blood.   5. Lipolysis produces fatty acids and glycerol. Only the glycerol can be converted directly to glucose by the liver. (Acetyl CoA, from fatty acid oxidation, is produced beyond the reversible steps of glycolysis and cannot be converted to glucose.)   6. The liver deaminates amino acids and converts the residues to glucose, which is released to the blood.   7. Fats   8. Ketone bodies from the oxidation of fats by the liver.   9. Epinephrine and glucagon   10. Alpha cells of pancreatic islets produce glucagon, which targets the liver and adipose tissue.   11. Falling glucose levels and rising amino acid levels.   12. High amino acid levels in blood stimulate release of insulin. Glucagon counteracts effects of insulin and prevents abrupt hypoglycemia.   13. Hypothalamic receptors sense declines in blood glucose levels. Stimulation of the adrenal medulla causes release of epinephrine, which produces the same effects as glucagon.

11.

Hormone	Blood glucose	Blood amino acids	Glycogenolysis	Lipogenesis	Protein synthesis
Insulin	↓	↓	↓	↑	↓
Glucagon	↑	XXX	↑	↓	XXX
Epinephrine	↑	XXX	↑	↓	XXX
Growth hormone	↑ (over the long term)	↓	↑	↓	↑
Thyroxine	↓	XXX	↑	↓	↑

12. 1. albumin   2. clotting proteins   3. cholesterol   4. hyperglycemia   5. glycogen   6. hypoglycemia   7. glycogenolysis   8. gluconeogenesis   9. detoxification   10. phagocytic   11. lipoproteins   12. insoluble   13. lower   14. high   15. chylomicrons   16. triglycerides (fats)   17. cholesterol   18. membranes   19. steroid hormones   20. liver   21. bile salts   22. atherosclerosis   23. unsaturated   24. H (high)   25. A, D, and B_{12} 26. iron   27. red blood

Energy Balance

1. 1. TMR   2. ↓ Metabolic rate   3. Child   4. Fats   5. Fasting   6. Body's core   7. Vasoconstriction

2. 1. C ↓   2. A ↓   3. B ↓   4. C ↑   5. D ↓↑   6. B ↑   7. C ↓   8. E ↓

3. 1. The intake of energy by the catabolism of food equals the total energy output of heat plus work plus energy storage.   2. heat   3. Body weight remains stable when energy intake equals energy outflow. Weight change accompanies energy inequality.

4. 1. D   2. B, K   3. A   4. F   5. J   6. C   7. H, I   8. G   9. E   10. J

5. 1. skeletal muscle   2. 37.8°C (100°F)   3. 10%   4. proteins   5. T   6. heat stroke

CHALLENGING YOURSELF

At the Clinic

1. Many vegetables contain incomplete proteins. Unless complete proteins are ingested the value of the dietary protein for anabolism is lost, because the amino acids will be oxidized for energy. Beans and grains.

2. "Empty calories" means simple carbohydrates with no other nutrients, such as candy, cookies, and soft drinks.

3. Glucagon; hypoglycemia.

4. Dieting triggers catabolism of proteins as well as fat, resulting in weight loss due to loss of muscle and adipose tissue. Subsequent weight gain without exercise usually means regaining only fat, not muscle. Continual cycling of muscle/adipose loss followed by adipose gain can significantly alter body fat composition and "rev up" metabolic systems that increase the efficiency of fat storage and retention.

5. Rickets; deficiency of vitamin D and calcium.

6. Ketosis; her self-starvation has resulted in deficiency of carbohydrate fuels (and oxaloacetic acid). This deficiency promotes conversion of acetyl CoA to ketone bodies such as acetone.

7. Heat exhaustion; they should drink a "sports drink" containing electrolytes or lemonade to replace lost fluids.

8. Bert has heat stroke. Heavy work in an environment that restricts heat loss results in a spiraling upward of body temperature and cessation of thermoregulation. Bert should be immersed in cool water immediately to bring his temperature down and avert brain damage.

9. Children have a greater requirement for fat than adults, particularly up to age 2 or 3 when myelination of the nervous system is still a major consideration.

10. Hypercholesterolemia; <200 mg/100 ml blood; atherosclerosis, strokes, and heart attacks.

11. Iron. She has hemorrhagic anemia compounded by iron loss.

12. Mr. Hodges has scurvy due to vitamin C deficiency. Recommend citrus fruits and plenty of tomatoes.

Stop and Think

1. Osmotic effect would be retention of water in cells maintaining a pool of amino acids; pH would decrease.

2. A higher concentration of glucose-phosphate in a cell would attract water, and the cell would swell.

3. Oxygen is required as the final electron acceptor in the electron transport chain. Lack of oxygen brings electron transport to a halt and backs up the Krebs cycle as well, since NAD^+ and FAD cannot be recycled. ATP production grinds to a halt in cells that cannot rely on anaerobic respiration (such as brain cells), and cell death occurs.

4. Urea production increases. Protein synthesis will not proceed unless all necessary amino acids are available. Hence, any amino acids that are not utilized are deaminated and oxidized for energy or converted to fat and stored. Excess amino groups will be converted to urea.

5. Absorption of simple sugars is quite rapid compared to absorption of complex carbohydrates, which must be digested first. The result is a much more rapid rise in blood glucose level when simple sugars are ingested.

6. No; the ability of brain cells to take in glucose is not regulated by insulin.

7. Since omega-3 fatty acids reduce the stickiness of platelets, excessive bleeding might result from ingesting an excess of these lipids.

8. Males tend to have a higher ratio of muscle to fat than females. Since muscle tissue has a higher BMR than fat, a higher proportion of muscle requires a higher calculation factor.

9. Since PKU sufferers cannot manufacture melanin, pigment in the interior of the eye could be deficient, resulting in poor vision. (Albinos likewise have poor vision.)

10. Depending on the diuretic, different electrolytes have an increased rate of excretion. A common type of diuretic promotes potassium excretion, requiring potassium supplementation.

11. The excess of glucose can form abnormal cross-bridges between protein fibers in the vessel walls, resulting in hardening of the arteries.

12. Hypothyroidism would result in hypothermia, since thyroid hormones are thermogenic (heat generating).

13. When muscles are "at work" they are generating and using large amounts of ATP to power the sliding of their myofilaments. Since some heat is "lost" in every chemical reaction, a large amount of heat is generated at the same time.

14. Graph C, because the sample with the highest concentration of succinic acid is decolorizing fastest, going from a high intensity, blue dye to a nearly colorless dye. A is wrong because the graph shows the color intensity of all the samples increasing with time. B is incorrect because the color intensities of the tubes are different to begin with and no differences in dye content of the samples was mentioned.

15. Nitrogen via the amine group.

COVERING ALL YOUR BASES

Multiple Choice

1. B, D   2. A, B, D   3. C   4. D   5. A, B, C, D   6. B   7. B, C   8. A, C   9. C, D   10. A, B, C, D   11. A
12. C, D   13. A, B   14. A   15. B, D   16. A   17. B, C, D   18. B, D   19. B, D   20. A   21. C   22. A, B, C
23. C   24. A, B, C   25. D   26. A, B, D   27. D

Word Dissection

	Word root	Translation	Example		Word root	Translation	Example
1.	acet	vinegar	acetyl CoA	6.	lecith	egg yolk	lecithin
2.	calor	heat	calorie	7.	linol	flax oil	linoleic acid
3.	flav	yellow	riboflavin	8.	nutri	feed, nourish	nutrient
4.	gluco	sweet	glucose	9.	pyro	fire	pyrogen
5.	kilo	thousand	kilocalorie				

Chapter 24 The Urinary System

[L1] Multiple Choice

1. A 2. B 3. C 4. D 5. C 6. B 7. D 8. C 9. A 10. A 11. C 12. B 13. D 14. C 15. C
16. B 17. D 18. A 19. D 20. A 21. B 22. B 23. D 24. B 25. D 26. A 27. B 28. C 29. B
30. A 31. B 32. C 33. B 34. A 35. C

[L1] Completion

1. kidneys 2. ureters 3. urethra 4. glomerulus 5. nephrons 6. interlobar veins 7. filtrate 8. loop of
Henle 9. secretion 10. renal threshold 11. composition 12. concentration 13. glomerular hydrostatic
14. glomerular filtration 15. parathyroid hormone 16. countertransport 17. countercurrent multiplication
18. antidiuretic hormone 19. internal sphincter 20. rugae 21. neck 22. micturition reflex 23. cerebral
cortex

[L1] Matching

1. I 2. F 3. G 4. K 5. A 6. H 7. J 8. B 9. E 10. D 11. C 12. N 13. T 14. R 15. Q
16. O 17. P 18. S 19. L 20. M

[L1] Drawing/Illustration Labeling

Figure 26.1 Components of the Urinary System

1. kidney 2. ureter 3. urinary bladder

Figure 26.2 Sectional Anatomy of the Kidney

1. minor calyx 2. renal pelvis 3. ureter 4. renal column 5. renal pyramid 6. major calyx 7. renal capsule 8. cortex

Figure 26.3 Structure of a Typical Nephron Including Circulation

1. efferent arteriole 2. glomerulus 3. afferent arteriole 4. proximal convoluted tubule (PCT) 5. peritubular
capillaries 6. distal convoluted tubule (DCT) 7. collecting duct 8. loop of Henle 9. proximal convoluted
tubule (PCT) 10. peritubular capillaries 11. Bowman's capsule 12. glomerulus 13. distal convoluted tubule
(DCT) 14. vasa recta 15. loop of Henle

[L2] Concept Maps

I Urinary System

1. ureters 2. urinary bladder 3. nephrons 4. glomerulus 5. proximal convoluted tubule 6. collecting
tubules 7. medulla 8. renal sinus 9. minor calyces

II Kidney Circulation

10. renal artery 11. arcuate artery 12. afferent artery 13. efferent artery 14. interlobular vein 15. interlobar vein

III Renin–Angiotensin–Aldosterone System

16. ↓ plasma volume 17. renin 18. liver 19. angiotensin I 20. adrenal cortex 21. ↑ Na^+ reabsorption
22. ↓ Na^+ excretion 23. ↓ H_2O excretion

[L2] Body Trek

1. proximal 2. glomerulus 3. protein-free 4. descending limb 5. filtrate 6. ascending limb 7. active
transport 8. ions 9. distal 10. aldosterone 11. ADH 12. collecting 13. urine 14. ureters 15. urinary bladder 16. urethra

[L2] Multiple Choice

1. D 2. C 3. B 4. D 5. C 6. D 7. B 8. D 9. C 10. B 11. A 12. A 13. B 14. D 15. C
16. A 17. C 18. D 19. A 20. C

[L2] Completion

1. retroperitoneal 2. glomerular filtration rate 3. osmotic gradient 4. transport maximum 5. macula densa
6. cortical 7. vasa recta 8. filtration 9. reabsorption 10. secretion 11. glomerular filtration 12. aldosterone 13. diabetes insipidus 14. angiotensin II 15. renin

[L2] Short Essay

1. (a) Regulates plasma concentrations of ions.

   (b) Regulates blood volume and blood pressure.

   (c) Contributes to stabilization of blood pH.

   (d) Conserves valuable nutrients.

   (e) Eliminates organic wastes.

   (f) Assists liver in detoxification and deamination.

2. kidney → ureters → urinary bladder → urethra

3. (a) renal capsule (fibrous tunic)

    (b) adipose capsule

    (c) renal fascia

4. glomerulus → proximal convoluted tubule → descending limb of loop of Henle → ascending limb of loop of Henle → distal convoluted tubule

5. (a) production of filtrate

    (b) reabsorption of organic substrates

    (c) reabsorption of water and ions

6.   (a)   (b)

    capillary endothelium   fenestrated capillaries

    basement membrane   dense and thick (lamina densa)

    glomerular epithelium   pedocytes with pedicels separated by slit pores

7. renin and erythropoietin

8. (a) Produces a powerful vasoconstriction of the afferent arteriole, thereby decreasing the GFR and slowing the production of filtrate.

    (b) Stimulation of renin release.

    (c) Direct stimulation of water and sodium ion reabsorption.

9. filtration, reabsorption, secretion

10. $P_f = G_{hp} - (C_{hp} + OP_b)$

$$\text{filtration pressure} = \begin{array}{c} \text{glomerular} \\ \text{blood} \\ \text{(hydrostatic)} \\ \text{pressure} \end{array} - \left\{ \begin{array}{c} \text{capsular} \\ \text{hydrostatic} \\ \text{pressure} \end{array} + \begin{array}{c} \text{blood} \\ \text{osmotic} \\ \text{pressure} \end{array} \right\}$$

11. Muscle fibers breaking down glycogen reserves release lactic acid.

    The number of circulating ketoacids increases.

    Adipose tissues are releasing fatty acids into the circulation.

12. (a) Sodium and chloride are pumped out of the filtrate in the ascending limb and into the peritubular fluid.

    (b) The pumping elevates the osmotic concentration in the peritubular fluid around the descending limb.

    (c) The result is an osmotic flow of water out of the filtrate held in the descending limb and into the peritubular fluid.

13. (a) autoregulation

    (b) hormonal regulation

    (c) autonomic regulation

14. (a) ADH—decreased urine volume

    (b) renin—causes angiotensin II production; stimulates aldosterone production

    (c) aldosterone—increased sodium ion reabsorption; decreased urine concentration and volume

    (d) Atrial Natriuretic Peptide (ANP)—inhibits ADH production; results in increased urine volume

[L3] Critical Thinking/Application

1. The alcohol acts as a diuretic. It inhibits ADH secretion from the posterior pituitary causing the distal convoluted tubule and the collecting duct to be relatively impermeable to water. Inhibiting the osmosis of water from the tubule along with the increased fluid intake results in an increase in urine production, and increased urination becomes necessary.

2. (a) If plasma proteins and numerous WBC are appearing in the urine, there is obviously increased permeability of the filtration membrane. This condition usually results from inflammation of the filtration membrane within the renal corpuscle. If the condition is temporary, it is probably an acute glomerular nephritis usually associated with a bacterial infection such as streptococcal sore throat. If the condition is long term, resulting in a nonfunctional kidney, it is referred to as chronic glomerular nephritis.

    (b) The plasma proteins in the filtrate increase the osmolarity of the filtrate, causing the urine volume to be greater than normal.

3. (a) Filtration

   (b) Primary site of nutrient reabsorption

   (c) Primary site for secretion of substances into the filtrate

   (d) Loop of Henle and collecting system interact to regulate the amount of water and the number of sodium and potassium ions lost in the urine.

4. (a)

$$\text{Effective filtration pressure (EFP)} = \left\{ \begin{array}{c} \text{Glomerular} \\ \text{hydrostatic} \\ \text{pressure} \end{array} + \begin{array}{c} \text{Capsular} \\ \text{osmotic} \\ \text{pressure} \end{array} \right\} - \left\{ \begin{array}{c} \text{Glomerular} \\ \text{osmotic} \\ \text{pressure} \end{array} + \begin{array}{c} \text{Capsular} \\ \text{hydrostatic} \\ \text{pressure} \end{array} \right\}$$

$$\text{EFP} = (G_{hp} + C_{op}) - (OP_b + C_{hp})$$

$$\text{EFP} = \left\{ \begin{array}{c} 60 + 5 \\ (\text{mm Hg}) \end{array} \right\} - \left\{ \begin{array}{c} 32 + 18 \\ (\text{mm Hg}) \end{array} \right\} = 15 \text{ mm Hg}$$

   (b) An EFP of 10 mm Hg is normal. A change in the EFP produces a similar change in the GFR.

   (c) A capsular osmotic pressure of 5 mm Hg develops in the capsular filtrate due to increased permeability of the glomerular endothelium, allowing blood proteins to filter out into the capsule. An EFP of 15 mm Hg indicates some type of kidney disease.

5. Strenuous exercise causes sympathetic activation to produce powerful vasoconstriction of the afferent arteriole, which delivers blood to the renal capsule. This causes a decrease in the GFR and alters the GFR by changing the required pattern of blood circulation. Dilation of peripheral blood vessels during exercise shunts blood away from the kidney and the GFR declines. A decreased GFR slows the production of filtrate. As the blood flow increases to the skin and skeletal muscles, kidney perfusion gradually declines and potentially dangerous conditions develop as the circulating concentration of metabolic wastes increases and peripheral water losses mount.

Chapter 25 Fluid, Electrolyte, and Acid–Base Balance

[L1] Multiple Choice

1. B 2. D 3. B 4. B 5. D 6. A 7. B 8. C 9. A 10. D 11. B 12. D 13. D 14. B 15. A
16. C 17. C 18. D 19. A 20. C 21. D 22. C 23. B 24. C 25. B 26. D 27. B 28. C
29. C 30. D 31. A 32. A 33. B

[L1] Completion

1. electrolyte 2. fluid 3. fluid shift 4. osmoreceptors 5. hypertonic 6. hypotonic 7. aldosterone
8. antidiuretic hormone 9. edema 10. net hydrostatic pressure 11. colloid osmotic pressure 12. kidneys
13. calcium 14. buffers 15. hemoglobin 16. respiratory compensation 17. renal compensation 18. acidosis 19. alkalosis 20. hypercapnia 21. skeletal mass

[L1] Matching

1. I 2. K 3. E 4. D 5. B 6. H 7. C 8. J 9. F 10. A 11. G 12. P 13. Q 14. L 15. N
16. U 17. R 18. T 19. M 20. O 21. S

[L1] Drawing/Illustration Labeling

Figure 27.1 The pH Scale

1. pH 6.80 3.   pH 7.35 5. alkalosis

2. acidosis 4.   pH 7.45 6. pH 7.80

Figure 27.2 Relationships among pH, P_{CO_2}, and HCO_3^-

pH	P_{CO_2}	HCO_3^-
1. ↓	5. ↑	9. N
2. ↓	6. N	10. ↓
3. ↑	7. ↓	11. N
4. ↑	8. N	12. ↑

[L2] Concept Maps

I Homeostasis of Total Volume of Body Water

1. ↓ volume of body H_2O 2. ↑ H_2O retention at kidneys 3. aldosterone secretion by adrenal cortex

II Fluid and Electrolyte Imbalance

4. ↓ pH   5. ECF hypotonic to ICF   6. ↓ ECF volume   7. ↑ ICF volume

III Respiratory Mechanisms for Control of pH

8. ↑ blood CO_2 9. ↑ depth of breathing   10. hyperventilation   11. ↑ blood pH   12. normal blood pH

IV Urinary Mechanisms for Maintaining Homeostasis of Blood pH

13. ↓ blood pH   14. HCO_3^- 15. ↑ blood pH

V Homeostasis—Fluid Volume Regulation—Sodium Ion Concentrations

16. ↓ B.P. at kidneys   17. ↑ Aldosterone release   18. ↓ H_2O loss   19. ↑ plasma volume   20. ↑ ANP release
21. ↓ ADH release   22. ↓ Aldosterone release   23. ↑ H_2O loss

[L2] Multiple Choice

1. B   2. D   3. C   4. A   5. D   6. D   7. B   8. D   9. A   10. B   11. C   12. D   13. B   14. C   15. C
16. A   17. C   18. B   19. C   20. D

[L2] Completion

1. kidneys   2. angiotensin II   3. volatile acid   4. fixed acids   5. organic acids   6. buffer system   7. respiratory acidosis   8. hypoventilation   9. hyperventilation   10. lactic acidosis   11. ketoacidosis   12. alkaline tide

[L2] Short Essay

1. (a) fluid balance

   (b) electrolyte balance

   (c) acid–base balance

2. (a) antidiuretic hormone (ADH)

   (b) aldosterone

   (c) atrial natriuretic peptide (ANP)

3. (a) It stimulates water conservation at the kidney, reducing urinary water losses.

   (b) It stimulates the thirst center to promote the drinking of fluids. The combination of decreased water loss and increased water intake gradually restores normal plasma osmolarity.

4. (a) alterations in the potassium ion concentration in the ECF

   (b) changes in pH

   (c) aldosterone levels

5. (a) an initial fluid shift into or out of the ICF

   (b) "fine tuning" via changes in circulating levels of ADH

6. $CO_2 + H_2O \ ´H_2CO_3 \ ´H+ + HCO_3^-$

7. (a) protein buffer system, phosphate buffer system, and carbonic acid-bicarbonate buffer system

   (b) respiratory mechanisms, renal mechanisms

8. (a) secrete or absorb hydrogen ions

   (b) control excretion of acids and bases

   (c) generate additional buffers when necessary

9. hypercapnia— ↑ plasma P_{CO_2}; Ø plasma pH—respiratory acidosis

   hypocapnia—Ø plasma P_{CO_2}; ↑ plasma pH—respiratory alkalosis

10. (a) impaired ability to excrete H^+ at the kidneys

    (b) production of a large number of fixed and/or organic acids

    (c) severe bicarbonate loss

[L3] Critical Thinking/Application

1. The comatose teenager's ABG studies reveal a severe respiratory acidosis. A pH of 7.17 (low) and a P_{CO_2} of 73 mm Hg (high) cause his respiratory centers to be depressed, resulting in hypoventilation, CO_2 retention, and consequent acidosis. His normal HCO_3^- value indicates that his kidneys haven't had time to retain significant amounts of HCO_3^- to compensate for the respiratory condition.

2. The 62-year-old woman's ABG studies reveal that she has metabolic alkalosis. A pH of 7.65 (high) and an HCO_3^- of 55 mEq/liter (high) are abnormal values. Her P_{CO_2} of 52 mm Hg indicates that her lungs are attempting to compensate for the alkalosis by retaining CO_2 in an effort to balance the HCO_3^- value. Her vomiting caused a large acid loss from her body via HCl, which means a loss of H^+, the acid ion. Predictable effects include slow respirations, an overexcitable CNS, leading to irritability and, if untreated, possible tetany and convulsions.

3. (a) metabolic acidosis

    (b) respiratory alkalosis

    (c) respiratory acidosis

    (d) metabolic alkalosis

4.

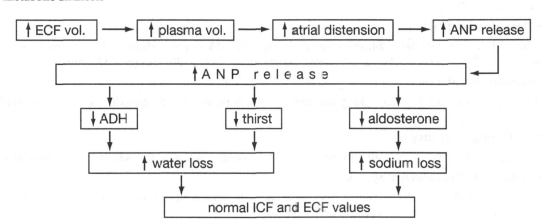

Chapter 26 The Reproductive System

[L1] Multiple Choice

1. D   2. B   3. D   4. C   5. A   6. A   7. B   8. C   9. C   10. D   11. D   12. A   13. D   14. B   15. C
16. C   17. B   18. A   19. C   20. B   21. C   22. B   23. C   24. A   25. C   26. D   27. D   29. D
28. B   30. A   31. A   32. B   33. C   34. B

[L1] Completion

1. fertilization   2. gonads   3. seminiferous tubules   4. testes   5. spermiogenesis   6. spermatids   7. ductus deferens   8. digestive   9. prostate gland   10. fructose   11. ICSH   12. ovaries   13. Graafian   14. ovulation   15. infundibulum   16. implantation   17. oogenesis   18. Bartholin's   19. progesterone   20. placenta   21. cardiovascular   22. menopause

[L1] Matching

1. J   2. F   3. C   4. G   5. E   6. A   7. I   8. B   9. K   10. D   11. H   12. N   13. P   14. T   15. L
16. R   17. M   18. O   19. Q   20. V   21. S   22. U

[L1] Drawing/Illustration Labeling

Figure 26.1 Male Reproductive Organs
1. prostatic urethra   2. pubic symphysis   3. ductus deferens   4. urogenital diaphragm   5. corpora cavernosa
6. corpus spongiosum   7. penile urethra   8. glans penis   9. navicular fossa   10. prepuce   11. testis
12. epididymis   13. urinary bladder   14. rectum   15. seminal vesicle   16. seminal vesicle   17. ejaculatory
duct   18. prostate gland   19. anus   20. anal sphincters   21. bulbourethral gland   22. membranous urethra
23. bulb of penis   24. scrotum

Figure 26.2 The Testes
1. septum   2. epididymis (head)   3. ductus deferens   4. rete testis   5. seminiferous tubule   6. tunica albuginea

Figure 26.3 Female External Genitalia
1. mons pubis   2. clitoris   3. labia minora   4. vaginal orifice   5. vestibule   6. perineum   7. prepuce
8. urethral orifice   9. labia majora   10. hymen

Figure 26.4 Female Reproductive Organs (sagittal section)
   1. uterus   **2.** urinary bladder   **3.** pubic symphysis   **4.** urethra   **5.** clitoris   **6.** labium minora   **7.** labium majora   **8.** cervix   **9.** vagina   **10.** anus

Figure 26.5 Female Reproductive Organs (frontal section)
   1. infundibulum   **2.** ovary   **3.** uterine tube   **4.** myometrium   **5.** cervix   **6.** vagina

[L2] Concept Maps

I Male Reproductive Tract

   1. ductus deferens   **2.** penis   **3.** seminiferous tubules   **4.** produce testosterone   **5.** FSH   **6.** seminal vesicles   **7.** bulbourethral glands   **8.** urethra

II Penis

   9. crus   **10.** shaft   **11.** corpus spongiosum   **12.** prepuce   **13.** external urinary meatus   **14.** frenulum

III Male Hormone Regulation

   15. anterior pituitary   **18.** interstitial cells   **21.** male secondary sex characteristics   **16.** FSH   **19.** inhibin   **17.** testes   **20.** CNS

IV Female Reproductive Tract

   22. uterine tubes   **23.** follicles   **24.** granulosa & thecal cells   **25.** endometrium   **26.** supports fetal development   **27.** vagina   **28.** vulva   **29.** labia majora and minora   **30.** clitoris   **31.** nutrients

V Female Hormone Regulation

   32. GnRH   **33.** LH   **34.** follicles   **35.** progesterone   **36.** bone and muscle growth   **37.** accessory glands and organ

VI Hormones During Pregnancy

   38. anterior pituitary   **39.** ovary   **40.** progesterone   **41.** placenta   **42.** relaxin   **43.** mammary gland development

[L2] Body Trek—Male Reproductive System

   1. seminiferous tubules and rete testis   **2.** body of epididymis   **3.** ductus deferens   **4.** ejaculatory duct   **5.** urethra   **6.** penile urethra   **7.** external urethral meatus

[L2] Multiple Choice

   1. A   **2.** C   **3.** A   **4.** C   **5.** D   **6.** B   **7.** B   **8.** C   **9.** B   **10.** D   **11.** D   **12.** C   **13.** B   **14.** D   **15.** A   **16.** D   **17.** A   **18.** B   **19.** D

[L2] Completion

   1. androgens   **2.** inguinal canals   **3.** raphe   **4.** cremaster   **5.** ejaculation   **6.** rete testis   **7.** acrosomal sac   **8.** prepuce   **9.** smegma   **10.** detumescence   **11.** menopause   **12.** zona pellucida   **13.** corona radiata   **14.** corpus luteum   **15.** corpus albicans   **16.** mesovarium   **17.** tunica albuginea   **18.** fimbriae   **19.** cervical os   **20.** fornix   **21.** hymen   **22.** clitoris   **23.** menses   **24.** ampulla

[L2] Short Essay

1. (a) maintenance of the blood–testis barrier

   (b) support of spermiogenesis

   (c) secretion of inhibin

   (d) secretion of androgen-binding protein

2. (a) It monitors and adjusts the composition of tubular fluid.

   (b) It acts as a recycling center for damaged spermatozoa.

   (c) It is the site of physical maturation of spermatozoa.

3. (a) seminal vesicles, prostate gland, bulbourethral glands

   (b) activates the sperm, provides nutrients for sperm motility, provides sperm motility, produces buffers to counteract acid conditions

4. Seminal fluid is the fluid component of semen. Semen consists of seminal fluid, sperm, and enzymes.

5. *Emission* involves peristaltic contractions of the ampulla, pushing fluid and spermatozoa into the prostatic urethra. Contractions of the seminal vesicles and prostate gland move the seminal mixture into the membranous and penile walls of the prostate gland.

   Ejaculation occurs as powerful, rhythmic contractions of the ischiocavernosus and bulbocavernosus muscles push semen toward the external urethral orifice.

6. (a) Promotes the functional maturation of spermatozoa.

   (b) Maintains accessory organs of male reproductive tract.

   (c) Responsible for male secondary sexual characteristics.

   (d) Stimulates bone and muscle growth.

   (e) Stimulates sexual behaviors and sexual drive.

7. (a) Serves as a passageway for the elimination of menstrual fluids.

   (b) Receives penis during coitus; holds sperm prior to passage into uterus.

   (c) In childbirth it forms the lower portion of the birth canal.

8. (a) *Arousal*—parasympathetic activation leads to an engorgement of the erectile tissues of the clitoris and increased secretion of the greater vestibular glands.

   (b) *Coitus*—rhythmic contact with the clitoris and vaginal walls provides stimulation that eventually leads to orgasm.

   (c) *Orgasm*—accompanied by peristaltic contractions of the uterine and vaginal walls and rhythmic contractions of the bulbocavernosus and ischiocavernosus muscles giving rise to pleasurable sensations.

9. Step 1: Formation of primary follicles

   Step 2: Formation of secondary follicle

   Step 3: Formation of a tertiary follicle

   Step 4: Ovulation

   Step 5: Formation and degeneration of the corpus luteum

10. Estrogens:

    (a) stimulate bone and muscle growth;

    (b) maintain female secondary sex characteristics;

    (c) stimulate sex-related behaviors and drives;

    (d) maintain functional accessory reproductive glands and organs;

    (e) initiate repair and growth of the endometrium.

11. (a) menses

    (b) proliferative phase

    (c) secretory phase

12. (a) human chorionic gonadotrophin (HCG)

    (b) relaxin

    (c) human placental lactogen (HPL)

    (d) estrogens and progestins

13. By the end of the sixth month of pregnancy the mammary glands are fully developed, and the glands begin to produce colostrum. This contains relatively more proteins and far less fat than milk, and it will be provided to the infant during the first two or three days of life. Many of the proteins are immunoglobulins that may help the infant ward off infections until its own immune system becomes fully functional.

[L3] Critical Thinking/Application

1. (a) The normal temperature of the testes in the scrotum is 1°–2° lower than the internal body temperature—the ideal temperature for developing sperm. Mr. Hurt's infertility is caused by the inability of sperm to tolerate the higher temperature in the abdominopelvic cavity.

   (b) Three major factors are necessary for fertility in the male:
   • adequate motility of sperm—30%–35% motility necessary
   • adequate numbers of sperm—20,000,000/ml minimum
   • sperm must be morphologically perfect—sperm cannot be malformed

2. The 19-year-old female has a problem with hormonal imbalance in the body. Females, like males, secrete estrogens and androgens; however, in females, estrogen secretion usually "masks" the amount of androgen secreted in the body. In females an excess of testosterone secretion may cause a number of conditions such as sterility, fat distribution like a male, beard, low-pitched voice, skeletal muscle enlargement, clitoral enlargement, and a diminished breast size.

3. The contraceptive pill decreases the stimulation of FSH and prevents ovulation. It contains large quantities of progesterone and a small quantity of estrogen. It is usually taken for 20 days beginning on day 5 of a 28-day cycle. The increased level of progesterone and decreased levels of estrogen prepare the uterus for egg implantation. On day 26 the progesterone level decreases. If taken as directed, the Pill will allow for a normal menstrual cycle.

4. In males the disease-causing organism can move up the urethra to the bladder or into the ejaculatory duct to the ductus deferens. There is no direct connection into the pelvic cavity in the male. In females the pathogen travels from the vagina to the uterus, to the uterine tubes, and into the pelvic cavity where it can infect the peritoneal lining, resulting in peritonitis.

Chapter 27 Development and Inheritance

[L1] Multiple Choice

1. B   2. D   3. C   4. A   5. C   6. B   7. A   8. D   9. C   10. B   11. A   12. C   13. B   14. C   15. D
16. D   17. B   18. D   19. A   20. C   21. D   22. A   23. C   24. D   25. A   26. C   27. C   28. D
29. C   30. A   31. B   32. D   33. A   34. B   35. C   36. A

[L1] Completion

1. development   2. embryological development   3. fertilization   4. capacitation   5. polyspermy   6. induction
7. thalidomide   8. second trimester   9. first trimester   10. chorion   11. human chorionic gonadotropin
12. placenta   13. true labor   14. parturition   15. expulsion   16. childhood   17. infancy   18. meiosis
19. gametogenesis   20. autosomal   21. homozygous   22. heterozygous

[L1] Matching

1. G   2. B   3. H   4. E   5. L   6. A   7. K   8. C   9. F   10. I   11. M   12. D   13. J   14. X   15. W
16. S   17. U   18. T   19. R   20. O   21. N   22. V   23. P   24. Q

[L1] Drawing/Illustration Labeling

Figure 27.1 Spermatogenesis
1. spermatogonia   2. primary spermatocyte   3. secondary spermatocyte   4. spermatids   5. spermatozoa

Figure 27.2 Oogenesis
1. oogonium   2. primary oocyte   3. secondary oocyte   4. mature ovum

[L2] Concept Maps

I Interacting Factors—Labor and Delivery
1. estrogen   2. relaxin   3. ↑ prostaglandin production   4. positive feedback   5. parturition

II Lactation Reflexes
6. anterior pituitary   7. prolactin   8. ↑ milk secretion   9. posterior pituitary   10. oxytocin   11. milk ejection

[L2] Body Trek
1. secondary oocyte   2. fertilization   3. zygote   4. 2-cell stage   5. 8-cell stage   6. morula   7. early blastocyst
8. implantation

[L2] Multiple Choice
1. B   2. C   3. D   4. C   5. A   6. B   7. D   8. B   9. A   10. D   11. C   12. C   13. B   14. D   15. C
16. A   17. D   18. B   19. D   20. B

[L2] Completion
1. inheritance   2. genetics   3. chromatids   4. synapsis   5. tetrad   6. spermatogenesis   7. oogenesis
8. spermiogenesis   9. alleles   10. X-linked   11. simple inheritance   12. polygenic inheritance   13. corona radiata   14. hyaluronidase   15. cleavage   16. chorion   17. differentiation   18. activation

[L2] Short Essay

1. In simple inheritance, phenotypic characters are determined by interactions between a single pair of alleles. Polygenic inheritance involves interactions between alleles on several genes.

2. Capacitation is the activation process that must occur before a spermatozoon can successfully fertilize an egg. It occurs in the vagina following ejaculation.

3. (a) cleavage (b) implantation (c) placentation (d) embryogenesis

4. (a) ectoderm (b) mesoderm (c) endoderm

5. (a)   (b)
    - yolk sac   - endoderm and mesoderm
    - amnion   - ectoderm and mesoderm
    - allantois   - endoderm and mesoderm
    - chorion   - mesoderm and trophoblast

6. (a) The respiratory rate goes up and the tidal volume increases.
    (b) The maternal blood volume increases.
    (c) The maternal requirements for nutrients increase.
    (d) The glomerular filtration rate increases.
    (e) The uterus increases in size.

7. (a) estrogens (b) oxytocin (c) prostaglandins

8. (a) Secretion of relaxin by the placenta—softens symphysis pubis.
    (b) Weight of the fetus—deforms cervical orifice.
    (c) Rising estrogen levels.
    (d) Both b and c promote release of oxytocin.

9. (a) dilation stage (b) expulsion stage (c) placental stage

10. infancy, childhood, adolescence, maturity, senescence

11. An Apgar rating represents an assessment of the newborn infant. It considers heart rate, respiratory rate, muscle tone, response to articulation, and color at 1 and 5 minutes after birth. In each category the infant receives a score ranging from 0 (poor) to 2 (excellent), and the scores are totaled. An infant's Apgar rating (1–10) has been shown to be an accurate predictor of newborn survival and the presence of neurological damage.

12. (a) Hypothalamus—increasing production of GnRH.
    (b) Increasing circulatory levels of FSH and LH (ICSH) by the anterior pituitary
    (c) FSH and LH initiate gametogenesis and the production of male or female sex hormones that stimulate the appearance of secondary sexual characteristics and behaviors.

13. (a) Some cell populations grow smaller throughout life.
    (b) The ability to replace other cell populations decreases
    (c) Genetic activity changes over time.
    (d) Mutations occur and accumulate.

[L3] Critical Thinking/application

1. Color blindness is an X-linked trait. The Punnett square shows that sons produced by a normal father and a heterozygous mother will have a 50 percent chance of being color blind, while the daughters will all have normal color vision.

Maternal alleles

		X^C	X^c
Paternal alleles	X^C	$X^C X^C$	$X^C X^c$
	Y	$X^C Y$	$X^c Y$ (color blind)

2. The Punnett square reveals that 50 percent of their offspring have the possibility of inheriting albinism.

Maternal alleles

	a	a
A	Aa	Aa
a	aa (albino)	aa (albino)

Paternal alleles

3. Both the mother and father are heterozygous-dominant.

T—tongue roller t—non-tongue roller

The Punnett square reveals that there is a 25 percent chance of having children who are not tongue rollers and a 75 percent chance of having children with the ability to roll the tongue.

Maternal alleles

	T	t
T	TT (yes)	Tt (yes)
t	Tt (yes)	tt (no)

Paternal alleles

4. Amniocentesis is a diagnostic tool to determine the possibility of a congenital condition. To obtain the sample of amniotic fluid, a needle is inserted into position using ultrasound. This represents a potential threat to the health of the fetus and mother. Sampling cannot be safely performed until the volume of amniotic fluid is large enough to avoid injury to the fetus. The usual time is at a gestational age of 14–15 weeks. By the time the results are available, the option of abortion may not be available. Chorionic villus sampling may be an alternative since it analyzes cells collected from the villi during the first trimester.